HARNESSING RENEWABLE ENERGY

in Electric Power Systems

HARNESSING RENEWABLE ENERGY

in Electric Power Systems

Theory, Practice, Policy

Edited by

**Boaz Moselle, Jorge Padilla
and Richard Schmalensee**

RFF PRESS
RESOURCES FOR THE FUTURE

Washington, DC • London

First published in 2010 by RFF Press, an imprint of Earthscan

Earthscan LLC,1616 P Street, NW, Washington, DC 20036, USA
Earthscan Ltd, Dunstan House, 14a St Cross Street, London EC1N 8XA, UK

Earthscan publishes in association with the International Institute for Environment and Development

For more information on RFF Press and Earthscan publications, see www.rffpress.org and www.earthscan.co.uk or write to earthinfo@earthscan.co.uk

ISBN: 978-1-933115-90-0

Copyedited by Joyce Bond
Typeset by KerryPress Ltd
Cover design by Circle Graphics

Library of Congress Cataloging-in-Publication Data

Harnessing renewable energy in electric power systems : theory, practice, policy/edited by Boaz Moselle, Jorge Padilla, and Richard Schmalensee.
        p. cm.
    Includes bibliographical references and index.
    ISBN 978-1-933115-90-0 (hardback : alk. paper)
1. Electric power production. 2. Electric power production—Environmental aspects. 3. Electric power production—Economic aspects. 4. Renewable energy sources. I. Moselle, Boaz. II. Padilla, Jorge 1983– III. Schmalensee, Richard.
    TK1001.H37 2010
    333.793'2--dc22
                        2010017827

A catalogue record for this book is available from the British Library

At Earthscan we strive to minimize our environmental impacts and carbon footprint through reducing waste, recycling and offsetting our CO_2 emissions, including those created through publication of this book. For more details of our environmental policy, see www.earthscan.co.uk.

Printed and bound in the UK by MPG Books

The paper used is FSC certified

Mixed Sources
Product group from well-managed forests and other controlled sources
www.fsc.org Cert no. SA-COC-1565
© 1996 Forest Stewardship Council

About Resources for the Future *and* RFF Press

Resources for the Future (**RFF**) improves environmental and natural resource policymaking worldwide through independent social science research of the highest caliber. Founded in 1952, RFF pioneered the application of economics as a tool for developing more effective policy about the use and conservation of natural resources. Its scholars continue to employ social science methods to analyze critical issues concerning pollution control, energy policy, land and water use, hazardous waste, climate change, biodiversity, and the environmental challenges of developing countries.

RFF Press supports the mission of RFF by publishing book-length works that present a broad range of approaches to the study of natural resources and the environment. Its authors and editors include RFF staff, researchers from the larger academic and policy communities, and journalists. Audiences for publications by RFF Press include all of the participants in the policymaking process—scholars, the media, advocacy groups, NGOs, professionals in business and government, and the public. RFF Press is an imprint of **Earthscan**, a global publisher of books and journals about the environment and sustainable development.

Contents

About the Contributors

Luis Agosti is a senior consultant at LECG, an economic and financial consulting firm, where he provides research and analysis in the field of applied microeconomics, including the economics of competition, regulation, and finance. He also belongs to the Energy Practice. During his years in consultancy, he has specialized in the electricity and gas sectors. His work has been focused in the analysis of regulation in the electricity and natural gas sectors, with special emphasis in the design of the wholesale power market in Spain.

Godfrey Boyle is a professor of renewable energy and director of the Energy and Environment Research Unit in the Faculty of Mathematics, Computing, and Technology at the UK Open University. He is also a visiting professor at The Energy and Resources Institute University in New Delhi. He is coauthor and editor of *Renewable Energy: Power for a Sustainable Future* (2004) and *Renewable Electricity and the Grid* (Earthscan 2009).

James Bushnell is an associate professor and the Cargill Chair in Energy Economics in the Department of Economics at Iowa State University, the director of the university's Biobased Industry Center, and a research associate of the National Bureau of Economic Research. He has served as a member of the Market Monitoring Committee of the California Power Exchange and is currently a member of the Market Surveillance Committee of the California Independent System Operator. He has testified on regulatory and competition policy issues before numerous state and federal regulatory and legislative institutions and consulted on energy issues throughout the United States and internationally. He has written extensively on the regulation, organization, and competitiveness of energy markets.

Kenneth Gillingham is an environmental and energy economist who worked for several years in Washington, DC, at the White House Council of Economic Advisers, Resources for the Future, and the Joint Global Change Research Institute. Following this, he was a Fulbright Fellow at the University of Auckland in New Zealand and is currently at Stanford University. He has published journal articles on topics such as solar energy policy, biofuels policy, energy efficiency, and transportation policy.

José Goldemberg, a physicist, is a professor emeritus of the University of São Paulo, Brazil, of which he was the rector between 1986 and 1990. He has served as president of the Energy Company of the State of São Paulo and Brazil's secretary of state for science and technology. He chaired the World Energy

Assessment of the United Nations Development Programme. *Time* magazine honored him as one of its "Heroes of the Environment," and the Asahi Glass Foundation of Japan awarded him its 2008 Blue Planet Prize.

Richard Green is the director of the Institute for Energy Research and Policy and a professor of energy economics in the Department of Economics at the University of Birmingham. He has held visiting positions at the Office of Electricity Regulation, University of California Energy Institute, and Massachusetts Institute of Technology. He is also an author or coauthor of numerous articles published in such journals as the *Journal of Political Economy*, *Journal of Industrial Economics*, *Oxford Economic Papers*, and *Fiscal Studies*.

Christian von Hirschhausen is a full professor of economic and infrastructure policy at Berlin University of Technology and a research professor at DIW Berlin. Before that, he held the chair of energy economics and public sector management at Dresden University of Technology. He is the scientific director of several programs that cover a wide range of research in energy and related fields. His recent research on contracts and institutions in the utilities was published in *The Energy Journal*. Additional research focuses on the European economy, energy policy, and economic policy in transitional countries.

William W. Hogan is the Raymond Plank Professor of Global Energy Policy at the John F. Kennedy School of Government, Harvard University, and the research director of the Harvard Electricity Policy Group, which is examining alternative strategies for a more competitive electricity market. He has been a member of the faculty of Stanford University, where he founded the Energy Modeling Forum, and is a past president of the International Association for Energy Economics. His current research focuses on major energy industry restructuring, network pricing and access issues, market design, and energy policy in nations worldwide.

Christopher Jones was the director of New and Renewable Sources of Energy, Energy Efficiency and Innovation at the Directorate-General for Energy and Transport, European Commission, until January 15, 2010, when he became the head of the cabinet of Commissioner Andris Piebalgs, responsible for EU development policy. He is also a visiting professor of law at the College of Europe in Bruges, Belgium. He has authored or coauthored and edited several books and numerous articles on EU energy law and competition policy. He is also a member of the advisory or editorial boards of a number of academic journals.

Florian Leuthold is a research associate at the chair of energy economics at Dresden University of Technology. His current research topics include renewable energy, environmental policies, and electricity market modeling. He coauthored several recent journal articles published in *Energy Economics*, *Energy Policy*, and *Utilities Policy*.

Erin T. Mansur is an associate professor in the Department of Economics at Dartmouth College and a faculty research fellow at the National Bureau of Economic Research. He has coauthored numerous articles published in economics journals, including the *American Economic Review*, *Review of Economics and Statistics*, *Journal of Law and Economics*, *Journal of Environmental Economics and Management*, *Journal of Industrial Economics*, and *Journal of Economics and Management Strategy*.

Boaz Moselle is an economist specializing in energy markets and a director of the economic and financial consulting firm LECG. He was previously a managing director at the UK energy regulator Ofgem. He has served as a consultant to governments and corporations in many countries on a wide range of energy policy, competition, and regulatory matters; testified before UK parliamentary committees on renewable generation, security of supply, and the structure of the British power market; and participated in a group advising the European Commission on energy, competitiveness, and environmental issues. He is a member of the Advisory Board of the Centre for Economic Learning and Social Evolution (ELSE) at University College London. He has written books and articles for scholarly journals, including the *Electricity Journal*; *Journal of Risk and Uncertainty*; *Journal of Law, Economics and Organization*; *Journal of Economic Theory*; *Northwestern Journal of International Law & Business*; *Economic History Review*; *Peace Economics, Peace Science and Public Policy*; and *Proceedings of the Edinburgh Mathematical Society*.

Jorge Padilla is the European chief executive officer of LECG and advises companies on a variety of competition policy and regulatory issues, covering a wide range of industries, including the electricity and natural gas sectors. He is a research fellow of the Centre for Economic Policy Research and the Centro de Estudios Monetarios y Financieros and is or has been a member of the editorial boards of *Competition Policy International*, *Review of Economic Studies*, *Spanish Economic Review*, and *Investigaciones Económicas*. He coauthored *The Law and Economics of Article 82 EC* (2006) and has written numerous articles on competition policy and industrial organization, published in such journals as the *Antitrust Bulletin*, *Economic Journal*, *European Economic Review*, *International Journal of Industrial Organization*, *Journal of Economics and Management Strategy*, *Journal of Economic Theory*, *RAND Journal of Economics*, *Review of Financial Studies*, and *World Competition*.

Michael G. Pollitt is an assistant director of the Economic and Social Research Council (ESRC) Electricity Policy Research Group, as well as a reader in business economics at Judge Business School, University of Cambridge, the director of studies in management and economics, and a fellow of Sidney Sussex College. He is currently an external economic adviser to Ofgem, the UK energy regulator, and has also advised the ESRC, Norwegian Research Council, DTI, World Bank, and European Commission. Additionally, he has consulted for National Grid, AWG, Eneco, Nuon, Roche, and TenneT.

Richard Schmalensee is the John C. Head III Dean Emeritus and the Howard W. Johnson Professor of Economics and Management of the Sloan School of Management at the Massachusetts Institute of Technology (MIT) and director of the MIT Center for Energy and Environmental Policy Research. He has served as a member of the President's Council of Economic Advisers and serves on the National Commission on Energy Policy and the National Academy of Sciences Committee on America's Climate Choices. He is an expert on regulation, antitrust, and energy and environmental policy.

James Sweeney is a director of the Precourt Energy Efficiency Center and a professor of management science and engineering at Stanford University. His professional activities focus on economic policy and analysis, particularly in energy, natural resources, and the environment. He has also advised in a number of energy litigations in natural gas, oil, and electricity industries in the United States and New Zealand. He was one of the editors of the three-volume *Handbook of Natural Resource and Energy Economics* (1985–1993).

Hannes Weigt is a research associate at the chair of energy economics at Dresden University of Technology. His current research topics include renewable energy and environmental policies. He is also a coauthor of numerous journal articles published in *Energy Economics*, *Energy Policy*, *Applied Energy*, and the *Electricity Journal*.

List of Figures and Tables

Figures

Tables

Acknowledgments

This book would not have been possible without the support of Luis Agosti, David Black, and Dhiren Patki. Special thanks go to Anne Layne-Farrar. They are owed a substantial debt of gratitude. Thanks also go to Don Reisman at Resources for the Future, who published the English version of the book, and Juan Jose Pons from Marcial Pons, in charge of the Spanish edition of the book, for their support. The views and opinions expressed in the chapters of this book are the sole responsibility of their authors.

List of Acronyms and Abbreviations

AC	alternating current
ACER	Agency for the Cooperation of Energy Regulators
AP	average participation
ARRA	American Recovery and Reinvestment Act of 2009
a-Si	amorphous silicon
AWEA	American Wind Energy Association
AZNM	southwest (Arizona–New Mexico) region (of WECC)
BAU	business-as-usual
BEITC	Business Energy Investment Tax Credit
BMU	Federal Ministry for the Environment, Nature Conservation and Nuclear Safety of Germany
BoS	balance-of-system
BPA	Bonneville Power Administration
Btu	British thermal unit
BWEA	British Wind Energy Association
CA	California region (of WECC)
CAES	compressed-air energy storage
CAISO	California ISO
CBA	cost–benefit analysis; cost–benefit analyses
CCC	Committee on Climate Change
CCGT	combined cycle gas turbine
CCS	carbon capture and storage
CDM	Clean Development Mechanism
CdTe	cadmium telluride
CECRE	Centre for the Control of the Special Regime
CEMS	continuous emissions monitoring system
CER	certified emission reduction
CERT	Carbon Emissions Reduction Target

CH_4	methane
CHP	combined heat and power
CIGS	copper indium gallium diselenide
CIS	copper indium diselenide
CO_2e	carbon dioxide equivalent
CPUC	California Public Utilities Commission
CRW	combustible renewables and waste
CSC	current source converter
CSP	concentrated solar power
DC	direct current
DLR	German Aerospace Center
DNA	designated national authority
DNI	direct normal irradiance
DOE	(U.S.) Department of Energy
EEA	European Environment Agency
EEA-MENA	European Economic Association–Middle East North Africa
EEG	Erneuerbare Energien Gesetz (Renewable Energy Source Act)
EEX	European Energy Exchange
EIA	(U.S.) Energy Information Administration
EJ	exajoule
ENTSO-E	European Network of Transmission System Operators for Electricity
EPA	(U.S.) Environmental Protection Agency
EPIA	European Photovoltaic Industries Association
ERU	emission reduction unit
ETS	(EU) Emission Trading System
EUMENA	Europe, the Middle East, and North Africa
EV	electric vehicle
EVA	Energy Ventures Analysis
FACTS	Flexible AC Transmission Systems
FERC	Federal Energy Regulatory Commission
FIT	feed-in tariff
FTR	financial transmission right
GaAs	gallium arsenide
GDP	gross domestic product
GHG	greenhouse gas
Gt	gigatons
GW	gigawatts
GWEC	Global Wind Energy Council
GWh	gigawatt-hours
GWP	global warming potential
GWth	gigawatts-thermal
HFCs	hydrofluorocarbons
HR	heat rate
HVAC	high-voltage alternating current

HVDC	high-voltage direct current
IEA	International Energy Agency
IER	Institute of Energy Economics and the Rational Use of Energy
IET	international emissions trading
IGBT	insulated gate bipolar transistors
IGCC	integrated gasification combined cycle
IHSGI	IHS Global Insight
IPCC	Intergovernmental Panel on Climate Change
IPP	independent power producer
ISO	independent system operator
ITC	investment tax credit
J	joule
JCSP'08	Joint Coordinated System Plan 2008
JI	joint implementation
kg_{CO2}/kWh	kilograms of CO_2 per kilowatt-hour
kWh	kilowatt-hour
kWy	kilowatt-year
LBD	learning by doing
LMP	locational marginal pricing
LNG	liquefied natural gas
LPG	liquefied petroleum gas
L-RES	large-scale renewable energy sources
m/s	meters per second
MAP	Market Incentive Program
MAPP	Mid-Continent Area Power Pool
mcm/day	million cubic meters per day
MENA	Middle East and North African region
MISO	Midwest ISO
MSP	Mediterranean Solar Plan
Mtoe	million tons of oil equivalent
MW	megawatts
MWh	megawatt-hour
MWh_{RES}	megawatt-hour of renewable energy
N_2O	nitrous oxide
NEMS	National Energy Modeling System
NERC	North American Electric Reliability Council
NETA	New Electricity Trading Arrangements
NFFO	Non-Fossil Fuel Obligation
NFPA	Non-Fossil Purchasing Agency
NHR	nonhydro renewable
NIMBY	not-in-my-backyard
NO_x	nitrogen oxides
NPV	net present value
NREL	National Renewable Energy Laboratory

NWPP   Northwest Power Pool region (of WECC)
NYISO   New York Independent System Operator
O&M   operation and maintenance
OECD   Organisation for Economic Co-operation and Development
OGT   open-cycle gas turbines
OMA   Office for Metropolitan Architecture
OR   Régimen Ordinario (Ordinary Regime)
ORC   organic Rankine cycle
OTC   over-the-counter
OTEC   ocean thermal energy conversion
OWC   oscillating water column
PER   Plan de Energías Renovables (Renewable Energy Plan)
PFCs   perfluorocarbons
PFER   Plan de Fomento de las Energías Renovables (Plan to Promote
              Renewable Energy)
PJM   Pennsylvania–New Jersey–Maryland Interconnection
POLES   Prospective Outlook on Long-term Energy Systems
ppm   parts per million
PTC   production tax credit; parabolic trough concentrator
PURPA   Public Utilities Regulatory Policies Act (of 1978)
PV   photovoltaic
PVPS   Photovoltaic Power Systems
R&D   research and development
RD   Royal Decree
RD&D   research, development, and demonstration
RDL   Royal Decree-Law
REC   renewable energy certificate; renewable energy credit
REE   Red Eléctrica de España
REPI   Renewable Energy Production Incentive
REPTC   Renewable Electricity Production Tax Credit
RES   renewable electricity standard
RGGI   Regional Greenhouse Gas Initiative
RHI   Renewable Heat Incentive
RMPP   Rocky Mountain Power Pool region (of WECC)
RO   Renewables Obligation
ROC   Renewables Obligation Certificate
RPS   renewable portfolio standard
RRETC   Residential Renewable Energy Tax Credit
RTO   regional transmission organization
RTP   real-time pricing
SEGS   Solar Energy Generating Systems
SERC   Southeastern Electric Reliability Council
SF$_6$ sulfur hexafluoride
SG   *Solar Generation*

SGIP	Self Generation Incentive Program
SHPPs	small hydroelectric power plants
SO	system operator
SO_2	sulfur dioxide
SO_x	sulfur oxides
SPP	Southwest Power Pool
SR	Régimen Especial (Special Regime)
StrEG	Stromeinspeisegesetz (Electricity Feed-In Act)
tcf	trillion cubic feet
tcm	trillion cubic meters
t_{CO2}	metric ton of CO_2
TD	technological development
TEAM	transmission expansion assessment methodology
TGC	tradable green certificate
TOU	time-of-use
TREC	Trans-Mediterranean Renewable Energy Cooperation
TSO	transmission system operator
TVA	Tennessee Valley Authority
TWh	terawatt-hours
UCTE	Union for the Co-ordination of Transmission of Electricity
UNFCCC	United Nations Framework Convention on Climate Change
VSC	voltage source converter
WECC	Western Electricity Coordinating Council
WECS	wind energy conversion system
WEM	World Energy Model
WETO	*World Energy Technology Outlook—2050*
WTO	World Trade Organization

Foreword

Energy is the foundation stone of prosperity, security, and peace. Yet the European Union's economic dependence on fossil fuels, of which the lion's share is imported, is exposing the EU to threats from climate change, global geopolitics, and resource competition from rising economies. These risks could undermine our industrial and social model and ultimately European stability itself.

In response to these challenges, the 27 member states of the European Union unanimously agreed in 2007 to binding targets to change the basis of Europe's energy supply. By 2020, the EU must reduce its greenhouse gas emissions by 20%—and by 30% when the conditions are right—and increase the share of renewable energy in energy demand to 20%. Energy efficiency must improve by one-fifth. These targets are at the heart of the European Commission's broad economic strategy for the year 2020, known as Europe 2020.

Meeting these targets not only is essential for the climate change challenge, but also will dramatically improve security of supply by making the EU economy more efficient, decoupling growth from resource use, and creating more than 1.5 million extra jobs. The EU economy will be strengthened, with savings of at least €60 billion ($81.6 billion) in decreased oil and gas imports, which can be invested in the domestic economy.

To do this, we must—within just a few years—generate more than one-third of our power from renewable sources of electricity. A significant part of our heating and transport must be based on renewable fuels. It is not enough to tinker around the edges. We need huge, practical, and concrete initiatives involving society as a whole. And we need to persuade our international partners to follow the same track.

The benefits are easy to see: lower imports, new jobs, cleaner air, more stable international energy markets and prices, lower energy bills, greater consumer empowerment. Renewable energy offers solutions to many of our problems—security, economic, and environmental. The switch to an economy with a large share of renewable and low-carbon sources is the only way to ensure sustainable economic growth that brings benefits to all parts of society.

Never before have businesses and consumers had to face such a daunting task. New energy sources call for new networks to bring them to customers. Intermittent generation requires new approaches to balancing demand and supply. New and renewable technologies must become much more efficient and commercially attractive. At the same time, we have to deal with economic uncertainty and growing global competitiveness.

It is unprecedented, even in a buoyant economy, for markets alone to make the types of investments and projects our system needs. The cost–benefit analysis for renewable energy is not simple for many investors. In addition, today's credit crunch risks undermining many advances industry has made in recent years. We also have to face up to the adverse impact on investment and investment planning that could ensue from the weak Copenhagen climate agreement.

Moving to a low-carbon economy calls for investments in the order of billions of euros. But climate and security risks also have a cost, which could be several times higher. There is a growing consensus that the investments we make today will pay for themselves many times over in the future, in terms of cheaper energy, greater energy security, new businesses and markets, a cleaner environment, and climate change mitigation. We cannot afford to miss out on the huge technology and employment opportunities and geopolitical security of renewable power.

Our 2020 targets are a stepping-stone toward the EU vision for a decarbonized power supply and transport sector by 2050. Let us not forget that the system we have in place today is largely a result of technologies and decisions from 40 years ago, or even more, so our 2050 timescale is not as ambitious as it sounds. It simply reflects the reality of how energy systems develop.

To get there, the commission is pursuing a number of interrelated priorities: to implement fully and effectively an internal market in Europe; to enforce renewables and greenhouse gas emission targets and strengthen the legislative framework to give greater certainty to investors; to create a solid framework for new network infrastructure investments; to promote greater collaboration and cohesion in research, including industry-led initiatives; to boost energy efficiency, notably in buildings, appliances, and transport; and develop partnerships with other countries, both producers and other consuming nations.

It is vital to inform, involve, educate, and motivate the widest possible public. Every citizen can play a part in the low-carbon revolution.

This book is therefore both timely and important. It is also highly educational. It can help us better understand the opportunities and challenges renewable energy creates and learn from the experience of others. In this way, we will all, whether in politics, business, education, or at home, be better equipped to make, with confidence, the vital decisions that will lead to the energy system we seek for the future—a system that is at once secure, sustainable, and economically robust.

Günther Oettinger
European Union Energy Commissioner

1

Toward a Low-Carbon Future in Electricity?

Boaz Moselle, Jorge Padilla, and Richard Schmalensee

Wide consensus exists that the world's energy system requires a significant transformation in order to address the issue of climate change. In particular, the electric power system needs to switch from its carbon-intensive present, where most electricity is produced using gas and coal, to a low-carbon future where electricity is produced using some combination of renewable sources, such as hydro, wind, biomass, tidal, and solar energy, along with nuclear power and carbon capture and storage (CCS) technology, which would allow the continued use of fossil fuels, with the carbon dioxide (CO_2) emitted from combustion being stored underground rather than escaping into the atmosphere. A radical change is needed because at present, power generation produces a major part of the world's anthropogenic (or human-caused) carbon dioxide emissions, reflecting its reliance on fossil fuels, and moreover because decarbonization is likely to require increasing electrification of other sectors of the economy—in particular, a switch to electric or plug-in hybrid vehicles.

Of the options for producing electric power without significant greenhouse gas emissions, renewable generation technologies such as hydroelectricity, wind power, solar power, and biomass are generally more attractive to policymakers than either nuclear power, which brings with it concerns about safety and waste storage as well as difficult political challenges, or CCS, a new and as yet unproven technology. Renewables are also perceived to have other important attractions: increased national self-reliance contributing to security of energy supply, industrial policy goals for countries that see themselves as leaders in developing new green technologies, and domestic job creation.

This book therefore addresses a set of key questions concerning the role of renewable electricity generation in addressing climate change—questions that are central to the current concerns of policymakers, the electric power industry, and economists who study energy and environmental issues:

- At the highest level, is it right to focus on renewable power as a primary tool for reducing greenhouse gas emissions? Although environmentalists and many politicians are strong supporters of renewable energy, many economists question whether it should be singled out for support rather than being encouraged through a broad approach to reducing carbon emissions (e.g., via a tax on CO_2 emissions).
- If renewable energy is to be given specific support, what form should that take? What is

the right balance between support for research and development and for deployment of renewable generation? Should all renewable technologies receive equal levels of support? If not, how should the system choose among technologies? What is the right mechanism for supporting renewable generation: straight financial payments, tax breaks, guarantees of prices at levels high enough to support investment, or a market-based method involving the trading of green certificates?

- At a more technical level—but of great importance—what are the implications for power markets of the widespread adoption of renewable generation? Is this trend compatible with the shift (or aspiration) toward liberalized, competitive markets that is seen in the European Union and much of the United States? What are the implications for system reliability of the use of intermittent resources, such as wind and sunshine, for a large part of generation capacity? Will markets provide needed backup generation, or is regulatory intervention required?

The various chapters in this book provide objective analysis of these questions, drawing on economic theory and evidence, including the experiences of U.S. states and EU member states that have devoted considerable resources to the promotion of renewable generation over the past decade or more. The focus is on the application of rigorous economic analysis to derive insights that have practical implications for policy in this area. The book is the result of a cooperative effort among a set of authors that includes both academics and policymakers, with a range of specialties covering renewable technology, environmental and natural resource economics, energy economics and industrial organization, and with specific knowledge of the energy sector, electric power markets, and renewables policy in Europe, the United States, and globally.

Although many books currently exist on climate change–related topics, most of these address different issues than this one. Many are focused on the scientific issues around global climate change

and its implications in such areas as agriculture, migration, or public health (see, e.g., Kruger 2006; Tester et al. 2005). Others focus on policy responses to climate change, often from a political science or international relations perspective (see, e.g., Dodds et al. 2009; Giddens 2009; Kalicki and Goldwyn 2005; Mitchell 2010; Stern 2009). Although a number of important texts have been written on the economics of global climate (e.g., Helm and Hepburn 2009), only a few address the role of renewable energy as part of climate change mitigation and the challenges that renewable generation poses for electricity markets (e.g., Grubb, Jamasb and Pollitt 2008).

This book differs from others on renewables in breadth and depth. It deals with technology issues, wide policy questions (such as the impact of renewables support on the climate change and security of supply goals of most governments), and practical implementation issues (e.g., the implications for system design, market performance, and policy design of massive deployment of renewable energy). It also describes the renewables policies and experiences of the United States, the European Union, the United Kingdom, Germany, and Spain and examines the lessons that can be extracted from them.

The book is organized into four parts. In Part I, Technology, Godfrey Boyle reviews in Chapter 2 each of the technologies covered in the book from both an economic and an engineering viewpoint, considering the impact of each on system operation, as well as its contribution to sustainability and economic efficiency.

Part II, Renewables, Climate Change, and Energy Policy, focuses on the high-level energy policy concerns that underlie renewables policy. In Chapter 3, Erin Mansur discusses how widespread concerns about climate change and policymakers' and voters' preferences will affect the development of renewable energy use. Boaz Moselle in Chapter 4 looks at the other main driver of renewables policy, the desire to develop indigenous sources of energy to meet security of supply concerns. He analyzes the main security of supply issues that drive the European debate, notably the question of reliance on Russian gas imports. Next, in Chapter 5, Kenneth Gillingham and James Sweeney delve into the economic motivation for renewable energy policies by highlighting the classes of relevant market failures. Key policy instruments are evaluated in the context of different market structures, with the goal of informing future policies in the renewable energy sector. Finally, José Goldemberg provides in Chapter 6 a broad economic analysis of the relationships among four important instruments that have become common in renewable energy policy: subsidies to renewable energy, emissions trading, the promotion of energy efficiency, and the Clean Development Mechanism developed under the Kyoto Protocol.

Part III, Renewable Generation and Electric Power Markets, focuses one level down, looking at the implications of renewable generation for electric power markets. In Chapter 7, William Hogan discusses the difficulties associated with deploying renewable electricity in large-scale wholesale electricity markets. He considers such issues as system design, transmission and distribution, and the development of smart grids, with special emphasis placed on the problems of integrating wind power into wholesale market design. Chapter 8, by Richard Green, considers the regulatory issues that will arise from the desire to integrate large-scale renewable energy deployment into existing electricity markets and discusses how these issues can be resolved. James Bushnell in Chapter 9 studies the intersection of two important trends: the restructuring of electricity markets and the growth of environmental regulation. He provides an empirical study that elucidates how the increasing penetration of intermittent renewable generation will alter the economics of investment in conventional thermal generation. Finally, in Chapter 10, Christian von Hirschhausen addresses the development of a 'supergrid', which is currently being debated in the context of harnessing renewable energy. Using one of the more advanced concepts for a 'supergrid' in the European/North African region, the discussion also highlights the practical obstacles in the way of the realization of such a project.

Part IV, National Experiences, offers insights from the experiences of various countries, with individual chapters on the United States,

the European Union, the United Kingdom, Germany, and Spain. The aim here is to capture lessons both from the different policies and policy instruments that have been applied and from differences in the policy concerns and debates across the various countries. In Chapter 11, Richard Schmalensee analyzes the development of renewable energy policies and deployment in the United States. He compares and contrasts the growth of renewable electricity deployment in Texas and California, highlighting the ability of well-tailored policy to advance the growth of renewable energy use, and discusses the difficulties of integrating wind power into the existing market framework. Christopher Jones in Chapter 12 provides an in-depth analysis of the emergence of the European Union's renewables policy, in the context of its wider climate change and energy security concerns. He describes the policy tools adopted and analyzes some of the key issues arising, such as the relationship with the EU Emissions Trading Scheme and the role of trading within the renewables promotion framework.

The remaining case studies concern three EU member states. Michael Pollitt in Chapter 13 examines the United Kingdom's renewable energy policy in the context of its overall decarbonization and energy policies. He explores the shortcomings of the UK renewables policy to date and suggests policy changes that would better suit the country's institutional and resource endowments. In Chapter 14, Hannes Weigt and Florian Leuthold discuss the development of renewable energy policy and deployment in Germany. In particular, they examine the implications of current policy for market design and future development, with a particular focus on the growing share of wind energy. Finally, Chapter 15, by Luis Agosti and Jorge Padilla, analyzes the regulatory schemes and market structure that have made possible the rapid growth of the Spanish renewables sector in recent years, as well as the consequences of this growth for the Spanish gas and power markets. The chapter focuses in particular on the impact of the large-scale deployment of wind generation on system operation and balancing, wholesale prices, competition, and investment incentives.

It is now widely accepted that a low-carbon world is technically feasible, and that renewables are likely to have a significant long-term role to play in the future energy system. The relevant question today is not whether renewables should be supported, but rather how to harness these technologies so that they can effectively and efficiently contribute to the ultimate goal of mitigating harmful climate change.

References

Dodds, Felix, Andrew Higham and Richard Sherman. Foreword by Achim Steiner. 2009. *Climate Change and Energy Insecurity*. London: Earthscan.

Giddens, Anthony. 2009. *The Politics of Climate Change*. Cambridge, UK: Polity Press.

Grubb, Michael, Tooraj Jamasb, and Michael Pollitt, eds. 2008. *Delivering a Low Carbon Electricity System*. Cambridge, UK: Cambridge University Press.

Helm, Dieter, and Cameron Hepburn, eds. 2009. *The Economics and Politics of Climate Change*. Oxford: Oxford University Press.

Kalicki, Jan H., and David L. Goldwyn, eds. 2005. *Energy & Security*. Baltimore: Johns Hopkins University Press.

Kruger, Paul. 2006. *Alternative Energy Resources: The Quest for Sustainable Energy*. Hoboken, NJ: Wiley-Blackwell.

Mitchell, Catherine. 2010. *The Political Economy of Sustainable Energy*. Basingstoke, UK: Palgrave Macmillan.

Stern, Nicholas. 2009. *A Blueprint for a Safer Planet*. London: The Bodley Head Ltd.

Tester, Jefferson W., Elisabeth M. Drake, Michael J. Driscoll, Michael W. Golay and William A. Peters 2005. *Sustainable Energy: Choosing Among Options*. Cambridge, MA: MIT Press.

Part I

Technology

2

Renewable Energy Technologies for Electricity Generation

Godfrey Boyle

It is tempting to imagine that the 17th-century poet and mystic William Blake was thinking of renewable energy when, in *The Marriage of Heaven and Hell,* he declared that "Energy is Eternal Delight" (Blake 1790). Renewable energy is usually described in more prosaic terms, however. According to the International Energy Agency's definition, "Renewable energy is derived from natural processes that are replenished constantly" (IEA 2002). Similarly, Twidell and Weir (1986) define it as "energy obtained from the continuous or repetitive currents of energy recurring in the natural environment."

How, then, should "renewable energy *technologies*" be defined? The following working definition may suffice: renewable energy technologies are those technologies that enable constantly replenished renewable energy flows to be harnessed to produce power in forms useful to humanity on a sustainable basis.

The sun is the source of the vast majority of the power that drives the abundant and varied sources of renewable energy that are available to humanity on the earth. The total quantity of solar power incident on our planet is approximately four orders of magnitude greater than our current rate of use of fossil and nuclear fuels.

Solar radiation can be used *directly*, to provide heating, lighting, and hot water in buildings and to generate electricity. The sun also powers the world's weather systems and is thus the *indirect* source of hydro, wind, and wave power. It also drives the process of photosynthesis in plants and so is the energy source underlying biofuels in their various forms.

Two other terms that should be defined here at the outset are "energy" and "power." Energy is defined as the *capacity to do work*: that is, to move an object against a resisting force. In everyday language, the word "power" is often used as a synonym for "energy," but this is not strictly correct. Power is defined as the *rate* of doing work—that is, the rate at which energy is converted from one form to another or transmitted from one place to another. The main unit of measurement of energy is the joule (J), and the main unit of measurement of power is the watt (W), which is defined as a rate of one joule per second.

Solar-Based Renewable Energy Sources

The Solar Resource

Solar energy makes an enormous but largely unrecorded contribution to our energy needs. It is the sun's radiant energy, aided by the atmospheric greenhouse effect, that maintains the earth's surface at a temperature warm enough to support human life.

The sun has a surface temperature of 6,000 degrees Celsius (°C), maintained by continuous nuclear fusion reactions between hydrogen atoms within its interior. This is a relatively slow process, and the sun should continue to supply power for another five billion years. The sun radiates huge quantities of energy into the surrounding space, and the tiny fraction intercepted by the earth's atmosphere 150 million kilometers (km) away is nonetheless equivalent to about 15,000 times humanity's present rate of use of fossil and nuclear fuels. Even though approximately one-third of the intercepted energy is reflected away by the atmosphere before reaching the earth's surface, this still means that a continuous and virtually inexhaustible flow of power, amounting to some 9,000 times our current rate of consumption of conventional fossil and nuclear fuels, is available in principle to human civilization.

Direct Uses of Solar Energy

Solar energy, when it enters our buildings, warms and illuminates them to a significant extent. When buildings are designed to take full advantage of the sun's radiation, their needs for additional heating and artificial lighting can be reduced. The sun's heat can also be harnessed by using solar collectors to produce hot water for washing and, in some circumstances, space heating in buildings. Such collectors are in widespread use in sunny countries, such as Israel and Greece, but are also quite widely used in less sunny places, such as Austria.

Solar radiation can also be concentrated by mirrors or lenses to provide high-temperature heat to drive heat engines that generate electricity. Such solar thermal-electric power stations are in operation in several countries. Solar radiation can also be converted directly into electricity using photovoltaic (PV) panels, usually mounted on the roofs or facades of buildings.

Indirect Uses of Solar Energy

Solar radiation can be converted to useful energy *indirectly*, via other energy forms. Sunlight falls in a more perpendicular direction in tropical regions and more obliquely at high latitudes, heating the tropics to a greater degree than polar regions. The result is a massive heat flow towards the poles, carried by currents in the oceans and the atmosphere. The energy in such currents can be harnessed, for example by wind turbines.

Where winds blow over long stretches of ocean, they create waves, and a variety of devices can be used to extract that energy.

Biofuels are another indirect manifestation of solar energy. Through photosynthesis in plants, solar radiation converts water and atmospheric carbon dioxide into carbohydrates, which form the basis of more complex molecules that constitute biofuels such as wood or ethanol.

A large fraction of the solar radiation reaching the earth's surface is absorbed by the oceans, warming them and adding water vapor to the air. This water vapor condenses as rain to feed rivers, in which dams and turbines can be placed to extract some of the energy of the flowing water, creating hydropower.

Nonsolar Renewables

Two other sources of renewable energy, tidal and geothermal energy, are not dependent on solar radiation. Tidal energy is sometimes confused with wave energy, but its origins are quite different. It arises from the gravitational pull of the moon (plus a small contribution from the sun) on the world's oceans. The source of geothermal energy is heat from within the earth caused mainly by the decay of radioactive materials within the earth's core.

Renewable Electricity Generating Technologies

This chapter concentrates on the use of renewables for electricity production, looking initially at solar, wind, and wave power, then turning to biofuels, hydro, tidal, and geothermal energy. It then analyzes the costs and economics of renewable electricity, and finally examines the challenges involved in integrating renewable electricity sources into current and future electricity supply systems.[1]

Solar Thermal Electricity

Greek legend relates that in 212 BC, Archimedes ordered his warriors to use their polished shields to concentrate the rays of the sun onto Roman ships besieging Syracuse, setting fire to them. As Everett observes: "Although long derided as myth, Greek navy experiments in 1973 showed that 60 men each armed with a mirror 1m by 1.5m could indeed ignite a wooden boat at 50m" (Everett, 2004, *51*).

Solar thermal electricity generating systems essentially use the sun's energy, in either direct or concentrated form, to drive a heat engine, which in turn drives an electrical generator. Heat engines (a steam engine, for example) convert heat to mechanical work by exploiting the temperature difference between a hot heat source and a cold heat sink, usually the ambient environment. The efficiency of a heat engine increases with increasing temperature difference between source and sink, so it is useful to rank the various technologies in order of their operating temperature.

Low-Temperature Solar Thermal-Electric Technologies

Solar Ponds

A solar pond is a very large pond filled with salt water and used to collect solar energy. The top layer has a low salt content, and the bottom layer has a high salt content. Between these is an intermediate layer with a varying salt concentration gradient, designed to prevent natural convection of heat from the bottom to the top. If the top layers of the pond are translucent, the bottom layer can absorb substantial quantities of solar energy and reach relatively high temperatures, around 90°C in sunny regions. As the temperature

at the top of the pond will remain at ambient levels, around 30°C, the difference in these temperatures can be used to power an organic Rankine cycle (ORC) heat engine, which in turn can power a generator to produce electricity.

An ORC engine operates on a cycle similar to that used in conventional steam turbines, except that the working fluid is not water (turned to steam) but an organic fluid, such as pentane or butane, which evaporates at lower temperatures. The vapor then drives a turbine. This cycle enables power to be produced from much lower-temperature sources than those used with steam turbines, though also with much reduced efficiency.

The low efficiency means that solar ponds need to be large to generate significant quantities of electrical power. (They are perhaps more suited to low-temperature heat production.) They also operate effectively only at low latitudes because the absorbing area is horizontal. In addition, the maintenance costs of replenishing the surface water and maintaining the salt gradient are significant.

Ocean Thermal Energy Conversion (OTEC)

In warm tropical regions of the world's oceans, the temperature of water at the surface can exceed 25°C, whereas at depths of around 1,000 meters, the water temperature can be below 5°C. This temperature differential can be used to drive a turbine employing an organic Rankine cycle heat engine, which in turn can power a generator to produce electricity, in what is called ocean thermal energy conversion (OTEC).

The potential resource of solar energy stored in the surface layers of the world's oceans and available to be tapped by OTEC systems is huge. Such systems should also be able to produce power on a continuous basis. Between the 1970s and the 1990s, several experimental plants were tested in Hawaii, and another in Japan. However, the engineering challenges involved in pumping huge quantities of water through extremely long, large-diameter pipes from the ocean depths to the surface are formidable, and considerable energy is required simply to pump the water.

The U.S. firm Lockheed Martin is currently developing plans for a new OTEC system taking advantage of modern materials and technology to generate power on a scale of approximately 100 megawatts (MW). Given adequate funding, the company foresees that a pilot 10 MW plant could be operating off Hawaii by 2013 (James 2009; Lockheed Martin n.d.).

Solar Chimney

The solar chimney concept involves heating large volumes of air in an extremely large "greenhouse" and allowing the warmed air to rise through a very tall chimney. The stream of rising air powers a wind turbine at the base of the chimney.

Such systems need to be very large if they are to generate significant quantities of power. In a 50-kilowatt experimental project at Manzanares in Spain, the greenhouse-type solar collector was 240 meters in diameter and the chimney was 195 meters high. Compared with concentrating solar collectors, the energy conversion efficiency of solar chimney systems is low, and the land area they occupy is correspondingly greater. They can produce power using diffuse as well as direct solar radiation, however, and some energy storage can be provided though heating the floor of the greenhouse (see Schlaich 1995).

Medium- and High-Temperature Solar Electric Technologies

Parabolic Trough Concentrators

Concentrating solar systems are normally practical only in relatively cloud-free regions of the world where the majority of solar radiation is direct. This is because the mirrors or lenses they use cannot concentrate the sun's indirect, diffuse radiation.

Parabolic trough concentrators (PTCs) incorporate trough-shaped parabolic mirrors that track the sun along a single axis, concentrating the sun's rays onto a tube at the focus containing a heat transfer fluid, usually a synthetic oil. The absorber tube is normally surrounded by a glass tube to reduce heat loss by re-radiation. The oil is then passed through a heat exchanger to produce high-temperature steam. This powers a turbine, which

in turn drives an electrical generator. Relatively high temperatures (around 400°C) can be attained, enabling fairly high energy conversion efficiencies (about 20%) to be achieved.

The world's longest-operating concentrating solar power plants are the nine Solar Energy Generating Systems (SEGS) established by the Luz Energy Corporation in California's Mojave Desert between 1984 and 1990. They use parabolic trough concentrators occupying several square kilometers of land, with a combined output of 350 MW. The plants were designed to help meet California's summer peak air-conditioning load. At night or in low-sun conditions, a natural gas boiler can be used to supply auxiliary steam to the turbines, enabling them to continue to supply power. Another, more recent, large parabolic trough concentrating solar system in the United States is the 64 MW Solar One, installed in the Nevada desert by Acciona Energy in 2007. The Israeli company Solel has signed a power purchase agreement with the California utility Pacific Gas and Electric to install some 553 MW of parabolic trough concentrating solar capacity in the Mojave Desert by 2011 (Hopwood 2009).

Europe's largest parabolic trough concentrating solar electric plants are the Andasol installations in southern Spain, each rated at 50 MW. The first is in commercial operation, the second entered its testing phase in 2009, and the third is due to be commissioned in 2011. They are located on the Guadix plateau in the province of Granada, an area with clear skies and very high annual solar radiation levels. Andasol 1 has 312 rows of collectors, totaling more than 500,000 square meters in area, and has an estimated annual output of 180 GWh. It includes a molten salt-based heat storage system that allows power production to continue for up to 7.5 hours after sunset.

A recent development in concentrator technology involves the use of lower-cost linear Fresnel reflectors instead of parabolic mirrors. These consist of flat or slightly curved mirrors arrayed in long rows and aligned so that they focus the sun's rays onto a long tube, with the aid of a small secondary reflector. Water in the tube is turned directly into high-pressure, high-temperature steam, which can be used to power a turbine. An experimental plant was set up in Almeria, Spain, in 2007 by researchers from the Fraunhofer Institute for Solar Energy Systems, based in Freiburg, Germany. The German company Novatec Biosol commissioned PE1, a 1.4 MW plant using Fresnel technology, in Spain in May 2009 and has commenced work on a larger, 30 MW plant.

Power Towers

An early example of the power tower approach from the 1980s and 1990s was the large installation at Barstow, California, now decommissioned. This used a field of tracking mirrors, or heliostats, to reflect the sun's rays onto a boiler at the top of a central tower. The first Solar One plant used high-temperature synthetic oils to transfer the heat to a boiler to raise steam. The later phase of the project, Solar Two, included high-temperature heat storage using molten salt, allowing electricity to be produced on a more continuous basis.

More recently, Abengoa Solar's 20 MW PS20 power tower near Seville in Spain (an uprated version of the company's earlier 10 MW PS10 design, installed nearby) became operational in summer 2009. The PS20 uses 1,255 movable heliostats, each 120 square meters in area, to focus the sun's rays onto a receiver and heat exchanger at the top of a 162-meter tower. The high-temperature solar heat produces steam to drive a turbine, which in turn powers a generator to produce electricity. Some of the steam is stored in insulated tanks, enabling generation to continue at night (Marsh 2009). The company is planning to construct larger power towers of up to 50 MW capacity as part of a solar electricity generating complex totaling 300 MW and incorporating a variety of solar electricity technologies, including parabolic trough and dish Stirling systems (described in the next section).

In the United States, Brightsource Energy, using its Luz Power Tower 550 system, aims to construct a number of power towers, each of 100 MW capacity, in projects for the utilities Southern California Edison and Pacific Gas and Electric. The aim is to have some 900 MW operational by 2013 (Hopwood 2009). Major concentrating solar power (CSP) plants are also planned in Israel, the United Arab Emirates, and other Middle Eastern countries (*Renew* 2009).

Dish Stirling Solar Concentrators

Another approach to concentrating solar power is to place a suitable small engine, such as a Stirling engine, at the focus of a dish-type solar concentrator. Dish Stirling solar systems can operate at around 1,000°C and deliver high energy conversion efficiencies, approaching 30%. The dish tracks the sun on two axes: azimuth and elevation. Practically, each individual unit can be constructed only on a relatively small scale, around 10 to 15 MW.

System Integration and Economics

The output of solar thermal-electric power plants is dependent on the solar input, which varies on a daily and seasonal basis. It is well matched to peak electric air-conditioning loads in many areas. Many systems incorporate thermal storage, and some include an auxiliary fossil-fueled plant, enabling their output to be dispatchable in a similar manner to conventional generating plants.

Electricity from concentrating solar thermal-electric systems is currently estimated to cost around 9 to 12 cents per kilowatt-hour (kWh), about two to three times the cost of conventional electricity (using normal accounting conventions, though these exclude the external costs of conventional generation). But with technological improvements and quantity production, CSP costs are expected to fall to about 6 cents/kWh within a decade (Marsh 2009).

Solar Photovoltaic Electricity

Physical Principles

The silicon solar photovoltaic (PV) cell is perhaps the ideal energy conversion device. Its "fuel" input, solar energy, is free; silicon is the second most abundant material in the earth's crust; its output is that most useful of energy forms, electricity; and, with no moving parts, it has extremely low operation and maintenance requirements.

Photovoltaic cells consist, in essence, of a junction between thin layers of two different types of semiconductor, known as p-type (positive) and n-type (negative). Semiconductors are materials whose electrical properties are intermediate between those of conductors, which offer little resistance to the flow of electric current, and insulators, which inhibit the flow of electricity. The semiconductors are usually made from silicon, although PV cells can be made from other materials. N-type semiconductors are made from crystalline silicon that has been "doped" with tiny quantities of an impurity, usually phosphorus, in such a way that the doped material possesses a surplus of free electrons. Because electrons possess a negative electrical charge, silicon doped in this way is known as an n-type semiconductor. P-type semiconductors are doped with very small amounts of a different impurity, usually boron, which causes the material to have a deficit of free electrons. These missing electrons are called "holes." Because the absence of a negatively charged electron can be considered equivalent to a positively charged particle, silicon doped in this way is known as a p-type semiconductor.

A p–n junction can be created by joining these dissimilar semiconductors. This sets up an electric field in the region of the junction, which will cause negatively charged particles to move in one direction and positively charged particles to move in the opposite direction. When photons of light of a suitable wavelength fall within the p–n junction, they can transfer their energy to some of the electrons in the material, causing an electric current to flow across the junction.

Photovoltaic Materials and Technologies

Crystalline Silicon

The most efficient silicon solar cells are made from extremely pure monocrystalline silicon— that is, silicon with a single, continuous crystal lattice structure with virtually no defects or impurities. Monocrystalline silicon is usually grown from a small seed crystal that is slowly pulled out of a molten mass of polycrystalline silicon, in a sophisticated process developed originally for the electronics industry. Polycrystalline silicon essentially consists of small grains of monocrystalline silicon.

Solar cell wafers can be made directly from polycrystalline silicon in various ways. These include the controlled casting of molten polycrystalline silicon into cube-shaped ingots, which are then cut into thin, square wafers and fabricated into complete cells in the same way as monocrystalline cells.

Polycrystalline PV cells are easier and cheaper to manufacture than their monocrystalline counterparts but are less efficient. Commercially available polycrystalline PV modules, sometimes called "multicrystalline" or "semicrystalline," can attain energy conversion efficiencies of around 14%, whereas monocrystalline module efficiencies can exceed 17%.

Gallium Arsenide

Another material suitable for PV is gallium arsenide (GaAs), a so-called compound semiconductor. It has a crystal structure similar to that of silicon but consisting of alternating gallium and arsenic atoms. In principle, it is highly suitable for use in PV applications because it has a high light absorption coefficient, so only a thin layer of material is required. GaAs cells are more efficient than those made from monocrystalline silicon. They can also operate at relatively high temperatures without substantial reduction in efficiency, which makes them well suited to use in concentrating PV systems.

But GaAs cells are more expensive than silicon cells, partly because the production process is not so well developed and partly because gallium and arsenic are not abundant materials. They are often used when very high efficiency is required, regardless of cost, as in many space applications.

Thin-Film Silicon PV

Solar cells can also be made from very thin films of silicon, in a form known as amorphous silicon (a-Si), in which the silicon atoms are much less ordered than in the crystalline forms described above. Amorphous silicon cells are much cheaper to produce than those made from crystalline silicon. This form of silicon is also a better absorber of light, so thinner, and therefore cheaper, films can be used. There are advantages in the manufacturing process as well: it operates at a much lower temperature than that for crystalline silicon, so less energy is required; it is suited to continuous production; and it allows quite large areas of cells to be deposited onto a wide variety of both rigid and flexible substrates, including steel, glass, and plastics.

But a-Si cells are currently much less efficient than their single-crystal or polycrystalline silicon counterparts. Commercially available a-Si modules achieve stable efficiencies in the range of 4% to 8%. A-Si cells are already widely used as power sources for a variety of consumer products, such as calculators, where the requirement is for low cost rather than high efficiency.

Other Thin-Film PV Technologies

Among the many other thin film technologies, some of the most attractive are those based on compound semiconductors, in particular, copper indium diselenide ($CuInSe_2$, usually abbreviated to CIS), copper indium gallium diselenide (CIGS), and cadmium telluride (CdTe). Modules based on all of these technologies are in production from various manufacturers. Thin-film CIGS cells have attained the highest laboratory efficiencies of all thin-film devices, around 17%, and CIGS modules with stable efficiencies over 10% are commercially available.

Cadmium telluride modules can be made using a relatively simple and inexpensive process, and efficiencies over 10% are claimed. However, the modules contain cadmium, a highly toxic substance, so stringent precautions need to be taken during manufacture, use, and eventual recycling.

Other thin-film and innovative technologies entering production or in development include multijunction PV cells, in which different p–n junctions are "tuned" to absorb light from different parts of the solar spectrum, and photoelectrochemical cells using dye-sensitized layers of titanium dioxide. Still at the R&D stage are third-generation photovoltaic systems based on nanotechnology or using organic materials.

Concentrating PV Systems

The energy output of PV cells can be increased by using mirrors or lenses to concentrate the incoming solar radiation onto the cells—an approach similar to that described above in the section on parabolic trough concentrators. The concentration ratio can vary from as little as two to several hundred or even several thousand times. The concentrating system must have an aperture equal to that of an equivalent flat plate array to collect the same amount of incoming solar energy. In concentrating PV systems, the cells are often cooled, either passively or actively, to prevent overheating.

Systems with the highest concentration ratios use sensors, motors, and controls to allow them to track the sun on two axes—azimuth (horizontal orientation) and elevation (vertical tilt)—ensuring that the cells always receive the maximum amount of solar radiation. Systems with lower concentration ratios track the sun on a single axis and can have simpler tracking mechanisms.

PV Systems for Remote Power

In many developing countries, electricity grids are often nonexistent or rudimentary, particularly in rural areas, and all forms of energy are usually very expensive. Here PV systems, usually incorporating battery storage, can be highly competitive with other forms of energy supply, and their use is growing rapidly.

Grid-Connected, Building-Integrated PV

In most parts of the developed world, grid electricity is easily accessible and can provide a convenient backup to PV or other fluctuating renewable energy supplies. In these grid-connected PV systems, a grid-commutated inverter, or synchronous inverter, transforms the DC power from the PV arrays into AC power at a voltage and frequency that can be accepted by the grid, while "debit" and "credit" meters measure the amounts of power bought from or sold to the utility.

PV arrays can be built into the roofs of houses. They can also be integrated into the roofs and walls of commercial, institutional, and industrial buildings, replacing some of the conventional wall cladding or roofing materials that would otherwise have been needed and reducing the net costs of the PV system. In the case of some prestigious office buildings, the cost of conventional cladding materials can exceed the cost of cladding with PV.

Commercial and industrial buildings normally are occupied mainly during daylight hours; this correlates well with the availability of solar radiation. Thus the power generated by PV can significantly reduce an organization's need to purchase power from the grid at the retail price and in some countries can be sold to the grid at a premium price (discussed in the section on Costs and Economics of Renewables below).

Large, Grid-Connected PV Power Plants

Large, centralized PV power systems, many at multimegawatt scale, have been built to supply power for local or regional electricity grids in a number of countries, including Germany, Switzerland, Italy, and the United States. Compared with building-integrated PV systems, large standalone PV plants can take advantage of economies of scale in purchasing and installing large numbers of PV modules and associated equipment, and they can be located on sites that are optimal in terms of solar radiation. On the other hand, the electricity they produce is not used on-site and has to be distributed by the grid, involving transmission losses.

Large plants also require substantial areas of land, which has to be purchased or leased, but in some cases low-value "waste" land, such as that alongside roads or railways, can be used. The land can also often be used for other purposes as well as PV generation. In the 1.7 MW installation at Sonnen in Germany, for example, the PV arrays have been mounted at least one meter above the ground, minimizing shading to the vegetation beneath and allowing sheep to graze beneath the panels. It would also, in principle, be possible to have other forms of renewable energy generation, such as wind turbines, alongside a large PV system.

Large PV power plants are more economically attractive in those regions of the world that have substantially greater annual total solar radiation,

and clearer skies, than northern Europe. In such regions, the majority of the radiation is direct, making tracking and concentrating systems effective and further increasing the annual energy output. The price of electricity from such PV installations is likely to be less than half of that from comparable non-tracking installations.

Kurokawa et al. (2007) give a detailed analysis of the feasibility and economics of very large-scale photovoltaic power plants in various regions of the world, including the Mediterranean, Middle East, Gobi Desert, and Oceania. Their report also examines the conditions under which very large-scale PV installations in deserts could contribute to sustainable community development in the surrounding regions and includes a comparison of the relative merits of concentrating solar thermal and concentrating PV systems.

System Integration of Grid-Connected PV

In northern European countries, most PV power would be produced in summer, when electricity demand is relatively low; much less would be produced in winter, when demand is high. But in many other regions, PV supply correlates well with summer daytime air-conditioning demand. PV power is quite reliable during daylight hours in climates with mainly clear skies, such as California and southern Spain; in more cloudy countries, it can be intermittent at times.

Cost of Energy from PV Systems

The Photovoltaic Power Systems (PVPS) task force of the International Energy Agency (IEA) regularly tracks the prices of PV modules and systems for a wide range of IEA member countries. System prices include both modules and the associated balance-of-system (BoS) costs—those of the array support structure, cabling, switching, inverters, and metering—plus the cost of connection to the grid. The trends in module and system prices (capital costs, adjusted for inflation) for 1997–2007 are shown in Figure 2.1.

As can be seen, PV module prices in the lowest-cost country (country 3, not identified but probably Germany) in 2007 were around $4 per installed watt, while system prices were around $6

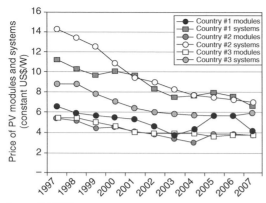

Source: IEA 2008

Figure 2.1. Evolution of price of PV modules and systems in selected IEA reporting countries, 1997–2007, allowing for the effects of inflation

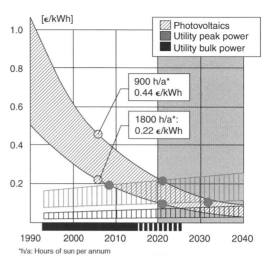

*h/a: Hours of sun per annum
900 h/a corresponds to northern countries of Europe
1800 h/a corresponds to southern countries of Europe

Note: the black band indicates that the market support programs will be necessary until about 2020 in some markets.

Source: EPIA/Greenpeace, 2008, 41

Figure 2.2. Projected convergence of utility prices and PV generation costs

per watt. The operation and maintenance (O&M) costs of PV installations are very low, and thus the main driver of the cost per unit of electricity produced is the capital cost. As the cost of electricity from PV systems continues to reduce and the cost of grid electricity from conventional fossil and nuclear sources continues to increase, many analysts expect the two to converge in the near future, leading to grid parity for PV power (see Figure 2.2).

Reducing the Costs of PV Power

The European Photovoltaic Industries Association suggests that electricity from PV could become "a mainstream power source in Europe by 2020" (EPIA 2009, *1*). The report outlines three possible scenarios for PV contributions to the electricity system by that year. In the "Baseline" scenario, few changes have been made to the existing electricity system, and by 2020, PV contributes only 4% of European electricity consumption. The "Accelerated Growth" scenario envisages minor changes to the electricity system, better cooperation from utilities, and optimized PV supply chains, with the result that PV provides 6% of Europe's electricity by 2020. In the "Paradigm Shift" scenario, PV provides 12% of Europe's electricity by 2020; this involves rapid and widespread adoption of "smart grid" and storage tech-

nologies, coupled with further improvements across the PV supply chain.

Looking beyond Europe to the potential for world-scale PV development, EPIA and Greenpeace International (2008) point out that the projections in their earlier *Solar Generation* reports (2001–2007) consistently underestimated the actual growth in world PV production (see Table 2.1). Growth in recent years has greatly exceeded expectations. The EPIA/Greenpeace projections for future world PV growth, shown in Table 2.2, therefore may not be as optimistic as they might seem. They suggest that by 2030, PV could be supplying some 2,600 terawatt-hours (TWh). This is 8.9% of the total world electricity demand forecast by the International Energy Agency in its Reference Scenario for that year; or 13.8% of world electricity demand if the energy efficiency improvements envisaged in Greenpeace's own *Energy Revolution* scenario (2005) are implemented.

Table 2.1. Annual PV capacity installed/predicted: market results versus *Solar Generation* (SG) scenario predictions since 2001 (in MW)

Year	2001	2002	2003	2004	2005	2006	2007	2008	2009	2010
Market result	334	439	594	1,052	1,320	1,467	2,392			
SG I 2001	331	408	518	659	839	1,060	1,340	1,700	2,150	2,810
SG II 2004					986	1,283	1,675	2,190	2,877	3,634
SG III 2006						1,883	2,540	3,420	4,630	5,550
SG IV 2007							2,179	3,129	4,339	6,650
SG V 2008								4,175	6,160	6,950

Source: EPIA/Greenpeace 2008
Note: The 2008 market result was 5,568 MW installed, again greatly exceeding the SG V 2008 projection of 4,175 MW

Table 2.2. Projected solar PV electricity output and detailed associated projections for 2030 in the SG V scenario

Global solar electricity output in 2030
8.9% of global electricity demand from PV[a]
13.8% of global electricity demand from PV[b]

Detailed projections for 2030	
PV systems cumulative capacity	1,864 GW
Electricity production	2,646 TWh
Grid-connected consumers	1,250 million
Off-grid consumers	3,216 million
Employment potential	10 million jobs
Market value	€454 billion ($618 billion) per annum
Cost of solar electricity	7–13 euro cents (10–18 U.S. cents) per kWh depending on location
Cumulative CO_2 savings	8,963 million metric tons of CO_2

Source: EPIA/Greenpeace 2008
[a]Demand forecast from IEA Reference Scenario
[b]Demand forecast from Greenpeace Energy (R)evolution scenario

Energy Balance of PV Systems

A common misconception about PV cells is that almost as much energy is used in their manufacture as they generate during their lifetime. This may have been true in the early days of PV, but a recent study (Alsema and Niewlaar 2000) found the energy payback time of PV modules, including frames and support structures, to be between two and five years in European conditions, and stated that with future improvements, this should reduce to one and a half to two years. The use of materials with low embodied energy (such as wood) in PV array support structures can also improve the overall energy payback time of PV systems.

Wind Power

When solar radiation enters the earth's atmosphere, because of the curvature of the earth, it warms different regions of the atmosphere to differing extents—most at the equator and least at the poles. Because air tends to flow from warmer to cooler regions, this causes what we call winds.

It is these air flows that are harnessed in windmills and wind turbines to produce power. Wind power, in the form of traditional windmills used for grinding corn or pumping water, has been in use for centuries. But in the past few decades, the use of wind turbines for electricity generation has been growing rapidly. This discussion will concentrate on modern, horizontal-axis wind turbines, installed on land and offshore.

It can be shown, using basic physical principles, that the power in a stream of flowing air—that is, in the wind—is proportional to the cube of the wind velocity. It can also be shown that the power produced by a wind turbine is proportional to the area swept by the blades, which for a conventional horizontal-axis turbine is proportional to the square of the rotor diameter.

A typical modern wind turbine starts producing power at wind speeds of around 5 meters per second (m/s). As wind speed increases, the power output increases steadily until it levels off at the rated power of the turbine, its maximum power output level. The wind speed at which it does this is called the "rated wind speed." The turbine is designed to continue producing power at this constant level at wind speeds above this rated level until it reaches an upper limit, the "shutdown wind speed." At this speed, the turbine is designed to stop rotating to avoid damage from excessive forces.

If a wind turbine could produce power continuously at its rated capacity for a year, its annual capacity factor would be 1.0. Clearly this is impossible, as the wind does not blow all the time. In practice, annual capacity factors range from about 0.2 to 0.4, depending on the frequency distribution and magnitude of the wind speeds at the site where a turbine is located.

European Wind Resources and Potential

A detailed study published by the European Environment Agency (EEA 2009) confirms that the wind energy resource available on land and offshore in the 27 European Union (EU) countries is enormous. The raw technical potential resource, excluding environmental and economic constraints, amounts to some 20 times Europe's projected electricity needs by 2020. As Table 2.3 shows, even when environmental and economic considerations are taken into account, the economically competitive potential, onshore and offshore, still amounts to three times the projected 2020 electricity demand and seven times that for 2030.

At the end of 2008, the EU's installed wind capacity was 65 GW, producing around 142 TWh of electricity, just over 4% of Europe's needs (EEA 2009). The EU has set a target to produce 20% of its primary energy from renewable sources by 2020, which will involve a substantial contribution from wind-generated electricity. Details of wind energy developments in Germany and Spain, the EU countries with the largest installed wind generating capacity, are discussed in Chapters 14 and 15.

U.S. Wind Capacity and Potential

According to the Global Wind Energy Council: "In 2008, the U.S. wind energy industry brought online over 8,500 megawatts (MW) of new wind power capacity, increasing the nation's cumulative total by 50% to over 25,300 MW. The new installations place the U.S. on a trajectory to generate 20% of the nation's electricity by 2030 from wind energy as long as the industry continues to garner long-term policy support" (GWEC 2009).

A U.S. Department of Energy study (NREL 2008) shows how the United States could rapidly expand its wind energy capacity to enable the achievement of this contribution. Regarding the economics of such a major expansion in capacity compared with a "No New Wind" scenario, it concluded:

Compared to other generation sources, the 20% Wind Scenario entails higher initial capital costs (to install wind capacity and associated transmission infrastructure) in many areas, yet offers lower ongoing energy costs than conventional power plants for operations, maintenance and fuel. Given the optimistic cost and performance assumptions of wind and conventional energy sources … the 20% Wind Scenario could require an incremental investment of as little as $43 billion NPV (Net Present Value) more than the

Table 2.3. Projected technically available, environmentally constrained, and economically competitive potential for wind energy in 27 EU countries in 2020 and 2030

		Year	TWh	Share of 2020 and 2030 demand[a]
Technical potential	Onshore	2020	45,000	11–13
	Onshore	2030	45,000	10–11
	Offshore	2020	25,000	6–7
	Offshore	2030	30,000	7
	Total	2020	70,000	17–20
	Total	2030	75,000	17–18
Constrained potential	Onshore	2020	39,000	10–11
	Onshore	2030	39,000	9
	Offshore	2020	2,800	0.7–0.8
	Offshore	2030	3,500	0.8
	Total	2020	41,800	10–12
	Total	2030	42,500	10
Economically competitive potential	Onshore[b]	2020	9,600	2–3
	Onshore[b]	2030	27,000	6
	Offshore	2020	2,600	0.6–0.7
	Offshore	2030	3,400	0.6–0.8
	Total	2020	12,200	3
	Total	2030	30,400	7

Source: EEA 2009
[a]European Commission projections for energy demand in 2020 and 2030 (European Commission 2008a, b) are based on two scenarios: "business as usual" (4,078 TWh in 2020 and 4,408 TWh in 2030) and "EC Proposal with RES trading" (3,537 TWh in 2020 and 4,279 TWh in 2030). The figures here represent the wind capacity relative to these two scenarios; e.g., onshore capacity of 45,000 TWh in 2020 is 11 to 12.7 times the size of projected demand.
[b]These figures do not exclude Natura 2000 areas

base-case No New Wind Scenario. This would represent less than 0.06 cent (6 one-hundredths of 1 cent) per kilowatt-hour of total generation by 2030, or roughly 50 cents per month per household. (NREL 2008)

The projections of the costs the Department of Energy made for its 20% Wind Scenario versus the No Wind Scenario, as described above, are shown in Figure 2.3.

World Wind Capacity and Potential

By the end of 2008, the total wind generating capacity installed worldwide was 120 GW. During 2008, about 27 GW of capacity was installed, valued at some $36 billion, and the average cumulative capacity growth rate during the preceding

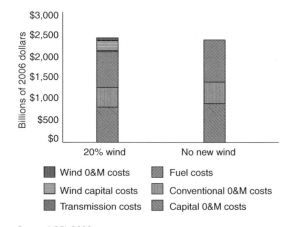

Source: NREL 2008

Figure 2.3. Incremental investment costs of a 20% wind contribution to U.S. electricity demand in 2030

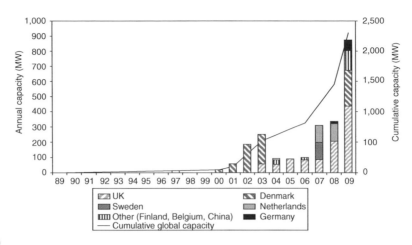

Source: BWEA 2009

Figure 2.4. Annual offshore wind capacity buildup in the United Kingdom, Sweden, Denmark, the Netherlands, and Germany, plus total cumulative installed capacity, 1989–2009

decade was 30% per annum. The wind industry now employs some 400,000 people worldwide (GWEC 2009).

According to a major study by the GWEC called Wind Force 12, by 2020, the world wind industry could be providing some 3,054 TWh of electricity, around 12% of world demand. This would involve an installation rate of about 158 GW per annum, culminating in a total installed capacity of 1,254 GW by 2020. The investment required would be approximately €80 billion ($109 billion) per annum, involving the creation of 2.3 million job-years of employment. The study estimates that the generation cost of electricity from wind in 2020 could reduce to 2.45 euro cents (U.S. 3.34 cents) per kWh (GWEC 2009). This may appear to be a best-case scenario but cost reductions of this order could be feasible, given the economies achievable through very large-scale production coupled with increases in turbine size and further improvements in turbine technologies.

Offshore Wind

Figure 2.4 shows the recent buildup of offshore wind generating capacity in Europe. Initially Denmark was the leading country, but since 2008 the United Kingdom has taken the lead, with some 1,000 MW installed by 2009. The United Kingdom has ambitious plans to install up to 29 GW of offshore capacity by 2020, though this may be constrained (Carbon Trust 2008; DECC 2009).

Wave Power

When winds blow over the world's oceans, they cause waves. The power in such waves as they gradually build up over very long distances can be great, as anyone watching that power eventually being dissipated on a beach will appreciate. A wide variety of technologies for harnessing the power of waves have been developed over the past few decades (see Duckers 2004). One example is the oscillating water column (OWC). Here the rise and fall of the waves inside an enclosed chamber alternately blows and sucks air through an air turbine, which is coupled to a generator to produce electricity. Another promising wave energy conversion system, currently undergoing tests off Portugal, is the Pelamis (sea snake), developed by the Scottish company Ocean Power Delivery. It is oriented head-on to the wave front and consists of a series of long, floating steel tubes connected by articulating hydraulic joints. The varying pressure in the hydraulic joints, as the passing waves move the cylinders relative to one another, powers hydraulic motors, which in turn drive electrical generators.

Biofuel

Since prehistoric times, human beings have harnessed the power of fire by burning wood to create warmth and light and to cook food. Wood is created by photosynthesis in the leaves of plants. Photosynthesis is a process powered by solar energy, in which atmospheric carbon dioxide and water are converted into carbohydrates (compounds of carbon, oxygen, and hydrogen) in the plant's leaves and stems. These, in the form of wood or other biomass, can be used as fuels—called "biofuels."

Wood is still widely used as a fuel in many parts of the developing world. In some countries, other biofuels, such as animal dung, are also used. These traditional biofuels are estimated to supply around 11% of world primary energy. If the forests that provide wood fuel are replanted at the same rate as they are cut down, then wood fuel use is in principle renewable. When forests are managed sustainably in this way, the CO_2 absorbed in growing replacement trees should equal the CO_2 given off when the original trees are burned.

A significant contribution to supplies now comes from modern bioenergy power plants. These feature the clean, high-efficiency combustion of straw, forestry wastes, or wood chips from trees grown in special plantations. The heat produced is used either directly or for electricity generation, and often for both purposes. Municipal wastes, a large proportion of which are biological in origin, are also widely used for heat or electricity production. Liquid wastes can also be processed in anaerobic digesters to produce methane, which can then fuel an internal combustion engine to produce electricity and heat. As a recent IEA report observes:

> *Technologies for producing heat and power from biomass are already well-developed and fully commercialised, as are first-generation routes to biofuels for transport. A wide range of additional conversion technologies are under development, offering prospects of improved efficiencies, lower costs and improved environmental performance. However, expansion of bioenergy also poses some challenges. The potential competition for land and for raw material with other biomass uses must be carefully managed. The productivity of food and biomass feedstocks needs to be increased by improved agricultural practices. Bioenergy must become increasingly competitive with other energy sources. Logistics and infrastructure issues must be addressed, and there is need for further technological innovation leading to more efficient and cleaner conversion of a more diverse range of feedstocks.* (IEA 2009, 2)

Hydroelectricity

Another energy source that has been harnessed by humanity for many centuries is the power of flowing water, which has been used for milling corn, pumping, and driving machinery. The original source of hydroelectric power is solar energy, which warms the world's oceans, causing water to evaporate from them. In the atmosphere, this forms clouds of moisture, which eventually falls back to earth in the form of precipitation. Rain flows down through mountains into streams and rivers, where its flow can be harnessed using water wheels or turbines to generate power. During the 20th century, hydropower has grown to become one of the world's principal electricity sources. In 2008, it contributed just over 6% of world primary energy (BP 2009).

Tidal Power

The physical principles underlying tidal energy are different from those underlying hydropower, but the technologies used in tidal "barrages" are similar to those employed in hydroelectric plants. Tides are caused chiefly by the gravitational pull of the moon on the oceans, although the sun's gravity also plays a minor role. The output from tidal energy systems is variable but highly predictable.

The principal technology for harnessing tidal energy essentially involves building a low dam, or barrage, across the estuary of a suitable river. The barrage includes inlets that allow the rising sea levels to build up behind it. When the tide has reached maximum height, the inlets are closed, and the impounded water is allowed to flow back to the sea in a controlled manner, via a turbine-generator system similar to that used in hydroelectric schemes.

The world's largest tidal energy scheme is at La Rance, France, with a capacity of 240 MW. There are a few other, smaller tidal plants in various countries, including Canada, Russia, and China. The United Kingdom has one of the world's best potential sites for a tidal energy scheme, in the Severn Estuary. If built, the largest of the various proposed Severn schemes would be rated at around 8,600 MW, much larger than any other single UK power plant, and could provide about 5% of current UK electricity demand (see DECC 2009; SDC 2007).

Another, newer tidal energy technology involves the use of underwater turbines, rather like submerged wind turbines, to harness the strong tidal and oceanic currents that flow in certain coastal regions. In the United Kingdom, a 10 kW prototype tidal current turbine was tested at Loch Linne, Scotland, in 1994; a larger, 300 kW prototype was tested off the Devon coast in 2002; and another 300 kW prototype is currently operational in Strangford Lough, Northern Ireland. The technology is still under development, but its prospects are promising.

Geothermal Energy

Geothermal energy is not derived from solar radiation. Its source is the earth's internal heat, which originates mainly from the decay of long-lived radioactive elements far below the surface. The most useful geothermal resources occur where underground bodies of water, or aquifers, can collect this heat, in areas where volcanic or tectonic activity brings it close to the surface. The resulting hot water, or in some cases steam, is used for electricity generation where its temperature is sufficiently high to make this feasible, such as in Italy, Iceland, New Zealand, the United States, and the Philippines, and for direct heating in many other countries.

If geothermal heat is extracted in a particular location at a rate that does not exceed the rate at which it is being replenished from deep within the earth, it is a renewable energy source. But in many cases, this is not so: the geothermal heat is in effect being "mined" and will be depleted locally in perhaps a few years or decades.

In regions of the world where geothermal aquifers are not readily accessible, it may nevertheless be possible to harness the earth's geothermal heat using enhanced geothermal, or "hot dry rock," technologies. These involve drilling down to considerable depths to access the hot rocks, then fracturing them using high-pressure water. This creates a form of heat exchanger into which cold water from the surface can be pumped and from which hot water can be extracted for heating or electricity production. The EU currently has a pilot project to develop this technique at Soulz, France (Dettmer 2009).

Costs and Economics of Renewables

The cost of energy generated by an energy source can be considered to be composed of three main elements: the capital costs, operation and maintenance (O&M) costs, and fuel costs. In the case of most renewable energy sources, the "fuel" is free (except for biofuels, which need to be grown and harvested), so the main cost elements are the capital and O&M costs.

The capital cost of a renewable energy plant is normally repaid over a period of years (often shorter than the plant lifetime), and interest is charged to give the capital provider a satisfactory rate of return on the investment. Private investors usually expect a higher rate of return and repayment over a shorter period than do public sector investors. To these regular repayments of capital costs, plus interest, must be added the O&M costs, which vary widely among different types of plant, to arrive at the total annual cost of operating the plant. This can then be divided by the annual energy output (say, in kWh) to give an average production cost of energy from the plant (say, in cents per kWh). However, this is not usually the cost paid by the final energy customer. The final retail price will include the costs of distribution

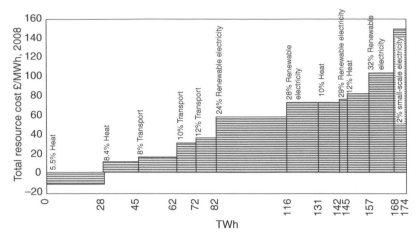

Sources: UK Department of Energy and Climate Change (DECC) and Department for Transport (DfT) internal analysis, based on Redpoint/ Trilemma 2009; NERA/AEA 2009; and Element/Pöyry 2009

Figure 2.5. Marginal resource costs for different levels of renewable generation by sector in the United Kingdom in 2020

and marketing, plus the profits made by the various intermediaries in the distribution chain from producer to consumer.

Calculations of the estimated future capital costs of renewable energy plant, or of the energy they generate, are often adjusted for the effects of inflation and are thus expressed in terms of costs or prices in a given year—for example, in 2009$. In a world of floating exchange rates, if cost calculations involve a conversion from one currency to another, they will be valid for only a limited time. In calculating the future capital costs of renewable energy equipment produced in substantial quantities, such as wind turbines or solar PV panels, analysts often assume that a reduction in unit costs will occur in the future as a result of the economies gained through volume production— sometimes called the "learning curve" effect.

It will be obvious from the above considerations that the wide variety of ways in which costs and prices can be calculated can give rise to confusion.

Resource-Cost Curves for Renewables

An insight into the likely costs of electricity from renewable sources can be gained by examining resource-cost curves. These show the quantity of the resource estimated to be available from selected renewables at various levels of cost. Figure 2.5 is a recent example (DECC 2009). This chart covers costs for heat and transport fuel, as well as for electricity. From this figure, it can be seen that 25% of UK electricity could be produced from renewables by 2020 for approximately £60 ($90) per MWh. Producing 28% of electricity from renewables would increase this to about £70 ($105) per MWh, and further increasing the proportion to 32% would cost around £100 ($150) per MWh.

The bar at the far right in the figure shows the cost of supplying 2% of electricity from small-scale renewable sources, estimated at about £150 ($225) per MWh. The price of electricity generation from small-scale sources varies widely, as can be seen from Table 2.4, which shows the prices proposed under new feed-in tariffs for small- and medium-scale electricity generation (under 5 MW) in the United Kingdom from 2010. The highest price is for domestic-scale photovoltaics under 4 kW, at 36.5 pence (54.8 cents) per kWh; the lowest is for medium-scale biomass, hydro, and wind plants, at 4.5 pence (6.8 cents) per kWh. These tariffs are designed to provide a reasonable rate of return to investors in the various

Table 2.4. Prices paid under proposed UK feed-in tariffs for electricity from 2010 and annual digression rates from 2010 onward

Technology	Scale	Proposed initial tariff (p/kWh)	Annual digression (%)
Anaerobic digestion	Electricity only	9.0	0
Anaerobic digestion	CHP	11.5	0
Biomass	< 50 kW	9.0	0
Biomass	50 kW–5 MW	4.5	0
Biomass	CHP	9.0	0
Hydro	< 10 kW	17.0	0
Hydro	10–100 kW	12.0	0
Hydro	100 kW–1 MW	8.5	0
Hydro	1–5 MW	4.5	0
PV	< 4 kW (new build)	31.0	7
PV	< 4 kW (retrofit)	36.5	7
PV	4–10 kW	31.0	7
PV	10–100 kW	28.0	7
PV	100 kW–5 MW	26.0	7
PV	Stand-alone system	26.0	7
Wind	< 1.5 kW	30.5	4
Wind	1.5–15 kW	23.0	3
Wind	15–50 kW	20.5	3
Wind	50–250 kW	18.0	0
Wind	250–500 kW	16.0	0
Wind	500 kW–5 MW	4.5	0
Existing microgenerators transferred from renewables obligation		9.0	N/A

Source: DECC 2009
Note: p/kWh = pence per kilowatt-hour; 1 pence = 1.5 cents (U.S.) as of this writing

technologies and should therefore give a reasonably good indication of the current costs/prices of electricity from small- to medium-scale plants in UK conditions.

The "Portfolio Effect" and the Economics of Renewables

Proponents of wind power and other forms of renewable energy have recently been pointing out that because their "fuel" is free, this has a significant effect on their economics—one that is not usually taken into account in conventional analyses. When wind electricity, for example, is available to the grid, its effective marginal cost to the electricity system is near zero; thus it should dis-

place more costly power from conventional plants. When wind power is contributing significant quantities of energy, it can also reduce the spot price of fossil fuels. Because it requires no fuel, wind energy if used significantly also reduces a nation's vulnerability to imported fossil-fuel price increases, with beneficial effects on GDP, and because of its fixed cost, it reduces the system risk in a nation's generation portfolio. (For further details, see Auwerbuch 2009; Bruce 2009).

Some of the key economic and technological characteristics of the renewable electricity generating technologies described above are summarized in Table 2.5: their cost drivers (the relative roles of capital, O&M, and fuel costs); their levels of maturity; the potential for scale economies; and

Table 2.5. Summary of economic characteristics of renewable electricity generation technologies

Technology	Cost drivers	Maturity level	Potential for scale economies	Potential for near-term technological advances
Solar ponds	Capital, O&M	High	Low	Low
Ocean thermal	Capital, O&M	Med	Med	Med
Solar chimney	Capital	Low	Med	Low
Concentrating solar: trough	Capital, O&M	Med	Med	Med
Concentrating solar: power tower	Capital, O&M	Med	Med	Med
Concentrating solar: dish Stirling	Capital, O&M	Med	High	Med
PV: crystalline	Capital	Med	High	Med
PV: thin film	Capital	Med	High	High
Concentrating PV	Capital, O&M	Med	Med	Med
Wind onshore	Capital	High	Med	Low
Wind offshore	Capital, O&M	Med	Med	Med
Wave	Capital, O&M	Low	Med	Med
Hydro (large)	Capital	High	Low	Low
Biofuel electricity	Capital, O&M, fuel	High?	Med	Med
Tidal barrage	Capital	High	Low	Low
Tidal stream	Capital, O&M	Low	Med	Med
Geo aquifers	Capital	High	Low	Low
Geo HDR	Capital	Low	Low	Med

Source: Author's estimates

the potential for near-term technological advances. The factors that are likely to lead to reductions in the cost of electricity from renewables vary widely among technologies: in some areas, significant potential exists for technological breakthroughs that could result in major cost reductions; in other, more mature areas, steady incremental improvements will gradually reduce costs. In addition, many renewable technologies benefit from economies of scale, including the economies of physical scale, such as those achievable from building larger wind turbines, and the economies of series production, which are achievable irrespective of physical scale.

Integration of Renewables into Electricity Systems

Some renewable electricity sources, such as bioenergy, hydroelectricity, and geothermal power, are dispatchable—in other words, like conventional power plants, their output can, within limits, normally be made available quickly to electricity system operators in response to demand. The outputs of other renewables, such as those based on wind, wave, and solar power, are not so readily dispatchable: they are weather-dependent and therefore variable—unless they incorporate storage, as is the case with some solar thermal-electric systems. Wind, wave, and solar power are sometimes described as intermittent, but a more accurate term for their output is variable. Tidal power is in an intermediate category: its output, though variable, is highly predictable.

But the variability of these renewable sources is not the major problem that some have suggested. National electricity systems are already designed to cope with the major fluctuations in both demand and supply that occur on various timescales, from minutes to years. Introducing a variable renewable source introduces an additional element of uncertainty into the system, but this is manageable by system operators in a manner similar to the way in which the uncertainty in both demand and conventional supplies is already managed. With low levels of penetration of variable renewables on the system, the additional level of uncertainty is small; it becomes larger as the penetration level increases.

For simplicity, this discussion will concentrate on the integration of *wind* power into electricity systems; the integration of other renewables, such as solar and wave power, is amenable to similar solutions. The topic of renewable electricity integration is covered in much greater detail in Boyle (2007).

In existing national electricity systems, various kinds of backup power supplies are already provided. In essence, these consist of short- and long-term supplies. Short-term backup supplies are provided to maintain frequency and voltage stability on the network. These include fossil-fueled spinning reserve plants, operating at below their rated power but able to increase output at very short notice; hydropower plants, including pumped storage schemes, the output of which can be made available quickly; and large diesel or gas turbine generators, which are able to be brought online within a few minutes.

Long-term backup supplies are those required to ensure security of supply in the event of major disruptions, such as the simultaneous failure of several large power stations. They include older fossil-fueled plants, usually less efficient than modern plants and therefore infrequently used, that can be brought back into operation if necessary within a few hours or days. In addition, many national systems have interconnectors to the electricity systems of nearby countries; these can be called on to provide additional power if needed.

How much would the additional backup supplies needed for substantial levels of wind contribution cost? A recent UK Energy Research Centre study (UKERC 2006) reviewed a wide range of evidence from around the world and concluded that for a 10% to 20% contribution of wind to the UK system, the additional cost would be £2.5 to £3 ($3.76 to $4.50) per MWh, rising to £3 to £3.5 ($4.50 to $5.26) per MWh for a 20% to 45%

wind contribution. These costs are relatively small in relation to total generation costs.

Wind Forecasting

The cost of providing additional backup to cope with the additional variability of substantial quantities of wind generation can be significantly reduced through the use of wind forecasting methods. Figure 2.6 shows an example of a day-ahead wind forecast for one month in Germany, using techniques developed at the University of Kassel. These employ a combination of techniques: numerical weather predictions; analysis of physical processes; statistical time series analysis; and learning techniques based on artificial neural networks (Lange et al 2007). As can be seen, the difference between forecast and monitored power output is relatively small. This enables backup plants to be scheduled efficiently and at minimum cost.

Storage

It is often asserted that energy storage is needed to cope with the variability of wind power and other fluctuating renewable energy sources, though this is not necessarily the case. Various large-scale storage technologies are available, ranging from pumped hydro schemes to compressed-air storage to vanadium redox (reduction-oxidation) battery storage, but their costs are high. However, electricity storage in large, integrated national electricity supply systems is desirable only if it costs less than providing more conventional backup supplies—or if storage can provide additional benefits to the system operator or to users, as may be the case with battery storage in electric vehicles.

Electricity storage in electric vehicle (EV) batteries may become increasingly attractive as such vehicles enter widespread use in order to reduce urban air pollution and emissions of greenhouse gases. EV batteries would be charged mainly at night, when electricity systems normally have spare capacity, and could readily absorb any surpluses of power from wind or other renewables. The batteries would be discharged

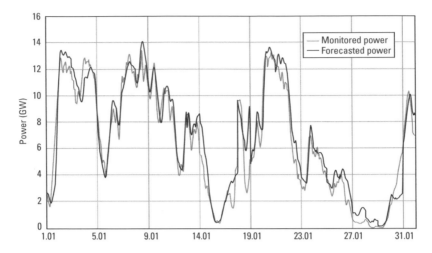

Source: Lange et al (2007)

Figure 2.6 Day-ahead forecast of wind power output compared with monitored output, for one month in Germany

when the vehicles are driven during the day, which should not make substantial demands on the electricity system, though some daytime charging would be inevitable.

Intercontinental Integration of Renewable Electricity: The European Supergrid and Desertec

The large-scale spatial dispersion of wind generation can markedly reduce the variability of the resource. The European supergrid is a proposal to create an electrical network linking large offshore wind farms in high-wind regions of Europe to neighboring countries and beyond. The links would use high-voltage direct current (HVDC) technology, which enables power to be transmitted over long distances with low losses. At the point of connection to a country's electricity network, the power would be converted to conventional alternating current (AC).

The proponents of the supergrid claim it is cheaper to generate electricity in high-wind areas and transmit it to the countries where it is needed than to generate it at lower-wind sites in areas with poorer resources. They also point out that a supergrid would facilitate a Europe-wide market for electricity (Hurley et al 2007). The govern-

ments of Germany, France, Belgium, the Netherlands, Luxembourg, Denmark, Sweden, Ireland, and the United Kingdom are developing plans, to be announced at the end of 2010, to build the first phase of the supergrid in the North Sea region.

Even greater smoothing effects may be achievable if wind power sources can be integrated over a still larger area. Gregor Czisch of the University of Kassel has modeled a series of detailed scenarios in which he has combined the monthly wind power production of good wind sites in the EU and Norway with sites in Northern Russia, western Siberia, southern Morocco, and Mauritania. When the combined output is compared with the average monthly electricity demand in the EU and Norway, supply and demand are quite well matched, except for a small shortfall around September–October (see Czisch 2006; Murray 2009).

A similarly ambitious proposal, the Desertec Industrial Initiative, has been put forward by the Trans-Mediterranean Renewable Energy Cooperation (TREC) and German Aerospace Center (DLR). The proposal, backed by 12 major European companies including Munich Re, the world's largest reinsurance company, involves linking a wide range of renewable electricity sources right across Europe, the Middle East, and

North Africa (EUMENA), again using HVDC links to minimize power losses in long-distance electricity transmission. The system would eventually combine the outputs of wind, biofuel, hydro, concentrating solar, photovoltaic, and geothermal power plants. The combined output would be sufficient to meet the total electricity needs of the entire area (see Desertec 2009; D-MTEC 2009). These proposals have recently been endorsed in principle by the European Union in its Mediterranean Solar Plan (Ferrero-Waldner 2009).

Conclusions

Renewable sources are in principle capable of supplying all of humanity's energy requirements many times over. Many relatively new technologies for renewable electricity generation, such as solar and wind power, are maturing and growing rapidly. Some others, such as hydroelectricity, are already mature. Renewables are already making significant inputs into the electricity supplies of some countries and have the potential to provide much more power worldwide in coming decades—provided that appropriate policy support measures are implemented (for examples, see REN21 2007, 2009).

The current costs of power from renewables are often higher than from conventional sources, but the costs of the former are steadily falling and those of the latter are likely to rise. In addition, the costs of conventional fossil fuels do not take into account the external costs to society of their use, such as their contribution to global climate change. If all such costs were included, most renewable energy sources would already be cost-competitive (see Sovakool and Watts 2009). Moreover, substantial future cost reductions may occur for many renewables as a result of mass production and improvements in technology.

Note

1. The subject of renewable energy is covered in much greater detail in Boyle (2004).

References and Further Information

AEE (Spanish Wind Association). 2009. *Wind Power 2008: Sector's Yearbook, Analysis and Data*. Madrid: Spanish Wind Association.

Alsema, E.A., and E. Niewlaar. 2000. Energy Viability of Photovoltaic Systems. *Energy Policy* 28: 999–1010.

Auwerbuch, S. 2009. Value of Wind Compared to Gas Generation: A Risk-Adjusted Approach. In *The Economics of Wind Energy*, edited by Krohn, S., Morthorst, P.E., and Auwerbuch, S. Brussels: European Wind Energy Association, 115–122, Section 5.1.

Blake, W. 1790. *The Marriage of Heaven and Hell*. Various editions: electronic edition available at www.gailgastfield.com/mhh/mhh.html (accessed 24 March 2010).

BMU (Federal Ministry for the Environment, Nature Conservation and Nuclear Safety). 2009a. *Development of Electricity Generation from Renewable Energy*. Bonn, Germany: BMU.

———. 2009b. *Renewable Energy Sources in Figures: Status, June 2008*. Bonn, Germany: BMU.

Boyle, G., ed. 2004. *Renewable Energy: Power for a Sustainable Future*. 2nd ed. Oxford. Oxford University Press.

———. 2007. *Renewable Electricity and the Grid: The Challenge of Variability*. London: Earthscan.

BP (British Petroleum). 2009. *BP Statistical Review of World Energy, June 2009*. London: BP.

Bruce, A. 2009. The Value of Wind: How More Renewables Means Lower Electricity Bills. *Real Power* (April–June): 9–11.

BWEA. 2009. *Offshore Wind: Staying on Track*. London: British Wind Energy, 8pp.

Carbon Trust. 2008. *Offshore Wind Power: Big Challenge, Big Opportunity*. London: Carbon Trust.

Czisch, G. 2006. *Least-Cost European/Transeuropean Electricity Supply Entirely with Renewable Energies*. Kassel, Germany: ISET.

DECC (Department of Energy and Climate Change). 2009. *Severn Tidal Power Consultation: Government Response*. London: DECC.

Desertec. 2009 12 Companies Plan Establishment of a Desertec Industrial Initiative. www.desertec.org/ (accessed January 15, 2010).

Dettmer, R. 2009. Return to Rock. *Engineering and Technology* 4 (16): 48–50.

D-MTEC (Department of Management, Technology and Economics). 2009. *The Vision of a Super Grid and*

Its Impact on the Market for Renewable Energy. Zurich: Swiss Federal Institute of Technology.

Duckers, L. 2004. Wave Energy. In *Renewable Energy: Power for a Sustainable Future*, 2nd ed., edited by G. Boyle. Oxford: Oxford University Press, 298–340.

EEA (European Environment Agency). 2009. *Europe's Onshore and Offshore Wind Energy Potential: An Assessment of Environmental and Economic Constraints.* Technical report 6/2009. Copenhagen: EEA.

Element/Pöyry. 2009. *Design of a Feed-In Target for Sub-5 MW Electricity in GB: Final Report.* London: Pöyry, 118pp.

EPIA (European Photovoltaic Industries Association). 2009. *Set for 2020: Executive Summary.* Brussels: EPIA.

EPIA/Greenpeace. 2008. *Solar Generation V—2008: Solar Electricity for Over One Billion People and Two Million Jobs by 2020.* Brussels: EPIA.

European Commission (EC). 2008a. *European Energy and Transport Trends to 2030 (update 2007).* http:// ec.europa.eu/dgs/energy_transport/figures/ trends_2030_update_2007/ energy_transport_trends_2030_update_2007_en.pdf

———. 2008b. *Model Based Analysis of the 2008 EU Policy Package on Climate Change and Renewables.* Brussels: Report to DG ENV.

Everett, R. 2004. Solar Thermal Energy. In *Renewable Energy: Power for a Sustainable Future*, 2nd ed., edited by G. Boyle. Oxford: Oxford University Press, 51.

EWEA (European Wind Energy Association). 2009. *Wind Energy: The Facts: Executive Summary.* Brussels: EWEA.

Ferrero-Waldner, B. 2009. The Mediterranean Solar Plan: A Necessity, Not an Option. Speech 09/60 by EU commissioner for External Relations and European Neighbourhood Policy, European Union Sustainable Energy Week, February 2009, Brussels.

Greenpeace. 2005. *Energy Revolution: A Sustainable Pathway to a Clean Energy Future for Europe.* Brussels, Greenpeace International.

GWEC (Global Wind Energy Council). 2009. *Global Wind 2008 Report.* Brussels: GWEC.

Hopwood, D. 2009. The New Hot Ticket. *Engineering and Technology* 15 (Sept. 12–25): 48–51.

Hurley, B. Hughes, P. and Giebel, G. 2007. Reliable Power, Wind Variability and Offshore Grids in Europe. In *Renewable Electricity and the Grid: The Challenge of Variability*, edited by G. Boyle. London: Earthscan, 181–199.

IEA (International Energy Agency). 2002. *Renewable Energy: Into the Mainstream.* Paris: IEA.

———. 2008. *Trends in Photovoltaic Applications: Survey Report of Selected IEA Countries between 1992 and 2007.* Paris: IEA.

———. 2009. *Bioenergy—A Sustainable and Reliable Energy Source: A review of Status and Prospects, Executive Summary.* Paris: IEA.

James, T. 2009. Energy from the Deep. *Engineering and Technology* 4 (14): 50–53.

Knies, G., Timm, G., Führ, F., Wolff, G., Schön, M., Straub, M., Nokraschy, H. and Steinmetz, O. (eds). 2009. *An Overview of the DESERTEC Concept.* DESERTEC Red Paper. Berlin: DESERTEC Foundation.

Kurokawa, K., Komoto, K., van der Vleuten, P. and Faiman, D. (eds). 2007. *Energy from the Desert.* London: Earthscan/International Energy Agency.

Lange, B., Rohrig, K., Schlögl, F., Cali, U. and Jursa, R. 2007. Wind Power Forecasting. In *Renewable Electricity and the Grid: The Challenge of Variability*, edited by G. Boyle. London: Earthscan, 95–120.

Lockheed Martin. No date. Ocean Thermal Energy Conversion (OTEC). www.lockheedmartin.com/ products/OTEC/ (accessed 26 March 2010).

Marsh, G. 2009. Power Stations: Can Solar Join the Big Hitters? *Renewable Energy Focus*, (May–June): 50–58.

Murray, J. 2009. Wind Holds Key to European Super Grid. Interview with Dr Gregor Czisch. *Real Power* 18 (Oct.—Dec.): 31–32.

NERA/AEA (NERA Economic Consulting/AEA Technology). 2009. *The UK Supply Curve for Renewable Heat.* Report for the Department of Energy and Climate Change, July 2009, Ref: URN 09D/689 (DECC). London: NERA Economic Consulting.

NREL (National Renewable Energy Laboratory). 2008. *20% Wind Energy by 2030.* NREL Report DOE/GO-102008–2567, July. National Renewable Energy Laboratory.

Redpoint/Trilemma. 2009. *Implementation of the EU 2020 Renewables Target in the UK Electricity Sector: RO Reform.* Report for the Department of Energy and Climate Change, June 2009, URN 09D/702. London: Redpoint Energy Ltd.

REN21 (Renewable Energy Policy Network for the 21st Century). 2007. *Renewables Global Status Report.* Paris: REN21.

———. 2009. *Renewables Global Status Report: 2009 Update.* Paris: REN21.

Renew. 2009. CSP Moves Ahead to 3GW. *Renew* 180: 12.

Schlaich, J. 1995. *The Solar Chimney: Electricity from the Sun.* Stuttgart: Edition Axel Menges.

SDC (Sustainable Development Commission). 2007. *Turning the Tide: Tidal Power in the UK*. London: SDC.

Sovakool, B., and C. Watts. 2009. Going Completely Renewable: Is It Possible (Let Alone Desirable)? *Electricity Journal* 22 (4): 95–111.

Twidell, J., and A. Weir. 1986. *Renewable Energy Resources*. London: E & FN Spon.

UKERC (UK Energy Research Centre). 2006. *The Costs and Impacts of Intermittency*. London: UKERC.

Part II

Renewables, Climate Change, and Energy Policy

3

Renewables Forecasts in a Low-Carbon World: A Brief Overview

Erin T. Mansur

This chapter examines how concerns for climate—coupled with policymakers' and voters' other preferences—are expected to affect the growth of renewables, particularly in the United States and European Union (EU). It begins with a review of the recent growth in renewables and a discussion of current carbon policies, then looks at predictions of levels of investment in renewables in a low-carbon world. Within the next 20 years, some authors predict that 20% to 40% of electricity will come from renewable resources, in an attempt to mitigate the impacts of climate change. Given the wide range of assumptions regarding carbon policies, economic growth, the responsiveness of the economy to carbon policy, innovation in renewables, and other modeling approaches, it is hard to generalize among these "black box" models. Their complexity and continuous updating make a detailed peer review process necessary, though this is beyond the scope of this chapter.

Under continued dependence on fossil fuels in a business-as-usual scenario, climate scientists predict significant increases in average temperature and sea level, as well as many other climatic responses. Climate change is expected to adversely affect many economic sectors, including agriculture, forestry, insurance, health, tourism, and energy. Furthermore, it is likely to have many notable nonmarket effects, such as the loss of flora and fauna and an increase in human morbidity and mortality. The Intergovernmental Panel on Climate Change (IPCC 2007) and Stern (2006) review the science and economic consequences of climate change.

These concerns may be addressed through several mechanisms for mitigating climate change. Broadly, we may change how we produce and use electricity, space heating, transportation, and other energy applications; we may sequester greenhouse gases (for example, by reducing deforestation or increasing reforestation); or we may even consider climate geoengineering.[1] Within the electricity sector, methods for reducing greenhouse gases, such as carbon dioxide (CO_2), include both demand-side (conservation and energy efficiency) and supply-side options. Supply options include switching from coal to less carbon-intensive conventional technologies such as natural gas, large hydroelectric, and nuclear power; continuing to use coal but reducing the carbon emissions with abatement technologies such as carbon capture and storage (CCS); or, the focus of this book, turning to alternative renewable sources of electricity, including wind, solar, geothermal, and small hydropower.

From an economic perspective, greenhouse gases are global, stock externalities. (Chapter 5 covers this topic in more depth.) In brief, an externality is a cost (or benefit) incurred by others not involved in a market transaction. Global externalities are those where the location of the source of the pollutant is irrelevant to the damages. For example, a coal-fired power plant in China may be the source of released carbon dioxide emissions, but the effects of these emissions will be experienced all over the world. Furthermore, these effects will be the same as had the carbon dioxide emissions come from natural gas power plants in, say, England. Stock pollutants are long-lived, and their damages from current emissions may continue for years to come. For example, carbon dioxide emitted today will remain in the upper atmosphere for 100 years or more (IPCC 2007).[2] For stock pollutants, the optimal policy is clear in theory: each ton of emissions released is charged the net present value of all future damages that it causes.[3] Specifically, a pollution tax can achieve the efficient outcome. A cap-and-trade regulation can also be efficient if the permit price equals this tax.

A pollution tax on greenhouse gases would give firms and consumers an incentive to change behavior in many ways: switching to less carbon-intensive technologies, conserving electricity, driving less, and so forth. Firms investing in renewables would be just one of many responses. Are renewables the best option for addressing climate change? In order to answer this question, one would need to know the relative marginal costs, both private and external, incurred by each option that reduces greenhouse gas emissions.

Whether or not producing electricity from renewable resources is the cheapest way to reduce greenhouse gas emissions, many government agencies and other authors predict that renewables will be a major contributor to a low-carbon future. Investing in renewables is a popular response to climate concerns, in part, perhaps, because of the other externalities that it addresses. First, other energy sources have additional negative externalities such as conventional air pollution, water pollution, and nuclear waste. Note that if regulation results in marginal social costs equaling marginal social benefits of these other energy sources, these externalities will be inter-nalized and no further regulation is required. Second, positive technological spillovers may result from investing in renewables from which other industries, or firms in the same industry, benefit.[4] Learning benefits within a firm, which may account for the largest gains, are not positive externalities. Finally, subsidizing technology is seemingly more politically palatable than taxing firms and consumers for polluting.

This chapter provides an overview of current electricity sources and energy and climate policies affecting the recent growth in investment in renewables, then looks at the direction of future carbon policies. This is followed by a review of the literature on predictions of investment in renewables under various low-carbon scenarios.

Current Energy Sources

Electricity production is dominated by fossil fuels. In the United States, coal accounts for more than 50% of electricity production, and natural gas accounts for another 20% (EIA 2009b). Conventional carbon-free technologies include nuclear power, which produces 20% of U.S. electricity, and hydroelectric power, which provides 6%. The European Union is less dependent on fossil fuels: here, only 54% of power comes from coal, oil, or natural gas (Eurostat 2009). Nuclear (28%) and hydropower (10%) are larger in the EU than in the United States.

Nonhydropower renewables, such as wind, solar, geothermal, tidal, and biomass, account for less than 7% of electricity produced in either the United States or the EU. In 2008, the United States produced 4,111 terawatt-hours (TWh) of electricity.[5] Of that, only 3% of was from nonhydropower renewables, including wind (52 TWh), wood (39 TWh), and other renewable sources (33 TWh) (EIA 2009b). In 2007, the European Union (EU-27) produced 6.5% of its electricity from wind (104 TWh), wood (52 TWh), and other renewables (55 TWh) (Eurostat 2009). Although the United States produces over 20% more total electricity than the EU, the European Union produced more power from renewable sources than did the United States.

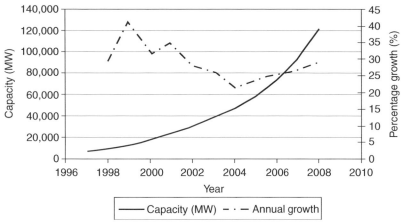

Source: WWEA 2009

Figure 3.1. Wind power worldwide capacity and annual growth rate, 1997–2008 (in MW)

While renewables are still a small share of total electricity production, they have seen enormous growth in the past two decades. In 1990, the Organisation for Economic Co-operation and Development (OECD) countries had a total capacity of 2.4 gigawatts (GW) of wind power and 0.5 GW of solar, including both photovoltaics (PV) and thermal (IEA 2004).[6] By 2008, however, wind capacity had reached 17 GW in Spain alone (WWEA 2009). Table 3.1 reports installed wind capacity for the 10 countries with the most wind capacity as well as worldwide totals for 2007 and 2008.

Worldwide, wind capacity reached 121 GW in 2008, an increase of 29% over the previous year (WWEA 2009). This annual growth rate is typical of this industry over the past decade. Figure 3.1 plots annual worldwide capacity and growth rate from 1997 to 2008.

Table 3.1. Total installed capacity of wind energy in 2007 and 2008 (in GW)

Country	2007	2008	Change	Growth rate
U.S.	16.8	25.2	8.4	50%
Germany	22.2	23.9	1.7	7%
Spain	15.1	16.7	1.6	11%
China	5.9	12.2	6.3	107%
India	7.9	9.6	1.7	22%
Italy	2.7	3.7	1.0	37%
France	2.5	3.4	0.9	39%
UK	2.4	3.3	0.9	38%
Denmark	3.1	3.2	0.0	1%
Portugal	2.1	2.9	0.7	34%
Rest of world	13.1	17.1	4.0	30%
Total	93.9	121.2	27.3	29%

Source: WWEA 2009

This impressive growth rate has also been exhibited in other renewables as well. As recently as 2003, worldwide capacity in solar PV was only 1.3 GW, but as of 2008, it had reached 13 GW. This tenfold increase can be attributed primarily to Germany and Spain, which account for two-thirds of the world's solar PV capacity. Overall, total renewables (excluding large hydropower) are now at 280 GW (REN21 2009). Table 3.2 reports the capacity of various renewable resources by country.

Historically, the two major impediments to renewables have been costs and intermittency. The cost of wind power has dropped substantially over the past decade (IEA 2004). Now, with the production tax credit (discussed below), wind power costs less than 5 cents per kWh in the United States and can compete with the cost of building new fossil-fuel-fired power plants (Wiser and Bolinger 2008). Photovoltaic solar power is an order of magnitude more expensive: the average installed cost (excluding direct financial incentives or tax credits) in 2007 was $7.60 per watt in the United States (Wiser et al. 2009), or about 30 to 50 cents per kWh, depending on the interest rate and capacity factor. These costs have fallen substantially over the past few decades. Even from summer 2008 to summer 2009, they fell another 40% with the entry of China into the market

(Galbraith 2009). Although dramatically cheaper than in the past, solar PV remains an expensive option for addressing climate change (Borenstein 2008). In comparison, the average installed cost of wind in 2007 was $1.70 per watt in the United States (Wiser and Bolinger 2008). The IPCC (2007) projects that the costs of renewables will continue to fall, and that by 2030, renewables (including wind, solar PV, and biomass) will see capital costs under $1.20 per watt. (See Chapter 2 for further discussion on renewable technologies and their costs.)

Recent Renewables and Climate Policy

The United States has been setting policies to promote investment in renewables for more than three decades. In 1978, the Public Utility Regulatory Policies Act first provided subsidies for investing in renewables. In some states, such as California, this led to substantial investments. (For a review of the history of U.S. renewables policies, see Chapter 11 of this book, as well as Martinot et al. 2005.)

The growth in U.S. renewables has been driven mainly by federal tax credit incentives.

Table 3.2. Capacity of renewable resources by type and country in 2008 (in GW)

	World	Developing countries	EU-27	China	U.S.	Germany	Spain	India	Japan
Wind	121	24	65	12.2	25.2	23.9	16.8	9.6	1.9
Small hydropower	85	65	12	60	3	1.7	1.8	2	3.5
Biomass	52	25	15	3.6	8	3	0.4	1.5	0.1
Solar PV	13	0.1	9.5	0.1	0.7	5.4	3.3	0	2
Geothermal	10	4.8	0.8	0	3	0	0	0	0.5
Solar thermal	0.5	0	0.1	0	0.4	0	0.1	0	0
Ocean (tidal)	0.3	0	0.3	0	0	0	0	0	0
Total renewables[a]	280	119	96	76	40	34	22	13	8

Source: REN21 2009
[a]Excluding large hydropower

With the passage of the American Recovery and Reinvestment Act of 2009 (ARRA; see U.S. Congress 2009), wind, small hydropower, geothermal, biomass, municipal solid waste, and marine energy sources may be eligible to earn a subsidy of $21/MWh under the production tax credit (PTC). Many of these renewable resources can forgo the PTC and become eligible for the 30% investment tax credit (ITC).[7] As a third option, a Department of Treasury cash grant can be selected in place of the PTC or ITC. Metcalf (2009b) provides greater detail on the tax incentives for renewables. U.S. wind investment is quite elastic to changes in the user cost of capital (Metcalf 2009a): the federal PTC has been a substantial driver of wind investment over the past two decades. How these incentives are expected to affect renewable investment is addressed in the next section.

A second major driver of renewable investment in the United States is the set of state-level renewable portfolio standards (RPSs, discussed in Chapter 11). To date, 28 states and the District of Columbia have implemented mandatory programs that require utilities to purchase a certain percentage of their power from renewable sources; the definition of the technologies that

comply with the regulation differs from state to state (see DSIRE 2009). Markets for renewable energy credits (RECs), or green tags, have arisen within some states. These allow firms to comply with the regulations by either directly investing in renewables or buying credits from other compliant sources.

In Europe, some countries have chosen renewable standards as a policy instrument to achieve the targets in the Renewable Electricity Directive (2001/77/EC). As in many U.S. REC markets, several European countries have implemented tradable certificates in order to reach these goals (European Commission 2009; Nielsen and Jeppesen 2003). Figure 3.2 reports the share of renewable electricity by country for large hydropower and other renewables in 2007. Notably, over half the electricity generated in Sweden is from large-scale hydropower or other renewables, and more than a quarter of Denmark's power is from nonhydro renewables. The figure also shows the 2010 objectives. Although these targets are greater than the share of electricity generation from renewable resources in 2007 for many countries, some, such as Denmark, have just reached the target, and Germany and Hungary have even exceeded it.

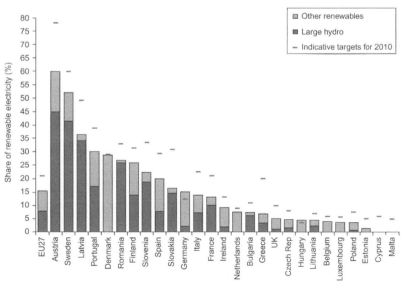

Source: Author's calculations based on European Commission 2009 and Eurostat 2009

Figure 3.2. Share of renewable electricity by EU country in 2007 and targets for 2010

In order to comply with these standards, many countries have used feed-in tariffs that have spurred investment in renewables. Many of these subsidies are on the order of hundreds of euros per MWh. For example, some solar power producers in Spain receive €340 ($463) per MWh under Real Decreto 1578/2008. In 2008, Germany's solar feed-in tariff was even greater: some solar producers received €574 ($782) per MWh under the Erneuerbare-Energien-Gesetz.[8] As a result, Spain and Germany have seen dramatic growth in renewable investments (see Tables 3.1 and 3.2). (Chapters 13 to 15 discuss the EU experience, focusing on the United Kingdom, Germany, and Spain.)

In addition to renewable standards and feed-in tariffs, the EU has implemented a multinational, multi-industry cap-and-trade policy for greenhouse gases. The EU Emission Trading System (ETS) began in 2005 and regulates about 2 billion metric tons of CO_2 each year. With permit prices fluctuating between €10 and €30 ($13 and $41) a ton, this market is valued at around €37 billion ($50 billion) per year.[9] (Chapter 6 further discusses emissions trading.)

In addition to costs, another major issue that renewable sources face is intermittency. Some renewable resources, such as wind and solar power, produce only some of the time and cannot be depended on to produce reliably. Intermittency will not be completely solved until a cheap, reliable mechanism of storing power is developed (NREL 2008). However, at a level of investment that is predicted over the next few decades (between 20% and 30% of electricity generation), geographic averaging and natural gas capacity that serves as backup reserve are likely to dampen the issue of intermittency. This may require new investment in natural gas power, especially in areas where renewables primarily produce off-peak (Campbell 2009). Complete dependence on current nonhydroelectric renewable technologies seems questionable, however, because of intermittency issues.[10]

A related issue concerns the development of grids. In the United States, many of the locations that have the most potential for renewables are far from population centers where electricity demand is greatest. Vajjhala et al. (2008) discuss how state RPSs would provide significantly different incentives for improving the transmission network than would a federal standard, which would allow for greater cost savings but would require more of a transmission build-out. State policies would be less cost-effective, as renewables would be built in many states that have high costs, but would require less investment in new transmission. (Chapters 7, 9, and 11 further discuss the important issues of intermittency and designing the transmission grid.)

Direction of Future Policy

Recently, carbon policy has become a central topic in both the United States and the EU. In the United States, while regional policies have been implemented in the Northeast, such as the Regional Greenhouse Gas Initiative (RGGI), or discussed in the West, such as California Assembly Bill 32 (AB 32), the focus has turned to a national cap-and-trade policy. In particular, Congress is considering the American Clean Energy and Security Act of 2009 (H.R. 2454), also known as the Waxman–Markey bill (U.S. House Committee 2009). If it were to pass, this bill would be the first U.S. national climate policy and would regulate multiple industries.[11] Its goal is to reduce greenhouse gas emissions by 17% of 2005 levels by 2020 and over 80% of 2005 levels by 2050, mainly through a national cap-and-trade system.

In addition to the tradable permit system, the Waxman–Markey bill contains a renewable electricity standard (RES) that would require that 15% of electricity purchased in the United States come from renewable resources (including solar, wind, biomass, landfill gas, and geothermal) by 2020.[12] This is in line with the White House agenda of 10% renewables by 2012 and 25% by 2025 (Heal 2009). Finally, the United States recently passed a short-term stimulus bill to help with economic recovery, the American Recovery and Reinvestment Act of 2009 (ARRA).

In Europe, both carbon policies and goals of renewable shares are expected to continue. The ETS is currently in its second phase, from 2008 to

2012. In June 2009, the new ETS Directive (2009/29/EC) committed the EU to reducing greenhouse gas emissions by 20% of 1990 levels by 2020 (see European Parliament and Council 2009 for more details). Furthermore, Directive 2009/28/EC states that 20% of the EU's total energy consumption must be from renewable resources by 2020. Note that this is a much larger commitment than in the United States, which seeks to have 20% of electricity production from renewables by 2020. In the United States, and in the rest of the world, about 40% of total energy consumption is used to generate electricity. So 20% of electricity generation in the United States is only 8% of total energy consumption.

These policies focus on the near future. In order to attain a low-carbon world, however, some believe we will need an even greater investment in renewables. The next section of this chapter examines the level of investment in renewables that is expected if we have carbon policies either like those described above or that call for even more dramatically reduced emissions. The focus remains on the United States and EU, but some models examine worldwide levels of investment in renewables.

Forecasts of Renewables in a Low-Carbon World

In examining the policies outlined above, as well as other possible policies, many authors have attempted to forecast what level of investment in renewables would be required in order to attain a low-carbon world. This section outlines the findings of some of the major studies in this area, including those by the International Energy Agency (IEA), European Commission, U.S. Department of Energy (DOE) and Environmental Protection Agency (EPA), FORRES 2020 Project, and a few others. For each model, when possible, both the expected capacity of and generation from renewables excluding large-scale hydropower, as well as total renewables, are reported. Each model has thousands of assumptions regarding economic growth, resource avail-

ability, technology, prices, and so forth. A careful comparison of the models requires an in-depth examination of each assumption and the modeling approach taken. However, the intent here is to give a brief overview of the findings so the reader can gain an appreciation of the range of estimates in the literature, rather than to provide a meta-analysis or pick a preferred model. The range of models discussed presents perspectives of worldwide, U.S., and EU investment over the next 20 to 40 years.

A Global Perspective

The IEA (2007) uses its World Energy Model (WEM) to examine long-run forecasts of emissions, energy supply and demand, and energy sources under various scenarios. In its annual report, the *World Energy Outlook*, IEA gives three scenarios: a reference or business-as-usual scenario; an alternative policy scenario that would include reducing greenhouse gas emissions by 19% *relative to the reference case* by 2030; and a 450 stabilization scenario. This last scenario is a low-carbon world in which carbon dioxide equivalent concentrations would be stabilized at levels ranging from 445 to 490 parts per million (ppm) (IPCC 2007). This would require emissions of carbon dioxide equivalent (CO_2e) to peak in 2015 and fall by up to 85% of 2000 levels by 2050.[13] For the year 2030, the reference scenario implies 42 gigatons (Gt, or billion metric tons) of CO_2 emissions, the alternative policy scenario implies 34 Gt, and the stabilization scenario implies 23 Gt.

In a low-carbon world, nonhydropower renewable resources would double their expected generation in 2030 relative to a business-as-usual scenario (see Table 3.3). This would include adding over 1,400 TWh per year from wind and solar power. Even in the reference case, the amount of wind power is expected to increase fivefold from current levels.[14] Overall, the IEA predicts that 40% of electricity could be produced from renewable resources, about half of which would be from nonhydropower resources.

The U.S. Department of Energy also publishes a global perspective of renewable investments in its *International Energy Outlook*. In the

Table 3.3. IEA world energy outlook predictions, showing generation by energy source (in TWh)

Source	2005	2030 reference case	2030 stabilization case	Change	Growth rate
Hydro	2,922	4,842	6,608	1,766	36%
Biomass	231	840	2,056	1,216	145%
Wind	111	1,287	2,464	1,177	91%
Geothermal	52	173	219	46	27%
Solar	3	161	406	245	152%
Tidal (wave)	1	12	28	16	133%
Nonhydro renewables	398	2,473	5,173	2,700	109%
Total renewables	3,321	7,315	11,781	4,466	61%
Total generation	18,197	35,384	29,300	−6,084	−17%
Percent renewable	18%	21%	40%		

Source: IEA 2007, *Table 5.6*

business-as-usual scenario, the DOE predicts a possible 6,724 TWh of renewables (21% of total generation) by 2030, including 1,951 TWh of nonhydroelectric generation (6.1% of total generation). Of this, most of the nonhydropower will be in the OECD countries (1,417 TWh).

A European Perspective

The European Commission's *World Energy Technology Outlook—2050* (WETO) forecasts three cases of world energy out to 2050: a reference case, carbon constraint case, and hydrogen case (European Commission 2006). The report uses a worldwide simulation model of various energy sectors, known as Prospective Outlook on Long-term Energy Systems (POLES), to look at both EU and global energy issues. The POLES model accounts for world population and GDP growth, as well as technological advancement lowering the costs of energy.[15] Table 3.4 reports WETO's predicted electricity generation by fuel type for each scenario in 2030 and 2050.

In the reference model, WETO forecasts that total renewables will account for 21% of electricity production by 2030 and 25% by 2050. By 2050, solar and wind are expected to produce more than half of the electricity generated from renewables, with wind (6,433 TWh per year), particularly offshore, becoming even larger than hydropower (4,853 TWh per year) worldwide.

This represents a 25-fold increase in wind power from 2008 levels. The increase to 1,493 TWh from solar is even larger in magnitude (the United States and EU produced about 4.5 TWh last year). Nuclear power is also predicted to increase rapidly. The reference case includes modest carbon policy akin to what is currently in place in those countries with such policy. For this case, the WETO reports substantial investment in renewables for the world as a whole. Nonetheless, carbon dioxide emissions are projected to be more than double today's levels by 2050 in this scenario.

The reference case is also reported by region. In Europe, WETO predicts even greater renewable penetration: 26% of electricity production could be from renewables in both 2030 and 2050. Solar, biomass, and wind power will account for approximately two-thirds of that generation. North America is similar, with an expected 20% of all electricity coming from solar, wind, or biomass.

The carbon constraint case seeks to stabilize carbon dioxide concentrations, though at levels greater than in the IEA study: the WETO case aims to stabilize CO_2e at 650 ppm. In 2030, WETO predicts 8,823 TWh of renewable production, about half from hydropower and a quarter each from wind and biomass. In 2050, wind is predicted to be dominant, accounting for 7,336 TWh of the 17,439 TWh that are renewable. This

Table 3.4. Electricity generation by fuel type for the three WETO scenarios (in TWh)

Panel A: year 2030	World			Europe			North America		
Energy source	Refer-ence	Carbon	Hydro-gen	Refer-ence	Carbon	Hydro-gen	Refer-ence	Carbon	Hydro-gen
Coal	12,689	9,114	8,205	1,551	969	794	2,944	1,208	1,491
Gas	8,760	9,438	8,851	1,319	1,545	1,540	1,836	2,281	2,186
Biomass	1,372	1,684	1,644	258	315	311	417	469	474
Nuclear	6,328	6,449	8,834	1,447	1,432	1,597	1,088	967	981
Hydro and geothermal	4,148	4,284	4,226	697	706	702	711	732	730
Solar	91	213	183	17	29	28	13	68	55
Wind	1,880	2,642	2,417	545	608	604	428	728	727
Hydrogen	39	56	44	9	15	12	4	9	7
Total electricity	36,295	34,587	35,039	5,932	5,673	5,642	7,560	6,548	6,714
Percent renewable	21%	26%	24%	26%	29%	29%	21%	30%	30%

Panel B: year 2050	World			Europe			North America		
Energy source	Refer-ence	Carbon	Hydro-gen	Refer-ence	Carbon	Hydro-gen	Refer-ence	Carbon	Hydro-gen
Coal	19,066	9,016	9,371	1,860	781	633	3,976	1,415	1,525
Gas	9,072	9,640	8,959	1,337	1,492	1,465	1,408	1,841	1,738
Biomass	2,246	2,649	2,584	328	361	360	598	680	685
Nuclear	14,866	19,862	21,426	2,931	3,612	3,942	2,014	2,509	2,474
Hydro and geothermal	4,853	5,128	4,998	738	746	743	764	784	782
Solar	1,493	2,326	2,058	344	593	591	308	590	523
Wind	6,433	7,336	6,799	817	859	838	1,115	1,337	1,352
Hydrogen	811	1,477	898	190	321	243	73	196	120
Total electricity	60,040	57,812	57,377	8,608	8,803	8,845	10,337	9,407	9,233
Percent renewable	25%	30%	29%	26%	29%	29%	27%	36%	36%

Source: European Commission 2006

implies that renewables will account for 30% of total electricity production, with wind (12.7%), solar (4.0%), and biomass (4.6%) all playing important roles. North America and Europe are expected to have similar levels of nonhydro renewable penetration: 14.2 and 9.8% wind, 6.3 and 6.7% solar, and 7.2 and 4.1% biomass for North America and Europe, respectively.

The hydrogen case continues with carbon policies to stabilize greenhouse gas concentrations but also assumes substantial breakthroughs in hydrogen technology. In particular, breakthroughs in the performance and cost of the distribution and consumption sectors of the hydrogen economy are identified as being of greatest importance. This scenario changes the mix of fossil fuels to nuclear power and changes transportation fuels: hydrogen provides 13% of final energy consumption (primarily for transport) in this case, compared with the 2% share in the reference case.

With respect to renewables, however, the hydrogen scenario is qualitatively similar to the carbon constraint case.

A U.S. Perspective

The DOE's Energy Information Administration (EIA) publishes the *Annual Energy Outlook*, which reports long-run projections of U.S. energy supply and demand. The EIA (2009a) uses the National Energy Modeling System (NEMS) to forecast scenarios relevant to investments in renewables. The reference case for 2030 predicts an increase in renewable capacity in the United States of 57 GW (+/− 10 GW, depending on scenario's assumptions regarding costs). This accounts for about 22% of all new capacity constructed over the next 22 years. Regardless of the cost scenario, the EIA expects 730 TWh of renewable generation in 2030. Nonhydropower resources are predicted to account for about 14% of U.S. total electricity generation (or 430 TWh). Costs do not change predictions much because the state renewable portfolio standards are assumed to bind. The mix of renewables does change, however: the EIA forecasts greater use of wind power relative to biomass if capital costs fall.

The EIA compares its reference case with some other studies. Namely, it notes that IHS Global Insight (IHSGI 2008) predicts similar levels of growth in renewables, with slightly more conservative estimates from Energy Ventures Analysis (EVA 2008). In the reference case, by 2015, the EIA predicts generation from hydroelectric and other renewables, including net imports, to be 555 TWh, while IHSGI predicts 537 TWh and EVA predicts 420 TWh, just slightly more than the 374 TWh generated in 2007. By 2030, the predictions increase to 758 TWh (EIA), 864 TWh (IHSGI), and 535 TWh (EVA). These correspond to 15%, 17%, and 11% of total generation for each model, respectively. EIA's projections of capacity are also in line with alternative models. In addition to IHSGI and EVA, the Institute of Energy Economics and the Rational Use of Energy (IER 2008) also forecasts renewable capacity for 2015 and 2030. The total capacity for hydroelectric and other renewables was 131 GW in 2007. In 2015, it is expected to increase to 157 GW (EIA), 160 GW (IHSGI), 115 GW (EVA), and 208 GW (IER). By 2030, the capacity is predicted to be 191, 232, 128, and 312 GW, respectively. In summary, the EIA reference case seems consistent with several other predictions by industry and academia.

The EIA predicts several counterfactuals relevant to a low-carbon future relative to a reference case that predated the recent stimulus bill, ARRA. The first counterfactual is to look at the effect of the bill, which extends two important subsidies: the PTC and the ITC. Figure 3.3 compares annual investment in nonhydropower renewables from 2006 to 2030 under the baseline reference case and under the ARRA. In 2012, the policy is expected to increase nonhydropower renewables from 195 to 310 TWh, a 59% increase. By 2030, total renewables are expected to account for 15% of electricity generation in the United States (two-thirds of which are from nonhydroelectric resources).

The increase in renewable capacity from the ARRA is even more substantial. By 2015, an additional 40 GW of renewable capacity is expected, mostly from wind (35 GW). The EIA anticipates that by 2030, wind power capacity (68 GW) will nearly rival that of conventional hydropower (78 GW) in the United States. Only some of the increase in renewables that is attributed to the ARRA is the result of simply extending the PTC.

In a simulation that extends the PTC through 2019, the EIA predicts that wind power would increase by 19 GW (while biomass, municipal solid waste, and geothermal power would be unchanged) by 2020 relative to the reference scenario. Although an increase of 19 GW may seem large, especially given that the United States had only 25 GW wind power capacity in 2008 (WWEA 2009), the EIA expects that the ARRA will increase renewable power by more than 33 GW in 2020, with wind accounting for all of the gain. The ARRA allows developers to convert the PTC into federal grants, thereby avoiding a major hurdle: namely, that only those with significant tax liability can benefit from the tax credit.

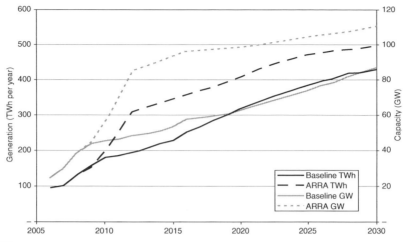

Source: EIA 2009a

Figure 3.3. Expected electricity generation and capacity from nonhydropower renewable sources with and without ARRA, 2006–2030

In a third scenario, the EIA examines a low-carbon case: the Lieberman–Warner bill, § 2191 (LW110). The EIA expected that the bill would result in the electric power sector's emissions falling by more than 50% relative to 2007 levels. Furthermore, the bill would have increased renewable generation in 2030 from 730 to 1,063 TWh (or 22% of total electric generation). Renewable capacity would nearly double from the reference case (57 to 103 GW). Nuclear power and advanced coal with carbon capture and storage (CCS) would also increase substantially: from 13/1 GW of nuclear/CCS capacity in the reference case to 47/99 GW in the LW110 case.

A Forecast of Proposed U.S. Carbon Policy

In a recent report, EPA (2009a) analyzed the Waxman–Markey bill. Although a federal carbon policy will almost surely differ from this exact bill, it is useful to examine nonetheless, as it is the most recent proposal as of this writing. This bill's cap-and-trade policy would result in greater costs for fossil-fuel electricity generation, making renewables more competitive. EPA estimated the initial cost of polluting to be around $13 per metric ton of CO_2e. From the cap-and-trade policy alone, EPA finds that investment in primary energy that has either no or low carbon

emissions—namely renewables, nuclear power, and advanced coal with CCS—would rise for the business-as-usual scenario of 14% of primary energy to 18% by 2020, 26% by 2030, and 38% by 2050.

Using the detailed Integrated Planning Model, EPA accounts for both the cap-and-trade program and the RES. Table 3.5 reports the expected investment in various sources of electric power under the reference case as well as under the Waxman–Markey bill. The reference case is based on the EIA's *Annual Energy Outlook 2009* (EIA 2009a). Relative to the reference case, the climate bill would increase electricity generated by renewables (excluding hydropower) by only 3% to 5%. Including hydropower, the EPA model predicts approximately zero change in generation from renewables in 2025. This status quo is due to a reduction in total electricity consumption, in part because of higher electricity prices but also because of economic incentives to conserve. One way utilities can comply with the RES is through energy efficiency programs.

Even though EPA does not predict that the bill will result in substantial *incremental* investment in renewables, the reference case includes 364 TWh produced by renewables in 2025. In contrast, current production from renewables is 124 TWh (EIA 2009b). In other words, based on cur-

Table 3.5 EPA analysis of the Waxman–Markey Bill, showing generation by energy source, 2020 and 2025 (in TWh)

Panel A: year 2020

Energy source	Reference case	H.R. 2454	Change	Growth rate
Coal	2,222	1,940	–282	–13%
Advanced coal (w/ CCS)	14	71	57	407%
Natural gas/oil	703	486	–217	–31%
Nuclear	816	816	0	0%
Hydropower	290	285	–5	–2%
Other renewables	334	351	17	5%
Total renewables	624	636	12	2%
Total electricity	4,379	3,949	–430	–10%
Percent renewable	14%	16%		

Panel B: year 2025

Energy source	Reference case	H.R. 2454	Change	Growth rate
Coal	2,312	1,851	–461	–20%
Advanced coal (w/ CCS)	14	184	170	1,214%
Natural gas/oil	788	544	–244	–31%
Nuclear	837	820	–17	–2%
Hydropower	292	282	–10	–3%
Other renewables	364	375	11	3%
Total renewables	656	657	1	0%
Total electricity	4,607	4,056	–551	–12%
Percent renewable	14%	16%		

Source: EPA 2009a

rent policies, EPA expects renewables to triple over the next 17 years. In the reference case, nonhydroelectric renewables would account for 8% of total electricity generation (or 9% under the Waxman–Markey bill). Including hydropower, this increases to 14% (16% with the bill). A final note regarding the Waxman–Markey bill: according to EPA's model, the bill is expected to cause substantial growth in "clean" coal (advanced coal with CCS), on the order of 400% to 1,200%, relative to the reference case.

In addition to the EPA study, the MIT Joint Program on the Science and Policy of Global Change has analyzed the bill (Paltsev et al. 2009). This analysis finds that annualized costs of the bill would be on the order of $400 per household with a permit price starting at just over $20 per ton of CO_2 in 2015 and reaching $38 by 2030.

The bill is expected to increase renewables only slightly: the share of power from nonhydroelectric renewables would increase from 10% to 11%.

A Forecast of EU Renewables Policy

In a report financed by the European Commission's Directorate-General of Energy and Transport, Ragwitz et al. (2005) examined how investment in renewables might proceed in the European Union through 2020. The authors use the Green-X model from the FORRES 2020 project, which assumes learning by doing and scale economies.

For the year 2020, their model suggests that the reference case could have 385 TWh from wind, 8.8 TWh from PV solar, and 607 TWh of total renewables (excluding large-scale hydropower). For comparison, the EU produced only 104 TWh from wind, 3.8 TWh from solar PV, and 212 TWh from nonhydropower renewables in 2007 (Eurostat 2009). As a share of overall gross electricity consumption in the EU countries, this is an increase from 6.5% in 2007 (16% if hydropower is included) to 15% (22%) in 2020.

The authors also examine a policy scenario whereby "best practices" of currently available strategies are applied across all 27 EU countries.[16] In this policy case, wind power is expected to produce 461 TWh, another 17.9 TWh from solar PV, and 928 TWh from total renewables (excluding large-scale hydropower), or 26% of expected total electricity generation. With hydropower, this increases to 1,234 TWh (34%). The authors conclude that following currently available best practices, renewables could account for a third of all electricity generation in the EU.

Other Models

The research of some academics, trade groups, and nonprofit organizations also has examined the question of what could be the long-run level of investment in renewables. Palmer and Burtraw (2005) use the RFF Haiku model of the U.S. electricity industry to analyze the effects of renewable portfolio standards (RPSs) and renewable energy production tax credits. In the reference case, the authors predict that in 2020, 151 TWh of nonhydropower could be generated, or only 3.1% of total generation (9.5% if hydropower is included). Under a general renewable production tax credit, which is set at current levels but applies to a much broader set of renewables, Palmer and Burtraw find that 729 TWh would be produced. This would result in 15% of electricity coming from nonhydropower renewables (with 43% of it from wind power). Total renewables, including hydropower, are predicted to account for 21% of electricity supply. Palmer and Burtraw look at several possible RPSs for 2020: 5%, 10%, 15%, and 20%. In each case, the standard is binding for nonhydropower renewables, and hydropower accounts for an additional 6.5% of total electricity generation. For the low-level RPS, nonhydropower renewables are dominated

by geothermal. However, a 20% RPS would require substantial investment in wind power, accounting for about half of all nonhydropower renewable generation (468 of 948 TWh).

Many other studies have examined this question. For example, the Intergovernmental Panel on Climate Change (IPCC 2007) notes that renewable electricity, including hydropower, was 18% of world electricity supply in 2005, and that with a carbon price of $50 per ton of CO_2e, it could reach a 30% to 35% market share by 2030. The Union of Concerned Scientists (Cleetus et al 2009) suggests a blueprint to reduce U.S. carbon dioxide emissions by 84% below 2005 levels by 2030. Through energy efficiency policies, the study suggests that electricity consumption could be reduced by 35% relative to the reference case. An RPS would result in wind, solar, geothermal, and biomass providing 40% of the total electricity, or about 21% of overall energy supply. The WWEA (2009) expects 1,500 GW of installed wind capacity producing 12% of electricity generation by 2020. The Energy Watch Group (Rechsteiner 2008) predicts that by 2025, the investment could be even greater, with 7,500 GW installed wind capacity producing 16,400 TWh a year. Furthermore, the study anticipates that total renewables could account for more than 50% of new power installations worldwide by 2019 and all of it by 2022. By 2037, it suggests that nonrenewable generation could be completely phased out.

Conclusions

Within 20 years, some authors predict that 20% to 40% of electricity could be produced from renewable resources. Some predict even higher levels. Table 3.6 draws together the medley of forecasts outlined above to show the range of model predictions as well as some important regional and policy differences.

Returning to an economist's perspective, one would need to know the relative net marginal social benefits for each type of renewable resource, at each location and point in time, in order to determine whether a 20%, 30%, 40%, or

Table 3.6. A summary of model predictions for 2030

Geographic scope	Modeling organization	Carbon policy	Generation percentage	
			Nonhydro renewables	All renewables
Worldwide	IEA	Business as usual	7%	21%
		450 stabilization	18%	40%
Worldwide	EC	Business as usual	11%	21%
		Carbon constraint	14%	26%
		Hydrogen	12%	24%
Worldwide	IPCC	$50/ton price	—	30%–35%
Europe	EC	Business as usual	15%	26%
		Carbon constraint	17%	29%
		Hydrogen	17%	29%
U.S.	EIA	ARRA	9%	15%
		Lieberman–Warner	—	22%
	EPA	Waxman–Markey	16%	26%

Sources: IEA 2009; European Commission 2006; EPA 2009b, *27*

even 50% market share for renewable electricity is optimal. This chapter focused, however, not on what *should* be the level of investment in renewables, but rather on what modelers predict *could* be the level of investment, based on either policies that are currently being discussed—such as the third phase of the EU Emission Trading System, EU Directive 2009/28/EC on renewables, or the U.S. Waxman–Markey bill—or future policy objectives, such as stabilizing carbon dioxide equivalent concentrations at 450 or 650 ppm.

By reviewing major studies on this topic, this chapter has provided a range of estimates of levels of investment in wind power, solar PV, nonhydropower renewables, and total renewables for the world overall, the EU, and the United States. The range of levels of investment reflects many differences regarding the assumptions in the models, the policies being analyzed, and the methodologies used by the researchers. This chapter has shown that although opinions are diverse on what might happen over the next 20 to 40 years, studies employing a variety of models and a range of assumptions regarding carbon policy forecast the likelihood of a significant increase in the role of renewables in meeting electricity demand.

Notes

1. Geoengineering includes methods such as stratospheric sulfur aerosols, which manage solar radiation. These methods do not reduce greenhouse gases, but rather limit their effects on global warming. Some also use this term to include carbon sequestration.

2. Not all greenhouse gases are as long-lived. Methane, for example, has a chemical lifetime in the atmosphere of approximately 12 years. Technically, a stock pollutant never expires; for example, lead is a true stock pollutant. However, the economic insights of stock pollutants help in thinking about regulating greenhouse gases.

3. More precisely, the optimal level of pollution at a point in time will be where present value marginal benefits of pollution (the avoided compliance costs) are equal to the present value marginal costs of pollution (the marginal damages). For further discussion, see Tietenberg (2006).

4. Fischer and Newell (2008) show that a policy promoting renewables may be more efficient than a carbon tax if these positive technology spillovers are large relative to the climate externalities. However, they find for a range of parameter values, a price on carbon is preferred even when there are knowledge spillovers.

5. One terawatt-hour is 1 million megawatt-hours (MWh) or 1 billion kilowatt-hours (kWh). One

TWh approximately equals the annual consumption of about 89,000 U.S. residential customers.

6. Electricity generation capacity is measured in watts (W), kilowatts (kW, 1,000 W), megawatts (MW, 1 million W), or gigawatts (GW, 1 billion W).

7. Some renewables, including solar, wind and geothermal energy, first became eligible for tax credits with the passage of the 1978 Energy Tax Act.

8. The EEG was further amended: as of January 2009, PV solar subsidies have been reduced to €330–€430 ($449–$586) per MWh.

9. The price on August 24, 2009 was €15.34 ($20.89) (Point Carbon n.d.).

10. Some express concern that predictions of substantial levels of investment in the future are not feasible, given the issue of intermittency. In a recent paper, Heal (2009) reviews the literature on the economics of renewables. He shares these concerns and concludes that nuclear and CCS are likely to be important sources of electricity in a low-carbon future.

11. It is unlikely that the Waxman–Markey bill will pass into law as it was written when the House passed it in the summer of 2009. As of this writing, Congress has not passed any climate bill.

12. The requirement is that 20% be from renewables or energy efficiency, but at least 75% of that amount must be through renewables. This constraint is expected not to be binding.

13. CO_2e is a measure for greenhouse gases whereby all gases are normalized by their global warming potential.

14. In 2008, wind power produced 260 TWh (WWEA 2009); in the reference case, the IEA (2007) predicts a possible 1,287 TWh by 2030.

15. The POLES model was developed by the Centre National de la Recherche Scientifique (CNRS) and is maintained by CNRS, UPMF University, Enerdata, and the Institute for Prospective Technological Studies. See Enerdata (2006).

16. Best practices are defined as those "strategies that have proven to be most effective in the past in implementing a maximum share of RES" (Ragwitz et al. 2005).

References

Borenstein, Severin. 2008. The Market Value and Cost of Solar Photovoltaic Electricity Production. Working paper 176. Berkeley, CA: University of California Energy Institute, Center for the Study of Energy Markets.

Campbell, Arthur. 2009. Government Support for Intermittent Renewable Generation Technologies. Working paper. Cambridge, MA: Massachusetts Institute of Technology. econ-www.mit.edu/files/3563 (accessed August 17, 2009).

DSIRE (Database of State Incentives for Renewables and Efficiency). 2009. Project of the North Carolina Solar Center and Interstate Renewable Energy Council funded by the U.S. Department of Energy's Office of Energy Efficiency and Renewable. Energy. www.dsireusa.org/ (accessed February 20, 2010).

EIA (U.S. Energy Information Administration). 2009a. *Annual Energy Outlook 2009: With Projections to 2030.* DOE/EIA-0383(2009). www.eia.doe.gov/oiaf/aeo/pdf/0383(2009).pdf (accessed August 19, 2009).

———. 2009b. *Short-Term Energy Outlook—August 2009.* www.eia.doe.gov/pub/forecasting/steo oldsteos/aug09.pdf (accessed August 29, 2009).

Enerdata. 2006. *POLES Model: Prospective Outlook on Long-term Energy Systems: A World Energy Model.* www.eie.gov.tr/turkce/en_tasarrufu/uetm/twinning/sunular/hafta_02/5_POLES_description.pdf (accessed August 29, 2009).

EPA (U.S. Environmental Protection Agency). 2009a. *EPA Analysis of the American Clean Energy and Security Act of 2009 HR 2454 in the 111th Congress.* www.epa.gov/climatechange/economics/economicanalyses.html (accessed August 20, 2009).

———. 2009b. *EPA Preliminary Analysis of the Waxman-Markey Discussion Draft: The American Clean Energy and Security Act of 2009 in the 111th Congress.* www.epa.gov/climatechange/economics/pdfs/WM-Analysis.pdf (accessed February 26, 2010).

European Commission. 2006. *World Energy Technology Outlook—2050.* Directorate-General for Research EUR 22038. ec.europa.eu/research/energy/pdf/weto-h2_en.pdf (accessed February 26, 2010).

———. 2009. *The Renewable Energy Progress Report.* Commission Staff Working Document SEC(2009) 503 final. http://eur-lex.europa.eu/LexUriServ/LexUriServ.do?uri=COM:2009:0192:FIN:EN:PDF (accessed August 19, 2009).

European Parliament and Council. 2009. Directive 2009/29/EC of the European Parliament and of the Council of 23 April 2009. eur-lex.europa.eu/LexUriServ/LexUriServ.do?uri=OJ:L:2009:140:0063:0087: EN:PDF (accessed February 26, 2010).

Eurostat (European Commission Eurostat). 2009. *Energy: Yearly Statistics 2007.*

EVA (Energy Ventures Analysis). 2008. *FUELCAST: Long-Term Outlook.*

Fischer, Carolyn, and Richard G. Newell. 2008. Environmental and Technology Policies for Climate Mitigation. *Journal of Environmental Economics and Management* 55 (2): 142–162.

Galbraith, Kate. 2009. More Sun for Less: Solar Panels Drop in Price. *New York Times*, Aug. 26, B1.

Heal, Geoffrey. 2009. The Economics of Renewable Energy. Working paper 15081. Cambridge, MA: National Bureau of Economic Research.

IEA (International Energy Agency). 2004. *Renewable Energy: Market and Policy Trends in IEA Countries.* Paris: OECD Publishing.

———. 2007. *World Energy Outlook 2007.* Paris: OECD Publishing.

———. 2009. World Energy Outlook 2009 Fact Sheet. www.worldenergyoutlook.org/docs/weo2009/fact_sheets_WEO_2009.pdf (accessed February 26, 2010).

IER (Institute of Energy Economics and the Rational Use of Energy). 2008. *TIAM Global Energy System Model.* Stuttgart: University of Stuttgart.

IHSGI (IHS Global Insight). 2008. *Global Petroleum Outlook.* Lexington, MA: IHSGI.

IPCC (Intergovernmental Panel on Climate Change). 2007. *Fourth Assessment Report.* www.ipcc.ch/publications_and_data/publications_and_data_reports.htm#1 (accessed August 10, 2009).

Martinot, Eric, Ryan Wiser, and Jan Hamrin. 2005. Renewable Energy Policies and Markets in the United States. Working paper. San Francisco: Center for Resource Solutions.

Metcalf, Gilbert. 2009a. Investment in Energy Infrastructure and the Tax Code. Working paper. Medford, MA: Tufts University.

———. 2009b. Tax Policies for Low-Carbon Technologies. Working paper w15054. Cambridge, MA: National Bureau of Economic Research.

Nielsen, Lene, and Tim Jeppesen. 2003. Tradable Green Certificates in Selected European Countries: Overview and Assessment. *Energy Policy* 31 (1): 3–14.

NREL (National Renewable Energy Laboratory). 2008. 20% Wind Energy by 2030. Increasing Wind Energy's Contribution to U.S. Electricity Supply. Technical paper. Golden, CO: NREL.

Palmer, Karen, and Dallas Burtraw. 2005. Cost-Effectiveness of Renewable Electricity Policies. *Energy Economics* 27: 873–894.

Paltsev, S., J.M. Reilly, H.D. Jacoby, and J.F. Morris. 2009. Appendix C: Cost of Climate Policy and the Waxman-Markey American Clean Energy and Security Act of 2009 (HR 2454). In *The Cost of Climate Policy in the United States*, edited by S. Paltsev, J.M. Reilly, H.D. Jacoby and J.F. Morris. MIT Joint Program Report Series No. 173, 1–21.

Point Carbon. No date. Point Carbon home page. www.pointcarbon.com (accessed February 26, 2010).

Ragwitz, Mario, Joachim Schleich, Claus Huber, Gustav Resch, Thomas Faber, Monique Voogt, Rogier Coenraads, Hans Cleijne, and Peter Bodo. 2005. Analysis of the EU Renewable Energy Sources' Evolution up to 2020 (FORRES 2020). www.emu.ee/orb.aw/class=file/action=preview/id=254843/FORRES_FINAL_REPORT.pdf 3563 (accessed August 25, 2009).

Rechsteiner, Rudolf. 2008. *Wind Power in Context: A Clean Revolution in the Energy Sector.* Basel, Switzerland: Energy Watch Group and Ludwig-Boelkow-Foundation.

REN21 (Renewable Energy Policy Network for the 21st Century). 2009. *Renewables Global Status Report: 2009 Update.* Paris: REN21 Secretariat.

Stern, Nicholas. 2006. *The Economics of Climate Change: The Stern Review.* Cambridge, UK: Cambridge University Press.

Tietenberg, Thomas. 2006. *Environmental and Natural Resource Economics.* 7th ed. Reading, MA: Addison-Wesley Longman.

U.S. Congress. 2009. *American Recovery and Reinvestment Act of 2009.* 111th Cong., 1st sess. frwebgate.access.gpo.gov/cgi-bin/getdoc.cgi?dbname=111_cong_bills&docid=f:h1enr.pdf (accessed August 25, 2009).

U.S. Congress House Committee on Energy and Commerce. 2009. *American Clean Energy and Security Act of 2009.* 111th Cong., 1st sess., HR 2454. energycommerce.house.gov/Press_111/20090515/hr2454.pdf (accessed August 20, 2009).

Vajjhala, Shalini, Anthony Paul, Richard Sweeney, and Karen Palmer. 2008. Green Corridors: Linking Interregional Transmission Expansion and Renewable Energy Policies. Discussion paper 08–06. Washington, DC: Resources for the Future.

Wiser, Ryan, and Mark Bolinger. 2008. *Annual Report on U.S. Wind Power Installation, Cost, and Performance Trends: 2007.* LBNL-275E. Berkeley, CA: Lawrence Berkeley National Laboratory.

Wiser, Ryan, Galen Barbose, and Carla Peterman. 2009. *Tracking the Sun: The Installed Cost of*

Photovoltaics in the U.S. from 1998–2007. LBNL-1516E. Berkeley, CA: Lawrence Berkeley National Laboratory.

WWEA (World Wind Energy Association). 2009. *World Wind Energy Report, 2008*.

www.wwindea.org/home/images/stories/worldwindenergyreport2008_s.pdf (accessed August 24, 2009).

4

Renewable Generation and Security of Supply

Boaz Moselle

A key question this book seeks to address is what justification exists for the promotion of renewable generation over other forms of low-carbon generation—in other words, for policies that specifically promote renewable generation rather than a technology-neutral approach such as a carbon tax or cap-and-trade mechanism. Simple economics suggests that the latter approach would be more effective in achieving carbon reductions at lowest cost, through competition between different carbon abatement mechanisms and technologies (e.g., renewable energy, nuclear, carbon capture and storage, reductions in non-generation sectors, energy efficiency).

In the European Union (EU), one of the most common responses is that renewable generation merits specific support because it enhances security of supply by reducing dependence on imported fuels. Concerns about import dependence refer particularly (though not exclusively) to dependence on natural gas imports from Russia and Algeria, which many observers view as potentially unreliable because of political instability and, in the case of Russia, a willingness to use energy supplies as a tool of geopolitics.[1] This concern has been greatly enhanced by interruptions in recent winters to the flow of gas from Russia into the EU via Ukraine, as a result of disputes between Russia and Ukraine.

At the same time, a commonly voiced concern with renewable generation is that it will endanger security of supply by leading to excessive dependence on intermittent sources such as wind and solar power. To some commentators, this argues against the promotion of renewable generation. To others, it implies the need for significant changes in power market design to ensure that sufficient backup capacity is available over various time frames.

This chapter therefore focuses on these two questions, examining to what extent security of supply concerns related to import dependence warrant additional support for renewable generation relative to other forms of low-carbon technology, and to what extent security of supply concerns related to intermittency undermine the case for supporting renewables at all or necessitate major changes in market design.

The focus is on the EU, where renewables deployment is most prominent on the policy agenda and is explicitly linked to security of supply by policymakers. However, many of the conclusions—in particular, those relating to intermittency—can be applied to other jurisdictions as well.

The chapter begins by examining the issue of import dependence. It assesses the extent of the problem and analyzes whether there are market or other failures that warrant intervention, and if so, whether the promotion of renewable generation is the most efficient form of intervention to address the problem. It then focuses on the problems posed by intermittency, again assessing the problem and analyzing the case for policy intervention and the most appropriate form that intervention might take.

EU Dependence on Imported Fuels

The need to reduce dependence on imported fuels is used to justify a range of EU policies, including not only the promotion of renewables, but also the promotion of energy efficiency and the provision by some national governments of subsidies to domestic coal production. In the past decade, these themes have been developed in numerous policy documents and pieces of legislation, including the European Commission's 2000 Green Paper on security of supply, the 2002 Regulation on State Aid in the coal sector, the 2008 Energy Security and Solidarity Plan, and the 2009 Renewables Directive (European Commission 2000; Regulation 1407/2002; European Commission 2008a; Directive 2009/28/EC).

This section therefore presents evidence on the extent of EU import dependence and the factors that have most given rise to concern with respect to power generation: the large and growing dependence on Russian gas imports and the effect of supply interruptions in recent winters. It also assesses the extent to which import dependence is a problem for the main fuels used for power generation and whether the promotion of renewable generation is the most appropriate policy response to any such problem.

Current and Projected Levels of EU Import Dependence

As Table 4.1 illustrates, the EU imports a large proportion of its primary energy sources, including the main fuels used for power generation. In 2006, around 80% of electricity was generated from coal (29%), gas (21%), and nuclear sources (30%) (European Commission 2008b).[2]

Imports are very significant for natural gas, which, as explained below, is the main source of concern among policy makers. The EU holds just 1.6% of the world's gas reserves and currently imports 58% of its natural gas demand, mainly from four countries: Russia, Norway, Algeria, and Nigeria.[3] Gas supplies 24% of total energy demand and 21% of electricity generation (European Commission 2008b). Gas import dependence is set to increase, as EU indigenous production is forecast to decline rapidly in the coming decade, from 176 million tons of oil equivalent (Mtoe) in 2010 to 131 Mtoe in 2019 (IEA 2009).[4] European Commission analysis forecasts net imports of natural gas increasing from 257 Mtoe in 2005 (58% of total consumption) to 390 Mtoe in 2020 (77% of total consumption) under a business-as-usual scenario, without taking into account the impact of the new energy policy adopted in 2009 (see European Commission 2008b, Annex 2).[5]

Table 4.1. EU import dependence, 2005

	EU primary energy demand (Mtoe)	EU primary production (Mtoe)	Net imports (Mtoe)	Import dependence (percentage)
Oil	666	133	533	80.0%
Natural gas	445	188	257	57.8%
Solid fuel	320	196	127	39.7%
Renewables	123	122	1	0.8%
Nuclear/ uranium	257	8	249	97.0%

Sources: European Commission 2008b, *65*; Euratom 2008
Note: Mtoe = million tons of oil equivalent

Winter Supply Interruptions

The heavy dependence of the EU on Russian gas has been brought home to the public and policymakers alike in recent years by interruptions to the supply of Russian gas at the start of the calendar year, arising from disputes between Russia and Ukraine. A number of such disputes have occurred since the breakup of the Soviet Union as a result of continuing difficulties in agreeing on the details of a new gas transit and supply regime, as well as deeper underlying differences. The most serious of these interruptions occurred at the beginning of 2006 and 2009. In January 2006, gas supplies to the EU were interrupted for one day; in January 2009, the interruption lasted 16 days (European Commission 2009a).

Ukraine's Role as a Gas Consumer and Transit Country

Ukraine is both a significant consumer of gas and a key transit country. Its daily consumption in winter is about 300 million cubic meters per day (mcm/day), and another 300 to 350 mcm/day of gas passes through Ukraine to the EU (European Commission 2009a). Imports from Russia via Ukraine constitute around 80% of EU imports of gas from Russia and about 20% of total gas demand in the EU (European Commission 2009a). The Ukrainian gas sector features below-cost pricing for domestic and government customers, and chronic underinvestment in its oil and gas sector, including the gas pipeline infrastructure (Chow and Elkind 2009).

Disputes between Ukraine and Russia over gas supplies, transit, and payment for gas have been a feature of this market since the early 1990s. Ukrainian inability to pay for the huge volumes of gas contracted (despite the very low prices Russia gave Ukraine) led to high levels of debt and unpaid bills on a continuous basis for many years (Stern 2005). The disputes remained unresolved despite a series of agreements covering the gas volumes and prices, the price of gas transit across Ukraine, and the level of debt owed to Gazprom by the Ukrainian gas company Naftokhaz, which

were characterized by low gas prices for Ukraine and low transit charges for delivery of Russian gas to Europe.[6]

In March 2005, Russia claimed that Ukraine was not paying for gas and was diverting gas intended for transit to the EU (BBC 2006). On January 1, 2006, Russia retaliated by cutting off gas supplies passing through Ukrainian territory.[7] Russia and Ukraine reached a preliminary agreement on January 4, and the supply was restored. The agreement provided for an increase in the nominal price of gas but did not provide an agreed pricing formula for future years or a transition period to higher prices. The new agreement was set to expire on December 31, 2008.

The 2009 crisis began on January 1, when Gazprom cut off suppliers (again, it stopped supplying gas for Ukrainian consumption while the supply of gas that was theoretically to be transited through for European consumption continued). Initially disruption of supply to the EU was only minor, but by January 7, all supplies from Russia to the EU were cut, and supplies were not resumed until January 20. This was the most serious gas supply crisis ever to hit the EU, depriving it of 20% of its total gas supply (European Commission 2009a). Within days of the supply disruption, 12 countries were affected. They responded by drawing on storage, importing additional LNG supplies, and fuel-switching by the use of fuel oil and coal. Increased supplies were sourced from Russia via Belarus and Turkey, as well as from Norway and Libya. Gazprom is estimated to have lost sales of $2 billion (European Commission 2009a).

Is Import Dependence Really a Problem?

Reliance on imported fuels is not, per se, a cause for concern. For policy intervention to be justified on security-of-supply grounds, a number of conditions must be satisfied, including that:

- The reliance on imports creates a genuine security-of-supply risk. This is unlikely to be the case for a fuel that can be imported easily from a number of different countries that are politically stable, friendly, and geographically diverse.

- There is good reason to think that the normal market response will not efficiently address any security-of-supply risks and that policy intervention can be expected to do better.

The first of these conditions is assessed below for each of the main fuels used for generation: coal, uranium, and natural gas. This is followed by a discussion of the potential for market or other failures that might justify intervention.

Coal

Globally, coal is much more abundant than oil or natural gas. There are proven coal reserves of 826 billion tons of coal, with a proven reserve-to-production ratio of 122 years (BP 2009).[8] Coal reserves are available in almost every country, with recoverable reserves in around 70 countries. Six countries together account for about 80% of coal reserves, as shown in Figure 4.1.

Given that world coal reserves are spread across a politically and geographically diverse set of countries, large in number and including some of Europe's closest political allies, the prospect of significant supply interruption seems relatively remote. It is therefore implausible to argue that dependence on coal imports is a significant threat to EU security of supply.

Uranium

The earth has 5.5 million metric tons of identified uranium resources, distributed widely around the world, as Figure 4.2 illustrates. At the current rate of consumption, this would constitute about 100 years' worth of supply.

Uranium's extraordinarily high energy density makes it practical to maintain large stockpiles (Euratom 2008), reducing the risks associated with a short-term interruption in supply. This factor and the diverse range of supply sources suggest that dependence on uranium imports is not a significant security-of-supply risk for Europe, despite the high level of import dependence, unavoidable given that Europe has less than 2% of the world's identified uranium resources (European Commission 2008b).

Gas

The picture for natural gas is very different than that for coal or uranium. Prima facie there is good reason to consider that the EU's import dependence does represent a potential threat to security of supply. As noted earlier, the EU imports more than half of its gas, of which a large proportion comes from Algeria and Russia, and gas imports are predicted to increase in coming years (European Commission 2007) as output continues to decline in the main EU producing nations.

Dependence on Algerian and Russian gas is of concern because of the absence or weakness of democratic institutions and transparent governance arrangements in these countries. Algeria has experienced recent civil war and ranks poorly on international league tables in terms of democracy

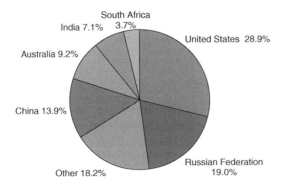

Figure 4.1. World coal reserves

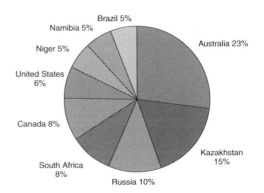

Figure 4.2. World uranium resources

and civil rights (World Audit 2010). Russia also has a low rank, and the poor climate for business investment raises questions as to whether new investment required to maintain and increase gas supply will be forthcoming. There is also a question as to how far the supply of gas is a commercial decision versus an instrument to exercise geopolitical influence. This means that the extent to which the supply of gas will respond to increased demand is unclear.

In addition, analysts have noted that Russia needs to replace declining fields with new production from the Yamal Peninsula and offshore fields and to refurbish a large, aging high-pressure pipeline network (Stern 2005). As mentioned above, there is also a need to invest in the Ukrainian pipeline network or construct new pipelines to maintain transit capacity to Europe.

Underlying these concerns is the absence of realistic alternative sources of natural gas. Relative to other fuels, the ability to bring gas from different sources is inherently limited by the more costly, capital-intensive and inflexible means of transportation required, in the form of long-distance pipelines or liquefied natural gas (LNG). Moreover, while gas remains abundant at global level, with world proven reserves as of 2007 standing at some 177 trillion cubic meters (tcm),[9] equivalent to some 60 years of consumption at current rates (BP 2009), those reserves are concentrated in a small number of countries, as shown in Figure 4.3. Of these, just three countries, Russia, Iran, and Qatar, hold about 53% of the total.

There is an unknown potential for European domestic gas supply to be boosted by unconventional or shale gas. In the United States, substantial discoveries of unconventional gas have been made.[10] However, estimates of the potential for unconventional gas in Europe are lower. One study estimates that Europe has 29 tcm, whereas the United States has around 233 tcm of unconventional gas (Holditch 2007).[11] Moreover, the ability to extract the resources will depend on environmental consents and the cost of extracting unconventional gas in Europe.

In conclusion, it seems that gas import dependence is a potentially significant security-

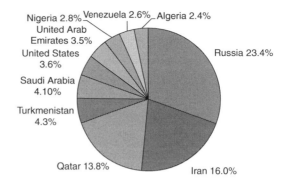

Figure 4.3. World gas reserves: top 10 countries

of-supply risk for the EU. It is possible that a combination of LNG imports and the arrival of unconventional gas (either in Europe or in the United States but "liberating" LNG flows that could come to the EU) will mitigate the problem. It is also possible that the risk is overestimated because of the mutual dependence between the EU and its suppliers: revenue from gas sales is of great importance to both Russia and Algeria, and indeed, they have been known to express concern about "security of demand" from the EU, mirroring the EU's concerns about security of supply (see, e.g., Yenikeyeff 2006). Neither of these possibilities can be viewed as certain, however, and the risk is therefore a real one, albeit difficult to assess or quantify.

The problem is particularly acute for eastern Europe. Estonia, Latvia, Lithuania, Bulgaria, Slovakia, and Finland are completely dependent on Russia for gas imports, while Greece, Hungary, and Austria are more than 80% dependent (European Commission 2008b). Among the seven new eastern European member states, dependence on Russian gas imports averages about 77% (European Commission 2009a). Eastern European commentators point to the experience in Lithuania—where oil supplies from Russia to the Mazeikiu refinery were halted because, it is claimed, Russia objected to its sale to a Polish refiner, PKN Orlen—as a sign of the potential risks they face (Geropoulos 2007). The political temperature is clearly at its highest with regard to eastern Europe, given Russian resentment at its loss of influence there since the breakup of the Soviet Union.

The Case for Policy Intervention

Gas import dependence is therefore an understandable source of concern for European policymakers. However, it does not automatically follow that policy intervention is warranted. Markets already provide strong incentives for market participants to appropriately ensure against unreliable supplies. Contracts between suppliers and consumers generally oblige suppliers to deliver energy, and suppliers that choose to contract with less reliable sources (in other words, are too reliant on gas from Russia and Algeria) will face whatever penalties their contracts contain. These penalties are negotiated on a bilateral basis and therefore represent accurately the costs to consumers of loss of supply, or the trade-offs consumers are willing to make between price and security of supply (for example, a consumer may be willing to sign a contract that has no penalties in the event of supply failure, such as through the operation of a force majeure clause, but in that case the supplier accepts a lower price in return). A similar logic applies for consumers that choose to rely on short-term contracts or spot markets: they accept the higher level of risk in return for greater flexibility or an expected lower price.

The key question therefore is whether these incentives are sufficient to provide an efficient[12] level of security—or, more accurately, whether they provide a more efficient level of security than can be expected from policy intervention, bearing in mind that real-world policy interventions and real-world markets are both inherently imperfect compared to any theoretical ideal.

In that context, a number of problems could undermine the ability of these market-based incentives to give an efficient outcome. These include some market failures that typically provide the theoretical justification for policy interventions, but also other issues that are arguably more important from both normative and positive perspectives (i.e., they should be taken more seriously, and they have a bigger impact on policy outcomes).

First, it may be that consumers (individuals and firms) are not good at making judgments of this kind, and that governments could make better judgments and use them to implement better policies. A case may therefore exist for intervention on essentially paternalistic grounds.

The second problem is the issue of politically motivated supply interruptions. Arguably, the risk of supply interruption by a hostile state actor is greater the more disruptive the effect of the interruption.[13] Thus, although ensuring against low rainfall in a hydro-dominated power system does not make rain more likely to fall, ensuring against gas supply interruptions in the EU actually reduces the threat of interruption, because if such interruptions are relatively painless, then a hostile state gets little strategic benefit from interrupting or threatening to interrupt supplies. If so, then individual investments in supply security (e.g., booking more gas storage or installing dual fuel capability at gas-fired power stations) create a positive externality, and as with any such externality, there will be an incentive to free ride: consumers will spend less than is socially optimal, because they face all the costs but only a small part of the benefits (the so-called "tragedy of the commons"). Moving down the chain, it follows that suppliers will not face appropriate incentives to ensure security, and the market will underprovide security.

Third, experience shows that in conditions of energy scarcity, regulatory or political intervention will almost certainly prevent the market from functioning efficiently. The prospect of such intervention will therefore undermine investment incentives. For example, a private investor might consider investing in a gas storage facility even if the market already appears well supplied with gas storage, on the basis that it would offer a very high return in the low-probability event that a major gas shortage leads to prolonged spikes in spot gas prices. Experience in Great Britain suggests that these spikes could involve prices many times as high as under normal conditions,[14] implying spectacular returns to anyone holding gas in storage.

In reality, however, the investor will be aware that many regulators or governments have arrangements in place that suspend the price mechanism in such emergencies. Such an investor will also be aware that even if those mechanisms are not yet in place, they could be introduced at short notice, and moreover, in the absence of price controls, they would be likely to suffer retribution if they were judged to have profiteered or "price-gouged" during a crisis.[15]

Conversely, market participants will also be aware that emergency arrangements typically involve the imposition of "shared pain" rules, which undermine private incentives to ensure against scarcity of supply. For example, scarce gas supplies might be allocated to all suppliers on a pro rata basis related to the size of their customer load. Such an outcome would do nothing to reward the supplier who had purchased gas from a more reliable source.

Examples of these two tendencies—nonreliance on the price mechanism and a "shared pain" approach—can be found in the gas "emergency cash-out" arrangements in Great Britain, which suspend the market-based determination of prices for the duration of the emergency (Ofgem 2006). The European Commission's proposed new legislation on gas security of supply provides for a variety of non-market-based measures including compulsory demand reduction and forced fuel switching (European Commission 2009c).

A fourth problem is a more conventional market failure: because security of supply is to some extent a public good, markets will tend to undersupply it.[16] Specifically, the issue arises for natural gas and electricity because they are transmitted via networks used by many consumers, and most individual consumers cannot be remotely interrupted when supplies are tight.[17] Domestic and commercial consumers generally do not have real-time metering and are not exposed to higher spot prices when supplies are scarce. There is therefore no incentive for individual consumers to ensure against supply risks, for example by paying more to purchase from a supplier that has more gas in storage.[18]

In particular, with electricity the absence of remote disconnection means that in the event of a blackout, all consumers will lose supply in an area, even though in general it would be possible to set a price—if all consumers were exposed to real-time prices—that would allow demand to match supply. An individual consumer therefore has no incentive to purchase energy from more reliable sources, as the higher levels of security are spread across all consumers. Purchasing from a more reliable source creates a positive externality but almost no private benefit (see Joskow 2007). Again, this gives rise to free riding and underprovision of security by the market.

Assessment

How material these problems are for security of supply is a difficult empirical question, both in absolute terms and because assessment should be against a counterfactual that is based on a realistic assessment of the likely intervention that the policy process would give rise to. Nonetheless, some simple observations are in order.

First, the paternalistic argument that consumers are unlikely to make wise decisions is at least plausible. Extensive research in psychology and behavioral economics shows that human beings have particular difficulty making decisions involving low-probability events that are well outside their normal range of experience (Tversky and Kahneman 1992). However, the claim that government intervention will lead to better outcomes is more contentious (apart from any other consideration, governments are made up of human beings subject to the same biases as others).

Second, the argument concerning politically motivated interruptions is also at least plausible. The key question for EU policymakers to answer is how likely Russia is to interrupt gas supplies for political reasons. On the one hand, instances have already occurred where Russia has cut off oil supplies to an EU member state for essentially political reasons. On the other hand, as noted earlier, profits from Gazprom are of great importance to Russia and members of its political elite, creating a relationship of mutual dependence between Russia and the EU.

Third, the combination of regulatory and market failures described above seems to imply that all but the very largest consumers are cut off from any of the upside from investing in enhanced security of supply.

Finally, whatever the objective merits, it is also clear that governments are increasingly set on intervention in this area, at EU and national levels. In the context of this book, it is therefore appropriate to ask whether, assuming that policymakers are intent on intervention, the promotion of renewable generation is the best form of intervention to address the EU's concerns about import dependence and its impact on security of supply.

Is Promotion of Renewables the Right Intervention?

It is natural to expect that the promotion of renewable generation will reduce gas consumption and hence gas import dependence, by substituting away from gas-fired generation. Analysis carried out for the European Commission is consistent with this logic. Table 4.2 shows the predicted effects of the EU's new 20–20–20 energy policy adopted in 2008, whose main components are commitments to achieve several goals by the year 2020: reduce demand, with an indicative target of 20% reduction in energy consumption relative to business as usual; increase the use of renew-able energy, with a binding target of 20% of final energy consumption; and reduce greenhouse gas emissions, with a 20% reduction relative to 1990 levels.

As the table shows, the combination of measures is predicted to reduce gas imports by about a quarter, relative to business-as-usual. However, this analysis also raises a number of questions.

First, it is clear that much of the reduction in gas consumption reflects the impact of energy efficiency measures that reduce total energy consumption, rather than the displacement of gas-fired generation by renewables. Indeed, one can see from the table (see the "Impact of new policy" rows), that the predicted reduction in gas consumption induced by the new energy policy (second column) is much larger than the induced increase in renewable energy (last column).

Second, although the analysis does not allow one to separate out these two effects, it is likely that the impact of renewables on gas-fired generation is materially affected by the need for continued use of gas to provide flexible backup for intermittent renewables. Recent analysis by Capros et al. (2008) suggests that the new energy policy will reduce coal-fired generation signifi-

Table 4.2. Energy consumption and import dependence by 2020

	Gas imports (Mtoe)	Gas con-sumption (Mtoe)	Gas imports/ consumption (%)	Solids imports (Mtoe)	Solids con-sumption (Mtoe)	Solids imports/ consumption (%)	Renewable energy production (Mtoe)
2005	257	445	57.8%	127	320	39.7%	122
2020 (oil $61/bbl)							
Business as usual	390	505	77.2%	200	342	58.5%	193
New policy (20-20-20)	291	399	72.9%	108	216	50.0%	247
Impact of new policy	−99	−106	−4.3%	−92	−126	−8.5%	54
2020 (oil $100/bbl)							
Business as usual	330	443	74.5%	194	340	57.1%	213
New policy (20-20-20)	245	345	71.0%	124	253	49.0%	250
Impact of new policy	−85	−98	−3.5%	−70	−87	−8.0%	37

Source: European Commission 2008b, *65*

cantly more than gas-fired, both because of the impact of carbon prices and because renewable power requires extensive support by flexible reserve power, supplied mainly by gas units. Indeed, the analysis in Table 4.2 also shows the impact of the new policy on coal (solids) to be equal to or larger than the impact on gas.

Third, it is unclear which gas sources are most likely to be affected by the reduction in gas imports. If the main effect of the policy is to displace imports of LNG from relatively friendly sources, then the effect on security of supply is small. However, this is likely to be the case. LNG is often viewed as the marginal source of gas, because of the relatively high cost of bringing LNG to the EU, and also because Algerian and Russian producers are to some extent captive suppliers, given the high cost of attempting to diversify away from their European customer base.[19]

Finally, the analysis described above suffers from a more fundamental flaw, in that the business-as-usual counterfactual is arguably something of a straw man. A more interesting counterfactual would be a scenario with a policy that involves the promotion of *all* forms of low-carbon energy on a technology-neutral basis: a carbon tax or cap-and-trade scheme (in this context, the EU ETS with a tighter cap) and no policies aimed specifically at promoting the large-scale deployment of renewables.[20]

The effect of such a policy would be to promote some combination of energy efficiency measures, nuclear power, coal-fired generation with carbon capture and storage (CCS), and renewables. The noteworthy point here is that of those four classes of technology, renewable generation—at least in the forms of wind, solar, or wave power—may well be the least suited to enhancing security of supply, because as noted earlier many renewable generation technologies are intermittent and will likely be associated with continued extensive use of gas-fired generation as "backup".[21] It is therefore likely that they will displace less gas-fired output than equivalent amounts of nuclear power or coal-fired generation (or investments in energy efficiency). Although increased use of nuclear power or coal-fired generation would probably entail increased

imports of uranium or coal, I have argued above that no significant security-of-supply issue should arise from such imports.

In conclusion, therefore, a policy that promotes low-carbon generation in general would probably be more effective in addressing gas import dependency and enhancing security of supply than the current policies that specifically promote renewable generation.

Intermittency

Some of the most prominent forms of renewable generation—in particular wind but also solar and wave power—are variable in output, with the level of production determined by exogenous factors such as wind speed, and also unpredictable to a lesser or greater degree. "Intermittency" is the term generally used to refer to this combination of variability and relative unpredictability.

Two concerns arise from the intermittent nature of renewable generation. A short-run concern is the impact on "system balancing"—ensuring that supply and demand of power are matched on a second-by-second basis. A long-run concern is whether a liberalized power market can be relied on to produce enough investment to meet the much greater need for backup generation—flexible capacity that will be used primarily when demand is high and wind output is low, and whose overall utilization will therefore be comparatively low.

System Balancing

The basic physics of electric power systems requires that production and consumption[22] are matched on a second-by-second basis. In any power system, a system operator (SO) is responsible for continuously ensuring this balancing. The SO has short-term control of certain generating assets, which it uses close to and in real time to correct any difference between the amounts of electricity supplied to the system and the amount being consumed.

Small deviations from perfect balance take place continuously and result in fluctuations in the frequency of AC power. Certain generating units are configured to react automatically and instantaneously to these deviations. This so-called "primary reserve" acts as a first line of defense against imbalances. In case of larger deviations, after the immediate response of the primary reserve, generators providing the so-called "secondary reserve" increase or reduce injections within seconds, following the instructions of a central device in a process known as automatic generation control. Secondary reserve is a scarce resource, because it is provided by units with specific technical capabilities. As soon as possible, therefore, typically with a lag of minutes, injections by units providing so called "tertiary reserve" are increased or decreased, following the instructions of the system operator, and secondary reserve capacity is restored to the pre-deviation level.

In a liberalized market, the SO generally contracts with generators, and sometimes large consumers, to procure these services.[23] The nature of the reserve contracts varies, but for the purpose of this chapter, it is sufficient to note that the SO will pay plants to be available to provide balancing services, as well as for the provision of the services when called on.

Clearly the task of system balancing becomes more difficult the greater the changes in the levels of output, especially if those changes are unpredicted or occur with only very short notice.[24] The prospect of high levels of penetration of intermittent generation therefore gives rise to concern that the job of system balancing will become more costly and less certain of success: the SO will have to purchase more balancing services, and if it fails to purchase enough, it could find itself overwhelmed by unexpectedly volatile shifts in output from intermittent generation, endangering security of supply.[25]

System Stability Implications

From a system stability perspective (i.e., in terms of the risk of supply disruptions), these concerns are probably exaggerated. The more technical aspects of the system-balancing challenges posed by intermittent generation are addressed in Chap-

ter 2 and references therein. In brief, it is clear that significant advances have been made in the ability to forecast wind speeds and the output from wind generation, such that while high levels of penetration of wind generation may add to the cost of system operation, they need not undermine system stability. Current evidence suggests this is the case at least for penetration up to 20% (i.e., with up to 20% of electric power being generated by wind).

The issue is at present less clear for other intermittent sources, and in climates with cloudy skies, solar photovoltaic (PV) power may present greater challenges, as cloud cover means the variability in output can occur over seconds rather than hours (although geographic dispersion will mitigate this to some extent). Nonetheless, Boyle argues in Chapter 2 that they can probably be dealt with in similar fashion (for more details, see also Boyle 2007).

The findings of a very comprehensive survey paper by Gross et al. are consistent with this conclusion: "none of the 200+ studies [we have] reviewed suggest that introducing significant levels of intermittent renewable energy generation on to the British electricity system must lead to reduced reliability of electricity supply" (2006, *iv*).

However, these conclusions do assume that advances in forecasting will be effectively incorporated into system operation procedures. Chapter 11 notes the example of Texas, where a much-discussed emergency occurred in 2008 following a rapid reduction in wind output. The reduction had been predicted by commercially available forecasts, but the SO had not purchased those forecasts.

Cost Implications

The same survey by Gross et al. (2006) also analyzes the cost implications of intermittency, looking at how much additional reserve capacity is likely to be required and how much this is likely to cost. The authors conclude that "for penetrations of intermittent renewables up to 20% of electricity supply, additional system balancing reserves due to short term (hourly) fluctuations in wind generation amount to about 5–10% of installed wind capacity. Globally, most studies estimate that the associated costs are less than £5/MWh of intermittent output, in some cases substantially less." Of course, an additional cost of £5 ($7.50) per MWh is a material issue,[26] but that forms part of a larger set of questions about the cost-effectiveness of renewable generation and is not really a security-of-supply issue.

All of this analysis assumes, however, that the necessary reserve will be there for the SO to call on. This naturally leads back to the question of investment incentives.

Investment in Backup Generation

Given the difficulty of storing electricity and the limited potential for shifting demand across time, the use of intermittent generation means that a large set of backup generation is required to ensure that demand can be met at times when the intermittent sources have low availability because of a lack of wind, sunshine, and so on. This need for spare capacity is not unique to systems with intermittent generation: no type of generation is available with 100% certainty, and conventional units also close down for planned and unplanned maintenance. Nevertheless, large-scale penetration of intermittent generation gives rise to a much higher requirement.

The size of this requirement will clearly depend on the level of penetration of intermittent generation, the technologies involved, the specific electricity system, relevant physical features (e.g., the geographic and temporal distribution of wind), and many other factors. This has been the object of many engineering studies. For the purpose of synthesis, it is convenient to summarize any such study in terms of its estimated "capacity credit," which measures how much conventional thermal generation is displaced by a unit of intermittent generation. So, for example, a capacity credit of 20% means that adding 100 megawatts (MW) of intermittent generation would allow one to retire 20 MW of conventional generation while maintaining the same overall level of system security.

A comprehensive survey of these studies can be found in Gross et al. (2006), whose summary of the estimates of the capacity credit from 19 of the studies is shown in Figure 4.4.

Clearly a capacity credit in the range implied by these studies would add significantly to the total capital costs of the system. With regard to security of supply, however, the concern is that a liberalized market will not have sufficient investment to provide the required level of generation capacity.

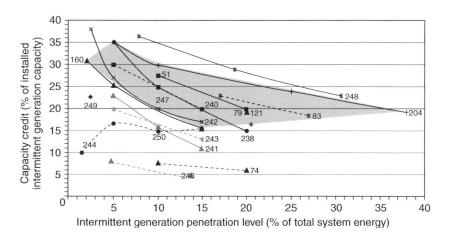

Source: Gross et al. 2006, *43*

Note: the shaded area refers to UK studies

Figure 4.4. Capacity credit values

Starting Point: Excess Capacity

In the short run, there may be little issue with the availability of reserves and peaking generation more generally, because as new intermittent capacity is added to the network, the existing conventional capacity remains available. Although generators could choose to retire this capacity, the incentives to do so are relatively weak, because the investment is already sunk and profits from operation need cover only annual fixed costs (such as transmission charges or taxes levied annually) to make it worth keeping the plant open.

Experience to date in Germany and Spain is consistent with these arguments. Sensfuß et al. (2008) note that for Germany, "the development of renewable electricity generation has had no major impact on investments into new generation capacity up to the year 2006. One reason is that the period after the liberalization of the electricity market was characterized by excess capacity and a subsequent decommissioning of power plants," while "most of the decommissioned capacity was decommissioned for economic reasons such as low efficiency of the plant, need for repairs or inefficient use of expensive fuels such as oil and gas." Chapter 15 in this book describes the evolution of Spanish capacity, characterized by high levels of excess capacity due in large part to the rapid expansion of renewable generation, and as yet without any consequent retirement or mothballing of plants.

In some markets, however, this initial overhang of excess capacity might erode relatively quickly, for a number of reasons:

- If there is too much capacity, then prices might fall to a level that induces plant mothballing or early retirement. Chapter 15 indicates that this situation may be developing in Spain.
- Generators with zonal or regional market power might have an incentive to retire some of these plants so as to raise peak prices and the price of reserve.
- Incentives for early retirement may be exacerbated by the costs of refurbishments, including those necessary to meet the requirements of new environmental legislation. So, for example, in the EU, the cost of adding "scrubbers" to coal-fired units by 2015, to comply with the Large Combustion Plant Directive, would have to be recovered through future profits, and this could be difficult if utilization is expected to be very low.

Investment Incentives in Energy-Only Markets

In the long run, however, there is a real question as to whether energy markets will deliver the needed investment. This question falls into a wider debate as to the ability of liberalized energy markets to provide sufficient levels of investment. The issue has been extensively discussed in academic and policy circles for some years (Cramton and Stoft 2005; Stoft 2002). This chapter can do no more than briefly sketch out the main positions taken.

The issue relates specifically to "energy-only" markets, where generators' only sources of revenue are the sale of electricity and the provision of reserves, as described earlier in this chapter.[27] Theoretical models suggest that although generators in a competitive energy-only power market can earn sufficient operating profits to cover their cost of capital (i.e., the variable profit from selling power can provide a sufficient return on investment), the requirements for that to happen are rather stringent and may not be met in practice in most real-world power markets.

The problem arises because if such a market is competitive, then the spot price of electricity will approximate the marginal cost of the most costly generator being called on—the "system marginal cost"—at any point in time except hours when demand (strictly speaking, demand for energy and operating reserves) exceeds available capacity. In those hours, it is possible for price to exceed system marginal cost, for example if it is set by price-responsive demand. The difference between price and system marginal cost is referred to as a "scarcity rent".

For peaking plants (the plants with the highest marginal cost on the system), these scarcity rents are the only way to create a return on capital. It is possible to show that at least in theory, scarcity rents are also necessary for plants with lower marginal cost, if they are to earn a sufficient return to cover their sunk costs. It is therefore necessary that prices in those hours be sufficiently high to provide an appropriate return on capital, i.e., one that will provide the right incentive for new generation in peaking plants.

Prices at times of scarcity should generally be set either by demand-side response or by actions of the system operator in its procurement of operating reserves (Hogan 2005). If those mechanisms work appropriately, then it can be shown that in theory, the level of scarcity rents will be efficient, in the sense of ensuring that generators earn their cost of capital and have appropriate incentives for new investment.

However, this outcome depends on the presence of flexible scarcity pricing mechanisms and the absence of market or regulatory imperfections that limit demand-side response or distort system operator decisions. In practice, such imperfections are endemic:

- The development of mechanisms to allow demand-side participation has been generally rather slow in most electricity markets, limiting the potential for demand-side response to set prices at times of scarcity.
- The protocols followed by many system operators at times of scarcity do not lead to the appropriate level of scarcity pricing.[28]
- The potential for prices to depart from generators' marginal costs at times of scarcity is often limited by administrative measures constraining prices, to mitigate market power or for other reasons. For example, many centrally organized markets ("pools") have explicit price caps in place,[29] and some limit the offer prices as a part of the ex ante market power mitigation process. In many markets, regulators monitor prices and perform ex post investigations of price spikes, with a chilling effect on scarcity pricing.

It is therefore argued that in practice, imperfections in energy-only markets will lead to underinvestment, particularly in peaking capacity. This issue is commonly referred to as the "missing money" problem.

On the other hand, proponents of a more market-oriented approach argue or assert that in the absence of price caps, the market can in practice be expected to provide sufficient capacity, theoretical models notwithstanding. In Great Britain, this view underlies the existing market design, the so-called New Electricity Trading Arrangements (NETA), which does not have any price caps in place. Practical experience in the decade since NETA was put in place is somewhat ambiguous. Despite many claims of imminent crisis, the lights have stayed on. However, this has been achieved with very little new investment in generation, indicating that the system may have enjoyed an overhang of excess capacity from the preceding decade.

In sum, there are theoretical reasons to believe that in the absence of some form of capacity mechanism, a competitive energy-only market without efficient scarcity pricing mechanisms may underdeliver on investment in reserve capacity (i.e., in flexible units that will experience low average utilization). Although the materiality of those concerns is open to debate, it is clear that any problems would be exacerbated considerably by the much greater need for such units that comes with high levels of penetration by renewable generation. Moreover, in practice, concerns about underinvestment are likely to be well founded because of the combination of explicit price caps and the implicit threat or shadow of future price regulation in most or all liberalized markets. Even in Great Britain, which until recently was viewed as the paragon of energy market liberalization, reregulation is now being openly discussed (see, e.g., Ofgem 2010).

The example of Great Britain also illustrates a deeper problem with investment incentives in the context of current energy policy, of which policy toward renewables forms only a part. The nature of the policy response to climate change, particularly in the EU, means that *all* forms of investment in new generation capacity are heavily influenced by government intervention. Thus renewables, nuclear, and CCS each attract technology-specific forms of support, whereas environmental regulation in the form of the EU Emissions Trading Scheme as well as non-climate-related measures[30] affect the relative and absolute returns on different technologies. Investments are thus arguably subject to very high levels of political risk, and it is by no means clear that markets are able to assess and bear these risks.

In conclusion, therefore, the possibility that competitive liberalized markets will struggle to provide sufficient peaking capacity to accommodate large amounts of intermittent generation is a very real one, for a variety of reasons. The biggest factor undermining investment incentives is the high level of uncertainty and political risk, which affects all generation investments to a lesser or greater degree, except for projects that can rely on explicit and iron-clad government guarantees.

The design of wholesale power markets may need to change to reflect these concerns, by providing stronger and more reliable incentives for investment, such as in the form of capacity payments or similar mechanisms. Capacity payments are widely used in the United States and have had some application in Europe (in Spain, for example, as well as in England and Wales in the 1990s) (Perekhodtsev and Blumsack 2009). These are payments to generators that are additional to the revenue they receive from the sale of energy. Different countries have taken alternative approaches toward implementing such a mechanism. In Europe, the approach generally has been for the transmission system operator (TSO) to make payments to generation on the basis of its availability to generate, recovering those payments as a surcharge on transmission tariffs. In the United States, regulators have tended to place obligations on demand-side participants to contract forward for capacity via organized "capacity markets". The level of the obligation then determines the demand for capacity in those markets, and that combines with supply to determine a capacity price. In either case, the details of design (including, for example, determining the appropriate level at which to place the price, or the quantity associated with an obligation) are extensive and potentially challenging (Harvey 2005). For the purposes of this chapter, it is sufficient to note that

high penetration of intermittent generation means that a number of EU regulators are likely to be addressing those challenges in the coming years.

Finally I note one caveat: the picture may be somewhat different in countries where generation investment decisions are more naturally influenced by informal ties between industry and government. For example, in Germany needed investments may take place as the outcome of informal (or at least non-contractual) agreements between government and industry, rather than being either a pure market outcome or one induced by regulatory mechanisms such as capacity payments.

Conclusions

Dependence on imported gas gives rise to real, albeit hard-to-quantify, security-of-supply issues for the EU, because of geopolitical concerns around both Russia and Algeria. Those problems are particularly acute for many of the new EU member states in eastern Europe, where dependence is highest and relations with Russia are most strained. Dependence on imported coal and uranium does not give rise to such concerns, because of the number, diversity, and friendliness of potential sources.

Market outcomes may not provide an efficient level of protection against the security-of-supply risks associated with gas import dependence, because of a variety of market and regulatory failures. However, the promotion of renewable generation is not the best policy response. Increased promotion of all forms of low-carbon energy (including energy efficiency) would appear to be at least as effective in enhancing security of supply, at lower overall cost.

Security-of-supply concerns related to intermittency and its impact on system operation and grid stability are exaggerated. In particular, recent improvements in wind forecasting mean that even rather high levels of penetration for wind generation can safely be accommodated by an efficiently run and appropriately regulated system operator. The impact is one of cost rather than a threat to stability. High levels of penetration of intermittent generation do, however, raise real questions about market design and security of supply—in particular, whether existing energy-only markets will provide strong enough incentives for the investment needed in peaking generation to cope with periods where high demand coincides with low intermittent output.

In principle, market mechanisms are sufficient to ensure the right levels of investment. In practice, however, the absence in most EU power markets of appropriate mechanisms for scarcity pricing, combined with very high levels of regulatory uncertainty and risk, suggests that there may be a need for some form of enhanced incentive such as capacity payments that reward generation for availability, except in markets where the level of investment is strongly influenced by implicit regulation and consensus-based decision-making involving industry, government, and other stakeholders.

Acknowledgments

Thanks to Luis Agosti, David Black, Godfrey Boyle, Toby Brown, Guido Cervigni, Dmitri Perekhodtsev, and Dick Schmalensee for many helpful suggestions and input. All errors and omissions are mine.

Notes

1. A parallel argument is made in the EU and the United States about the benefit of renewable fuels in reducing the risks arising from dependence on imported oil for transportation. The focus of this book, however, is on renewable generation.
2. The bulk of the remainder was from renewables (14%).
3. Russia provides 42% of the EU's gas imports, Norway 24%, Algeria 18%, and Nigeria 5%.
4. A more recent forecast is even more dramatic, showing a fall from 166 Mtoe in 2010 to 113 Mtoe in 2019 (ENTSOG 2009); all figures

converted from billion cubic meters (bcm) to Mtoe using 1 bcm = 0.90 Mtoe (www.bp.com/conversionfactors.jsp).
5. The 390 Mtoe figure assumes an oil price of $61 per barrel (bbl). A second business-as-usual scenario has an oil price of $100/bbl and forecasts net imports of 330 Mtoe (75% of total consumption).
6. Some observers note that the actual price paid by Ukraine is higher than the contracted price because of an agreement due to arrangements to provide free gas in exchange for delivery of gas into Ukraine. However, even allowing for the additional cost, the price remains well below European levels. See Chow and Elkind 2009.
7. In principle, Gazprom did not cut off supplies to the EU; it reduced the level of flows by the amount of gas that previously would have been intended for Ukraine, while continuing to flow gas for transit across Ukraine to the EU. However, it was easily predictable that Ukraine would continue to consume gas, with the effect of reducing transit flows significantly.
8. Corresponding figures are 42 years for oil and 60 years for gas (BP 2009).
9. The corresponding figure for 1987 was 70 tcm.
10. The U.S. Energy Information Agency (EIA 2008) has reported increases in the level of proven gas reserves as a result of the development of unconventional gas resources. The Potential Gas Committee (2009) reported an increase in reserves, (including proven, possible and speculative reserves) in 2008 to the highest level in its 44-year history.
11. Figures converted from trillion cubic feet (tcf) to tcm using 1 tcm = 35.3 tcf (www.bp.com/conversionfactors.jsp).
12. Here "efficiency" refers to the trade-off between cost and risk. Arrangements are efficient if the additional cost of investing to increase security outweighs the additional benefit (and the saving from spending less does not justify the increased level of risk).
13. So either supply interruptions become more probable/frequent, or society pays a higher price to avoid them, in the form, for example, of higher national security costs or unwanted changes in foreign policy to appease the potential interrupter. This argument has been used in the past to justify the requirements for strategic oil storage.
14. For example, in 2005, a combination of factors temporarily reducing supplies to the United King-

dom led to price spikes of up to 500% between February 23 and March 11 (Trade and Industry Committee 2005).

15. Some U.S. states even have legislation specifically prohibiting price-gouging. For example, Florida Statute 501.160 states that during a state of emergency, it is unlawful to sell "essential commodities" for an amount that grossly exceeds the average price for such commodities during the preceding 30 days.

16. A public good is a good that is non-rivalrous and non-excludable. This means that consumption of the good by one individual does not reduce availability of the good for consumption by others, and that no one can be effectively excluded from using the good.

17. In other words, it is not possible for the system operator to cut off supply to individual consumers, other than very large consumers (who often have "interruptible supply" contracts that allow for such actions).

18. Given metering technologies currently in place, it is not possible to create such an incentive. For example, gas meters typically record only cumulative consumption, and unless they were read on a daily basis—which would clearly be impossibly costly—there would be no way to know how much has been consumed by an individual customer on a day when supplies were particularly scarce.

19. This is a general analysis; individual import contracts can vary significantly.

20. Another interesting counterfactual, and one that in principle should be the starting point for the design of any intervention, would be to use taxation to correct for any security-of-supply externalities. In theory, this might lead to different levels of taxation applied to gas from different sources, with Russian gas probably incurring the highest tax. In practice, this could create difficulties with World Trade Organization (WTO) rules, and it would also raise difficult questions about the quantitative assessment of the size of the externality. A more realistic approach would be to tax all gas. However, this would also be politically difficult because of the aversion of key member states (notably the United Kingdom) to EU-level taxes, and because the United Kingdom and the Netherlands are both major gas producers.

21. This is not to assert that intermittency per se is a security-of-supply risk (see next section), but merely to observe that all else being equal, inter-

mittent generation will displace less gas-fired generation than will non-intermittent. Clearly this would not apply to hydro generation or to biomass. The potential for new hydro is relatively limited, however, and intermittent sources (in particular wind) are forecast to be the dominant form of new installed renewable generation capacity in the coming decade at least.

22. Including consumption in the form of losses arising from transmission and distribution.

23. With the exception of primary reserve, whose provision is typically an obligation placed by administrative means on generators connected to the system.

24. An important distinction must be made here between wind and solar photovoltaic (PV) power. Wind variability occurs over a matter of hours and is relatively amenable to forecasting. Except in climates with cloudless skies, solar PV can vary over seconds and is therefore more difficult to forecast.

25. This account has greatly simplified the complexities of running an electric power system. As well as the need to match total supply with total demand, the system has a number of other technical requirements, including so-called "voltage regulation", and the need to respect transmission constraints. The latter task in particular is likely to become more costly and challenging with the addition of large amounts of new intermittent generation, as discussed in a number of the case study chapters in this book.

26. As of February 2010, this is about €5.70 ($7.75) per MWh.

27. This is in contrast to markets where generators also receive payments for being available to generate, via "capacity payment" mechanisms or capacity requirements and auctions, as discussed later in this chapter.

28. Mechanisms allowing the scarcity of operating reserves to set the price in the energy market are not in place in most EU markets. Such mechanisms require an advanced level of integration between the markets for energy and the markets for reserves, as well as between the spot and balancing markets. Market designs allowing such integration can be seen mostly in the United States. See, e.g., Kranz et al. 2003.

29. For example, the markets in Alberta and Ontario have price caps of C$1,000 ($979) and C$2,000 ($1,958) per MWh (Adib et al, 2008), and Texas (ERCOT) has a price caps of $2,250 (ERCOT 2008). In Europe, Nordpool caps the day-ahead

price at €2,000 ($2,720) per MWh (Nordpool 2008). As discussed in Chapter 15 of this book, Spain has a very low cap of €180 ($245) per MWh, but it is not an energy-only market, as generators also receive capacity payments.

30. Notably the Large Combustion Plant Directive (Directive 2001/80/EC) and the Industrial Emissions Directive (still under negotiation in the European Parliament at the time of this writing).

References

Adib, P., E. Schubert, and S. Oren. 2008. Resource Adequacy: Alternate Perspectives and Divergent Paths. In *Competitive Electricity Markets: Design, Implementation, Performance*, edited by F. P. Sioshansi. Oxford, UK: Elsevier, 327–362

BBC. 2006. *Ukraine Gas Row Hits EU Supplies*. January 1.

Boyle, Godfrey, ed. 2004. *Renewable Energy: Power for a Sustainable Future*. 2nd ed. Oxford: Oxford University Press/Open University.

———. 2007. *Renewable Electricity and the Grid: the Challenge of Variability*, London: Earthscan

BP. 2009. *Statistical Review of World Energy*. London: BP. June.

Bushnell, James. 2005. Electricity Resource Adequacy: Matching Policies and Goals. CSEM Working paper 146. www.ucei.berkeley.edu/PDF/csemwp146.pdf (accessed February 26, 2010).

Capros, P., L. Mantzos, V. Papandreou, N. Tasios. 2008. Model-Based Analysis of the 2008 EU Policy Package on Climate Change and Renewables. E3MLab/NTUA. ec.europa.eu/environment/climat/pdf/climat_action/analysis.pdf (accessed February 26, 2010).

Chow, Edward, and Jonathan Elkind. 2009. Where East Meets West: European Gas and Ukrainian Reality. *Washington Quarterly 32 (1) (January): 77–92.*

CNE (National Energy Commission). 2010. Información Estadística sobre las Ventas de Energía del Régimen Especial (Statistical Information on Special Regime Sales, January). www.cne.es/cne/Publicaciones?id_nodo=143&accion=1&solo Ultimo=si&sIdCat=10&keyword=&auditoria=F (accessed in January 2010).

Cramton, Paul and Steven Stoft. 2005. A Capacity Market That Makes Sense. *Electricity Journal* 18 (7): 43–54.

EIA (U.S. Energy Information Administration). 2008. U.S. Crude Oil, Natural Gas, and Natural Gas Liquids Proved Reserves. www.eia.doe.gov/oil_gas/natural_gas/data_publications/crude_oil_natural_gas_reserves/cr.html (accessed February 26, 2010).

ENTSOG (European Network of Transmission System Operators for Gas). 2009. European Ten Year Network Development Plan 2010–2019. www.entsog.eu/download/ENTSOG_TYNDR_MAIN_23dec2009.pdf (accessed February 26, 2010).

ERCOT (Electric Reliability Council of Texas). 2008. www.ercot.com/news/press_releases/2008/pr_print_1_173287_173287 (accessed January 6, 2010).

Euratom. 2008. *Annual Report*. Luxembourg: European Union.

European Commission. 2000. Towards a European Strategy for the Security of Energy Supply. COM/2000/0769 final. http://europa.eu/legislation_summaries/energy/external_dimension_enlargement/l27037_en.htm (accessed February 26, 2010).

———. (2007). *European Energy and Transport Trends to 2030 – Update 2007*. Luxembourg: European Commission.

———. 2008a. EU Security and Solidarity Action Plan. http://eur-lex.europa.eu/LexUriServ/LexUriServ.do?uri=COM:2008:0781:FIN:EN:HTML (accessed February 26, 2010).

———. 2008b. Second Strategic Energy Review: Europe's Current and Future Energy Position. http://europa.eu/energy/strategies/2008/2008_11_ser2_en.htm (accessed February 26, 2010).

———. 2009a. The January 2009 Gas Supply Disruption to the EU: An Assessment. Commission staff working document. http://ec.europa.eu/energy/strategies/2009/doc/2009_ser2_documents_travail_service_part1_ver2.pdf (accessed February 26, 2010).

———. 2009b. Proposal for Regulation to Safeguard Security of Gas Supply. http://ec.europa.eu/energy/security/gas/new_proposals_en.htm (accessed February 26, 2010).

———. 2009c. Proposal for Regulation to Safeguard Security of Gas Supply and Repeal Directive 2004/67/EC. http://eur-lex.europa.eu/LexUriServ/LexUriServ.do?uri=CELEX:52009PC0363:EN:NOT (accessed February 26, 2010).

Geropoulos, Kostis. 2007. Druzhba: The Not-So-Friendly Russian Oil Pipeline. www.neurope.eu/

articles/Druzhba-The-notsofriendly-Russian-oil-pipeline/73863.php (accessed February 25, 2010).

Gross, Robert, Philip Heptonstall, Dennis Anderson, Tim Green, Matthew Leach, and Jim Skea. 2006. *The Costs and Impacts of Intermittency: An Assessment of the Evidence on the Costs and Impacts of Intermittent Generation on the British Electricity Network*. A report of the Technology and Policy Assessment Function of the UK Energy Research Centre, with financial support from the Carbon Trust. London: UK Energy Research Centre.

Harvey, Scott. 2005. ICAP Systems in the Northeast: Trends and Lessons, California Independent System Operator, September 19.

Hogan, William. 2005. *On an "Energy Only" Electricity Market Design for Resource Adequacy*. Cambridge, MA: John F. Kennedy School of Government, Harvard University.

Holditch, Stephen. 2007. NPC Global Oil and Gas Study. Topic Paper 29. National Petroleum Council, Washington. www.npchardtruthsreport.org/topic_papers.php (accessed February 26, 2010).

IEA (International Energy Agency). 2009. *World Energy Outlook 2009*. Paris: IEA.

Joskow, Paul. 2007. Competitive Electricity Markets and Investment in New Generating Capacity. In *The New Energy Paradigm*, edited by Dieter Helm. Oxford: Oxford University Press, 76–122.

Kranz, Bradley, Robert Pike and Eric Hirst. 2003. Intergrated Electricity Markets in New York. *Electricity Journal* 15 (2): 64–65.

Nordpool. 2008. Adjustment of Elspot Technical Price Ceiling in NOK and SEK. No. 98/2008. www.nordpoolspot.com/Market_Information/Exchange-information/No9808-Adjustment-of-Elspot-technical-price-ceiling-in-NOK-and-SEK/ (accessed February 19, 2010).

Ofgem. 2006. Emergency Arrangements—Open Letter. www.ofgem.gov.uk/Pages/MoreInformation.aspx?docid=5&refer=MARKETS/WHLMKTS/COMPANDEFF/GASEMERG (accessed February 26, 2010).

———. 2010. *Project Discovery: Options for Delivery Secure and Sustainable Energy Supplies*. London: Ofgem.

Perekhodtsev, Dmitri and Seth Blumsack. 2009. Wholesale Electricity Markets and Generators' Incentives: An International Review. In *International Handbook on the Economics of Energy*, edited by Joanne Hunt and Lester Evans. Northampton, MA: Edward Elgar, 722–768.

Potential Gas Committee. 2009. Potential Gas Committee Reports Unprecedented Increase in Magnitude of U.S. Natural Gas Resource Base. Colorado School of Mines. www.mines.edu/Potential-Gas-Committee-reports-unprecedented-increase-in-magnitude-of-U.S.-natural-gas-resource-base (accessed February 26, 2010).

Sensfuß, Frank, Mario Ragwitz, and Massimo Genoese. 2008. The Merit-Order Effect: A Detailed Analysis of the Price Effect of Renewable Electricity Generation on Spot Market Prices in Germany. *Energy Policy* 36: 3086–94.

Stern, Jonathan. 2005. *The Future of Russian Gas and Gazprom*. Oxford: Oxford Institute of Energy Studies.

Stoft, Steven. 2002. *Power System Economics: Designing Markets for Electricity*. New York: IEEE/Wiley.

Trade and Industry Committee, House of Commons. 2005. *Security of Gas Supply: First Report of Session 2005–06. Vol. 2, Written Evidence*. London: TSO (The Stationery Office).

Tversky, A. and D. Kahneman. 1992. 'Advance in Prospect Theory – Cumulative Representations of Uncertainty', *Journal of Risk and Uncertainty*, 5: 297–323.

World Audit. 2010. Freedom House Annual Survey Political Rights Checklist. www.worldaudit.org/polrights.htm (accessed March 28, 2010).

Yenikeyeff, Shamil Midkhatovich. 2006. *The G8 and Russia: Security of Supply vs. Security of Demand?* Oxford: Oxford Institute for Energy Studies.

5

Market Failure and the Structure of Externalities

Kenneth Gillingham and James Sweeney

Policy interest in renewable energy technologies has been gathering momentum for the past several decades, and increased incentives and funding for renewable energy are often described as the panacea for a variety of issues ranging from environmental quality to national security to green job creation. Sizable policies and programs have been implemented worldwide to encourage a transition from fossil-based electricity generation to renewable electricity generation, and in particular to fledgling green technologies such as wind, solar, and biofuels.

The United States has a long history of policy activity in promoting renewables, including state-level programs, such as the California Solar Initiative, which provides rebates for solar photovoltaic purchases, as well as federal programs, such as tax incentives for wind. Even in the recent stimulus package, the American Recovery and Reinvestment Act of 2009, $6 billion was allocated for renewable energy and electric transmission technology loan guarantees (U.S. Congress 2009). (See Chapter 11 for further discussion of the U.S. experience.) Moreover, such policies are not restricted to the developed world. For example, China promulgated a National Renewable Energy Law in 2005 that provides tax and other incentives for renewable energy and has succeeded in creating a burgeoning wind industry (Cherni and Kentish 2007).

Advocates of strong policy incentives for renewable energy in the United States use a variety of arguments to justify policy action, such as ending the "addiction" to foreign oil, addressing global climate change, or creating new technologies to increase U.S. competitiveness. However, articulation of these goals leaves open the question of whether renewable energy policy is the most sensible means to reach these goals, or even whether renewable energy policy helps meet these goals. Furthermore, many different policy instruments are possible, so one must evaluate what makes a particular policy preferable over others.

Economic theory can provide guidance and more rigorous motivation for renewable energy policy, relying on analysis of the ways privately optimal choices deviate from economically efficient choices. These deviations are described as market failures and, in some cases, behavioral failures.[1] Economic theory indicates that policy measures to mitigate these deviations can improve net social welfare, as long as the cost of implementing the policy is less than the gains if the deviations can be successfully mitigated.

Under this perspective, policy analysis involves identifying market failures and choosing appropriate policy instruments for each. While an almost unlimited number of different possible policy instruments can be envisioned, an analysis of relevant market failures allows us to identify which instruments are most likely to improve economic efficiency. This endeavor is complicated by the complexity of some market failures, which may vary intertemporally or geographically.

This chapter explores these issues in the context of renewable energy, with a particular focus on renewable energy used for electricity generation. It first sets the stage with a brief background on the fundamental issues inherent in renewable energy. Next, it elaborates on the concepts of competitive markets and resource use, and how the deviations found in reality from the assumptions of perfect markets may result in market failures. This leads naturally to articulating the classes of possible deviations from perfect markets. A discussion follows of the use of policy instruments to help mitigate or correct for these market failures, with a particular focus on how the structure of the failure influences the appropriate policy approach.

Fundamental Issues in Renewable Energy

Renewable energy, including wind, solar, hydro, geothermal, wave, and tidal, offers the possibility of a large, continuous supply of energy in perpetuity. Analysis of the natural energy flows in the world shows that they provide usable energy many orders of magnitude greater than the entire human use of energy (Hermann 2006). For example, the amount of sunlight reaching the earth is more than 10,000 times greater than the total human direct use of energy, and the amount of energy embodied in wind is at least 4 times greater (Archer and Jacobson 2005; Da Rosa 2005; EIA 2008). In principle, renewable energy offers the possibility of a virtually unlimited supply of energy forever.

In contrast, most of the energy sources we rely on heavily today, such as oil, natural gas, coal, and uranium, are depletable resources that are present on the earth as finite stocks. As such, eventually these stocks will be extracted to the point that they will not be economical to use, because of

either the availability of a substitute energy source or scarcity of the resource. The greater the rate of use relative to the size of the resource stock, the shorter the time until this ultimate depletion can be expected.

These simple facts about the nature of depletable and renewable resources point to a seemingly obvious conclusion: the United States and the rest of the world will eventually have to make a transition to alternative or renewable sources of energy. However, the knowledge that the world will ultimately transition back to renewable resources is *not* sufficient reason for policies to promote those resources. Such transitions will happen regardless of policy, simply as a result of market incentives.

The fundamental question is whether markets will lead the United States and the rest of the world to make these transitions at the appropriate speed and to the appropriate renewable resource conversions, when viewed from a social perspective. If not, then the question becomes, why not? And if markets will not motivate transitions at the appropriate speed or to the appropriate renewable supplies, the question becomes whether policy interventions can address these market failures so as to make the transitions closer to the socially optimal.

The question of why not may seem clear to those who follow the policy debates. Environmental and national security concerns are foremost on the list of rationales for speeding up the transition from depletable fossil fuels to renewable energy. Recently there have also been claims that promoting new renewable technologies could allow the United States, or any country, to become more competitive on world markets or could create jobs.

But much national debate often combines these rationales and fails to differentiate among the various policy options, renewable technologies, and time patterns of impacts. The rest of the chapter explores these issues in greater detail in order to disentangle and clarify the arguments for renewable energy policy.

Resource Use and Deviations from Perfectly Functioning Markets

Welfare economic theory provides a framework for evaluating policies to speed the transition to renewable energy. A well-established result from welfare economic theory is that absent market or behavioral failures, the unfettered market outcome is economically efficient.[2] Market failures can be defined as deviations from perfect markets due to some element of the functioning of the market structure, whereas behavioral failures are systematic departures of human choice from the choice that would be theoretically optimal.[3]

A key result for analysis of renewable energy is that if the underlying assumptions hold, then the decentralized market decisions would lead to an economically efficient use of both depletable and renewable resources at any given time. Moreover, the socially optimal rate of transition from depletable energy supplies to renewable energy can be achieved as a result of decentralized market decisions, under the standard assumptions that rational expectations of future prices guide the decisions of both consumers and firms (Heal 1993).

Although markets are not perfect, the concept of perfectly competitive markets provides a benchmark for evaluation of actual markets. Identification of market imperfections allows us to evaluate how actual markets deviate from the ideal competitive markets and thus from the economically efficient markets. Hence with economic efficiency as a policy goal, we can motivate policy action based on deviations from perfectly competitive markets—as long as the cost of implementing the policy is less than the benefits from correcting the deviation.[4]

For renewable energy, market failures are more relevant than behavioral failures, as most energy investment decisions are made by firms rather than individuals, so some of the key decisionmaking biases pointed out in the behavioral economics literature are likely to play less of a role. However, behavioral failures may influence consumer choice for distributed genera-

tion renewable energy (e.g., residential solar photovoltaic investments) and energy efficiency decisions.[5] These could imply an underuse of distributed generation renewable energy—or an overuse of all energy sources (including renewables) if energy efficiency is underprovided.

Both market failures and behavioral failures can be distinguished from market barriers, which can be defined as any disincentives to the use or adoption of a good (Jaffe et al. 2004). Market barriers include market failures and behavioral failures, but they also may include a variety of other disincentives. For example, high technology costs for renewable energy technologies can be described as a market barrier but may not be a market failure or behavioral failure. Importantly, only market barriers that are also market or behavioral failures provide a rationale based on economic efficiency for market interventions.

Similarly, pecuniary externalities may occur in the renewable energy setting and also do not lead to economic inefficiency. A pecuniary externality is a cost or benefit imposed by one party on another party that operates through the changing of prices, rather than real resource effects. For instance, if food prices increase because of increased demand for biofuels, this could reduce the welfare of food purchasers. However, the food growers and processors may be better off. In this sense, pecuniary externalities may lead to wealth redistribution but do not affect economic efficiency.

Nature of Deviations from Perfectly Functioning Markets

It is useful to consider deviations from perfectly functioning markets based on whether the market failure is atemporal or intertemporal.

Atemporal deviations are those for which the externality consequences are based primarily on the rate of flow of the externality. For example, an externality associated with air emissions may depend primarily on the rate at which the emissions are released into the atmosphere over a period of hours, days, weeks, or months. Such externalities can be described statically. They may change over time, but the deviation has economic consequences that depend primarily on the amount of emissions released over a short time period (e.g., hours, days, weeks, or months). These may have consequences that are immediate or occur over very long time periods.

Intertemporal deviations are those for which the externality consequences are based primarily on a stock that changes over time depending on the flow of the externality. The flows lead to a change in the stock over a relatively long period of time, typically measured in years, decades, or centuries. The stock can be of a pollutant (e.g., carbon dioxide) or of something economic (e.g., the stock of knowledge or of photovoltaics installed on buildings). If the flow of the externality is larger (smaller) than the natural decline rate of the stock, the stock increases (decreases) over time. Intertemporal externalities can best be described dynamically, for it is the stock (e.g., carbon dioxide), rather than the flow, that leads to the consequences (e.g., global climate change).

For some environmental pollutants (e.g., smog), the natural decline of the stock is rapid—perhaps over the course of hours, days, weeks, or months. For these pollutants, the stock leads to the damages, and the stock is entirely determined by the flow over this short time frame. These can be treated as atemporal deviations, as the dynamic nature of the externality is less important with such a rapid natural decline rate.

For atemporal externalities, the appropriate magnitude of the intervention depends primarily on current conditions. Thus, because conditions can change over time, the appropriate magnitude could increase, decrease, or stay constant over time. For intertemporal externalities, the appropriate magnitude of the intervention depends more on the conditions prevailing over many future years than on current conditions or those at one time. As time passes, the appropriate magnitude of the intervention changes but, more predictably, based on the stock adjustment process. Therefore, the appropriate price or magnitude of the intervention will have a somewhat predictable time pattern.

Atemporal (Flow-Based) Deviations from Economic Efficiency

Atemporal deviations from economic efficiency fall into several categories: labor market supply–demand imbalances, environmental externalities, national security externalities, information market failures, regulatory failures, market power, too-high discount rates for private decisions, imperfect foresight, and economies of scale.

Labor Market Supply–Demand Imbalances

Unemployment represents a situation in which the supply of labor exceeds demand at the prevailing wage structure, perhaps because of legal and institutional frictions slowing the adjustment of the wage structure. In the United States, such unemployment does not occur very often, typically only during recessions. At times of full employment,[6] abstracting from the distortionary impacts of income or labor taxes,[7] the social cost of labor (i.e., the opportunity cost and other costs of that labor to the employee) would be equal to the price of labor (i.e., the wage an employer must pay for additional labor), and hence there is no room to improve economic efficiency through green jobs programs.

With unemployment, however, the price of labor exceeds the social cost of that labor. This difference represents a potential net economic efficiency gain, and thus any activity that employs additional workers may improve economic efficiency. For example, if an additional amount of some economic activity produced no net profit, and therefore would not be privately undertaken, the net social economic gain would be equal to the differential between the price of labor and its social cost.

With unemployment, the opportunity cost (and other cost) of labor to the person being employed could be expected to vary substantially across individuals. Some unemployed persons may use their free time productively to perform work at home or improve skills, so that the opportunity cost of labor might be only slightly below the wage. Others may not be able to make such productive use of their time, so that the opportunity cost might be virtually zero, significantly below the wage. Thus the potential net social gain from additional employment could range from nearly the entire wage to zero.

Little evidence exists to suggest that additional employment in renewable energy can provide larger net social gains than any other industry, including the fossil-fuel industry. Moreover, such gains must be seen as transient possibilities in an economy such as that of the United States, which regularly is near full employment.

Environmental Externalities

Environmental externalities are the underlying motivation for much of the interest in renewable energy. The discussion here focuses on general issues in environmental externalities; specific issues inherent in intertemporal environmental externalities are addressed below in the section titled "Stock-Based Environmental Externalities". Combustion of fossil fuels emits a variety of air pollutants, which are not priced without a policy intervention. Air pollutants from fossil-fuel combustion include nitrogen oxides, sulfur dioxide, particulates, and carbon dioxide. Some of these pollutants present a health hazard, either directly, as in the case of particulates, or indirectly, as in the case of ground-level ozone formed from high levels of nitrogen oxides and other chemicals.

When harmful fossil-fuel emissions are not priced, the unregulated market will overuse fossil fuels and underuse substitutes, such as renewable energy resources. Similarly, if the emissions are not priced, firms will have no incentive to find technologies or processes to reduce the emissions or mitigate the external costs. The evidence for environmental externalities from fossil-fuel emissions is strong, even if estimating the precise magnitude of the externality for any given pollutant may not be trivial.

In some cases, there may also be significant environmental externalities from renewable energy production, such as hydroelectric facilities that produce methane and carbon dioxide emissions from submerged vegetation, or greenhouse gas emissions and nitrogen fertilizer runoff from the production of ethanol biofuels. In many other cases, these environmental externalities are relatively small. Whether renewable energy resources are underused or overused relative to economically efficient levels depends on which of the two environmental externalities is greater: those from fossil fuels or from the renewable energy resources. In most, but by no means all, cases, the externalities from the fossil fuels are greater, implying that the market will underprovide renewable energy.

Unpriced environmental externalities from either fossil fuel or renewable energy use would imply either an overuse of energy in general or an underuse of potential energy efficiency improvements.

National Security Externalities

Oil production around the world is highly geographically concentrated, with the bulk of the oil reserves in the hands of national oil companies in unstable regions or countries of the world, such as the Middle East, Nigeria, Russia, and Venezuela. Oil-importing countries, such as the United States, European nations, and China, have seen large security risks associated with these oil imports. In response, they have laid out substantial diplomatic and military expenditures in these regions, at least partly in order to ensure a steady supply of oil. If increases in oil use lead to additional security risks, these risks represent an externality associated with oil use. Moreover, if the additional security risks are met with increases in diplomatic and military expenditures, then these added expenditures can be used as an approximate monetary measure of the externalities.

However, it appears unlikely that a modest increase or decrease in oil demand will influence these expenditures due to the lumpiness of the expenditures, even though the increases in oil use could lead to additional security risks. Conversely, long-term large changes in oil demand may reduce national security risks and the corresponding military and diplomatic expenditures.

In many countries around the world, such as those in Europe, the use of natural gas may have national security externalities because of similar issues. Quantifying the national security externalities associated with oil or natural gas consumption is more fraught with difficulties than doing so with environmental externalities, yet some analysts have suggested that the magnitude may be substantial (Bohi and Toman 1996). Others are more sanguine and believe that global energy markets can substantially buffer national security risks.

In the U.S. context, natural gas and some renewable energy resources, such as biofuels, are substitutes for oil with few or no energy security externalities and thus would be underused relative to the economically efficient level. Improving the energy efficiency of vehicles and furnaces is also a substitute for oil and would also be underused. Most renewable energy resources produce electricity, so until electric vehicles are a viable large-scale substitute for conventional vehicles fueled by refined oil products, national security externalities apply only indirectly to such renewable energy resources. However, these national security externalities, although indirect, can be important. For example, the production of electricity from renewables could lead to reductions in natural gas used for electricity production. This reduction would lead to more availability of natural gas for other purposes, such as heating, where it could substitute for oil in some locations. For biofuels, national security externalities are of foremost consideration. Moreover, in the European context, renewable energy directly substitutes for natural gas.

Information Market Failures

Information market failures relate most directly to the adoption of distributed generation renewable energy by households, such as solar photovoltaic systems or microgeneration wind turbines. If households have limited information about the effectiveness and benefits of distributed generation renewable energy, an information market failure may occur. In a perfectly functioning market, one would expect profit-maximizing firms to undertake marketing campaigns to inform potential customers. However, for nascent technologies that are just beginning to diffuse into the market, economic theory suggests that additional infor-

mation can play an important role (Young 2010). Information market failures are closely related to behavioral failures. Reducing information market failures would also be expected to reduce behavioral failures associated with heuristic decisionmaking.

Imperfect foresight by either firms or consumers (or investors in the stock market who influence firms) suggests an inability to predict future conditions accurately, which may lead to an underestimate or overestimate of how energy prices may rise in the future. If firms systematically under- or overestimate future energy prices, then there may be an underinvestment or overinvestment in research and development (R&D) for renewable energy technologies relative to the economically efficient level.

Although it certainly seems plausible that firms have imperfect foresight, it is less plausible to believe that this imperfect foresight will systematically lead to an underestimate of future energy prices, rather than random deviations that are sometimes underestimates and other times overestimates. Even if firms have imperfect foresight, as long as the firms' estimates of future prices are not systematically biased, then on average investment in renewable energy technologies would still follow the economically efficient path. In this situation, errors leading to overinvestment would be balanced by those leading to underinvestment. At present, there is little evidence either for or against the hypothesis that firms systematically underestimate future price increases.

Another information market failure is the classic principal-agent or split-incentive problem, which may influence renewable energy adoption in two ways. First, in many cases for rental properties, landlords make the decision about whether to invest in distributed generation renewable energy, while tenants pay the energy bills (Jaffe and Stavins 1994; Murtishaw and Sathaye 2006). Second, if landlords are not compensated for their investment decisions with higher rents, then they would tend to underinvest in distributed generation renewable energy. This market failure has been most carefully examined in the context of energy efficiency and heating (e.g., see Levinson and Niemann 2004), but the extent to which this market failure is important for renewable energy has not yet been empirically examined.

Finally, there may be a principal-agent problem relating to managerial incentives. In many cases, managers have their compensation tied to the current stock price, rather than the long-term performance of the company (Rappaport 1978). However, investors may have difficulty distinguishing between managerial decisions that boost short-term profits at the expense of long-term profits and those that boost both short- and long-term profits. In the context of renewable energy, the emphasis on short-term performance may lead to underinvestment in R&D for renewable energy technologies, for the benefits of developing such technologies are likely to be received over the long term, while the costs are borne in the short term. Of course, this issue may occur in any industry and is not unique to renewable energy resources.

Regulatory Failures

In some cases, the regulatory structure can create perverse incentives. For example, average cost pricing of electricity implies that consumers often face a price of electricity that does not reflect the marginal cost of providing electricity at any given time. This may influence the adoption of distributed generation renewables, such as residential solar photovoltaic (PV) systems. In many locations, electricity output from a solar PV unit tends to be higher during the day, corresponding to times of high electricity demand. To the extent that the solar PV output is correlated with high wholesale electricity prices, consumers and firms deciding whether to install a new solar PV unit will undervalue solar PV absent tariffs that account for the time variation. Borenstein (2008) quantifies this effect in California, finding that solar is currently undervalued by 0% to 20% under the current regulatory framework, and that this could rise to 30% to 50% if the electricity system were managed with more reliance on price-responsive demand and peaking prices, because solar output would be concentrated at times with even higher value.

Too-High Discount Rates

In some cases, the discount rate for private investment decisions may be higher than the social discount rate for investments with a similar risk profile. For example, the corporate income tax distorts incentives for firms to invest, effectively implying that they require a higher rate of return on investments than they would otherwise. Alternatively, credit limitations may also occasionally lead to a higher rate of return required for investments. These credit limitations may be due to macroeconomic problems, such as the recent liquidity crisis in the United States, or individual limitations on the firm involved in the renewable energy investment. Individual credit limitations may also apply in cases where consumers are interested in installing distributed or off-grid generation.

Discount rates that are too high may lead to two effects. First, if firms investing in renewable energy technologies have distorted discount rates, this could lead to underinvestment in renewable energy resources relative to the economically efficient level. Second, if discount rates are too high for firms extracting depletable resources, such as fossil fuels, then the fuels are extracted too rapidly, leading to prices that are lower than economically efficient. Because the depletable resource would be depleted too rapidly, the transition to renewable energy technologies may then be hastened relative to the efficient transition. However, investment in renewables may be second best, in that it would still be optimal to invest more, conditional on the too-rapid extraction of depletable resources.

This phenomenon is applicable not only to energy-related investments, but also to investments throughout the economy. Thus this issue provides reasons for changing incentives for investment throughout the economy, but it does not provide a particular reason for shifting investments from other parts of the economy to renewable energy, unless evidence suggested that high discount rates are particularly important for renewable energy. However, we are aware of no evidence that could give a sense of the magnitude of this distortion.

Economies of Scale

Economies of scale, particularly increasing returns to scale, refers to a situation where the average cost of producing a unit decreases as the rate of output at any given time increases, resulting from a nonconvexity in the production function for any number of reasons, including fixed costs. This issue may inefficiently result in a zero-output equilibrium only when we have market-scale increasing returns, where the slope of the average cost function is more negative than the slope of the demand function, and the firm cannot overcome the nonconvexity on its own.

Market-scale increasing returns refer to a nonconvex production function at output levels comparable with market demand. Figure 5.1 graphically illustrates the second condition. If the quantity produced is small (e.g., quantity *a*), then no profit-seeking firm would be willing to produce the product, but if production could be increased to some level above the crossing point (e.g., at the quantity *b*), then it would be profitable for the firm to produce: price would exceed average cost.

Usually a firm could overcome the situation in Figure 5.1 on its own simply by selling at a low price. Even if this is a risky endeavor, it is not likely that all firms would ignore this opportunity. However, firms may not be able to take advantage of the opportunity because of capital constraints or a simultaneous coordination problem.

Capital constraints may be a problem only if the aggregate investment required is extremely large; otherwise, it is likely that some firm could be expected to raise the necessary capital. Capital constraints facing an economy, as occurred in the 2008–2009 recession, could limit such capital investments for an entire economy. Because such events tend to be transient, however, these constraints at most could be expected to delay the investments.

Often economies of scale are accompanied by a "chicken-and-egg" problem, wherein multiple actors must simultaneously invest and ramp up production in order to commercialize a new technology. This may be most relevant in technologies that require a new infrastructure, such as hydrogen-fueled vehicles, which may or may not use renewable energy depending on the hydrogen generation source. Such possibilities require interindustry cooperation and thus may greatly delay investments. Similar chicken-and-egg problems have been overcome in the past, as with personal computers, operating systems, and application software or automobiles, gasoline, service stations, and roads, but these problems greatly complicate investments.

It should be noted that the equilibrium that would occur with market-scale increasing returns would unlikely be a workable competitive equilibrium, but rather a single-firm monopolistic equilibrium. In fact, the situation of market-scale increasing returns is often referred to as a "natural monopoly." This situation raises the possibility of market power.

Market Power

Uncompetitive behavior may influence the adoption of renewable energy technologies in several ways. First, market power in substitutes for renewable energy can influence the provision of renewable energy through two channels. Firms effectively exercising market power in substitutes for renewable energy (e.g., at times the OPEC cartel) would raise the price of energy above the economically efficient level, making investment in

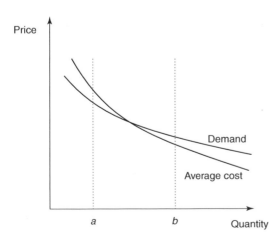

Figure 5.1. Economies of scale: slope of average cost function is more negative than slope of demand function

renewable energy more profitable and leading to an overinvestment in renewable energy. On the other hand, firms that have market power in substitutes for renewable energy may have an incentive to buy out fledgling renewable energy technologies to reduce competitive pressures—leading to a possible underprovision of renewable energy resources if that purchasing firm "buries" the renewable technology. However, the prospect of being bought by a competitor could provide a strong incentive for a new firm to be created with the explicit intention of selling itself to a larger company. Which effect dominates and whether there is market power in substitutes for renewable energy can be determined only empirically.

Market power may also influence the adoption of renewable energy resources by influencing the rate and direction of technological change. If less competition exists in a market, firms are more likely to be able to fully capture the benefits of their innovations, so incentives to innovate are higher (e.g., see Blundell et al. 1999; and Nickell 1996). Conversely, if more competition exists, firms may have an incentive to try to "escape" competition by investing in innovations that allow them to differentiate their product or find a patentable product. Some evidence suggests that the relationship between competition and innovation may be an inverted U-shaped curve, with a positive relationship at low levels of competition and a negative relationship at higher levels of competition (Aghion et al. 2005; Scherer 1967). This relationship likely holds in all industries, not just the renewable energy industry.

Finally, in some cases, vertically integrated utilities may effectively exercise market power by favoring their own electricity generation facilities over other small generation facilities, including renewable energy facilities. This was a concern for the implementation of renewables when utilities invested mostly in nonrenewable energy, but utilities now typically invest in renewable energy along with conventional generation plants.[8]

Intertemporal (Stock-Based) Deviations

An important intertemporal deviation may occur with the existence of stock-based environmental externalities. A second intertemporal deviation may occur if an imperfect capture of the stock of knowledge is created as a result of current actions, leading to underinvestment or underproduction of those activities that lead to growth of the knowledge stock. These can occur with knowledge generation processes, such as learning by doing or research and development; market diffusion of a new technology; or network externalities. Intuitively, when others can capture some of the benefits from the choice made by a firm or consumer, the uncaptured benefits will be socially valuable but will not be taken into account by the firm or consumer.

Stock-Based Environmental Externalities

As discussed above, some environmental externalities have consequences based on the stock of the pollutant, rather than the flow, and the stock adjusts only slowly over time. For such environmental externalities, the intertemporal nature of the damages from the stock imposes additional structure on the time pattern of deviations.

Particularly relevant to renewable energy supplies are carbon dioxide and other greenhouse gases. For CO_2, every additional metric ton emitted remains in the stock for more than a century. Thus emitting a ton today would have roughly the same cumulative impacts as emitting a ton in 20 years. This implies that, absent changes in the regulatory environment, the magnitude of the deviation for emissions now will be the same as the magnitude of the deviation for emissions 20 years from now. Economic efficiency implies that a society should be almost indifferent between emitting a ton of CO_2 now, 20 years from now, or any year in between.[9] As will be discussed below in the section titled "Policies for Stock-Based Environmental Externalities: Carbon Dioxide", it is this relationship that imposes a structure on the time pattern of efficient policy responses.

Similar issues arise for toxic metals released into the waterways, radioactive nuclear waste, mercury in waterways and oceans, sequestration of carbon dioxide in the deep oceans, and rainforest land degradation.

Imperfect Capture of Future Payoffs from Current Actions

R&D

When firms invest in increasing the stock of knowledge by spending funds on R&D, they may not be able to perfectly capture all of the knowledge gained from their investment. For example, successful R&D (e.g., creating a new class of solar photovoltaic cells) by a particular firm could be expected to result in some of the new knowledge being broadly shared, through trade magazines, reverse engineering by its competitors, or technical knowledge employees bring with them as they change employment among competitive firms. In addition, patent protection for new inventions and innovations has a limited time frame (20 years in the United States), so after the patent lapses, other firms may also benefit directly from the invention or innovation.

Fundamentally, R&D spillovers can be thought of as an issue of imperfect property rights in the stock of knowledge: other firms can share that stock without compensating the original firm that enhanced the knowledge stock. To the extent that those spillover benefits occur, the social rate of return from investment in R&D is greater than the firm's private rate of return from investment in R&D. Indeed, although estimates differ by sector, there appears to be substantial empirical evidence that the social rate of return is several times that of the private rate of return. For example, in the United States, the social rate of return is estimated in the range of 30% to 70% per year, while the private rate of return is 6% to 15% per year (Nordhaus 2002). However, the magnitude of the R&D spillovers depend on the stage in the development of a new technology, with more fundamental research having significantly greater R&D spillovers than later-stage commercialization research (Nordhaus 2009).

Evidence of high social returns to R&D is found not just in the renewable energy sector, but throughout the economy. Thus, to the extent that some R&D in renewable energy technologies comes at the expense of R&D in other sectors with a high social rate of return, the opportunity cost of renewable energy R&D may be quite high (Pizer and Popp 2008). Empirical work suggests that additional R&D investment in renewable energy will at least partly displace R&D in other sectors. Popp (2006) finds that approximately half of the energy R&D spending in the 1970s and 1980s displaced, or crowded out, R&D in other sectors. Part of the rationale for this may be that years of training are required to become a competent research scientist or engineer, and therefore the supply of research scientists and engineers is, at least in the short term, relatively inelastic. In the longer term, crowding out is less likely to be an issue, as universities train more scientists and engineers.

Learning by doing

A similar intertemporal market imperfection due to a knowledge stock spillover may also occur if there is a significant learning-by-doing (LBD) effect that cannot be captured by the firm. LBD has a long history in economics, dating back to Arrow (1962). The basic idea behind LBD is that the cost of producing a good declines with the cumulative production of the good, corresponding to the firm "learning" about how to produce the good better.[10] One interpretation is that with LBD, the cost is dependent on the stock of knowledge, which is proxied by the stock of cumulative past production. In the standard model of LBD, the firm today bears the up-front cost of producing an additional unit and thereby also increasing the knowledge stock, while all firms in the industry benefit from the increased stock of knowledge, leading to reduced costs in the future for all firms—an intertemporal spillover.

Importantly, LBD alone does not necessarily imply a market failure. In some situations, one could imagine that all knowledge leading to cost reductions could be used only by the single firm making the decision. In this special case, there are no spillovers, and the firm would have the incentive to produce optimally, weighing the up-front cost of learning against the benefits of the cost reductions in the future as it would any investment decision.[11]

Outside of this special case, the existence of LBD can represent an externality with the potential to be an important market imperfection in renewable energy markets. There is little or no empirical evidence on the degree of spillovers from LBD, but ample evidence exists that the cost of several important renewable energy technologies tends to decline as cumulative production increases (Jamasb 2007). This evidence alone does not prove the existence of a market failure, for other factors may also be able to explain the cost decreases (e.g., R&D or even time-dependent autonomous cost decreases).

The magnitude of a LBD market failure is specific to each technology, and each has to be assessed on a case-by-case basis. Moreover, much like R&D spillovers, LBD spillovers are not unique to renewable energy technologies, but may also be present in any number of fledgling technologies as they diffuse into the market. Hence both R&D and LBD spillovers can be considered broader innovation market failures that lead to underinvestment in or underproduction of certain renewable energy resources.

Network externalities

Network externalities occur when the utility an individual user derives from a product increases with the number of other users of that product. The externality stems from the spillover one user's consumption of the product has on others, so that the magnitude of the externality is a function of the total number of adoptions of the product. Often quoted examples of network externalities include the introduction of the "QWERTY" typewriter keyboard, telephone, and fax machine (David 1985).

An important caveat about network externalities is that the externality may already be internalized. For example, the owner of the network may recognize the network effects and take them into account in his or her decisionmaking (Liebowitz and Margolis 1994). Alternatively, in some cases, the recipients of the network spillover may be able to compensate the provider. For example, for network effects in home computer adoption, the new adopter might take the previous adopter to lunch as thanks for teaching him or her how to use the computer (Goolsbee and Klenow 2002). When the externality is already internalized, net-

work externalities are more appropriately titled "network effects" or "peer effects" and do not lead to market failures (Liebowitz and Margolis 1994).

In the context of renewable energy, network externalities may play a role in the adoption of distributed generation. This may come about if consumers believe that installing renewable energy systems on their homes sends a message to their neighbors that they are environmentally conscious—and that more installations in the neighborhood will increase this "image motivation" or "snob effect." Evidence for this effect has been shown in Sacramento for solar panels (Lessem and Vaughn 2009). Little evidence is available to indicate whether this is truly a network externality or just network effects in distributed generation renewable energy.

Policy Instruments

Each of the failures described above can provide motivation for policy to correct the failure, but it is not always a simple task to appropriately match the policy to the failure. Table 5.1 lists some of the more common classes of policy instruments available to address failures relevant to renewable energy. This table is meant to be illustrative, as there exist an almost uncountable variety of different policy instruments.

How do we choose among the policy instruments? Economic theory along with careful analysis can provide guidance. First, both theory and evidence indicate that multiple market failures will likely require multiple interventions, so a sensible policy goal involves matching the most appropriate intervention to the failure (Aldy et al. 2009; Goulder and Schneider 1999). In some cases, several policy instruments can address, or partly address, a given market failure. In these cases, if economic efficiency is the goal, the combination of policy instruments that provides the greatest net benefits should be chosen. In addition, many of the market failures relevant to renewable energy are broader market failures that may apply to a wide range of markets or technologies. Therefore, economic efficiency would

Table 5.1. Some potential policy instruments

Direct regulation	Command-and-control methods (e.g., requiring firms to generate electricity from renewable energy resources)
Direct government-sponsored R&D	Government funding for scientists and engineers working on improving different renewable energy technologies, support for national laboratories, funding research prizes such as "X prizes"
R&D tax incentives	Subsidies for private renewable energy technology R&D
Instruments to correct market prices: excise taxes, cap-and-trade, subsidies	"Get prices right" by adding to the cost of goods (e.g., through a tax or a permit price) or reducing the cost of goods (e.g., through a subsidy)
Feed-in tariffs	Require electric utilities to purchase electricity from other generators (often small renewable energy generators) at a specified price
Information programs	Education campaigns and required labels
Product standards	Require firms to improve their product characteristics to meet a specified goal (e.g., efficiency of solar PV cell or energy efficiency of lighting)
Marketable marketwide standards: renewable portfolio standards, low-carbon fuel standards, corporate average fuel, economy standards	Require firms (e.g., utilities) to meet a specified standard (e.g., produce a specified amount of electricity from renewables) or purchase permits or certificates from other firms that overcomply with the standard
Transparency rules	Require firms to provide more information about their current conditions to investors
Macroeconomic policy	Fiscal or monetary policies to stabilize the economy and provide liquidity to markets to reduce credit constraints
Corporate taxation reform	Adjusting the corporate income tax to improve corporate incentives
Competition policy/laws	Reduce the exercise of market power through antitrust action
Restructured regulation	Reduce regulatory failures and loopholes in regulations that allow for market power
Intellectual property laws	Laws to encourage innovation by allowing innovators to appropriate the benefits of their work

be further enhanced if the interventions to address these market failures were not focused solely on renewable energy.

Several concerns warrant careful attention in this matching process. First, we care about how effective the intervention will be at actually correcting the market failure. Second, the benefits from the intervention must be weighed against the costs of implementing the policy, including both government administrative costs and individual compliance costs—taking into account the risk of poor policy design or implementation. In addition, careful consideration of any equity or distributional consequences of the intervention is important, both for ethical reasons and for gaining the political support for passage of the policy.

Uncertainty about the magnitude of the market failure and the effectiveness of the interventions is another important concern. In some cases,

potential damages from a market failure may be large enough that the most sensible intervention is direct regulation, so that we can be certain the risk is mitigated. For example, if a toxin is deemed to have sufficiently high damages with a high enough probability, it may be sensible for the government to simply ban it. A comprehensive analysis of the costs and benefits of different policy options that explicitly includes uncertainty, in this case could be expected to reveal the need for simply banning the toxin.

Finally, the temporal structure of the market failures may have a profound influence on the temporal structure of optimal intervention. Economic theory suggests that not only should an intervention be matched to the failure, but also the temporal pattern of the intervention should be matched to the temporal pattern of the failure. For example, the optimal correction for failures that decrease in magnitude and eventually vanish over time would be a transient intervention.

Table 5.2 summarizes the matching, with the various market failures listed as rows and policy instruments from Table 5.1 as the columns. For those instruments that appear to be potentially well matched to the market failures, the letters *P* and *T* indicate whether the instrument could be expected to be permanent or transient. Of course, the particular circumstances of each market failure and the potential policy must be assessed. Some potential policies may be useful only under limited circumstances, and the evidence for some market failures in renewable energy is much weaker than others. Moreover, some of the policy options listed may be reasonably well matched with a market failure but may be second best to other policy options.

Policy Instruments for Atemporal (Flow-Based) Deviations

Atemporal deviations lend themselves to policy interventions that vary, perhaps greatly, with changing external conditions. If the underlying market deviation is a continuing problem, then the policy interventions can be expected to have a relatively permanent nature. If the deviation is transient, the appropriate policy intervention would likewise be transient.

Table 5.2. Sources of market failure and some illustrative potential policy instruments

	Direct regulation	Direct government-sponsored R&D	Competitions, such as X prize	R&D tax incentives	Excise taxes	Production subsidies	Feed-in tariffs	Information programs	Product standards	Cap-and-trade	Marketable marketwide standards	Transparency rules	Macroeconomic policy	Corporate taxation reform	Competition policy/laws	Restructured regulation	Intellectual property law
Labor supply/demand imbalances						T							T				
Environmental externalities	P	P	P	P	P	P	P	P	P	P	P	P					
National security externalities	P	P	P	P	P	P	P	P	P	P	P	P					
Information market failures								P	P			P					
Regulatory failures																P	
Too-high discount rates				P										P	P		
Imperfect foresight								P									
Economies of scale						T	T								P		
Market power									P						P	P	
R&D spillovers		P	P	P											P		P
Learning-by-doing						T	T										
Network externalities						T									P		

Note: P indicates permanent change or instrument; T indicates transient instrument

Policies for Labor Market Supply–Demand Imbalances

Labor market unemployment in well-functioning developed economies can be expected to be a transient problem, associated with economic recession. Typically, policies are crafted at the national or international level and focus on economywide transient monetary or fiscal policies that are terminated when the economy returns to full employment.[12] However, it is often asserted that subsidizing new renewable technologies is advantageous because it would create jobs.

In theory, in order to align private incentives with socially optimal incentives, the labor cost of providing renewable energy could be subsidized by the difference between the market price of labor and the social cost of that labor. Thus in order to improve economic efficiency, such a labor subsidy must vary sharply over the course of the business cycle; be zero during times of full employment; and differ across employees, depending on the options facing the unemployed person. This set of conditions may make it extremely difficult to implement such a policy.

Moreover, and perhaps most important, unemployment is an economywide phenomenon, so an equally valid argument could be made for subsidizing labor throughout the economy, including in the fossil fuels sector. Thus the "creating jobs" argument does not clearly justify targeting the labor subsidies to the renewable energy industry, unless a particularly large deviation existed between the social cost of the labor and the market price relative to the rest of the economy.

Policies for Environmental Externalities

Table 5.2 lists a wide variety of different policy instruments to address environmental externalities. The most straightforward of these is to simply price the environmental externality, following the theory first developed by Pigou (Baumol 1972). In doing so, firms and consumers will take into account the externality in their decisions of how much to produce and consume. The price could be imposed directly as a pollution tax or pollution

fee, with the optimal tax set at the magnitude of the externality. Or a cap-and-trade system could impose a marketwide limit on the emissions, in which case trading of the allowances under a cap-and-trade system would lead to a market-clearing price for the allowances. The cap should be set so that the resulting permit price is equal to the magnitude of the externality.[13] The magnitude of the externality can be estimated based on damage estimates from scientific and economic literature.

In some cases, the risk from particularly severe pollutants (e.g., possibly some criterion air pollutants) may be sufficiently high that the marginal damage associated with the release of the pollutant would always exceed the economic costs of reducing that pollution—implying that direct regulation could be an economically efficient policy. Direct regulation would entail the government setting strict limits on the amount of the severe pollutant emitted or, in some cases, possibly even banning emission of the pollutant entirely.

Environmental externalities from renewable energy can be treated the same way as environmental externalities from fossil-fuel combustion. For most renewables, the environmental externalities are small, so the appropriate tax would be small. A few, such as corn-based ethanol and palm oil biodiesel, may have significant emissions of some pollutants, and the damages from these should be added to the price of the resource.

A second tax or subsidy approach to addressing environmental externalities more closely follows the policies in many countries. Rather than putting a price on both fossil fuel and renewable energy generation corresponding to the magnitude of each externality, the same cost differential could be maintained by subsidizing low-emitting resources and not subsidizing (or taxing) high-emitting resources. However, this approach would have the unintended consequence of making energy use less expensive than its actual social cost, because the external costs would remain unpriced. An additional subsidy on energy efficiency investment can correct for the overuse of energy, removing the primary distortion in energy markets. Unfortunately, this may still lead to a distortion through an overinvestment in the subsidized energy-efficient technologies, because the optimal choice may have involved more energy conservation and less investment in energy-efficient technologies.[14] In addition, such a combination of subsidies may lead to further distortions in factor markets, such as markets for the inputs in the production of energy efficiency equipment. Thus the economic theory suggests that the first-best approach to addressing environmental external damages is through taxes or permits, and the subsidy approach outlined above can be considered a second-best approach to be pursued if the first-best approach is not politically feasible.

Other approaches rely on the idea that if firms must clearly disclose their environmental impacts, they will be motivated to reduce those impacts, and consumers will be motivated to shift their purchases away from damaging products and toward those that are environmentally benign. Information programs designed to publicize the environmentally damaging product or transparency rules designed to document and communicate the environmental damages are prompted by this idea. Enterprise software available from companies such as Hara Software[15] have made it possible to document and broadly communicate carbon dioxide and other environmental impacts in a transparent manner.

Policies for National Security Externalities

Each of the policy instruments available for responding to environmental externalities is also available for responding to national security externalities. Again, the first-best policy intervention works by getting prices right. By pricing the external costs imposed by the consumption of the fuel, firm and consumer decisions will take into account the externality, resulting in an economically efficient outcome. In this case, getting the price right inherently involves taking into account the full external effect, such as the externality that one country's spending an extra dollar on defense causes other countries to spend more on defense. With a correct price on the fuel, firms and consumers will substitute other energy resources that do not lead to national security risks, such as coal or renewable energy, or will find ways of reducing energy use.

Just as for environmental externalities, a second approach would be based on maintaining a price differential between fuels with high and low national security external costs. This approach would face the same issues: overuse of fuel with high external costs and overuse of energy in general. Policies to subsidize energy efficiency would help but may come at the cost of distortions through overinvestment in energy efficiency or overconsumption in some factor markets.

Other policy instruments may also improve economic efficiency by reducing consumption of oil, such as product standards (e.g., for fuel economy), but these approaches inherently lead to additional economic distortions and thus are also not a first-best approach. For example, fuel economy standards lower the effective cost per mile of driving and thus induce more driving, a reaction known as the rebound effect. The additional driving may increase the use of oil, reducing the energy security (and environmental) benefits and at the same time increasing the external costs from accidents and congestion.

Policies for Information Market Failures

Information market failures stem from a variety of sources, and some may be very difficult to address. Those that lead to an underinvestment in distributed generation renewable energy by households may be addressed through information programs to raise awareness. Similarly, consumers typically cannot readily obtain information about their instantaneous use of electricity; they normally receive only a monthly bill for their total electricity use. Programs to provide households with feedback on the price and usage of electricity (e.g., "smart" meters or in-home dashboards to display instantaneous energy use) can help consumers make more informed choices relating to use of energy. Both feedback and information programs may also reduce behavioral failures, possibly providing an additional benefit.

For interventions to address imperfect information, such as imperfect foresight for firms, the intervener—presumably a government agency—would have to possess better information. In situations in which a government agency has superior knowledge, such as of future probable energy prices, an obvious intervention is for the agency to share that information. The Energy Information Administration of the U.S. Department of Energy provides exactly such data and projections accessible to anyone. In fact, given the ability for a government agency to share information broadly,[16] and at low cost, it is very unlikely that imperfect foresight about future energy conditions would provide a strong case for other governmental interventions.

In cases when information is particularly difficult to process or a principal-agent issue exists, consumers may be unable to make informed decisions, suggesting that the government can improve economic efficiency by using its superior information-processing ability to make sensible choices. This reasoning underlies appliance energy efficiency standards and may perhaps pertain to distributed generation renewables in limited cases.

If managerial incentives are misaligned because of the imperfect knowledge of stock market investors, accounting and information rules to promote transparency and a clearer flow of information may be warranted. These accounting and information rules are not specific to renewable energy and may also improve economic efficiency in general.

In addition, if the managers of some firms take a short-term perspective and underinvest in renewable energy, then other firms with a longer-term perspective may invest more to take advantage of the long-term profit opportunities. If other firms with a longer-term perspective do not step in, then there may be motivation for public support for R&D, either through public R&D or subsidies for private R&D. This may not be a very likely outcome, but it could occur in the presence of behavioral failures on the part of stock market investors that lead to a systematic bias toward rewarding short-term performance.

Policies for Regulatory Failures

Policy interventions to reduce regulatory failures involve simply changing the regulatory structure to reduce perverse incentives. For example, to improve on average cost pricing of electricity,

real-time pricing (RTP) of electricity at the wholesale level could be expanded to the retail level.[17] However, the benefits of RTP or time-of-use (TOU) pricing would have to be weighed against the technology and implementation costs, however.

Policies for Too-High Discount Rates

If the discount rate is too high because of the corporate income tax, then the failure here is a regulatory failure, and the appropriate response would be a tax reform. One tax reform that would alleviate this issue would be to allow for the expensing of capital investments. Other options include accelerated depreciation for investments, tax credits for research and development, or the elimination of the corporate income tax entirely.[18] These issues are not particular to renewable energy development, however, and a deeper examination of tax reform is beyond the scope of this chapter.

If the discount rates are too high because of credit limitations, then the appropriate government response involves macroeconomic policy actions, primarily by the central bank. Both tax reforms and macroeconomic policy actions are economywide policy actions that may affect renewable energy, but they are unlikely to have a disproportionate effect on the renewable energy sector in particular.

Policies for Imperfect Foresight

If the evidence is sufficiently strong that a systematic bias exists as a result of imperfect foresight, this would imply a variety of government interventions designed to provide information about possible future states of the world in order to improve long-term decisionmaking. Government information programs that involve data collection and possibly forecasting reports may help alleviate the systematic bias by improving firms' ability to predict future conditions. Increasing regulatory consistency by governments implementing clear, predictable long-term renewable energy policies could also help improve long-term decision-making by firms.

Policies for Economies of Scale

Although economies of scale are not likely to play a significant role for renewable energy in general, it may play a role in specific areas. One approach to address economies of scale would be a temporary direct subsidy sufficient to induce firms to produce at the higher level. Once a sufficiently high level of production is achieved such that the positive competitive equilibrium can be reached, the subsidy can be removed. As indicated above, because in many cases firms can individually overcome problems of economies of scale, it is unlikely that such approaches are in fact needed.

Policies for Market Power

For market power relating to the possibility of firms buying out competing technologies, possibly including renewable energy technologies, enforcement of antitrust laws is likely to be the most effective intervention. In some cases, vertical disintegration may be warranted to ensure a competitive market. Direct government subsidies for private R&D investment, coupled with limitations on the sale of the subsidized company, are another possible alternative to address market power.

For market power motivating utilities to favor their own generation over that from outside suppliers, a feed-in tariff or equivalent policy may increase economic efficiency if the price is set appropriately. The appropriate price would be the wholesale market price for electricity, adjusted for risk and intermittency. Such a price would prevent utilities from favoring their own generation, but it also would prevent any distortions from a price that does not correspond with the market.[19]

As an alternative to a feed-in tariff, regulators can restructure utilities to ensure that they do not favor their own generation over that from outside suppliers. Alternatively, careful oversight of utilities by public utility commissions can also help address market power.

Policies for Intertemporal (Stock-Based) Deviations

Intertemporal deviations are those in which the external costs are based primarily on a stock that changes over time. Individuals influence these stocks only indirectly, by altering the flows into or out of the stock. But once the flow is determined, those individuals have no further control of the stock. For that reason, policy instruments cannot be directed toward the stock but must be directed toward influencing the flow. For economic efficiency, the strength of the incentives must be guided by the intertemporal nature of the stock externality and can be determined from the discounted net present value of the entire flow of future impacts.

Policies for Stock-Based Environmental Externalities: Carbon Dioxide

Carbon dioxide is perhaps the most important stock-based environmental externality, and therefore the following discussion focuses on this pollutant, but a similar result would hold for any stock-based pollutant.

In any given year, a firm can alter the amount of carbon dioxide it releases into the atmosphere, but once the carbon dioxide is released, the firm has no further control. That additional carbon dioxide remains in the atmosphere, increasing the stock of carbon dioxide for the next century. The economically efficient carbon price in any given year (e.g., 2010) can be determined by taking the damages each subsequent year and discounting them back to the chosen year using the social discount rate. In this sense, the optimal carbon price is still the magnitude of the external cost, just as with atemporal environmental externalities.

The calculated optimal carbon price differs by year (e.g., in 2010 compared with 2020) in three ways. First, and most important, the damages are discounted back further at the earlier date, implying that the carbon price is lower at the earlier time.[20] Second, some damages occur during the time between the two dates. Depending on the damage function, this difference may be small (perhaps as it is between 2010 and 2020) and may not change the increase over time of the optimal carbon price. Third, a natural rate of decline of the stock occurs from dissipation of emissions in the atmosphere. This fact would slightly increase the rate of growth of the optimal carbon price.

The magnitude of the damages from carbon dioxide is controversial, and estimates will improve with increased scientific knowledge. Different time patterns of damages would lead to different time patterns of the carbon price, based on the three points discussed above. For example, if the damages from an additional metric ton of carbon dioxide grow (in real terms) at the social discount rate, then the optimal carbon price will also grow (in real terms) at approximately the social discount rate. Under the unlikely assumption that the incremental damages are constant in real terms into the future, we could find a nearly constant (in real terms) economically efficient carbon price.

Policies for Imperfect Capture of Future Payoffs from Current Actions

R&D

When a market failure occurs as a result of R&D spillovers from imperfect property rights in knowledge generation, several possible government interventions might increase economic efficiency. The government could directly subsidize private R&D to bring the private rate of return from R&D closer to the social rate of return, an example of getting the prices right. Such a subsidy would continue as long as a deviation exists between the private and social rate of return, and perhaps indefinitely. The economically efficient subsidy would be set equal to the present discounted value of the spillovers from R&D. Importantly, R&D spillovers are likely to exist in more than just the renewables sector, so an appropriate policy would also provide the subsidy to private R&D in these other sectors.

The government could also directly fund R&D in sectors where spillovers are particularly high. For example, the U.S. government directly funds research in renewable energy in national laboratories, universities, and some research institutes. Theoretically, public R&D can improve economic efficiency if it is focused on research areas where the social rate of return is sufficiently high relative to the private rate of return. In these cases, little R&D would have been undertaken by firms relative to the economically efficient amount, so public R&D complements private R&D. On the other hand, public R&D can crowd out the private, depending on the nature of the R&D. For example, pure science public R&D would be much less likely to crowd out private R&D than would demonstration projects. The empirical evidence on public R&D is not clear-cut. David et al. (2000) review the empirical evidence on whether public R&D complements or crowds out private R&D and find an ambiguous result, suggesting that the result is situation-dependent and underscoring the importance of the nature of the R&D in the social rate of return of public investment.

Intellectual property law plays a key role in how well firms can capture the rents from their innovative activity. Determining the direction in which to change intellectual property law is not simple. If intellectual property law is tightened (e.g., by increasing the length of time patents hold force), then two opposing effects would exist. Firms could capture more of the benefits of R&D and thus would have a greater incentive to invest in it. But fewer spillover benefits may result from the R&D activity, so the social rate of return from the activity would be lower. Little empirical evidence is available to suggest that either a tightening or loosening of intellectual property law would increase economic efficiency.

LBD

If learning by doing occurs in the production of a new technology (e.g., solar photovoltaic installations), then the act of producing increases the firm's stock of cumulative experience and thus leads to declines in future costs. The stock of cumulative experience grows when insights from previous production by that or another firm allows it to improve its production techniques. The stock also may decline if some of these techniques are forgotten. Theories of LBD often proxy all of these complex dynamics by postulating that the cost of future production for *all* firms at any time will be a function of the cumulative stock of experience from production in the market. But the market failure can be thought of in a more general sense as a spillover from the stock of any single firm's cumulative experience from production to other firms.

Once a firm chooses how much to produce at any given time (i.e., the flow into the stock of experience), it subsequently has no further control over the stock of experience and its impact on future costs. Thus economically efficient policies for LBD must focus on the quantity produced, while taking into account the fact that experience is a stock. The most straightforward policy instrument to address LBD spillovers is a subsidy. The economically efficient per-unit subsidy equals the discounted present value of all future cost reductions resulting from the additional production that cannot be captured by the individual firm.

However, a second element to the economic theory behind LBD also may affect the economically efficient policy: the spillovers from LBD are postulated to decline along with the costs. For example, in the standard formulation, as illustrated in Figure 5.2, the percentage cost decrease depends on the percentage increase in the stock, so every additional unit has a progressively decreasing percentage impact on costs. Consequently, as cost decreases with a greater stock, a given percentage cost decrease leads to a smaller absolute cost decrease. These factors together imply that the LBD externality—and hence the

appropriate magnitude of the intervention—will be declining over time. Acting in the opposite direction, if the sales are growing rapidly, the cost reduction is applied to a larger amount of production, reducing the rate of decline of the intervention.

Thus optimal subsidies for LBD will likely be transient and decline over time as LBD runs its course. The speed at which the subsidies are phased out will depend on the particular technology and may require adjustment if different conditions arise than were initially expected. In one example, the optimal solar PV subsidies for California calculated under the baseline assumptions in van Benthem et al. (2008) follow a declining path and are phased out over 15 years.

Network externalities

Network externalities may play a role in the adoption of distributed generation renewable energy. If it can be demonstrated that a network externality truly exists, rather than network effects, then one approach to correct for this externality would be a temporary production subsidy (Goolsbee and Klenow 2002). Once a product has taken over (nearly) the entire market, there would be no room for further spillovers and thus no need for the subsidy policy.

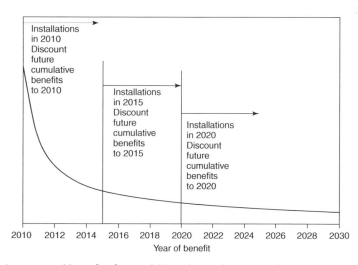

Figure 5.2. Illustrative incremental benefits from additional cumulative installations: LBD

Conclusions

Renewable energy has an immense potential to serve our energy needs, and in the long run, a transition from depletable fossil fuel resources to renewable energy is inevitable. This chapter has delved into reasons why policymakers should be interested in policies to promote renewable energy, pointing to a variety of market failures that may lead to a divergence between the optimal transition to renewables and the observed transition. Economic theory suggests that we can improve economic efficiency by matching the policy instrument to the market failure.

The structure and nature of each market failure have important ramifications for the appropriate policy actions to correct for the market failure and move closer to an optimal transition to renewable energy. The discussion above distinguished between atemporal market failures and intertemporal (i.e., stock-based) market failures. In either case, the economically efficient policy action matches the temporal pattern of the market failure. This implies a temporary policy (e.g., LBD spillovers) in some cases and a permanent policy (e.g., R&D spillovers) in others.

Renewable energy policy is likely to require several different policy instruments to address the various kinds of market failures. When the market failures are closely related, a single policy instrument can address, or partly address, more than one market failure. For instance, provision of information about low-cost or low-effort opportunities to save energy and help preserve the environment may reduce the informational market failure and also influence consumers to partly internalize the environmental externalities (Bennear and Stavins 2007).

For renewable energy, the most important market failures, with the strongest empirical evidence, appear to be environmental externalities, innovation market failures, national security market failures, and regulatory failures. Only a few of the market failures identified in this chapter are unique to renewable energy. Environmental externalities due to fossil-fuel use are the most important of these, but if policy action is already under way to correct for externalities from fossil-

fuel emissions, then we must look to other market failures for motivation for renewable energy policy. As these other market failures often apply to other parts of the economy, addressing them may entail policy actions that extend much beyond renewable energy.

Political feasibility is a final consideration with important ramifications for renewable energy policy. In some cases, the first-best policy approach may not be politically feasible. A second-best approach may involve multiple instruments, even in cases when the first-best approach involved only a single instrument. For example, rather than a single tax to internalize environmental externalities, the same price differential can be achieved by combining a smaller tax (or no tax) on fossil fuels with a subsidy for renewable energy. Similarly, a cap-and-trade system may not be politically feasible because of uncertainty about how high the costs of abatement might be, so a more viable option might be to use two instruments in a hybrid cap-and-trade and tax system, commonly known as a cap-and-trade with a safety valve (Jacoby and Ellerman 2004; McKibbin and Wilcoxen 2002; Pizer 2002).

In other cases, the only politically feasible options for addressing the market failures relevant to renewable energy are not the first-choice instruments, but rather second-choice instruments that address the market failures indirectly. Renewable portfolio standards (RPSs) are one of the most prominent examples of a policy instrument that only indirectly addresses the market failures relevant to renewable energy. By setting a requirement on the amount of renewable energy in each utility's electricity generation mix, an RPS adds an implicit subsidy on renewable energy, with the magnitude of the subsidy directly related to the stringency of the cap. If the RPS is carefully set, this implicit subsidy could act just like an appropriately set actual subsidy—leading to the second-best outcome described above. However, finding this appropriate level for an RPS may be exceedingly difficult and subject to intense political disputes.

A sensible set of policies to address the market failures relevant to renewable energy has the potential to greatly improve economic efficiency—and at the same time would have other benefits, such as improving air quality and mitigating the risk of catastrophic global climate change. Much future work remains to better quantify the most relevant market failures and further improve our understanding of how to develop policies to best address these market failures.

Acknowledgments

The authors thank Richard Schmalensee, Boaz Moselle, Arthur van Benthem, Douglas Hannah, and Jonathan Leaver for very helpful comments. Any remaining errors are the sole responsibility of the authors.

Notes

1. The concept of behavioral failures stems from behavioral economics and is quite new to environmental economics. See Shogren and Taylor (2008) and Gillingham et al. (2009) for recent reviews discussing the concept in the context of environmental economics.

2. Economic theory defines "economically efficient" in technical terms as an allocation of resources where no potential Pareto improvement exists, which refers to a reallocation of resources that benefits at least one individual and imposes no costs on any others. Note that economic efficiency is a distinct concept from the equity or fairness of an allocation of resources.

3. It is still theoretically unclear how to disentangle systematic biases in decisionmaking from inherent preferences, but behavioral welfare analysis is an area of active theoretical development and may eventually shed light on this issue. See, e.g., Bernheim and Rangel (2009).

4. Important equity or fairness concerns may also be involved. This chapter focuses on economic efficiency as a policy goal, while noting that equity considerations, in theory, can often be dealt with through lump-sum transfers of wealth that do not distort incentives or through modifications of the income tax rates. If the policy goal is reducing

global inequity, other distributional policies are likely to be more effective than renewable energy policy.

5. It is important to note that unless a behavioral failure is a systematic, rather than random, departure of observed choice from a theoretical optimum, it may be very difficult to formulate policies. If the systematic departure is in a consistent direction, the intervention can work in the opposite direction to correct this deviation. But random deviations would require an intervention contingent on the deviation. For example, poor information about the operating characteristics of distributed photovoltaics could lead some people to install these devices even though they would ultimately come to regret the decision and other people not to install them even though the devices would have turned out to be beneficial. In such circumstances, development and dissemination of information about photovoltaic operating characteristics for alternative locations could improve such decisions. For the most part, however, policy options designed to compensate for random deviations would be difficult to formulate and effectively implement.

6. "Full employment" for a well-functioning developed economy refers here to "at the natural rate of unemployment." Some unemployment will always exist as a result of transitions between jobs and mismatches of available and needed skills.

7. Personal income taxes or labor taxes, such as the U.S. Social Security tax, provide incentives to reduce the supply of labor, so that the marginal social value of labor exceeds the value of that labor to the worker. However, issues of the distortions associated with and the reform of such tax systems go well beyond the scope of this chapter.

8. This remains a concern for the overall economic efficiency of investment, even when it does not distort the mix of renewables versus nonrenewable technologies.

9. "Almost indifferent" because the cumulative impacts of emitting a ton now may be somewhat different from the impacts of emitting a ton in 20 years and because the regulatory environment could change in that period.

10. LBD is closely related to economies of scale, except that learning by doing has a distinctly different intertemporal relationship, where costs decline as a function of cumulative production, and increasing returns to scale implies that average costs decline with production at a given time.

11. If the knowledge leading to cost reductions by one firm could have been used by other firms, but that firm somehow manages to keep all the knowledge private, even if it does not use it (so it is effectively "wasted knowledge"), there would still be a market failure in that some of the potential benefits of the learning would not be captured by anyone.

12. As noted above, this does not deal with the labor market problems associated with income taxes or labor taxes that provide incentives to reduce the supply of labor.

13. A substantial literature addresses the trade-offs between a tax and a cap-and-trade system, particularly relating to policymaking under uncertainty. For a recent review discussing these issues, see Aldy et al. (2009).

14. If behavioral failures have caused an under-investment in energy efficiency, then there may not be an overinvestment in energy efficiency from the subsidy.

15. Information available at www.hara.com.

16. In some cases, release of information is not possible or is undesirable, such as when it involves weapons programs or other programs closely related to national security.

17. In order to be effective, RTP would have to be complemented with real-time feedback on the electricity price at the current time.

18. Note that reducing taxes in some areas may require increasing taxes in others, so a full analysis should examine the relative distortions from each of the different taxes.

19. For example, in the United States, the Public Utility Regulatory Policies Act (PURPA) of 1978 required electric utilities to buy power from small-scale nonutility producers at the avoided cost rate, which is the cost the utility would incur were it to acquire the electricity from other sources. Choosing the appropriate price turned out to be remarkably problematic.

20. For instance, the 2020 efficient tax would be greater than the 2010 efficient tax by a factor of $(1 + r)^{10}$, where r is the annual social discount rate. At a 5% discount rate, the 2020 carbon tax would be 63% greater than the 2010 carbon tax.

References

Aghion, P., N. Bloom, R. Blundell, R. Griffith, and P. Howitt. 2005. Competition and Innovation: An Inverted-U Relationship. *Quarterly Journal of Economics* 120: 701–728.

Aldy, J., A. Krupnick, R. Newell, I. Parry, and W. Pizer. 2009. Designing Climate Mitigation Policy. Discussion paper 08–16. Washington, DC: Resources for the Future.

Archer, C., and M. Jacobson. 2005. Evaluation of Global Wind Power. *Journal of Geophysical Research D* 110: 1–20.

Arrow, K. 1962. The Economic Implications of Learning by Doing. *Review of Economic Studies* 29: 155–173.

Baumol, W. 1972. On Taxation and the Control of Externalities. *American Economic Review* 62: 307–322.

Bennear, L., and R. Stavins. 2007. Second-Best Theory and the Use of Multiple Policy Instruments. *Environmental and Resource Economics* 37: 111–129.

Bernheim, D., and A. Rangel. 2009. Beyond Revealed Preference: Choice-Theoretic Foundations for Behavioral Welfare Economics. *Quarterly Journal of Economics* 124: 51–104.

Blundell, R., R. Griffith, and J. Van Reenen. 1999. Market Share, Market Value and Innovation in a Panel of British Manufacturing Firms. *Review of Economic Studies* 66: 529–554.

Bohi, D., and M. Toman. 1996. Economics of Energy Security. Norwell, MA: Kluwer Academic Publishers.

Borenstein, S. 2008. The Market Value and the Cost of Solar Photovoltaic Electricity Production. CSEM Working paper 176. Berkeley, CA: University of California Energy Institute.

Cherni, J., and J. Kentish. 2007. Renewable Energy Policy and Electricity Market Reforms in China. *Energy Policy* 35: 3616–3629.

Da Rosa, A. 2005. *Fundamentals of Renewable Energy Processes*. Amsterdam; Elsevier Academic Press.

David, P. 1985. Clio and the Economics of QWERTY. *American Economic Review* 75: 332–337.

David, P., B. Hall, and A. Toole. 2000. Is Public R&D a Complement or Substitute for Private R&D? *Research Policy* 29: 497–529.

EIA (Energy Information Administration). 2008. *International Energy Annual 2006*. Washington, DC: Department of Energy, EIA.

Gillingham, K., R. Newell, and K. Palmer. 2009. Energy Efficiency Economics and Policy. *Annual Review of Resource Economics* 1: 597–619.

Goolsbee, A., and P. Klenow. 2002. Evidence on Learning and Network Externalities in the Diffusion of Home Computers. *Journal of Law and Economics* 35: 317–343.

Goulder, L., and S. Schneider. 1999. Induced Technological Change and the Attractiveness of CO_2 Emissions Abatement Policies. *Resource and Energy Economics* 21: 211–253.

Heal, G. 1993. The Optimal Use of Exhaustible Resources. In *Handbook of Natural Resource and Energy Economics*, Vol. 3, edited by A. Kneese and J. Sweeney. Amsterdam: Elsevier.

Hermann, W. 2006. Quantifying Global Exergy Resources. *Energy* 31: 1685–1702.

Jacoby, H., and A. D. Ellerman. 2004. The Safety Valve and Climate Policy. *Energy Policy* 32: 481–491.

Jaffe, A., R. Newell, and R. Stavins. 2004. The Economics of Energy Efficiency. In *Encyclopedia of Energy*, edited by C. Cleveland. Amsterdam: Elsevier, 79–90.

Jaffe, A., and R. Stavins. 1994. The Energy Paradox and the Diffusion of Conservation Technology. *Resource and Energy Economics* 16: 91–122.

Jamasb, T. 2007. Technical Change Theory and Learning Curves: Patterns of Progress in Electricity Generation Technologies. *Energy Journal* 28: 51–71.

Lessem, N., and R. Vaughn. 2009. Image Motivation in Green Consumption. Working paper. Los Angeles: University of California–Los Angeles.

Levinson, A., and S. Niemann. 2004. Energy Use by Apartment Tenants When Landlords Pay for Utilities. *Resource and Energy Economics* 26: 51–75.

Liebowitz, S., and S. Margolis. 1994. Network Externality: An Uncommon Tragedy. *Journal of Economic Perspectives* 8: 133–150.

McKibbin, W., and P. Wilcoxen. 2002. The Role of Economics in Climate Change Policy. *Journal of Economic Perspectives* 16: 107–129.

Murtishaw, S., and J. Sathaye. 2006. *Quantifying the Effect of the Principal-Agent Problem on US Residential Use.* LBNL-59773. Berkeley, CA: Lawrence Berkeley National Laboratory.

Nickell, S. 1996. Competition and Corporate Performance. *Journal of Political Economy* 104: 724–746.

Nordhaus, W. 2002. Modeling Induced Innovation in Climate Change Policy. In *Technological Change and the Environment*, edited by A. Grubler, N. Nakicenovic, and W. Nordhaus. Washington, DC: Resources for the Future Press.

Nordhaus, W. 2009. Designing a Friendly Space for Technological Change to Slow Global Warming. Snowmass Conference on Technologies to Combat Global Warming. August 2009, Snowmass, CO.

Pizer, W. 2002. Combining Price and Quantity Controls to Mitigate Global Climate Change. *Journal of Public Economics* 85: 409–434.

Pizer, W., and D. Popp. 2008. Endogenizing Technological Change: Matching Empirical Evidence to Modeling Needs. *Energy Economics* 30: 2754–2770.

Popp, D. 2006. R&D Subsidies and Climate Policy: Is There a "Free Lunch?" *Climatic Change* 77: 311–341.

Rappaport, A. 1978. Executive Incentives vs. Corporate Growth. *Harvard Business Review* 56: 81–88.

Scherer, F. 1967. Market Structure and the Employment of Scientists and Engineers. *American Economic Review* 58: 524–531.

Shogren, J., and L. Taylor. 2008. On Behavioral-Environmental Economics. *Review of Environmental Economics and Policy* 2: 26–44.

U.S. Congress. 2009. *American Recovery and Reinvestment Act of 2009.* 111th Cong., 1st sess.

van Benthem, A., K. Gillingham, and J., Sweeney. 2008. Learning-by-Doing and the Optimal Solar Policy in California. *Energy Journal* 29: 131–151.

Young, P. 2010. Innovation Diffusion in Heterogeneous Populations: Contagion, Social Influence, and Social Learning. *American Economic Review* 99: 1899–1924.

6

Renewable Energy, Energy Efficiency, and Emissions Trading

José Goldemberg

The present energy system is based primarily on the use of fossil fuels. In 2008, total primary energy consumption was 516 exajoules (EJ)—corresponding to 12.32 billion tons equivalent of petroleum—of which coal, oil and gas represented 81% (Figure 6.1). The remaining 19% originated in traditional biomass (8%), used mainly in developing countries; nuclear (6%); large hydropower (2%), which is a renewable source of energy; and "new renewables" (3%), which include modern biomass, geothermal, solar, wind, small hydro, and marine energy.[1] Large hydropower and new renewables together are referred to as "modern renewables."

The 20th century marked the emergence of fossil fuels, which represented less than 20% in the middle of the 19th century. Until then, renewables—mainly fuelwood—supplied the bulk

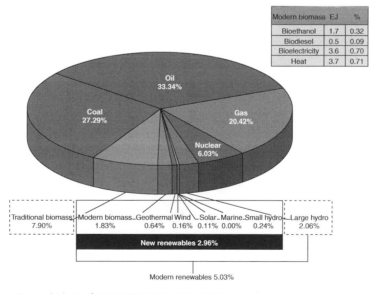

Modern biomass	EJ	%
Bioethanol	1.7	0.32
Biodiesel	0.5	0.09
Bioelectricity	3.6	0.70
Heat	3.7	0.71

Sources: Author's elaboration on the basis of UNDP 2000, 2004; REN21 2009

Figure 6.1. World primary energy supply shares of 516 exajoules (EJ)

of the energy needed for all purposes ranging from home heating to cooking to manufacturing (Figure 6.2).

These energy sources allowed the industrialized countries to achieve a high level of development benefiting at least one-third of the world's population. Fossil fuels were cheap and abundant throughout most of the 20th century, which discouraged efforts to optimize energy systems and reduce energy losses. The continued heavy reliance on fossil fuels today as the main source of energy is creating serious problems, which are becoming increasingly evident as time goes by:

- Reserves of fossil fuels are finite and by the end of the 20th century were showing signs of exhaustion.
- Impurities of fossil fuels, such as sulfur oxides and particulate matter, became a main source of pollution at the local and regional levels.
- The combustion of fossil fuels has the unavoidable result of producing carbon dioxide (CO_2), which is changing the composition of the atmosphere, as well as other greenhouse gases (GHGs). Before the industrial age, at the end of the 17th century, the amount of CO_2 in the atmosphere was 0.027%, or 270 parts per million (ppm), but it has been growing steadily and reached 0.0338%, or

338 ppm, in 2008. Such increase is the main source of global warming and associated climate changes.

Figure 6.3 shows the evolution of CO_2 emissions resulting from the present energy system. Carbon dioxide emissions from Annex B countries (of the Climate Convention) have stabilized since 1990 but are growing rapidly in developing (non-Annex B) countries (of the Climate Convention) at a rate of approximately 4% per year; this is reflected in world emissions, which are growing roughly 600 million tons of CO_2 per year.

Carbon dioxide emissions are the dominant component of greenhouse gas emissions, but in 2006, they represented only 69.6% of total emissions. The remaining 30.4% were methane (CH_4), nitrous oxide (N_2O), and fluorinated gases with high global warming potential (GWP), which are sulfur hexafluoride (SF_6), hydrofluorocarbons (HFCs), and perfluorocarbons (PFCs) (Figure 6.4).

GHG emissions are usually expressed in CO_2 equivalent. Total emissions in 2005 were approximately 45 gigatons (Gt) of CO_2 equivalent. To reduce CO_2 and other GHG emissions thus became one of the most urgent tasks we face today. There are two approaches to this problem: use energy more efficiently, consequently emit-

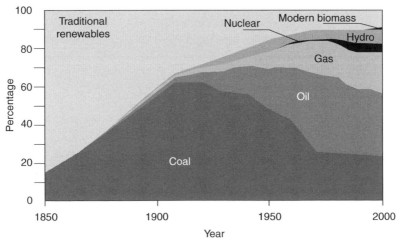

Source: UNDP 2000

FIGURE 6.2. World energy consumption, 1850–2000

ting less CO_2 and extending the life of fossil-fuel reserves; and increase the contribution of renewable energy in the world energy matrix.

National governments, as well as some sectors of the productive system, such as industry, transportation, and residential, can adopt these solutions to varying degrees. In industrialized countries, which have already reached a high level of energy consumption per capita, energy efficiency can be implemented more easily, but renewable energy can also play a significant role. In developing countries, where energy consumption per capita is low and growth in energy services is inevitable, clean and efficient technologies and renewable energy can be incorporated early in the process of development, following a different path than that taken in the past by today's industrialized countries.

Against this background, this chapter discusses the potential of energy efficiency, renewable energy, and emissions trading schemes in achieving the objective of reducing greenhouse gas emissions.

Renewable Energy

Table 6.1 lists the energy from various types of renewable sources used in the world at the end of 2008, as well their yearly growth rates. Traditional biomass is left out of this table because it is used mainly in rural areas as cooking fuel or charcoal in ways that are frequently nonrenewable, leading to deforestation and soil degradation.

Some of the renewable energy sources are developing rapidly, with impressive growth rates of 38% per year for photovoltaic (PV) and 25% per year for wind (see Figure 6.5).

In 2008, renewables (including large hydro) represented approximately 5% of the world's total primary energy consumption, but they are growing at a rate of 6.3% per year, whereas total primary energy supply is growing at a smaller rate of approximately 2% per year. Taking into account the appropriate efficiency and capacity factors,[2] the numbers in Table 6.1 can be converted into the total primary energy contribution from renewables, as shown in Table 6.2 and Figure 6.6.

An extrapolation of the contribution of renewables up to 2030 on the basis of the rates of growth in the last 10 years is shown in Figure 6.7.

To give an idea of the effort that would be needed to curb CO_2 emissions up to 2050, the

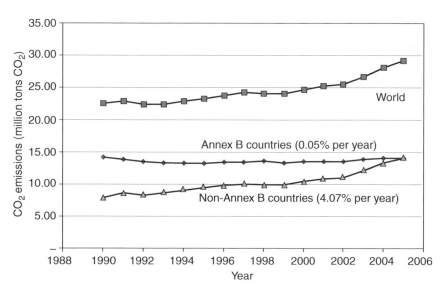

Source: CDIAC 2009

Figure 6.3. World fossil-fuel CO_2 emissions and growth rate, 1990–2005

Table 6.1. Electricity, heat, and transport fuel from renewable sources

	Year				Growth rate per year
	Electricity (GW)				
	end 1998 [a]	end 2001 [b]	end 2006 [c]	end 2008 [d]	
Large hydropower	640	690	774	860	3.00%
Wind power	10	23	74	121	28.32%
Small hydropower	23	25	73	85	13.96%
Biomass power	40	40	45	52	2.66%
Solar PV	0.5	11	7.8	13	38.52%
Geothermal	8	8	9.5	10	2.26%
Solar thermal power	0.4	0.4	0.4	0.5	2.26%
Ocean (tidal) power	0.3	0.3	0.3	0.3	0.00%
	Hot water/heating (GWth)				Growth rate per year
Biomass heating	200	210	235	250	2.26%
Solar collectors	18	57	105	145	23.20%
Geothermal	11	11	33	50	16.35%
	Transport fuels (billion liters/year)				Growth rate per year
Ethanol	18	18	39	57	12.22%
Biodiesel	0	1.2	6	12	38.95%

Sources: [a]UNDP 2000; [b]UNDP 2004; [c]REN21 2007; [d]REN21 2009
Note: GW = gigawatts; GWth = gigawatts-thermal

International Energy Agency (IEA) recently produced two scenarios of what would be required in terms of renewables in the electricity sector. In one, called the ACT Scenario, global CO_2 emissions would be returned to current levels by 2050; in the other, the BLUE Scenario, CO_2 emissions would be reduced by 50% from current levels. The results are shown in Table 6.3.

In the IEA scenarios, nuclear energy and coal- and gas-fired thermal power plants with carbon capture and storage (CCS) are included. These numbers are very large but give an idea of the effort required to prevent catastrophic climate change.

The main policy instruments used to accelerate the introduction of renewables in the energy systems of a number of countries are feed-in tariffs and renewable portfolio standards (RPSs). Feed-in tariffs are a policy adopted by governments to accelerate the introduction of renewable energy sources in their matrixes. They obligate utilities to purchase the output of renewable generators at a fixed price, which is set high enough to ensure that the renewable generation in ques-

tion is profitable. The costs of the feed-in tariff are generally passed on to consumers via regulated charges. Feed-in tariffs have been used in Germany and Spain (see Chapters 14 and 15), and in both countries, they have been associated with rapid growth in renewable generation. Under the

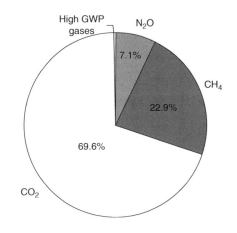

Source: UNFCCC 2009a

Figure 6.4. Contributions of greenhouse gases to global warming in 2006

Table 6.2. Primary energy production from new renewables

Source/technology		Energy production (EJ)				Growth rate
		1998	2001	2004	2008	
Modern biomass energy	Total	6.033	6.369	7.001	9.422	4.56%
	Bioethanol	0.450	0.45	0.763	1.675	14.05%
	Biodiesel	0.000	0.045	0.079	0.45	38.95%
	Electricity	2.618	2.782	2.921	3.616	3.28%
	Heat	2.965	3.092	3.238	3.681	2.19%
Geothermal	Total	1.800	2.106	2.604	3.285	6.20%
	Electricity	1.656	1.908	2.147	2.385	3.72%
	Heat	0.144	0.198	0.457	0.900	20.11%
Small hydropower	Total	0.324	0.36	0.878	1.224	14.22%
Wind electricity	Total	0.065	0.155	0.32	0.814	28.76%
Solar	Total	0.056	0.212	0.280	0.573	26.18%
	Low-temp heat	0.050	0.205	0.270	0.522	26.44%
	PV grid	0.002	0.004	0.007	0.047	37.12%
	PV off-grid			0.000	0.000	
	Thermal electricity	0.004	0.003	0.003	0.004	0.00%
Marine energy	Total	0.009	0.009	0.009	0.009	0.00%
	Tidal	0.009	0.009	0.009	0.009	0.00%
Total new renewables	Total	8.29	9.21	11.09	15.33	6.34%
Large hydropower	Total	8.98	9.09	9.29	10.12	1.20%
Total renewables		17.27	18.30	20.38	25.45	3.95%

Sources: UNDP 2000, 2004; REN 21 2007, 2009

German system, the rates paid for new contracts decline annually, forcing the green energy sector to innovate.

Renewable portfolio standards (RPSs) require energy suppliers to purchase a proportion of their electricity (typically 10% to 20%) from renewable

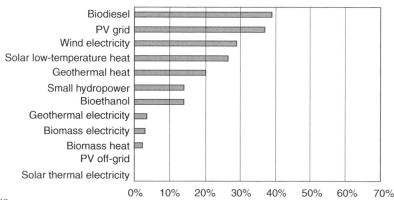

Source: REN21 2009

Figure 6.5. Annual growth rates of renewable energy capacity, 1998–2008

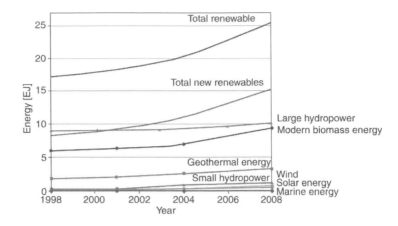

Sources: Author's elaboration on the basis of UNDP 2000, 2004; REN 21 2007, 2009

Figure 6.6. Contribution of renewables to the total energy supply (EJ)

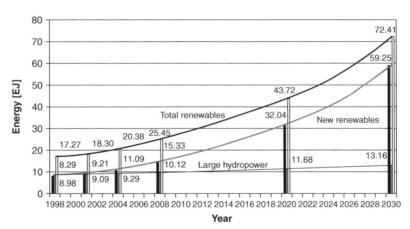

Sources: UNDP 2000, 2004; REN 21 2007, 2009

Figure 6.7. Projection of renewable energy production up to 2030

energy sources. This enables renewable generators to charge higher prices for their electricity. In practice, the policy is implemented by having renewable energy generators earn certificates for every unit of electricity they produce. They then sell these along with their electricity to supply companies. As discussed in Chapters 13 and 11 of this book, RPS mechanisms have been used in the United Kingdom and in many U.S. states.

Renewable energies are being introduced in a significant way in many countries, particularly in Europe in the form of "distributed generation" (Bayod-Rújula 2009), which is mostly renewable

and seems to be the approach that will be used on a large scale in the future (Figure 6.8).[3]

Energy Efficiency

The amount of energy required to provide the energy services needed depends on the efficiency with which the energy is produced, delivered, and used. Gains in energy efficiency are usually measured by indicators, one of which is called energy intensity (I) and defined as the energy (E) neces-

Table 6.3. Additional rate of investment in power generation technologies needed in the electricity sector every year until 2050

	ACT scenario	BLUE scenario	Normalized plant size
Coal-fired with CCS	30	35	500 MW plants
Gas-fired with CCS	1	20	500 MW plants
Nuclear	24	32	1,000 MW
Hydro	1/5 of Canada's hydropower capacity		
Biomass plants	30	100	50 MW plants
Wind: inshore	2,900	14,000	4 MW wind turbines
Wind: offshore	775	3,750	4 MW wind turbines
Geothermal	50	130	100 MW plants
Solar PV	115	215	Million solar panels
Solar CSD	45	80	250 MW plants

Source: OECD/IEA 2008a, 2008b

sary per unit of gross domestic product (GDP): I = E/GDP. Reductions in the energy intensity of economies over time indicate that the same amount of GDP is obtained with a smaller energy input, as shown in Figure 6.9.

Figure 6.10 shows the impressive improvements in energy efficiency made in the OECD countries in the period 1973–1998; without these gains, energy consumption would be 49% higher than it was in 1998, which means a decline in energy use of 2.3% per year. In terms of CO_2 emissions for the OECD countries, this means a reduction of roughly 350 million metric tons of CO_2 per year.

Such decline can be attributed to a combination of the following structural factors:

- improvements in efficiency of use of materials and manufactured goods in industrialized and transition countries, such as increased recycling, substitution away from energy-

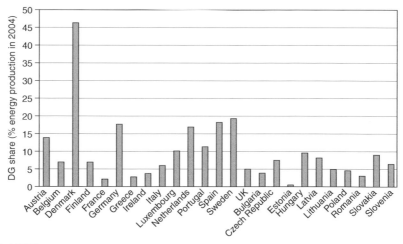

Source: Cossent et al. 2009

Figure 6.8. Energy produced from distributed generation (**DG**) in European countries

Table 6.4. The carbon market: Volumes and values for emissions trading, 2006–2007

Allowances	2006		2007	
	Volume (MtCO$_2$e)	Value ($ million)	Volume (MtCO$_2$e)	Value ($ million)
EU ETS	1,104	24,436	2,061	50,097
New South Wales	20	225	25	224
Chicago Climate Exchange	10	38	23	72
UK ETS	N/A	N/A		
Total	1,134	24,699	2,109	50,393

Source: World Bank 2008
Notes: The New South Wales scheme and the Chicago Climate Exchange, for voluntary trading of emissions, were set before the EU scheme; MtCO$_2$e = metric tons of carbon dioxide equivalent.

intensive materials, improved material efficiency, and intensified use of durable and investment goods;
- shifts in the mix of activities undertaken in the economy toward services and types of industrial production that are less energy-intensive; and

- saturation effects, whereby societies are approaching natural limits on the number of certain goods in the residential and transportation sectors (e.g., refrigerators, television sets, cars) that they can absorb, resulting in energy usage growing at a slower rate than GDP. (UNDP 2004)

Because more than 80% of the energy used in the world today comes from fossil fuels, the reduction in energy intensity is reflected in a reduction in carbon intensity ($I = CO_2/GDP$), defined as the amount of CO_2 emitted per unit of GDP (in parity purchasing power) as shown in Figure 6.11.

As can be seen, the OECD countries have experienced a steady decline in the carbon intensity. Non-OECD countries also had a decline, but carbon intensity stabilized after the year 2000. Figure 6.12 shows the energy intensities for different industrial sectors, indicating that some of them have been declining more rapidly than others. This clearly points out the most interesting sectors from the viewpoint of optimizing energy savings.

Over the next 20 years, there is significant scope for improvements in energy efficiency, which may largely be attained by replacement of the existing capital stock. It is estimated that within the next two decades, energy efficiency in industrialized countries could be cost-effectively reduced by 25% to 35%, whereas in transitional economies, reductions of more than 40% could be achieved. Developing countries, which typically have high economic growth and dated capi-

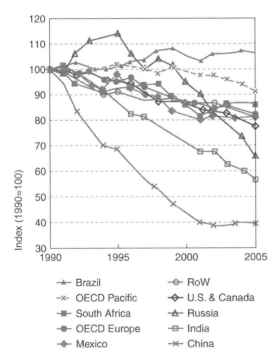

Source: OECD/IEA 2008a, 2008b
Note: RoW = Rest of the world

Figure 6.9. Evolution of energy intensity in a number of countries and regions, 1990–2005

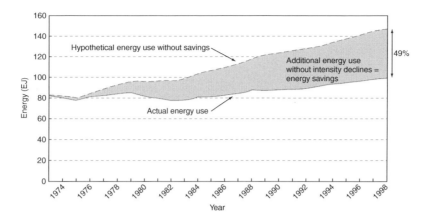

Source: OECD/IEA 2004

Figure 6.10. Energy savings in the OECD countries, 1973–1998

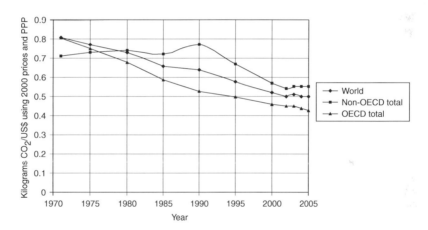

Source: OECD/IEA 2007
Note: PPP is the purchasing power parity, adjusting nominal GDP figures according to the living conditions of each country

Figure 6.11. Carbon intensity: CO_2 emissions per GDP (PPP), 1970–2005

tal and vehicle stocks, could achieve cost-effective improvement of 30% to more than 45%

Global energy intensity could decline by as much as 2.5% per year as a result of a combination of structural changes and efficiency improvements. The extent to which this will be achieved depends on the effectiveness of government policy, adaptation of attitudes and behaviors, and the level of entrepreneurial activity in energy conservation and material efficiency.

Policymakers play a central role in driving energy efficiency improvements by setting stand-

ards, such as building codes; market-based incentives, including certificate markets; and adequate payment systems (World Bank 2008) for energy that are applied by well-informed consumers, planners, and decisionmakers.

Emissions Trading

The discussions above have given brief overviews of two of the main classes of technology that are

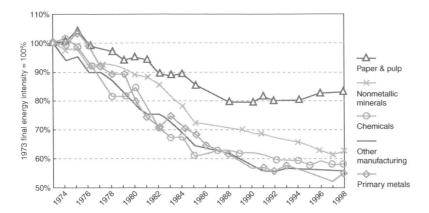

Source: UNDP 2004

Figure 6.12. The evolution of industrial subsector energy intensities, 1974–1998

available to reduce GHG emissions: improvements in energy efficiency and the increased use of renewable energy. Emissions trading, frequently known as cap-and-trade, is a technology-neutral tool to incentivize efficient emissions reduction by companies and countries. Several emissions trading schemes are currently in place and generally function as follows:

- Setting of a cap. A government or international body sets a limit on the total amount of pollutants that can be emitted in a specific period.
- Allocation of allowances. Participants in the scheme are allocated allowances to pollute a certain quantity. Allowances can be allocated on a number of bases, such as historical emissions, or through an auction of rights. The total number of allowances allocated cannot exceed the cap set by the governing body.
- Emissions trading. Scheme participants that emit more than their allocations must purchase additional allowances, while those that have an excess number of allowances may sell these. Participants that can reduce their emissions at low cost have an incentive to do so, and sell allowances, whereas those that face high costs of abatement that exceed the costs of allowances must pay to pollute more.

One such scheme was implemented in the United States under the 1990 Clean Air Act to curb emissions of sulfur dioxide (SO_2; a local pollutant, not a greenhouse gas). By 2007, the scheme succeeded in reducing annual SO_2 emissions to approximately 50% of 1980 levels (EPA 2009).

Another emissions trading scheme was implemented at the international level by the Kyoto Protocol, which came into force in 2005. This binds the participants to a cap-and-trade system covering the six major greenhouse gases. The scheme covers only developed nations, in recognition of the fact that they are principally responsible for the majority of the past global emissions. Notably, the United States, which is responsible for a significant proportion of world emissions, is the only developed nation that signed the UNFCCC that is not participating in the scheme.

The participants agreed to an average overall reduction in emissions of approximately 5% relative to 1990 levels by the end of 2012 (UNFCCC 2009b). During the five-year compliance period between 2008 and 2012, participants can earn and trade credits through three market-based mechanisms: international emissions trading (IET), joint implementation (JI) projects, and Clean Development Mechanism (CDM). IET involves trading of allowances among countries as described above; JI and CDM are means for countries to earn allowances by reducing emissions in other countries, as explained later in this chapter. The second commitment period of the Kyoto Protocol, together with a long-term cooperative action under the UNFCCC, were discussed at the end of 2009 in the 15th Conference of the Parties to the Climate Convention in Copenhagen but no general agreement of the type reached in Kyoto was achieved. It was decided instead that the industrialized countries, including the United States, commit to implement individually or jointly quantified economy wide emissions targets for 2020 to be submitted to Secretariat of the Convention by January 31, 2010. The developing countries would present voluntary non-mandatory pledges which will be subject to measurement, reporting and verification.

The European Union Emissions Trading System

Under the Kyoto Protocol, the European Union (EU) committed to an 8% reduction of emissions relative to the 1990 level by 2012 (EU 2003).[4] The responsibility for meeting this commitment is shared among member states, based on agreed national allocations. Pursuant to this, the EU has set a target for a reduction in emissions of GHGs of at least 20% of 1990 levels by 2020. Central to its strategy for achieving this target is the EU Emissions Trading System (ETS), the largest multinational emissions trading scheme in the world.

Under the ETS, member states agree to legally binding national emissions targets with the European Commission. Each country allocates its national emissions target among the companies in those emissions-producing sectors of the economy covered by the scheme. Currently, these allowances are distributed to companies by member governments free of charge. In the first phase of operation, the scheme included more than 10,000 industrial plants, comprising steel factories, power plants, oil refineries, paper mills, and glass and cement installations, which accounted for almost half of EU CO_2 emissions, 2.4 billion tons of CO_2 equivalent (CO_2e) (European Council 2009). The emissions allowances could be traded to allow abatement to occur at the lowest cost. The total number of allowances is reduced in each year of the scheme in order to achieve the desired overall reductions in emissions.

The scheme, which initially covered the 15 then-existing member states, began its first trading period on January 1, 2005. The first trading period lasted until the end of 2007 and was primarily intended to ensure that the ETS was functional by the start of the first commitment period under the Kyoto Protocol in 2008. The second trading period commenced in January 2008 and will end in December 2012, coinciding with the end of the first commitment period of the Kyoto Protocol. Table 6.4 shows the volume of CO_2 equivalent and volumes (in dollars) which were object of transaction in 2006 and 2007.

As shown in Figure 6.13, the price of allowances fell dramatically twice during the first period. The first fall occurred following the peak in April 2006, when it was discovered that some countries had overallocated allowances to industry, creating a substantial excess supply of allowances. Subsequently, prices faced another dramatic decline to approximately €1.20 ($1.63) per ton in March 2007 and later fell to around 10 euro cents (14 U.S. cents) in September 2007, because existing allowances expired at the end of the first phase and could not be carried over into subsequent periods. The initial overallocation of allowances dampened the incentives to abate and created a windfall for many industrial companies. The subsequent collapse in the price of allowances reduced the incentives for abatement.

The collapse of prices at the end of the first phase did not directly affect prices for contracts for 2008, the first year of the second phase. Market participants knew already in 2007 that this phase would be more stringent in regard to the cap and less lenient toward allowances, which explains the high prices for 2008 allowances.

In April 2009, the European Commission announced a number of changes to the scheme that will be effective from the third trading period, commencing in January 2013 (European Council 2009):

- Member states will introduce auctioning of allowances, which will be introduced gradu-

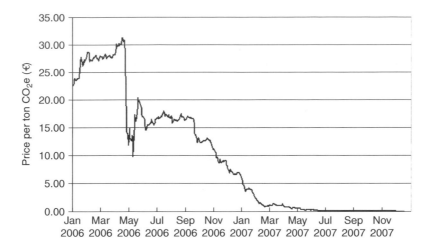

Source: ECX 2009
Note: €1 = $1.36 as of this writing

Figure 6.13. Carbon price, January 2006–November 2007 (settlement price of December 2007 ECX futures)

ally into most sectors, with plans to auction all allowances by 2020. Following the primary auction, allowances can be traded among companies as before.

- Nitrous oxides and perfluorocarbons will be added to the list of GHGs covered by the scheme.
- The scheme will be extended to include the aviation industry.
- The number of credits that can be earned through CDM and JI activity will be limited in order to motivate member states to reduce emissions domestically.

The proposed caps for the third trading period target an overall reduction of greenhouse gases for the sector of 21% in 2020 relative to 2005 emissions (European Council 2009). In addition, the third trading period will be both more economically efficient and environmentally effective. It will be more efficient because trading periods will be longer (eight years instead of five) and have a substantial increase in the amount of auctioning (from less than 4% in the second phase to more than half in the third). Environmental effectiveness will be guaranteed by a robust and annually declining emissions cap (21% reduction in 2020 compared with 2005) and a centralized allocation

process within the European Commission. Figure 6.14 shows the cap on emissions set by the EU as well as actual (and future) emissions.

A robust secondary market for carbon certificates exists through which investors bank on the future value of the ETS certificates changing many times. The ETS does not include transport, however, and thus this action is limited to the industrial process and energy sectors.

Joint Implementation

Joint implementation (JI) is one of the flexibility mechanisms included in the Kyoto Protocol as a means for developed nations with emissions reduction commitments (Annex I countries) to meet their obligations at the lowest possible cost.[5] JI allows an Annex I country to reduce its domestic emissions reduction requirements by undertaking projects to reduce emissions in another Annex I country. This allows Annex I countries to reduce their cost of emissions reduction.

A key requirement for a JI project is that it must provide an emissions reduction, or a removal of carbon from the atmosphere that is demonstrably additional to what otherwise would have occurred. This is known as "additionality." If a project can be shown to be additional and meet

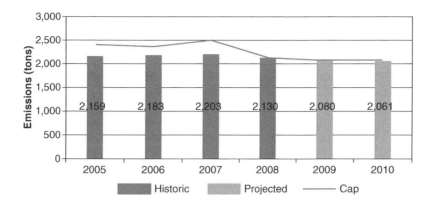

Source: New Energy Finance 2009a

Figure 6.14. Cap and ETS emissions in the European Union

other requirements set out by the UNFCCC, the project owner can earn credits called emission reduction units (ERUs) from the host country. Each ERU represents an emissions reduction equivalent to 1 ton of CO_2 and can be set against the domestic emissions reduction requirement.

After a long preparatory process, JI projects began to take shape, and as of March 2010, 207 projects had been submitted. If all were implemented, they would lead to an emissions reduction of 363,355 million tons of CO_2 equivalent in the period 2008–2012. The great majority of the projects are in the Russian Federation and eastern European countries.

So far very few ERUs have been issued.

Clean Development Mechanism

The Clean Development Mechanism (CDM) is another flexibility mechanism included in the Kyoto Protocol.[6] Under the CDM, Annex I countries can reduce their domestic emissions reduction requirements by undertaking projects to reduce emissions in developing countries. This allows Annex I countries to reduce their cost of emissions reduction, and global emissions to be reduced at a much lower global cost, by financing emissions reduction projects in developing countries where costs are lower than in industrialized countries. Furthermore, this encourages technology transfer and stimulates investment in sustainable development in less developed countries.

The CDM is administered by a designated national authority (DNA) in the country where the project takes place and is supervised by the CDM executive board at the international level. For projects to be approved, they must demonstrate additionality and meet the other requirements set forth by the UNFCCC. If a project is approved, the project owner is granted a certified emission reduction (CER), each of which represents an emissions reduction equivalent to 1 ton of CO_2. This can be counted toward the domestic emissions reduction target.

By June 1, 2009, 4,417 projects had been submitted; if all implemented, these would correspond to 2,931,813 million tons of CO_2e, representing roughly 1% of the total necessary effort to curb GHG emissions until 2050. (Roughly 75% of the CDM projects are in China.) Table 6.6 shows the number of CDM projects of each type, along with the 2012 CERs granted.

The distribution of CDM projects from different sectors are shown in Figure 6.15.

In contrast to emissions trading schemes, which are actively traded in the stock market, JI and CDM are project-based transactions. Annual volumes for 2006–2007 are given in Table 6.7.

Figure 6.16 gives estimates of the total amount of emissions transactions of the EU ETS, CDM, and JI for the years 2002 to 2008.

Table 6.5. Distribution of JI projects by type

Type	Number		2012 ERUs (000)	
HFCs, PFCs & N$_2$O reduction	31	13%	96,223	27%
CH$_4$ reduction & cement & coal mine/bed	115	49%	166,302	46%
Renewables	78	33%	32,058	9%
Energy efficiecncy	54	23%	71,053	20%
Fuel switch	9	4%	10,896	3%
Afforestation & reforestation	1	0%	410	0%
Total	233	100%	362,355	100%

Source: UNEP RISO 2010

Table 6.6. CDM projects grouped by type

Type	Number		2012 CERs (000)	
HFCs, PFCs & N$_2$O reduction	106	2.1%	741,442	26%
Renewables	2,959	60%	980,433	35%
CH$_4$ reduction & cement & coal mine/bed	989	20%	576,142	20%
Supply-side energy efficiency	540	11%	375,976	11%
Fuel switch	111	2.2%	172,894	6.1%
Demand-side energy efficiency	190	3.8%	25,420	0.9%
Afforestation & reforestation	52	1.0%	15,224	0.5%
Transport	21	0.4%	8,076	0.3%
Total	4,968	100%	2,835,607	100%

Source: UNEP RISO 2010

Table 6.7. Volumes and values for CDM and JI, 2006–2007

	2006		2007	
	Volume (MtCO$_2$e)	Value ($ million)	Volume (MtCO$_2$e)	Value ($ million)
Project-based transactions				
Primary CDM	537	5,804	551	7,426
Secondary CDM	25	445	240	5,451
JI	16	141	41	499
Other compliance and voluntary transactions	33	146	42	265
Total	611	6,536	874	13,641

Source: World Bank 2008

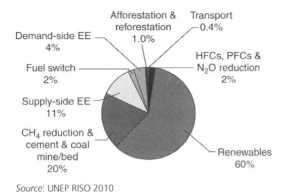

Source: UNEP RISO 2010

Figure 6.15. Distribution of CDM projects by type

Stimulus Packages

A significant amount of the stimulus packages adopted by a number of governments to face the financial crisis of 2007–2008 consists of investments in green activities. These amount to 6% of the total recovery packages announced by governments. Figure 6.17 shows how much 12 different countries invested in green stimuli. The estimated amounts announced by these economies total $184.9 billion invested in green stimuli. China

and the United States are the leaders, in nominal terms, of the green stimuli activities, earmarking $68.7 billion and $66.6 billion, respectively.

The sector breakdown in Figure 6.18 shows that energy efficiency remains at the heart of the low-carbon fiscal stimuli. Accounting for as much as 36% of the total $184.9 billion, this sector will receive a boost of some $65.7 billion globally, mainly via building efficiency projects. In addition, $7.9 billion has been announced for research and development in energy efficiency. The second major winner is electricity grid infrastructure. More than $48.7 billion has been earmarked for grid development and upgrade, accounting for some 26% of the total funds.

The U.S. Department of Energy has already disbursed $41.9 million in grants for fuel cell energy projects. Furthermore, $101.5 million has been directed to wind energy research, and detailed plans have been disclosed on $2.4 billion to be spent on carbon capture and storage and $4 billion for grid upgrades. Out of a total of $2 billion to support energy science research, the breakdown of almost $1.3 billion have also been confirmed, and only some $725 million remains to be allocated.

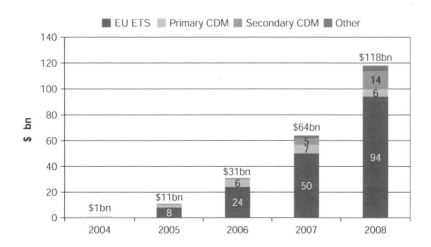

Source: New Energy Finance 2009b

Figure 6.16. Carbon market estimates, 2002–2008

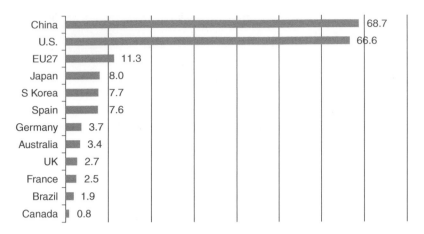

Source: ECX 2009

Figure 6.17. Investments in green stimuli (**$ billion**)

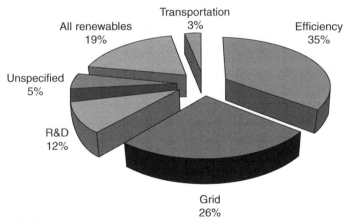

Source: New Energy Finance 2009b

Figure 6.18. Sector breakdown of global green stimuli

Notes

1. "Traditional biomass" is used to denote locally collected and often unprocessed biomass-based fuels, such as crop residues, wood, and animal dung, most of which are used noncommercially. Sometimes these lead to deforestation and therefore are not renewable. "Modern biomass" refers to biomass produced in a sustainable way and used for electricity generation, heat production, and transportation (liquid fuels). International Energy Agency (IEA) statistics lump together traditional and modern biomass under the heading of "combustible renewables and waste" (CRW).

2. Average conversion efficiency: heat, 85%; biomass electricity, 22%; combined heat and power, 80%; geothermal electricity, 10%; all others, 100%.

3. The main sources of distributed generation are reciprocating engines (internal combustion engines), gas turbines, microturbines, fuel cells, photovoltaic systems, thermoelectric solar plants, wind energy conversion systems (WECSs), biomass to energy power plants, and small hydroelectric power plants (SHPPs).

4. Article 17 of the Kyoto Protocol. The Conference of the Parties shall define the relevant principles, modalities, rules and guidelines, in particular for verification, reporting and accountability for

emissions trading. The parties included in Annex B may participate in emissions trading for the purposes of fulfilling their commitments under Article 3. Any such trading shall be supplemental to domestic actions for the purpose of meeting quantified emissions limitation and reduction commitments under that Article.

5. Article 6 of the Kyoto Protocol. For the purpose of meeting its commitments under Article 3, any Party included in Annex I may transfer to, or acquire from, any other such Party emissions reduction units resulting from projects aimed at reducing anthropogenic emissions by sources or enhancing anthropogenic removals by sinks of greenhouse gases in any sector of the economy, provided that: (a) any such project has the approval of the Parties involved; (b) any such project provides a reduction in emissions by sources, or an enhancement of removals by sinks, that is additional to any that would otherwise occur; (c) it does not acquire any emission reduction units if it is not in compliance with its obligations under Articles 5 and 7; and (d) the acquisition of emission reduction units shall be supplemental to domestic actions for the purposes of meeting commitments under Article 3.

6. Article 12 of the Kyoto Protocol. (1) A Clean Development Mechanism (CDM) is hereby defined. (2) The purpose of the clean development mechanism shall be to assist Parties not included in Annex I in achieving sustainable development and in contributing to the ultimate objective of the Convention and to assist Parties included in Annex I in achieving compliance with their quantified emission limitation and reduction commitments under Article 3. (3) Under the clean development mechanism: (a) Parties not included in Annex I will benefit from project activities resulting in certified emission reductions; and (b) Parties included in Annex I may use the certified emission reductions accruing from such project activities to contribute to compliance with part of their quantified emission limitation and reduction commitments under Article 3, as determined by the Conference of the Parties to this Protocol.

References

Bayod-Rújula, Angel A. 2009. Future Development of the Electricity Systems with Distributed Generation. *Energy* 34: 377–383.

CDIAC (Carbon Dioxide Information Analysis Center, Oak Ridge National Laboratory). 2009. Fossil-Fuel CO_2 emissions, cdiac.ornl.gov (accessed January 10 2010).

Cossent, Rafael, Tomás Gómez, and Pablo Frías. 2009. Towards a Future with Large Penetration of Distributed Generation: Is the Current Regulation of Electricity Distribution Ready? Regulatory Recommendations under a European Perspective. *Energy Policy* 37: 1145–1155.

ECX (European Climate Exchange). 2009. ECX EUA Futures Prices. www.ecx.eu/ (accessed December 21, 2009).

EPA (U.S. Environmental Protection Agency). 2009. Acid Rain Program 2007 Progress Report. www.epa.gov/airmarkets/progress/arp07.html (accessed January 10, 2010).

European Council. 2009. Directive 2009/29/EC of the European Council. Press release. ec.europa.eu/ environment/climat/emission/ ets_post2012_en.htm (accessed December 21, 2009).

EU (European Union). 2003. Kyoto Protocol. europa.eu/rapid/pressReleasesAction.do?reference= MEMO/03/154&format=HTML&aged= 0&language=EN&guiLanguage=en (accessed December 15, 2009).

New Energy Finance. 2009a. EU ETS – Analyst Reaction (April 3, 2009). Available at carbon.newenergyfinance.com/ (accessed April 3, 2009).

———. 2009b. Carbon Industry Intelligence Research Note. October 2008. Available at carbon.newenergyfinance.com/ (accessed May 22, 2009).

OECD/IEA (Organisation for Economic Co-operation and Development/International Energy Agency). 2004. Oil Crises and Climate Challenges: 30 Years of Energy Use in IEA Countries. www.iea.org/textbase/nppdf/free/2004/30years.pdf (accessed December 21, 2010).

———. 2007. *CO_2 Emissions from Fuel Combustion, 1971–2005*. Paris: OECD Publishing.

———. 2008a. *Energy Technology Perspectives. In Support of the G8 Plan of Action. Scenarios & Strategies to 2050*. Paris: OECD/IEA Publishing.

———. 2008b. *Worldwide Trends in Energy Use and Efficiency. Key Insights from IEA Indicator Analysis. In Support of the G8 Plan of Action*. Paris: OECD Publishing.

REN21 (Renewable Energy Policy Network for the 21st Century). 2007. Renewables 2007: Global Sta-

tus Report. www.ren21.net/pdf/
RE2007_Global_Status_Report.pdf (accessed
December 10, 2010).

———. 2009. Renewables Global Status Report: 2009
Update. www.ren21.net/pdf/
RE_GSR_2009_Update.pdf (accessed December
10, 2010).

UNDP (United Nations Development Programme).
2000. *World Energy Assessment: Energy and the Challenge of Sustainability*. New York: UNDP.

———. 2004. *World Energy Assessment: Overview 2004
Update*. New York: UNDP

UNEP RISO. (2010). CDM/JI Pipeline Analysis and
Database http://cdmpipeline.org/cdm-projects-
type.htm (accessed January 11, 2010).

UNFCCC (United Nations Framework Convention
on Climate Change). 2009a. Greenhouse Gas Inventory Data. unfccc.int/ghg_data/items/3800.php
(accessed January 11, 2010).

———. 2009b. Kyoto Protocol. unfccc.int/
kyoto_protocol/items/2830.php (accessed January
11, 2010).

World Bank. 2008. State and Trends of the Carbon
Market 2008. siteresources.worldbank.org/NEWS/
Resources/State&Trendsformatted06May10pm.pdf
(accessed January 11, 2010).

Part III

Renewable Generation and Electric Power Markets

7

Electricity Wholesale Market Design in a Low-Carbon Future

William W. Hogan

Policy to convert the energy system to a low-carbon configuration involves a central focus on the electricity sector. Electricity generation is a major use of fossil fuels and therefore accounts for a large fraction of the emissions of carbon dioxide; reducing carbon emissions in other sectors, such as transportation, may involve increased electrification; and electricity can be and has been generated without carbon emissions. In addition, electricity generating facilities burning fossil fuels are large and easy to identify and thus a natural focus for regulation and policy to reduce carbon emissions.

Designing policy for a low-carbon electricity sector depends on the nature of the technology and institutions in that sector. In many countries, the electric power system is already involved in a major restructuring process. Critical technological and institutional features of that reform process center on wholesale market design elements that have important implications for expansion of reliance on low-carbon energy sources. The wholesale market covers bulk generation, dispatch, and transport of electric power for ultimate delivery to retail customers. Although the details and jurisdictional rules differ in the United States and the European Union (EU), a common distinctive feature of the wholesale market is the interaction through the interconnected transmission grids that transcend states and countries. The complementary rules for retail supply or distribution of electricity are important, but the emphasis here is on electricity wholesale market design in a low-carbon future. The main theme emphasizes the strong interaction between market design and policies for achieving a low-carbon future.

Electricity System Fundamentals

All electricity systems share certain fundamental characteristics. Efficient power generation benefits from substantial economies of scale. The result of more than a century of evolution of sophisticated power systems is a fleet of relatively large generating plants.

To enjoy the benefits of these economies of scale, traditional power plants have not been located near the ultimate load. Moving power from the generating plants to the ultimate consumer requires high-voltage transmission lines. Because of the nature of electricity transmission, the higher the voltage, the lower the required current and the resulting transmission losses. Transformers convert the relatively low voltage at the point of generation to allow for high-voltage transmission to another set of transformers that lower the voltage for retail distribution to factories, businesses, and homes.

Typically the local retail distribution system is simpler in its design than the transmission system. In particular, the distribution network is more decentralized or radial in the sense that electrical power problems in one distribution network, the principal cause of power outages, can be isolated from the rest of the system.

The interconnected transmission network is another story. The transmission network initially developed organically as individual companies sought to connect their generators to their loads. One of the features of the electric power system is the speed of adjustment when a change occurs in load, generation, or transmission connections. With present technology and little storage, to a first approximation, electricity is the limiting case of same-time production. The power produced and consumed must maintain instantaneous balance throughout the system, and any disruption of the transmission grid results in instantaneous redistribution of the flow of power in the system. The system is not controllable in the same ways as we imagine for a network of pipelines with valves and relatively slow-moving fluids. Power flows at the speed of light.

Companies building bulk transmission facilities consequently relied on redundant pathways in the transmission grid to ensure reliability. In addition, the power system required standby generating capacity that could be called on immediately in order to replace a lost generating unit. As neighboring electricity companies would be unlikely to face disruptions at the same instant, redundant transmission and generation in one system could help other systems and lower the total cost of maintaining reliability. This confluence of technology and economics led to the gradual development of interconnected alternating current (AC) transmission grids linking loads to thousands of generators through tens of thousands of individual transmission links.

Throughout such an interconnected grid, all of the generators and load must be synchronized. The resulting ensemble has been called the "largest machine in the world" (Amin 2000, *264*). For example, the North American continent from Mexico to Canada is dominated by only three synchronous grids in the Eastern, Western, and Texas Interconnections, operating with limited exchange through direct current (DC) interconnections between them. (Alaska and Quebec have their own separated grids as well.) Similarly, a large synchronized grid covers 24 European countries (ENTSO-E 2008).

The complexity of a large synchronized grid is well known to electricity system operators but not most customers. Traditionally, the electricity company was vertically integrated from generation through transmission to distribution. Customers faced a monopoly that provided the power and charged a price only loosely coupled to actual contemporaneous costs. The company made its own investment plans for generation and wires, often through joint investments with other vertically integrated monopolies. Control of the interconnected transmission grid was handled through an array of bilateral and multilateral agreements among the members of the "club," but with strict exclusion of potential new competitors. These club agreements worked reasonably well, although below the surface, difficult problems often occurred at the seams between regions or when one member of the group was "leaning" too much on the system.

The club agreements involved coordinated planning and expansion of the transmission grid, always an opaque and arcane process. It was difficult to define the resulting rights to transmit power and determine how these rights would be allocated in the interconnected grid, and real-time dispatch of power plants had to be coordinated in order to maintain the grid's reliability.

The rules and incentives for operation of this system were complicated by the nature of electricity regulation and its focus on cost recovery. The emphasis of regulation or government ownership was on control of the average costs, with relatively little attention paid to the role of marginal costs and the connection to incentives that could or should govern operations and efficient investment. This history would be a major hurdle to overcome in the development of electricity market reforms.

Economic efficiency always played a secondary role to maintaining system reliability, keeping the lights on. Gold plating the system a little might produce some inconvenient questions on occasion, but major blackouts or even relatively minor but frequent local supply interruptions could limit a career and were deemed unacceptable. The common approach for the wholesale power system was, and continues to be, treating reliability as a constraint and economic efficiency as a goal to be sought subject to that constraint. (Because of the lower availability of redundancy and greater expense of reliability, a more nuanced trade-off is seen at the retail distribution level.)

In real time, the variable cost of generating power ranges from virtually zero for run-of-the-river hydropower, to moderate for nuclear and coal plants, to expensive for natural gas and oil plants. With load changing rapidly over the day and total generation at the trough during the night at as little as 30% of the peak during the day, it makes sense to choose the cheapest generators available to produce at any time (Monitoring Analytics 2009).

The basic idea is to operate as closely as possible to the security-constrained (respecting all the many reliability constraints on the grid) economic dispatch that provides the necessary ancillary services and minimizes the cost of meeting a given electric load at any moment and over the course of the day. Under the traditional electricity model, the aggregate cost of this economic dispatch would be recovered through preset customer charges that muted or completely ignored the dramatic changes in opportunity costs over the day and season. As a result, the traditional system often provided adequate cost recovery but did little to reveal or communicate incentives to guide either operations or investment. Rather, investment decisions relied on and defaulted to the expert assessments of the established electricity companies and left few opportunities for innovation by new entrants.

Although the operating decisions were neither open nor transparent, a reasonable case can be made that traditional reliance on the framework of security-constrained economic dispatch produced efficient operating decisions and certainly contributed to the reliability of the system. The signals sent for investment and innovation were an entirely different matter, however. The system depended on the planning decisions of the protected monopolies, and the lack of transparency coupled with major construction delays and cost increases precipitated deep concern with investment choices.

Electricity Market Design

As long as the natural benefits of economies of scale produced steady reductions in the real and nominal average price of electricity, as was true for decades, the vertically integrated model with franchise monopolies worked well. Rapid growth in electricity demand hid mistakes. Average costs were declining, and the big concern was to invest rapidly enough to stay ahead of growing demand. However, this system began to break down when the returns to increasing scale declined, electricity growth patterns changed, and mistakes were made that resulted in large cost overruns. The long-running good news that new investment would lower average electricity costs was soon replaced with the bad news that new investment was more expensive and would raise average costs (Hogan 2009).

Electricity Market Reform

These changes accompanied a general interest in reducing reliance on regulation and turning more to market forces to guide investment and operations. For example, in the 1980s, the United States eliminated regulation of natural gas production, and a great boom of activity and improved economic efficiency ensued. Policymakers in the United Kingdom and Chile turned attention to similar reforms of electricity systems. In the United States, successful experiments with limited introduction of generation investment by companies outside the monopoly club had demonstrated that new entrants could be accommodated without compromising efficiency or reliability. In 1992, the United States adopted the

Energy Policy Act (EPAct92), which included provisions for open access to the transmission grid.

Authorities in Australia, Argentina, most of Europe, New Zealand, the United States, and elsewhere were experimenting with new structures for organizing the electricity system. Many recognized or assumed that economies of scale in generation had largely been exhausted, and new and more loosely regulated entrants were just as capable of building and operating successful power plants as had been the incumbent electric utilities. This precipitated the notion that vertical separation of generation, transmission, low-voltage distribution, and supply would be at least possible and perhaps desirable. Existing generators, perhaps divided and divested from existing electric companies, could compete against each other and against new entrants to construct power plants and sell electricity to others, including final customers. Local distribution facilities would continue to operate more or less under the old regulated monopoly model, albeit often as a wires-only business with suppliers acquiring electricity from generators and selling on to final customers.

A key requirement for this vertical separation and competition in generation would be open access to the common integrated transmission grid and associated unbundling of critical services. The best form of organization for the common interconnected grid with the unbundling of services was not immediately apparent. In the United States, the emphasis was soon on transmission open access and nondiscrimination in prices and services for all participants in the electricity market. As it turned out, these seemingly innocuous requirements had profound implications for the nature of electricity market design.

The details of the story and the alternative market approaches are many, and an extensive literature exists on alternative market designs (Sioshansi 2008). The purpose here is not to recite these details, but to emphasize certain features that are salient for the discussion of a low-carbon electricity system that relies heavily on technologies such as solar, wind, and demand-side man-

agement, which differ substantially from the legacy portfolio of fossil-fuel generation.

Alternative Market Designs

For this purpose, electricity system market designs can be divided into three categories. First are the legacy systems that continue to be organized around the model of vertical integration and closed transmission access.[1] This would include many of the Southeast regulated utilities and Northwest municipal and public power systems in the United States. Second are the organized countertrade markets with aggregate zonal transmission systems that support sometimes separate trading platforms and scheduling procedures that are only partially integrated with system operations. The countertrade refers to the activities of the transmission system operator, who must conduct offsetting transactions that undo the schedules of market participants to bring the net schedules in line with the capabilities of the transmission system. This describes many systems, including most of the electricity markets in the EU. Third are the organized spot markets under independent system operators (ISOs) that coordinate dispatch but do not own the grid and integrate real-time trading and dispatch with system operations. This integration includes the full locational granularity of the actual grid for determining energy flows and locational prices. This would include the multistate regional transmission organizations (RTOs) or equivalent single-state ISOs that together cover approximately two-thirds of the U.S. load.

To a significant degree, the vertically integrated systems are similar to those of the past, and we can think about how regulated utilities would be likely to adapt to a low-carbon future. The countertrade systems include many market innovations and allow a great deal of flexibility in trading arrangements, operations, and investment incentives. At their core, however, these markets are incompatible with the requirements of system operations. The aggregate trading arrangements ignore many of the relevant constraints on the grid. The associated nominal schedules are thus often not collectively feasible, and countertrade is necessary to undo what the nominal market has done. Countertrade, or some other system redispatch intervention like it, is necessary whenever the market schedules do not reflect system operation reality. Furthermore, workable countertrade market designs and interventions are necessarily discriminatory in selectively choosing and paying for redispatch of some generators but not others similarly situated, as shown by experience in the United States (Hogan 2002). This countertrade design has implications for the treatment of renewables and other low-carbon energy sources. In order to understand the implications, it is convenient first to sketch out the essential features of the RTOs and organized spot markets that integrate market design and system operations.

Integrated Locational Electricity Market Design

The U.S. RTOs have regular market monitoring organizations that prepare extensive evaluations of the design and operation of their markets (see HEPG, various dates). The critical design criterion is to structure the spot market products and services as much as possible to conform to actual system operations, and then price those products and services to reflect the marginal costs that would drive market clearing competitive prices.

The initial focus is on the spot market. The forward markets play a critical role, but forward market participants will look ahead to the anticipated operation of spot markets. Thus efficient design of forward markets depends in significant measure on a good design for spot markets. Further, a focus on competitive market design is not intended to overlook the possibility of the existence and exercise of market power. Rather, a good competitive spot market design greatly simplifies possibly necessary regulatory intervention to mitigate market power. For electricity systems, a necessary condition for good market design is good design of the spot market.

When closely tied to system operations, good spot market design can be integrated with bilateral or multilateral trading. The organized spot market does not preclude decentralized trading. Transac-

tions through the spot market can be gross, without separate bilateral transactions and schedules, or net, covering only imbalances relative to bilateral transactions and schedules. The differences are largely semantic, despite heated arguments in the past for the merits of gross or net market design.

The principal market design problem that arises in all electricity systems follows from the nature of the interconnected transmission grid. In addition to being large, interconnected, fast responding, and contingency constrained, electricity transmission grids have an unusual feature that follows from the need for fast response. The redundancies and contingency constraints arise because it is not possible to use valves to control the flow of power. To a good first approximation, once the pattern of load and generation is set, the flow of power through the grid is determined by physical laws that distribute the power over the system to (more or less) minimize losses. It turns out that power flows to varying degrees on every available path between generation and load. This means that control of power plant dispatch and control of transmission flows are two sides of the same coin. Changing the dispatch changes the power flows, and changing the power flows requires changing the dispatch.

This technological fact has profound implications. For example, it means that it is impossible to operate the system with only decentralized decisions about generation and load. There must be central coordination of everything and central control of enough of the dispatch to meet the requirements of system operations. The parallel flow of power means that any trading system must confront material externalities as the real flows for one transaction interfere with the real flows of other transactions. In the United States, the electric utilities struggled for decades to design a workable system of transmission flow accounting that would support physical transmissions rights, and never succeeded in working around the inconvenient fact that power flows everywhere (Lankford et al. 1996).

The design solution to this otherwise intractable problem is to recognize that the framework of security-constrained economic dispatch, already familiar to system operators, provides the foundation for a coordinated spot market (Schweppe et al. 1988). This spot market inherently respects the requirements of system operations and provides a convenient connection to electricity markets and forward trading.

Recognizing that there must be a system operator, this design asks for bids and offers for power at the physical locations, schedules between locations, or schedules with bids and offers for deviations from the schedules. Thus the structure of the information provided to the system operator is the same as under a vertically integrated system, only now the engineering estimates of loads and costs are replaced by the bids and offers for power.

As before, the system operator selects the changing pattern of economic dispatch to meet load and provide ancillary services subject to the (many) security constraints and the complex flows of power on the transmission grid. In economic terms, the independent system operator internalizes the major transmission externalities so that transmission and transaction schedules can be point-to-point and be silent on the path between the points.

The quantity result of the security-constrained economic dispatch for any interval is a schedule of generation and load at each electrical location. Hand in hand with the quantity dispatch is a set of market-clearing prices for settlement purposes that capture the system marginal cost of meeting increased load or decreased generation at each location. The term of art is locational marginal pricing (LMP). These locational marginal prices provide an immediate definition of the appropriate spot price of transmission between any two locations: a straightforward arbitrage argument dictates that the competitive spot price of transmission between any two locations is the difference in the energy spot prices at the locations.

When there is no congestion in the system, the market clearing prices would be the same as the normal single market clearing price of simpler models, except for differences in marginal transmission losses. But when transmission constraints are binding, the locational prices differ according to the marginal impacts of activity at each location on system congestion. These congestion-induced differences can be surprisingly large and sometimes counterintuitive. Simultaneous market clearing prices can often be well above the marginal cost of the most expensive generation running at some locations and well below marginal cost or even negative elsewhere (Hogan 1999). This is a material effect of the complicated electrical interactions made visible in the spot market but previously hidden in system operations.

Once this security-constrained economic dispatch framework is adopted, with accompanying locational prices applied in market settlements, it is a simple matter for market participants to schedule or otherwise arrange transactions. For example, a bilateral transaction can be scheduled between any two locations, for a charge at the difference in locational prices. Any imbalances in actual delivery would be paid for at the relevant locational prices. With security-constrained economic dispatch and locational prices, the imbalance market merges with the spot market. All parties can participate, so there is open access. And all parties face the same scheduling rules and resulting prices, so there is nondiscrimination. No provision exists for countertrading through market positions taken by the system operator, because countertrades are not needed to bring the spot market into conformance with system operations. This results in less concern over conflicts of interest for the system operator. By construction, security-constrained economic dispatch is consistent with system operations and the spot market.

In addition, the existence of the spot market and locational prices provides the foundation for the financial transmission right (FTR) (Hogan 1992). In the simplest form, an FTR calls for paying to the right holder the (congestion) difference between the corresponding locational prices. Absent grid outages, the FTR is a long-term instrument that provides a perfect hedge for the short-term congestion fluctuations in transmission spot prices. With a matching FTR between generation and load, a supplier can sign a fixed price contract for delivered power and be sure that the system will always allow fulfillment of the contract through either physical delivery or offsetting purchases and sales with no incremental charges for volatile transmission congestion. This workable financial transmission right provides the functionality sought without success in unworkable systems of physical transmission rights.

Concerns early on were that this integrated locational model could not work well with very many locations. The United States went through the agony of forcing aggregations across zones to reduce the granularity of the market representation. Zonal aggregation subject to rules of open access and nondiscrimination was tried and abandoned in the PJM system, a large RTO that covers the Mid-Atlantic states in the United States, the corresponding New England RTO, the California RTO, and the Texas RTO (Hogan 2002; Potomac Economics 2009). This zonal aggregation inherently suppressed the detail of real system operations and thereby lost the efficient pricing signals, which in turn required complex rules to bridge the constructed gap between the spot market and system operations. Painful experience made it clear that the simplest system is to go as far as possible to match temporal and locational granularity with real operations and the associated system opportunity costs. The integrated locational design with very many locations works. For example, in the Mid-Atlantic states, PJM updates the coordinated dispatch and prices every five minutes for approximately 8,000 locations. This granularity means that geographically proximate locations that are electrically distant can have very different prices, and these prices reinforce rather than contravene the imperatives of efficient and reliable system operations. One of the regular reports from system operators newly adopting this model is that it greatly simplifies and improves dispatch operations, because market participants have strong economic incentives to follow dispatch instructions.

Some contend that a more geographically aggregated system would be easier and cheaper to implement. This might be correct if an alternative were available that could avoid the need to attend to all the detail in real operations.[2] No such alternative is available, however. If the system operator is applying the basics of security-constrained economic dispatch, then all the essential information

on transmission lines and multiple locations must already be available. The distinctive feature of the integrated locational market design is that it makes the locational marginal opportunity costs visible and applies these as the prices used in the settlements system. The incremental costs of using the full granularity are modest, or even negative when considering the costs of imposing rules and procedures to overcome the effects of artificial aggregation.

Aggregate Regional Countertrade Market Design

The countertrade markets differ from the integrated locational markets described above in a variety of ways (Boucher and Smeers 2002). A typical feature is an attempt to separate spot market trading from the actual details of system operations. The energy product is defined according to inputs and outputs at some level of regional aggregation. Trading reaches an equilibrium in these aggregate products, and this is turned into a set of schedules for implementation by the transmission system operator. The nominal equilibrium schedules determined in the market are seldom if ever strictly feasible for implementation on the actual grid, because they ignore many or all of the constraints on grid operations. The transmission system operator has available essentially two broad strategies for bridging the gap between the nominal market equilibrium and physical system: applying either ex ante limits or ex post countertrading.

An ex ante limit would be to define different regional aggregations for the energy products and pretend there is a simple pipeline between the two regions. Transfers through the pipeline would be limited to a conservative estimate of the real capacity, and transfers from anywhere in the first zone to anywhere in the second zone would be (artificially) treated as having the same effect. The conservative capacity cushion would help limit problems caused by trades that would appear identical in the pipeline model but would have different impacts on capacity in the real system. This approach ensures underutilization of the grid by all parties that must use this mechanism for trading. The same conservative assumptions create opportunities for transmission owners to exploit transmission capacity that is in effect withheld from the rest of the market.

Other forms of ex ante rules required by the disconnect between market design and system operation may include restrictions on the lead time for changing energy schedules. Physical operation of plants and control mechanisms often allow for changes up to minutes before real time, but formal market schedules may foreclose changes an hour or more ahead of operations. This scheduling lag could be particularly important for highly variable energy resources.

Despite the conservative capacity restrictions and other ex ante rules, market schedules may still violate the physical limits of the system. Even though generation and load may balance within the boundaries of an aggregate zone used to define a common energy product, for instance, intrazonal power flows may violate transmission constraints. There is no way to set an ex ante rule that maintains the aggregation of the zone and reflects the impacts of the intrazonal limits on the transmission system. The trade-determined schedules cannot be honored without some redispatch of the system, and this provides a need for countertrade. Typically the initial schedules are honored, but the system operator arranges a generation redispatch that involves the equivalent of purchases and sales of energy at different locations in the system and creates counterflows that relieve the transmission constraints. In principle and in practice, this countertrade redispatch may involve the very trades and generators that created the potential overload. In effect, a generator may be paid in the first instance to provide energy as part of the nominal market equilibrium schedule, and then be paid not to generate the same energy in order to accommodate the counterflow and relieve the transmission constraints.

As might be expected, the incentive effects of these aggregation and countertrade arrangements can be perverse in the extreme. The zonal aggregation models in the PJM system, New England, California, and Texas all faced these perverse incentives, which precipitated abandonment of the zonal aggregation and countertrading market design.

Other markets have implemented countertrade systems that work much better. For instance, the EU universally employs aggregate regions for defining energy products, and it uses pipeline models with conservative transmission capacity assumptions. All these workable systems find it necessary to dispense with principles of nondiscrimination. The transmission system operator is able to make onetime arrangements for countertrades that relieve transmission constraints and balance the system without having to offer the same deal to every other participant in the market. This reduces the ability of generators to extract payments for not running. Although necessary, this selective participation in the market by the transmission operator creates its own set of incentive problems.

The cost allocation mechanisms for these countertrade systems are varied. In some cases, such as in the United Kingdom, the transmission system operator absorbs the costs under a price cap regime and therefore internalizes incentives to minimize the countertrade costs. However, this same system requires the operator to take on the sole responsibility for transmission expansion, as the aggregate price signals in the market do not provide sufficient incentive or information to guide detailed transmission investments.

Market Design for a Low-Carbon Future

In the United States, installations of wind energy are disproportionately found in the RTO markets because of the greater ease of integration (EPSA 2008). As would be apparent from the summary of key features presented here, there are net benefits to moving away from either vertical integration or regional aggregation with countertrade and toward the integrated locational market design. Similar conclusions can be found in other important reviews looking toward a low-carbon future in the United States (Helman et al. 2010; Joskow 2008) and United Kingdom (Grubb et al. 2008). As summarized by the International Energy Agency in its review of market experience across its member countries: "Locational marginal pricing (LMP) is the electricity spot pricing model that serves as the benchmark for market design—

the textbook ideal that should be the target for policy makers. A trading arrangement based on LMP takes all relevant generation and transmission costs appropriately into account and hence supports optimal investments" (IEA 2007, *16*).

Connection Standards

The rules for generator grid interconnection play a major role in affecting the integration of new capacity. In the case of the integrated locational market design, there is fundamental simplicity in theory that can be reasonably approximated in reality. In the other market designs, system connection rules confront the challenge of designing protocols to overcome the perverse incentives created in the market.

The simplicity of the integrated locational market design is illustrated in the rules for "energy resource" interconnection in the PJM system (PJM 2009). An investor that has a site with the required permits and wants to build a new facility to sell energy into the PJM market has to meet only a minimal set of requirements. Primarily these are technical constraints to ensure that the connection to the grid will satisfy electrical characteristics so that connection and charging of the line, with no material power generation, do not compromise the rest of the system. In effect, the generator interface is an extension cord to the rest of the grid that has to meet certain standards, and the generator has to pay for the equipment and extension line.

This form of interconnection allows the generator to produce, buy, and sell energy in the spot market at the locational marginal price at its point of interconnection. There is no guarantee about the price or profitability of the energy produced, nor any guarantee that access to the grid at the point of connection provides transmission rights to hedge the cost of delivery to other locations in the grid. When the transmission system is constrained, the locational marginal price at the point of connection might be very low, and the generator may choose not to run. The generator can have the system operator make these decisions in real time by simply offering to produce with a minimum acceptable price. There would be no need to arrange advance schedules or bilateral transactions.

Although the generator could participate in forward markets, arrange long-term contracts, and purchase FTRs to hedge transmission costs, these are not necessary conditions of the connection rule, and immersion in trading would not change the incentives for the price-taking generator to make simple offers into the real-time market to allow the system operator to take the energy when available and when the locational price is at least equal to the minimum bid.

As discussed below, in PJM, most generators choose a more complicated form of interconnection in order to participate in the capacity market that operates on top of the energy market. However, the simple ideal of the energy-only interconnection is available and is used by some generators.

The countertrade markets face a quite different situation when considering the rules for connecting new generators. The generators do not see the costs of transmission constraints obscured by zonal aggregation of energy product definitions. Hence they may choose to locate where costs are actually higher but are imposed on someone else. Furthermore, the typical countertrade market design carries with it an explicit or implied obligation to accept the generators' energy output and deliver it to some loads. In effect, in the terms of the integrated locational market design, new generators acquire a bundle of transmission rights by virtue of their interconnection. The connection of new generators may imply that the transmission owner must make sometimes substantial transmission investment to support these new rights. Similarly, for all generators, but particularly for highly variable wind and solar plants, there must be increased operating reserves or other controls needed to support energy delivery. The transmission system operator will have to make these investments or impose constraints on the interconnection.

This gap between the incentives for the new entrant and the real costs of interconnection creates a need for rules and regulations to overcome the incentive effects. For example, new generators may be required to make so-called deep transmission investments elsewhere in the network in order to accommodate their new production without undoing the implicit rights of other generators. Alternatively, the costs of reliability and transmission upgrades to support the expanded set of transmission rights are imposed on the transmission system operator or somehow collected in socialized charges applied to all customers.

Smart Grids and Smart Pricing

The notion of the smart grid typically implies a mix of control technologies, information systems, and information distribution that allows for much finer control of all the devices connected in the largest machine in the world. This would include more flexible controls in the transmission grid, better monitoring of grid and distribution flows, real-time status and fault monitoring, automatic meter reading, and importantly, real-time automation of end-use devices. Signals from the central system operator would communicate through the network to change the settings on transformers deeply embedded in the grid or trigger customers' settings to turn down the air-conditioners in their homes.

The evolution of the smart grid will be particularly relevant in the development of dispersed generation, end-use efficiency, and load management. An important question is what information is provided and who decides how to use it. Consumers are unlikely to surrender their ability to control the temperature in the house or to decide whether to run a factory. However, it is easy to imagine widespread adoption of smart devices that implement instructions as to when to curtail usage and when to run as needed.

For these smart systems to be successful, consumers must receive a signal that aligns their incentives to behave in a way that reflects the opportunity costs in the system. This is a challenge in the vertically integrated and aggregated countertrade systems, because under these market designs, prices facing the consumer do not reflect the granular detail of system operations. Command and control under the vertically integrated model and countertrading under the aggregated

market models can in principle provide an efficient dispatch for generators and respect the transmission constraints, but they do not by themselves align the incentives of customers.

By contrast, the integrated locational market design provides a straightforward alignment of incentives. With a retail rate design that passes through the locational price of energy, the smart device would have smart prices that aligned with the incentives of the consumer and the system's costs. Some distortions would remain to the extent that distribution or other customer service fixed costs are collected in variable rates, but the distortions would be small given the large changes in energy prices that would or should be the norm during peak periods.

The smart grid needs smart pricing. Market models that suppress price information, especially in prices of final delivery to the consumer, would require new and sometimes complex rules to undo the consequent perverse incentives. By contrast, the integrated locational market design intentionally links the market and operations in order to provide the right price signals.

Resource Adequacy

A central function for vertically integrated electric utilities has always been to invest in anticipation of electricity demand. The club members of vertically integrated companies developed rules for investing while sharing the responsibility to maintain reliability. In practice, this amounts to a responsibility to build or contract for energy generation capacity adequate to provide a specified planning reserve margin (e.g., 15% of estimated peak load) that would ensure sufficient capacity in the event of normal outages for maintenance and some temporary equipment failures.

This obligation continues for the vertically integrated utilities. However, the situation has become more complicated in the market models where generation has been separated from transmission, distribution, and final supply to the customers. The success of these models in achieving resource adequacy is neither certain nor resolved. The early days of restructuring, at least in the United States, saw a surge of new construction of more efficient generating plants. This created excess capacity. When coupled with bad market design and rising oil and natural gas prices, this capacity was not economic, and the result was a major contraction in investment and significant financial losses for some generators. In one sense, this was the intended consequence of electricity restructuring in shifting the burden of risks to voluntary investors rather than imposing them on customers. The excess investment was not a good thing, even if a good deal of the problem was caused by the incentives of bad market design rather than the reliance on markets per se.

The result has been a concern that in the future, investment in generating capacity in electricity markets would not be adequate. This concern has been strongly reinforced by the regular demonstration that the returns to investors in the energy and ancillary services prices have not been adequate to support new investment.[3] Although it is the anticipated returns that should govern, not the realized returns in a market with excess capacity, the low realized returns are sobering. The consensus analysis is that energy prices in many electricity markets have been too low, and they are especially low during periods of capacity scarcity, such as during the peak hours of the day.

The response to this concern has been varied. In some markets, notably New York, PJM, and New England, a "capacity" product and an associated capacity market have been created. The essence of the capacity market has been to construct a forecast of future loads and investments, and then conduct an auction for existing and new generators, or demand response, to offer capacity to meet those requirements. The full description of how to define "capacity" and ensure its future deliverability on the grid is another task. However, it is clear that this capacity construct is an attempt to re-create something like the responsibility of the vertically integrated utility, but now under the management of the independent system operator.

The difficulties of defining and measuring capacity for new low-carbon technologies such as wind, solar, and load management are particularly relevant. As discussed below, the variable availability of renewable resources and the problem of

defining baseline load make it hard to map them into the equivalent savings in conventional fossil-fuel generation capacity. In part, the problems are inherent in capacity markets where the product is not easy to define or measure, but the difficulties are exacerbated by the substantial differences in the technologies.

At the other end of the spectrum has been the recognition that inadequate scarcity pricing is the root cause of the deficient incentive for investment.[4] Markets such as in Australia and Texas have mechanisms to allow prices to rise during times of scarcity on the assumption that this will be sufficient to meet the needs of resource adequacy.

Nothing fundamental requires a choice between improved scarcity pricing and adopting well-designed capacity markets. Better scarcity pricing would provide benefits in improved operations as well as market incentives for investment. Furthermore, better scarcity pricing in markets would complement the designs of capacity markets to account for actual or expected scarcity payments (Hogan 2006). The design of better scarcity pricing systems is an active agenda item in the RTO markets in the United States (ISO-NE 2006; MISO 2009; NYISO 2008).

The concern with resource adequacy may be more acute in the United States than in the EU market design models. All of the U.S. models include procedures to monitor and mitigate the exercise of market power, primarily through the application of offer caps. These procedures, coupled with many other market design nuances, accumulate to depress energy market prices. By comparison, the EU market is more opaque in this dimension, more inclined to structural interventions such as divestiture, and less inclined to directly intervene in the bidding process. The incentive to exercise market power is material, and the opportunity may be greater in the EU context. The net result is a more mixed picture about the adequacy of incentives for new generation investment. Furthermore, at the moment, the more aggressive policies in some EU countries for introducing renewable energy sources, particularly wind, have produced excess capacity and raised total system costs, but the increase in capacity depresses energy prices as they appear in the nominal market (Traber and Kemfert 2009).

Infrastructure Investment

Providing generation resource adequacy is only part of the necessary development of the electricity system. Other necessary infrastructure development includes transmission grid expansion and deployment of system upgrades in the form of better information, smarter controls, and smarter metering. In the vertically integrated electric system, these investment decisions were and remain primarily the responsibility of the electricity monopoly, subject to regulatory approval. The restructured markets, however, present a different mix of choices, and in many respects responsibility for infrastructure investment is unresolved.

A principal purpose of development of electricity markets was to provide better incentives and opportunities for decentralized decisions with a corresponding allocation of risk and reward for investments in generation plants and end-use efficiency. In an idealized electricity market structure, energy market prices would be sufficient drivers of generation and end-use investment. As discussed above in the section titled Resource Adequacy, the less-than-ideal reality has not yet achieved this goal for generation, and similar problems arise in providing the incentives for end-use investment.

The case for transmission and related infrastructure investment is even more of a challenge. The transmission grid and associated dispatch functions of the system operator continue as natural monopolies. Even in the idealized version of electricity market design, it could be difficult to fashion a regime that relied on market-based transmission infrastructure investment (Hogan 2009). Accordingly, it is widely (but not universally) assumed that some residual monopoly—a transmission owner, system operator, or hybrid special-purpose organization—must make infrastructure investment decisions, cause the expansion to be implemented, and then use the compulsion through regulation to make the erstwhile unwilling beneficiaries pay.

If the beneficiaries were willing to pay, they could in principle organize to make the transmission investment without the coercive power of regulation. In some cases, market participants do make their own decisions to invest and acquire incremental transmission rights (Hogan 2009). In other cases, however, it may well be that no coalition of beneficiaries could be assembled to undertake desirable transmission investment. In these cases, a transmission company, the system operator, and the regulator must cooperate to implement investment plans.

Designing a hybrid system that could accommodate both market-based and regulatory-driven infrastructure investment is a major challenge for liberalized electricity markets. In some regions, the assumption is that such a hybrid system is impossible and only the transmission company can or will make investments. Other regions have seen a struggle to find a workable compromise. An interesting case is the hybrid transmission expansion framework adopted under the New York Independent System Operator (NYISO), modeled after the transmission investment experience in Argentina. In essence, the NYISO model allows for decentralized investment when the beneficiaries voluntarily assume the responsibility to pay. In cases where the dispersion of benefits makes it difficult or impossible to assemble a coalition of the beneficiaries, the system operator and regulators can go forward subject to a supermajority endorsement where the beneficiaries vote and pay for the investment in proportion to the estimated benefits (Budhraja et al. 2008; NYISO 2007). An important feature of both investment avenues is that beneficiaries pay and the costs are not socialized, which provides good incentives and is compatible with the framework for investment in generation and end use without creating conflicting subsidy regimes.

The ability to develop an adequate hybrid infrastructure investment framework depends on the rest of the market design. In systems with broad energy regions with a common nominal energy product and a single price, the details of transmission congestion are hidden and market signals are weak (between regions) or absent (within regions). In these cases, market participants have no incentive to invest, and a transmission company monopoly may be the only workable system. For example, in England and Wales, the single transmission owner National Grid is responsible for designing, implementing, and charging for transmission investment under the supervision of the regulator. The United States, on the other hand, has a mixture of evolving infrastructure investment schemes. New England follows close to a central-planning and full-cost socialization system, whereas New York, PJM, Texas, the Midwest, and California have various hybrid models in place or in flux.

The details of each of these systems can be complicated, but a general principle connects to the underlying market design. By construction, the more aggregated the market design, the less articulated the investment incentives for transmission. Within aggregated zones, market participants have no incentive to invest because transmission constraints are assumed away. Between aggregate zones, transmission investment incentives may exist, but the price information in the market would only dimly reflect the underlying reality of the transmission interactions. Only in the case of the fully locational integrated market designs could energy prices furnish accurate information about transmission congestion that provides a framework for awarding feasible transmission rights. But these market designs result in efficient infrastructure investment decisions only when the investment itself has relatively limited impact on market prices. Larger investments that could materially change expected market prices may then require a hybrid framework like the New York model.

Green Energy Resources

Green energy resources include a diverse array of technologies. Nuclear power and large-scale hydro provide energy without producing material carbon emissions, and their impacts on the electrical system are well understood. Newer low- or zero-carbon generation technologies such as wind, solar thermal, solar photovoltaic, tidal system, biomass, and fossil fuels with carbon capture

and storage offer a variety of nontraditional operating characteristics that could affect electricity systems and markets. Energy efficiency and load management investments could materially alter the load profile and interact strongly with the portfolio of generation and transmission assets.

Desirable policy for pursuing low-carbon technologies depends in large part on the associated choices in market design. In some cases, such as nuclear and hydropower, the technology is familiar and well understood. In others, such as carbon capture and storage (CCS) or expanded cofiring of biomass, although costs may be different, nothing is obviously fundamentally different from existing fossil-fuel generation that could alter market design. In still other cases, such as wind or solar, the operating characteristics are significantly different. At a small scale, almost any new generation technology can be absorbed, but large-scale integration of the newer low-carbon technologies is more complex. And some anticipated changes, such as the development of smart grids, smart appliances, and electrification of the transportation sector, could require or facilitate major changes in system operations and market design.

Uncertainty and Technology Choice

If you know what to do, do it![5] If we knew which technologies to embrace, which infrastructure investments to support, and how opportunities would evolve, then the low-carbon investment problem would be simple, and the vertically integrated monopoly electric utility model would have much to recommend it. Regulators would continue to oversee the investment choices and set rates for cost recovery. With little uncertainty, the task would be relatively easy, risks would be low, and the lack of efficient incentives for market participants would be less problematic.

Unfortunately, we do not know exactly what to do. By the late 1980s, partly as a result of changes in technology, vertically integrated electric utilities around the world were saddled with high costs and unwanted assets. The resulting pressure led to reform of electricity markets to change the incentives, locus of decisions, and allocation of risks. Part of the animating idea was to promote innovation, entry, and flexibility in the electricity system. New technologies and new operating procedures would arise as a result of market incentives and decentralized decisions. Incentives would be better aligned to support innovation in both end use and generation facilities, and innovation would increase. Rewards would go with the risks, and the market participants would do a better job of euthanizing bad investments as well as capitalizing on what works.

The more innovative the idea, the less likely it would be adopted under the regulated vertically integrated organization. Regulation works better when the choices are highly standardized and easy to evaluate. But when the product includes many moving parts or involves a great deal of uncertainty, it can be much harder to write down the rules. In these cases, business judgments can be made and the uncertainty priced, with the associated risks and rewards. For example, consider the case of EnerNOC, an innovative aggregator of demand response services, and its demand product, which provides operating reserves in markets such as PJM (EnerNOC n.d.). The de facto product provided to PJM behaves essentially like reliable standby generating reserve that can be called on to meet gross load or reduce net load at a set of locations. The actual service, hidden from view of the system operators, is a complicated array of contracts and operating agreements with end users that allow a variety of interventions with various technologies to reduce or temporarily shift electricity load. These contracts are negotiated privately, and voluntarily, to share risks and rewards. There is no need for regulators to approve the complex and varied terms and conditions of the individual contracts. EnerNOC takes a reasonable business risk, constrained in its returns through the possibility of competition from others in providing similar services. PJM gets innovative access to cost-effective operating reserves that fit naturally under the market design. The market design stimulated a market response, but the rules did not prescribe the result.

This broad motivation for electricity market reform is greatly reinforced by the challenges of developing a low-carbon electricity system. Car-

bon emissions have a long duration in the atmosphere and will affect the climate for centuries after their sources have been retired, and generating plants may operate for many decades. Hence we are interested in impacts over very long timescales, and we are hoping for and expecting dramatic innovations in technology and operating procedures. Over this timescale, enormous uncertainty exists about what will work and how the system will operate in practice. The biggest surprise would be if there were no major surprises.

In this setting, it is even more important to engage the creativity and innovations of the many current and potential market participants rather than rely on the wisdom of a few central planners. If we knew what to do, the central planners could execute. But because we do not know exactly what to do, we need an electricity market design that facilitates learning.

In the face of great uncertainty, the signals and incentives should be as technology-neutral as possible. Rather than prescribe or constrain the choices of technology, market operations and prices should reflect the real costs incurred. To the extent possible, externalities should be internalized. For example, rather than mandate technologies, we should put a price on carbon that should affect technology choices.

Among the three market models, the vertically integrated model is most like central planning, and the integrated locational market design is most attuned to reflecting real costs associated with system operations. The aggregated countertrade models fall somewhere in between, with more opportunities for decentralized investment decisions but more muted incentives to guide those investments.

The need to support innovation, to pursue technologies, investments, and consumption choices not yet envisioned by anyone—including by the central planner—provides a powerful motivation for getting the signals and incentives aligned to support decentralized decisions. By contrast, the more the electricity market design relies on socialized costs, muted incentives, and regulatory mandates, the more the central planner assumes the burden for making investment decisions and applying regulatory compulsion to recover the costs.

Investment and Operating Costs

There would not be much policy concern with low-carbon technologies if they did not appear to be more expensive than fossil-based alternatives. With a price on carbon emissions, the cost differential between fossil-fuel plants and low-carbon alternatives may be overcome. However, material differences in costs may remain for nascent technologies entering the market.

The response to any remaining cost differential would depend on the nature of the higher costs and the structure of the market design. If a price is put on carbon, but the price is not sufficient to induce adoption of a particular technology, there could be several explanations. For example, it may be that the technology is simply too expensive compared with other alternatives. In this case, no real problem exists, and the failure to embrace the particular low-carbon investment is the correct solution.

Another possibility is that the price of carbon is too low. The best response would be to raise the price of carbon. Absent an adequate carbon price, if a policy decision is made to invest in low-carbon technologies that are not cost-competitive, the nature of the cost differential would have different impacts under alternative market designs.

An alternative case would be that the price of carbon is appropriate, the current cost of the new low-carbon technology makes it not competitive, but learning by doing could lower the costs enough to make the low-carbon technology competitive. Again, the impacts will be different under alternative market designs.

A market design based on a vertically integrated monopoly will face familiar issues of technology adoption and investment in all three cases. The regulator would oversee investment choices and provide rates for cost recovery. Low-carbon technologies could be adopted as a matter of policy, despite their costs. The particular nature of the cost differentials would not be a first-order concern.

In the other market models, relying more on prices and other market incentives, the nature of the cost differential would matter more. With higher costs, adoption will require some form of subsidy. If the higher cost is in the form of high investment costs, tax credits or other capital subsidies could be offered in many ways. Once the subsidy is provided, the new generation plant or end-use investment can participate in the ongoing electricity market on the same basis as other investments.

If the source of the higher cost is a higher operating cost, the interaction with the market design may be more immediate. Consider, for example, an end-use technology such as load management to reduce consumption when the avoided cost of electricity is very high. If the market design does not provide the appropriate price signals that capture the avoided cost in the system, often over relative short intervals, enough incentive may not exist to pursue load management even if the up-front investment cost is low or subsidized. Here both the temporal and locational granularity of prices would be important. Similar challenges would arise for generation investments such as pump storage, flywheel storage, or pondage hydro, which could smooth out effective load curves but face high effective operating costs. If the market design does not offer sufficient granularity of price determination, then other cost-effective low-carbon technologies would be too expensive to operate or would require regulatory mandates for adoption.

Intermittency and Reliability

Of the many technical characteristics of certain low-carbon technologies, the feature that draws the most attention is intermittency of the supply and the implications for reliability and meeting system load. The canonical concern is for wind and solar photovoltaic (PV) panels. Once constructed, the variable operating cost of these generation plants is effectively zero. But if the wind does not blow or the sun does not shine, no power is generated.

This intermittency gives rise to two related but different problems. The first is the availability of the power when it is needed. With traditional nuclear, hydro, and fossil-fuel plants, required maintenance can be scheduled to minimize the impact on peak hours, and the random outages that cannot be controlled have a relatively low probability. By contrast, the implied effective capacity factor of 30% or below for individual renewable facilities is equivalent to random outage probabilities of 70% or more. The correlation of these outages with peak and near-peak loads would be important, but the basic intermittency is a hurdle for some low-carbon technologies.

Another aspect of variable availability of low-carbon technologies is the speed at which they come on or, more important, go off the system. This "ramp rate" can present material operational challenges for the system. For small-scale penetration of the low-carbon technologies, not much more need be done than include this variability as part of the natural variability of residual load. But on a large scale, the challenge would be different depending on the dispatchability of the plant.

A common answer is that the individual variability of solar or wind facilities is less of a problem when regional diversification of sources is sufficient where winds speeds are not correlated. It is true that the correlation reduces across wider areas (Holttinen et al. 2009).[6] However, exploiting this portfolio effect depends importantly on the configuration of the transmission grid as discussed below under Green Infrastructure Development.

In principle, for the integrated locational market design, variability in production does not present much of a design problem. Security-constrained economic dispatch would impose limits on the output of the plants and reduce prices for energy the more that capacity has to be reserved to meet the potential changes in production. For example, this might involve restricting output from wind facilities when the wind is blowing hard to keep the combined output of the wind farm below the level that the system could handle if the wind suddenly drops. The net effect would be to reduce the locational price of energy and increase the locational price of operating reserves. Most of the cost of variability would then fall on the wind supplier, with the associated incentives to invest in storage or other backup options.

This appeal to the theory of integrated locational market design contradicts the common assumption that windmills should generate whenever the wind is blowing. Although this is not correct as an economic matter, because at times free energy is too expensive, widespread concern exists that investment in low-carbon technologies should be combined with other investments to ensure that the power can flow when it is available.

The market design implications of the intermittency of supply are familiar. The more granularity, over time and location, in the prices and dispatch, the easier it is to integrate low-carbon technologies. The better the prices reflect avoided costs, the easier it would be to integrate such technologies, especially those with high operating costs.

The greater variability of supply for key low-carbon technologies and increased end-use response become more and more important the greater the investment in smart grids. As discussed above, smart grids require smart prices. Smarter prices would better reflect scarcity conditions, locational differences, and dynamic response. In the absence of sufficiently granular prices and quantity definition, incentives for low-carbon investment diverge from the real costs of system operations. The details will be different in different markets, but the greater the gap, the more the reliance on regulation and central mandates to support low-carbon technologies.

Green Infrastructure Investment

The places where the wind blows and the sun shines are not always where people congregate. Hence, from a strictly technical perspective, some of the best locations for siting low-carbon technologies like wind and solar energy are far from loads. West Texas has a great deal of wind, but the load is in Dallas and Houston. The result is a substantial need for transmission investment. In Texas, a policy decision has been made to move ahead with transmission expansion to enable greater utilization of the wind resources and socialize the cost through additional charges to all customers.[7]

In other regions, the justification for additional transmission and the associated cost allocation are more problematic. In the case of New York, the large potential wind resources are in the northwestern region of the state, and the major load center is around New York City. Controversy has arisen about whether to build new transmission and who should pay. The integrated locational pricing design sends clear signals about the potential benefits of expanded transmission, but so far the benefits have not been seen as worth the costs. Under the innovative New York transmission investment rules, the beneficiaries must pay and must approve in advance according to supermajority voting. In the case of the proposed New York Regional Intertie, designed to exploit upstate wind, the developers withdrew the plan on the grounds that it would not receive sufficient support from the putative beneficiaries to obtain approval (Puga and Lesser 2009).

One of the challenges for transmission investment is the intermittency of wind and solar energy production. A standard argument is that diversification of sources of supply across large regions where wind and cloud cover are not perfectly correlated would provide a sufficient portfolio effect to mitigate the intermittency. What this argument must confront is the level of transmission investment required. For the diversification argument to hold fully, transmission capacity must be sufficient to accommodate the maximum output of all of the sources. In the case of dedicated long-distance lines to bring power to load, each line must be sized to be fully utilized only a fraction of the time. Otherwise the full diversification benefit would not be realized. This surge capacity investment in transmission, and planned underutilization, could materially add to the costs of interconnection for remote low-carbon energy technologies (NAS Committee 2009).

The more the market design adheres to the granularity of time and location, the greater will be the transparency of incentives for transmission investment. The more the market design aggregates across time and location, the more hidden will be the benefits of transmission. The higher the degree of aggregation, the greater will be the tendency to socialize the cost of transmission.

Movement toward the integrated locational market design facilitates a beneficiary-pays system

of transmission expansion and supports other features of market investment decisions. Without a beneficiary-pays protocol, there is no principled answer to why the subsidies to transmission should not be extended to demand and production alternatives that are partial substitutes for transmission expansion. A beneficiary-pays protocol for transmission is an important long-term component of market design. As ready examples in Texas and New England demonstrate, however, the use of an integrated locational market design for the energy market is no guarantee that transmission investment will be market-driven and not socialized.

Green Policy Mandates

Many policies have arisen or might arise to support development and deployment of low-carbon technologies. In some cases, these policies would complement broader market decisions. In other cases, the efforts to internalize carbon externalities might conflict with market design features.

Carbon Emission Caps

By far the most important component of an efficient and effective policy to internalize the climate impacts of carbon emissions is to put a price on carbon, as has been done in the EU and is likely in the United States. For all the usual reasons, the carbon pricing regime should, to the extent possible, be economywide and global in its coverage (Stavins 2007). The details of the policy choice of a carbon tax versus a cap-and-trade proposal are important and raise many other issues.

A carbon cap with trading of emission permits is widely accepted as being more politically feasible because of the greater opacity of the revenue transfers inherent in allocation of the permits. A principal feature of a good allocation design is to break any connection between actual energy production and the aggregate allocation of the permits.[8] In this event, free permit allocations involve a transfer of wealth but provide no reduction in the cost of carbon emissions on the margin.

A key element of a workable policy will be the credibility of the carbon regime and the exposure to future political risk (Neuhoff et al. 2009). Major investments in expensive low-carbon technologies would be profitable only if sustainable public policy ensures a significant implicit or explicit price on carbon emissions that is expected to remain high enough for long enough to recover the substantial investment.

Sustainability of public policy will depend in part on compatibility with the basic market design. For example, an economywide cap on carbon emissions would be largely technology-neutral and would integrate well with efficient market operations. Investors in a particular technology would not need to worry as much that their specific venture would be subject to idiosyncratic subsidy changes. In order to change the economics of the individual investment, the carbon cap would need to be changed for all emissions, and this is less likely than a change in a targeted subsidy. By contrast, the boom-and-bust cycle of solar deployment in the United States, driven by the dependence on periodic reauthorization of targeted tax credits for solar investments, illustrates the risk of developing a sustained commitment to investment based on special-purpose support (NAS Committee 2009). Comprehensive carbon emission caps and good market design would reinforce the sustainability of the system.

Research, Development, and Demonstration

The usual arguments imply that major spillover benefits should accrue to research, development, and even early demonstration (RD&D) efforts to discover and refine better low-carbon technologies. Instituting policies to put a price on carbon would reinforce incentives for private RD&D, but there is no reason to believe that the full externalities of the public-good aspect of RD&D would be overcome by putting a price on carbon. Mounting an RD&D program to support energy innovation (Anadon and Holdren 2009) has major challenges. However, the challenges are not much affected by different wholesale electricity market designs.

Infant Industries and Learning by Doing

Commercialization beyond RD&D and learning by research interact with deployment and learning by doing. A major argument in favor of public investment to support early adoption of low-carbon technologies is the ability to capture the benefits of early investment, which accumulate to reduce the going-forward cost of the technology. The externality arises when the benefits of information about the success of the technology and the improved understanding of how to build and operate cannot be captured by the investor. Thus learning by doing is a type of infant industry argument, where early support is needed to launch the technology, but once mature, the technology is able to compete on its own without further subsidy.

An interesting feature of the application of learning-by-doing analysis to energy technologies is the substantial nature of the putative benefits. High learning rates generate such substantial reductions in total electricity generation cost that most of the benefit comes from improved efficiency of the electricity system, and carbon emission reduction benefits are a small component of the gain. In some cases, if the claimed learning rates are true, it would pay to provide public support for the technology even if carbon emissions posed no cost (van Benthem et al. 2008).

This argument about large potential cost reductions might apply to wind and solar generation technologies that are alternatives to fossil-fuel generation but cannot apply to CCS technologies. Although substantial learning may come in CCS design and deployment, the remaining costs will always be in addition to the cost of fossil-fuel generation. Even if CCS were effectively free, it would not be cheaper than using the fossil-fuel plant without CCS. Hence all the benefits for CCS come from the carbon reduction.

Policies to support learning by doing should be structured to recognize the distinction between supporting learning about the technology through early cumulative investment, and supporting the technology by offering sustained subsidies with little or no further learning. Quantitative targets for low-carbon technology investment may have little connection with the public benefits of learning. For instance, the case of the California solar rooftop initiative is instructive. Launched with a promise to install solar PV on a million rooftops by 2015, the idea was to both reduce carbon emissions and capture the benefits of learning by doing. However, whereas the assumed learning rate is an input, the necessary scale of the investment should be an output of the analysis and not a constraint on the policy. In the California case, further analysis revealed both the implied trajectory of the optimal subsidies and investment profiles as a function of the assumed learning rate. A central conclusion was that the optimal subsidies would be associated with investment at only about a quarter of the scale of the nominal million-rooftop target. Higher learning rates needed less initial subsidy, and lower learning rates might not produce enough benefit to justify any material subsidy (van Benthem et al. 2008).

Proper design of support policies to capture the benefits of learning by doing interact with market design in straightforward ways. The more transparent the market design and the clearer the market signals, the easier to achieve the benefits of the learning and know whether the benefits are appearing. In the energy market, the better the price signals, to include scarcity costs, the better the opportunity for private investment to drive the benefits of lower costs.

Renewable Energy Standards

The competition between incentives and targets appears most starkly in the case of renewable energy standards (also known as renewable portfolio standards, or RPSs). Motivated by the market model of the vertically integrated electric utility, with a single buyer, the idea is to promote penetration of low-carbon technologies by setting mandates for the percentage of electricity generation that must be provided by defined categories of renewable or low-carbon energy sources. Such goals supported by feed-in tariffs have been adopted as targets throughout the EU and as quantity mandates in many states in the United States. Experience with this policy instrument

presents a number of difficulties, some of which interact with the nature of the market design.

The standards often lack a principled basis. A cap on carbon emissions, where the emissions of carbon can be measured and controlled, is technology-neutral. By contrast, renewable energy standards require selecting the acceptable technologies. The result has been a substantial degree of political bargaining, with variation across jurisdictions revealing the fundamental disagreements about goals and means. For instance, in the United States, state programs define a wide array of more than a dozen possible renewable technologies, yet "states agree on only three technologies: biomass conversion, solar photovoltaic and wind" (Michaels 2008, *10*).

The renewable energy standards also suffer from confusion about objectives and a poor mapping between policy and goals. Requiring minimum penetration standards to support early development of expensive or risky renewable technologies is akin to the quantity target and subject to the comments above about the mismatch between learning-by-doing justification and quantitative targets.

Or consider the justification that the technology would never be competitive on its own, and the minimum standard is intended to reduce carbon emissions. Although this approach may have an appeal in the absence of a carbon cap, the argument no longer applies in the presence of a cap. As soon as there is a binding cap on carbon emissions, a renewable electricity standard (RES) produces no incremental carbon emission benefits. If the cap is binding, the effect of an RES is to require more expensive investments that reduce carbon emissions and therefore lower the cost for everyone else and every other technology in meeting the carbon cap. Hence the proposed 33% RES by 2020 in California should raise costs of control in the state, to the benefit of the rest of the country.[9] But once a cap-and-trade system is in place, carbon emissions would be the same as without the RES. In effect, the RES lowers the market price for carbon emission permits and raises the social cost of reducing carbon emissions but does not lower carbon emissions.[10]

In market designs without vertical integration, an RES presents the challenge of how to implement and enforce the technology constraint. One approach is to create RES certificates and require all buyers or generators to redeem a certain percentage of RES generation credits or pay a tax (RECS n.d.). The price of the credits is then a factor in the price of electricity and alters the economic dispatch. However, the connection with carbon emissions is imperfect, as low-carbon technologies such as nuclear are often excluded from RES credits. Thus the preferred cap-and-trade system would have parallel trading systems to control emissions and promote renewability. There is nothing inherently infeasible about having multiple permits systems. For example, the carbon permit would be layered on top of tradable sulfur dioxide emission permits. But the added complexity does raise a question about the incremental benefits of RES mandates.

Green Uneconomic Dispatch

Another approach to promoting green energy resources would be to mandate priority for low-carbon technologies to be selected first in energy dispatch (Dubash 2002). This idea presents more complications than might first appear, because of the nature of the transmission system interaction with electricity market design.

The complex interaction of power flows in the transmission system can produce cases where actions at a location to reduce energy use or increase emission-free electricity production can actually increase carbon emissions in the overall system (Rudkevich 2009). Meeting electricity load at certain locations creates counterflow in the grid, which reduces congestion. Reducing that counterflow can create a requirement for a multiplant redispatch that increases overall carbon emissions. The technical condition is similar to the effects of transmission counterflow, which can drive locational energy prices negative even when all generation offers are positive. Hence the system impacts on carbon emissions are not always easily predictable.

This might support a call for a green energy dispatch protocol in place of economic dispatch,

but the interaction with energy market design would be disruptive. In the case of the vertically integrated monopoly, there would be less of a problem. By assumption, the monopoly can internalize all the untoward effects in the production and delivery chain and ignore the internal transfer prices.

By contrast, the market structures now based on bid and offers in a framework of security-constrained economic dispatch would confront a substantial disconnect between the economic prices applied in the settlements system and the opportunity costs of changes in the dispatch. As much experience has shown, whenever market prices used in settlements systems diverge materially from the costs of real system operations, arbitrage opportunities and temptations are created that could undermine the dispatch and the market.

It would be possible to impose a constraint on emissions in the dispatch (over very short intervals), and then apply the usual principles of economic dispatch subject to the emissions cap. This would produce consistent market prices with scarcity components reflecting the cost of carbon emissions implied by the constraint. In effect, this would replace an economywide cap on emissions, allowing implicit trading across time and space, with a new cap-and-tax system with short-term caps and implicit taxing at the implied variable carbon price. Absent a formal electricity-only cap-and-trade system that allowed intertemporal balancing, the system operator would have to decide on the limit for virtually every dispatch period. It would be reasonable to anticipate that the implicit (very) short-term carbon price would be highly volatile.

A far simpler approach would be if the cap on aggregate emissions and the implied carbon price in the economywide cap-and-trade system were sufficient to internalize the cost of carbon. Then the carbon emission permit costs, along with all other costs for fuels and other emissions, would be treated the same in the security-constrained economic dispatch. In the integrated locational market design, the associated locational marginal prices would include the effects of carbon emissions. There would be no additional need for an incremental green dispatch that could break the connection between market design and real operations.

Feed-In Tariffs

Green energy mandates that require system operators to accept energy from approved technologies at approved fixed prices, known as feed-in tariffs, have been widely adopted in the EU. Not surprisingly, with high enough prices, such mandates have been highly successful at increasing the market share of approved sources such as wind and solar installations (Muñoz et al. 2007). However, the structure of the feed-in tariff creates collateral damage similar to the effects of green uneconomic dispatch, and it is not clear whether the model is consistent with developing sustainable growth of low-carbon investments.

Set aside the issue that the new technologies are expensive and the expense is becoming a matter of policy concern in the EU.[11] The feed-in tariff interacts poorly with the rest of the market design in terms of system operations, price signals, and infrastructure investment.

The problem with system operations appears because the system operator must take the energy input, even when the resulting power flow might foreclose other generation alternatives, except in emergency conditions. In the case of wind, for example, the variable cost of wind energy may be zero, but this does not mean that it is always cost-effective to accept the wind energy. Conditions occur on the grid where the value of the wind energy is negative. In effect, the feed-in tariff forces wind energy onto the grid and drives the implicit (in the EU) or explicit (in the U.S. RTOs) locational price of energy substantially below zero. This is a regular event in PJM, for example.

Because the mandate is to take the green energy, the burden of investing in transmission connections and upgrades falls on someone else, either on the transmission company or by some method of cost socialization through the system operator. Besides the obvious total cost inefficiencies, this cost socialization distorts the choices among renewable energy resources.

The simple alternative to the feed-in tariff would be some mix of investment tax credit or direct subsidies that reduce the cost of investment (but not operations). In order to provide incentives for operations, collection of the subsidy could be conditioned on offering the capacity in the real-time market, whereupon the usual principles of security-constrained economic dispatch would apply.

Note that conditioning the subsidy on offering the energy to the market is not the same thing as conditioning the subsidy on the energy actually produced. System operators have good experience in discriminating good-faith offers of energy and need not actually dispatch the plant whenever it is offered to verify its bona fides. But if the subsidy is conditional on producing the energy, the effect would be to convert the fixed investment subsidy into a variable opportunity cost. In this case, the wind or solar plant could profitably enter a negative bid (bounded below by minus the variable subsidy value) to ensure it was dispatched. This would distort prices and exacerbate the problem of the technology subsidies sending the wrong signals to the market.

Transmission Investment

A major challenge remains in defining the appropriate protocols for transmission investment. The general problems of constructing a satisfactory hybrid system, as outlined above, are magnified by the perception of many that a major expansion of transmission capacity is required to build the long-distance connectors between loads and the major potential sources of renewable energy (NAS Committee 2009).

The principal implication for green energy mandates would be to decide on the degree to which transmission costs are considered in the competition among green energy resources. Which major expansions of transmission systems are necessary is far from obvious. Solar rooftop installations may require relatively little, and certainly different, transmission investments than distant wind or solar installations. Renewable energy sources are partial substitutes for each other, and there is no reason to believe that every renewable option should be pursued. It follows that the model for transmission investment and cost allocation could have a major impact on the choice of renewable technologies. If transmission investment cost is socialized, for everything or even only for renewable sources, then distant wind will look cheaper and nearby rooftop solar more expensive, even when the opposite ranking may be true.

An obvious principle to apply to green transmission investment, as for any transmission investment, would be to adhere to a beneficiary-pays system (Hogan 2009). If the requirement to pay for transmission makes a preferred renewable technology more expensive, then this can be addressed directly in the balance of subsidies. In the presence of a carbon cap, with the cap accepted as the proper balance of carbon costs and benefits, no good reason exists to treat green transmission investment any differently than other transmission investment.

Conclusions

Policy supporting low-carbon technologies and end-use choices in the electricity sector interacts with electricity market design. Great uncertainty remains about the appropriate investments, and the consensus is that achieving a low-carbon future will require innovation and invention. Success is more likely if appropriate price signals and incentives appear to drive decentralized decisions of the many participants in electricity markets. Placing a price on carbon is a critical step. Getting the resulting incentives right will be easier the closer the electricity market design reflects the reality of electricity system operations. The experience with electricity market alternatives points to the integrated locational electricity market design as the only workable model that is compatible with open transmission access and nondiscrimination.

Notes

1.   In the U.S. case, vertically integrated utilities are subject to certain open-access provisions, but these

open-access rules lack the critical ingredient of nondiscriminatory access to economic dispatch.

2.   Likewise, administrative aggregation without changing the underlying grid does not increase competition or reduce market power.

3.   PJM reports that on average between 1999 and 2008, a combustion turbine would have earned 43% of its fixed charges in energy net revenue (Monitoring Analytics 2009).

4.   The causes of inadequate scarcity pricing are many, including but not limited to regulatory offer caps on supply (Hogan 2005).

5.   "If you know what to do, do it! If you don't know what to do, decision analysis can help you decide." Aphorism from Professor Ron Howard of the Department of Management Science and Engineering at Stanford University.

6.   This portfolio effect does not eliminate cases such as a night when the sun is down nor necessarily when even a large area can be becalmed and remove all the wind generation (NERC 2009).

7.   Texas Utilities Code § 36.053 (d), available at http://codes.lp.findlaw.com/txstatutes/UT/2/B/36/B/36.053 (accessed February 20, 2010).

8.   Initial designs in the EU included allocations for new power plants as a set-aside under the total cap. This creates the incentive to build new plants and raises the cost for existing plants by reducing the net cap for the existing fleet.

9.   California Executive Order S-14–08, November 17, 2008, available at www.gov.ca.gov/executive-order/11072/ (accessed February 20, 2010).

10.   The argument is slightly different for a carbon tax, where the price of carbon is fixed. Then an RES adds to costs by requiring use of more expensive low-carbon technologies, but it does reduce carbon emissions.

11.   According to ENDS Europe (2009): "The new German coalition government will cut feed in tariffs for solar power by more than the planned 8% reduction for 2010, according to a 128-page policy document published on Friday [October 23, 2009]. The tariffs will now be reviewed every three years."

References

Amin, M. 2000. National Infrastructures as Complex Interactive Networks. In *Automation, Control, and*

Complexity: An Integrated Approach, edited by Tariq Samad and John Weyrauch. New York, John Wiley and Sons, 263–286.

Anadon, Laura Diaz, and John P. Holdren. 2009. Policy for Energy Technology Innovation. In *Acting in Time on Energy Policy*, edited by Kelly Sims Gallagher. Washington, DC: Brookings Institution Press, 89–127.

Boucher, Jacqueline, and Yves Smeers. 2002. Towards a Common European Electricity Market Paths in the Right Direction Still Far from an Effective Design. *Journal of Network Industries* 3 (4): 375–424.

Budhraja, Vikram, John Ballance, James Dyer, Fred Mobasheri, Alison Silverstein, and Joseph H. Eto. 2008. Transmission Benefit Quantification, Cost Allocation and Cost Recovery. Sacramento, CA: California Energy Commission, Energy Research and Development Division.

Dubash, Navroz K. 2002. The Changing Global Context for Electricity Reform. In *Power Politics: Equity and Environment in Electricity Reform*, edited by N.K. Dubash. Washington, DC: World Resources Institute, 11–30.

ENDS Europe (Environmental Data Services Europe). 2009. New German Coalition Confirms Solar Subsidy Cuts. www.endseurope.com/22460 (accessed February 20, 2010).

EnerNOC (Energy Network Operations Center). No date. EnerNOC: Get More from Energy. www.enernoc.com/ (accessed February 20, 2010).

ENTSO-E (European Network of Transmission System Operators for Electricity). 2008. *Regional Group Continental Europe, Statistical Yearbook*. Brussels, European Network of Transmission System Operators for Electricity.

EPSA (Electric Power Supply Association). 2008. EPSA Statement on Renewable Energy in Organized Electricity Markets. Press release. Washington, DC: EPSA.

Grubb, Michael, Tooraj Jamasb, and Michael G. Pollitt. 2008. A Low-Carbon Electricity Sector for the UK: What Can Be Done and How Much Will It Cost? In *Delivering a Low-Carbon Electricity System*, edited by Michael Grubb, Tooraj Jamasb, and Michael G. Pollitt. Cambridge, UK: Cambridge University Press, 462–497.

Helman, Udi, Harry Singh, and Paul Sotkeiwicz. 2010. RTOs, Regional Electricity Markets, and Climate Policy. In *Generating Electricity in a Carbon-Constrained World*, edited by Fereidoon P. Sioshansi. Burlington, MA: Academic Press, 527–563.

HEPG (Harvard Electricity Policy Group). Various dates. RTO annual reports. www.hks.harvard.edu/hepg/rlib_rp_RTO_ISO_reports.html (accessed February 20, 2010).

Hogan, William W. 1992. Contract Networks for Electric Power Transmission. *Journal of Regulatory Economics* 4: 211–242.

———. 1999. Getting the Prices Right in PJM: Analysis and Summary: April 1998 through March 1999, the First Anniversary of Full Locational Pricing. Cambridge, MA: Harvard University. www.hks.harvard.edu/fs/whogan/pjm0999.pdf (accessed April 16, 2010).

———. 2002. Electricity Market Restructuring: Reforms of Reforms. *Journal of Regulatory Economics* 21 (1): 103–132.

———. 2005. On an "Energy Only" Electricity Market Design for Resource Adequacy. Cambridge, MA: Center for Business and Government, John F. Kennedy School of Government, Harvard University. www.hks.harvard.edu/fs/whogan/Hogan_Energy_Only_092305.pdf (accessed April 16, 2010).

———. 2006. Resource Adequacy Mandates and Scarcity Pricing ("Belts and Suspenders"). Comments submitted to the Federal Energy Regulatory Commission. Docket Nos. ER05-1410-000 and EL05-148-000. www.hks.harvard.edu/fs/whogan/Hogan_PJM_Energy_Market_022306.pdf (accessed April 16, 2010).

———. 2009. Electricity Market Structure and Infrastructure. In *Acting in Time on Energy Policy*, edited by Kelly Sims Gallagher. Washington, DC: Brookings Institution Press, 128–161.

Holttinen, Hannele, Peter Meibom, Antje Orths, Bernhard Lange, Mark O'Malley, John Olav Tande, Ana Estanqueiro, Emilio Gomez, Lennart Söder, Goran Strbac, J. Charles Smith, and Frans van Hulle. 2009. Impacts of Large Amounts of Wind Power on Design and Operation of Power Systems, Results of IEA Collaboration. 8th International Workshop on Large Scale Integration of Wind Power into Power Systems as Well as on Transmission Networks of Offshore Wind Farms. October 2009, Bremen, Germany.

IEA (International Energy Agency). 2007. *Tackling Investment Challenges in Power Generation in IEA Countries: Energy Market Experience*. Paris: OECD Publishing.

ISO-NE (ISO New England). 2006. FERC Electric Tariff No. 3, Market Rule I, Section III.2.7.

Joskow, Paul. 2008. Challenges for Creating a Comprehensive National Electricity Policy. Speech given to the National Press Club. September 2008, Washington, DC. www.hks.harvard.edu/hepg/Papers/Joskow_Natl_Energy_Policy.pdf (accessed February 20, 2010).

Lankford, Craig B., James D. McCalley, and Narinder K. Saini. 1996. Bibliography on Transmission Access Issues. *IEEE Transactions on Power Systems* 11 (1): 30–40.

Michaels, Robert J. 2008. A Federal Renewable Electricity Requirement, What's Not to Like? Policy Analysis No. 627. Washington, DC: Cato Institute.

MISO (Midwest ISO). 2009. FERC Electric Tariff, Vol. No. 1, Schedule 28.

Monitoring Analytics. 2009. *2008 State of the Market Report for PJM.* Vol. 2, *Detailed Analysis.* www.monitoringanalytics.com.

Muñoz, Miquel, Volker Oschmann, and J. David Tábara. 2007. Harmonization of Renewable Electricity Feed-In Laws in the European Union. *Energy Policy* 35: 3104–3114.

NAS Committee (Committee on America's Energy Future). 2009. *National America's Energy Future: Technology and Transformation.* Washington, DC: National Academy of Science.

NERC (North American Electric Reliability Corporation). 2009. *Special Report: Accommodating High Levels of Variable Generation.* Princeton: NERC.

Neuhoff, Karsten, Sam Fankhauser, Emmanuel Guerin, Jean Charles Hourcade, Helen Jackson, Ranjita Rajan, and John Ward. 2009. Structuring International Financial Support to Support Domestic Climate Change Mitigation in Developing Countries. Cambridge, UK: Climate Strategies, www.climatestrategies.org.

NYISO (New York Independent System Operator). 2007. Order No. 890 Transmission Planning Compliance Filing. Docket No. OA08-13-000. Cover Letter Submitted to Federal Energy Regulatory Commission, December 7, 14–15.

———. 2008. Ancillary Service Manual, Vol. 3.11, Draft, 6-19–6-22.

PJM 2009. PJM Open Access Transmission Tariff, Subpart A: Interconnection Procedures. 6th Rev. Vol. No. 1, Para. 36.1.

Potomac Economics. 2009. *2008 State of the Market Report for the ERCOT Wholesale Electricity Markets.* www.hks.harvard.edu/hepg/Papers/RTO-ISO_reports/2008_ERCOT_SOM_REPORT_Final.pdf (accessed April 16, 2010).

Puga, J. Nicolas, and Jonathan Lesser. 2009. Public Policy and Private Interests: Why Transmission Planning and Cost-Allocation Methods Continue to Stifle Renewable Energy Policy Goals. *Electricity Journal*, 22 (10) (December): 7–19.

RECS (RECS International Association). No date. Renewable Energy Certificate System. www.recs.org (accessed February 20, 2010).

Rudkevich, Aleksandr. 2009. Economics of CO_2 Emissions in Power Systems. Boston: CRA International. www.hks.harvard.edu/hepg/ (accessed February 20, 2010).

Schweppe, F. C., M. C. Caramanis, R. D. Tabors, and R. E. Bohn. 1988. *Spot Pricing of Electricity.* Norwell, MA: Kluwer Academic Publishers.

Sioshansi, Fereidoon P. 2008. *Competitive Electricity Markets: Design, Implementation, Performance.* Oxford: Elsevier.

Stavins, Robert N. 2007. A U.S. Cap-and-Trade System to Address Global Climate Change. Hamilton Project discussion paper 2007–13. Washington, DC: Brookings Institution.

Traber, Thure, and Claudia Kemfert. 2009. Gone with the Wind? Electricity Prices and Incentives to Invest in Complementary Thermal Power Plants under Increasing Wind Energy Supply. Berlin: German Institute for Economic Research.

van Benthem, Arthur, Kenneth Gillingham, and James Sweeney 2008. Learning-by-Doing and the Optimal Solar Policy in California. *Energy Journal* 29 (3): 131–152.

8

Energy Regulation in a Low-Carbon World

Richard Green

Increasing the use of renewable energy will have significant impacts on the operations of energy utilities, the companies that deliver electricity and gas to consumers using networks of wires and pipes. As discussed in Chapter 2, many renewable energy technologies are very different from the traditional large-scale, centralized technologies that utilities have relied on for more than 100 years. Electricity transmission and distribution system operators will have to become used to taking power from many smaller generators, distributed around the system, while larger-scale renewable generators are often sited far away from the major loads. Other renewable electricity may be self-generated by consumers and firms, and electric utilities would then provide a residual service or perhaps install and maintain the self-generators. Gas utilities may find that the demand for their product falls significantly as consumers switch to renewable sources of heat.

If the utilities' operations are changing, should this affect their regulation? Some principles of regulation, such as the need for transparency and stability, will surely remain unchanged. What about the way in which these principles are put into practice? Should the scope of regulation, the activities subject to an economic regulator, be broadened (or narrowed) as the amount of renewable generation grows? Should the regulator's objectives, or the factors it takes into account when deciding how to achieve those objectives, change? How are its decisions likely to change?

This chapter begins with a discussion of the scope of economic regulation and its interaction with energy policy. It then presents four models of economic regulation for energy utilities: a retail competition model, used in the Nordic countries, the United Kingdom, and some U.S. states (such as Texas), in which only the natural monopoly in delivery (transmission and distribution) is regulated; a wholesale competition model, in which unregulated generators provide power, but the prices paid by (at least some) retail customers are regulated (as in France, Spain, and some other U.S. states); a single buyer model, in which a regulated entity is responsible for procuring power through competitive tenders (as in some developing countries); and an integrated firms model, in which regulators have to oversee most of the industry's value chain (as in those parts of the United States that have not adopted liberalization policies).

The chapter subsequently goes into more detail about how the increase in renewable energy will affect the electricity industry, then draws out some general implications of these changes for economic regulation, which will apply regardless of the specific model chosen. This is followed by a discussion of lessons that are specific to the particular tasks facing regulators, which vary according to the regulatory model chosen. Although the electricity industry will see the biggest changes, the chapter ends with a look at possible impacts on the gas industry and lessons for its regulation.

The Scope of Economic Regulation and Energy Policy

This discussion of economic regulation concentrates on government or government agency regulation of the prices and service standards offered by an industry that is perceived as constituting a natural monopoly. It is thus distinct from competition policy, which applies to industries where competition is believed to be possible; health and safety standards; and environmental regulation.

Traditionally, the concerns of an economic regulator have been to protect consumers from high prices and protect investors in the utilities from low prices. This does not mean that consumers and investors have diametrically opposing interests, however. In the short term, it might be possible to reduce the utilities' prices without ill effects, but in the long term, this is likely to make the companies unsustainable, unable to raise the funds needed to expand or even maintain their capital equipment. Spiller and Viana Martorell (1996) document what happened when some governments in Latin America reduced electricity prices below the level of long-term viability: the eventual outcome was nationalization. Only when new systems of regulation were created, with sufficient protection for investors, was it possible to reprivatize the companies.

From this perspective, the regulator can be seen as balancing two objectives, both of which are actually in the interests of consumers. One is to minimize the price of energy. The other is to ensure a secure supply of energy, and the need to give the utilities sufficient funds can be seen as contributing toward this objective. To achieve this objective, it is necessary to go beyond simply providing them with adequate funds, and beyond the

scope of regulation, as for example the security of supply of imported energy is a foreign policy concern for many countries. Nonetheless, if the industry's capital stock suffers because the utilities lack resources, the country's security of energy supply will quickly fall.

An emphasis on security of supply may be an unusual way of framing a regulatory issue, but this is a key objective of energy policy for governments. The U.S. Department of Energy has five strategic themes, the first of which is energy security, defined as "promoting America's energy security through reliable, clean and affordable energy" (DoE, 2006, 7). The European Union's 2006 Green Paper on Energy set three core objectives: sustainability, competitiveness, and security of supply. The United Kingdom has four goals for energy policy, including goals related to the environment ("to put the UK on a path to cut our carbon dioxide emissions by some 60% by about 2050, with real progress by 2020"), security of supply ("to maintain reliable energy supplies"), and the cost of energy ("to ensure that every home is adequately and affordably heated") (DTI 2003).[1]

Energy policy thus commonly adds a third goal—achieving a low environmental impact—to the two that have traditionally concerned regulators: achieving low prices while ensuring sufficient investment to maintain security of supply. These three goals may often appear to conflict and are frequently portrayed as the corners of a triangle. Diversifying energy sources can increase security of supply, but if it involves raising the share of higher-cost resources, it will act against the objective of keeping prices down. Adding pollution control equipment will reduce environmental impacts and raise prices. In some countries, coal is seen as a more secure primary fuel than oil and gas, but the carbon dioxide (and local pollutant) emissions from burning coal, and hence its environmental impact, are higher. At other times, however, a new development, and particularly a new technology, may further all three goals at once. The introduction of combined cycle gas turbine generators in the United Kingdom in the 1990s raised security of supply by diversifying away from coal (which then dominated the industry's fuel mix),[2] reduced the environmental impact from sulfur emissions (and also from carbon dioxide, which was not then a priority for environmental policy), and was also cheaper than building coal-fired stations when new investment was required (Newbery 1999).[3] Increasing the efficiency with which energy is used will tend to reduce the cost and environmental impact of a given level of energy services—that is, heat and light, rather than gas or electricity. This generally leads to lower overall levels of energy consumption, which will increase security of supply by cutting the amount of primary energy required.[4]

Models of Regulation

The way an industry is regulated has to reflect its structure. In the past, this did not in itself cause any variation in practice, because practically all of the energy utilities were either vertically integrated monopolies or part of a chain of monopolies. Several stages can be distinguished: electricity generation (or the production of gas) is the first, followed by high-voltage or high-pressure transmission over potentially long distances. Distribution at lower voltages or pressures takes the electricity or gas to the consumer and was traditionally defined to include the sales transaction as well. (Full energy liberalization, however, is based on the idea that retailing, called "supply" in the United Kingdom, can be separated from distribution.) Gas utilities might buy their product from oil companies, and some industrial self-generators would sell surplus power to the electricity grid, but the rest of the industry was monopolized. Regulators accordingly concerned themselves with the final prices charged to end consumers and the intermediate prices used when a regional or national utility sold gas or power to a smaller firm for local distribution.

This started to change when competition was introduced to the energy utilities. Once it was realized that the natural monopoly at the heart of each industry covers only its network, then other companies could be allowed to use that network, whether they were producing energy or selling it to consumers. The first experiments were for limited competition in electricity generation in the United States, where the Public Utilities Regulatory Policies Act of 1978 required utilities to buy power from certain kinds of rival generators at their avoided cost of generation, and in Chile, where the 1982 Electricity Act led to the creation of several regional spot markets (Pollitt 2004).[5] The privatization of the gas industry in Great Britain went further, as independent companies were meant to compete to sell gas to large consumers, and the privatization of electricity included a timetable that would culminate in every consumer in the country having a choice of electricity supplier (retailer).

Many other countries followed suit, and the European Union (EU) adopted a pro-liberalization policy in 1996 and committed itself in 2003 to introducing full retail competition by 2007 at the latest. Despite this commitment, not all member states have achieved, or perhaps do not wish to achieve, the same level of competition in practice. Similarly, in the United States, 13 states and the District of Columbia have implemented retail competition, and others participate in regional transmission organizations that run organized wholesale markets, but nearly half do not (EIA 2009).[6] This means that moves to increase the share of renewable energy need to be studied in the context of a range of regulatory systems.

These systems differ in terms of the activities that the regulators have to carry out. Do they need to regulate the prices paid by consumers? Are separate prices incurred for using the network that need to be regulated, or are the costs of the networks simply bundled into the consumers' prices? Are the costs of generation subject to regulation?

Figure 8.1 shows four different models of regulation defined below for the purposes of discussion in this chapter: retail competition, wholesale competition, single buyer, and integrated firms.

The first, retail competition, is the minimalist model of regulation, in which the regulator's activities are largely confined to the natural monopoly of the network of pipes and wires and the system operation. For this model to work

	Generation	Transmission/distribution	Retail
Retail competition	Competitive	Regulated prices	Competitive
Wholesale competition	Competitive	Regulated prices	Regulated prices
Single buyer	Tendered	Regulated	Regulated prices
Integrated firms	Regulated		Regulated prices

Figure 8.1. Models of regulation

well, effective competition must exist both in electricity generation or gas production and in retailing. If retail competition is effective, then prices to end consumers do not need to be regulated, as retailers will be forced to set prices close to their costs of buying energy, paying to use the network and dealing with their customers. Similarly, prices in the wholesale market can generally be set by the normal processes of competition. The caveat is needed because of the special features of electricity, a nonstorable product that must be delivered through a transmission network subject to complicated and interacting physical limitations. The demand for electricity is very inelastic in the short term, not just because it cannot be stored, but also because most customers do not see the real-time price of power. These features make it possible for even companies with low market shares to exercise market power at particular times or in particular parts of the country, and thus a system of wholesale market monitoring is often needed to ensure that this is not abused. Even so, this market monitoring should be seen as a special form of competition policy, rather than of economic regulation.

The regulator's role under the retail competition model is to ensure that the prices for using the network are appropriate, and that all companies have equal access to it. If the network owner is still integrated into the other stages of the industry, this can be hard to ensure, as an unscrupulous operator can limit its competitors' access to the network in many ways.[7] The best solution to this problem is to separate the role of system operator from any commercial user of the network, either

by banning network owners from the other stages of the industry or by creating an independent system operator (ISO) to control the network assets owned by companies active in production, generation, or retailing. An ISO has the advantage that it can coordinate operations over a wider area than a single company, which will be useful if the historic pattern of asset ownership has created a patchwork of systems that would be inefficiently small if operated separately. At the same time, an ISO may not be as effective in pushing through a program of capital investment in the networks of independent firms as a single network company would be.

It is worth noting that the problem of discrimination among network users has historically been much less important at the distribution level than in transmission. Energy sources (power stations or gas fields) are usually connected to the transmission system rather than to distribution. Even when a large power station was connected to the distribution system, it was usually the transmission operators that controlled its ability to operate. At the retail level, it was practically impossible for a distribution system operator to discriminate among customers of different retailers in terms of the quality of energy supply, as all the customers connected to the same segment of the network would receive their supply under the same physical conditions. The regulatory requirements for keeping distribution networks separate have therefore typically been weaker than with transmission, particularly for smaller utilities.[8]

The second model, wholesale competition, has effective competition in generation, based around an active wholesale market, but competition in retailing is limited or nonexistent, so final prices to consumers are regulated, as well as the charges for using the networks. This might be a transitional phase; if competition has recently been introduced and is becoming stronger, but most customers are still with the original incumbent retailers, then some protection can be appropriate.[9] Some EU countries have so little competition to serve domestic customers that this transitional phase may appear permanent, even though the market is officially open. It is also possible as a permanent policy to restrict competition to the wholesale market only, if policymakers are uncertain of the benefits of retail competition and do not wish to incur the transaction costs of implementing it. The wholesale market needs to have enough separate buyers to avoid a monopsony, but a market covering several regional or subregional retail monopolies will meet this condition. In the United States, Vermont and West Virginia participate in regional wholesale markets (ISO New England and PJM, respectively) without opening their retail markets to competition.

A third model, which has been applied in a number of developing countries, is to have a single buyer. This is a regulated entity that is responsible for procuring electricity from generators, but through contracts rather than a wholesale market. The industry may be too small for adequate competition among generators, or policymakers may distrust the market's ability to deliver enough capacity, particularly in a system facing high demand growth. The use of long-term contracts is important, as electricity generation has very high sunk costs, and a producer selling to a single organization without the protection of a contract risks being held up for a lower price once its investment is complete. When the European Commission designed a single buyer model, it made it equivalent in its effects to limited retail competition, but most countries that actually use this model combine it with monopolies in retailing.

This means that prices to end consumers must be regulated, as with the wholesale competition model. It is likely, however, that prices no longer need to be regulated for transmission and distribution, for these prices may not exist. Generators will have agreed to the terms for connecting to the network as part of their long-term contracts, and as this would be done before an investment decision is made, the contracts should provide sufficient protection to both parties. If the generators know that they will have to make payments to use the network, they will seek higher prices from the single buyer.

Although there may not be formal prices for using the network, the regulator will still have to oversee its revenue requirements, ensuring that the amount recovered from consumers is reasonable. Figure 8.1 thus describes this part of the industry as regulated without specifying that it has regulated prices. The cost of generation should be kept down by competitive tendering, and then passed on to consumers (just as adequate competition in a wholesale market should keep down the amount that regulated retailers could charge in the second model).

The fourth and final model of regulation is one of integrated firms. This does not mean that a vertically integrated monopoly is responsible for every stage of gas or electricity supply. It may well be that vertical separation exists between the utilities responsible for energy production (or import) and transmission, and those responsible for distribution and retailing. The German electricity industry has a three-layer system of interconnected, regional, and municipal utilities, with the interconnected utilities owning almost all of the transmission system and much of the generation, but regional and municipal utilities delivering energy to about two-thirds of customers (Schulz 1995). The model is also compatible with a utility that buys some of its gas or power from third parties, but without the separation implied by a formal single buyer. Independent power producers that sell power as their main businesses would need the protection of long-term contracts, but industrial self-generators with occasional surpluses of power could sell these under short-term deals.

In this model, generation is now regulated, as are the networks. The regulator must oversee final prices for all consumers, and there may be no intermediate prices to regulate, although if a large utility sells gas or electricity to a smaller one, the regulator may also need to oversee this transaction to ensure that excessive costs are not passed on.

The main challenge for regulators—under any model—is to ensure that prices are high enough for the utility to recover efficiently incurred costs, but not so high that consumers are exploited. The regulator can generally measure what a utility's costs actually are (assuming that competent accountants are available, and with a caveat concerning the cost of capital), but it is a different matter to measure what the costs *could be*. When just one firm is being regulated, the regulator can only extrapolate from past trends, adjust for predicted changes in the future, commission efficiency studies from consultants, and perhaps make comparisons with firms in other jurisdictions, hoping that their environments are sufficiently similar to make the comparisons valid. When the regulator must deal with several firms, it is possible to make comparisons among them on the principle of yardstick regulation (Shleifer 1985). If the firms face sufficiently similar operating environments, then there should be no reason why all firms could not reach the level of the best performers, and their prices should be set to reflect this. Good performers could expect to receive more than the cost of capital, whereas firms with higher costs would not be able to do so until they cut those costs. In practice, some of the differences in operating environments will be significant, and regulators will have to adjust for these (Jamasb and Pollitt 2007; Pollitt 2005). The difficulty of doing so is why competition, where possible, generally gives better incentives to firms than does even the most enlightened regulation.

Utilities in a Low-Carbon World

How will the move to a lower-carbon energy system affect the energy utilities? Many countries, as well as individual U.S. states, have adopted targets for renewable energy, and the European Union now has a legally binding target for 2020 that 20% of its final energy consumption shall come from renewable sources, as discussed in Chapter 12. Given the resources available for renewable heat and transport, and their costs, the proportion of renewable electricity will need to be well above 20%.

Humans have been using renewable generation for as long as the electricity supply industry has existed—the world's first public electricity supply, installed in 1881 in the English village of Godalming, was hydroelectric (Hannah 1979). A number of countries, both developed and developing, get much or all of their electricity from hydropower. Most developed countries, however, have developed most of their available large-scale hydro resources, prohibiting some potential

developments for environmental reasons, though opportunities still exist to develop small-scale schemes. Further increases in renewable energy therefore are likely to come largely from burning biomass (including waste) and from wind power. In some countries, solar photovoltaic power may be a sensible option, though not in northerly, frequently cloudy regions like the UK; other countries are surrounded by seas containing significant energy in their currents, tides, and waves. Devices to harvest this energy are being developed but are still mostly in the prototype stage.[10]

Most renewable generation will cost more than conventional alternatives, excluding externalities, unless the price of fossil fuels rises dramatically. In most cases, this is because of high capital costs—several renewable technologies get their "fuel" for free. Biomass generation is the main exception for which fuel costs are a significant part of the whole. Large-scale hydroelectric generation was generally a low-cost energy source, although few sites remain available, and wind turbines at particularly good, windy locations onshore appeared quite competitive with fossil-fueled power stations at the high energy and carbon prices of early 2008. These high costs mean that companies will not be willing to build most types of renewable generators unless required or they are offered financial support. Chapter 6 and the various country studies discuss the mechanisms that can be used to achieve this.

The EU target for renewable energy leads to a wide range of national targets, related to each country's income and existing level of renewable energy, and the mix of renewable sources used will vary among countries. Table 8.1 gives a set of estimates prepared for the European Commission, giving a mix of sources predicted to minimize the cost of meeting the 20% target for renewable energy.

The use of biomass and hydroelectricity will increase, but their percentage share of renewable generation would fall. Solar and marine energy would increase from very low levels at present. By far the greatest increase would come from wind generation, which might provide more than one-sixth of Europe's electricity in 2020.[11]

Table 8.1. EU electricity generation from renewable sources

	Generation in 2006		Potential for 2020, Green-X model, least-cost scenario	
	TWh	Percentage	TWh	Percentage
Biomass	90	17%	186	14%
Geothermal	6	1%	7	1%
Hydro	344	66%	398	30%
Solar	2	0.1%	62	5%
Marine	1	0%	124	9%
Wind	82	16%	545	41%
Total	525	100%	1,322	100%

Source: European Commission 2007
Note: TWh = terawatt-hours

This level of wind generation will lead to significant challenges in dealing with intermittency. Large-scale wind generators reach full output only at wind speeds between around 12 and 25 meters per second (m/s), shutting down at higher speeds and losing power rapidly when the wind is low.[12] A well-sited turbine might have an average output equal to 30% of its rated capacity over the year, but the actual output will vary sharply over time, and meaningful predictions are impossible more than a few days in advance. In regions where clouds are rare, the main factor affecting the output from solar power will be the earth's predictable rotation (although in regions with variable cloud cover, this will have a significant effect on solar output), and tidal energy can be predicted years in advance but will sometimes be highest at off-peak times. Biomass generators can run when the user chooses, but if these users are households or small businesses with combined heat and power units, they may choose a heat-led operating pattern that does not necessarily produce power at the times when it would be most useful for the electricity industry (Hawkes and Leach 2007).

Intermittent outputs from renewable generators cause two main problems. First, the system operator will need to keep more plants in reserve for times when the level of renewable output suddenly falls. This particularly applies to wind out-

put, as most other renewables are more predictable over the relevant timescales (of a few hours).[13] Gross et al. (2006) have estimated that these reserves would cost £2 to £3 ($3.05 to $4.58) per megawatt-hour (MWh) of intermittent renewable energy if the United Kingdom were to get 20% of its electricity from wind. Note that the system operators always have to keep some plants in reserve in order to respond instantly if a power station fails, but it has traditionally been sufficient to set this reserve equal to the size of the largest unit running on the system—the worst case for a single failure. If the wind drops over a large area, many separate wind turbines, with a greater collective capacity, could be affected. The level of reserve generation (or demand reduction potential) needed to cover this risk naturally grows with the amount of wind generation, and the system reserve requirement is the greater of that required by wind stations and by conventional plants. The rules of the system—either those of the wholesale market or the regulations of the system operator, depending on where the responsibility for providing these reserves lies—will have to ensure that these can be paid for.

The second problem is that the wind or tide may not be available at the time of peak electricity demand, which is what determines the total amount of capacity needed on the system. Not all of the capacity of a conventional plant can be counted against this need, as it may be unavailable at the critical time, but it is generally sensible to assume that more than 80% will be. The risk that many wind generators will be becalmed at the same time is greater, however, and the effective contribution of a portfolio of wind power stations to ensuring ability to meet peak demand has been estimated at only 20% (or less) of their total capacity.[14] This means that 10 gigawatts (GW) of additional wind power could replace only 1 to 2 GW of conventional stations, in terms of planning to meet the peak demand. The energy produced by the wind stations could actually replace the output of around 3.5 GW of conventional plants, if the time of delivery were irrelevant.[15] In other words, between 1.5 and 2.5 GW of conventional plants would be needed per 10 GW of wind, because we cannot know whether wind stations will produce when we most want them to. Gross et al. (2006) predict that this would cost £3 to £5 ($4.58 to $7.63) per MWh of wind energy in UK conditions. The wider the geographic dispersion of the wind stations, the lower this penalty will be—as long as this dispersion reduces the correlation among their outputs and enough transmission is available.

Note that both of these problems are far less severe in a system with, or connected to, large amounts of hydro generation with reservoir storage. The output from hydro generators can respond inversely to the output from wind, storing energy in the form of water until it is needed. The cost of short-term reserve to cover variations in wind output is very low, as it costs almost nothing to keep a hydro station ready to increase output at short notice. At most hydro stations, the reservoir is not large enough to keep the generator running throughout the year, so the system can provide enough energy over the year as a whole only if it has more than enough capacity to meet the peak demand. In this context, the risk that a wind generator will not be available at the peak time is less important.

In a system with little hydro generation, the inevitable consequence of increasing the variable output from wind generators is that the output from conventional generators will also tend to be more volatile, except to the extent that demand-side response takes up the slack. Sometimes the output from wind stations will rise at the same time as demand, reducing the increase required from conventional stations; at other times, demand and renewable outputs will move in opposite directions, increasing the strain on the system. There will also be some stations that are needed for the times when high demand levels coincide with low wind speeds but do not run very often. It will be important to ensure that these generators can cover their costs.

Demand response can reduce the need for peak capacity, cutting the industry's costs (Borenstein 2005). Some response can be made without consumers noticing, such as delaying the start of water heaters or refrigerator motors when prices are particularly high, or responding to some other signal such as system frequency. Some

industrial customers have long been used to scheduling energy-intensive processes away from the times when power is most expensive, although this rescheduling is likely to involve some costs. The likely growth of electric vehicles offers a good opportunity to increase the "unnoticed" element of demand response, simply by ensuring that the vehicles mainly charge themselves during low-demand periods overnight, although it will be important to ensure that the vehicle is sufficiently charged by the time it is needed. Electric vehicles have a significant advantage over most other forms of energy storage, in that the battery is needed in any case, and this kind of use by the electricity industry is essentially a free good. Car batteries could also be discharged when the industry is particularly short of power, but imposing additional cycles of deep discharging and recharging would shorten the battery's life. Given the cost of batteries, this would be an expensive source of electricity.

Moving on to network issues, in many countries significant investments will be needed to accommodate an increase in renewable generation (Pollitt and Bialek 2008). Many of the best sites for renewable generators are remote from the centers of demand, and transmission lines will be needed to move the electricity to where it is needed. Most renewable generators are on a much smaller scale than conventional centralized power stations, so many separate schemes, each with its own grid connection, may be needed to replace a single large conventional station. Because the renewable schemes are generally smaller, their connections will often be to the distribution networks rather than the transmission system. This will certainly be the case where self-generation or community-owned small-scale generation is concerned.

Connecting large amounts of generation to the distribution networks will require significant changes in their operating practices. Broadly speaking, transmission networks have always been operated to accept two-way flows across every line in the system, but distribution systems have generally been designed to take power in one direction only—from the connection with the transmission system to the customer.[16] If power always flows in one direction, the design of the system is simpler, and protection equipment against power surges is needed on only one side of the substation it is intended to protect. If power could suddenly flow from a generator located on the customer side of the substation, then extra protection equipment is needed, and it will be necessary to manage the flows on the distribution network in a much more active manner. This requires additional equipment to monitor conditions in real time and operating practices that respond to them. Local generators and loads may have to change behavior in order to keep power flows within acceptable limits. Greater monitoring, however, can also change those limits. For example, windy conditions allow the heat from power flowing through the network to dissipate more easily, increasing the safe operating limit at the very times when the output from nearby wind farms will be at its greatest (Douglas 2005).

Finally, it is worth mentioning another change that is not directly connected to the growth in renewable energy but is clearly linked to the move toward a low-carbon energy system. This is the adoption of carbon trading, first in the European Union, and now in parts of the United States.[17] The need to buy permits raises the marginal cost of generation from fossil fuels, even if the generator receives those permits for free.[18] This will tend to raise the wholesale price of power produced by a given capital stock; in a fully competitive market, the price would rise by the price of emissions multiplied by the carbon content of the marginal plant.

In the longer term, the level and composition of the industry's capital stock may change because of carbon trading. First, if generators receive some permits free of charge, contingent on the existence of a power plant, then the value of those permits can be offset against the cost of keeping the station open. This may allow the station to remain open when its revenues from the electricity market alone would not justify this. This could lead to a market equilibrium with a greater amount of capacity, which would tend to depress the price of power, partly offsetting the impact of the carbon price (Green 2005).

A more significant change to the capital stock should be that compared with high-carbon power stations, low-carbon generators become relatively more attractive. Natural gas will gain relative to coal, and there is already talk of nuclear power enjoying a renaissance in the United States and United Kingdom. Many countries are promoting demonstration schemes for carbon capture and sequestration and, once the technology is proven, could compel generators to fit this to new plants and perhaps even retrofit it to existing ones. If the carbon price rose to a sufficiently high level and was expected to remain there, carbon capture would be economic without government compulsion. The price within the ETS, however, has never reached this level, let alone stayed there long enough to make such investments attractive.

This also applies to renewable generators. If they receive a wholesale price that has been increased by the cost of carbon emissions, this will reduce their need for additional support. Likely levels of carbon prices, however, are unlikely to make most renewable generators competitive with gas-fired or nuclear generators, at least given the costs expected in the United Kingdom (DECC 2009a).

General Implications for Regulation

How do these trends affect the task of regulation? First, it is clear that the cost of energy is going to rise. Most renewable energy costs more than conventional sources at current fuel prices, even before considering the costs of investment in the networks and changed operating requirements. If fossil-fuel prices were to rise significantly, then a move to renewable energy would not lead to a further increase, and might in extreme cases reduce costs, but this would be little comfort to energy consumers. The EU has estimated that meeting its 20% target for renewable energy will cost an extra €24 billion to €31 billion ($32.7 billion to $42 billion) in 2020, against a predicted energy bill of around €350 billion ($476.7 billion) (European Commission 2007). This assumes an oil price of $48 per barrel; if the oil price rises to $78 per barrel, energy costs will be much higher, but the additional cost of renewable energy will fall to at most €11 billion ($15 billion) and would be zero in one scenario. Some of these costs may be borne by taxpayers, but the remainder will have to come from energy consumers, and regulators will need to allow the utilities to collect these—as with any other efficiently incurred cost increase. Where parts of the industry have been liberalized, the regulators will not determine prices directly, but regulators that have oversight of these competitive areas must not intervene to suppress necessary increases.

Second, the electricity industry will need a lot of capital investment, both in renewable generation (many technologies are capital-intensive) and in changes to the network to accommodate it. This will affect the weight that regulators should place on the different cost components when setting incentives for network companies and for generators, if they are regulated. A regulated firm's costs can be broken down into its cash operating costs (labor, materials, and bought-in services), the return on its new investments, and the return on its existing assets. The firm is assumed able to control both its operating costs and its investment in new assets, but its existing capital stock is, naturally, fixed. The required return on both new and existing assets depends on the cost of capital, which is affected by the perceived risk of the business.

High-powered incentives to reduce costs will increase the company's risk, as success or failure to do so will feed through to the company's profits. Standard models of financial economies, such as the capital asset pricing model, suggest that diversifiable risks should not affect a company's cost of capital. Nonetheless, the level of incentives might have an impact through two routes. First, if the company's profits become more sensitive to the overall state of the economy, and are positively correlated with it, then its beta will rise, increasing the cost of its equity. Second, if favorable tax treatment reduces the cost of debt and a company with risky cash flows has to reduce its gearing, this will increase its weighted average cost of capital.

An optimal regulatory scheme would balance the expected savings from strengthening the incentive on the volume of operating costs, or of investment, against the cost of having to pay a higher expected rate of return. In other words, although it is possible to give the firm very high-powered incentives to reduce both its operating costs and its investment (such as a pure price cap regime does), this would be undesirable if it caused too great an increase in the cost of capital. If the industry's cost structure shifts away from operating costs, then optimal regulation would imply paying more attention to the rate of return on capital and less to the level of operating costs. An increase in the volume of investment will mean that more weight should be placed on incentives for efficient investment than on the impact of a higher cost of capital on payments for existing assets. In other words, incentives for efficient operation might be relaxed, and those for efficient investment should be strengthened.

One way of doing this in practice is to offer the firm a menu of regulatory contracts (Laffont and Tirole 1993; Sappington 1982). In the United Kingdom, the regulator has given distribution companies such menus for their investments over the next price control period (Pollitt and Bialek 2008). The regulator uses consultants to assess the necessary level of investment, but the firm can propose a higher base figure. The firm's allowed revenues are then linked to this proposal and its outturn expenditure. Whatever the outturn level of expenditure, the firm's revenues are highest if this was the level that it actually proposed, providing an incentive for truthful cost revelation. The allowed revenues increase by less than a unit for each unit increase in the firm's actual expenditure, however, so the firm has to bear a share of any cost overrun and keeps a share of any savings. This provides an incentive to keep actual costs down, and one that is greater the tougher the target that the firm accepts. Accepting a tough target thus allows the firm the chance to benefit from high-powered incentives. A firm that accepts and meets the regulator's target will be allowed revenues of more than the amount it spends, which gives a margin of error in case the regulator's target is too tough. Under Ofgem's scheme, which differs from some versions of the menu of contracts approach, the allowed revenues also increase by less than a pound for each pound that the firm proposes to spend above the regulator's target. The greater the firm's proposal, the less revenue the firm will be allowed for any outturn spending below this proposal.[19] Overall, the scheme gives the firm an incentive to reveal the truth about its expected capital needs and to keep its costs down, while allowing it to pass part of any genuine overrun on to consumers.

A final general implication is that the number of small electricity generators that wish to inject energy into the network will increase. Any energy producer connected to the network must be subject to the network operator's technical standards and the industry's commercial arrangements—purely bilateral transactions are impossible in an interconnected system. Energy regulators are often involved in overseeing the details of such standards and arrangements to ensure that these do not discriminate against particular network users. If we wish to further the development of microgeneration (and the high costs of many microgenerators should be taken into account in that decision), then the regulators will have to ensure that the technical standards are not too onerous and the commercial arrangements are suitable for nonspecialists.

Accommodating these generators will be helped by a variety of so-called smart grid technologies. Traditionally, system operators have had little real-time information on the actual state of the distribution network, which forces them to run it in a relatively conservative manner. More information can be used to increase the allowable power flows. Furthermore, some small-scale generators and loads can be dispatched, responding to instructions based on the state of the system—both the overall balance between generation and demand and conditions on the local distribution network. Regulators will have to ensure that companies are rewarded for innovations such as these, and that the boundaries among generation, retailing, and networks do not act as barriers. This is potentially a disadvantage of the retail competition model, which sometimes severs the relationship between a customer and its network operator

(although in some countries, the customer continues to receive a bill for network services).

The need to give incentives for innovation has emerged as a key theme of the British regulator Ofgem's 2008–2010 review of network regulation, known as RPI-X@20.[20] Spending on research and development by the distribution network operators in Great Britain has risen dramatically since a separate revenue stream to fund it was created in 2005 (Ofgem 2009). One key issue is that spending may have to be incurred well before customers see any benefit from it, and regulators must allow companies to fund this.

Implications for the Regulator's Tasks

How will the general implications of an increasing share of renewable energy change what regulators need to do? The following analysis is broken down by the major tasks regulators must undertake: regulating the wires, regulating generation revenues, and regulating retail prices.

Regulating the Wires

In both the retail and wholesale competition models, the regulator has to oversee the prices, and other terms, for companies wishing to use the network; in the retail competition model, this is the only area of ex ante regulation. This may include the rules of the wholesale market (discussed in Chapter 7). A liquid multilateral market with prices that reflect the changing state of supply, demand, and the transmission system will be far more effective than a bilateral market with prices that ignore the fact that generators in some locations may be unable to get their power to consumers. The transmission system operators already have to undo some trades of this kind to make the European wholesale markets work properly, and the scale of the task will increase with the level of renewable generation.[21]

Price regulation has two key aspects. One is the average level of prices, and the other is their distribution among customers. As discussed above, the average level of prices is linked to the industry's expected costs, and a key aspect of these is the level of investment. Investment in the electricity networks will need to rise, increasing costs and hence prices. Strong incentives to minimize investment costs might keep prices down but could jeopardize investment in renewable energy if insufficient grid capacity is available. For an extreme example, new generators inquiring about connecting to the transmission system in Scotland were told that they might have to wait more than 10 years for capacity to become available (House of Lords 2008a, *para. 133*).

The primary cause of such delays is the long lead time for transmission investment, typically greater than that for generation. In part, this time depends on the process of obtaining planning permission for new transmission lines, which has become a lengthy one in many countries. Sometimes it will not be possible to develop a line in time to meet an unanticipated need for capacity, and the regulator (and would-be generators) will have to accept this—although reforms to speed the planning process would make this less common.

The impact of this lead time is worsened because it will not always be clear in advance exactly where capacity will be needed, or how much, even if the general requirement is clear. If the network owner is worried that it will be penalized for spending that turns out to be unnecessary, it will not wish to start the detailed investment process until the needs are clear and, preferably, contracts are signed with users. This is likely to impose significant delays, which would be unnecessary in cases where it had earlier become clear that some investment was likely to be required. Regulators should allow companies to recover the cost of making plans, and even seeking planning permission, for new lines that appear likely to be needed but are later abandoned as circumstances change. To reduce the risk that too many unwanted lines are planned, wider consultation should be done on network investment plans. Pollitt (2008) calls for a process of "constructive engagement" already used abroad and in the regulation of UK airports, where users and the airport owner could jointly agree on a pro-

gram of capital investment. Littlechild (2008) describes the negotiations used to decide on transmission investments in Chile, where transmission users were able to insist on a cheaper alternative to the line originally proposed by the transmission utility. A balance is needed between making a timely start to investment and not authorizing projects with insufficient demand. The California Independent System Operator's Location Constrained Resource Interconnection Policy requires financial commitments from renewable generators to use at least 60% of a new line's capacity, but then incorporates the line's costs in its general transmission tariff.[22] A more prescriptive approach would imply the creation (or empowerment) of some kind of national planning agency to coordinate generation and network investment and act as a "guiding mind," as Ofgem puts it in its RPI-X@20 review.

It is also important to ensure that the investment needs in the grid are not increased by inflexible procedures. Traditionally, transmission companies have been reluctant to connect generators unless they are certain they can almost always accept their output. This is a sensible policy for conventional generators, as, if the investment is desirable, they can expect to be needed to meet peak demand, and preventing them from generating could risk power cuts. Wind generators, in contrast, may not generate at the time of the peak; if they do, some other stations, which need to be available, will not be running. The transmission system does not need to accept every generator's output simultaneously, and investment rules should be altered accordingly. It is important, however, to allocate access to the grid efficiently—something achieved automatically in a wholesale market based on locational marginal prices.

The second aspect of price regulation is the distribution of payments among network users. In particular, how should they vary over time and space? A partial answer is that if the wholesale market adopts nodal marginal pricing, then cost-reflective variations will occur over time and space, and these will be passed on to network users. The prices at nodes with net generation are, on average, below those with net demand, because the costs of transmission are incurred as power flows from generation to demand nodes. The transmission operator can therefore "buy low and sell high," retaining the surplus. The problem is that other charges will have to be added, for these net revenues from nodal marginal prices generally recover just a small part of the total cost of transmission—often only around 20% (Pérez-Arriaga et al. 1995). It is possible to derive an optimality condition for transmission investment, under which the marginal cost of expanding transmission capacity should just equal the marginal benefit of doing so, which is given by the difference in prices at each end of the line. With constant returns to scale and perfectly divisible capital, this suggests that nodal pricing would completely recover the costs of an optimal system. Perez-Arriaga et al. suggest that this result does not hold because of economies of scale and indivisibilities, because it is often sensible to build a line that is currently too large, in order to accommodate future growth, and because changing patterns of generation and demand mean that the inherited transmission system will inevitably be suboptimal. This suggests that the missing revenue should not be seen as related to identifiable costs of transmission, but as a lump sum that has to be recovered with the minimum of distortion.

Given this, how should the remaining network costs be recovered across time? Should generators (and customers) pay whenever they are sending power to (or taking power from) the grid? Should they pay based on the maximum cost that they could impose on the grid or based on the cost they impose when the load on the grid is heaviest? Given that capital costs form a high proportion of the total, this would argue for some form of peak load pricing, rather than recovering costs evenly over time. Peak load pricing is based on charging users at the time when the load on the grid is heaviest, as capacity built to cope with these times is effectively "free" at times with lower loads.

The issue is that with this kind of peak load pricing, renewable generators would tend to face much lower transmission payments per kW of capacity than would conventional generators, but those payments would be variable over time. In some years, a renewable generator would be able to generate at the time of the system peak and would be assessed for transmission charges on the basis of this. In other years, the system peak would come when the local wind was low, and the generator would have little output and would pay little for transmission. This is unlikely to be politically acceptable and could also produce perverse incentives not to generate at the system peak—transmission charges per MW can be an order of magnitude above all but the very highest electricity prices, and if just one or two hours of generation creates a liability to those charges, it will not be worthwhile.[23]

This suggests that transmission charges should be based on either the capacity of a power station or the energy it generates over the year, perhaps weighted according to the time of production. If the charges are capacity-related, intermittent renewable generators will pay much more per MWh actually generated than conventional stations able to run at base load. Conventional generators that are needed to meet peak demands, but rarely run at other times, will be in a similar situation. Both may claim this to be discrimination. Furthermore, they will need some revenue source to cover these costs if they are to remain available in a long-term equilibrium. For peaking generators, this is likely to be reflected either in the prices for peak power or in a capacity market, if one exists. For renewable generators, less able to rely on peak prices or capacity markets, the remainder will have to come from their support scheme. Charging intermittent renewable generators on the basis of their capacity, but adjusted for their relatively low expected output, might be a politically acceptable way of reducing the cost of this—effectively, using a hybrid scheme.

If transmission charges are energy-related, the impact on peak prices and the cost of supporting renewables will be lower, though electricity prices will be slightly higher throughout the year as generators pass through this additional marginal cost. Furthermore, wholesale prices may not accurately reflect the marginal cost of expanding transmission to accommodate more generation (even with nodal marginal prices, indivisibilities might mean that the system has to be expanded to the point where the price differences at each end of the line are quite low), or wholesale prices may not include any transmission component. In this case, the transmission charges should signal the cost of expanding the system, and capacity-related charges will send a more accurate signal than energy-based ones.

Similar considerations apply to the decision about how network charges should vary over space. The overall system of transmission charges (including transmission-related elements in any wholesale market) should signal the costs of using the transmission system and ensure that the network companies recover their efficiently incurred costs (Green 1997). If other parts of the pricing system send adequate locational signals, so that network charges are purely to recover a lump sum of missing revenue, then a uniform national or systemwide charge is appropriate. If generators and customers do not otherwise face charges that reflect the spatial variation in transmission costs, however, then transmission charges should vary over space.

The implications of this may depend on factors specific to each market. In Great Britain, for example, transmission charges are highest in Scotland (which is bad news for wind farms sited there) and lowest in southwest England (which will be good news for marine energy schemes located off the coast of that region). In general, however, it seems likely that renewable generators located in rural areas will face higher transmission charges than conventional generators closer to the loads. Once again, this will affect the cost of supporting renewable energy. The higher the transmission charges paid by the marginal generator (the one whose needs just determine the level of support required), the greater the support it will need. Unless the support scheme separates out and pays each generator's individual transmission charge, this will raise the rents obtained by generators in more favorable locations.

Transmission charges may not, in fact, have much impact on the locational choices made by renewable generators, which need to choose sites that maximize their output. A 1% difference in the load factor achieved by a British wind farm,

for example, would largely offset the difference in transmission charges between the north and south of Scotland or central and southwest England.[24] In this case, minimizing the rents obtained by well-sited generators might be more important than sending precise signals. However, the impact on conventional generators must also be taken into account. These have more flexibility to choose their sites and should be sent signals of transmission costs—either through spatially varying wholesale prices or through transmission charges.

The final issue involved in regulating the wires is how to regulate the transmission system operator, as distinct from the transmission owner. The transmission owner receives payments for having built the transmission wires and keeping them in good repair; the transmission operator is responsible for managing their daily use to move power. Sometimes both functions are combined in a single company, but an independent system operator can be used when it is most effective to run a single market over several transmission owners' grids or when regulators want to ensure that the grid is operated independently of generation interests, without ordering an integrated company to divest any assets.

The system operator will need to buy operating reserves and, in markets without nodal pricing, will resolve congestion by buying and selling power on either side of a constraint. As the amount of renewable energy increases, so will these costs. This implies that the benefits from giving the system operator strong incentives to control them are likely to rise. It may be difficult to give strong financial incentives, relative to the costs involved, to an independent system operator, for organizations like these have few assets to cushion them against unforeseen events that would lead to a bad outturn, and hence performance penalties, even in a single year. If significant transmission assets are owned by an independent company that is also the system operator, however, then the revenue stream for these assets provides a suitable cushion against which to strengthen the system operator's incentives.[25] The increase in renewable energy therefore provides an additional argument for establishing independent transmission companies, as opposed to independent system operators.

Regulating Generation Revenues

In the model of integrated firms, the regulator is responsible for overseeing each stage of the industry's value chain, from generation onward. It is no longer necessary to oversee a transmission or distribution tariff, as there would be no independent generators or retailers to use it, but the issues surrounding investment in the networks remain. The one simplifying factor is that the regulated firm can coordinate investment in generation and the networks internally, rather than rely on the price mechanism to persuade generators to favor sites that are helpful to the transmission company.

Against this, the regulator now has some responsibility for the level of investment in generation. As discussed earlier, most forms of renewable generation are good substitutes for conventional generators in providing energy (measured in MWh of power at some point during the year) but are poor at providing capacity (measured in MW of ability to provide electricity when it is really needed). Regulators will have to allow utilities to add renewable generation to their portfolios without retiring many conventional stations. If the conventional fleet is aging, new construction of both renewable and conventional power stations may be needed. The regulator will then have to accept that some of the conventional capacity will rarely be required—it is needed to ensure that peak demand can be met when this coincides with low availability of renewable generators, and this will not happen every year. Too much pressure to demonstrate that reserve stations are "used and useful" will make utilities reluctant to keep this reserve at a suitable level.

Regulators could also face challenges of a different kind if they face a rapid rise in renewable output when conventional capacity was already adequate. In this case, some of that capacity truly would be surplus to requirements. Should the regulator eliminate it from the rate base so that consumers do not have to pay for assets they are not using? The regulatory compact adopted in many jurisdictions that have liberalized the energy

industries has been to allow utilities to recover the cost of such stranded assets, in the interest of long-term investment incentives. This would also be appropriate in this case but will increase the apparent cost of renewable energy. With a liberalized wholesale market, the cost of stranded assets is absorbed by their owners, but the risk that something like this would happen should have been taken into account when those owners calculated their cost of capital, which would normally be higher than in a regulated system.

The cost of generation will also be affected by the cost of carbon in countries with a system of carbon trading. If generators have to buy all their permits, then this will be a cost of business that the regulator should include in their allowable revenues. If generators receive some permits for free, however, then the regulated firm's revenue requirements should take this into account, muting the increase in price. Politically, this may be an advantage, but it implies that the impact of carbon pricing will have to come entirely from the supply side, rather than from both supply- and demand-side responses.

It is worth pointing out that where generation is traded in a wholesale market, regulators are often responsible for market monitoring, even though this is really an aspect of competition policy rather than of economic regulation. Market monitors need to know when to intervene to stop the abuse of market power, which typically manifests itself as high prices. The challenge in electricity markets is that some periods of high prices may be essential if generators are to recover their fixed costs,[26] and market monitors must not intervene to suppress these necessary peaks. A system with a high proportion of intermittent renewable generators may find that the residual load on thermal generators becomes much more uneven, with periods of zero (or negative) marginal costs. If the market is so competitive that prices can rise above marginal cost and pay for capacity only in the few hours when demand is high enough to create scarcity rents, prices at these times will have to be extremely high. An oligopoly with moderate price-cost margins for a larger number of hours might produce a more stable outcome. In either case, the need to differentiate between high and excessive prices, and perhaps respond to political pressure to keep prices down, will make the task of the market monitor more demanding.

Regulating Retail Prices

In three of the models described earlier, the regulator is responsible for overseeing the prices charged to at least some energy consumers, either because there is no retail competition (although there may be wholesale competition) or because policymakers judge that it is not yet sufficiently effective to protect consumers. The combination of regulation and a partially competitive market offers particular challenges, as a danger exists that if the regulator puts too low a cap on the incumbent's prices, then entrants will not be able to win customers, and competition will never develop to the point where it becomes self-sustaining (Joskow 2008).

If regulators wish to develop retail competition, and the costs of renewable energy are significant, then it is important that they be shared across customers regardless of their choice of retailers. If the costs were small, it might be possible to assign them all to the incumbent retailer, on the basis that this would do no more than partially offset the advantages of incumbency; most EU countries have taken a similar approach to the cost of universal postal service obligations. The likely excess costs of renewable energy, however, are too great for this approach to be workable. This means that the costs must be recovered either across all energy retailers or via distribution tariffs, which must also be nondiscriminatory across retailers.

One of the standard mechanisms for supporting renewable energy does this automatically. If all retailers are obligated to obtain a set proportion of their power from renewable generators, usually administered by a system of tradable certificates, then this should be neutral across competitors. If a high proportion of the renewable generators able to provide eligible power are integrated with incumbent retailers, then this could form a barrier to entry in retailing;[27] however, the rapid increase in renewable energy that most countries are tar-

geting should allow plenty of room for entry in generation to relax this constraint.

The other standard mechanism is to pay renewable generators a feed-in tariff that offers them a premium price for their power. Some organization has to make these payments and recoup the cost of doing so. A distribution company might appear to be well placed to do this. First, most renewable generators will be connected to its system, which gives it the knowledge of which generators are eligible for support and what they produce. Second, it already bills either consumers or their retailers for distribution services in a nondiscriminatory manner and can add the cost of the feed-in tariff to these bills. In a system with more than one distribution utility, however, there will almost certainly be a mismatch between each utility's share of renewable energy sources (and hence payments) and energy consumption (and hence receipts). On the basis that the cost of supporting renewable energy should be shared over a wider area, side payments among distributors would be needed. This means that the scheme would have to be overseen by a government agency or the regulator's office to ensure that the correct payments were made. It might be best for this agency to actually calculate those payments, using information provided by the distribution companies.

These points also apply in the retail competition model, because that depends on retailers facing similar obligations. They would not apply if no retail competition existed, because then no distortion could arise. In the absence of retail competition, the regulator has more ability to influence which customers actually have to pay for renewable energy. If regulators have a particular duty to protect selected groups of customers, this raises the issue of whether the price rises should be skewed toward others. The problem with this approach is that it can be difficult to ensure that such help is actually given to those who need it most. Keeping down tariffs for those who use very little electricity may benefit the owners of second homes, for example. Many "fuel-poor" households have relatively high energy consumption, often because their homes are poorly insulated.[28]

The distribution of price increases among customer classes is also relevant here: commercial and (particularly) industrial customers facing international competition might claim that they should not be exposed to unnecessary price rises, suggesting that domestic customers should face a high proportion of the support costs. For most industrial and commercial customers, energy costs are not significant; Yago et al. (2008) found that a 30% increase in the price of electricity would raise costs by less than 1% in sectors making up 90% of the UK economy. The remaining sectors will be more affected, however, and some of those are exposed to international competition—particularly aluminum smelting. Should regulators try to design tariffs that will shield such energy-intensive industries from price increases? The general thrust of liberalization policy has been to reduce such political interference in markets, as benefits often go to the best lobbyists rather than the most deserving causes, and align prices to costs.

The Natural Gas Industry

What about the gas industry? There is some scope to replace natural gas with biogas from plant or animal waste, but otherwise, the impact of renewable energy on the gas industry will come from the demand side rather than the supply side. In the medium term, natural gas is likely to be favored over coal as a fuel for electricity generation. This is both because of its lower carbon emissions and because gas turbines can be more flexible in operation, and better able to respond to intermittent renewable sources, than large coal-fired units. Although the shift to renewables would crowd out fossil fuels, a large enough move away from coal could still cause an increase in gas demand, as could the increased use of gas-fired combined heat and power to increase energy efficiency. The first would require large quantities of gas to be delivered to a few sites, whereas the second would increase the quantity sent to many separate sites around the country. In both cases, additional capacity in the network might be required.

When it comes to the growth of renewable energy, however, this could lead to a reduction in end users' demand for natural gas. The use of renewable heat sources—biomass and heat pumps[29]—could double as part of the EU's drive to obtain 20% of its energy from renewable sources, displacing natural gas and other fossil fuels (European Commission 2007). In the long term, the need to reduce CO_2 emissions by 80% or more is likely to be incompatible with burning natural gas without carbon capture, which will probably be impractical for small-scale heating systems.

Gas industry regulators may thus face the challenging task of managing both growth and decline. If the demand for gas for electricity generation continues to grow, then the issues involved will be similar to those facing electricity networks where more investment is needed. However, the networks involved will mainly be the high-pressure pipelines, delivering large amounts of gas to large generators. If renewable heat and renewable sources of electricity reduce the demand for gas by end users, then the utilities will have to face this, even though the capital (and some operating) costs of their distribution networks will not be declining. This would imply a rising per-unit price, just as the price of natural gas may also be increasing. The process would not be sudden, and a switch to biogas might boost demand, but the potential exists for a vicious circle of rising prices and falling demand. In extremis, regulators or governments might need to consider giving gas utilities additional support to ensure that they can still manage their distribution networks safely while reducing sales.

Conclusions

This chapter has suggested specific ways regulators will need to respond if the energy utilities are to absorb large amounts of renewable energy. What about the broader questions posed at the outset?

Should regulators' objectives change, or the factors they take into account when deciding how to achieve those objectives? Regulators doubtless will have to consider their impact on the environment when making decisions. If they did not, they would find it hard to justify the investments needed to accommodate renewable electricity generation, for example. Should protecting the environment be seen as an objective to place alongside consumer and producer protection or a constraint on how the regulator goes about its other duties? A mathematical problem can be set up to give the same results whether environmental protection is included as something to maximize or a constraint that must be met, if the constraint is set at the right level. In the real world, however, regulators would probably have to act in different ways if they were to give environmental protection the same priority as their other duties. We do not want them to damage the environment, but their relative expertise is not in this area, and it would be preferable if economic regulators were not designing environmental policy. It would seem best for regulation to continue to prioritize consumer protection and ensuring that firms can finance their activities, but to do so in light of government environmental policies, and promoting their achievement.[30]

Should the scope of regulation be broadened or narrowed? Regulators will need to make different decisions on specific issues, but there will be no step changes in the kinds of questions they must address. The bulk of the evidence so far is that well-designed liberalization programs offer superior performance to the traditional utility model (Joskow 2008).

Would the growth of renewable energy overturn this result? Integrated firms can coordinate the development of the network to accommodate renewable generation. The single buyer model allows the policymaker to choose a mix of low-carbon generators in a coordinated manner to meet its targets. Wholesale market monitoring to guard against the exploitation of market power will be more challenging in an industry with a high proportion of intermittent generation with very low marginal costs. Retail competition may act as a barrier to the development of smart grid technologies that coordinate devices for consumers and on the network. Competitive models that raise the cost of capital will be more costly for an industry that is becoming more capital-intensive.

These are significant arguments, all suggesting that liberalization will be less successful at dealing with the challenges of renewable energy. They are not likely conclusive, however. The great advantage of competition is that it can allow new entrants to spot opportunities that incumbents have not exploited. If we want many consumers to generate part of their own electricity, then a model with free entry for competing retailers that could provide and maintain generating equipment on a customer's premises could further this. Even though the retail competition model often severs the direct link between the customer and distribution network operator, it should be possible to find a business model through which retailers or others that install a smart grid application on a customer's premises can share in the resulting benefits. Regulators may have to help the industry develop the essential information protocols and compatibility standards to make this possible, but competitive environments are generally more innovative than monopolies.

As the level of renewable generation increases, less of the market may be truly competitive. Governments may reserve part of the market for renewable generators, either implicitly or explicitly. Other support schemes may be needed to persuade companies to invest in carbon capture and storage or nuclear power. The danger would be that if the market for unsupported generation became a small rump, competition within it would no longer act as sufficient discipline on the participating firms, and the prices set there would lose their ability to send meaningful signals.

Helm (2008) has suggested that a "utility" should be created to tender for these stations, financing them in a way that minimizes the cost of capital. This is effectively a variant of the single buyer model. If sufficient competition exists among developers to win the tenders and build the stations, it might achieve the best of both worlds. The danger, however, is that the single buyer would end up favoring particular technologies that turned out to be unsuccessful, and that there would be no checks and balances to prevent this. It would be better to establish a long-term carbon price and use this to provide incentives for investment in low-carbon generation on the level playing field of a competitive wholesale market. Similarly, efforts to provide a "guiding mind" to coordinate investment in generation and the networks should be based on constructive engagement among the relevant parties, sharing information on their plans and needs, rather than on prescriptive central planning.

At the same time, competitive models do involve greater risks, and thus a higher cost of capital, than the alternatives. In a more capital-intensive industry, the cost of capital will make a greater contribution to consumer prices, but the importance of choosing an efficient amount of capital will also rise—particularly during a period of high investment, such as most countries are now facing. Again, competitive mechanisms generally lead to better investment decisions than regulatory ones; even when investors have indulged in excessive plant building, this has not been at the cost of electricity consumers.

Therefore, although the detailed decisions economic regulators need to make will change, and they will have to take more account of the environment as a constraint on what they expect companies to do, the shift to renewable energy will not change the fundamental tasks or nature of economic regulation. We may need to adapt our existing tools but can continue to use them to build a low-carbon energy system.

Acknowledgments

Thanks go to the editors, Chris Hemsley and Andrew Quinn, and participants at the Centre for Competition and Regulation Policy Workshop held at Aston Business School in July 2009, for helpful comments. The author also thanks Boaz Moselle for directing him to the relevant part of the California ISO's website.

Notes

1. The fourth goal, "to promote competitive markets in the UK and beyond, helping to raise the rate of sustainable economic growth and to improve our productivity," is also related to the price of energy, although one might argue that a competitive market is a means to an end rather than an end in itself.

2. Although an indigenous source of supply would normally be seen as secure, miners' strikes caused major power cuts in the 1970s and threatened them in 1984–1985, thus diversification away from coal reduced the risk of a recurrence.

3. In practice, much of the new investment was made before additional capacity was actually needed, because market power raised prices and made entry attractive, and it also may have raised the industry's costs in the short term.

4. The demand for energy services is likely to increase because of their lower effective price (the so-called direct rebound effect—as comfort becomes cheaper, people like to be more comfortable) and because the money saved in one area typically will be spent on other goods and services that also consume energy (an indirect effect). Sorrell (2007) reviews the evidence for this and concludes that in developed countries, the direct rebound effect is between 10% and 30% of the energy saving per unit of energy services. The evidence on indirect effects is inconclusive, but they may be quite large (more than 50% of the initially predicted energy saving).

5. The prices in these spot markets, and for longer-term sales, were calculated based on estimated marginal costs, rather than freely submitted price offers.

6. The map of regional transmission organizations, which do not correspond neatly with state boundaries, shows 20 states with little or no coverage. Even in those states, however, some bilateral trading may occur.

7. For example, the network operator might deny access on spurious grounds of system security (i.e., claiming that the network would be vulnerable to failure if power flows from the entrant's area increased), fail to invest in new infrastructure that would facilitate access, or institute a "margin squeeze" through setting excessive prices for ancillary services.

8. The EU's second electricity and gas directives, for instance, allow member states to choose whether to exempt utilities serving fewer than 100,000 customers from the requirements for legal separation between distribution and retailing that are otherwise compulsory (European Commission 2003a, b).

9. In Great Britain, the incumbent retailers faced price controls when selling to domestic customers until 2002, even though all customers had a choice of retailers by mid-1999. In contrast, price controls for medium-size commercial and industrial electricity customers were lifted as soon as this market was opened to competition in 1994, in the belief that these buyers were more sophisticated and could protect themselves by shopping around.

10. An exception is the tidal barrage at La Rance, France, which is effectively a hydroelectric scheme—a very mature technology—built across an estuary rather than an inland river. A similar scheme across the Severn Estuary in the United Kingdom could generate 5% of the country's electricity (DECC 2009b) at the cost of significant changes to the local ecosystem and £21 billion ($32 billion).

11. While wind energy would be 41% of renewable generation in this scenario, 43% of electricity generation would be renewable, giving an overall penetration of more than 17%.

12. The range can vary among turbine designs. For example, GE's 3.6-megawatt (MW) offshore wind turbine does not need to cut out until the wind reaches 27 m/s but needs a speed of 14 m/s to reach full output, whereas its 1.5 MW 1.5xle onshore design can reach full power at a speed of 11.5 m/s but cuts out after 10 minutes averaging 20 m/s.

13. Individual photovoltaic units could have volatile outputs on a partly cloudy day, producing much less when a cloud moves overhead.

14. Gross et al. (2006) give a range from 19.1% to 26% for Great Britain, if it were to get 20% of its energy from wind—somewhat less than is now planned. The UK government uses a range of 10% to 20% for the larger quantities expected (House of Lords 2008b, *484*), and E.ON UK, an integrated power and gas company, has suggested that the figure should be less than 10% (ibid., *107*).

15. This assumes that the wind generators have a load factor of 28% and the conventional generators one of 80%, which is rather low but produces round numbers in the example: both sets of stations would produce an average output of 2.8 GW.

16. Some power stations have been connected at distribution voltages, particularly at the higher voltages close to the transmission system, but on a limited scale compared with the likely growth of distribution-connected renewable generation.

17. Federal legislation for a nationwide scheme is being debated at the time of writing (November 2009).

18. A generator with a surplus of permits, albeit free, still faces the opportunity cost of not selling the spare ones.

19. If the firm spends more than it proposed, however, it would have been better off had it proposed a higher level of spending.

20. Because Great Britain follows the model of retail competition, formal regulation covers only the transmission and distribution networks, and this review does not deal with issues related to generation or retailing, even though many network innovations will also affect these sectors. For documents related to the review, see www.ofgem.gov.uk/Networks/rpix20/Pages/RPIX20.aspx.

21. This is because many renewable generators will be located far from demand, and their low load factors mean that it would not be economic to build enough transmission capacity to accommodate all their output at the rare times when they are producing at close to full output, leading to an increase in transmission constraints.

22. For more information, see the California ISO's website at www.caiso.com/1816/1816d22953ec0.html.

23. If this behavior allowed a generator to avoid building the extra transmission, and the generator could still meet the peak demand, it would be efficient.

24. These transmission charges vary by around £7.00 ($10.68) per kW per year, whereas a forward wholesale price for 2010 (at the end of June 2009) was £51.25 ($78.17) per MWh, and a renewable generator would also receive Renewables Obligation Certificates that were selling for around £52.00 ($79.32) per MWh (*UK Powerfocus* 2009). A 1% change in load factor leads to an increase in output of 88 MWh (for a 1 MW unit), and hence an extra £4.70 ($7.17) per kW per year in income.

25. A state-owned transmission company potentially has the best financial cushion of all, but it may well be less receptive to financial incentives than a private-sector organization.

26. The alternative paradigm uses a capacity market to recover generators' fixed costs, sometimes coupled with payments linked to spot prices that should act to restrain those prices (Cramton and Stoft 2008).

27. If a high level of integration between retailing and renewable generation extended to the generation

sector overall, then the barrier to entry in retailing would be severe. If several regional incumbents exist within a larger market, however, effective competition among them is possible, though not inevitable.

28. In the United Kingdom, fuel-poor households are defined as those that need to spend more than 10% of their income to achieve acceptable standards of heat and light.

29. Heat pumps basically use refrigerator technology in reverse to extract heat from the environment, chilling a fluid so that it is colder than conditions outside (or underground) and can absorb heat from its surroundings. Compressing the fluid then raises its temperature to a point where the heat can be extracted and used. The gross energy delivered by a heat pump can be four times that used for pumping, in which case 75% of the energy delivered would be counted as renewable by the EU.

30. In countries where the regulator is constrained to closely follow specific laws, this implies that those laws should give the regulator tasks that achieve these same aims.

References

Borenstein, S. 2005. The Long-Run Efficiency of Real-Time Electricity Pricing. *Energy Journal* 26 (3): 93–116.

Cramton, P., and S. Stoft. 2008. Forward Reliability Markets: Less Risk, Less Market Power, More Efficiency. *Utilities Policy* 16 (3): 194–201.

DECC (Department of Energy and Climate Change). 2009a. *Consultation on Renewable Electricity Financial Incentives 2009*. London: DECC.

———. 2009b. *The UK Renewable Energy Strategy*. Cm 7686. London: Stationery Office.

DoE (Department of Energy). 2006. *U.S. Department of Energy Strategic Plan*. Washington, DC: Department of Energy.

Douglas, J. 2005. In the Zone. *Power Engineering International* 13 (12): 45–47

DTI (Department of Trade and Industry). 2003. *Our Energy Future: Creating a Low Carbon Economy*. Cm 5761. London: Stationery Office.

EIA (Energy Information Administration). 2009. US Independent System Operators. www.eia.doe.gov/cneaf/electricity/page/channel/fig8.html (accessed March 22, 2010).

European Commission. 2003a. *Directive 2003/54/EC of the European Parliament and of the Council of 26 June 2003 concerning Common Rules for the Internal Market in Electricity and Repealing Directive 96/92/EC*. Brussels: Commission of the European Communities.

———. 2003b. *Directive 2003/55/EC of the European Parliament and of the Council of 26 June 2003 concerning Common Rules for the Internal Market in Natural Gas and Repealing Directive 98/30/EC*. Brussels: Commission of the European Communities.

———. 2007. *Renewable Energy Road Map: Renewable Energies in the 21st Century: Building a More Sustainable Future: Impact Assessment. Accompanying Document to the Communication from the Commission to the Council and the European Parliament*. SEC (2006) 1719/3. Brussels: Commission of the European Communities.

Green, R. J. 1997. Electricity Transmission Pricing: An International Comparison *Utilities Policy* 6 (3): 177–184.

———. 2005. Electricity and Markets *Oxford Review of Economic Policy* 21 (1): 67–87.

Gross, R., P. Heptonstall, D. Anderson, T. C. Green, M. Leach, and J. Skea (2006) *The Costs and Impacts of Intermittency: An Assessment of the Evidence on the Costs and Impacts of Intermittent Generation on the British Electricity Network*. London: Imperial College.

Hannah, L. 1979. *Electricity before Nationalisation*. London: MacMillan.

Hawkes, A., and M. Leach. 2007. Cost-Effective Operating Strategy for Residential Micro-combined Heat and Power. *Energy* 32 (5): 711–723.

Helm, D. R. 2008. Renewables—Time for a Rethink? www.dieterhelm.co.uk/node/488 (accessed March 22, 2010).

House of Lords. 2008a. *The Economics of Renewable Energy, Economic Affairs Select Committee Fourth Report of Session 2007–8*. HL195-I of 2007–8. London: Stationery Office.

———. 2008b. *The Economics of Renewable Energy, Economic Affairs Select Committee Fourth Report of Session 2007–8*. Vol. 2, *Evidence*. HL195-II of 2007–8. London: Stationery Office.

Jamasb, T., and M. G. Pollitt. 2007. Incentive Regulation of Electricity Distribution Networks: Lessons of Experience from Britain. *Energy Policy* 35 (12): 6163–6187.

Joskow, P. L. 2008. Lessons Learned from Electricity Market Liberalization. *Energy Journal* 29, Special Issue in Honor of David Newbery, 9–42.

Laffont, J.-J., and J. Tirole. 1993. *A Theory of Incentives in Procurement and Regulation*. Cambridge: MIT Press.

Littlechild, S. C. (2008) Some Applied Economics of Utility Regulation. *Energy Journal* 29, Special Issue in Honor of David Newbery, 43–62.

Newbery, D. M. (1999) *Privatization, Restructuring and Regulation of Network Utilities*. Cambridge, MA: MIT Press.

Ofgem. 2009. *Innovation in Energy Networks: Is More Needed and How Can This Be Stimulated? Regulating Energy Networks for the Future: RPI-X@20*. Working paper 2. London: Office of Gas and Electricity Markets.

Pérez-Arriaga, I. J., F. J. Rubio, J. F. Puerta, J. Arceluz, and J. Marin. 1995. Marginal Pricing of Transmission Services: An Analysis of Cost Recovery. *IEEE Transactions on Power Systems* 10 (1): 546–553.

Pollitt, M. G. 2004. Electricity Reform in Chile: Lessons for Developing Countries. *Journal of Network Industries* 5 (3–4): 221–262.

———. 2005. The Role of Efficiency Estimates in Regulatory Price Reviews: Ofgem's Approach to Benchmarking Electricity Networks. *Utilities Policy* 13 (4): 279–288.

———. 2008. The Future of Electricity (and Gas) Regulation in a Low-Carbon Policy World. *Energy Journal* 29, Special Issue in Honor of David Newbery, 63–94.

Pollitt, M. G., and J. Bialek. 2008. Electricity Network Investment and Regulation for a Low-Carbon future. In *Delivering a Low Carbon Electricity System: Technologies, Economics and Policy*, edited by M.

Grubb, T. Jamasb and M. Pollitt. Cambridge: Cambridge University Press, 183–206.

Sappington, D. 1982. Optimal Regulation of Research and Development under Imperfect Information. *Bell Journal of Economics* 13 (2): 354–368.

Schulz, W. 1995. Restructuring the Electricity Market: A German View. In *Competition in the Electricity Supply Industry: Experience from Europe and the United States*, edited by O. J. Olsen. Copenhagen: DJØF Publishing.

Shleifer, A. 1985. A Theory of Yardstick Competition. *RAND Journal of Economics* 16: 319–327.

Sorrell, S. 2007. *The Rebound Effect: An Assessment of the Evidence for Economy-wide Energy Savings from Improved Energy Efficiency*. London: UK Energy Research Centre.

Spiller, P. T., and L. Viana Martorell. 1996. How Should It Be Done? Electricity Regulation in Argentina, Brazil, Uruguay and Chile. In *International Comparisons of Electricity Regulation*, edited by R. J. Gilbert and E. P. Kahn. Cambridge: Cambridge University Press: 82–125.

UK Powerfocus. 2009. Month at a Glance. *UK Powerfocus* 109: 1.

Yago, M., J. P. Atkins, K. R. Bhattarai, R. J. Green, and S. D. Trotter. 2008. Modelling the Economic Impact of Low-Carbon Electricity. In *Delivering a Low Carbon Electricity System: Technologies, Economics and Policy*, edited by M. Grubb, T. Jamasb, and M. Pollitt. Cambridge: Cambridge University Press, 394–413.

9

Building Blocks: Investment in Renewable and Nonrenewable Technologies

James Bushnell

Within a span of 20 years, the electric power industry has become the central focus of two extraordinary policy trends, each one significant enough to fundamentally reshape the industry. One of these trends is liberalization, a term that has come to encompass both privatization and regulatory restructuring. Beginning with the visions articulated in such works as Joskow and Schmalansee (1985) and Schweppe et al. (1988), the restructuring movement in electricity can be viewed as an extension of the trend toward market liberalization that had previously transformed the airline, communications, and natural gas industries. The generation sector of the industry has undergone a sporadic but inexorable transition from economic regulation under cost-of-service principles to an environment in which markets heavily influence, if not dominate, the remuneration and investment decisions of firms.

The second trend to engulf the electricity industry has been the growth of the environmental movement. More specifically, the growing alarm over the threat of global climate change, and the more recent engagement of policymakers in combating it, is likely to dominate decisionmaking in the power industry over the next several decades. Electricity and heat production are responsible for 40% of CO_2 emissions in the United States and about 31% worldwide (Stern 2006).

Although not obvious at first glance, these two trends, restructuring and environmental regulation, share many common ideological roots. In the United States, the growing stringency in air quality regulation was accompanied by an increased acceptance of market-based environmental regulations. These include cap-and-trade mechanisms, such as the program put in place to limit SO_2 emissions under the 1990 amendments to the Clean Air Act (Ellerman et al. 2000). Regulators were also interested in experimenting with market-based incentives to promote alternative energy sources. Many trace the birth of the U.S. independent power industry to the passage of the Public Utilities Regulatory Policies Act (PURPA) in 1978. The PURPA legislation established mandates for the purchase of energy produced by qualifying small and renewable sources of generation (Joskow 1997; Kahn 1988). Although inspired largely by environmental and energy security goals, the largest impact of PURPA is arguably in the resulting demonstration of the viability of smaller-capacity generation technologies and the nonutility generator business model.

One important aspect of the independent power producer business model was the relative freedom—and risk—allowed in investment of new facilities. Investments are based on market-based long-term contracts and projections of market revenues, rather than regulatory findings of need and guaranteed cost recovery. The restructuring movement in the United States was led by states with the worst track records in utility investment (Ando and Palmer 1998). Although evidence suggests that operations have become more efficient in these states (Wolfram 2005), restructuring was primarily intended to improve the incentives of firms to make prudent investments (Borenstein and Bushnell 2000). In some parts of the world, this general approach to investment has come to dominate the industry. In many others, policymakers continue to search for the proper tools for balancing market incentives with concerns over reliability and adequacy of investment (Joskow 2005; Oren 2005). One central aspect of this search concerns the design of wholesale electricity markets and the payment streams they provide to suppliers. Markets can differ greatly on the primary sources of remuneration for generators, with some relying on energy and ancillary services markets, while others have established mechanisms for compensating suppliers for their installed or available capacity (Bushnell 2005; Cramton and Stoft 2005).

This chapter studies the intersection of these two trends as they come to dominate the economics of the industry. In particular, it examines how the increasing penetration of intermittent renewable generation can change the economic landscape for merchant power investment in conventional thermal generation. Currently, renewable generation earns revenues from a wide range of sources, from energy markets to government tax credits. The impact of renewable generation on the electricity markets in which they participate has to date been relatively modest outside of regions of high concentration such as west Texas. That will almost certainly change, however, as state and federal policies considerably ramp up the amount of renewable generation throughout the country. This can have a profound impact on prices and the economics of supply for both renewable and nonrenewable generation.

An equilibrium model of generation investment is developed, based on the long-standing principles of finding the optimal mix of capital-intensive and higher-marginal-cost resources to serve a market with fluctuating demand. This model is then applied to data on electricity markets from several regions of the western United States to examine how the interaction of increasing wind capacity and electricity market design affects the equilibrium mix of thermal capacity and the revenues earned by renewable suppliers. The chapter first provides a brief background on this question, then describes the equilibrium conditions that form the stylized investment model. Next, it details the data and assumptions used in the study. The final section contains the bulk of the results and analysis.

Background: Renewable Energy in Restructured Electricity Markets

Renewable, or green, power is viewed by many policymakers as the key to combating greenhouse gas emissions within the power sector. Explicit and implicit subsidies for renewable power continue to grow. By the end of 2007, 25 U.S. states and Washington, DC, had some form of renewable portfolio standard (RPS), which requires purchasers of wholesale electricity to procure some percentage of their power from renewable sources (Wiser and Barbose 2008). The long-standing, but intermittent and precarious, production tax credit (PTC) for wind energy in the United States pays wind producers 2.1 cents/kWh for energy production. The American Recovery and Reinvestment Act of 2009 contained several provisions favorable to renewable generation, including the extension of the PTC until 2012 and alternative investment tax credits for facilities constructed in 2009 and 2010 (Wiser and Bolinger 2009).

For the industry as a whole, the growth of nonutility generation has coincided with the expansion of renewable generation sources. This is not the product of happenstance; from the passage of PURPA, various legislative purchasing mandates and tax incentives played a dominant role in the growth of both renewable and nonutility generation. To this day, the renewable industry is dominated by nonutility producers.[1]

The subsidization of renewable generation is expanding in parallel with efforts to create cap-and-trade programs for CO_2. This can be seen as antithetical to the spirit of a cap-and-trade program, where promoting flexibility in compliance options is a central ideal. Unlike the SO_2 program, cap-and-trade is but one of a broad set of policy tools being brought to bear against greenhouse gas (GHG) emissions. Some view this as undermining the strength of cap-and-trade regulation. The cap has less incremental impact if much of the GHG reductions are already accounted for under various more directed measures and regulations. In regions such as California, cap-and-trade is viewed more as a backstop than as a bulwark in combating climate change.

Although policies that promote renewable generation sources are extremely popular with regulators, politicians, and the general public, their continued expansion to unprecedented levels does raise some concerns. One source of concern is cost. Although the technological frontier continues to advance, much controversy exists over the appropriate timing and form of policy intervention to promote renewable generation. Most accept that renewable generation would not be a significant source of supply today if not for some form of public support. The fact that the external cost of GHG emissions have not yet been priced into the investment decisions of fossil-based generation firms certainly provides justification for support of renewable power, but the prospect of regional and possibly national caps on CO_2 emissions undermines that justification. A common argument for support of renewable generation is the hope that expansion of supply will yield learning benefits, thereby lowering costs of future supply. However, a market failure exists only if that learning cannot be appropriated for private gain. Although the bulk of public support for renewable generation has taken the form of production mandates or credits, it is not clear whether commercialization is the point in the supply chain where the problem of intellectual property is most acute. Further, the evidence to date indicates that cost reductions in alternative energy sources can be driven as much by exogenous technology developments as by the expansion of installed capacity (Nemet 2006).

The most commonly heard concern over the rapid expansion of renewable electricity supply is over the fact that this supply is available only intermittently (NERC 2009). With the prospect of one-fifth or more of electrical energy coming from intermittent sources, many in the industry are confronting the fact that the traditional tools for planning for and providing reliable electric service may prove inadequate. In fact, as discussed below, the traditional utility planning paradigm has been disrupted by market liberalization over the last 10 years. The industry has yet to settle on a single framework to replace utility planning. The large-scale addition of intermittent resources is therefore happening against a backdrop in which the mechanisms through which generators are compensated are very much in flux.

Investment in Restructured Electricity Markets

Since the onset of market liberalization, concerns have been raised that the newly formed market regimes would fail to produce adequate investment in generation capacity. Ironically, in many parts of the world, it was the cost of excess capacity that provided the impetus for liberalization. The safety net of guaranteed capital cost recovery in both publicly owned and rate-of-return regulated utilities had provided a high degree of reliability. Indeed, the reliability of electric supply in most OECD countries is so high that it is often taken for granted. U.S. electricity consumers, unlike those in many developing countries, fully expect to be able to consume as much electricity as they need whenever they desire.

These high levels of reliability came at a high cost, however, particularly when combined with the weak incentives for cost control provided by public ownership and regulation. Under the traditional model, a utility and its regulators jointly forecast a "need" for investment, and the regulator would guarantee the recovery of costs undertaken to meet that need. In the liberalized market, private firms no longer receive a guaranteed recovery of their investments. One of the hopes for liberalization was that this market-based risk would lead to more prudent and cost-effective investment decisions. At the very least, it was observed, the costs of overinvestment would be borne by investors rather than ratepayers under the new market regime. In many markets, this latter belief has been supported by the fact that many of the firms that procured or expanded capacity in liberalized markets experienced severe financial difficulties during the early part of this decade.

Whereas a transition away from payments based on a cost-of-service framework is shared by all liberalized markets, the revenue streams that replaced these payments differ greatly. Many markets focus the remuneration of generators on the provision of energy and related services. In the jargon of the U.S. electricity industry, this conceptual framework has been referred to as an "energy-only" framework. The name, which is somewhat inaccurate, refers to the fact that contributions against fixed and sunk costs arise only from payments for the provision of either energy or associated operating reserve services. Although no market is fully unconstrained in this way, markets such as those found in the United Kingdom, Australia, Texas, New Zealand, and Norway operate under general energy-only principles to the extent that they have no or relatively high price caps and provide no other specific payments for the supply of capacity.

In many markets, however, the revenues provided from the provision of energy and ancillary services appear to be insufficient to cover the fixed cost of new entry (Joskow 2005). Myriad reasons can be given for this, including the existence of price caps, the subtle but significant impact of the decisions of system operators on market prices, and simply the overinvestment of capacity. This and other factors have led to a level of discomfort among many policymakers over leaving investment decisions entirely up to the market. Therefore, many electricity markets, including several in the United States, provide payments for capacity "availability" that supplement revenues received

for the provision of energy and ancillary services. This feature is not unique to the United States, as capacity payments played a significant role in the early years of market liberalization in the United Kingdom and continue to be a significant factor in Spain and Colombia.

The details of these capacity payments vary, but the general common features that are represented in the stylized model used here are a formal or informal constraint on energy prices combined with a fixed payment (here assumed to be in dollars per megawatt-year) based on installed capacity. The fixed payments can be scaled according to the expected or historic availability of generation, a fact most significant for wind generation sources.

In many restructured markets, some form of payment for installed or available capacity is made to producers as a supplement to the revenues they earn through the sale of energy and ancillary services. These payments are not without controversy, however, as debate continues over how exactly to measure and remunerate the provision of "reliable" capacity (Cramton 2003; Hogan 2005; Oren 2005).

One aspect of this debate is how to deal with unconventional sources of generation. Resources, such as hydroelectric facilities, that are energy-limited cannot produce at their full capacity all the time. Many renewable resources can supply power only intermittently, and their supply is dependent on ambient conditions rather than under the control of the operator. In general, the capacity payments made to resources such as these are scaled downward according to rough probabilistic measures of their potential availability. As explored below, the specification of such rules will interact with the level of penetration of renewable generation to shift the relative value of different types of payment streams for intermittent producers.

The power industry today therefore features two contrasting models for financing new investment: the energy-only model, which relies on periodic, extremely high prices for energy and ancillary services to provide the scarcity rents that are applied to the recovery of capital costs; and the capacity payment model, in which a large portion of the capital costs are recovered through capacity payments. Under energy-only markets, the choice and profitability of specific generation sources will depend on the degree and timing of high prices. Under capacity markets, the spot energy prices are somewhat less critical, but the specific implementation of capacity payments is very important to the relative profitability of technologies.

The large-scale deployment of intermittent resources can imply a major paradigm shift for both investment models. Electric systems will likely experience a massive addition of renewable generation capacity that is largely motivated by nonmarket considerations such as climate change. This will result in an influx of energy with extremely low marginal cost, but only during some time periods. As a result, the remaining need for thermal generation capacity could look very different than it would in the absence of the renewable capacity. In market terms, the levels and patterns of energy prices could be quite different with the addition of renewables. The months and hours that experience peak prices will be driven as much by the availability of intermittent resources as by the fluctuations in end-use demand. These questions are explored empirically in the following section.

Equilibrium Model of Electricity Investment

This section uses a long-run equilibrium model of investment to explore the ramifications of greatly expanded intermittent supply. A technical formulation of the model is provided in the appendix at the end of this chapter. The model draws from the classic framework of utility investment, which applies a mix of technologies of varying capital intensity to satisfy fluctuating demand (see Kahn 1988). This demand is often represented in a load-duration curve, which illustrates a cumulative distribution of demand levels over some time period, such as one year. This basic model is expanded to incorporate elements of peak load pricing as articulated in theory by Borenstein (2005). The model examines the mix and cost of technologies

that achieve the break-even point where annual energy revenues for each technology equal their annualized cost of capacity. As in Borenstein (2005), these values depend on prices rising above the marginal cost of the highest-cost technologies where, in effect, demand sets the market price. This process has come to be called "scarcity pricing" in wholesale electricity markets. Similar to Lamont (2008), the model also incorporates intermittent resources. As described below, the wind production profiles used here are based on specific projections of wind production profiles, rather than the stylized correlation coefficients used by Lamont.

The model here assumes perfect competition, essentially free entry into any generation technology in the markets, and also disregards concerns of "lumpiness" of capacity. Firms are free to install any combination of capacity sizes that satisfy differentiable equilibrium conditions. This greatly simplifies computational concerns and, in light of the size of the markets being examined here, is not an unreasonable assumption. As this is a long-term model, it also ignores operational constraints such as minimum run times, start costs, and ramping rates. These are obviously important considerations of operating an electricity system that will be affected by the expansion of intermittent technologies, but they are beyond the capabilities of the model used here.

The approach of the model is to examine the actual load profiles or hourly distributions of demand of certain markets, and then impose varying levels of intermittent wind production on those demand distributions. In other words, the wind investment is considered exogenous to the equilibrium investment model, having been implemented through nonmarket constraints such as a renewable portfolio standard. The model then derives the mix of thermal technologies that would be constructed to serve the resulting residual demand that is left over after accounting for wind production. The equilibrium resulting from an assumption of competitive entry and no lumpiness is equivalent to the optimal, or least-cost, set of technologies. The intuition behind the equilibrium constraints described in the appendix is straightforward. Firms will continue to construct additional capacity in a given thermal technology as long as the revenues implied by the residual demand are sufficient to cover a levelized cost of investment, as well as operating costs.

The empirical calculations are based on data taken from the Western Electricity Coordinating Council (WECC) for the reference year 2007. These data are in turn subdivided into the four WECC subregions: the California (CA) region; the Northwest Power Pool (NWPP) region; the southwest (AZNM) region, made up mostly of Arizona and New Mexico; and the Rocky Mountain Power Pool (RMPP) region (see Figure 9.1).

The general approach is to ask how electricity load would have looked during 2007 under various levels of wind penetration. The model then solves for the equilibrium investment mix of conventional technologies that optimally serves the resulting load shape. This section includes descriptions of the data sources and assumptions used in implementing this calculation.

It is important to keep in mind that this is not a simulation of the *incremental* investment required going forward in these markets, but rather an exercise that examines how the long-run equilibrium mix of generation and costs would change. Thus it is not meant to be predictive of these actual markets, but uses these market data to

develop calculations for a range of possible representative markets. The market-based model assumes that all regions are restructured (when in fact, only California is currently even partially restructured) and that the investment choices are starting from a clean slate of no existing capacity.

One difficulty with simulating electricity markets in a high level of detail is that, although data on most fossil-fuel-based generation units are quite extensive and reliable, far less data exist on the activities of hydroelectric plants, renewable generation, and the substantial amount of power generated from combined heat and power (CHP) or cogeneration plants. When building a counterfactual re-creation of an electricity market, these data gaps make assumptions about the missing production necessary.

This chapter takes the approach of restricting the construction of a counterfactual market outcome to the portion of resources for which detailed data are available. In effect, it assumes that, under the counterfactual assumptions of wind penetration, the operations of nonmodeled generation plants would not have changed. The total production from "clean" sources is unlikely to change in the short run. The production of electricity missing from the data is driven by natural resource availability (rain, wind, sun) or, in the case of CHP, to nonelectricity production decisions. The economics of production are such that these sources are essentially producing all the power they can. However, it is important to recognize that this modeling approach assumes that existing unconventional sources will not change not only *how much* they produce, but also *when* they produce it. This is a problematic assumption in regions with substantial hydro resources, such as the Pacific Northwest. Ideally, an investment analysis would involve a co-optimization of hydro, wind, and thermal electric production. This is beyond the scope of this chapter. For this reason, the results pertaining to the Pacific Northwest region should be interpreted with this shortcoming in mind.

In any event, the goal here is not to reproduce the electric system as it actually operated in 2007, but rather to assess how investment decisions would play out if the industry were starting from a

Figure 9.1. The four WECC subregions

completely clean slate and faced the residual (after existing unconventional generation) load shapes of 2007. The data used here are meant to convey conditions present in representative electricity systems, rather than completely reproduce a specific system.

Demand Data

The primary data source for this discussion is the BASECASE dataset from Platts, which is in turn derived primarily from the continuous emissions monitoring system (CEMS) used by the U.S. Environmental Protection Agency (EPA) to monitor the emissions of large stationary sources.[2] Almost all large fossil-fired electricity generation sources are included in this dataset, although hydroelectric, renewable, and some small fossil generation sources are missing. The CEMS reports hourly data on several aspects of production and emissions. Hourly data on nuclear generation plants are included with fossil generation data in the BASECASE dataset. The model here uses the hourly generation output and carbon emissions for available facilities.

These hourly output data are aggregated by firm and region to develop the demand in the simulation model. As described above, this is in fact a residual demand: the demand that is left after applying the output from non-CEMS plants. Plant cost, capacity, availability characteristics, and regional fuel prices are then taken from the Platts POWERDAT dataset. These data are in turn derived from mandatory industry reporting to the Energy Information Administration (EIA) and North American Electric Reliability Council (NERC).

These data are then combined to create a demand profile and supply functions for periods in the simulation. Although hourly data are available, for computational reasons these are aggregated into representative time periods. Each of the four seasons has 50 such periods, yielding 200 explicitly modeled time periods. The aggregation of hourly data was based on a sorting of the California residual demand. California aggregate production was sorted into 50 bins based on equal MW spreads between the minimum and maximum production levels observed in the 2007 sample year. A time period in the simulation therefore is based on the mean of the relevant market data for all actual 2007 data that fall within the bounds of each bin. For example, every actual hour (of which there were 14) during spring 2007 in which California CEMS production fell between 7,040 and 7,243 MW were combined into a single representative hour for simulation purposes.

The number of season-hour observations in each bin is therefore unbalanced; there are relatively few observations in the highest and lowest production levels, and more observations closer to the median levels. The demand levels used in the simulation are then based on the mean production levels observed in each bin. In order to calculate aggregate production and revenues, the resulting outputs for each *simulated* demand level was multiplied by the number of *actual* market hours used to produce the input for that simulated demand level. Table 9.1 presents summary statistics of CEMS load levels for each of the four WECC subregions.

Table 9.1. Summary statistics of demand

Region	CEMS load (MW)			
	Mean	Min.	Max.	S.D.
CA	13,216	6,022	29,985	3,626
NWPP	15,334	9,670	18,884	2,400
AZNM	17,942	13,626	25,586	2,706
RMPP	6,986	5,531	9,141	723

Note: MW = megawatts; S.D. = standard deviation

Wind Generation Data

The wind generation profiles used in this chapter come from WECC transmission planning studies. The WECC studied several scenarios for renewable energy penetration (see Nickell 2008), with particular focus on an assumption of 15% of total WECC energy being provided from renewable sources. This modeling effort employed a dataset from the National Renewable Energy Laboratory (NREL) that provides 10-minute wind speeds with a high level of geographic resolution throughout the U.S. portion of the WECC system. The WECC study combines these wind potential data with other local sources of information to construct projections of new wind development, as well as of hourly wind production from those potential new sources.

This chapter draws on the hourly load profiles of the projected wind facilities from the WECC study and aggregates these profiles according to the four WECC subregions described above. Because of the focus here on the investment impacts of wind penetration, this section looks at the baseline level of estimated production used in the WECC study and also a level that is double that used in the WECC study. The aggregate generation levels are summarized in Table 9.2. As a portion of CEMS load, the new wind sources would account for about 15% of 2007 CEMS energy, although these resources are not evenly distributed across the WECC.[3] The RMPP area, which includes the wind-rich areas of Wyoming, has a great deal of wind potential, whereas the desert Southwest has much less.

When the projected additional wind production is combined with and assumed to displace CEMS production, the result is a sharply shifted residual load profile that must be served by conventional generation sources. Figures 9.2 and 9.3 illustrate the hourly CEMS load, both before and

Table 9.2. Aggregate generation levels

	Hourly averages				
	Load	Wind		High wind	
Region	(MWh)	(MWh)	Share	(MWh)	Share
CA	13,216	1,866	14%	3,733	28%
NWPP	15,334	2,229	15%	4,458	29%
AZNM	17,942	1,445	8%	2,891	16%
RMPP	6,986	1,902	27%	3,804	54%
Totals	53,479	7,443	14%	14,885	28%

Note: MWh = megawatt-hours

after accounting for the additional wind resources for the months of August and December.

The aggregate effects are well summarized by load duration curves presenting the cumulative distribution of CEMS load and residual demand after new wind sources. Figure 9.4 presents these load duration curves for the four subregions.

The CEMS load profile in California is much more variable than in other regions, while CEMS load levels in the Pacific Northwest are relatively constant because of the abundance of hydro energy in that region. In all cases, the increasing penetration of wind resources makes the load profiles steeper. This reflects the fact that wind pro-

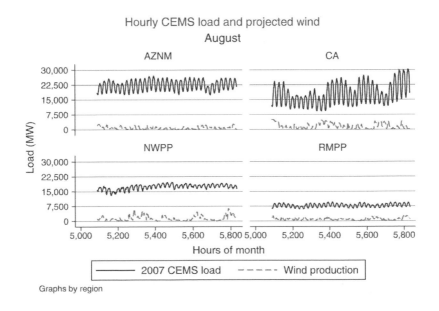

Figure 9.2. CEMS load and wind production for August

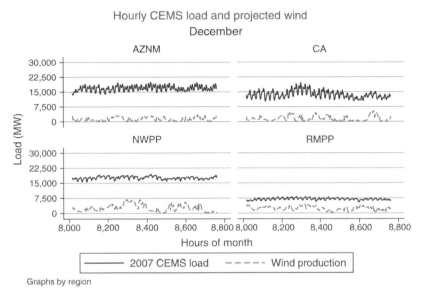

Figure 9.3. CEMS load and wind production for December

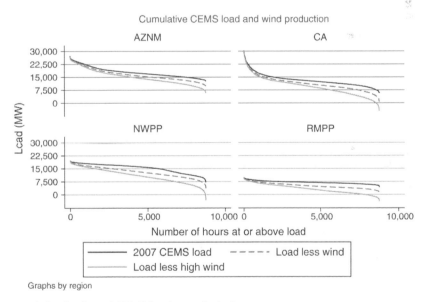

Figure 9.4. Annual distribution of CEMS load net of wind

duction is not correlated with CEMS load. To the extent that more wind production is generated in low CEMS load hours, the residual load becomes more variable and the load duration curve steeper. This effect is most pronounced in the RMPP region, where CEMS load was relatively constant but which experiences the highest degree of wind penetration.

The market implications of Figure 9.4 are central to the results of this chapter, so they deserve a little further discussion. The increasing penetration of wind resources in the WECC will create a surge of energy supply, much of which will be uncorrelated with end-use demand. The net result is a residual load shape that is more "peaky." As will be demonstrated in the results of the simulations, the optimal mix of resources to serve this profile of residual demand will be composed of a far greater share of low-capacity-cost, high-marginal-cost peaking resources.

Thermal Generation Cost Data

The model here examines the optimal possible mix of generation technologies, assuming it starts from a clean slate, with no sunk (or stranded) investment decisions. This section examines the optimal mix of three basic technologies that form the backbone of most U.S. electric systems. Each represents different levels of the trade-off between capital costs and marginal costs. Included are a base load pulverized coal technology, a midmerit combined cycle gas turbine (CCGT) technology, and a peaking gas combustion turbine (CT). The costs of construction and operation for each of these technologies are taken from the Energy Information Administration's 2007 *Annual Energy Outlook* (EIA 2007). The basic cost characteristics, taken from the EIA study, are summarized in Table 9.3. To convert these costs to an annualized fixed cost, a 15-year payback period and 10% financing cost are assumed. Fuel costs are taken from the EIA's figures for 2007. The resulting aggregate (including operating and maintenance) costs are summarized in Table 9.4.

Table 9.3. Thermal generation costs from EIA

	Total overnight cost ($/kW)	Fixed O&M ($/kW)	Variable O&M ($/MWh)	HR Btu/kWh
Scrubbed new coal	2,058	27.53	4.59	9,200
CCGT	962	12.48	2.07	7,200
CT	670	12.11	3.57	10,800

Source: EIA 2007
Notes: O&M = operating and maintenance costs; HR = Heat Rate

Analysis and Results

Using the data described in the previous section, the resulting optimal mix and level of generation capacity are calculated for each of the four WECC subregions. For the purposes of this study, each

Table 9.4. Thermal generation costs used in simulations

	Total annual fixed cost ($/kWy)	Fuel costs ($/MMBtu)	Total marginal cost ($/MWh)
Coal	282.17	1.74	20.60
CCGT	136.57	7.06	52.90
CT	98.51	7.06	79.82

Note: kWy = kilowatt-year

region is treated as isolated from the others. This is equivalent to assuming that transmission flows among the regions do not change from their 2007 levels. As described above, the four regions represent a wide spectrum in terms of current demand for generation and future wind potential.

Energy-Only Market

The results are first examined under an assumption that each region operates under an energy-only market paradigm, with no price cap and no capacity payments. The analysis begins with the equilibrium energy prices in each market. Figures 9.5 and 9.6 illustrate the hourly market-clearing energy prices in each market for the final week of August and first week of December. Note that these prices are plotted on a logarithmic scale, reflecting the highly volatile nature of equilibrium electricity prices in an energy-only market. Although significant differences in energy prices are difficult to detect in CA, the impact of wind penetration is clear on the pricing patterns in regions such as the NWPP and RMPP.

The changes in the residual demand profiles and the resulting equilibrium prices do have a significant effect. Figure 9.7 summarizes the equilibrium investment levels under three wind scenarios: wind at 2007 levels, wind at 14% of CEMS load, and wind at 28% of CEMS load.

Several aspects of the results are reflected in Figure 9.7. First, the already volatile CA load profile implies an optimal mix of relatively little base load generation compared with the other regions, whereas the very consistent load of the NWPP implies an optimal mix that is heavily base load,

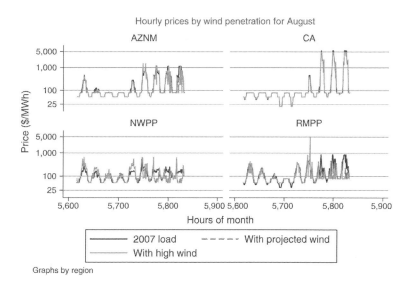

Figure 9.5. Energy market prices for August

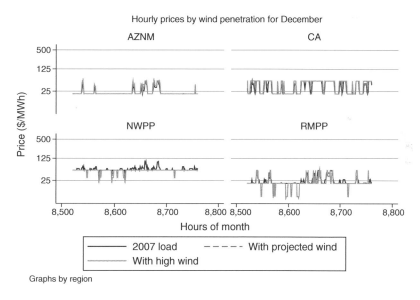

Figure 9.6. Energy market prices for December

with no peaking resources at all under the baseline scenario. Second, the increasing penetration of wind resources produces a clear shift of investment toward less capital-intensive peaking resources in every market. This shift is most pronounced in the RMPP region, where wind penetration is the greatest as a percentage of baseline

CEMS load. Third, less thermal capacity is needed in every market as a reflection of the fact that wind generation has lowered the residual demand required to be served by thermal sources. However, the equilibrium thermal capacity requirement is reduced only modestly by the entry of new wind capacity.

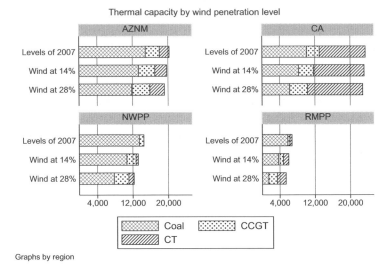

Figure 9.7. Equilibrium capacity for energy-only market

These factors are summarized in Table 9.5. For each region, the aggregate equilibrium thermal capacity and assumed wind capacity are given in the first two columns of figures. The assumed average capacity factor, taken from the wind profiles from the WECC study is given in the next column, and the shares of thermal capacity that are base load and peaking are given in the last two columns. Note that the large levels of new wind capacity, those of more than 10 gigawatts (GW), result in reductions of equilibrium thermal capacity of only 1 to 2 GW.

Across the regions, the reduction in thermal capacity averages about 15% of the new installed wind capacity, with relatively little variation across regions. It is important to mention again, however, the strong assumption made here that hydro output, particularly in the NWPP region, would

Table 9.5. Equilibrium results for energy-only market

	Thermal Capacity (MW)	New wind Capacity (MW)	Wind capacity factor	Share Coal	Share CT
CA	23,308	NA	NA	43%	44%
	22,753	5,670	33%	36%	50%
	22,442	11,340	33%	28%	55%
NWPP	14,472	NA	NA	93%	0%
	13,188	7,890	28%	81%	4%
	12,237	15,780	28%	64%	10%
AZNM	20,276	NA	NA	73%	11%
	19,691	3,840	39%	68%	14%
	19,141	7,680	39%	62%	17%
RMPP	6,751	NA	NA	86%	7%
	6,000	4,650	41%	61%	20%
	5,374	9,300	41%	26%	37%

not adjust to the new intermittent capacity. By taking advantage of the implicit storage potential of the hydro resources, one would expect the equilibrium capacity needs in this region to be reduced quite a bit more than implied by this calculation.

Capacity Market Results

As in the appendix, the simulation of a capacity market requires two important parameters to be specified. The first is the energy market price cap, set here to be $1,000/MWh. The second important parameter is the capacity market payment made to the generation sources. In order to calculate the capacity payment, the implied shortfall that would be created by capping prices at $1,000/MWh is first estimated.[4]

In practice, capacity payments are intended to replace the revenues necessary for investment that are in principle denied to suppliers through either explicit or implicit restraints on energy prices (see Joskow 2005; Oren 2005). For this study, this was accomplished by calculating the total revenues of peaking generation sources under the energy-only scenarios described above. Next, a counterfactual level of income for a 1 MW peaking generator that would have resulted from the same investment levels is calculated, but with prices earned by generators capped at $1,000. The difference, sometimes known in industry jargon as the "missing money" caused by price caps, can be expressed as a dollars-per-kilowatt-year ($/kWy) value. This value was used as the capacity payment in the second set of simulations. These payments are summarized in Table 9.6.

Table 9.6. Capacity payments resulting from $1,000 price cap (in $/kWy)

	No new wind	14% of CEMS	28% of CEMS
CA	58.41	54.58	55.84
NWPP	0.00	0.00	0.00
AZNM	1.15	1.57	12.06
RMPP	0.00	2.53	24.80

It is worth noting that these values are quite a bit lower than those currently seen in U.S. electricity markets. One reason for this is that the investment numbers from the EIA represent generic investment costs for the country, while capacity markets tend to operate in regions of the United States, such as California and New York, where investment can be much more costly. Another more important driver is that these equilibrium simulations are allowing the price to rise above the marginal cost of a peaking plant more frequently than has been historically seen in these markets. This is a reflection of the fact that the model determines the equilibrium, break-even level of capacity, whereas today's markets tend to feature more capacity than this level. In practice, today's capacity markets do not attempt to differentiate among causes of revenue shortfalls; they usually calculate net costs of entry based on historic energy prices.[5] Therefore, the revenues lost to the price cap in this simulation produce less missing money than has been estimated from current capacity market proceedings.

Next, the above simulations are repeated, with two adjustments to the original model summarized by equations (9.4) and (9.5) in the appendix at the end of this chapter. The most striking results are naturally found in the hours that were formerly those with prices significantly above $1,000. Figures 9.8 and 9.9 illustrate the changes to the peak hour price duration curves for the CA and RMPP regions because of both wind penetration and the capacity market policies. These figures summarize the 150 highest price hours in each market, in order from highest to lowest. Note that prices in these figures are on a logarithmic scale because of the high volatility.

For the wind scenarios, the same hours are plotted. As is clear from these figures, the highest price hours in the baseline simulations are not those producing the highest prices as wind investment increases. This reflects that fact that as wind investment increases, prices are increasingly driven by wind availability as well as total end-use demand. This is particularly true for the RMPP region, where the highest price hours under high levels of wind investment rank below the 100th highest price hours without the wind investment.

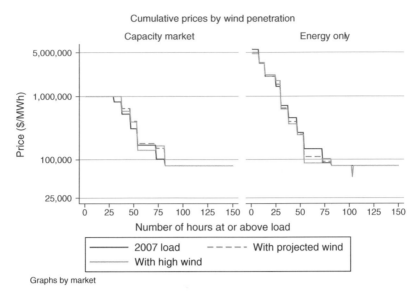

Figure 9.8. Highest 150 prices CA

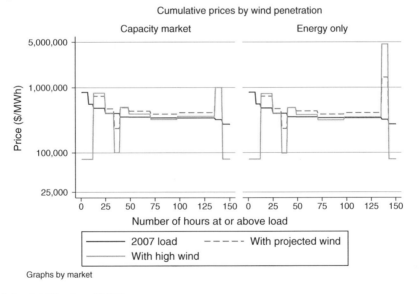

Figure 9.9. Highest 150 prices RMPP

These figures also illustrate the impact that the price cap has on these "scarcity price" hours. In general, the highest price hours are reduced to the cap levels, and price levels in most other hours remain unchanged. The resulting impact of these capacity market elements on investment levels are summarized in Table 9.7.

Revenues of Wind Resources

Because individual wind plants will have varying profiles across and within regions, it is difficult to make general statements about the equilibrium revenues of wind plants. Nevertheless, the earnings are estimated of a hypothetical 1 MW "port-

Table 9.7. Investment levels with a capacity market

	Thermal Capacity (MW)	New wind Capacity (MW)	Wind capacity factor	Share coal	Share CT
CA	23,421	N/A	N/A	43%	44%
	23,141	5,670	33%	36%	50%
	22,817	11,340	33%	28%	55%
NWPP	14,472	N/A	N/A	93%	0%
	13,188	7,890	28%	81%	4%
	12,237	15,780	28%	64%	10%
AZNM	20,282	N/A	N/A	73%	11%
	19,691	3,840	39%	68%	14%
	19,168	7,680	39%	62%	17%
RMPP	6,751	N/A	NA	86%	7%
	6,001	4,650	41%	61%	20%
	5,383	9,300	41%	26%	37%

Note: MW = megawatts.

folio" of plants that features the same production profile as the regional aggregate profile used to construct the residual demand.

In order to evaluate the revenues of intermittent resources under a capacity market paradigm, further assumptions are needed about how the reliable capacity of those resources, on which the capacity payment is based, is measured. The most basic, and clearly overgenerous, method would be to assume that 100% of the installed capacity was eligible for capacity payments. Given the intermittent availability of wind resources, this is not the usual approach. A more conventional approach is to discount the installed capacity according to a historical measure of the capacity factor (average energy output divided by capacity) of either the specific unit or the class of technologies from which the unit is drawn. Even this approach can overstate the "value" of capacity if the production profile of a generation unit is negatively correlated with total system load. A third approach, similar to one recently adopted for the purposes of measuring wind and solar capacity in California, is to measure the production of resources only during high demand hours, discarding production statistics for other hours.[6]

For purposes of comparison, revenues have been calculated under a capacity market in two ways, roughly following the options outlined above. The first approach discounts the capacity payment according to the annual capacity factor, derived from the wind profile data. The second approach calculates a capacity factor only for hours 14 through 17 of each day. The results for the two alternative calculations of capacity factor (using annual average and peak hour average) were very similar, so only the revenues are reported, assuming capacity payments are based on the peak hour average capacity factor.

Table 9.8 summarizes the revenues of this hypothetical average wind turbine for each region. These values are given in terms of $/kWy. By comparison, the peaking units are earning $95.82/kWy, while coal plants are earning $282.17/kWy.[7] To the extent that actual costs of new wind facilities would exceed these equilibrium investment revenue levels, the difference would have to be captured in subsidies—either through the production tax credit or through price premiums paid by utilities in order to comply with their renewable portfolio standards. As further reference, using the same assumptions and cost estimates from the EIA as were used to calculate thermal annual fixed costs, wind costs would be roughly $231/kWy.

Table 9.8. Summary of the revenues of the hypothetical "average" wind turbine ($/kWy)

Region	CEMS load	Energy-only New wind 14% of CEMS	New wind 28% of CEMS
CA	113.24	112.11	109.27
NWPP	123.49	106.48	105.17
AZNM	138.31	135.00	132.75
RMPP	158.39	142.03	135.17
Region	CEMS load	Capacity Market New Wind 14% of CEMS	New Wind 28% of CEMS
CA	126.74	124.82	122.31
NWPP	123.49	106.48	105.17
AZNM	138.35	135.59	136.27
RMPP	158.39	143.02	144.36

Note that under the energy-only market, the revenues for an average profile wind plant decline in each region. This is because prices are being influenced increasingly by wind availability, and a profile that mirrors the system wind profile would be producing during hours of glut and not producing during hours of wind production shortfall. If revenues are instead based on a combination of capped energy market revenues and capacity payments, wind producers do a little better than under the energy-only paradigm. This is a much stronger effect under the high wind penetration scenarios.[8] Revenues in the RMPP area are about 5% higher with a capacity payment. This is in part because the capacity payment rewards production during high-*demand* hours, whereas the energy-only market rewards production during high-*price* hours. As wind penetration increases, the high-price hours are relatively more focused on low-wind hours than on high-demand hours.

Impact of a Carbon Market

The last scenario examined is the application of a price of CO_2 onto the electricity sector. For the purposes of this discussion, the source of the CO_2 price could be either a cap-and-trade mechanism or a CO_2 tax. Rather than try to calculate a closed-loop equilibrium price for CO_2, it is assumed that these regions participate in broader

CO_2 markets with a price of $25/metric ton. This value is approximately the 2012 futures price for one ton in the European Union's Emissions Trading System (ETS) market for CO_2. It is also assumed that the imposition of CO_2 prices affects only marginal and not capital or fixed costs of any of the thermal generation technologies.

The same approach as before can be used to calculate the resulting equilibrium investment levels of thermal capacity and revenues for wind facilities. Only the equilibrium is calculated under the energy-only market paradigm. Figure 9.10 illustrates the equilibrium investment capacities under the different wind scenarios. Note that coal is much less used in all markets and is driven out of the CA and RMPP markets completely under high wind penetration.

Table 9.9 summarizes the energy market revenues earned by the hypothetical wind plant under various levels of wind penetration. With the $25/ton carbon price, wind revenues are substantially higher overall. The degradation of these revenues with increasing wind penetration is also more pronounced, however. With a price on CO_2, revenues in the RMPP region are only 5% lower per kilowatt-year under high wind penetration than they would be for the first megawatt of wind capacity added to that region. This is contrasted to the almost 15% decline in revenues for the same comparison in the absence of a carbon

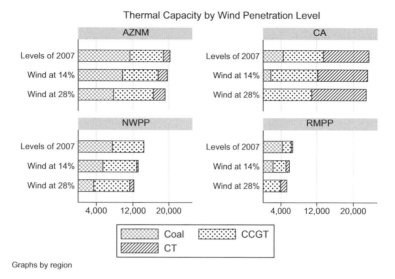

Figure 9.10. Equilibrium capacity investment with $25/ton CO_2

market. With carbon at $25/ton, wind resources are able to earn relatively more revenues during even off-peak hours when coal would be setting the price. Increasing wind penetration leads to more of these hours, but the differential between these off-peak and on-peak hours is smaller than in the absence of a carbon price.

Table 9.9. Wind revenues with carbon price at $25/ton (in $/kWy)

Region	CEMS load	New wind 14% of CEMS	New wind 28% of CEMS
CA	194.15	193.00	185.29
NWPP	188.06	173.46	172.81
AZNM	231.09	228.41	227.96
RMPP	251.85	246.10	238.87

Estimating the Cost of Energy Availability Profiles

Given that the equilibrium mix of generation resources can be quite different with high penetration of wind resources, it is natural to ask what the costs impacts of this changing mix might be. This question is addressed by comparing two hypothetical scenarios. First the total and average

costs of serving the *residual* demand (e.g., that which is left over after the new energy is applied) are calculated under the assumption that new energy appears in a manner consistent with the two wind penetration scenarios described above. In other words, the average cost of constructing and operating thermal plants to meet the demand that is not met by the renewable production is calculated. Second, the same amount of energy is used as in the wind scenarios, but instead assuming that it is applied as a base load supply source. In other words the "new" energy is distributed evenly across all hours.

The results of this calculation are summarized in Table 9.10. The columns labeled "As wind" refer to the same wind distributions that have been applied to previous results, and those labeled "as base load" show the results for the evenly distributed energy. Because the more volatile wind profiles require the construction of fewer base load plants and less frequent operation of peaking plants, average costs are higher under the wind profiles. In California, average costs from the variability of supply increase about 4% ($3/MWh) under 14% wind penetration and close to 9% ($7/MWh) with high wind penetration. In the high-penetration RMPP region, costs rise close to 25% under the high-wind-penetration scenario.

Table 9.10. Impact of intermittency on average thermal costs ($/MWh)

	New energy 14% of CEMS load		New energy 28% of CEMS load	
	As base load	As wind	As base load	As wind
CA	75.73	78.61	81.87	88.92
NWPP	57.70	59.20	59.02	63.56
AZNM	59.89	61.05	60.71	63.37
RMPP	57.71	63.09	62.28	85.11
	With carbon at $25/ton			
CA	100.26	102.78	106.46	107.18
NWPP	82.16	83.57	83.15	87.31
AZNM	84.82	85.76	85.56	87.61
RMPP	83.43	88.20	88.43	104.92

Conclusions

The increasing deployment of renewable resources whose intermittent production is determined by natural forces will reshape the economics of power generation in developed electricity markets. This chapter has presented calculations on what the optimal mix of major conventional generation sources would be under various assumptions of end-use demand and penetration of wind generation. Data on actual demand for thermal generation in the western United States were combined with highly detailed estimates of production from new wind resources for this region of the country. The result is a load shape with relatively higher spreads between peak and average demand for thermal production. As demonstrated in the equilibrium model, the amount of coal-fired base load production that would be an economical equilibrium investment steadily declines as wind penetration increases. The reliance on the low-capital-cost combustion turbine technology increases.

Another key change in the economics of power systems will come from the rising importance of intermittent production as a driver of market prices. As these simulations demonstrate, the availability (or lack) of wind resources will be an important contributor to market clearing prices. The normal relationship between end-use demand levels and market prices becomes redefined as wind resources grow to take a substantial share of the market. Implications of this are

that wind resources that are "typical," in the sense that their output is correlated with the bulk of other wind resources, will earn less, and the total capacity of wind resources is ramped up. Their production will be correlated with hours of surplus and therefore increasingly less correlated with prices. In the presence of a capacity market, this effect is more muted. This is because capacity markets—at least at present—award capacity payments based on availability during high-demand periods, rather than high-price periods. This too may change, however, as the underlying economics of the energy markets become more strongly influenced by the ebbs and flows of intermittent generation.

Overall, increasing reliance on intermittent resources creates, or increases, costs in a fashion similar to that caused by fluctuating end-use demand. In planning to serve a system where consumption fluctuates widely, firms must turn to resources that are more flexible, but also more expensive on an average cost basis. While the added costs associated with fluctuating end-use demand can be greatly mitigated by enabling price-responsive consumption, the intermittency of renewable supply is a fact of nature. Storage technologies can play a valuable role here, and estimates such as those developed in this chapter can provide an indication of the potential value of such storage options.

Although the analysis in this chapter was grounded in data taken from actual energy markets, it is important to recognize the limitations of this exercise. Two important elements of some electricity markets are missing here, although their effects work in opposite directions. The short-term operational constraints of thermal generation units have not been modeled. The presence of such constraints would tend to favor the nimble combustion turbine technology even more heavily. Also not modeled is the potential reallocation of production from energy-limited resources, namely hydroelectric. In the Pacific Northwest in particular, this will be an important resource that can go a long way toward counteracting the effects of intermittent generation. In fact, even with these limitations, the effects of wind penetration in the NWPP region are relatively minor in contrast to the wind-rich but hydro-poor Rocky Mountain region. The potential for increased trade among the regions also has not been modeled, although such trade will be limited by the availability of transmission capacity.

Of course, the real western United States is not starting from scratch in building its investment portfolios. Outside of California, coal-fired generation is currently a mainstay of electric companies west of the Mississippi. To the extent that these results portend changes in the economics of these technologies, they would affect the earnings of the owners of these technologies more than the actual mix of generation resources.

Appendix: An Equilibrium Model of Generation Investment

This appendix describes the technical derivation of the equilibrium investment model employed for the results presented above. Each conventional generation technology, indexed by i, features a marginal cost c_i and fixed cost of capacity F_i. Firms invest in capacity that serves a market with demand that fluctuates over time periods $t \in (1 \ldots T)$ with some degree of price elasticity. Demand at time period $Q_t(p_t)$ is represented as:

$$Q_t(p_t) = a_t - f(p_t)$$

where a_t is an additive shift of demand and $f(p_t)$ is a function of market price p_t.

The perfectly competitive firms in the model continue to add production in any given hour, and capacity overall, as long as the revenues from adding the production or capacity exceed the costs. In equilibrium, therefore, production levels in any hour will be set such that the marginal cost of production equals the market price. This equilibrium point can be represented with the following complementarity condition:

$$q_{it} \geq 0 \perp p_t - c_i - \psi_{it} \leq 0 \; \forall \; i, t \quad (9.1)$$

where ψ_{it} represents the equilibrium shadow value of the capacity of technology i and will never be positive if price is below marginal costs c_i. This is the shadow price on the constraint that production be no greater than installed capacity, as reflected in the following condition:

$$\psi_{it} \geq 0 \perp q_{i\,t} - K_i \leq 0 \; \forall \; i, t \quad (9.2)$$

Equation (9.1) is therefore equivalent to setting price equal to marginal operating costs as long as production quantities are below the capacity constraint K_i. The equilibrium level of investment will arise from the condition that the value of a marginal unit of capacity equals the cost of that capacity.

$$K_i \geq 0 \perp F_i - \Sigma_t \psi_{it} \leq 0 \; \forall \; i \quad (9.3)$$

where $\Sigma_t \psi_{it}$ represents the cumulative value of an extra unit of capacity type i aggregated over all time periods. Recall that this value is zero for a given period if the capacity is unneeded in that period, which in this model is equivalent to prices falling below the marginal cost of production of technology i.

The equilibrium level of investment and production can be found by simultaneously solving for the above three conditions. These conditions form a complementarity problem (see Cottle et al. 1992) of size $t \times i$. The following sections describe the data used in formulating the empirical model.

Market Demand

Demand is represented with the partial-log function:

$$Q_{rt}(p_{rt}) = a_{rt} - b_r \ln(p_{rt})$$

where *r* is used to denote the region. The value for *b* was set at 800 for CA, NWPP, and AZNM, and a value of 400 was used for the smaller RMPA. The price elasticity for this functional form of demand is equal to b_r / Q_r, so at the mean observed demand level (summarized in Table 9.1), elasticity is about 0.05 in each market. In other words, a nonzero but still very modest level of demand response is assumed. One advantage of this functional form of demand is that its convexity implies little price response at levels around the marginal costs of generation, but more response when prices reach "scarcity" levels over \$500/MWh.

Price Caps and Capacity Payments

The above modeling framework imposes two significant assumptions to reach its equilibrium. First, at least some degree of price response from end-use demand is assumed. Second, equilibrium energy prices are not constrained in any way and are allowed to rise in order to balance supply and demand.

In modeling a stylized capacity market, the above model is modified in several ways. First, the price cap is represented with the addition of a large capacity "fringe" technology with a marginal cost of \$1,000/MWh. In other words, in addition to actual thermal technologies, *i*, there is an additional complementarity condition similar to equation (9.1) without the capacity constraint on production:

$$q_{CAPt} \geq 0 \perp c_{CAP} - p_t \leq 0 \ \forall \ t \quad (9.4)$$

where q_{CAPt} is positive only if the price cap level c_{CAP} is binding. The quantity q_{CAPt} can be thought of as the energy shortfall caused by the price cap, to be dealt with through either demand rationing or out-of-market transactions. To allow for capacity payments, equation (9.3) is modified so that the annual fixed costs of entry equal energy market revenues *plus* the capacity payment:

$$K_i \geq 0 \perp F_i - CAP\_PAY - \Sigma_t \psi_{it} \leq 0 \quad (9.5)$$

The capacity market equilibrium is therefore represented by the simultaneous solution of conditions (9.1), (9.2), (9.4), and (9.5).

Revenues to Wind Producers

Earnings of the average wind profile are calculated by multiplying the output of wind production by the market price for each period. In other words, the energy market earnings of such a portfolio can be expressed as

$$\Sigma_t \, p_{rt} \star CF_{rt} \star Capacity_r \quad (9.6)$$

where CF refers to the capacity factor of wind in region *r* at time *t*.

Notes

1. Private independent power producers (IPPs) own 83% of cumulative wind capacity in the United States (Wiser and Bolinger 2009). The passage of the Emergency Economic Stabilization Act in November 2008 could constitute a major shift in this trend. Among the act's many provisions was the extension of investment tax credit (ITC) for certain forms of renewable generation. The act also allows, for the first time, utility companies to take advantage of the ITC, which had previously been reserved only for nonutility producers.

2. The CEMS data are available at www.epa.gov/cems. The Platts datasets, POWERDAT and BASECASE, are available via paid subscription service at www.platts.com.

3. The study assumes a 15% total renewable penetration, but only half of that is estimated to come from wind. However, in 2007, about half of the existing energy currently generated in the WECC came from non-CEMS sources. So the wind portion of our residual demand profiles is roughly 7.5% of total load in the base case, and 15% under the assumption of doubled wind capacity.

4. The mechanisms and levels for limiting prices varies by market. Markets in the eastern U.S. technically limit offer prices to \$1,000/MWh. In theory market clearing prices can rise above this level, but they have not in practice done so. One hypothesis (Joskow 2005) is that actions taken by operators to preserve reliability also coincidently limit prices below "scarcity" levels required to recoup investment costs.

5. An example of such a calculation for the New York ISO region can be found in NERA (2007).

6. The newly adopted California rule also uses an *exceedance* measure, rather than a capacity factor.

This means that the capacity payment is based on the percentage of peak hours in which production exceeds a given threshold (e.g., 70%) of nameplate capacity. Using the data in this discussion, this measure gave extreme results, so instead the focus here is on a measure of peak hour capacity factor.

7. Recall that these are their annual entry costs, and the equilibrium conditions equilibrate net operating costs with these annual fixed costs.

8. The $1,000/MWh price cap was almost never binding in the NWPP and AZNM regions; therefore, the results for the energy-only market and capacity markets are virtually the same. These markets have no "missing money," and thus no capacity payment was necessary even with the price cap in place.

References

Ando, Amy W., and Karen L. Palmer. 1998. Getting on the Map: The Political Economy of State-Level Electricity Restructuring. Working paper 98–19-REV. Washington, DC: Resources for the Future.

Borenstein, Severin. 2005. The Long-Run Efficiency of Real-Time Electricity Pricing. *Energy Journal* 26 (3): 93–116.

Borenstein Severin, and James B. Bushnell. 2000. Electricity Restructuring: Deregulation or Reregulation? *Regulation* 23 (2).

Bushnell, James. 2005. Electricity Resource Adequacy: Matching Policies and Goals. *Electricity Journal* 18 (8): 11–21.

Cottle, R. W., J.-S. Pang, and R. Stone. 1992. *The Linear Complementarity Problem*. London: Academic Press.

Cramton, Peter. 2003. Electricity Market Design: The Good, the Bad, and the Ugly. Presented at the 36th Annual Hawaii International Conference on Systems Science. January 2003, Hawaii.

Cramton, Peter, and Steven Stoft. 2005. A Capacity Market that Makes Sense. *Electricity Journal* 18 (7): 43–54.

Ellerman, A. D, P. L. Joskow, Richard Schmalensee, J. P. Montero and E. Bailey 2000. *Markets for Clean Air*. Cambridge: Cambridge University Press.

EIA (Energy Information Administration). 2007. *Annual Energy Outlook*. Washington, DC.

Hogan, William H. 2005. On an "Energy Only" Market Design for Electricity Resource Adequacy. Working paper. Cambridge, MA: Harvard University. http://ksghome.harvard.edu/~whogan/Hogan_Energy_Only_092305.pdf (accessed 12 October, 2009).

Joskow, Paul L. 1997. Restructuring, Competition and Regulatory Reform in the U.S. Electricity Sector. *Journal of Economic Perspectives* 11 (3): 119–138.

———. 2005. The Difficult Transition to Competitive Electricity Markets in the United States. In *Electricity Deregulation: Choices and Challenges*, edited by James Griffin and Steve Puller. Chicago: University of Chicago Press, 31–97.

Joskow, Paul L., and Richard Schmalensee. 1985. *Markets for Power: An Analysis of Electrical Utility Deregulation*. Cambridge, MA: MIT Press.

Kahn, Edward E. 1988. *Electric Utility Planning and Regulation*. Washington, DC: American Council for an Energy-Efficient Economy.

Lamont, Alan D. 2008. Assessing the Long-Term System Value of Intermittent Electric Generation Technologies. *Energy Economics* 30: 1208–1231.

Nemet, Gregory F. 2006. Beyond the Learning Curve: Factors Influencing Cost-Reductions in Photovoltaics. *Energy Policy* 34: 3218–3232.

NERA (National Economic Research Associates). 2007. Independent Study to Establish Parameters of the ICAP Demand Curve for the New York Independent System Operator. www.nyiso.com/public/webdocs/committees/ (accessed October 14, 2009).

NERC (National Electricity Reliability Council). 2009. 2009 Long-Term Reliability Assessment. www.nerc.com/files/2009_LTRA.pdf (accessed October 14, 2009).

Nickell, Bradley M. 2008. TEPPC Renewable Energy Cases: Renewable Generation Information. Salt Lake City: Western Electricity Coordinating Council.

Oren, Shmuel S. 2005. Ensuring Generation Adequacy in Competitive Electricity Markets. In *Electricity Deregulation: Choices and Challenges*, edited by James Griffin and Steve Puller. Chicago: University of Chicago Press, 388–414.

Schweppe, Fred C., Michael C. Caramanis, Richard D. Tabors, and Roger E. Bohn. 1988. *Spot Pricing of Electricity*. Boston: Kluwer Academic Publishers.

Stern, Nicholas. 2006. *The Stern Review: The Economics of Climate Change*. London: HM Treasury.

Wiser, Ryan, and Galen Barbose. 2008. Renewable Portfolio Standards in the United States, Berkeley, CA: Lawrence Berkeley National Laboratory. http://eetd.lbl.gov/ea/ems/re-pubs-html (accessed September 9, 2009).

Wiser, Ryan, and Mark Bolinger. 2009. *2008 Wind Technologies Market Report*. DOE/GO-102009–2868. Washington, DC: U.S. Department of Energy.

Wolfram, Catherine. 2005. The Efficiency of Electricity Generation in the U.S. after Restructuring. In *Electricity Deregulation: Choices and Challenges*, edited by James Griffin and Steve Puller. Chicago: University of Chicago Press, 227–255.

10

Developing a Supergrid

Christian von Hirschhausen

Harnessing renewables effectively requires transporting electricity generated by renewable energy to centers of demand. The difficulty of doing this is sometimes underestimated in the policy debate on renewable targets. Renewable energy sources are "fuel from heaven" only if the derived products, mainly electricity, are delivered to the customer's locale on demand. In this context, the concept of a "supergrid," or transmission overlay network, is being intensely debated on both sides of the Atlantic. This concept has been propelled to center stage by politically bold statements about the future share of large-scale renewable energy sources in a carbon-constrained world. In addition, China has recently started to develop long-distance high-voltage direct current transmission to transport more hydroelectricity from the center of the country to demand locations on its east coast. As the political debate accelerates, however, the pros and cons of supergrids must be objectively assessed and the different, sometimes competing, visions put into a comparative perspective.

This chapter discusses issues related to the development of supergrids that are currently debated in the context of harnessing renewable energy. The term "supergrid" refers to the assimilation of a high-voltage direct and alternating current (HVDC and HVAC) network overlay with the existing traditional alternating current (AC) network, with the objective of integrating large-scale renewable energy sources (L-RES) into the grid. This chapter does not address the link between renewables and existing low-voltage networks, nor does it cover operational issues, balancing, or other topics at the local low-voltage level. Instead, it highlights some of the key issues, conceptually and by using a variety of existing concepts for potential supergrids. A distinction is made between studies focusing more on the harnessing aspect of renewables, such as the Solar Grand Plan, and those that include a more serious network component, such as the Joint Coordinated System Plan developed for a group of North American system operators. An inverse relation exists: the more a supergrid study looks at the obstacles to developing the appropriate transmission infrastructure, the less such studies tend to prefer supergrids, instead arguing in favor of more decentralized, regional solutions.

If it is commonly accepted that network development is important for harnessing L-RES, few researchers to date have looked closely at the engineering-economic aspects of expansion projects on both sides of the Atlantic. The concept of linking European electricity markets to renewable energy potential in the Middle East and North African (MENA) region via HVDC transmission is particularly interesting and is presented as an in-depth case study. The European Economic Association–Middle East North Africa (EEA-MENA) supergrid interconnection plan for 2050 is a variant of the Desertec project and the Mediterranean Solar Plan (MSP), but with its own distinctive features. Thus, in addition to including different amounts of concentrated solar power (CSP) electricity imported from the MENA region to Europe by constructing a supergrid, the study also considers northern European offshore wind and hydro resources and finds that the consideration of a truly European market for renewable electricity changes the topology of the optimal supergrid significantly, tending toward more regional clustering. Also highlighted is an important distributional issue that arises between "winners" of more transmission lines, whose electricity prices fall, and "losers," whose prices increase.

Next, several critical issues for the further development of supergrids are examined. Transmission investment has been problematic in both the United States and Europe, and the development of a supergrid poses even more complex long-term challenges to industry and policymakers. For industry, a balance has to be struck between lucrative investments in generation and transmission assets and the economic, political, and regulatory risks related thereto. Policymakers, on the other hand, face the challenge of having to design instruments and regulatory frameworks to achieve very long-term objectives given high uncertainty and widely diverging incentives between stakeholders, such as federal versus regional levels and producers versus consumers. Surprisingly little attention has been given to long-term planning mechanisms, a critical element in such complex projects. Planning and regulatory issues are closely related to financing issues, and the optimal organizational structure for a supergrid has yet to be identified. The discussion also includes a political economy interpretation of the obstacles to overcome, among other compensating mechanisms between potential winners and losers.

The chapter therefore concludes on a skeptical note. The findings that have been presented temper the enthusiasm that generally accompanies supergrid concepts: although the underlying objectives for their development may be well founded, the large number of obstacles makes a rapid emergence of supergrids unlikely. Instead, it seems more reasonable to focus on a stepwise, bottom-up approach by which transmission expansion follows a gradual, more traditional path.

Stylized Supergrid Projects in the United States and Europe/North Africa

Typology of Supergrids

The concept of supergrids is closely related to attempts to tap distributed renewable energy sources and thus pave the way to a low-carbon electricity system. All studies on sustainable energy systems acknowledge the need for large-scale high-voltage transmission. Jacobsen and Delucchi (2009) have sketched out "a path to sustainable energy by 2030 in which wind, water, and solar technologies could provide 100% of the world's energy, eliminating all fossil fuels." This vision also includes a decarbonized transportation sector. The authors stress the importance of transmission: "each nation needs to be willing to invest in a robust, long-distance transmission system that can carry large quantities of wind, water, and solar technologies from remote regions, where it is often greatest—such as the Great Plains for wind and the desert South West for solar in the United States—to centers of consumption, typically cities" (65).

Although a precise definition for the term "supergrid" does not exist, this chapter follows the Jacobsen–Delucchi suggestion of what is required to make a large-scale renewables-based energy system workable in terms of transmission capacity. More generally, there is a common understanding that supergrids have become synonymous with transcontinental electricity networks, tying in the existing high-voltage grid.

Also, the term "transmission overlay" is used to characterize a portfolio of high-voltage transmission additions to existing electricity networks that together serve and link entire regions and markets (Kaupa 2009; Midwest ISO et al. 2008). Supergrids are thus characterized by the following:

- flexibility in system balancing;
- high capacity for bulk power transmission; and
- geographically long distances.

In addition to the prevailing alternating current (AC) technology in power transmission, HVDC or Flexible AC Transmission Systems (FACTS)[1] technologies are increasingly used in supergrids. These hybrid systems can improve transmission capacity and system stability by bypassing heavily loaded AC systems. The relevance of these features increases with the prospective integration of large-scale renewable generation capacities that produce higher fluctuations in loads. Moreover, power generation becomes increasingly distributed and a growing number of generation capacities are located far from load centers, leading to greater transmission distances. In this context, HVDC offers two important advantages over AC technologies:

- On the one hand, higher bulk power capacities can be realized per line. Thus fewer lines are necessary, an important factor in the public's acceptance of new transmission projects, which is often low because of the not-in-my-backyard (NIMBY) mindset.
- On the other hand, HVDC lines have lower power losses over long distances, as shown in Table 10.1. Despite the higher initial investment costs of HVDC and FACTS, these characteristics make DC bulk power transmission (≥ 1,000 megawatts) more economical than AC for transmission distances above 600 kilometers (Claus et al. 2008). HVDC transmission technology is rapidly evolving. It allows longer water crossings and does not require phase synchronization.[2]

Table 10.1. Characteristics of high-voltage transmission technologies

Voltage	735 kV AC	500 kV DC	800 kV DC
Power losses per 1,000 km line	6.7%	6.6%	3.5%
Transmission capacity	3 GW	3 GW	6.4 GW

Source: Siemens 2009, *4*

The multiple visions of future supergrid developments can be classified according to technical, economic, or institutional criteria. To structure the subsequent discussion, electricity generation and transmission are differentiated as follows:

- generation: supergrid projects that rely on one source of renewable generation (singlesource) or integrate a variety of L-RES (multiple sources); and
- transmission: gradual extension of existing AC with additional local and interregional power lines or radical changes that include a transmission overlay with multigigawatt "highways" interconnecting entire continents.

Table 10.2 classifies the major existing visions and concepts for the United States and Europe based on these criteria. The subsequent sections review studies with different grades of detail and focus, ranging from conceptual ideas to more detailed calculations, and outline some of the most relevant supergrid visions. This discussion follows the structure in the table, starting with the U.S. projects and then looking at those in Europe and North Africa.

Supergrid Projects in the United States

Following are some of the major supergrid projects in the United States. For other U.S. supergrid projects, see the survey by Tierney (2008).

The Solar Grand Plan

Zweibel et al. (2008) and Fthenakis et al. (2009) developed a vision of a solar-based supergrid

Table 10.2. Studies for large-scale integration of renewable energy sources

Energy Source	Geographic approach	
	Continental	Regional
Single	Zweibel et al. (2008), A Solar Grand Plan	Midwest ISO et al. (2008), Joint Coordinated Sys-tem Plan 2008
	Trieb et al. (2009), Characterisation of Solar Electricity Import Corridors from MENA to Europe (Desertec, Mediterranean Solar Plan)	Office for Metropolitan Architecture (OMA 2009), Masterplan Zeekracht
	Airtricity (2006), European Offshore Supergrid Proposal	
Multiple	Trieb et al. (2006), Trans-Mediterranean Inter-connection for Concentrating Solar Power	Krapels (2009), Integrating 200,000 MWs of Renewable Energy into the US Power Grid
	AWEA and SEIA (2009),[a] Green Power Superhighways	Egerer et al. (2009), Sustainable Energy Networks for Europe

[a]This study builds on a wind-only study for the United States; see AEP 2007.

across the United States, called the "Solar Grand Plan." In essence, it is based on a combination of photovoltaic (PV) facilities spread across different areas and concentrated solar power (CSP) systems in the Southwest, where the highest average solar irradiation in the country can be harnessed (Figure 10.1).

The Solar Grand Plan also includes a substantial amount of compressed-air energy storage (CAES) located close to demand. New HVDC lines would connect the Southwest to the rest of the country. The technologies, scale, and learning for a project of this size are substantial; thus 2,940 GW of PV should be developed through a national energy plan built around solar power. Increased thin-film module efficiency from 10% to 14% and reduced installation costs from $4 to $1.20 per watt (W) in 2050 would lead to levelized electricity costs of $0.05 per kilowatt-hour (kWh). A corresponding development is also expected for CSP, though at a somewhat smaller scale: cumulated 558 GW in 2050 will lead to

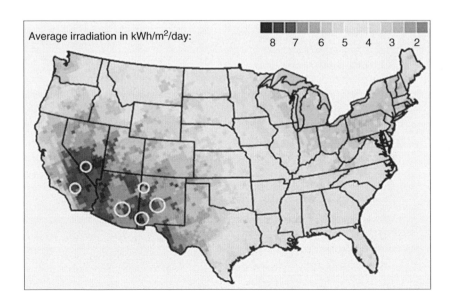

Source: Zweibel et al. 2008, *53*

Figure 10.1. Solar radiation in the United States

decreasing installation costs from $5.30 to $3.70/W. Thus electricity generation costs for CSP drop to $0.09/kWh. By 2050, solar power would provide 35% of total energy consumed in the United States and 70% of electricity. If implemented, the Solar Grand Plan would substantially reduce fossil-fuel consumption, CO_2 emissions, and U.S. import dependence. The plan's total costs sum up to $420 billion until 2050.[3] Fthenakis et al. (2009) concentrate on the feasibility of the vision laid out by Zweibel et al. (2008). They refine the proposal of a two-step implementation plan: Stage I (from the present to 2020) comprises a 10-year solar deployment and incentive program that includes guaranteed loans, a mandatory solar portfolio standard for electric utilities, and a solar feed-in tariff scheme. Costs are estimated at $300 billion; this amount would ensure a transition to self-sustained growth in the CSP and PV markets after 2020. Nevertheless, Stage II (from 2020 to 2050) should include a commitment to an annual deployment schedule to sustain growth for renewable technologies.

It is evident that HVDC transmission is a crucial part of the Solar Grand Plan, as 90% of the plan's solar energy production is located in the Southwest. Transmission-wise, the Solar Grand Plan therefore proposes a radical approach: an entirely new HVDC power transmission backbone. Interestingly, no major technical advances are deemed necessary. During Stage I, the first expansion of the DC transmission system would occur, extending the network via existing rights-of-way along interstate highway corridors, which would minimize land acquisition and regulatory hurdles.[4] In Stage II, the remaining extensions would occur. The HVDC transmission companies would not need to be subsidized, because "they would finance construction of lines and converter stations just as they now finance AC lines, earning revenues by delivering electricity" (Zweibel et al. 2008, 57).[5]

However, three issues are not addressed by the authors. First, the role of other L-RES, such as wind power in the Great Plains, as potential competitors to solar power is underrepresented. In this context, it appears questionable that solar power from the Southwest will serve the majority of the U.S. electricity supply until 2050. Second, nationwide transmission planning is key, yet Fthenakis et al. (2009) give a vision of HVDC transmission only for the Southwest. The anatomy of their HVDC transmission overlay does not take into account storage sites, also a key element of the plan. Third, economic analyses of the welfare effects as well as profit considerations have not been included so far.

Wind-Based Transmission Expansion Plan

The Joint Coordinated System Plan 2008 (JCSP'08) contains a wind-based regional transmission expansion plan developed by the system operators Midwest ISO (MISO), Pennsylvania–New Jersey–Maryland Interconnection (PJM), Southwest Power Pool (SPP), Tennessee Valley Authority (TVA), Mid-Continent Area Power Pool (MAPP), and several key members of the Southeastern Electric Reliability Council (SERC). The JCSP evaluates scenarios of a grid overlay in the year 2024 for the Eastern Interconnection. An optimal transmission grid overlay has been modeled for two scenarios of power generation capacity developments: a reference scenario and a 20% wind energy scenario. In both scenarios, the transmission overlay includes 800 kilovolt (kV) HVDC as well as 765 kV, 500 kV, and 345 kV AC lines, but the transmission expansion differs. The reference scenario assumes that the present renewable portfolio standard (RPS) requirements are met in 2024 with local onshore wind resources. The wind scenario assumes a significant enlargement of wind power capacities contributing to 20% of the U.S. Eastern Interconnection energy use.[6] The two scenarios' main assumptions and results are displayed in Table 10.3.

The reference scenario suggests primarily 345 kV line extensions in the Northwest.[7] Preliminary analyses show that the potential benefits from reduced energy costs for consumers in the East exceed incurred costs of approximately $50 billion on an aggregate interregional level in comparison with the present grid configuration. The 20% wind energy scenario shows significantly more high-voltage transmission capacity (see Figure 10.2). Approximately 75% of the conceptual

Table 10.3. JCSP'08 main scenario assumptions and results

		Reference scenario		Wind scenario	
			Percentage		Percentage
New generation expansion capacity (MW)	Wind	58,000	31%	229,000	67%
	Base load steam	76,800	40%	37,200	11%
	Gas CT	49,200	26%	69,600	20%
	Gas CC	4,800	3%	4,800	1%
	Other fossil	1,200	1%	1,200	0%
	Total	190,000	100%	341,800	100%
Transmission overlay (miles)	HVAC	7,109	71%	6,898	48%
	HVDC	2,870	29%	7,582	52%
	Total	9,979	100%	14,480	100%
Transmission capital cost (2024 million $)	Transmission overlay	42,159		72,825	
	Transmission substations	6,401		7,074	

Source: Midwest ISO et al. 2008, 6

transmission overlay consists of 765 kV AC or 800 kV DC. Supported by a network of 345 and 500 kV AC lines as well as several 800 kV DC feeder lines, seven major HVDC lines will trans-port electricity from renewables and thermal plants in the Midwest to the load centers in the East and Southeast.

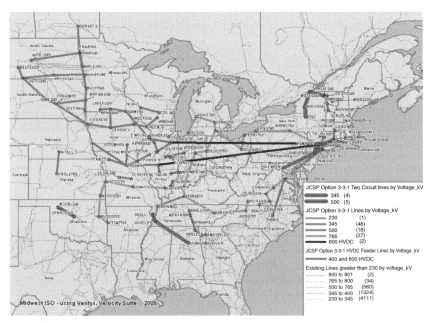

Source: Midwest ISO et al. 2008, 9

Figure 10.2. JCSP'08 wind energy scenario conceptual transmission overlay

Methodologically advanced, the high-renewables scenario for transmission planning can be critically assessed with respect to the concentration on onshore wind. Canadian hydro potential as well as offshore wind capacities should be more strongly reflected in such a scenario to determine future transmission expansion. Midwest ISO et al. (2008) also recommend that future analyses should pay more attention to local and decentralized energy generation scenarios rather than long-distance production and transmission; this would affect the type, location, and cost of necessary transmission infrastructure and could change the associated social benefits.

Integrating Wind, Solar, and Biomass Generation

AWEA and SEIA (2009) and Krapels (2009) are prominent examples of multisource studies, with a focus on wind and solar energy, as well as some geothermal and biomass. In contrast to the Solar Grand Plan project, Krapels adopts a bottom-up, regional approach to transmission expansion based on the belief that "the structure and governance of the power industry in the United States falls along regional lines, strongly suggesting efforts to meet the environmental goals should be regional" (2009, 4). The diversity of the states' interests, political alignments, and resources suggests that any federal policy should only define broad objectives and allow the states and regions to determine how to achieve the target.

Krapels's analysis assumes that a national RPS of 20% would require about 200,000 MW of wind, solar, and biomass generation capacities. This, in turn, would necessitate significant investment in generation facilities and an overhaul of the transmission systems to take the renewable energy to market and achieve the following:

1. on the East and West Coasts, connect nearby terrestrial and offshore wind resources to the population centers;
2. in the Midwest and Southwest, connect the highest-quality wind to inland population centers on both sides of the Continental Divide;
3. in Texas, connect the wind and solar in the North and West to the population centers in the Center and South; and
4. in the South, where wind resources are meager, allow nuclear power plants to meet RPS and carbon targets (Krapels 2009, *4*).

Krapels rejects the economic and political feasibility of a coast-to-coast "electricity superhighway" and argues for a series of initiatives from coastal states that would essentially confine the superhighway to a smaller area complemented with a system enabling the coastal states to harness near-terrestrial and offshore wind (see Figure 10.3). This coastal complement would eliminate the need for midwestern wind delivered via the proposed national electricity superhighway. According to Krapels, regional transmission planning in the United States has not led to the desired interstate transmission expansion to increase competition, improve security of supply, and lower average consumer prices.[8] These traditional mechanisms will not allow L-RES to be built at the envisioned scale and thus must be addressed in detail. Despite the regional approach, institutional hurdles remain the most challenging part of transmission expansion.

Supergrid Projects in Europe/North Africa

This section looks at some of the major supergrid projects in Europe and North Africa. Several European Union-sponsored projects also assess some supergrid proposals, such as SUSPLAN and the SOLID-DER project. Other ongoing or recent studies include WIND FORCE 12 by Greenpeace, Tradewind, and DENA 2.[9]

Submarine Wind Energy Superhighways for Europe

In Europe, different projects for large-scale wind integration are currently on the agenda, based on offshore transmission lines. The vision by Airtricity (2006), a wind power developer and operator, integrates large offshore wind capacities along the continent's coastlines into the European electricity system via a submarine grid of HVDC

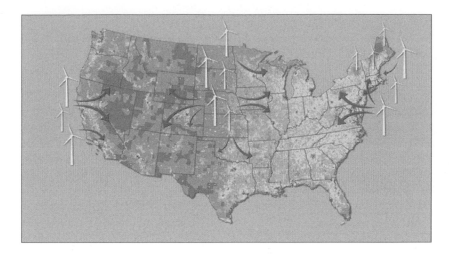

Source: Krapels 2009, *4*

Figure 10.3. Integrating 200,000 MW of renewable energy in the U.S. grid **(exemplified for wind power)**

lines (see Figure 10.4). The connection of distributed wind over long distances reduces wind
farms' power variability. It has been shown that
power output correlation decreases as distance
between wind farms increases (see, e.g., Sinden,
2007), because wind patterns are regional and
change over longer distances as a result of areas of
high and low barometric pressure. The question,
however, is to what extent wind power will prove
to be a reliable and predictable source of energy
(Airtricity 2006). Considering the demand side,
the differences in lifestyles, time zones, and uses of
electricity will lead to elongated peak demand and
therefore result in a greater capacity credit for the
supergrid than for offshore wind farms being connected to a single national electricity system.
Moreover, the study argues that the HVDC submarine grid would resolve much of the complexities associated with achieving a single European
electricity market, as the supergrid would serve as
an interconnector among national markets.

The study delivers neither capacity projections nor cost estimations for the proposed pan-
European submarine supergrid. Instead, it suggests an initial project in the North Sea as a
nucleus for further HVDC expansion.[10]
Airtricity's (2006) calculation for this 10 GW initial project deserves critical evaluation with
respect to two issues. First, the project's economics are strongly dependent on the assumed finance

Source: Airtricity 2006, *9*

Figure   10.4.   Airtricity's   European   offshore
supergrid proposal

structure, but the proposed debt interest rate of
5.5% per annum seems rather low for a project of
this size and scope. Hence it implicitly requires
financial guarantees by public institutions to leverage private capital. Second, because a predictable
yield for investors is necessary to attract investment, it will likely require a fixed electricity price
for wind power and preferred feed-in guarantees.
Institutional and political barriers will remain the
major roadblocks to such supranational agreements.

The North Sea Wind Energy Super Ring

A less ambitious and more focused project is the North Sea Wind Energy Super Ring. The idea is to develop a meshed transmission grid in the North Sea to better connect the grids of north-west Europe, the United Kingdom, and Scandinavia. This interconnection should facilitate exploiting the potential of the North Sea's wind resources, as well as reducing the problem of intermittent wind availability.

One of several concepts has been designed by the Office for Metropolitan Architecture (OMA) for the Society for Nature and Environment (Natuur en Milieu 2009). The authors calculate a theoretical annual electricity generation potential of 13,400 terawatt-hours (TWh) from wind power in the North Sea. The Master Plan for the North Sea develops the structure of a HVDC ring to harness the wind potential by connecting to the load centers on the European continent and the British Isles (Figure 10.5). Including seven countries, the ring structure allows flexible dispatch and integrates Scandinavian pump storage facilities. Moreover, exploited submarine gas and oil fields in the North Sea could potentially serve as compressed air storage facilities. The meshed structure increases security of supply in comparison with single transmission lines. If the Energy Super Ring were implemented, it is estimated that Europe could reach energy independence from Russia and the Gulf states in 2050 (Natuur en Milieu 2009).

Although this is an interesting approach, several questions remain concerning its implementation according to OMA (2009). The plan includes no projections about the actual wind power capacity needed, nor does it specify the necessary transmission line capacity. It also does not consider the possible use of submarine gas and oil fields for future carbon capture and storage (CCS). Hence compressed air storage capacity could be less than expected. Finally, the plan does not indicate the extent to which Scandinavian hydropower reservoirs are able to store wind capacity from the proposed project.

The Desertec Project

The Desertec concept, a mainly solar-based, radical transmission expansion project, is being devel-

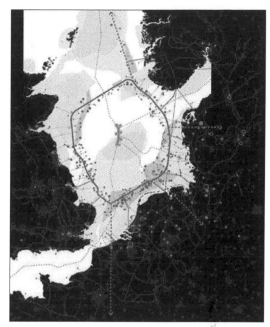

Source: OMA 2009, 9

Figure 10.5. The North Sea wind power transmission ring

oped jointly by the Trans-Mediterranean Renewable Energy Cooperation (TREC), a network of scientists, politicians, businesspeople, and the German society of the Club of Rome.[11] The technical studies were carried out by the German Aerospace Center (DLR) and financed by the German Ministry for the Environment (BMU) (see Trieb et al. 2005, 2006).[12]

The Desertec project focuses on the generation of about 2,400 TWh per year of mainly CSP by 2050. This is based on generation cost reductions for CSP, where electricity costs are expected to drop from 9.8 euro cents (U.S. 13.3 cents) per kWh in 2015 to 5.5 euro cents (7.5 cents) per kWh in 2050.[13] About 700 TWh of this solar electricity will be supplied to the European Union (EU) via a new HVDC overlay network. For this, Trieb et al. (2009, 5) assume an HVDC transfer capacity of 20 × 5 GW cables. Investment is in the same range as for the U.S. Solar Grand Plan, €400 billion ($545 billion) until 2050, of which €45 billion ($61 billion) is dedicated to the HVDC overlay network. Figure 10.6 shows the structural network that has been developed using

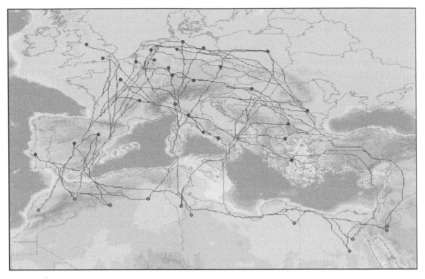

Source: Trieb et al. 2009, *124*

Figure 10.6. The Desertec HVDC overlay network **(physical map)**

least-cost algorithms with several constraints. An HVDC core connects 11 CSP production sites in the MENA region with 27 European demand centers, including corridors for exports of Saudi Arabian CSP to destinations as far away as Milan, Paris, and even London.

The Desertec project is more explicit about the institutional structure of the transmission lines than its U.S. equivalent, the Solar Grand Plan. It proposes the creation of an international transmission association to be owned by the companies participating in the construction and operation of the HVDC lines. The Nabucco Gas Pipeline International GmbH, a project company set up to develop a multinational natural gas pipeline from Turkey to Austria, is considered a role model. The transmission project association would be responsible for planning, financing, constructing, operating, and marketing of the supergrid. A close relation between the national and interregional transmission system operators (TSOs) would need to be ensured either through direct ownership or contractual arrangements.

The main criticism of the trans-Mediterranean supergrid as proposed in Trieb et al. (2009) is related to other L-RES deployment. The proposed HVDC network overlay does not take wind and hydropower in the North Sea and Scandinavia into account. Thus the authors imply that solar power from the MENA region can compete with these renewables in the United Kingdom and the countries adjacent to the North Sea. Considering the potential for other L-RES, the supergrid's layout (as shown in Figure 10.6) appears questionable. In addition, the implementation of the proposed HVDC grid overlay, stretching from Saudi Arabia to the United Kingdom, seems challenging in terms of its institutional and political obstacles even under the proposed institutional design.

Evaluating the Supergrid Proposals

The concepts of the supergrids reviewed here show differing foci and grades of detail. Some studies (AWEA and SEIA 2009; Zweibel et al. 2008) concentrate on renewable energy capacity development and address transmission expansion for integrating L-RES into the existing grid as a necessary side condition. Other studies (e.g., Midwest ISO et al. 2008) explicitly model future transmission overlays for different generation scenarios, accounting for consumer benefits and reliability issues.

While none of these studies is beyond criticism, all make one point clear: the supergrid projects require reaching an operational level of transmission planning and regulation. Surprisingly, in none of the numerous studies surveyed for this chapter is there any reference to technology as an obstacle. There is also a large consensus that transmission issues are critical, whereas expanding the use of renewable energy sources as such is less difficult. This holds even though the pure investment sums for tapping the renewable energies significantly exceed the transmission investments.

Few studies surveyed include an economic analysis beyond some rough financial indicators, such as costs. In the United States, Midwest ISO et al. (2008) calculate consumer benefits under constraints of security of supply. For Europe, Trieb et al. (2009) provide some cost predictions but do not address welfare considerations. The next section therefore explores these aspects in the analysis of another specific project, the EEA-MENA supergrid, before the discussion turns to the general issues faced by all of the supergrid projects.

Case Study: EEA-MENA 2050 Supergrid

This case study is an engineering-economic analysis of the European–North African Supergrid (EEA-MENA 2050). It proposes a welfare-optimal HVDC extension plan under assumed CSP capacity deployment in the MENA region, using a network model of the European electricity market. The model maximizes the value of total welfare less the annuity for the selected transmission lines to determine optimal transmission corridors. It also mirrors the evolution of a trans-Mediterranean supergrid in discrete time steps of 10 years until the year 2050.[14]

Modeling Approach

The subsequent simulation, applies an engineering-economic DC load flow model based on ELMOD (Leuthold et al. 2008). ELMOD is a welfare maximization model with technical constraints, including thermal limits, electricity losses, loop flows, and security constraints. The applied model consists of 105 regional zones, represented by nodes. The grid consists of interzonal high-voltage lines connected to the nodes by auxiliary nodes and lines. Each main node has its own demand and generation portfolio. The existing European electricity grid, comprising the UCTE region, NORDEL, the United Kingdom transmission system operator, and other UKTSO members, is modeled, with the model limited to the high-voltage level (132 to 750 kV). The existing AC grid includes all existing interzonal links and high-voltage AC lines according to ENTSO-E (2008) and the other European TSOs. Concerning the future development of the AC grid, all projects planned by the European system operators until 2030 are assumed to be completed (ENTSO-E 2009).[15] Further AC grid expansion is not implemented because of the lack of available information beyond 2030. In addition to the AC grid, existing DC connections are implemented in the model with its technology-specific parameters.[16]

Electricity demand is characterized by a reference demand and a reference price. While the reference demand is given by the scenarios, the reference price equals the costs of the marginal plant under base load conditions. A linear inverse demand function is determined for each region with an assumed price elasticity of 0.1. The CSP-exporting regions are modeled as simple export nodes.

Generation capacities comprise 14 types of plant according to three groups: fuel-fired (nuclear, lignite, hard coal, gas-fired combined cycle gas turbines [CCGT], gas, oil, and biomass); renewable generation (run of river, wind on- and offshore, PV, CSP, and geothermal plants); and storage (hydropower reservoirs). As the fluctuating character of wind generation cannot be determined by season or time of day, three cases—high, medium, and low—are included for each load level. This leads to a total of 24 model cases, distinguishing among seasons, day and night, demand, and wind availability. All model cases have equal weights.[17] An overview of the endogenous and exogenous model parameters is presented in Table 10.4.

Table 10.4. Exogenous and endogenous parameters of the model

Exogenous	Zonal demand and generation capacity
	CSP generation expansion in MENA and number of HVDC lines
	Marginal costs for generation technologies including CO_2 price[a]
	Extension of AC grid according to existing extension plans until 2030
	Scenario-based evaluation: influence of stronger integration of Scandinavia to Continental Europe via HVDC connections
Endogenous	Determination of the welfare optimal integration strategy for CSP by an assessment of connections from 3 MENA regions to 30 different demand centers in Europe
	Allocation of yearly seasonal hydro storage (reservoirs) generation budget for balancing purposes (wind, demand levels, etc.)

[a] Prices for emissions certificates are based on a review of price projections (see Egerer et al. 2009, *44*). CO_2 prices have been allocated to generation costs for different technologies via technology-specific emission factors.

Scenarios

Given the high variance in any of the parameter estimations until 2050 (e.g., demand, technologies, climate policy), the study is limited to a business-as-usual (BAU) scenario as the reference case and a technological development (TD) scenario that captures the main characteristics of a renewable future as possible boundaries for the EEA-MENA supergrid. Figure 10.7 provides an overview of the generation capacities for the BAU and TD scenarios for 2010–2050. Fossil-fuel price developments are based on current market prices and develop according to fuel-specific escalation rates ranging between 1% and 2.5% per annum (in real terms). In both scenarios, slightly increasing electricity demand is expected, from 3,500 TWh (2008) to 4,200 TWh (2050).

In the BAU scenario, coal, lignite, and nuclear remain almost on the same level as today except in Germany, where nuclear is phased out. The appearance of L-RES is limited: only 60% of European offshore wind and no Scandinavian hydropower potentials are exploited, and CSP

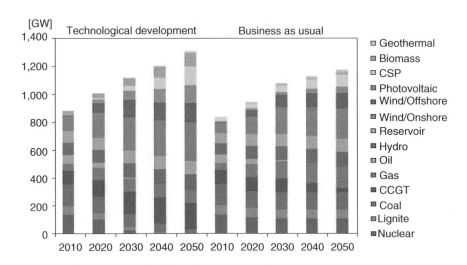

Source: Egerer et al. 2009, *42*

Figure 10.7. Installed capacities for the BAU and TD scenarios, 2010–2050

capacity in the MENA region does not exceed 12 GW until 2050. This development assumes moderate CO_2 certificate prices, with €24 ($33) per metric ton in 2030 and €30 ($41) per ton in 2050. In contrast, the TD scenario adopts a perspective of an 80% reduction of CO_2 emissions by 2050 (base 1990). To realize these targets, an increase of the CO_2 price to €57 ($78) per ton in 2030 and €100 ($136) per ton in 2050 is assumed. Also assumed are intensive technology R&D and that the technical potentials described in terms of harnessing renewables, particularly wind, are attained. Nuclear is phased out, and any potential hydrogen developments are ignored. The deployment of smart grids allows a higher share of local decentralized renewables in addition to the L-RES that are modeled explicitly. Natural gas serves as backup capacity.

In addition to CSP integration in North Africa, other L-RES potential in Europe is reflected, in the TD scenario, by two subscenarios for the integration of wind and hydropower capacities. The first subscenario, A, assumes reinforcement of the grid in addition to the modeled network described above to transport the vast amount of future offshore wind from the North Sea to demand centers in the United Kingdom, France, and Germany. This is reflected in the model by additional transmission in the countries adjacent to the North Sea. In the second subscenario, B, the HVDC lines connecting Scandinavia to the rest of Europe are expanded exogenously to a capacity of 8 GW per connection in 2050. These lines are modeled in addition to the transmission capacity according to subscenario A. Thus subscenario B can be considered to be close to the concept of the North Sea Energy Super Ring discussed above.[18] These two subscenarios allow an examination of the welfare benefits of seasonal hydropower generation from reservoirs as possible balancing power to offshore wind.

Results

Following are the results of the model. First, generation capacities and prices for the BAU and TD scenarios are discussed. The second part proposes welfare maximizing paths for grid expansion in the EEA-MENA supergrid. Third, effects from a stronger integration of the Scandinavian electricity market are considered.

Generation and Prices

In the BAU scenario, coal remains a cheaper alternative to natural gas. With the stronger growth of the CO_2 certificate price in the TD scenario, coal loses its competitiveness against CCGT generation. As the model structure allows only limited peak demand, the gas share in reality might increase as a result of the need for open-cycle gas turbines (OGT) to serve as suppliers for peak demand with only a few full load hours. Whereas in the BAU scenario, 60% of the electricity demand is supplied by fossil fuels, this value decreases to about 35% in the TD scenario. In 2050, CSP delivers about two-thirds of the electricity provided by nuclear today. Biomass as a CO_2-neutral fuel becomes an important source of electricity too. Wind generation is only 25% higher than in the BAU scenario. Being less affected by high CO_2 prices, CCGT becomes the dominant fossil plant in the TD scenario. Its share does not decrease until 2040, as RES capacities continue to grow.

Because of the stronger growth of the price for CO_2 certificates, the TD scenario leads to a stronger increase in the average electricity price,[19] exceeding €120 ($163) per MWh in 2050, almost double the price in the BAU scenario. For the BAU scenario, the remaining CCGT is used only for mid and peak load, where prices are higher than the average electricity price. In the TD scenario, CCGT plants have lower marginal generation costs and replace coal in the mid and base load. The high electricity price can be explained by more frequent use of backup OGT, which have higher marginal costs as a result of their lower efficiency. Finally, the prices also indicate the strong increase of biomass capacity in the TD scenario favored by the steep growth of the CO_2 certificate price.

HVDC Grid Expansion

In the BAU scenario, a CSP capacity of 11.8 GW is installed in Morocco, Algeria, Tunisia, and Libya by 2050. For this limited electricity generation capacity, four transmission cables are built, and the capacity is split in half between the Moroccan and Tunisian export nodes. The first two lines are built in 2030, and the other two are installed in 2050. In 2030, CSP electricity exports from Tunisia to Italy yield only 3.8 euro cents (U.S. 5.2 cents) per kWh cost coverage and, because of higher electricity prices in Spain, 4.4 euro cents (6 cents) per kWh cost coverage for Moroccan CSP plants. Rising electricity prices in Spain until 2050 will lead to 6 euro cents (8.2 cents) per kWh cost coverage.[20] These figures indicate that CSP will not become competitive in the BAU scenario.

For the TD scenario, more lines—30 connections until 2050 with a capacity of 4 GW each—need to be built to transmit the 113.8 GW of peak export CSP generation from the MENA region in 2050 (Table 10.5). The TD scenario assumes extensive CSP generation in Morocco, Tunisia, and the Middle East. For 2020, the first line is built from Morocco to southern France; interestingly, it does not supply the Spanish market, as the Iberian electricity market has large shares of less expensive CCGT compared with more expensive coal from Italy and Germany that influences the electricity price in France. The other two MENA export nodes, Tunisia and the Middle East, choose one of the closest demand nodes for the HVDC connection because of lower line costs.

Although the model is welfare-maximizing, CSP's profitability is crucial to potential investors. With the assumed price path for gas and coal, electricity price in the targeted sales market is around 5 euro cents (6.8 cents) per kWh. Considering transmission costs of roughly 1 to 2 euro cents (1.4 to 2.7 cents) per kWh, the amount left for generation is far from the break-even point of about 9 euro cents (12 cents) per kWh for CSP in

2020. Therefore, the first installations must either be subsidized or be built in the expectation of future profitability from rising electricity prices. A decade later, CSP reaches its break-even point. In 2030, CSP generators in the three exporting regions can sell electricity at prices of 7 to 7.7 euro cents (9.5 to 10.5 cents) per kWh net of transmission costs. By then, CSP plants built in the MENA region are assumed to have levelized generation costs of 7 euro cents (9.5 cents) per kWh.[21] Continuously rising electricity prices would lead to even higher profits over the lifetime of the CSP facilities. Thus a rapid diffusion of CSP starting in 2030 seems possible.

Under profitable generation conditions for CSP, transmission lines develop according to Figure 10.8 until 2050. However, no transmission is realized to any node of the reinforced northern European grid. This result suggests that a more regional integration of CSP generation capacity is the preferred mechanism. CSP from the export node in Morocco is connected to Spain and France, Tunisia delivers most of its exported electricity to Italy, and the CSP generation from the Middle East is connected to the southeastern part of Europe. No lines connect to Germany, the Benelux, or the United Kingdom.[22]

Stronger Integration of the Scandinavian Electricity Market

The integration of the Scandinavian market is examined via a comparison of subscenarios A and B in the TD scenario, assuming that Scandinavia is connected to the United Kingdom and central Europe by six large-scale HVDC cables. Repeating the welfare optimization yields the following results:

Table 10.5. Number of HVDC transmission cables and CSP generation capacity in MENA (TD scenario)

	2020		2030		2040		2050	
Morocco	1	1.9 GW	2	7.8 GW	5	18.5 GW	9	32.7 GW
Tunisia	1	1.4 GW	4	5.7 GW	4	13.4 GW	6	23.6 GW
Middle East	1	3.5 GW	4	14.4 GW	9	33.9 GW	15	57.5 GW

Source: Egerer et al. 2009, *53*

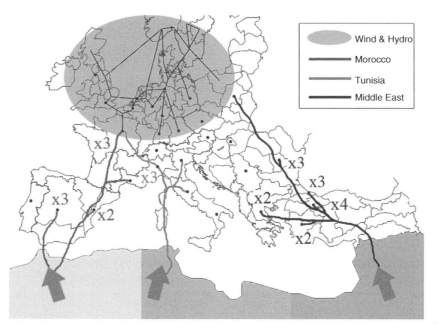

Source: Egerer et al 2009, 57
Note: Each line has a capacity of 4 GW unless a higher number indicates multiple lines.

Figure 10.8. HVDC grid in 2050 (TD scenario)

- The welfare increase for the exogenous expansion scenario for HVDC connections outweighs the associated cost. Therefore, an endogenous optimization could be even more profitable (this has not been modeled here because of the increasing complexity).
- Electricity prices are converging: by 2050, prices in Scandinavia increase by 4 euro cents (5.4 cents) per kWh (price increase by 50%) and decrease in the rest of Europe by about 1 euro cent (1.4 cents) per kWh.
- Lower prices in the entire European electricity market (continental Europe) lower the profits of CSP generation in MENA.
- The welfare optimal expansion paths for HVDC connections from MENA to Europe remain the same until 2050.

On the one hand, a stronger integration of northern Europe's electricity markets has a positive impact on the total welfare by balancing wind from the North Sea with reservoirs in Scandinavia. With the additional integration of the Scandinavian electricity markets, the annual welfare gains increase strongly over time. In 2050, the annual welfare benefit exceeds €3 billion ($4 billion), while the levelized annual cost of the necessary connectors between Scandinavia and continental Europe is about half that amount. Therefore, a more detailed analysis of concepts like the North Sea wind power transmission ring seems reasonable.

On the other hand, changes in welfare are accompanied by a modified distribution of consumer and producer surplus. Thus prices increase in Scandinavia when a higher share of inexpensive hydro can be exported to the United Kingdom and central Europe. Consequently, Scandinavian consumer surplus decreases while producer surplus increases. In the United Kingdom and central Europe, lower electricity prices have the opposite effect. Figure 10.9 presents estimated zone-specific price differences from the reinforced interconnections to Scandinavia in 2050. It becomes obvious that customers in the Nordic

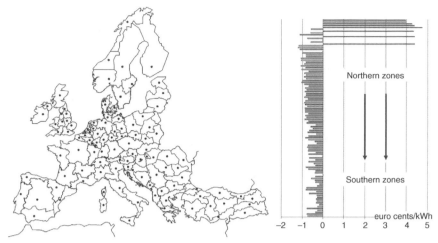

Source: Egerer et al. 2009, *60*

Figure 10.9. Electricity price changes with reinforced interconnectors to Scandinavia in 2050

countries have good reasons to favor a low integration of the Scandinavian electricity market, despite reduced welfare for the rest of Europe.

The integration of Scandinavia and the lower prices in central and southern Europe are bad news for a rapid diffusion of CSP and, in fact, could postpone its development for years because of the lower prices in the zones connected to MENA by HVDC. It seems probable that an isolated analysis of CSP generation without considering electricity system developments, such as the integration of available potential for wind and balancing hydro capacity, may result in misleading forecasts. Thus a single focus on L-RES from the MENA region seems inappropriate.

Financial Requirements and Sources

The investment volume for the CSP generation capacity in the TD scenario is about €390 billion ($531 billion) until 2050. This amount can be allocated to each decade as shown in Figure 10.10.[23] The total investment of €63 billion ($86 billion) for transmission expansion is derived from the HVDC lines for CSP integration according to Figure 10.8. The investment projections according to Figure 10.10 show that the project's major costs are attributed to generation capacity investment. All in all, the share of transmission investment is only about 14% of the total investment

volume. Nevertheless, generation and transmission have to be taken into account equally, because both stages in the value chain are intertwined: as long as generation capacity has not been built up, transmission lines are not necessary and vice versa. Not only because of this "chicken and egg" problem, it should also be determined how best to finance generation and transmission expansion.

Several public and private initiatives are under way, such as the Trans-Mediterranean Energy Cooperation/Desertec Initiative, Union for the Mediterranean, and bilateral technology agreements. However, common institutional and regulatory platforms among the EEA and MENA countries need to be further developed to finance

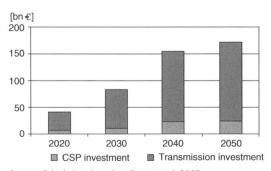

Source: Calculations based on Egerer et al. 2009

Figure 10.10. Required generation and transmission investment for the EEA-MENA supergrid

such large transnational infrastructure projects. This includes coordinated funding schemes by the EEA member states' national development banks, multilateral development banks (European Bank for Reconstruction and Development, African Development Bank), the MENA states in close cooperation with the UNFCCC, the World Bank Group, private investors (private equity funds, venture capital firms, private-public partnership entities), and other stakeholders. In this context, the importance of a stable regulatory framework as a prerequisite for leveraging private capital should be kept in mind.

Apart from institutions, funding could be provided for an EEA-MENA supergrid by several mechanisms:

- Extending transferability of certified emission reductions (CERs) from clean development mechanism (CDM) projects within the EU Emission Trading Scheme (EU-ETS); a less probable alternative is the de facto integration of MENA countries into the EU-ETS via direct substitutability of European emissions allowances by CERs from MENA countries.
- Establishing new, or actively exploiting, existing international technology transfer programs and funds, including the World Bank's and multilateral development banks' Climate Investment Funds and Clean Technology Fund, bilateral clean energy and technology funds, and future United Nations Framework Convention on Climate Change (UNFCCC) Multilateral Clean Technology Funds as proposed by the G77+ countries (see World Bank 2008; Seligsohn et al. 2009).
- Granting financial guarantees or extending policy instruments for renewable energy technology deployment (e.g., feed-in tariffs, tax incentives) by EEA countries to energy projects in the MENA region.
- Setting a generous limit for the upcoming determination of allowed renewable energy imports from joint projects between EU member states and third countries to meet the national targets on the promotion of

renewable energies according to the recent EU Directive 2009/28/EC (EU 2009a, Article 9, 2009/28/EC).

Assessment

The EEA-MENA case study provides insights into the potential unfolding of a supergrid and the related technical and economic aspects. Clearly, there may be economic benefits from developing a supergrid, such as the use of less carbon-intensive sources of electricity and higher reliability within the transmission network. The EEA-MENA case study showed welfare benefits of the grid development starting in 2030, given assumptions that do not seem to be outside the realm of reality. Transmission expansion develops gradually from a nucleus of point-to-point relations and spreads over the region over time. Taken as a whole, the project is profitable, but this ignores risk assessment and an analysis of real business cases. Similar results might be expected from welfare assessments or cost–benefit analyses (CBA) of the other projects presented in this chapter.

The assumptions of the model and the choice of technologies and regions considered have a significant effect on the results, and thus the results discussed here differ somewhat from those obtained in the Desertec study by Trieb et al. (2009). The model of the European electricity system applied here allows for a spatial and temporal resolution of demand, generation capacities, and electricity prices. In particular, applying a multisource approach (solar, wind, and hydro) in a truly pan-European context yields quite different results in terms of network design and prices. Thus the North Sea Energy Super Ring or any other North Sea energy grid topology ("Seatec") may become a "competitor" to the solar-founded Desertec project. The results underline that the project needs to be seen in the context of other transmission expansion projects, capacity replacements, and evolving generation from L-RES. Compensation mechanisms need to be put in place as a cooperation scheme between the losers (transit countries) and the winners from lower electricity prices. The above discussion has touched on these institutional obstacles, including financing problems.

One issue that needs further exploration is the multiple incentive structure of the actors involved in the process. In particular, the North African countries may face conflicts of interest in considering the supergrid option. Previous rent earners, such as electricity consumers in the Nordic countries and the natural gas industry, may oppose the project. The domestic nonenergy industry has argued for the deployment of energy-intensive industries in the MENA region, using electricity from L-RES and exporting the products, such as "green aluminium"; this is expected to favor the emergence of new industries and employment. Also, instead of transmitting electricity physically to the EEA, natural gas could serve as a "currency" for electricity from L-RES in MENA countries with natural gas resources, such as Libya and Algeria. Some actors have indeed argued that the EEA countries could pay a fixed price for CSP-generated electricity, which can be converted to an amount of gas with equivalent energy content. Exporting gas through existing pipelines and via LNG terminals might avoid the need for extensive electricity transmission expansion. Thus it is not clear whether the supergrid idea is the preferred solution of all players involved.

Challenges for Developing Supergrids

What are some general challenges and problems related to the deployment of supergrids? In particular, recent difficulties faced by transmission expansion projects on both sides of the Atlantic show that a cost–benefit ratio below one or positive welfare effects do not suffice to make supergrids "fly." Instead, questions regarding the institutional structure of a further supergrid architecture abound. Many of them touch on the issue of institutional design, or what 2009 Nobel Prize winner Oliver Williamson calls the choice between "markets and hierarchies," referring to which element of the value-added chain can be developed with the use of market signals, and for which a more hierarchical or planning approach is more appropriate. In fact, most institutions used in transmission expansion might combine elements of both markets and hierarchies, becoming hybrid organizational forms.

Planning Issues

Any supergrid requires long-term planning to create the conditions under which large-scale transmission investment can unfold. Transmission planning arrangements include, among others, the planning process itself, the implementation and mechanisms for cost recovery, the role of markets (price signals) as a decision support, and trade-offs between transmission and non-transmission investment (Moselle and Brown 2007). Note that the supergrid planning process stretches well beyond conventional transmission planning procedures. Time horizons projected forward are much longer, and system changes must be considered. Moreover, the maximum span of demand and generation forecasts used in traditional national planning procedures is 7 to 10 years (e.g., in the United Kingdom), with the maximum of (less-detailed) forecasts of 20 years in Alberta (Moselle and Brown 2007). This is significantly shorter than the three- to four-decade horizon adopted by most supergrids.

Clearly, the institutional framework for planning and developing the supergrid is not yet available in the United States and Europe. The United States is more advanced with respect to interregional transmission development. However, the Federal Energy Regulatory Commission (FERC) cannot impose the development of a supergrid on any of the regional transmission organizations (RTOs) or the individual independent system operators (ISOs). Neither can it, for the time being, consider RPS obligations as legitimate criteria for the development of new transmission (Krapels 2009).

In Europe, there is still less ground on which the planning process for a supergrid could be based. Contrary to many restructured electricity systems, continental Europe lacks a regional transmission development plan (Moselle and Brown 2007). Transnational transmission expansion is only beginning to be coordinated at the European level. An emerging European regulatory agency, the Agency for the Coordination of Energy Regulators (ACER), is set to negotiate planning ideas with its counterpart, the European Network of Transmission System Operators for Electricity (ENTSO-E).[24] Given the lack of institutional support, it seems that without federal or European-wide planning procedures and some implementing power, the development of any supergrid is unlikely. Whether any such planning processes can reasonably be implemented is yet another open question.

Cost Allocation

Cost allocation and cost recovery are crucial in any transmission regime, but they become particularly difficult in the supergrid context, where more than one ISO or TSO is involved. A restructured market with open access requires some form of cost allocation mechanism for transmission expansion. Baldick et al. (2007) identify principles to follow: they propose using a standard measurement for societal benefits that incorporates economic values and having in place an open, transparent, and inclusive process for regionally based transmission planning and analysis. New transmission investment should be supported in federal or other wholesale rates, instead of in the retail rate base, and free entry should be permitted in transmission investment.

There are two main approaches to allocate costs. First, those who clearly benefit from the investment are identified and consequently pay for it; note that the question of who benefits is not trivial either, particularly in a dynamic context with a changing network topology. Second, the cost of new transmission investment is socialized among all users in a region or market (Baldick et al. 2007). Another key issue of cost allocation is the ability of the institutional system to compensate parties who "lose" from transmission investment. Besides the question of cost allocation, other issues, such as consumer concerns about price development, can arise. Namely, parties protecting consumers in regions with low-cost generation may fear that transmission investment will cause generation-related prices to equalize over a larger geographic region and thus increase for a specific region.[25]

Vertical or horizontal coordination, or both, would make cost allocation for a supergrid even more complex. In the United States, the dual pricing regime, a structure of transmission cost recovery that is affected by both state and federal ratemaking practices, complicates the appropriate cost allocation. Currently, FERC, the federal regulator, must consider both the allocation of costs among different generators and load, and the reflection of those costs in retail rates. Obviously, this dual-pricing regime has a rather complicating effect. Europe has been slow to develop an inter-TSO compensation mechanism (Moselle 2008), which complicates any supergrid development. In addition, the atomization of European TSOs makes successful cooperation more difficult. The three Scandinavian system operators have developed a voluntary compensation mechanism (Nylund 2009). But even this relatively small jointly managed grid illustrates the weakness of voluntary approaches to inter-TSO cooperation in Europe and seems to suffer from the absence of legally binding arrangements. As the number of participating TSOs increases, transaction costs increase exponentially.

Market Design

Both gradual transmission expansion and supergrids should deploy a market-oriented market design that is conducive to socially optional investment decisions. A critical element thereof is bid-based, security-constrained economic dispatch with locational marginal pricing (LMP), or nodal pricing, as proposed by Hogan (2008), to achieve welfare maximization and identify potential transmission bottlenecks. In many instances, LMP is the most cost-efficient solution to transmission problems because the prices identify the true scarcities in the system. Thus longer-term planning for a supergrid should incorporate this welfare-maximizing algorithm. In the United States, these principles are fulfilled in the more reform-oriented regions, most of which are also elaborating on supergrid proposals. Note that while LMPs are useful in providing locational signals for placing generation and load, their value for establishing transmission investments is more doubtful; therefore, financial transmission rights (FTRs) based on LMP differences have not fully resolved the issue of transmission investment, as was initially hoped for.

In Europe, no electricity system has a nodal pricing system in place, not even the United Kingdom, which applies static G-components, with generators compensated for relieving network congestion or penalized for contributing to it. Continental Europe is still largely dominated by uniform transmission pricing. Hence the conditions under which efficient supergrid investment could occur are not really in place.

A critical issue in any intermittent-based system is the design of the balancing market and creating incentives for investment in backup capacity for intermittent generation from renewables. Most of the scenarios discussed early in this chapter have not gone the full way of installing storage capacity for the intermittent large-scale renewables (wind and solar), primarily because of cost. In this case, the generators themselves will need to analyze other technologies to cope with the intermittency of the renewables portfolio. Thanks to their high ramping flexibility, relatively low capital costs, widely available fuel, and ease of operation, gas turbines are likely to be the most economic backup technology.

Cost–Benefit Analyses

Even if a workable long-term planning process is in place, with cost recovery and price signals defined, an institutional design regarding the assessment of transmission expansion would be required. Long-term planning can define the "big picture" of generation and transmission expansion, but it cannot provide an assessment of whether an individual line, or a certain part of the network, should or should not be extended. For this, some form of cost–benefit comparison might be useful. As a rule of thumb, three approaches can be applied:

- Traditional net present value (NPV) assessment of individual transmission investments, by relating (expected) private revenues to costs; this business perspective adheres to the logic of an investor but ignores larger economic benefits and costs.

- Calculating cost changes by producers and consumers as a result of the expansion of transmission lines; this corresponds to a more economic approach, as it approximates the welfare effects of investments by the change in producer and consumer surpluses. For example, PJM values the economic benefit of additional transmission investment by $0.7 \, \Delta \, PC + 0.3 \, \Delta \, LP$, where $\Delta \, PC$ is the change of production costs and $\Delta \, LP$ is the change in load payments (Lin 2009).

- A comprehensive, sophisticated cost–benefit analysis that also takes into account indirect effects of transmission expansion, such as increased system reliability or competition in one of the zones. For example, the California ISO (CAISO) uses a comprehensive transmission economic assessment methodology (TEAM) as a decision support tool for transmission planners, in which the annual benefits from an expansion include production cost benefits, competitivity benefits, operational benefits, generation investment cost savings, reduced losses, and emission benefits (California ISO 2004).[26]

All substantial public policy interventions of the type required for the supergrid projects discussed require justification, and a sound, transparent cost–benefit analysis provides just that. Thus the CAISO-TEAM methodology might be developed further to become applicable to longer-term supergrid developments as well. This CBA framework could then be applied to the projects under discussion. This is particularly important for Europe, where the 10-year EU-wide plans are not yet systematically subject to cost–benefit analysis. The normative aspects (yes or no) of such analysis have a strong positive effect, increasing transparency and accountability of the actors involved.

Regulatory Options

While the "optimal" regulation of transmission expansion is already a controversial issue, this is even more the case for the regulatory framework of any supergrid. The following issues merit consideration and await solutions:

- Regulated versus merchant transmission investment: in general, the more meshed a transmission network, the more difficult it is to isolate the effects of a specific newly constructed line, and hence the more difficult it is to apply merchant investment. Krapels (2009) suggests that HVDC lines are able to attract private merchant investment because of the point-to-point character of these lines. The empirical underpinning related thereto is scarce, however: except for a few local transmission lines, there is little independent transmission expansion in the United States and Europe. It seems that the need for coordinated, long-term planning and inter-TSO coordination, information asymmetries between the incumbent network owner/operator and the market entrant, and scale and scope effects are arguments in favor of regulated investment by the incumbent ISOs, RTOs, or TSOs. This does not exclude tendering of a large share of the activities that will be subject to market forces.

- Incentive versus cost-based regulation: opting for a regulatory approach necessitates determining the "power" of the incentive scheme, in other words the degree to which the network tariffs are fixed by the regulator, and thus does not correspond to some approximation of costs (cost-based regulation). Whereas incentive regulation has resulted in increased static allocative efficiency, its benefits in terms of dynamic investment efficiency are unclear. Although a general consensus exists that an incentive-based regulatory regime can theoretically induce an "optimal" level of transmission expansion under certain conditions, the real-world implementation of these mechanisms has not followed suit. The Hogan-Rosellon-Vogelsang mechanism (Hogan et al. 2007) is an example of such a traditional, non-Bayesian incentive scheme. However, it assumes constant demand and has difficulties accommodating intermittent renewable electricity sources. Finally, the danger of regulatory discretion and limited commitment, and the potential instability of the political and institutional framework, would suggest a reduction of the incentive power of the regulatory regime for a supergrid.

Political Economy Arguments: Achieving Consensus and Compensating Losers

The case studies examined earlier suggest that technology per se is not a real obstacle. Also, a lack of long-term planning might be overcome at the operational level, albeit at higher transaction costs and potential losses in efficiency. The real challenge for the implementation of a supergrid, or any other megaproject of that type, is how to reach consensus among a very large group of stakeholders, in this case generators, system owners, TSOs, consumers, and the decisionmaking entities at all levels of government.

In some settings, one can use force to obtain consensus, such as in the case of large-scale infrastructure projects in the former Soviet Union. Another way of pushing megaprojects through is to dedicate unlimited financial resources, as in the U.S. space race in the 1960s. Closer to our field of infrastructure development, the top-down approach by which the United States implemented its interstate highway program beginning in the 1950s can also be considered a historic example, whatever the driving force behind it (e.g., transport or national defense) might have been. These examples do not directly apply to supergrids, however, as centralized, top-down interventionism is not an option in a democracy, financial means are very limited, and siting and implementation of large-scale infrastructures are much more difficult today than 60 years ago.

Instead, the key to implementing such large-scale projects is to create a consensus, in particular about the sharing of the gains and the compensation of losers by the winners. It is not yet clear how the welfare gains that any supergrid is likely to achieve can be divided among the participating parties to make the project become a reality. At least three levels need to be considered:

- On the producer side, and even assuming that transmission can be treated as a cost block, allocating producer rent among the players depends on the behavioral assumptions—in other words, whether one assumes cooperative or noncooperative behavior—and the allocation of grandfathered rights. In addition, established incumbent electricity producers may hesitate to invest in low-cost capacity abroad that might undermine the price in their home markets as well (cannibalizing effect).

- On the consumer side, there will be clear winners and losers from the additional generation and transmission capacities. As the case study demonstrates, former locked-in low-price consumers tend to be adversely affected, while consumers in former high-price zones clearly benefit.

- Last but not least, the sharing of rents among different federal levels is a potential source of conflict as well. Welfare maximization over the entire supergrid region is, in fact, an oversimplification, because U.S. states and European nations are likely to influence decisions and seek to optimize only their own welfare. As in the planning process, this would speak in favor of centralization of decisionmaking with flexible side payments and compensation.

Conclusions

The main message of this chapter is that harnessing renewable energy to generate electricity is relatively simple in comparison with transporting that electricity over long distances to large-scale demand centers. The idea of developing large-scale supergrids, or transmission overlay grids, may be appealing, judging by the mushrooming number of pilot studies. However, large-scale harnessing of renewables may be limited by transmission bottlenecks that will be difficult to overcome in the current market and institutional environment:

- Few of the reviewed case studies deal with transmission issues in a serious way, and those that do tend to prefer decentralized, regional network integration to supergrids.

- The case study in this chapter, the EEA-MENA project, indicates that large-scale CSP generation in MENA countries and its HVDC transmission to Europe may increase welfare and even become profitable under certain conditions. However, a pan-European perspective is required, and it is currently unclear whether the institutional arrangements necessary for the project, including adequate financing mechanisms, will be put in place in time.

- All supergrid projects also face several cross-cutting issues: the necessity of efficient long-term planning procedures, the simplification of cost allocation issues, market-oriented pricing where possible, a comprehensive cost–benefit analysis to identify economic solutions, and adequate regulatory incentives.

Potential investors face a multitude of market, policy, and regulatory risks; technological uncertainties; coordination problems; and other barriers, such as local resistance. The current lack of business cases for network expansion can be overcome only if a clear, stable, and equitable long-term policy framework is in place. Welfare benefits of network expansion projects should be distributed in an incentive-compatible fashion. Hence an institutional analysis is required to determine opportunities and challenges in the development of such scenarios.

Several issues that should be addressed in more detail include timing, irreversibility of investment, and risk considerations. This chapter has only touched on issues of the appropriate regulatory setting, the most critical being today's policy of favoring national subsidies over federal regulation. On both sides of the Atlantic, transmission planning competence and the ability to develop and install supergrids are limited. The most important issues to resolve are those linked to rent sharing. Thus future research should investigate the distributional effects of different scenarios on producer and consumer rents in each of the regions concerned, as well as ponder the proper compensation mechanisms to overcome local resistance to welfare-improving projects.

Acknowledgments

This chapter is based on the research program Electricity Markets at the Dresden University of Technology (TU Dresden). The author thanks Jonas Egerer and the study project 2050 for background research, and Florian Leuthold, Christina Beestermöller, Johannes Herold, Robert Wand, and Hannes Weigt for comments and suggestions; thanks also to two referees for constructive comments.

Notes

1. According to IEEE (1997), FACTS are defined as "alternating current transmission systems incorporating power electronic-based and other static controllers to enhance controllability and increase power transfer capability." FACTS comprise a number of technologies, which are used to stabilize the frequency, control the real and reactive power flow, or compensate and manage the effective power flow. Improving the static stability of a multiline transmission system, FACTS can increase the power flow on existing AC lines.

2. HVDC can be connected to AC networks via a converter station, using conventional line-commutated current source converters (CSCs), or self-commutated voltage source converters (VSCs). The latter are based on insulated gate bipolar transistors (IGBT) and can be adjusted with respect to load flows. These components also offer black start capacity. Whereas traditional HVDC was mainly limited to point-to-point operation, VSCs enable HVDC systems to work in more complex structures. This development offers the possibility to create entire HVDC transmission overlays as a supergrid.

3. The Solar Grand Plan even stretches to the end of this century: by 2100, the L-RES could generate 100% of U.S. electricity and more than 90% of total U.S. energy (Zweibel et al. 2008).

4. "This backbone would reach major markets in Phoenix, Las Vegas, Los Angeles and San Diego to the west, and San Antonio, Dallas, Houston, New

Orleans, Birmingham (Ala.), Tampa (Fla.), and Atlanta to the east" (Zweibel et al. 2008, *54*).

5. For an average transmission distance of 1,500 miles, one converter per line, and a capacity utilization factor of 27%, Fthenakis et al. (2009) estimate a levelized transmission cost of $0.024/kWh on average. Investment and operation costs for transmission will be included in grid developers' royalties.

6. For a U.S.-wide study on large-scale wind integration, see the transmission plan by American Electric Power (AEP 2007) at the request of the American Wind Energy Association, suggesting a 765 kV AC overlay grid.

7. The Midwest and the East Coast are connected by 765 kV AC lines and two 800 kV DC lines, with major reinforcements between Massachusetts and New Jersey. The two HVDC lines are fed by additional 400 and 800 kV DC lines. Moreover, two-circuit 500 kV AC lines build up the existing grid in Oklahoma and connect Arkansas and Alabama as well as Maryland and New York. A new 345 kV two-circuit line will be built in New York.

8. This is also reflected in the introduction of incentive-based rate treatments for transmission in interstate commerce by FERC as a measure to stimulate interstate transmission expansion (Energy Policy Act 2005, Section 1241, and amendment to the Federal Power Act, Section 219).

9. For more information on SUSPLAN (PLANning for SUStainability), see www.susplan.eu/; for the SOLID-DER project (Coordination Action to Consolidate RTD Activities for Large-Scale Integration of Renewable Energy into the European Electricity Market), see www.solid-der.org/; for WIND FORCE 12 by Greenpeace, see www.ewea.org/fileadmin/ewea_documents/documents/publications/reports/wf12-2005.pdf; for Tradewind, see www.trade-wind.eu/; and for DENA 2, see www.dena.de/de/themen/thema-reg/projekte/projekt/netzstudie-ii.

10. The initial project is supposed to be connected to the United Kingdom, the Netherlands, and Germany.

11. The overall objective of the Desertec Foundation is to make productive use of the largest source of energy, solar, as a basis for electricity consumption and sustainable development around the globe, with a focus on desert countries. Besides the energy problem, the Desertec consortium also addresses issues of water supply, food security, and climate change.

12. Since the summer of 2009, the project has been accelerated by the Desertec Industrial Initiative (DII), a consortium of utilities, equipment producers, banks, and insurance companies. At the EU level, there is also activity in the form of the Union for the Mediterranean, which has developed the Mediterranean Solar Plan (MSP). The MSP is organized in three phases: building an institutional structure (ongoing); developing a Master Plan Study (until 2010); and implementing the plan until 2020. The following discussion refers to the most recent study at the time of this writing, Trieb et al. (2009).

13. Being highly site-dependent, this calculation is based on a solar direct normal irradiance (DNI) of 2,700 kWh/m²/a and a CSP design for extensive heat storage (solar multiple of 4).

14. For technical calculations on the EEA-MENA project, we refer to an ongoing research project at the Chair of Energy Economics and Public Sector Management at Dresden University of Technology (see Egerer et al. 2009).

15. This includes the high-priority "projects of European interest for inter-European electricity interconnection, and linkage with neighboring regions": according to the Trans-European Energy Projects (TEN-E) and Priority Interconnection Plan (PIP) (EC, 2006).

16. Compare Leuthold et al. (2008) and Egerer et al. (2009) for a detailed technical discussion.

17. For a detailed description, see Egerer et al. (2009, *32*).

18. For the spatial configuration of the additional lines, see Egerer et al. (2009, *46*).

19. The average electricity price (system price) is calculated from the model's demand-weighted zonal prices.

20. Cost coverage is calculated by subtracting transmission costs from electricity prices in the export electricity market.

21. For a detailed overview of prices, transmission costs, and cost coverage for generation, see Egerer et al. (2009, *56*).

22. In addition to zones with large wind capacity, zones with large hydropower capacity (e.g., Switzerland, Austria, and Serbia) are not served by CSP-generated electricity. Although these zones have seasonal storage capacity (reservoirs), for welfare purposes it seems preferable to substitute fossil-fueled base load capacity elsewhere.

23. These cost estimates are based on decreasing average investment cost for CSP from €5,300 ($7,220)

per kW in 2020 to €3,944 ($5,373) per kW in 2030 to €3,429 ($4,671) per kW in 2050 (Trieb et al. 2009, *83*).

24. As a first step, Regulation 714/2009/EC (EU 2009b) requires that ENTSO-E adopt a nonbinding communitywide 10-year network development plan every 2 years, which is then assessed by the agency (ACER), consistent with the national 10-year development plans provided by the member states.

25. Beyond the underlying principles, a concrete cost allocation is the method of average participation (AP) (Pérez-Arriaga and Olmos 2009). AP can track the actual upstream and downstream flows to the generators, and loads that can be associated plausibly with them. Theoretically, the cost of the "used" fraction of each line can be apportioned to generation and load in proportion to the aggregate economic benefits.

26. An essential component of the CAISO-TEAM is that it implements a market simulation model based on dynamic supply bids and incorporating a detailed physical transmission modeling capability for a reliability region. Besides, CAISO-TEAM includes uncertainty and risks about the future that can partly be quantified. Apart from these benefits, cross-sectoral positive externalities comprise simplified rights-of-way for the use of other network infrastructure being built, once the land is assigned to transmission purposes (such as optical fiber telecommunications), reflecting a positive externality of transmission expansion. Additionally, long-term resource cost advantages, synergies with other transmission projects, fiscal benefits from construction and taxes, and impacts on fuel markets should be taken into consideration according to Pfeifenberger and Newell (2007).

References

AEP (American Electric Power). 2007. Interstate Transmission Vision for Wind Integration. www.aep.com/about/i765project/docs/WindTransmissionVisionWhitePaper.pdf (accessed December 3, 2009).

Airtricity. 2006. European Offshore Supergrid Proposal: Creating a More Powerful Europe. www.trec-uk.org.uk/resources/airtricity_supergrid_V1.4.pdf (accessed December 2, 2009).

AWEA/SEIA (American Wind Energy Association/ Solar Energy Industries Association). 2009. Green

Power Superhighways: Building a Path to America's Clean Energy Future. www.awea.org/GreenPowerSuperhighways.pdf (accessed December 3, 2009).

Baldick, Ross, Ashley Brown, James Bushnell, Susan Tierney, and Terry Winter. 2007. *A National Perspective on Allocating the Costs of New Transmission Investment: Practice and Principles.* Blue Ribbon Panel on Cost Allocation. www.puc.nh.gov/Transmission%20Commission/120108%20Progress%20Report/Attachment%20M.pdf (accessed March 18, 2010).

California ISO (California Independent System Operator). 2004. Transmission Economic Assessment Methodology (TEAM). Folsom, CA: California ISO.

Claus, M., D. Retzmann, S. Sörangr, and K. Uecker. 2008. Solutions for Smart and Super Grids with HVDC and FACTS. 17th Conference of the Electric Power Supply Industry. October 2008, Macau. www.ptd.siemens.de/CEPSI08_Art.pdf (accessed December 1, 2009).

EC (European Commission). 2006. Decision No. 1364/2006/EC of the European Parliament and of the Council of 6 September 2006 Laying Down Guidelines for Trans-European Energy Networks and Repealing Decision 96/391/EC and Decision No. 1229/2003/EC. *Official Journal of the European Union:* L262/1-23.

Egerer, Jonas, Lucas Bückers, Gregor Drondorf, Clemens Gerbaulet, Paul Hörnicke, Rudiger Säurich, Claudia Schmidt, Simon Schumann, Sebastian Schwiedersky, Thorsten Spitzel, and Anja Thanheiser. 2009. Sustainable Energy Networks for Europe: The Integration of Large-Scale Renewable Energy Sources until 2050. www.tu-dresden.de/wwbwleeg/publications/wp_em_35_Egerer_et_al_2050.pdf (accessed March 1, 2010).

ENTSO-E (European Network of Transmission System Operators for Electricity). 2008. ENTSO-E GridMap. www.entsoe.eu/index.php?id=77 (accessed November 10, 2009).

———. 2009. UCTE Transmission Development Plan 2009. www.entsoe.eu/fileadmin/user_upload/_library/publications/ce/otherreports/tdp09_reporr_ucte.pdf (accessed November 10, 2009).

EU (European Union). 2009a. Directive 2009/28/EC of the European Parliament and of the Council of 23 April 2009 on the Promotion of the Use of Energy from Renewable Sources and Amending and

Subsequently Repealing Directives 2001/77/EC and 2003/30/EC. *Official Journal of the European Union* L140/16–62.

———. 2009b. Regulation No. 714/2009 of the European Parliament and of the Council of 13 July 2009, on Conditions for Access to the Network for Cross-Border Exchanges in Electricity and Repealing Regulation (EC) No 1228/2003. *Official Journal of the European Union:* L211/15–35.

Fthenakis, Vasili, James Mason, and Ken Zweibel. 2009. The Technical, Geographical, and Economic Feasibility for Solar Energy to Supply the Energy Needs of the US. *Energy Policy* 37 (2): 387–399.

Hogan, William. 2008. Electricity Market Design: Coordination, Pricing and Incentives. Presentation at the Toulouse Conference on Energy Economics. www.energypolicyblog.com/wp-content/uploads/2008/06/20080623_hogan.pdf (accessed December 8, 2009).

Hogan, William, Juan Rosellon, and Ingo Vogelsang. 2007. Toward a Combined Merchant-Regulatory Mechanism for Electricity Transmission Expansion. Paper presented at the IAEE European Conference. April 2007, Florence, Italy.

IEEE (Institute of Electrical and Electronics Engineers). 1997. Proposed Terms and Conditions for FACTS. *IEEE Transactions on Power Delivery* 12 (4): 1848–1853.

Jacobsen, Mark Z., and Mark A. Delucchi. 2009. A Path to Sustainable Energy by 2030. *Scientific American* 299 (November): 58–65.

Kaupa, Heinz. 2009. Smart Grids and/or Super Grid? Presentation at the Alpbacher Technologiegespräche conference. August 2009, Vienna. www.bmvit.gv.at/service/publikationen/innovation/downloads/3kaupa.pdf (accessed December 3, 2009).

Krapels, Edward. 2009. Integrating 200,000 MWs of Renewable Energy in the US Power Grid. www.hks.harvard.edu/hepg (accessed November 3, 2009).

Leuthold, Florian, Hannes Weigt, and Christian von Hirschhausen. 2008. ELMOD – A Model of the European Electricity Market. Electricity Markets working papers WP-EM-00. www.tu-dresden.de/wwbwleeg/publications/wp_em_00_ELMOD.pdf (accessed November 13, 2009).

Lin, Jeremy. 2009. Market-Based Transmission Planning Model in PJM Electricity Market. Energy Markets 2009. Paper presented at the EEM 2009 (6th Conference on European Electricity Markets). May 2009, Leuven, Belgium.

Midwest ISO, PJM, SPP, TVA, and MAPP. 2008. Joint Coordinated System Plan 2008: Economic Assessment. Report, Vol. 1. www.jcspstudy.org (accessed December 7, 2009).

Moselle, Boaz. 2008. Reforming TSOs: Using the "Third Package" Legislation to Promote Efficiency and Accelerate Regional Integration in EU Wholesale Power Markets. *Electricity Journal* 21 (8): 9–17.

Moselle, Boaz, and Toby Brown. 2007. *International Review of Transmission Planning Arrangements.* Brussels: Brattle Group.

Natuur en Milieu (Netherlands Society for Nature and Environment). 2009. Office for Metropolitan Architecture Presents Master Plan Offshore Wind in the North Sea. Utrecht, Netherlands: Natuur en Milieu.

Nylund, H. 2009. Sharing the Costs of Transmission Expansion: A Cooperative Game Theory Approach Applied on the Nordic Electricity Market. Proceedings of the IAEE 10th European Conference. September 2009, Vienna, Austria.

OMA (Office for Metropolitan Architecture). 2009. Masterplan Zeekracht. www.zeekracht.nl/sites/default/files/oma.pdf (accessed November 29, 2009).

Pérez-Arriaga, Ignacio, and Luis Olmos. 2009. *A Comprehensive Approach for Computation and Implementation of Efficient Electricity Transmission Network Charges.* Cambridge, MA: Center for Energy and Environmental Policy Research.

Pfeifenberger, Johannes, and Sam Newell. 2007. Evaluating the Economic Benefits of Transmission Investments. Paper presented at EUCI's Cost-Effective Transmission Technology Conference. May 2007, Nashville, TN.

Seligsohn, Deborah, Lutz Weischer, Shane Tomlinson, and Pelin Zorlu. 2009. Key Functions for a UNFCCC Technology Institutional Structure: Identifying Convergence in Country Submissions. Working paper. Washington, DC: World Resources Institute. www.wri.org/climate/cop-15 (accessed December 3, 2009).

Siemens. 2009. Ultra HVDC Transmission System, Newsletter Issue 0910. www.trec-uk.org.uk/resources/siemens_uhvdc_october_2009.pdf (accessed December 1, 2009).

Sinden, Graham. 2007. Characteristics of the UK Wind Resource: Long-Term Patterns and Relationship to Electricity Demand. *Energy Policy* 35 (1): 112–127.

Tierney, Susan. 2008. *A 21st Century "Interstate Electric Highway System": Connecting Consumers and Domestic Clean Power Supplies.* Boston: Analysis Group.

Trieb, Franz, Christoph Schillings, Stefan Kronshage, Uwe Klann, Peter Viebahn, Nadine May, Regina Wilde, Christian Paul, Malek Kabariti, Abdelaziz Bennouna, Hani El Nokraschy, Samir Hassan, Laila Georgy Yussef, Tewfik Hasni, Nasir El Bassam, and Honorat Satoguina. 2005. Concentrating Solar Power for the Mediterranean Region. Final Report. Stuttgart: German Aerospace Center (DLR) Institute of Technical Thermodynamics Section Systems Analysis and Technology Assessment.

Trieb, Franz, Christoph Schillings, Stefan Kronshage, Peter Viebahn, Nadine May, Christian Paul, Malek Kabariti, Khaled M. Daoud, Abdelaziz Bennouna, Hani El Nokraschy, Samir Hassan, Laila Georgy Yussef, Tewfik Hasni, Nasir El Bassam, and Honorat Satoguina. 2006. Trans-Mediterranean Interconnection for Concentrating Solar Power. Final Report. German Aerospace Center (DLR) Institute of Technical Thermodynamics Section Systems Analysis and Technology Assessment, Stuttgart. www.dlr.de/tt/Portaldata/41/Resources/dokumente/institut/system/projects/TRANS-CSP_Full_Report_Final.pdf (accessed December 1, 2009).

Trieb, Franz, Marlene O'Sullivan, Thomas Pregger, Christoph Schillings, and Wolfram Krewitt. 2009. Characterisation of Solar Electricity Import Corridors from MENA to Europe. Stuttgart: REACCESS Report, German Aerospace Center (DLR) Institute of Technical Thermodynamics Section Systems Analysis and Technology Assessment.www.dlr.de/tt/Portaldata/41/Resources/dokumente/institut/system/publications/Solar_imimpo_DLR_2009_07.pdf (accessed December 1, 2009).

World Bank. 2008. Illustrative Investment Programs for the Clean Technology Fund. http://siteresources.worldbank.org/INTCC/Resources/Illustrative_Investment_program_May_15_2008.pdf (accessed November 26, 2009).

Zweibel, Ken, James Mason, and Vasilis Fthenakis. 2008. Solar Grand Plan. *Scientific American* 298 (1): 48–57.

Part IV

National Experiences

11

Renewable Electricity Generation in the United States

Richard Schmalensee

Thomas A. Edison's Pearl Street Station in New York, the first permanent, commercial electric generating plant, began operation on September 4, 1882 (IEEE 2008b). Just 26 days later, the first commercial generating plant using renewable energy—a hydroelectric facility—began operation in Appleton, Wisconsin (IEEE 2008a). The United States has considerable hydroelectric potential and moved aggressively, particularly in the 1930s, to exploit it. By 1949, hydropower accounted for just under a third of U.S. electricity generation (EIA 2009b, *Table 1.1*).

Since then, however, the relative importance of hydropower has waned, as potential dam sites were of lower quality than those already employed, the performance of other generating technologies improved, and the public became increasingly concerned about the environmental impacts of dams. In recent years, more attention has been given to the possible demolition of hydroelectric dams than to their possible construction. Hydropower accounted for only about 6% of U.S. electricity generation in 2007 (EIA 2009b, *Table 1.1*).

Renewable generation technologies other than hydroelectricity, referred to in this chapter as nonhydro renewable (NHR) technologies, began to attract significant attention from public and private decisionmakers in the United States and abroad after the energy crises of the 1970s. As environmental concerns, particularly those related to climate change, have become more important, support for these technologies has generally increased. In the United States the result has been a complicated saga of erratic and unfocused federal policy and widely divergent state policies, with results that have not surprisingly varied considerably over time and among the states.

The chapter begins with a brief quantitative overview of the actual and potential importance of nonhydro renewable energy over time in the United States, until recently a leader in NHR generation of electricity. Lately, other nations have provided more effective support of these technologies and accordingly have taken the lead in using them. Next, the chapter outlines rationales and policy tools for supporting NHRs and examines policy at the federal level in the United States. It then considers state-level policies and their effects, with brief discussions of experiences in two major states that have played very different leadership roles in this area: California and Texas. This is followed by a look at the most rapidly growing NHR technology in the United States—wind—and some of the issues and concerns its growth has raised.

Nonhydro Renewables in the United States

Between 1949 and 2008, both total U.S. energy consumption and consumption derived from NHRs grew at about 1.95% annually on average. In the first half of this period, from 1949 to 1978, total energy consumption grew at a 3.21% average annual rate, while energy from NHRs grew only about a third as fast—at a 1.06% annual rate. Thereafter, the growth of total energy consumption slowed dramatically to a 0.72% annual rate, while the growth of energy from NHRs accelerated to a 2.82% annual rate. Despite this impressive growth, however, NHRs have never accounted for more than 4.5% of total U.S. energy consumption (EIA 2009a, *Table 1.3*).

Figure 11.1 gives a breakdown of total energy consumption from nonhydro renewables over the 1978–2008 period by source. In the early years, the only important source in this category was biomass, mainly wood and wood waste, used to generate heat rather than electricity. In recent years, biofuels, chiefly ethanol, have become of comparable importance. Together with a small

contribution from what is termed "other solar"—the use of solar energy to produce heat, mainly to warm swimming pools—these three nonelectric uses of renewable energy are much more important than the use of NHRs to generate electricity.

Since the late 1970s, NHRs have been of interest to policymakers primarily because of their perceived potential to displace fossil fuels (and in some jurisdictions, nuclear energy) in electricity generation. Despite this interest, however, and a wide variety of policies aimed at encouraging the use of NHRs, these technologies have accounted for only 2% to 2.5% of total U.S. electricity generation since 1989, as Figure 11.2 shows. For all of the 1990s, NHRs played a more important role in generating electricity in the United States than in Europe. But major European nations, particularly Germany, were much more aggressive in promoting NHRs over most of this period, and the share of these technologies in European electricity generation has accordingly been rising. It is now almost double that in the United States.

Figure 11.3 shows the contributions of the various NHR technologies to electricity generation since 1990. About 70% of biomass generation

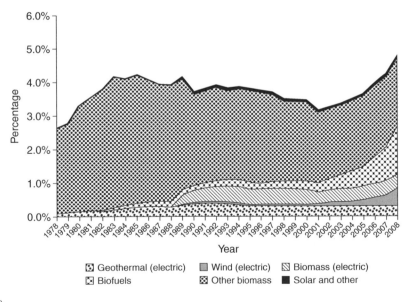

Source: EIA 2009a

Figure 11.1. Nonhydro renewable energy consumption as a percentage of total U.S. energy consumption, 1978–2008

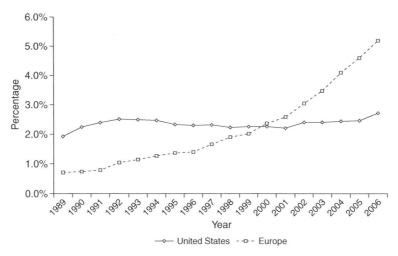

Source: EIA n.d.b

Figure 11.2. Share of nonhydro renewable electricity in total generation, 1989–2006

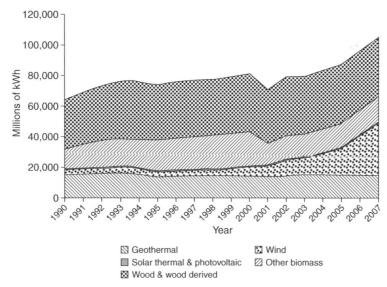

Source: EIA 2009b, *Data Table EIA-906*

Figure 11.3. U.S. electricity generation from nonhydro renewable energy, 1990–2007

is fueled by wood and wood waste; the remainder is fueled by biogenic municipal solid waste, landfill gas, and a variety of other substances. Between 1990 and 2007, geothermal generation declined slightly, and biomass-fueled generation grew at only a 1.1% average annual rate. In these data, solar generation grew at an average annual rate of 3%, but from a tiny base. Because the U.S. Energy Information Agency (EIA) tracks genera-

tion only from solar installations with capacities above 1 megawatt (MW), it seems likely that solar generation at the end of this period was understated by at least 60%.[1] Even correcting for this bias, however, solar's share remains tiny. Wind, which grew at an average annual rate of 15.9%, accounted for the bulk of NHR growth over this period.

Table 11.1. Actual and potential NHR generation in the United States

Resource	Estimated total realizable potential by 2020 (TWh)	Actual 2007 gross generation (TWh)	Actual as a percentage of potential
Biomass	501.6	58.6	11.7
Wind	300.4	32.3	10.8
Solar	85.2	0.7	0.8
Geothermal	36.0	16.9	47.0
Tidal & wave	2.3	0.0	0.0
Total	925.5	108.4	11.7

Sources: Estimated potentials from IEA 2008a, *65*; generation from IEA 2008c, *396*
Note: TWh = terawatt-hours

Many analysts contend that even with current technology, nonhydro renewables have the potential to play a much larger role in the United States than they do at present. Table 11.1 compares actual generation from nonhydro renewables in the United States in 2007 with estimates by the International Energy Agency (IEA) of "total realizable potential by 2020."[2] These estimates are intended to reflect both natural endowments (e.g., average solar radiation) and the relative costs of current NHR technologies, but they are inevitably imprecise and should accordingly be treated with caution. It is worth noting, however, that even though the IEA believes that solar generation has not even reached 1% of its potential, despite decades of attention by policymakers, the agency also estimates that its ultimate potential is much less than either biomass or wind.

There has been a great deal of variation in state-level experience with NHRs. In 2007, NHRs accounted for 2.53% of total U.S. net generation, but more than 5% in seven states and less than 1% in eleven states. This variation reflects differences in both the potential for various renewable technologies and state-level policies toward renewables. To shed quantitative light on the relative importance of these two sources of variation would require plausible estimates of state-level, technology-specific potentials comparable to the IEA estimates in Table 11.1, but no such estimates appear to exist.[3]

Table 11.2 provides information on the seven states for which NHR generation accounted for more than 5% of total generation, as well as the two states not in this set that were in the top five in terms of total NHR generation. These nine

Table 11.2. Leading NHR generation states

State	2007 NHR generation Percent of state total	2007 NHR generation TWh	Main NHR technology or technologies
Maine	26.1	4.21	Wood/wood waste
California	11.8	24.85	Geothermal
Vermont	8.0	0.65	Wood/wood waste
Minnesota	7.2	3.93	Wind
Hawaii	6.6	0.75	Wind, geothermal
Iowa	5.8	2.91	Wind
Idaho	5.7	0.65	Wood/wood waste
Texas	2.5	10.29	Wind
Florida	1.9	4.30	Wood/wood waste, other biomass

Source: EIA 2009c

states accounted for 92% of U.S. NHR generation in 2007. For most states, one technology is the dominant contributor to NHR generation, but two are nearly tied in both Hawaii and Florida. The importance of wood and wood waste is clear here, as it was in Figure 11.3, particularly in heavily forested states like Maine, Vermont, and Idaho. The so-called "wind belt," extending northward from Texas to the Canadian border, is visible here, though some states in that belt are conspicuous by their absence. (The wind belt is discussed below in the section on Wind Power in the United States.) It is also interesting to note the unimportance of solar power, even in states with abundant solar resources such as California, Hawaii, and Texas.

Federal Policies in Support of NHRs

The U.S. federal government has long supported research and development (R&D) aimed at advancing NHR technologies and has more recently moved to subsidize their deployment. Motivations for such support have varied over time; energy security is less important now than earlier, and environmental concerns, particularly those associated with global climate change, have become more important in recent years.

Research and Development

Government financial support for basic research and precommercial development aimed at advancing NHR, or almost any other, technology can be justified by the positive externalities that knowledge spillovers produce. Despite this rationale and strong rhetorical support for NHRs, however, the data reveal that U.S. policymakers have historically allocated more generous R&D support to fossil-fuel and nuclear technologies, which are generally much more mature than NHRs. Between 1978 and 2007, federally sponsored R&D on renewable technologies amounted to 17.8% of total energy-directed R&D, while 39.3% was spent on nuclear technologies and 32.1% on fossil-fuel technologies (EIA 2008a, 40).[4] Figure 11.4 graphs federal expenditure on renewables during this period.

Not only has federal R&D support for NHRs lagged behind that for more conventional technologies, but it has also varied substantially over

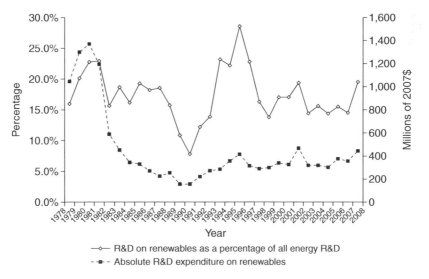

Source: EIA 2008a

Figure 11.4. Federal expenditure on R&D in renewable technologies, 1978–2007

time in both relative and absolute terms, as Figure 11.4 shows. R&D for NHRs, and for most other energy technologies, peaked in 1980, fueled by intense concerns over energy security and rapidly rising oil prices. As oil prices receded, so did energy-related R&D. Since the early 1980s, R&D funding in support of NHRs has been both modest and variable from year to year—hardly conducive to long-term, sustained efforts aimed at major breakthroughs.

Support for NHR Deployment: Conceptual Overview

Before examining actual federal and state policies to support the deployment of existing NHR technologies, it is worth noting that such policies are difficult to justify economically. In the presence of a binding cap on carbon dioxide emissions, for instance, a subsidy to NHR deployment will have no impact on total emissions but will raise the total social cost of meeting the cap. And although many claim that widespread deployment of NHRs will lower their costs through learning by doing, they rarely note that firm-specific learning that does not lower the costs of other firms does not justify subsidies. Rigorous empirical support for the importance or even existence of such spillover benefits is lacking. Other arguments for subsidizing NHR deployment, such as capital market imperfections (which somehow permit large, risky investments in other sectors), infant industry considerations (which logically should apply across the economy and have supported policies with a terrible historical record), and job creation (which lacks rigorous support and runs counter to historical progress by favoring labor-intensive over labor-saving technologies), are even less persuasive.

Nonetheless, subsidies of four basic sorts have been adopted in the United States and abroad: feed-in tariffs, output subsidies, investment subsidies, and output quotas. Feed-in tariffs, which guarantee a predetermined, above-market price for power over a period of years, are the most popular policy device outside the United States (BMU 2007; Coenraads et al. 2008; EREC 2007; European Commission 2008; IEA 2009).[5] They

provide strong incentives for minimizing costs and maximizing production. Feed-in tariffs, however, generally do not provide stronger incentives for generating electricity when it is more valuable (e.g., by scheduling maintenance accordingly), and they provide an invisible subsidy by shifting all risk related to the supply of and demand for electricity to other market participants. An output subsidy, paid on top of market price, can eliminate both of these shortcomings while retaining the other good incentive properties of a feed-in tariff. Output subsidies are not widely employed, however, and like feed-in tariffs, they can provide incentives to operate NHR facilities even when the marginal value of their generation is negative (e.g., see the discussion of Texas in the section on State Policies and Experience).

Investment subsidies are not particularly attractive economically, because they provide weaker incentives for reducing initial cost than do feed-in tariffs or output subsidies. Nonetheless, governments in the United States and abroad that promote deployment of NHRs almost all use investment subsidies as part of their policy packages. Finally, output quotas, known in the United States as renewable portfolio standards (RPSs), typically require load-serving entities to generate or procure a minimum fraction of energy from NHRs. This approach is not as popular as feed-in tariffs abroad, but it is very popular at the state level in the United States and is part of legislation being actively debated at the federal level.[6] Not only has the United States adopted a different mix of policies than most other wealthy nations, but it also has implemented those policies in ways that significantly limit their efficiency and effectiveness.

Federal Support of NHR Deployment

Somewhat ironically, in light of subsequent developments, the first federal initiative that supported deployment of NHRs did so almost unintentionally and led to the establishment of generous feed-in tariffs in several states. The Public Utilities Regulatory Policies Act of 1978 (PURPA) was primarily aimed at opening electric utilities to competition and increasing efficiency in electricity markets. PURPA required utilities to purchase electricity generated from certain defined "qualified facilities" at the utilities' avoided costs. Qualified facilities could be either cogeneration facilities, which produced both useful heat and electricity, or certain small NHR generators. Because electric utilities at that time were almost all vertically integrated, avoided costs were to be determined by state regulators rather than market prices, and regulators in some states (notably California, as discussed later in the section on State Policies and Experience) responded by establishing feed-in tariffs that were based on the expectation of high and increasing generation costs. As costs of conventional generation in fact came down, this system became unsupportable, and it was largely dismantled by the early 1990s (Borenstein and Bushnell 2000, *48*).

Since then, federal policy has promoted NHR deployment primarily through favorable corporate income tax provisions: accelerated depreciation and tax credits for production and investment. After 1986, most NHR generating assets, which had been depreciated over 15 years for tax purposes, could be written off over 5 years. (The list of eligible NHR technologies was expanded in 2005 and 2008.) This increased the present value of tax deductions for depreciation by around half.[7]

The Renewable Electricity Production Tax Credit (REPTC) was first established by the Energy Policy Act of 1992.[8] It provided for a corporate income tax credit of 2.1 cents per kilowatt-hour (kWh; 1.5 cents/kWh in 1993$, indexed for inflation) for generation using some technologies and half that for others for (generally) the first 10 years of operation. Favored NHR technologies are currently wind, closed-loop biomass, and geothermal; other eligible technologies include open-loop biomass, landfill gas, municipal solid waste, and certain hydroelectric, marine, and hydrokinetic facilities. The legislation establishing the REPTC also established a Renewable Energy Production Incentive (REPI) program, which authorized payments roughly equivalent to the production tax credit to entities such as state and local governments that were not corporate income tax payers.

This output subsidy policy has not been consistently or predictably implemented over time. Payments actually made under the REPI must be appropriated annually and thus are far from certain. Solar facilities were eligible for the REPTC only briefly—if they began operation in 2005. The REPTC expired at the end of 2001 and was then extended in March 2002. It then expired at the end of 2003 and was not renewed until October 2004, in legislation that extended it until the end of 2005. Legislation passed in 2005 extended it through the end of 2007, legislation passed in 2006 extended it through 2008, and laws passed in 2008 and 2009 revised and extended it through 2012 for wind and 2013 for other technologies. Figure 11.5 shows a surge in installation of wind capacity during 2001 before the REPTC expired, followed by a drastic drop-off during 2002, reflecting the uncertain status of the REPTC until March and the lag between project initiation and completion. Similarly, the unavailability of the REPTC during 2004 shows clearly in the figure. If investors cannot rely on a subsidy's remaining in place, that subsidy provides at most weak incentives for long-term investments in such things as technology development and efficient production capacity.

The Energy Tax Act of 1978, which was passed along with PURPA, established investment tax credits for a variety of NHR technologies. These were modified several times in the ensuing years (EIA 1999). Since 2005, the Residential Renewable Energy Tax Credit (RRETC) has provided personal income tax credits for up to 30% of investments in solar electric systems, solar hot water systems, wind turbines, fuel cells, and geothermal heat pumps. Also since 2005, the Business Energy Investment Tax Credit (BEITC) has provided a 30% corporate income tax credit for investment in essentially all solar systems except those used to heat swimming pools, as well as for fuel cells and small wind turbines. It provides a 10% investment tax credit for certain other technologies. Both of these provisions were initially scheduled to expire at the end of 2008, but legislation that year extended them to 2016.

For solar systems, the initial investment accounts for most of the life cycle cost, so a 30%

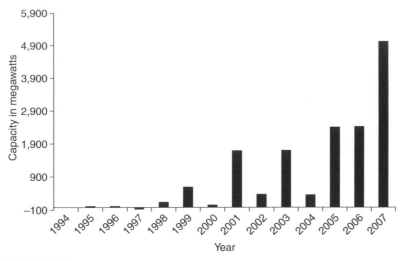

Source: EIA 2009b, *Table EIA-860*

Figure 11.5. Wind electricity capacity addition, 1994–2007

investment tax credit is a very large subsidy indeed. The Interstate Renewable Energy Council (Sherwood 2009) reports that the annual growth rate of photovoltaic capacity installed doubled in 2006, and capacity installed in 2008 was triple that in 2005. Similar dramatic growth occurred in solar hot water and space heating. It is important to note, however, that an investment tax credit is most valuable when it is less than current taxable income. This condition is probably satisfied for most homeowners who can seriously consider installing a solar system, but it is unlikely to be satisfied for any corporation specializing in grid-scale solar power. The need for such firms to use joint ventures and other devices to ensure that the full value of the investment tax credit is received can add significant friction to the process of financing solar projects.

The REPTC and BEITC have been the most important sources of support for renewables deployment. In FY2007, the reductions in tax revenue caused by subsidized financing of renewables facilities under other programs was $100 million, compared with $690 million in such tax expenditures for the REPTC and BEITC. But programs supporting fossil fuels were considerably more costly, resulting in $2.7 billion in tax revenue reductions (GAO 2007, *37*).

The American Recovery and Reinvestment Act of 2009, generally known as the stimulus bill, allows taxpayers eligible for the BEITC or the REPTC for facilities entering service or, generally, beginning construction in 2009 or 2010 to elect to receive a BEITC-equivalent cash grant instead. The rationale is that tax credits are of limited value during a period of unusually low corporate profits; but on the other hand, entitlement to a grant is of no value if Congress does not appropriate sufficient funds.

Several relatively small federal grant and loan guarantee programs also exist, each targeted at certain classes of entities (e.g., municipal governments) and technologies. These programs are modified from time to time, and the actual funding available is determined each year by the appropriations process. In FY2006, excluding energy efficiency, the federal government made only $16.7 million in grants to support renewables and guaranteed just $23.8 million in loans (GAO 2007, *50*).

As with R&D, it is interesting to compare federal subsidies for the use of NHRs with subsidies for other generation technologies. Table 11.3 shows EIA estimates of total subsidies and support by technology for 2007, both in absolute dollar terms and per megawatt-hour (MWh) of genera-

Table 11.3. Subsidies and support to electricity production by technology, 2007

Fuel/end use	2007 net generation (million MWh)	2007 subsidy ($ million)	Subsidy ($/MWh)
Coal & refined coal	2,018	3,010	1.49
Natural gas & oil	919	227	0.25
Nuclear	794	1,267	0.16
Hydroelectric	258	174	0.67
Solar	1	14	24.34
Wind	31	724	23.37
Other NHR[a]	70	59	0.84

Source: EIA 2008a, *xvi*
[a]Includes biomass (and biofuels), landfill gas, municipal solid waste, and geothermal

tion. In absolute terms, coal (especially clean coal) and nuclear power were the most heavily subsidized, while per unit of output, solar and wind were by far the biggest winners. It is interesting to note that wind, in particular, received more than 12 times as much support as "other NHR," even though those technologies accounted for more than twice as much generation.

State Policies and Experience

This section begins with an overview of state policies in support of NHR deployment and then provides brief discussions of the California and Texas experiences. It focuses initially on what is generally considered to be the most important state-level NHR policy and is certainly one of the most popular: renewable portfolio standards.[9]

Renewable Portfolio Standards

Renewable portfolio standards require that a minimum percentage of electricity generated or sold by a covered entity come from sources designated as renewable. Compliance is usually measured on an annual basis, and the required percentage typically increases over time. Iowa enacted the first RPS in 1983, and Nevada adopted the second in 1998. Since then, the pace has increased dramatically, and 29 states plus the District of Columbia now have RPSs. These include all the states listed in Table 11.2 except Vermont (which has a voluntary standard), Idaho, and Florida.

States with RPSs accounted for 62% of U.S. net electricity generation in 2007. Table 11.4 lists these states in order of their initial RPS adoption and gives some of their most important current features. Five additional states have voluntary goals for renewable energy; these are listed in Table 11.5.

While all RPS programs have the common goal of increasing the share of renewable resources, they differ considerably along multiple dimensions. One important difference is how compliance is to be achieved. In states with organized wholesale markets, entities that distribute power are generally responsible for meeting RPS targets and are given considerable freedom to choose how to do so. In states that have regulated, vertically integrated utilities, regulators oversee contracting and utility procurement. In New York and Illinois, a state agency has direct responsibility for the procurement of renewables under the RPS (Wiser and Barbose 2008). Some states have legislated explicit per-MWh penalties for noncompliance, whereas others allow the state's public utility commission to determine the appropriate penalty.

Differences also exist in the definition of resources that are deemed renewable and whether the RPS is applicable solely to investor-owned utilities or is extended to smaller retail suppliers with a lower target, as is the case in Colorado and Oregon. In some instances, the size of a facility is an important determinant of whether its output counts toward RPS requirements. Maine, for instance, requires facilities to be 100 MW or

Table 11.4. State renewable portfolio standards (RPSs)

State	First RPS adoption	Current target	Other requirements
Iowa	1983	105 MW	
Nevada	1997	6% by 2005, 20% by 2015	5% of RPSs to be solar in each year
Massachusetts	Nov. 1997	15% by 2020 (Class 1) and 1% each year thereafter, 3.5% of sales each year starting in 2009 (Class 2)[a]	To be determined
Connecticut	July 1998	27% by 2020	20% Class 1, 3% Class 2, 4% Class 3[b]
New Jersey	Jan. 1999	22.5% by 2021	2.12% solar by 2021
Texas	Sept. 1999	2,280 MW by 2007, 5,880 MW by 2015	500 MW from sources other than wind
Maine	1999	30% by 2000 (Class 2), 10% by 2017 (Class 1)[c]	
Hawaii	2001	20% by 2020	
Wisconsin	Oct. 2001	10% by 2015	
California	2002	20% by 2010	
Maryland	May 2004	20% by 2022 (Tier 1), 2.5% 2006–2018 (Tier 2)[d]	2% solar by 2022
Rhode Island	June 2004	16% by 2020	
New York	Sept. 2004	24% by 2013	Not specific
Colorado	Nov. 2004	20% by 2020	4% of RPSs to be solar in each year
Pennsylvania	Nov. 2004	18% by 2020 (8% Tier 1, 10% Tier 2)[e]	0.5% solar by 2020
DC	April 2005	20% by 2020	0.4% from solar by 2020
Montana	April 2005	5% in 2008, 10% in 2010, 15% in 2015	
Delaware	July 2005	20% by 2019	2.005% photovoltaic by 2019
Arizona	Nov. 2006	15% by 2025	30% of RPSs from distributed renewables after 2012
Washington	Nov. 2006	15% by 2020	
Minnesota	Feb. 2007	25% by 2025, Xcel Energy 30% by 2020	Xcel Energy 25% of RPSs from wind in each year
New Hampshire	May 2007	23.8% by 2025	0.3% solar, 6.5% existing biomass, 1% existing small hydro
Oregon	June 2007	25% by 2025	Varies by utility
Illinois	August 2007	25% by 2025	75% from wind
North Carolina	Aug. 2007	12.5% by 2020	0.2% solar & thermal by 2018, 0.2% swine waste by 2018, 900,000 MWh from poultry waste by 2014
New Mexico	Aug. 2007	20% by 2020	4% solar, 4% wind, 2% geothermal & biomass, 0.6% distributed renewables
Michigan	Oct. 2008	10% by 2015	Varies by utility
Missouri	Nov. 2008	15% by 2021	0.3% solar by 2021
Ohio	Jan. 2009	12.5% by 2025	0.5% solar by 2025
Kansas	May 2009	20% by 2020	

Source: DSIRE 2009a

[a]Class 1: (in-state, on-site) solar, wind, ocean thermal, wave and tidal, fuel cells, landfill gas, qualifying hydroelectric, qualifying biomass, geothermal; Class 2: (in-state, on-site) systems dating prior to December 1997 using the same technologies as Class 1

[b]Class 1: solar, wind, fuel cell, landfill gas, small hydroelectric, wave, tidal and ocean thermal, sustainable biomass; Class 2: trash to energy, biomass not included in Class 1; Class 3: customer-sited cooling-heating-power systems, recent savings from conservation and load management, recycled energy from heat pipes

[c]Class 1: RPS mandate to provide 30% of sales through renewables; Class 2: portfolio goal to increase new renewable capacity by 10% by 2017

[d]Tier 1: solar, wind, qualifying biomass, landfill gas, geothermal, wave, tidal and ocean thermal, small hydroelectric, fuel cells; Tier 2: trash to energy, hydroelectric other than pump storage

[e]Tier 1: new and existing solar, wind, small hydro, geothermal, biomass, fuel cells, qualifying gas; Tier 2: new and existing waste coal, large hydro, waste to energy, distributed generation, demand-side management, certain biomass

Table 11.5. State voluntary renewables goals

State	Date goal adopted	Current goal
North Dakota	August 2007	10% by 2015
South Dakota	February 2008	10% by 2015
Vermont	March 2008	20% by 2017
Utah	March 2008	20% by 2025
Virginia	July 2009	15% by 2025

Source: DSIRE 2009a

smaller. In other states, the age of a facility determines whether it is considered eligible. For example, in Massachusetts, only capacity installed after 1997 is considered eligible. Hydroelectric facilities are generally eligible subject to the capacity constraint that each state sets on facilities. Some states, such as New Hampshire, are explicit in their consideration of small hydroelectric facilities. A number of states have tiers or set-asides, often with different time frames or target levels. Fifteen states and the District of Columbia have provisions favoring solar power or distributed generation; nine have minimum solar requirements of various sorts; and the others give extra credit for solar or distributed generation. Illinois, on the other hand, requires that 75% of renewable generation come from wind. Nine of the RPS jurisdictions give at least some credit for solar hot water systems as displacing nonrenewable generation, and Hawaii, Nevada, and North Carolina have provisions that allow demand-side efficiency to be used to meet a part of the RPS requirements (Wiser and Barbose 2008).

The most common mechanism for demonstrating compliance with RPSs is the purchase of renewable energy certificates (RECs) (Corey and Swezey 2007). Renewable generators sell power at the market price and then also sell, in effect, a 1 MWh REC for each MWh of electricity they have sold. Distribution utilities and others obliged to obtain a minimum percentage of their electricity from NHRs demonstrate compliance by purchasing an appropriate number of RECs and surrendering these to the authorities. The ability to trade RECs ensures that costs are minimized within the state, as there are economic incentives to, in effect, produce the certificates using the cheapest available NHR technology. (This regime does not, however, create any incentive to favor technologies with large spillover benefits.) Because the potential for NHR generation differs widely among states, even in the absence of a nationwide RPS, interstate trading of RECs would potentially be an important way of reducing the cost of meeting the states' goals. But unfortunately, state RPS programs differ in so many dimensions—including the precise definition of an REC—that interstate trading is virtually impossible. Indeed, some state RPS programs prohibit it altogether.

At the federal level, in 2005, the Senate passed a bill containing a national RPS that would have required 10% of electricity in the country to be generated by renewables by 2020, but the bill died in the House. In 2007, the House passed legislation containing a national RPS of 15% by 2020; this bill died in the Senate. Most recently, the American Clean Energy and Security Act of 2009, or Waxman–Markey bill, passed by the House in June 2009, contains a national RPS with nationally tradable RECs. The bill's standard, which could be met with a combination of energy efficiency savings and NHR generation, would start at 6% in 2012 and rise to 20% by 2020. As of this writing, the fate of this provision is yet to be determined.

A majority of state RPS programs have only recently become operational—10 of them are less than three years old, and 19 are less than five years old. Furthermore, RPSs are just one of the many state-level policies that have been adopted to promote renewable energy. As a consequence, it is difficult to make confident statements about the effectiveness of RPSs in increasing NHR generation, let alone assess their costs. A significant impact is suggested by the fact that in 2007, states with RPS programs accounted for an overwhelming 86% of new NHR generating capacity, as compared with just 22% of all new generating capacity (EIA 2009b, *Data Table EIA-860*). In a multivariate statistical analysis, Menz and Vachon (2006) find that RPS programs effectively encourage cumulative renewable energy investment and capacity deployment. However, in a later analysis using additional control variables, including the environmental orientation of each state's legislators and the size of each state's agencies concerned with natural resources, Carley (2009) finds that the adoption of RPS mandates does not effectively increase the share of renewable electric generation. There are at least reasons to be concerned that some of these programs may fail to meet their goals.

Other State Policies

In addition to RPSs of various shapes and sizes, state governments have adopted a wide variety of other measures aimed at promoting NHR generation. Table 11.6 provides some information regarding their popularity. As with RPSs, no two state policies for a particular type of incentive are identical.

Table 11.6. Other state policies to promote NHR generation

Type of incentive	Number of states
Personal tax: credits or other	21
Corporate tax: credits or other	23
Sales tax: exemption or deduction	25
Property tax: exemption or special assessment	32
Rebates programs	19
Grant programs	22
Subsidized bond or loan programs	34
Production incentives	9
Public benefit funds	18
Net metering	43

Source: DSIRE 2009a
Note: The District of Columbia is counted as a state in this table

The IEA lists the three most important state policies promoting renewables as RPSs, public benefit funds, and tax incentives (IEA 2008a). Public benefit funds are generally financed by a small surcharge on retail electric rates and are used to support renewable energy in a wide variety of ways. They are projected to total $7.3 billion by 2017 (DSIRE 2009a). All states except Arkansas offer some subsidy for investment in NHR generation, but the design and impact of tax benefits, rebates, grant, and subsidized bond or loan programs vary enormously.

Beginning with Massachusetts and Wisconsin in 1982, 42 states and the District of Columbia have established net metering policies, and the Energy Policy Act of 2005 requires all utilities to provide net metering to customers that request it. Net metering allows utility customers with some NHR generators, generally only small residential or commercial installations, to sell electricity to the distribution entity that serves them at the retail rate the customer pays for electricity, not the typically much lower wholesale rate the distribution entity pays for other power. In Massachusetts in 2007, for instance, retail rates averaged $0.152 per kWh, while the average wholesale price in the New England market was only $0.068 per kWh (EIA n.d.b; FERC 2009). A small part of this difference reflects power losses in transmission and distribution, but these losses average only about 7% of net generation in the United States (see, e.g., EIA 2009b). Most of the wholesale–retail difference arises simply because regulated prices do not reflect incremental costs: retail rates are generally set to recover the fixed costs of distribution systems through a per-kWh charge added to wholesale electricity rates rather than through fixed charges of one sort or another.

Although net metering programs are popular in state capitals, they are not yet widely used. Only 48,280 utility customers participated in net metering programs in 2007; 95% were residential, and 72% were in California (which established its program in 1995). But participation did grow at a 46% annual rate over the 2004–2007 period (EIA 2007, 2008b).

Ten U.S. states—Connecticut, Delaware, Maine, Maryland, Massachusetts, New Hampshire, New Jersey, New York, Rhode Island, and Vermont—have recently signed the Regional Greenhouse Gas Initiative (RGGI) agreement.[10] The agreement obliges these states to cap their total CO_2 emissions from the electric power sector through 2015, and then reduce them by 10% by 2018. Beginning at the start of 2009, electric utilities in these states have had to obtain and surrender allowances equal to their CO_2 emissions. These allowances are mainly auctioned by the governments of the 10 states involved. In principle, this system caps utility CO_2 emissions in the affected region, but allowance prices have so far been quite low: $2 to $3 per ton of CO_2, a fraction of prices in the European Union's Emissions Trading System for CO_2. It thus seems unlikely that this system has so far had much effect on the deployment of nonhydro renewables.

Finally, it is interesting to note the relative unpopularity of production incentives such as feed-in tariffs and output subsidies in the United States. Perhaps the most important in this country is the California feed-in tariff discussed below, but it is available only to small generators.

California: A Long History of Carrots

California was an important early leader among U.S. states in promoting NHR generation. Despite generating only 5.5% of the nation's electricity in 1990, California accounted for 37% of U.S. NHR generation that year. As Figure 11.6 shows, however, California's share of NHR generation has declined over time as other states have moved to promote renewables, but in 2007, California still accounted for just under 24% of national NHR generation.

California's early high share of national NHR generation is mainly due to its response to PURPA. In 1983, the California Public Utilities Commission (CPUC) developed policies that guaranteed qualifying facilities generous feed-in rates for a period of 10 years. These policies were based on assumptions that oil prices (and therefore avoided costs) would continue to rise from what were then already high levels (Hirsh 1999). The result was a boom in construction of small NHR generators and other qualifying facilities. Even though the CPUC suspended further contracts

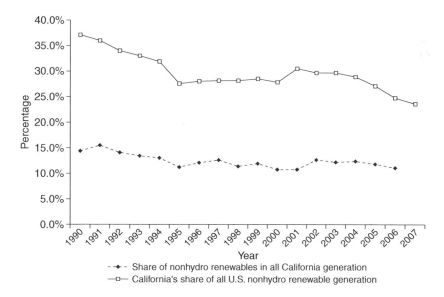

Source: EIA 2009b, *Data Table EIA-906*

Figure 11.6. Nonhydro renewables in California, 1990–2007

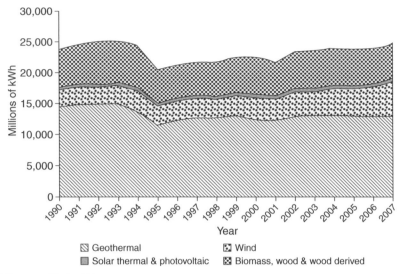

Source: EIA 2009b, *Data Table EIA-906*

Figure 11.7. Electricity generation by nonhydro renewable sources in California, 1990–2007

for power generation in 1985, qualifying facilities that had already contracted with the CPUC were permitted to sell power at high rates. By 1986, California had nearly 90% of *global* wind generating capacity (DOE 2008, *6*). Figure 11.7 shows that the bulk of the resulting NHR generation was powered by geothermal energy and biomass. It also shows that a number of these facilities shut down when their PURPA contracts expired between 1993 and 1995, though most continued to operate.

In the ensuing years, California adopted a wide variety of policies to promote solar and other NHR generation, relying more heavily on subsidies of various sorts than on regulation or mandates, but Figures 11.6 and 11.7 show that these policies did not produce significant increases in the NHR share of total generation or even the absolute amount of NHR generation.[11] In 1995, for instance, the CPUC proposed an RPS regime to increase renewable generation, but the following year, the legislature adopted a production-based auction funded by surcharges on electric utility bills instead (Wiser et al. 1996). This program ran from 1998 to 2001, provided between $540 million and $640 million in funding each year, and supported 4,400 MW of existing and

1,600 MW of new renewable capacity (Ritschel and Smestad 2003; Wiser et al. 1996).[12]

Between 1998 and 2007, California's Emerging Renewables Program, funded by the ratepayers of California's four largest investor-owned utilities, has funded roughly 130 MW of capacity additions from smaller wind, solar, and fuel cell facilities (CEC 2009). The Self Generation Incentive Program (SGIP), funded at roughly $83 million each year, supports customer-generated renewable energy via wind, solar, and fuel cell sources. Between 2001 and 2007, the SGIP funded over 300 MW of total capacity additions.[13]

In 2006, California adopted the California Solar Initiative (CSI), a 10-year $3.2 billion program to fund the development of 3,000 MW of solar capacity (DSIRE 2009c). Part of the CSI is the New Solar Homes Partnership, a 10-year $400 million incentive-based program aimed at constructing homes with solar energy systems with a focus on energy efficiency (DSIRE 2009d).

Beyond the big-ticket subsidy programs described above, the state of California runs a slew of smaller, more localized funding programs for renewable energy development. These include 5

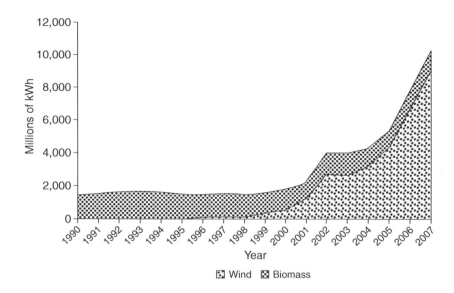

Source: EIA 2009b, *Data Table EIA-906*
Note: Solar-generated electricity accounted for up to 385,000 kWh of generation in 1990, but that number decreased to zero in 2001

Figure 11.8. Electricity generation by nonhydro renewable sources in Texas, 1990–2007

utility-specific grant programs, 11 utility-specific loan programs, and 94 utility-specific rebate programs and other smaller financial incentives. And solar systems are exempted from local property taxes.

Following eight earlier adopters, California enacted an RPS in 2002. The California RPS requires electric utilities to acquire 20% of their electricity from renewable sources by 2010. More recently, the state has adopted a nonbinding goal of 33% by 2020. Of the 7,000 MW of contracts for renewable generation signed between 2002 and 2007, 53% is wind, 23% solar, 12% geothermal, 7% biomass, and less than 1% small hydro and ocean energy (Wiser and Barbose 2008). It should be clear from the foregoing, however, that the RPS is but one in a large set of policies aimed at promoting NHR generation in California.

In 2008, California established a feed-in tariff for small renewable energy facilities with capacities of 1.5 MW or less. It has the efficiency-enhancing feature that rates are to vary by time of day. Facilities that sell power under this tariff are not eligible for additional state incentives and programs (DSIRE 2009b).

Texas: RPS-Driven Wind Energy Development

In contrast to California, Texas was slow to embrace NHR generation, and it does not seem to have made much use of explicit subsidies. In 1990, Texas accounted for less than 2% of national NHR generation, even though it generated 9.3% of the nation's electricity. Dramatic changes began to occur in 1999, when Texas adopted an RPS program with binding obligations beginning in 2002 and extending (as amended) to 2015. As Figure 11.8 shows, the result was extraordinary growth in wind power, dwarfing the California growth shown in Figure 11.7. In 2007, Texas accounted for 9.8% of U.S. electricity generation and an identical percentage of NHR generation. And in 2008, Texas accounted for 31% of new U.S. wind generation capacity, more new capacity than any *country* except China and the United States (AWEA 2009). Texas currently has about 8,800 MW of wind generating capacity (AWEA 2009; ERCOT 2009a), which is about 12% of total capacity, and is projected to have 18,500 MW of wind generating capacity by 2015 (O'Grady 2009).

Observers who have analyzed Texas's RPS attribute its strong impact to several factors. At least initially, the system was technology-neutral,[14] so the most economical resource—wind in this case—could be used most intensively. As discussed below in the section on Wind Power in the United States, Texas, along with a few other states, is blessed with excellent wind resources. This is particularly true of western Texas, where wind speeds average 8 meters per second year-round, and wind power facilities can operate at capacity factors of 40% or more (Langniss and Wiser 2003), at the upper end of the 25%–40% range commonly cited for wind generators (see, e.g., AWEA 2009). The remote location of these sites and the lack of transmission infrastructure initially inhibited exploitation of their potential. Subsequent legislation required utilities to upgrade their transmission systems as necessary to meet the state's RPS goals and allowed them to recover the costs in retail rates (DSIRE 2009a; Langniss and Wiser 2003). As discussed further below, however, transmission from these sites nonetheless remains a problem.[15]

It is also important that the Texas RPS program applies to most of the state's retail electricity load in a way that permits these remote sites to be fully exploited. While most RPS programs set generation requirements, Texas's RPS sets requirements for capacity and thus for capacity additions year by year. Owners of renewable generating capacity can sell both electricity and renewable energy credits to any electricity retailer in the Texas market, and retailers can freely buy, sell, and bank these credits. A capacity conversion factor, now based on performance of renewable generating units in the two prior years, is used to convert capacity requirements into MWh requirements, which are allocated to retailers based on their shares of statewide electricity sales. The relatively large, organized, competitive wholesale power market in Texas (Potomac Economics 2009) has enabled an effective market for renewable energy credits.[16]

In addition, the structure of the Texas RPS enables renewable energy suppliers to sign long-term (10- to 25-year) contracts, which reduces their risk and makes it easier to raise capital, thus lowering costs. Because the law sets annual requirements, each retailer can forecast how many credits it will need in the future and can thus confidently sign long-term contracts with renewables suppliers.[17]

Finally, the Texas RPS legislation provides strict, automatic penalties for noncompliance, while providing flexibility to electricity retailers through the ability to trade and bank renewable energy credits (Langniss and Wiser 2003). The California program, in contrast, seems to rely on the general enforcement powers and discretion of the Public Utility Commission to deal with any instance of noncompliance.

Wind Power in the United States

According to the IEA (2008a, *65–66*), the potential for wind-powered electricity generation in the United States substantially exceeds that in any other Organisation for Economic Co-operation and Development (OECD) nation, as well in Brazil, Russia, India, and China. In 2008, the U.S. Department of Energy published a detailed analysis of a scenario under which wind would account for 20% of U.S. electricity generation by 2030 (DOE 2008). And, as noted earlier in the section on Nonhydro Renewables in the United States, wind-powered generation grew at a 15.9% average annual rate during 1990–2007 and accounted for the bulk of NHR growth over that period. That growth has not been geographically uniform, however. Additionally, because wind, like solar but unlike some other NHR technologies, is intermittent, that growth is raising new issues of power system design and operation.[18]

According to the American Wind Energy Association, 12 states in the so-called Wind Belt, stretching northward from Texas to the Canadian border, have 93% of the wind energy potential in the United States (AWEA n.d.).[19] Table 11.7 provides information on these states, as well as 3 states on the Pacific Coast that have substantial wind generation despite having considerably less potential than the Wind Belt states. Together, the 15

Table 11.7. Leading wind generation states

| State/region | Estimated wind potential (TWh) | 2007 Wind generation | | | Initial RPS year |
		TWh	% of est. potential	% of total generation	
North Dakota	1,210	0.62	0.05	1.99	
Texas	1,190	9.01	0.76	2.22	1999
Kansas	1,070	1.15	0.11	2.30	2009
South Dakota	1,030	0.15	0.01	2.44	
Montana	1,020	0.50	0.05	1.71	2005
Nebraska	868	0.22	0.03	0.67	
Wyoming	747	0.76	0.10	1.65	
Oklahoma	725	1.85	0.26	2.54	
Minnesota	657	2.64	0.40	4.84	2007
Iowa	551	2.76	0.50	5.65	1983
Colorado	481	1.29	0.27	2.40	2004
New Mexico	435	1.39	0.32	3.87	2007
Wind Belt total	9,984	22.33	0.22	2.58	
California	59	5.59	9.47	2.65	2002
Oregon	49	2.44	2.56	2.28	2006
Washington	37	1.25	6.52	2.26	2007
Pacific total	161	9.27	6.39	2.49	
Total Wind Belt + Pacific	10,129	31.60	0.31	2.55	
Rest of U.S.	648	2.85	0.44	0.10	

Sources: Estimated potentials are from AWEA n.d. and, for Washington and Oregon, personal communication with AWEA. Generation data are from EIA 2009c, and RPS dates are from Table 11.4

states listed in the table accounted for 30% of all U.S. electricity generation in 2007 and 92% of wind-powered generation. The table also shows when the states that have RPSs initially enacted them.

Table 11.7 reveals a number of interesting patterns. First, all these states look very different from the rest of the country in terms of their potential for and use of wind generation. Second, Texas and California stand out in terms of total wind generation, together accounting for just over a third of the U.S. total. Third, there is enormous variation in the extent to which the potential for wind generation is exploited, with the three Pacific Coast states generating much larger percentages of their estimated potentials than any of the Wind Belt states. In the case of California, this is clearly attributable to very generous early subsidies for renewable generation. Oregon and Washington are also well known as green states, but they were not early adopters of RPSs, nor do they have sub-

sidy programs with California-like levels of generosity. Part of the reason for their relatively intensive exploitation of their wind potential may be that California utilities have taken advantage of their ability to meet their RPS obligations by purchasing NHR power generated elsewhere.

Within this group of states, the share of total generation accounted for by wind also shows substantial variation. Here, though, neither Texas nor the Pacific states are outliers. On the high side, Iowa and Minnesota are the most reliant on wind generation. Iowa was an early RPS adopter, but Minnesota was not. On the low side, both in terms of reliance on wind generation and exploitation of wind potential, Nebraska, Wyoming, Montana, and North Dakota stand out. Among these four, only Montana had an RPS in 2007. Perhaps more important, all are relatively small in terms of population and total electricity generation, and all are distant from major population centers, so that the wind integration problems discussed below are unusually difficult. More generally, the Wind Belt suffers from the fact that only 7% of the U.S. population lives in the top 10 states for wind potential (NERC 2009a).

As mentioned earlier, the rapid growth and significant penetration of wind power are raising important issues in power system design and implementation. Wind power is intermittent, meaning both that the output of wind-powered generators is *variable* over time and that it is *uncertain*—it cannot be perfectly forecast. The output of hydroelectric facilities is also variable and uncertain because rainfall cannot be perfectly forecast, but these features manifest themselves over timescales of months or years. The output of wind facilities is variable and uncertain over timescales of hours; the output of solar facilities can vary from minute to minute as clouds pass by overhead. Because residential, commercial, and industrial demands also vary over these timescales, at small levels of penetration wind power poses no new issues. At large scales, however, an influential industry group has concluded that "reliably integrating high levels of variable resources [including wind and solar] into the North American bulk power system will require significant changes to traditional methods used for system planning and operations" (NERC 2009a).[20]

Perhaps the most talked-about manifestation of the variability of wind power took place in Texas on February 26, 2008 (ERCOT 2008; Galbraith 2008; Grant et al. 2009, *51–52*). As the evening electricity load was increasing, wind generation dropped from over 1,700 MW to 300 MW in a three-hour period because wind speeds decreased. This was roughly equivalent in magnitude to a single large fossil-fuel generating unit going offline—not a rare event—and it happened gradually. (Moreover, commercial forecasts, not available to the grid operators, had predicted the fall in wind speeds.) This emergency, which was exacerbated by the unforeseen unavailability of some fossil-fuel-fired capacity, was mainly handled by curtailing service to large industrial and commercial users that had contracted for interruptible power, reducing system loads by 1,100 MW within a 10-minute period. Although wind provides only a few percent of generation in Texas

on average, winds in the western part of the state generally blow the strongest at night, when demand is low. As a result, wind can provide more than 10% of power in Texas on some occasions, making its variability a potentially more serious issue. In fall 2008, the operators of the Texas grid increased backup power requirements, particularly at night.

With wind generation in Texas expected to more than double by 2015, wind's variability is projected to be a more serious concern going forward, and more flexible gas-fired capacity will likely be needed. Since power prices tend to be low at night, however, and the gas-fired units used to provide backup power tend to have high marginal costs, some observers worry that the Texas market may not provide sufficient backup capacity (see O'Grady 2009 and Chapter 9 of this volume).[21]

Similar issues have confronted the Bonneville Power Administration (BPA), which operates the grid in the Pacific Northwest with about 41,000 MW of peak generating capacity. During one 24-hour period in December 2008, BPA received near-zero levels of wind generation early and late in the day, punctuated by nearly 1,600 MW around midday. Between January 5 and 14, 2009, wind output varied from 500 MW to 1,500 MW—followed by two weeks of zero output. In part, this high degree of variability has arisen because most of the relevant capacity is geographically concentrated along the Washington–Oregon border—just as much of Texas's wind generation capacity is concentrated in the western portion—and thus wind conditions are highly correlated within the generating fleet (Riner 2009, *8*).[22]

As wind power gains in importance, it will become more important to enhance the flexibility of the overall electric power system (Grant et al. 2009; IEA 2008b; Milligan et al. 2009; NERC 2009a). The basic methods for doing this are well known. One can, in principle, increase demand responsiveness to supply conditions and go well beyond what was possible in the Texas emergency discussed above. A variety of institutional, regulatory, and technological barriers make this far from straightforward, however. On the supply side, one can add generating units that can increase or decrease output rapidly (mainly gas-fired under current technology) or add grid-level storage (generally too expensive with current technology). Alternatively, one can use transmission and operational integration to create large power systems, taking advantage of the fact that "the correlation between production from multiple wind plants diminishes as those plants are geographically farther apart" (Kirby and Milligan 2008, 3). It is often difficult to get permission to build transmission capacity in this country, however, and geographic averaging is inherently expensive in areas that are thinly populated and distant from major load centers, like many of the states in the Wind Belt.

In addition, some utilities (and their regulators) have been reluctant for a variety of reasons to join the large integrated regional systems operated by regional transmission operators (RTOs) and independent system operators (ISOs) that currently meet about two-thirds of U.S. electricity demand (IRC 2007). The open, flexible wholesale electricity markets operated in those systems help integrate wind generation economically and reliably. In light of these advantages, it is not surprising that as of the end of 2007, 74% of U.S. installed wind generating capacity was located in ISO and RTO regions, even though those areas had only 44% of the nation's wind energy potential (Kirby and Milligan 2008). Nor is it surprising that Minnesota and Iowa, which have the highest levels of wind energy penetration (see Table 11.7) and do not appear to have experienced serious operational problems, are part of the Midwest ISO. So is North Dakota, but this state has not actively promoted renewable generation, and it is distant from the major load centers in this ISO. On the other hand, Nebraska and Wyoming, which make conspicuously little use of their abundant wind resources, are not in an organized regional market, and neither is most of Montana.

Finally, a number of observers have commented on the fact that spot electricity prices in west Texas are often negative, particularly at night, when the wind is strongest and demand is lowest (Lively 2009; Wang 2008; see also Lawhorn et al. 2009, 86–87). This generally happens when the power lines connecting the wind generators in the west to the major load centers elsewhere in the state are operating at capacity, and spot prices in the rest of the state are positive. Negative prices would induce conventional thermal generating units to shut down, unless the energy cost of ramping up when demand rises would exceed the costs of paying the grid operator to take power. Wind units do not generally incur ramp-up costs, and when there is an excess of power, it would commonly be more efficient for wind units to cease production than for, say, a base load coal plant with significant ramp-up costs to do so. (There are currently no costs of CO_2 emissions to factor into this comparison in most of the United States.) But if a wind-powered generator remains in operation, it earns both the federal REPTC of 2.1 cents/kWh and the value of the renewable energy credits to which its output entitles it. In Texas, it is apparently a better deal for wind generators to pay the grid operator 4 cents/kWh to take their output than to shut down. In the case of Texas, adding transmission capacity seems the best way to deal with this problem, and the state plans to add more than 2,300 miles of new transmission capacity by 2015, about a 6% increase (ERCOT 2009b; O'Grady 2009). More generally, output subsidies and feed-in tariffs can be expected to raise operating issues of this sort from time to time.

Conclusions

Though it is far from certain as this is written that the United States will soon adopt a cap-and-trade system to limit CO_2 emissions from the combustion of fossil fuels, there seems a fair chance that it will do so within, say, the next decade. Whether or not this happens, and even though supporting the deployment of NHR generation would make little economic sense if a CO_2 cap were in place, it seems close to certain that, as in Europe, U.S. governments will nonetheless continue to support both the development and deployment of NHR technologies. And, absent a dramatic change in the nature of support policies, it also seems close to certain that wind will account for the dominant share of new NHR generating capacity in the United States for some years to come.

As the References section at the end of this chapter indicates, much attention is currently being paid, in the United States and abroad, to the challenges posed by large-scale integration of wind and other intermittent generation technologies. But it seems that almost no attention is being devoted to increasing the economic efficiency of state and federal policies that subsidize development and deployment of NHR technologies. Among the issues raised by the current U.S. regime and discussed above that deserve serious thought are the following:

- Federal R&D support has tended to favor relatively mature fossil and nuclear technologies, and support for NHR technologies has been far from steady over time.
- Channeling federal support for NHR deployment primarily through the corporate income tax disadvantages small firms without substantial income streams and complicates project financing generally.
- The variability of federal subsidy programs over time discourages investments in long-lived tangible and intangible capacity by producers of NHR generating equipment.
- Subsidies tied to the level of initial investment provide weak incentives for cost containment or efficient and reliable operations.
- When transmission capacity is inadequate, output subsidies (and feed-in tariffs) can create perverse incentives to generate power when it is not needed.
- The variation in state-level renewable portfolio standards almost entirely prevents interstate trading, which would lower total national costs of meeting state-specific targets.
- Although states have adopted a variety of different RPS designs, little systematic analysis has been done of the performance implications of these design differences.
- Federal policy toward the electric power sector has ignored the evidence that organized ISO/RTO wholesale power markets facilitate deployment of NHR generation.

- The myriad state and federal (and other) NHR programs and policies confront a would-be NHR generator with unproductive complexity.

The last of these issues is not likely to go away, as complete preemption of state and local authority in this area is hard to imagine. Nor would the ideal way forward be simply to adopt some other nation's policy regime. Other chapters in this volume make it clear that no perfect solution to the problem of efficiently subsidizing NHR deployment has yet been implemented. But as in other areas of public policy, careful economic analysis could at least increase the returns from investments in deployment subsidies.

Acknowledgments

The author is indebted to Dhiren Patki for superb research assistance and Boaz Moselle for exceptionally useful comments on an earlier draft. This chapter also benefited from the author's participation in the MIT Future of Solar Energy study, in which Kevin J. Huang provided excellent research assistance.

Notes

1. According to the International Energy Agency (IEA 2008c), which bases its U.S. figures on data submitted by the EIA, solar-thermal installations accounted for 97.4% of 2007 U.S. solar-electric generation, whereas according to the Interstate Renewable Energy Council (Sherwood 2009), which measures all grid-connected solar electric capacity, solar thermal units accounted for only 49.2% of average solar generating capacity in 2007 (taking the average of solar thermal and photovoltaic (PV) capacities at the end of 2006 and the end of 2007). If PV units had the same capacity factor as solar thermal units on average, total U.S. solar generation was 98% above the IEA figures. It was at least 60% above the IEA figures if PV units had at least 62% of the capacity factor of solar thermal units, and this seems a conservative assumption.

2. Two clarifying observations are in order. First, the IEA's data are based on reports submitted to it by national statistical agencies such as the EIA, so the IEA understates U.S. solar generation just as the EIA does. Second, the IEA reports gross electricity generation, including estimated in-plant losses, whereas all EIA numbers are for net generation. Net generation is about 5% below gross generation for the United States as a whole.

3. Estimates of the state- and technology-specific potentials have been published by the Union of Concerned Scientists (UCS; see Deyette et al. 2003). The UCS estimates did not take into account costs, however, and they imply total national potential roughly 20 times as large as the IEA's and with a very different pattern across technologies. The UCS estimate of solar potential was 3 times as large as that of biomass potential, and estimated wind potential was 19 times as large.

4. The remainder (10.9%) was devoted to end-use technology.

5. At least 16 of the 30 OECD nations have feed-in tariffs, as do 7 of the 8 European Union (EU) member states that are not OECD members.

6. Only seven EU members employ this device, three of which also use feed-in tariffs. Two non-EU OECD nations also employ this mechanism. (Coenraads et al. 2008; EREC 2007; European Commission 2008; IEA 2009)

7. Conventional generation assets are depreciated using 150% declining balance over 15 years, with the option to switch to straight-line depreciation at any point. Qualifying NHR generating assets can be depreciated using 200% declining balance over 5 years, with the same option. The figure in the text was computed by assuming the switch occurs when it is most profitable and employing a 10% discount rate. For more details, see Metcalf (2009a, b).

8. Except where noted in the following discussion, all information on state and federal policies is from DSIRE (2009a).

9. Rabe (2007) suggests that these policies are popular because they are seen to rely on market forces. A more cynical assessment would be that their costs are less visible than those of other subsidy types.

10. A good source of information on this initiative is its website, www.rggi.org/home.

11. For an interesting discussion on this topic, see Taylor (2008).

12. The surcharge has been estimated to have added between 2% and 3% to the price of a kWh. The proceeds were aimed at production credits for biomass, wind, solar, geothermal, and small hydroelectric facilities.

13. Like the Emerging Renewables Program, funding for solar and PV projects for the SGIP was taken over by the California Solar Initiative in 2007.

14. As noted above, Texas has given a premium for nonwind renewable generation since 2005 (DSIRE 2009a).

15. Observers have also noted that the use of a zonal pricing system within Texas, rather than a nodal pricing system, contributed to inefficient use of transmission capacity; see Potomac Economics (2009).

16. Connecticut is one example of a state where the RPS applies to such a small section of the electricity market as to be rendered marginal (Langniss and Wiser 2003).

17. In contrast, in some states, considerable uncertainty exists around the size and scope of the RPS, as well as its end date. For instance, in Maine, the RPS is slated to be reviewed every five years, and in Connecticut and Massachusetts, the end date of the RPS is unclear.

18. These issues have also been encountered in other countries with high levels of wind penetration. For an interesting discussion of the experience in four such countries, see Ackerman et al. (2009).

19. The AWEA's total estimated U.S. potential is 36 times the IEA estimate, indicating that the former includes sites that the latter does not deem economic by 2020. The AWEA numbers are used here on the assumption that they are correlated with potentials that would be estimated using the IEA's assumptions and methods.

20. For illuminating recent discussions of wind integration issues, see Grant et al. (2009) and Milligan et al. (2009).

21. A similar problem has recently been analyzed quantitatively in the German context; see Traber and Kemfert (2009).

22. For an interesting discussion and graphical depiction of wind variability, see NERC (2009b).

References

Ackerman, Thomas, Graeme Ancell, Lasse Diness Borup, Peter Børre Ericksen, Bernhard Ernst, Frank Groome, Matthias Lange, Corinna Möhrlen, Antje

G. Orths, Jonathan O'Sullivan, and Miguel de la Torre. 2009. Where the Wind Blows. *IEEE Power & Energy Magazine* 7: 65–75.

AWEA (American Wind Energy Association). 2009. Annual Wind Industry Report: Year Ending 2008. www.awea.org/publications/reports/AWEA-Annual-Wind-Report-2009.pdf (accessed February 22, 2010).

———. No date. Top 20 States with Wind Energy Resource Potential. www.awea.org/newsroom/pdf/Top_20_States_with_Wind_Energy_Potential.pdf (accessed February 22, 2010).

BMU (Federal Ministry for the Environment, Nature Conservation and Nuclear Safety). 2007. *EEG—The Renewable Energy Sources Act: The Success Story of Sustainable Policies for Germany.* Berlin: BMU. www.gtai.com/uploads/media/EEG_Brochure_01.pdf (accessed September 3, 2009).

Borenstein, Severin, and James Bushnell. 2000. Electricity Restructuring: Deregulation or Reregulation? *Regulation* 23: 46–52.

Carley, Sanya. 2009. State Renewable Energy Electricity Policies: An Empirical Evaluation of Effectiveness. *Energy Policy* 37: 3071–3081.

CEC (California Energy Commission). 2009. Emerging Renewables Program. www.energy.ca.gov/renewables/emerging_renewables/index.html (accessed July 17, 2009).

Coenraads, R., G. Reece, C. Klessmann, M. Ragwitz, A. Held, G. Resch, and C. Panzer. 2008. *Renewable Energy Country Profiles: Final Version February 2008.* Utrecht, Netherlands: EU Commission.

Corey, Karlynn, and Blair Swezey. 2007. Renewable Portfolio Standards in the States: Balancing Goals and Rules, *Electricity Journal* 40: 21–32.

Deyette, Jeff, Steve Clemmer, and Deborah Donovan. 2003. *Plugging in Renewable Energy: Grading the States.* Washington: Union of Concerned Scientists.

DOE (U.S. Department of Energy). 2008. 20% Wind Energy by 2030: Increasing Wind Energy's Contribution to U.S. Electricity Supply. DOE/GO-102008–2567. Washington, DC: DOE. www.20percentwind.org/20percent_wind_energy_report_revOct08.pdf (accessed February 22, 2010).

DSIRE (Database for State Incentives for Renewables and Efficiency). 2009a. Project of the North Carolina Solar Center and Interstate Renewable Energy Council funded by the U.S. Department of Energy's Office of Energy Efficiency and Renewable Energy. www.dsireusa.org (accessed February 22, 2010).

———. 2009b. California Feed-In Tariff. www.dsireusa.org/incentives/incentive.cfm?Incentive_Code=CA167F&re=1&ee=1 (accessed February 22, 2010).

———. 2009c. California Solar Initiative. www.dsireusa.org/incentives/incentive.cfm?Incentive_Code=CA134F&re=1&ee=1 (accessed February 22, 2010).

———. 2009d. CEC: New Solar Homes Partnership. www.dsireusa.org/incentives/incentive.cfm?Incentive_Code=CA150F&state=CA&CurrentPageID=1&RE=1&EE=1 (accessed February 22, 2010).

EIA (Energy Information Administration). 1999. *Federal Financial Interventions and Subsidies in Energy Markets 1999: Primary Energy.* Washington, DC: EIA.

———. 2007. *Green Pricing and Net Metering Programs, 2005.* Washington, DC: EIA.

———. 2008a. *Federal Financial Interventions and Subsidies in Energy Markets 2007.* Washington, DC: EIA.

———. 2008b. *Renewable Energy Annual 2007.* Washington, DC: EIA.

———. 2009a. *Annual Energy Review 2008.* Washington, DC: GPO. www.eia.doe.gov/aer/overview.html (accessed February 22, 2010).

———. 2009b. *Electric Power Annual 2007.* Washington, DC: EIA.

———. 2009c. *State Renewable Energy 2007.* Washington, DC: EIA.

———. No date, a. Electricity. www.eia.doe.gov/fuelelectric.html (accessed November 14, 2009).

———. No date, b. International Energy Statistics. http://tonto.eia.doe.gov/cfapps/ipdbproject/IEDIndex3.cfm?tid=6&pid=29&aid=12 (accessed February 22, 2010).

ERCOT (Electricity Reliability Council of Texas). 2008. ERCOT Demand Response Program Helps Restore Frequency Following Tuesday Evening Grid Event. www.ercot.com/news/press_releases/2008/nr02-27-08 (accessed February 22, 2010).

———. 2009a. ERCOT Expects Adequate Power Supply for Summer: Update. www.ercot.com/news/press_releases/2009/nr05-29-09 (accessed February 22, 2010).

———. 2009b. ERCOT Quick Facts. www.ercot.com/content/news/presentations/2009/ERCOT_Quick_Facts_February_2009.pdf (accessed February 22, 2010).

EREC (European Renewable Energy Council). 2007. National Policy: Overview of EU Member States. www.erec.org/policy/national-policy.html (accessed September 3, 2009).

European Commission. 2008. *Commission Staff Working Document: The Support of Electricity from Renewable Sources.* SEC(2008) 57. Brussels: EU Commission. http://ec.europa.eu/energy/climate_actions/doc/2008_res_working_document_en.pdf (accessed February 22, 2010).

FERC (Federal Energy Regulatory Commission). 2009. Electric Power Markets: New England (ISO-NE). www.ferc.gov/market-oversight/mkt-electric/new-england.asp#prices (accessed November 14, 2009).

Galbraith, Kate. 2008. Texas Adjusts Its Grid for Wind. *New York Times*, Nov. 13. http://greeninc.blogs.nytimes.com/2008/11/13/texas-adjusts-its-grid-for-wind/ (accessed February 22, 2010).

GAO (U.S. Government Accountability Office). 2007. *Federal Electricity Subsidies: Information on Research Funding, Tax Expenditures, and Other Activities that Support Electricity Production.* Washington, DC: GAO.

Grant, William, Dave Edelson, John Dumas, John Zack, Mark Ahlstrom, John Kehler, Pascal Storck, Jeff Lerner, Keith Parks, and Cathy Finley. 2009. Change in the Air. *IEEE Power & Energy Magazine* 7: 47–58.

Hirsh, Richard F. 1999. PURPA: The Spur to Competition and Utility Restructuring. *Electricity Journal* 12: 60–72.

IEA (International Energy Agency). 2008a. *Deploying Renewables: Principles for Effective Policies.* Paris: IEA.

———. 2008b. *Empowering Variable Renewables.* Paris: IEA. www.iea.org/g8/2008/Empowering_Variable_Renewables.pdf (accessed February 22, 2010).

———. 2008c. *Renewables Information 2008.* Paris: IEA.

———. 2009. Global Renewable Energy: Policies and Measures. www.iea.org/textbase/pm/?mode=re (accessed September 3, 2009).

IEEE (IEEE Global History Network). 2008a. Milestones: Vulcan Street Plant, 1882. www.ieeeghn.org/wiki/index.php/Milestones:Vulcan_Street_Plant,_1882 (accessed September 3, 2009).

———. 2008b. Pearl Street Station. www.ieeeghn.org/wiki/index.php/Pearl_Street_Station (accessed September 3, 2009).

IRC (ISO/RTO Council). 2007. Progress of Organized Wholesale Electricity Markets in North America: A Summary of 2006 Market Data from 10 ISOs & RTOs. www.isorto.org/atf/cf/{5B4E85C6–7EAC–40A0–8DC3–003829518EBD}/IRC_State_of_the_Markets_Report_103007.pdf (accessed February 22, 2010).

Kirby, B., and M. Milligan. 2008. *Facilitating Wind Development: The Importance of Electric Industry Structure.* NREL Technical Report NREL/TP-500–43251. NREC.

Langniss, Ole, and Ryan Wiser. 2003. The Renewables Portfolio Standard in Texas: An Early Assessment. *Energy Policy* 31: 527–535.

Lawhorn, John, Dale Osborn, Jay Caspary, Bradley Nickell, Doug Larson, Warren Lasher, and Manzar Ea. Rahman. 2009. The View from the Top. *IEEE Power & Energy Magazine* 7: 77–88.

Lively, Mark B. 2009. Renewable Electric Power—Too Much of a Good Thing: Looking at ERCOT. *USAEE Dialog* 17 (2): 21–26.

Menz, Frederic C., and Stephan Vachon. 2006. The Effectiveness of Different Policy Regimes for Promoting Wind Power: Experiences from the States. *Energy Policy* 34: 1786–1796.

Metcalf, Gilbert E. 2009a. *Investment in Energy Infrastructure and the Tax Code.* Tufts University, Department of Economics.

———. 2009b. Tax Policies for Low-Carbon Technologies. *National Tax Journal* 62: 519–533.

Milligan, Michael, Kevin Porter, Edgar DeMeo, Paul Denholm, Hannele Holttinen, Brendan Kirby, Nicholas Miller, Andrew Mills, Mark O'Malley, Matthew Schuerger, and Lennart Soder. 2009. Wind Power Myths Debunked. *IEEE Power & Energy Magazine* 7: 89–99.

NERC (North American Electric Reliability Corporation. 2009a. Accommodating High Levels of Variable Generation. www.nerc.com/files/IVGTF_Report_041609.pdf (accessed February 22, 2010).

———. 2009b. How BPA [Bonneville Power Administration] Supports Wind Power in the Pacific Northwest. www.nerc.com/docs/pc/riccitf/BPA_supports_wind_power_for_the_Pacific_Northwest_Mar_2009.pdf (accessed February 22, 2010).

O'Grady, Eileen. 2009. Texas Power Suppliers Facing Wind Challenges. www.reuters.com/article/idUSTRE59701B20091008 (accessed February 22, 2010).

Potomac Economics. 2009. 2008 State of the Market Report for the ERCOT Wholesale Electricity Market. www.puc.state.tx.us/wmo/documents/annual_reports/2008annualreport.pdf (accessed February 22, 2010).

Rabe, Barry. 2007. Race to the Top: The Expanding Role of U.S. State Renewable Portfolio Standards. *Sustainable Development Law and Policy* 10: 10–16.

Riner, Bobette. 2009. BPA Struggling with Vagaries of Wind Power. *Natural Gas Week*, July 29.

Ritschel, Alexander, and Greg P. Smestad. 2003. Energy Subsidies in California's Electricity Market Deregulation. *Energy Policy* 31: 1379–1391.

Sherwood, Larry. 2009. U.S. Solar Market Trends 2008. Interstate Renewable Energy Council (IREC). www.irecusa.org/fileadmin/user_upload/ NationalOutreachDocs/SolarTrendsReports/ IREC_Solar_Market_Trends_Report_2008.pdf (accessed March 19, 2010).

Taylor, Margaret. 2008. Beyond Technology-Push and Demand-Pull: Lessons from California's Solar Policy. *Energy Economics* 30: 2829–2854.

Traber, Thure, and Claudia Kemfert. 2009. Gone with the Wind? Electricity Market Prices and Incentives to Invest in Thermal Power Plants under Increasing Wind Energy Supply. DIW Berlin Discussion Paper No. 852. http://ssrn.com/abstract=1430905 (accessed February 22, 2010).

Wang, Ucilia. 2008. Texas Wind Farms Paying People to Take Power. *Greentech Media*, Dec. 10. www.greentechmedia.com/articles/print/texas-wind-farms-paying-people-to-take-power-5347/ (accessed February 22, 2010).

Wiser, Ryan, and Galen Barbose. 2008. *Renewable Portfolio Standards in the United States: A Status Report with Data through 2007.* Berkeley, CA: Lawrence Berkeley National Laboratory.

Wiser, Ryan, S. Picker, and C. Goldman. 1996. *California Renewable Energy Policy and Implementation Issues—An Overview of Recent Regulatory and Legislative Action.* Berkeley, CA: Lawrence Berkeley National Laboratory.

12

The European Union's Policy on the Development of Renewable Energy

Christopher Jones

This chapter discusses policy in the European Union (EU) toward renewable energy. It begins with a general history of the development of EU policy, then looks more specifically at the main elements of the Renewable Energy Directive adopted by the EU at the beginning of 2009. This is followed by a discussion of future energy targets, as well as issues and challenges the EU will face in meeting them. Finally, grid and energy security issues are examined.

The Gradual Development of an EU Policy on Renewable Energy

Although it is generally considered that the European Union's push toward developing an ambitious policy to support the growth of renewable energy is recent, in fact this development began as early as 1996, when, in a Green Paper on renewable energy, the European Commission suggested an indicative target for a share of renewable energy of 12% for 2010, equivalent to a doubling of share in the EU at the time (European Commission 1997). It is interesting to note that the reasons why the commission proposed this target focused on the issue of energy security (the EU was steadily becoming more dependent on imported energy from Russia and the Middle East) at least as much as, if not more than, environmental issues.

This target was endorsed by the European Council in its resolution on the matter from June 1997, stating that a target of 12% renewable energy by 2010 "is ambitious and could give useful guidance for increased efforts at Community as well as at Member State level" (European Council 1997). The European Parliament, for its part, proposed a goal of 15% and also called on the commission to submit specific measures, including the setting of targets per member state.

The next step was the commission's White Paper of 1997,[1] which argued that "an indicative target is a good policy tool, giving a clear political signal and impetus for action." At the time, however, no attempts were made to divide the target among the member states, and the target was not given a legal status in community legislation. The White Paper went no further than to suggest that "targets in each Member State could stimulate the efforts towards increased exploitation of the available potential" and that it would be important that each define its own strategy and "within it propose its own contribution towards the overall 2010 objective" (European Commission 1997, 10).

The White Paper led to the proposal and subsequent adoption on September 27, 2001, of the

Renewable Electricity Directive (2001/77/EC), which laid down indicative minimum targets for the share of renewable energy in electricity generation in each member state and introduced provisions that did the following:

- obliged member states to introduce guarantees of origin for renewable electricity, with some (rather general) requirements regarding their format and operation;
- required member states to actively consider how to reduce administrative burdens applicable to production plants for renewable electricity;
- set forth rather general requirements regarding grid connection and operation in an attempt to eliminate any potential discrimination that renewable electricity producers might face in getting access to the grid, including a provision stating that member states "may also provide for priority access to the grid system of electricity produced from renewable energy sources" and that "when dispatching generating installations, transmission system operators shall give priority to generating installations using renewable energy sources insofar as the operation of the national electricity system permits"; and
- laid down various reporting obligations on both member states and the commission.

Although the text of the final directive seems to provide very little in terms of concrete and legally binding obligations on member states, a careful reading of its Article 3(2) makes it clear that member states have to take "appropriate steps" to achieve the targets given in the Directive and publish a report setting out how they intended to achieve this. Logically, therefore, if such a report was clearly inadequate in terms of the measures proposed in order to meet the target, the member state would have failed to have met its obligation in 3(2). Indeed, the commission has commenced investigations into certain member states for failing to comply with this provision of the directive.[2]

However, it is clear that the burden of proof was on the commission to demonstrate that the member state's plan could not have any reasonable chance of meeting its 2010 target. In fact, various commission reports indicated that the EU was not likely to meet its overall target of 21% of the EU's total electricity supply coming from renewable sources by 2010. A result of 19% was considered more likely.

The second piece of legislation flowing from the White Paper was the 2003 "Biofuels" Directive (2003/30/EC), which required member states to set targets for renewable energy in transport in 2005 and 2010, taking the reference values of 2% and 5.75% into account. The commission began infringement proceedings against nine member states that initially failed to properly fulfil the first of these obligations. All subsequently set targets for 2005, 2010, or both that the commission considered appropriately ambitious in relation to the requirements of the directive. The text does not, however, require member states to achieve the targets they have set themselves. As with the Renewable Electricity Directive, commission reports have indicated that many member states, and thus the EU as a whole, are unlikely to meet their targets by 2010. A result of 4.2% has been considered more likely (European Commission 2009a).

Following the period when these directives were adopted, the EU's energy position changed considerably. Although groundbreaking at the time, it rapidly became clear that these measures were inadequate to meet the needs of Europe's energy and climate policy for the 21st century. Three developments in particular can be identified as leading to this change.

First, the price of oil increased from $23/barrel in 2001, when the Renewable Electricity Directive was adopted, to between $50 and $65/barrel in the period 2005–2007, then to $126/barrel in June 2008. Second, it was becoming more and more evident that the EU was becoming overwhelmingly dependent on imports, especially of oil and gas, for its energy; and higher prices and volatility of imports were increasingly viewed as a threat to the EU's prosperity. Finally, the EU's heads of state and government became convinced that climate change was such a threat that it demanded immediate and determined action by the EU, even though much of the rest of the world was failing to take equivalent action, notably in the case of the U.S. Bush administration.

The European Council at Hampton Court in October 2005 discussed the need for the EU to develop a new European energy policy to meet three core objectives: sustainability, security of energy supply, and competitiveness. It invited the commission to put forward a blueprint for change. At that time, the price of oil had recently doubled over two years, and a gas dispute between Russia and the Ukraine looked increasingly likely. Indeed, such a dispute erupted shortly after the council, in December 2005, leading to limited interruptions to the EU's gas supplies. In the light of these developments, the council invited the commission to propose a new energy policy for Europe.

The commission presented its First Strategic EU Energy Review in January 2007, titled "An Energy Policy for Europe" (European Commission 2007b). The key elements of this review appear in the appendix at the end of this chapter. The review explains the EU's rationale for all subsequent changes in its energy policy and then details the concrete proposals, which were later endorsed by the EU's heads of state and government, as well as the European Parliament.

In essence, the review unequivocally accepts the need for the EU to act to limit the global temperature increase to 2°C compared with preindustrial levels, and it identifies and accepts the existence of growing threats to the EU's energy security. It considers that dealing with these challenges could provide a major opportunity for the EU in terms of competitiveness, jobs, and growth, and then proposes the following strategic energy objectives for the EU:

- *an EU objective in international negotiations of 30% reduction in greenhouse gas emissions in developed countries by 2020 compared to 1990. In addition, 2050 global GHG emissions must be reduced by up to 50% compared to 1990, implying reductions in industrialised countries of 60–80% by 2050;*

- *an EU commitment now to achieve, in any event, at least a 20% reduction of greenhouse gases by 2020 compared to 1990.*

In order to achieve these goals, the commission proposed the revision of the emissions trading system to bring it into line with the 20% objective by 2020 and to improve its functioning; the agreement of an objective for the EU to improve its energy efficiency by 20% by 2020 (meaning that, if achieved, the EU would reduce its energy consumption by some 13% compared with 2005 levels); and finally, that the EU should agree on a 20% target for renewable energy in its total energy mix (compared with about 8.5% in 2005). These proposals have become known as the "20-20-20" package.

It is worth reflecting on quite how ambitious this package of measures was and remains. First, 20% greenhouse gas cut by 2020—a unilateral commitment irrespective of action outside the EU—would be far from simple to achieve and would require difficult actions. Second, the 20% renewable energy objective should be seen in light of recent developments in the EU's energy mix. Of the 8.5% renewable energy in the EU's energy mix at the time, some 7% came from biomass and hydro, established for purely commercial reasons. The additional 1.5% from wind, PV, solar, and other renewables had been added over the course of a decade and meant that the EU had been by far the world leader in installing new renewable capacity. In essence, therefore, the 20% target meant that in just 11 years, the EU would commit to installing more than 10 times the renewable capacity that it had achieved over the previous decade. Or to put it another way, every year over the next decade, the EU would install the same renewable energy capacity that it had achieved over the entire last decade. Furthermore, it was proposed that this 20% target would not simply be a vague political commitment, but would be enforced thorough legally binding commitments placed on every single EU member state.

The first significant step toward the agreement on the "new directive" referred to in the commission's Energy Review—the future Renewable Energy Directive—was taken by the European

Council of March 2007, under the German presidency and a very determined Chancellor Angela Merkel. The chancellor considered it vital for the EU's credibility in ongoing attempts to promote an international agreement on climate change that a real commitment to the commission's proposals be reached at the council.

The council formally endorsed the commission's "20-20-20" proposal, including the principle of legally binding targets for renewable energy for each member state. It invited the commission to submit concrete proposals to make the "20-20-20" approach a reality. In addition, it agreed with the commission's proposal that 10% of all transport fuels must come from renewable energy sources by 2020 in every member state.[3] It is probably fair to say that the commission's approach regarding the overall renewable energy targets, asking the council to endorse the principle and the overall EU target while deferring the question of how the target would later be shared among the member states, facilitated agreement.

The commission proposed a package of measures on January 23, 2008, including a revision of the EU Emission Trading System (ETS) for the period 2013–2020 so that it would achieve cuts commensurate with the EU's political commitments to reduce greenhouse gases by 2020 and to include the principle of auctioning allowances rather than free allocation (with some exceptions); legally binding greenhouse gas targets on member states for non-ETS sectors; and a new Renewable Directive.

It is worth highlighting the fact that the EU has taken the approach of having a specific target for renewable energy in addition to binding measures on ETS and non-ETS sectors. It is true that some argued that separate renewable energy targets were unnecessary, even counterproductive. Given the existence of an ETS regime that would cover the electricity sector, surely, it was argued, this should set the level of renewable energy compared with nuclear, carbon capture and storage (CCS), and so forth. Indeed, according to the modeling work undertaken by the commission in preparing its 20-20-20 proposal, the ETS system would be expected to produce about 14% of

renewable energy in the EU's energy mix by 2020, without the need for further action.

However, the member states took the view that such an approach would not meet the EU's wider energy policy aims, for several reasons. First, the EU considered that it was in its interests in terms of energy supply security to ensure that a greater proportion of its energy was generated indigenously, via renewables. The EU already had the position of world leader in renewable energy installations, notably wind and PV, and this was providing considerable employment in the EU and creating an important export industry. According to Energy Commissioner Andris Piebalgs at a technology conference in Stockholm in October 2009:

> *Sixty per cent of the world's wind capacity was installed in Europe at the end of 2007, and European companies had a global market share of 66 per cent of turbine sales … Our low-carbon energy industry today, which exists quite simply because we have invested where others watched, has produced 1.4 million jobs, a figure that could double by 2020, and exports of a value of 3.7 b€ … We are exporting our 3, and 5 MW windmills. These probably would not have been developed in the EU were it not for our determination to take a risk by supporting these technologies before they were mature. We are exporting our leading-edge PV panel systems, our bio-gas plants, our biofuel expertise, and our concentrated solar technologies.*

Second, there was real concern that the ETS system alone would not provide the necessary incentives to maintain a thriving renewable energy industry in the EU, and many doubted that it would in reality lead to even 14% of renewable energy in the EU's energy mix by 2020. These doubts followed from the EU's experience in support schemes for renewable electricity to date. Three types of support schemes have been operating in the EU:

- Tendering schemes, where a government determines how much renewable electricity (or any other form of renewable energy) it wants and tenders for the company willing to construct and operate the capacity for the lowest subsidy.

- Green certificates, where a government places an obligation on electricity retailers to ensure that a minimum percentage of their sales are renewable in origin. They are obliged to acquire enough green certificates to demonstrate that this minimum level is achieved, and producers of renewable electricity are allocated certificates for their production, which they can then sell. The price is thus set by the market, based on the cost of the marginal certificate necessary to meet the required level of demand.

- Feed-in tariffs, where a government decides what level of subsidy should be given to the different forms of renewable energy, and producers are paid this subsidy for each unit produced (such as kilowatt-hours). It is usually electricity distributors that are given an obligation to purchase and then resell to final customers the renewable electricity produced in their catchment areas, and to pay the feed-in tariff subsidy to the generator, financing it through a customer charge on the distribution tariff. Normally a mechanism exists to compensate distributors in areas that have a greater level of renewable energy than others. One advantage of such a system is that it enables a government to give different subsidies to different technologies, such as a lower price to onshore wind than to photovoltaics (PV) or offshore wind, eliminating windfall profits that might result when prices are set by the marginal, most expensive unit of production.

The commission has carefully followed the relative success of each system, as have many others. In principle, one would expect that the tendering option and green certificate system would lead to the lowest prices because of the competition among producers that would result. However, this has not proven to be the case. Perhaps because of the immature nature of green certificate markets that have operated to date in the EU, it appears that the uncertainty regarding future price levels that is inherent in a green certificate system (given the speed of technological development, it is normal to assume that the price will reduce over time), the risk premium demanded under such systems appears to be high. In any event, green certificate systems have typically led to higher prices than have feed-in tariffs. In addition, green certificate and tendering systems have had problems in catalyzing the actual construction of the level of renewable energy that has been desired, apparently because of the difficulty in attracting financing to what is inherently a more risky investment than a feed-in tariff system. Green certificate schemes have never been introduced at the size necessary to create a truly liquid market, however, nor with the long-term certainty needed for them to develop optimally.

Another reason why a feed-in tariff may be cheaper than a green certificate system stems from the ability to differentiate among the costs of different forms of renewable energy in the feed-in tariff system, which is not typically a feature of a green certificate system.[4] One could argue that a green certificate system based on the price of the marginal unit will result in pushing producers into more of the cheaper technologies, where they make more profit, thereby bringing down the price. However, the ability to move into these cheaper technologies is constrained by planning and environmental constraints; it is this element that differentiates renewable energy from other markets, where competition will always push producers to install cheaper production techniques.

An additional concern for green certificate systems results from the speed of increase in demand that will result from the new Renewable Energy Directive. Supply for renewable energy can be "lumpy" because of the difficulty in getting planning permission for new, large projects. There is genuine concern that supply will have difficulty in keeping up with exponentially growing demand, enabling the price for the price-setting marginal (and scarce) unit to be very high. This is not an inherent feature of the feed-in tariff system. One answer to this problem is to have separate green certificates for different forms of renewable electricity, so that each will reach its own competitive price level. However, this would require that the government decide how much of each type of renewable energy it desires when setting the green certificate requirements on distributors, which is not necessary under the feed-in tariff system.

These issues were considered vital when determining whether the EU should rely on the ETS mechanism to support the development of renewable electricity, or whether it should continue its approach with separate EU and national renewable targets. As the ETS system is economically the same as a green certificate system, some questions remain as to its effectiveness on an imperfect renewable electricity market, and it brings the same level of risk, in terms of both cost and its ability to actually deliver the amount of renewable energy needed.

At the end of the day, it is these reasons that have led the EU to establish a separate renewable energy target, partly a rational response to the EU's emerging energy security vulnerability, and partly an industrial policy consideration based on the beliefs that the global market for renewable facilities would continue to expand greatly over the coming decades, and that the continued growth of installed capacity in the EU would underpin its industry's continued major role. Indeed, this objective has been underlined by the EU's recent focus on increasing its support to emerging low-carbon energy technology with the Strategic Energy Technology Plan and the Financing Communication (European Commission 2009b). In the Financing Communication, the commission has set out a series of Technology Road Maps identifying the concrete research projects that will need to be undertaken in the EU up to 2020 and proposing a doubling of the current levels of public support to such research and development (R&D).

The European Council and Parliament agreed on the 20-20-20 package, with its formal adoption taking place on December 11–12, 2008, less than one year after its presentation by the commission. The Renewable Directive has the following key elements:

- A community decision to ensure that by 2020, 20% of the EU's total energy needs will come from renewable energy sources. It is notable that the directive refers to renewable energy as a proportion of the EU's total energy consumption and not just its electricity production, as was the case in the existing Renewable Electricity Directive.

- Division of this target among the EU's 27 EU member states in the form of separate, legally binding minimum renewable energy targets on a state-by-state basis. It is this legally binding nature that marked the biggest departure from earlier renewable energy legislation.

- A method to permit one member state to invest in the production of renewable energy in another member state or, under different rules, in a third country, with the resultant energy counting toward the investing member state's target.

- Rules to overcome administrative barriers to the development of renewable energy and ensure access to the grid, in particular for electricity from renewable sources.

- An obligation on all member states to ensure that at least 10% of their energy needs for road transport are met through renewable energy sources. This does not mean a 10% biofuel obligation, as alternatives might be used, such as cars powered by renewable electricity or renewably produced hydrogen. It is clear, however, that much of the 10% will come from biofuels. The directive prescribes minimum sustainability criteria that must be respected for any biofuels counting toward the target, to ensure that they effectively contribute to a real and important reduction in carbon dioxide compared with burning gas or diesel fuel.

The Main Elements of the New Directive

Following is a short summary of the new Renewable Energy Directive adopted by the EU at the beginning of 2009.[5]

Legally Binding National Targets

In reaching agreement on the directive, one of the most difficult issues was the division of the 20% target among the individual member states. As the target was to be legally binding in nature, if a member state fails to meet it, the commission may, through an infringement procedure, bring the country in question before the European Court of Justice for failing to meet its EU law obligations. Given the fact that meeting the target would imply the granting of subsidies by member states, the division of the 20% was of central importance in the negotiations.

The European Council conclusions of December 11–12[6] specifically referred to the need to set the national targets "with a view to sharing efforts and benefits fairly and equitably among all Member States, taking into account different national circumstances, starting points and potentials." The commission considered two basic approaches for sharing the target among member states: sharing the effort on the basis of member states' national resource potential; or sharing on the basis of a flat-rate increase in the share of renewable energy (measured in percentage points) in each member state weighted by gross domestic product (GDP) per capita.

Under the first approach, each member state's renewable energy resources and costs were estimated, together with a forecast for total energy consumption in 2020. On the basis of this, an economic modeling exercise was carried out to determine the effort sharing. This would result in lower cost for the EU, because the targets would reflect the potential for producing renewable energy in each member state.

Under the second approach, each member state would have to increase its share of renewable energy by a fixed number of percentage points, to which a modulated contribution defined according to a set of objective criteria, most importantly GDP per capita, would be added. This would lead to targets that would reflect the economic strength of the member states rather than the potential for increasing the share of renewable energy.

Although both approaches obviously have merit, at the end of the day the commission concluded that the latter approach would be appropriate, finally assigning targets partly on a pro rata basis, all member states contributing equally to achieve half the target, and partly on a GDP per capita basis. This mixed approach was considered to be a simple and fair distribution of the effort, in which the wealth of the different member states would be reflected through a GDP per capita criterion. In detail, this approach was applied by the commission as follows:

- First, the existing share of renewable energy as a percentage of the total energy mix was calculated for each member state for 2005. The share was then adjusted to reflect efforts already made: those member states whose growth in renewable energy was more than 2% over 2001–2005 received a reduction of a third of that growth from the 2005 base year share (referred to as an "early-starter bonus"). In total, the EU needs to increase the share of renewable energy in its energy mix by 11% to meet the 20% by 2020 target. For the pro rata part of the target, 5.5% was added to each member state's existing share of renewable energy in 2005.
- For the remaining 5.5% of the EU's energy mix to be met by renewable energy, this was allocated on the basis of a contribution per EU citizen, weighted by a GDP per capita index to reflect different levels of wealth across member states, and multiplied by each one's population.
- The next step was to add together these two elements to derive the full renewable energy share of total final energy consumption in 2020.
- Finally, a cap was introduced to ensure that no target would be 50% or more of the total national energy mix for any member state.

The targets per member state, as adopted by the European Council and Parliament, are shown in Table 12.1.

Table 12.1. Member state targets

	Share of energy from renewable sources in gross final consumption of energy, 2005	Target for share of energy from renewable sources in gross final consumption of energy, 2020
Belgium	2.2%	13%
Bulgaria	9.4%	16%
Czech Republic	6.1%	13%
Denmark	17.0%	30%
Germany	5.8%	18%
Estonia	18.0%	25%
Ireland	3.1%	16%
Greece	6.9%	18%
Spain	8.7%	20%
France	10.3%	23%
Italy	5.2%	17%
Cyprus	2.9%	13%
Latvia	32.6%	40%
Lithuania	15.0%	23%
Luxembourg	0.9%	11%
Hungary	4.3%	13%
Malta	0.0%	10%
The Netherlands	2.4%	14%
Austria	23.3%	34%
Poland	7.2%	15%
Portugal	20.5%	31%
Romania	17.8%	24%
Slovenia	16.0%	25%
Slovak Republic	6.7%	14%
Finland	28.5%	38%
Sweden	39.8%	49%
United Kingdom	1.3%	15%

In addition to these targets, the directive also provides requirements regarding the trajectory that member states should respect over time. This is important. As mentioned above, the member state targets are legally binding. In other words, each member state accepts a community law obligation to ensure that its share of renewable energy meets the above levels by 2020. Failure to do so would result in legal sanction by the European Court for failure to have met its obligation. However, if the commission could take action only for failure of a member state to meets it obligation at the end of

the 2020 period, it would be a rather theoretical exercise, as it would be too late for the country in question to do anything to meet the target at that stage.

While in many respects the ideal approach would have been to have had both a legally binding end target and a binding minimum trajectory, it was felt that this did not give member states enough flexibility. Thus an indicative trajectory was agreed on, whereby member states should achieve 20% of their target by 2012 (i.e., 20% of the difference between the level of renewable energy in their energy mix in 2005 and their 2020 target) and 30% by 2014. It is true that this minimum trajectory is rather flat, and it was agreed upon on the basis that expected cost reductions for renewable energy, particularly for PV and offshore wind, mean that it makes sense to focus most efforts during the period 2015–2020. Achieving 30% of the target by 2014, however, would put member states in a reasonable position by that date to make the final target a realistic proposition.

Member states are not subject to infringement proceedings solely for not meeting the minimum indicative trajectory. Regardless, this does not make the trajectory ineffective. In combination with another obligation contained in Article 3(2) of the directive, which requires member states to take "measures effectively designed to ensure that the share of energy from renewable energy sources equals or exceeds that shown in the indicative trajectory," the indicative trajectory becomes important. The explicit connection between these two elements—the indicative trajectory and the effectively designed measures—was designed to allow the commission to use the trajectory as a series of benchmarks for individual member states when assessing compliance with the obligation to take measures effectively designed to increase the share of renewable energy.

The directive does not define what kind of effectively designed measures will be required. It is obvious that they will need to include appropriate renewable energy support schemes, as well as measures when necessary on grid connection, planning, and the availability of adequate finance.[7]

It therefore seems clear that the requirement for member states to adopt effectively designed measures, combined with the indicative trajectory, will be effective in ensuring that the aims of the directive will be met in practice. Member states are obliged to submit national action plans to the commission on a regular basis, the first by June 2010. These will be produced according to an agreed standard format, explaining the measures that member states have taken and intend to adopt in order to ensure that they will meet their final targets as well as their indicative trajectories. Where these plans manifestly put a member state on a path whereby it will be unrealistic for it to achieve its final target, one may reasonably assume that the commission could already bring an action against the country in question before the European Court of Justice, on the grounds that the member state in question had infringed Article 3(2) of the directive, as it had not taken "measures effectively designed to ensure that the share of energy from renewable energy sources equals or exceeds that shown in the indicative trajectory."

In conclusion, therefore, the directive sets ambitious, legally binding, and effectively enforceable targets for member states that should be achieved in practice.

Trade in Renewable Energy Credits

Renewable energy is a good. The EU has been built on four fundamental freedoms: trade, labor, capital, and services. This is based on the belief that competition and the law of comparative advantage will push the production of goods and services in the EU to the point where it is economically most beneficial to produce them. The law of comparative advantage applies to few products more strongly than renewable energy. It makes as much sense to put PV panels on houses in northern Europe when roofs in southern Europe have none as to produce olives in greenhouses in Finland.

Logically, the EU should support renewable energy where it is the cheapest to produce it, as in fact the Common Agricultural Policy in principle supports the production of food in the EU where it is most advantageous to do so in climatic and soil terms.

Nonetheless, the manner in which the national targets have been allocated, as explained above, was in the end not based on where the economic potential for renewable energy in the EU exists. Roughly speaking, much of the best renewable potential in the EU is concentrated in the south (sun), at the northern periphery (offshore wind), and in the eastern member states (biomass). Allocating targets solely on the basis of economic renewable energy potential in many cases would have placed the highest burden on the poorest countries. The final compromise, allocating targets on a split pro rata–GDP per capita basis, means that targets are allocated irrespective of economic potential, and often countries with the highest targets have relatively limited renewable economic potential.

In such circumstances, it can clearly be argued that trade in renewable certificates, or guarantees of origin (which the directive requires member states to issue to renewable energy producers on request in a standardized manner to enable mutual recognition), should be a basic principle underlying the directive. Member states would meet their national targets by offering support to generators regardless of where they are located. Generators and producers would then establish themselves where it would be the cheapest to produce, meaning that national subsidy schemes would be as limited as possible.

It is with this in mind that the commission originally proposed elements of a free trade approach for renewable energy. During negotiations with the council and parliament, however, this was rejected in favor of a more restricted approach, for two reasons. First, the market for renewable energy is special in that it relies on subsidies for its existence (at least at present; costs are coming down and the ETS is increasing the cost of fossil-fuel-based generation). Many member states consider that their citizens would be less likely to be willing to pay extra for renewable energy if it is produced and consumed, and the jobs are created, elsewhere. And second, a free trade approach will not permit, or will make very difficult, the contemporaneous existence of different types of support systems in the member states. As discussed above, three types of support system for renewable energy have been developed in the EU: green certificates, tendering, and feed-in tariffs.

During the negotiations on the directive, member states with a feed-in tariff expressed the concern that the existence of free trade would cause their system to implode. They argued that where other member states operate green certificate systems, the prices in those countries would be set by the marginal units, likely to be PV or offshore wind. This would be higher than the price offered in feed-in tariff countries to cheaper forms of renewable energy, such as onshore wind, large-scale PV, or small hydro. If renewable generators from feed-in tariff countries would be free to sell into green certificate systems, these low-cost producers would obviously choose to export their energy to higher-cost support systems. Feed-in tariff countries thus would be unable to maintain their approach of differentiating their support depending on the actual cost of producing the different forms of renewable energy.

These arguments were considered to be persuasive, and in the final text of the directive, a more restrictive form of trade in renewable credits was introduced. As mentioned above, it makes sense to envisage the possibility of one member state acquiring green credits from renewable energy produced in another country, particularly as some member states have high targets and relatively little indigenous renewable energy potential. However, the need to envisage the possibility of trade was made subject to the right of member states to limit support to renewable energy to that produced and consumed within its territory, and to limit trade by national producers.

The final approach thus allows a member state to prohibit generators of renewable electricity from selling their production into support schemes of other member states. Nevertheless, if a member state has excess renewable energy potential, it may agree with another country to sell that potential. This could be done, for example, by the exporting country establishing its own support scheme such that the amount of renewable energy generated and consumed domestically exceeded its national target, selling the resultant statistical transfers to another country, which could then

account for the latter's target. Alternatively, through bilateral agreement, companies from the importing member state might produce and sell renewable electricity in the exporting member state but be subsidized directly by the importing country's support scheme, with statistical transfers accounting for the importing country's target.

Similar arrangements are also possible with non-EU countries, whereby an EU member state may invest in major new renewable projects in countries with major untapped potential, such as solar in deserts, wind in Northern Africa, or biomass in the Ukraine. In this case, however, the renewable energy must come from a facility constructed after the date of entry into force of the new directive, and the resultant electricity must be physically imported into the EU. These constraints on third-country projects underline that one of the main objectives of the Renewable Energy Directive is security of supply. The production of renewable energy will displace EU imports only if it is actually consumed within the EU.

Notwithstanding the existence of these mechanisms for enabling trade, initial expectations are that most member states will, at least in the short to medium term, choose to support domestically produced renewable energy, and trade will be the exception rather than the rule.

Other Policy Considerations

Several other questions have arisen regarding EU policy toward renewable energy, or more precisely ones that will inevitably become increasingly important as the new Directive is implemented. These include the issue of whether the trading system provided by the new legislation is adequate to enable member states with limited competitive renewable potential to really import credits from other member states or third countries, and what should be the EU's longer-term approach to ensuring the appropriate level of renewable energy in its overall energy mix in order to meet its objectives of competitiveness, sustainability and security.

Should the EU Move Toward a Trading System That Is More Open?

With a 20% target for renewable energy in the EU's overall energy mix, it is expected that 35% of the EU's total electricity supply will come from renewable energy sources, compared with 16% today. As discussed in more detail below, by 2050, one can expect a significantly higher percentage than this, probably 60% or more, in the context of the action that will be needed to achieve an 80% cut in EU greenhouse gas emissions. If the current situation remains, with renewable energy being produced nationally with national support schemes, then this major part of the EU's electricity supply will be removed from the competitive internal energy market,[8] making it so distorted as to be incapable of operating reasonably efficiently.

Potential medium-term solutions to this problem that would not destroy the effectiveness of the support schemes for renewable energy that have worked well for many years might include a regional, and then an EU-wide, feed-in tariff. There are strong grounds to argue that work should now commence on the development of an EU-wide renewable support mechanism that would enable renewable energy to be traded across borders as an integral part of the internal energy market. This work should have certain preconditions from the start, however, to ensure that it does not result in a wait-and-see approach to investments in the meantime. For example, a guarantee could effectively be given that any future system would not affect the support schemes applicable to existing investments prior to the introduction of any new EU-wide approach; in other words, they should have guaranteed "grandfathering" rights. In addition, any new approach must be as effective as the existing mechanisms presently operating in the EU in terms of ensuring that renewable energy grows to meet the EU's targets.

Should the EU's Approach to Imports from Third Countries Evolve over Time?

Already today, under the Renewable Energy Directive, renewable energy produced outside the EU, but resulting from new facilities constructed as a result of EU investment, can count toward a member state's national target if that electricity is physically delivered into the EU. Moving toward 2050, it makes sense to reexamine this approach in the medium term, given the significantly greater level of renewable energy that will be required by the EU; the enormous cheap renewable energy potential in neighboring countries and the cost of building interconnectors and the losses that result when transporting electricity over long distances.

For example, a regional wider European renewable energy market agreement could be pursued, whereby neighboring countries would agree to make some form of commitment regarding renewable energy development, and this would open the possibility for the EU to build facilities and receive the renewable energy, and greenhouse gas (GHG), credits. This in turn would enable the EU to use some of the gas and oil that otherwise would have been used in these neighboring countries for the parts of its economy difficult to replace with carbon-free energy services, such as planes, heavy goods vehicles, and maritime vessels, and provide important inward investment in these countries. Such a development, based on the model of the Energy Community, under which the countries of southeast Europe become part of the EU's internal energy market, clearly will take time to negotiate and would be far from simple. Given the mutual advantage that would result, however, it is an objective worth pursuing.

Further Renewable Energy Targets to 2030 and 2050

It is evident that the EU's climate change objectives do not stop at a 20% greenhouse gas reduction by 2020. Indeed, the EU has already accepted that in the context of an international deal on climate change it would accept a 30% cut by 2030. On many occasions, national EU prime ministers, chancellors, and presidents, as well as the commission president, have spoken of an 80% cut by 2050. Others have even considered a 95% cut for the EU by 2050. Similar issues apply with respect to energy security; the EU's policies on energy efficiency and indigenous energy production will continue as a form of insurance policy against price volatility.

The practical consequences of an 80% to 95% cut in greenhouse gas emissions for the EU have to be seen in the context of the expected global growth in energy demand over the next 40 years. Given the anticipated 40% to 50% increase in global population during this period, and the improving standards of living in the developing world, energy use and greenhouse gas emissions are widely predicted to increase by 40% to 60% by 2050 compared with today's levels on a business-as-usual scenario. The challenge of preventing this growth in emissions in developing countries from rendering irrelevant any efforts in the developed world to reduce carbon emissions is huge. Investments in these developing countries in energy efficiency and low-carbon energy will need to be as great as those in the developed world, if not greater. Given this, it is clear that the overwhelming bulk of any EU 80% reduction commitment will have to be realized within the EU. It may well be that the developed world will have to contribute to making the needed cuts in the developing world, but these will need to be in addition to reductions at home, not instead of them. Put simply, there will be no "low-hanging fruits" in the developing world that might allow the EU to achieve its own reduction target cheaply; it will have to realize an 80% or more cut in Europe.

An 80% cut in the EU is a huge challenge. Today almost 20% of the EU's greenhouse gases come from agriculture (methane from livestock) and industrial emissions (nitrous oxide). Both of these are difficult and expensive to reduce substantially, as are, potentially, emissions from air transport, maritime, and large freight vehicles. So to achieve an 80% cut, the EU will have to invest heavily in energy efficiency, and then move to a zero-carbon electricity system, a zero-carbon heating and cooling system for buildings, and a zero-carbon road and rail transport system. Put simply, the EU will have to have a more or less zero-carbon energy system by 2050. There are limited ways to achieve this: renewable energy,

nuclear power, and coal and gas power generation combined with carbon capture and storage (CCS).[9]

How Might the EU Move to a Zero-Carbon Energy System by 2050?

Today nuclear energy meets around 15% of the EU's total energy demand. There are reasonable grounds to believe that this level will be maintained in the EU, perhaps even increased somewhat, as some countries such as Italy are seriously considering nuclear power. It remains to be seen, however, whether this 15% level will be significantly increased. In any event, even were it to be doubled, it would still fall far short of what is needed.

Renewable energy currently accounts for slightly less than 9% of the EU's energy needs. This will increase to 20% by 2020. Even with this huge growth in renewable energy, and maintaining or somewhat increasing the levels of nuclear power in the EU, a large gap will still remain.

According to most studies, CCS offers huge potential for low-carbon energy production. It will be particularly important for countries with vast cheap coal reserves, such as China and South Africa. Without effective CCS technologies, climate change will be very difficult to address. Nearly all studies conclude that CCS will be far from a cheap technology, however, and that renewable energy will be at least as competitive, and probably more so, especially where good renewable energy potential exists (see, e.g., IEA 2008). Furthermore, CCS will remove around 80% of greenhouse gas emissions, not 100%.

In fact, the EU is blessed with excellent renewable energy potential: onshore wind, offshore wind in the North and Baltic Seas, solar and PV in the south, biomass particularly in the east. Many studies indicate that with large-scale investment and a determined approach to energy efficiency, the EU could meet all its energy needs by 2050 from renewable energy. In fact, after considering the EU's options in producing a near zero-carbon energy sector by 2050, one comes to the conclusion that it will certainly include a high proportion of renewable energy. It is difficult to paint a realistic scenario where renewable energy will (or at least should) account for less than 50% of the EU's energy mix by 2050, and 60% to 80% seems perfectly reasonable. Such predictions are less surprising when one considers the direction of the EU's energy mix today. In 2009, new renewable energy installed capacity surpassed that from traditional forms of electricity, with wind taking by far the largest share. If this trend continues, renewable energy will already meet around 30% of the EU's energy needs by 2020, way above the 20% target.

In the event, therefore, that the post-Copenhagen process reaches an agreement that is sufficiently robust to permit the EU to formally revise its 2020 target to a 30% cut and accept an 80% or more reduction figure for 2050, the question will clearly be posed whether the 20% 2020 renewable energy target should be increased. In this respect, it is worth noting that the EU's new ETS Directive already provides for an adjustment of the available carbon credits from 2013 onward in the event that the EU accepts a 30% greenhouse gas cut, to bring the reduction trajectory for ETS into line with this new objective. In addition, it is reasonable to expect that if the EU accepts a binding 80%+ emissions cut for 2050, it will equally revise the ETS Directive accordingly, providing its industry—and in particular, its electricity industry—with the long-term certainty and predictability that it needs to make the necessary investments to achieve such radical cuts.

Although the EU has never seriously debated whether renewable energy targets should follow suit for 2020 or a legally binding minimum target should be set for 2050 for renewable energy, good grounds exist for such a move. Important arguments can be made in favour of using the ETS mechanism only to ensure the necessary (80% to 95%) reductions, widening its scope in terms of the industries and sectors covered, and permitting the electricity industry to adapt in the most cost-effective manner, which would result in a greater or lesser proportion of nuclear, renewable energy, and fossil-fuel electricity production combined with CCS.

A number of important counterarguments also can be made, however. These were already considered above but merit further discussion regarding the future. It is clear that from the perspectives of energy policy, industrial policy (i.e., a focus on jobs in the EU), and energy security, so long as renewable energy is competitive compared with CCS or nuclear, there is merit in ensuring a significant proportion of renewable energy in the EU's mix. A concern, however, is that this significant proportion may not result from a simple application of the ETS system, even if renewable energy would be a relatively cheap source compared with CCS and even nuclear.

First, the ETS system is economically the same as a green certificate system and therefore results in the same level of risk, in terms of both cost and its ability to actually deliver the amount of renewable energy needed. Renewable projects are typically small undertakings, as local knowledge is often necessary to secure planning permission and the small scale of many projects excludes large undertakings. These small companies have difficulty in attracting financing in a market where profitability depends on a support mechanism characterized by fluctuating prices and thus high levels of risk. The result of an ETS-only system may be lost investment opportunities at these levels, with consequently more focus on large CCS projects by major utilities that can secure financing.

Second, the ETS system relies on—in fact, is based on—the principle that it is operating on a reasonably functioning market. Thus in principle, in determining how to react to increasing carbon prices, generators should be able to freely choose among nuclear, investing in energy efficiency, coal and gas with CCS, and renewable energy. However, the ability to construct most nuclear and large renewable-energy-based plants is dependent on planning and environmental permission for often highly controversial projects, such as onshore wind, large-scale solar PV, or hydropower, and most important, permission to build new overhead lines. To enable the choice to move into renewable electricity to be made, governments will also have to undertake massive infrastructure investments, such as smart grids, offshore grids, and pumped storage, which will result in increased transmission charges to customers. These are difficult political decisions and typically subject to very long delays, if approved at all. Indeed, the result of simply relying on the ETS system may, perversely, be that because there are no minimum renewable targets, it becomes more politically expedient to take no action on permitting, planning, and investment, forcing generators down the coal and CCS route, which may well be more expensive, produce less jobs in the EU, and not have the same positive effects in terms of promoting the EU's energy independence as would result from the cheaper renewable energy.

These issues are very important for the development of renewable energy in the EU and for its ability to meet its climate change commitments.

Under any scenario, it is difficult to envisage a future zero-carbon electricity industry that does not figure at minimum around 50% renewable electricity. It will almost certainly be more. In order to ensure that member states concentrate on ensuring the development of appropriate planning laws, as well as the cross-border regulatory rules and financial incentives and guarantees necessary to enable the development of large multicounty projects in due time, there are therefore strong grounds for agreeing to minimum binding 2050 targets on a member state by member state basis for these (conservative) levels in the event of an agreement resulting from the Copenhagen process. However, this issue has hardly been debated at the EU level.

Grid and Energy Security Issues

Meeting the 20% 2020 target will lead to a massive change in the EU's electricity system, notably in terms of the number of generators (from hundreds to millions), the number of sites, the distance of much of the generation from load (large renewable generation facilities are often considerable distances from major centers of demand), and the difficulty of ensuring that the system is kept in balance. Much renewable energy is intermittent; the wind does not blow or the sun does not shine according to schedule.

This gives rise to three major challenges. First, many new transmission lines will be needed to reflect the changing topography of EU generation. The need for such investment is already being felt in the EU; when the wind blows unexpectedly hard in Germany, which has much of the EU's installed wind capacity, transmission operators struggle to bring the energy generated securely and effectively to demand centers. Second, with many millions of more or less predictable generators, in order to have a cost-effective approach to balancing, a smart grid is imperative. And third, many large-scale renewable projects will be cross-border in nature, such as offshore wind parks. These will require common regulatory and grid access rules to enable them to operate effectively.

Regarding the first challenge, the need for new overhead lines, it is already clear that the difficulty in acquiring permission to build new high-voltage electricity lines threatens to be a major bottleneck to the development of many of the most cost-effective forms of renewable electricity, notably onshore wind farms, large-scale PV parks, and offshore wind farms. Almost by definition, these installations are situated away from large population centers and industrial demand, and new lines are thus essential. Already in the EU, the failure to approve such overhead lines at the same time that renewable capacity has been added has led to considerable grid problems, as capacity is built before the necessary lines are constructed to efficiently carry it to demand. Underground lines are becoming more cost-effective, but they remain more expensive than overhead AC lines by a factor of 5 to 10. This has to be addressed—it is not possible in the medium term to continue constructing large wind farms without, at the same time that the farms are approved, agreeing to the construction of the necessary grid reinforcements.

A new approach to infrastructure planning is foreseen in the third internal energy market package, which sets the rules for the liberalization of the EU's electricity market. Under this recently adopted legislative package, the new European Agency for the Cooperation of Energy Regulators (ACER) has to regularly adopt a 10-year rolling infrastructure plan on the basis of a proposal prepared by the transmission companies through a new association, the European Network of Transmission System Operators for Electricity (ENTSO-E). This has great potential to address this priority. It will, however, need to be followed up with real determination at the national political level to ensure that the necessary planning permission is granted sufficiently quickly for either overhead lines or "undergrounding," financed through transparent and expensive public subsidies, before permission is given to construct renewable capacity. Any other approach is likely to result in unacceptable grid security risks in the medium term.

One possible approach is to require national energy regulators to approve new renewable capacity projects above a given size (5 MW, for example) before construction to ensure that the necessary grid capacity exists. Some argue, however, that this will simply result in an insurmountable barrier to new large-scale renewable energy plants: because of the political difficulty in approving new overhead transmission lines, planning permission will not be forthcoming in any event, and projects will simply be blocked by the regulator's veto. It is far better, goes the argument, to let the new renewable capacity build up until network security becomes a pressing and unavoidable issue; only then will planning permission for the overhead lines be granted. While such an approach cannot be described as good governance, it may, regrettably, be true. This is a real problem, but pursuant to the subsidiarity principle, planning permission is an issue that can be addressed only at the member state level.[10]

In regard to the second issue, the need for adequate balancing, it is vital that a clear and predictable framework be developed at the EU level to ensure that the necessary capacity is available when it is needed to deal with rapidly increasing levels of renewable energy, not after. The EU has many potential sources of balancing capacity, such as pumped storage, compressed air, and gas-fired generation including CCS. Over the next years, therefore, the EU should give priority to determining a clear set of rules on issues such as whose responsibility it is to ensure that adequate balanc-

ing capacity exists—whether this should simply be left to the market, a supplier of last resort, the national energy regulator or the relevant transmission company—and equally important, who pays.

In addition, one very important source of balancing capacity will need to come from the development of a smart grid. In essence, this means the ability of electricity distribution companies, through smart meters in every home and business, to control a number of sources of energy demand, such as refrigerators, freezers, and most important, electric car batteries. In the third internal energy market package, member states have accepted an obligation to install such meters in all buildings when it is cost-effective to do so. A smart grid requires a great deal more than this, however, and its establishment must be a priority of the commission, national energy regulators, transmission companies, distributors, and member states over the coming years.

Finally, the third issue with a new and comprehensive regulatory framework for renewable energy concerns common regulatory rules for grid access regarding projects broader than a single member state. As projects such as the North Sea Offshore Ring further develop, this will need to be another priority for the commission, national energy regulators, and transmission companies.

Conclusions

This short tour of the EU's new renewable energy policy is far from exhaustive, yet it does illustrate some important truths. Though the policy is bold and ambitious, it represents but the first steps down what will be a very long road. The clearest conclusion to be drawn at present is that there is a pressing need to develop a clear, transparent, and predictable regulatory regime at the EU level. Infrastructure and grid access rules must be put into place rapidly to ensure that along with the growth in renewable energy, adequate infrastructure is built to make the best use of available capacity. This will be a major challenge, but given the emergence of an increasingly mature regulatory environment at the EU level with the creation of ACER and ENTSO-E, there are good grounds to believe that with determination, it will be possible to meet this challenge.

Appendix: Key Excerpts from the First Strategic Energy Review

Following are excerpts containing the key elements from the First Strategic EU Energy Review, titled "An Energy Policy for Europe," presented by the European Commission in January 2007 (European Commission 2007b). Unless noted otherwise, the European Commission was the source of all data except for the percentage given in the first sentence, which was from the European Environment Agency. The review also had a footnote stating that the assumed dollar exchange rate was $1.25 per euro, and that it was using for comparison an oil price of $60 (in 2007$) in 2030. First, in terms of the rationale for change, the commission stated the following:

1.1. Sustainability

Energy accounts for 80% of all greenhouse gas (GHG) emission in the EU; it is at the root of climate change and most air pollution. The EU is committed to addressing this – by reducing EU and worldwide greenhouse gas emissions at a global level to a level that would limit the global temperature increase to 2°C compared to pre-industrial levels. However, current energy and transport policies would mean EU CO_2 emissions would increase by around 5% by 2030 and global emissions would rise by 55%. The present energy policies within the EU are not sustainable.

1.2. Security of supply

Europe is becoming increasingly dependent on imported hydrocarbons. With "business as usual" the EU's energy import dependence will jump from 50% of total EU energy consumption today to 65% in 2030. Reliance on imports of gas is expected to increase from 57% to 84% by 2030, of oil from 82% to 93%.

This carries political and economic risks. The pressure on global energy resources is intense. The International Energy Agency (IEA) expects global demand for oil to grow by 41% by 2030. How supply will keep up with this demand is unknown: the IEA in its 2006 World Energy Outlook stated that "the ability and willingness of major oil and gas producers to step up investment in order to meet rising global demand are particularly uncertain" [EIA/DOE 2006, 4]. The risk of supply failure is growing.

In addition, the mechanisms to ensure solidarity between Member States in the event of an energy crisis are not yet in place and several Member States are largely or completely dependent on one single gas supplier.

At the same time, EU electricity demand is, on a business as usual scenario, rising by some 1.5% per year. Even with an effective energy efficiency policy, investment in generation alone over the next 25 years will be necessary in the order of €900 billion. Predictability and effective internal gas and electricity markets are essential to enable the necessary long term investments to take place and for user prices to be competitive. These are not yet in place.

1.3. Competitiveness

The EU is becoming increasingly exposed to the effects of price volatility and price rises on international energy markets and the consequences of the progressive concentration of hydrocarbons reserves in few hands. The potential effects are significant: if, for example, the oil price rose to 100 $/barrel in 2030, the EU-27 energy total import bill would increase by around €170 billion, an annual increase of €350 for every EU citizen. Very little of this wealth transfer would result in additional jobs in the EU.

Providing that the right policy and legislative frameworks are in place, the Internal Energy Market could stimulate fair and competitive energy prices and energy savings, as well as higher investment. However, all the conditions to achieve this do not yet exist. This prevents EU citizens and the EU economy from receiving the full benefits of energy liberalisation. A longer time horizon in the area of carbon constraints is required in order to promote the necessary investments in the electricity sector.

Boosting investment, in particular in energy efficiency and renewable energy should create jobs, promoting innovation and the knowledge-based economy in the EU. The European Union is already the global leader in renewable technologies, accounting for a turnover of €20 billion and employing 300,000 people [European Union

Committee 2008]. It has the potential to lead the rapidly growing global market for low carbon energy technologies. In wind energy, for example, EU companies have 60% of the world market share. Europe's determination to lead the global fight against climate change creates an opportunity for us to drive the global research agenda. All options should be kept to ensure the development of emerging technologies.

At the same time, the social dimension of Europe's energy policy needs to be taken into account throughout all stages of designing and implementing the individual measures. While this policy should overall contribute to the growth and jobs in Europe on the long term, it may have a significant impact on some internationally traded products and processes in particular in the area of energy-intensive industries.

The relevant parts of the review concerning renewable energy and ETS are as follows:

2. A STRATEGIC OBJECTIVE TO GUIDE EUROPE'S ENERGY POLICY

The point of departure for a European energy policy is threefold: combating climate change, limiting the EU's external vulnerability to imported hydrocarbons, and promoting growth and jobs, thereby providing secure and affordable energy to consumers.

In the light of the many submissions received during the consultation period on its Green Paper [European Commission 2006b], in this Strategic Energy Review the Commission proposes that the European Energy Policy be underpinned by:

- an EU objective in international negotiations of 30% reduction in greenhouse gas emissions in developed countries by 2020 compared to 1990. In addition, 2050 global GHG emissions must be reduced by up to 50% compared to 1990, implying reductions in industrialised countries of 60–80% by 2050;
- an EU commitment now to achieve, in any event, at least a 20% reduction of greenhouse gases by 2020 compared to 1990.

These form a central part of the Commission Communication "*Limiting Climate Change to 2°C – Policy Options for the EU and the world for 2020 and beyond.*"

Meeting the EU's commitment to act now on greenhouse gases should be at the centre of the new European Energy Policy for three reasons: (i) CO_2 emissions from energy make up 80% of EU GHG emissions, reducing emissions means using less energy and using more clean, locally produced energy, (ii) limiting the EU's growing exposure to increased volatility and prices for oil and gas, and (iii) potentially bringing about a more competitive EU energy market, stimulating innovation technology and jobs.

Taken together, this strategic objective and the concrete measures set out below to make it a reality represent the core of a new **European Energy Policy** …

3.3. A long-term commitment to greenhouse gases reduction and the EU Emissions Trading System

The EU traditionally favours the use of economic instruments to internalise external costs as the [*sic*] allow the market to determine how to react most efficiently and with limited costs. More particularly, in its Communication *Limiting Climate Change to 2°C – Policy Options for the EU and the world for 2020 and beyond*, the Commission has set out how the emissions trading mechanism is and must remain a key mechanism for stimulating reductions in carbon emissions and how it could be used as a basis for international efforts to fight climate change. The Commission is reviewing the EU ETS to ensure that emissions trading reaches its full potential: this is critical to creating the incentives to stimulate changes in how Europe generates and uses its energy.

3.4. An ambitious programme of energy efficiency measures at Community, national, local and international level

For Europe's citizens, energy efficiency is the most immediate element in a European Energy Policy. Improved energy efficiency has the potential to make the most decisive contribution to achieving sustainability, competitiveness and security of supply.

On 19 October 2006 the Commission adopted the Energy Efficiency Action Plan [European Commission 2006a], containing measures that would put the EU well on the path to achieving a key goal of reducing its global primary energy use by 20% by 2020. If successful, this would mean that by 2020 the EU would use approximately 13% less energy than today, saving €100 billion and around 780 millions tonnes of CO_2 each year. However, this will require significant efforts both in terms of behavioural change and additional investment ...

3.5. A longer term target for renewable energy

In 1997, the European Union started working towards a target of a 12% share of renewable energy in its overall mix by 2010, a doubling of 1997 levels. Since then, renewable energy production has increased by 55%. Nevertheless the EU is set to fall short of its target. The share of renewable energy is unlikely to exceed 10% by 2010. The main reason for the failure to reach the agreed targets for renewable energy – besides the higher costs of renewable energy sources today compared to "traditional" energy sources – is the lack of a coherent and effective policy framework throughout the EU and a stable long-term vision. As a result, only a limited number of Member States have made serious progress in this area and the critical mass has not been reached to shift niche renewables production into the mainstream.

The EU needs a step change to provide a credible long term vision of the future of renewable energy in the EU, building on the existing instruments, notably the Renewable Electricity Directive. This is essential to realise present targets [European Commission 2007c] and trigger further investment, innovation and jobs. The challenge for renewables policy is to find the right balance between installing large scale renewable energy capacity today, and waiting until research lowers their cost tomorrow. Finding the right balance means taking the following factors into account:

- Using renewable energy today is generally more expensive than using hydrocarbons, but the gap is narrowing – particularly when the costs of climate change are factored in;
- Economies of scale can reduce the costs for renewables, but this needs major investment today;
- Renewable energy helps to improve the EU's security of energy supply by increasing the share of domestically produced

energy, diversifying the fuel mix and the sources of energy imports and increasing the proportion of energy from politically stable regions as well as creating new jobs in Europe;
- Renewable energies emit few or no greenhouse gases, and most of them bring significant air quality benefits.

In the light of the information received during the public consultation and the impact assessment, the Commission proposes in its Renewable Energy Roadmap [European Commission 2007d] a binding target of **increasing the level of renewable energy in the EU's overall mix** from less than 7% today **to 20% by 2020**. Targets beyond 2020 would be assessed in the light of technological progress ...

This 20% target is truly ambitious and will require major efforts by all Member States. The contribution of each Member State to achieving the Union's target will need to take into account different national circumstances and starting points, including the nature of their energy mix. Member State should have the flexibility to promote the renewable energies most suited to their specific potential and priorities. The way in which Member States will meet their targets should be set out in National Action Plans to be notified to the Commission. The Plans should contain sectoral targets and measures consistent with achieving the agreed overall national targets. In practice, in implementing their Plans Member States will need to set their own specific objectives for electricity, biofuels, heating and cooling, which would be verified by the Commission to ensure that the overall target is being met. The Commission will set out this architecture in a new renewables legislative package in 2007.

A particular feature of this framework is the need for a minimum and coordinated development of biofuels throughout the EU. While biofuels are today and in the near future more expensive than other forms of renewable energy, over the next 15 years they are the only way to significantly reduce oil dependence in the transport sector. In its Renewable Energy Roadmap and Biofuels Progress Report [European Commission 2007a], the Commission therefore proposes to set a binding minimum target for biofuels of 10% of vehicle fuel by 2020 and to ensure that the biofuels used are sustainable in nature, inside and outside the EU. The EU should engage third countries and their producers to achieve this. In addition, the 2007 renewables legislative package will include specific measures to facilitate the market penetration of both biofuels and heating & cooling from renewables. The Commission will also continue and intensify the use of renewable energy through other policies and flanking measures with the aim of creating a real internal market for renewables in the EU.

Notes

1. European laws are adopted by codecision, which means that that the council, a body composed of representatives of the EU's 27 member states, has to agree on new laws with the European Parliament, comprising 785 directly elected members from all EU countries. The council agrees on the text mostly under a qualified majority voting system (which applied, for example, to the renewable energy and electricity texts discussed in this chapter), meaning that larger countries get more votes than smaller ones, taking into account inter alia their greater populations. However, it is important to understand the role of the European Commission, an administrative body of 27 headed by a president (currently Manuel Barroso) with 26 commissioners, thus one representative per member state. The commission has the sole right of initiative on new legislative proposals and is very important when negotiating the final text with the council and parliament.

2. The commission's progress report on renewable energy (European Commission 2009a) found that Cyprus, Finland, Latvia, Malta, Romania, and Slovenia were all showing low levels of recent growth and of progress toward the 2010 targets.

3. This was the only element of the commission's proposals that, in fact, the council could formally agree on; it concerned an equal target for all member states. The other elements proposed an overall EU target (20% renewable energy in the overall EU energy mix) without giving a member state by member state breakdown of the target.

4. To illustrate this, on the basis of the figures outlined in the IEA Energy Technology Perspectives Report and taking the lowest figure in the range for each technology, the current cost of onshore wind is 4.6 euro cents (6.23 U.S. cents) per kilowatt-hour (kWh), offshore wind 5.3 (7.2), solar PV 21.2 (28.7), concentrated solar power 8.8

(11.92), and biomass 4.2 (5.7). Although onshore wind and biomass are among the cheapest, supply is limited because of planning constraints and is unlikely to meet all the demand for renewable electricity, certainly given the level of future demand resulting from the new Renewable Energy Directive. Thus under a green certificate system, the overall price will be set by the cost of the marginal unit necessary to meet the level of demand set (or at least the price that the marginal unit is willing to bid into the price-setting mechanism, which in times of shortage can be considerably higher than the actual cost; see the discussion immediately below). This may be photovoltaics, for example, which would mean that all other producers would benefit from a windfall profit, all being paid 21.2 euro cents (28.7 U.S. cents) per kWh.

5. For a more complete account of the directive, see Hodson et al. (forthcoming).

6. See www.consilium.europa.eu/ueDocs/ cms_Data/docs/pressData/en/ec/104692.pdf.

7. Indeed, the directive recognizes that public support is necessary to reach the community's objectives for renewable energy.

8. The internal energy market is the name given to the liberalized electricity market in the EU. It is based on the principles that customers may purchase from any electricity supplier in the EU, and generators can establish themselves in any EU country and export to any customer regardless of where they are situated in the EU. For a detailed analysis of the market, see Jones (2010b) .

9. A more detailed analysis of this discussion can be found in Jones (2010a).

10. The subsidiarity principle states that action can be taken at the EU level only when it is essential to achieve a given (and recognized as a legitimate) objective of the EU Treaty and equivalent results cannot be achieved adequately by action at the national level. For further information on this concept, see European Commission (2001).

References

EIA/DOE (Energy Information Administration/U.S. Department of Energy). 2006. International Energy Outlook. http://161.116.7.34/conferencies/ viitrobada/ INTE.%20ENEREG.%20AGC.%20resum%20angl %C3%A8s.pdf (accessed February 20, 2010).

European Commission. 1997. Communication from the Commission, Energy for the Future: Renewable Sources of Energy, White Paper for a Community Strategy and Action Plan. http://europa.eu/documents/comm/white_papers/pdf/com97_599_en.pdf (accessed February 20, 2010).

———. 2001. White Paper on European Governance. http://eur-lex.europa.eu/LexUriServ/site/en/com/2001/com2001_0428en01.pdf (accessed February 20, 2010).

———. 2006a. Action Plan for Energy Efficiency: Realising the Potential. http://ec.europa.eu/energy/action_plan_energy_efficiency/doc/com_2006_0545_en.pdf (accessed February 20, 2010).

———. 2006b. Green Paper: A European Strategy for Sustainable, Competitive and Secure Energy. http://ec.europa.eu/energy/green-paper-energy/doc/2006_03_08_gp_document_en.pdf (accessed February 20, 2010).

———. 2007a. Biofuels Progress Report. http://ec.europa.eu/energy/energy_policy/doc/07_biofuels_progress_report_en.pdf (accessed February 20, 2010).

———. 2007b. An Energy Policy for Europe. http://europa.eu/legislation_summaries/energy/european_energy_policy/l27067_en.htm (accessed February 20, 2010).

———. 2007c. Follow-Up Actions of the Green Paper: Report on Progress in Renewable Electricity. http://ec.europa.eu/energy/energy_policy/doc/06_progress_report_renewable_electricity_en.pdf (accessed February 20, 2010).

———. 2007d. Renewable Energy Roadmap: Renewable Energies in the 21st Century; Building a Sustainable Future. http://ec.europa.eu/energy/energy_policy/doc/03_renewable_energy_roadmap_en.pdf (accessed February 20, 2010).

———. 2009a. Renewable Energy Progress Report. http://eur-lex.europa.eu/LexUriServ/LexUriServ.do?uri=COM:2009:0192:FIN:EN:PDF (accessed February 20, 2010).

———. 2009b. Strategic Energy Technology Plan (SET Plan). http://ec.europa.eu/energy/technology/set_plan/set_plan_en.htm (accessed February 20, 2010).

European Council. 1997. Council Resolution of 27 June 1997 on Renewable Sources of Energy. *Official Journal* C 210.

European Union Committee. 2008. The EU's Target for Renewable Energy: 20% by 2020. Vol. 1, 27th Report of Session 2007–08. http://www.publications.parliament.uk/pa/ld200708/ldselect/ldeucom/175/175.pdf (accessed February 20, 2010).

Hodson, Paul, Christopher Jones, and Hans van Steen, eds. Forthcoming. *EU Energy Law. Vol. III, Book 1, Renewable Energy Law and Policy in the European Union.* Leuven, Belgium: Claeys & Casteels Publishing.

IEA (International Energy Agency). 2008. *Energy Technology Perspectives: Scenarios and Strategies to 2050.* Paris: OECD Publishing.

Jones, Christopher. 2010a. A Zero Carbon Energy Policy for Europe: The Only Viable Solution. In *EU Energy Law. Vol III, Book 3, The European Renewable Energy Yearbook.* Christopher Jones (ed). Leuven, Belgium: Claeys & Casteels Publishing, 21–100.

Jones, Christopher, ed. 2010b. *EU Energy Law.* Vol. I, *The Internal Energy Market.* 3rd ed. Leuven, Belgium: Claeys & Casteels Publishing.

Piebalgs, A. 2009. http://europa.eu/rapid/press ReleasesAction.do?reference=SPEECH/09/488 (accessed April 6, 2010).

13

UK Renewable Energy Policy since Privatization

Michael G. Pollitt

This chapter reviews the progress with increasing renewable energy supply in the United Kingdom since 1990, with a particular focus on recent developments. This country is regarded as one where the considerable potential for renewable energy,[1] relative to other major European countries, has failed to be realized. It is also frequently suggested that the United Kingdom needs to change its policies to renewables to look more like those in Germany or Spain (e.g., Mitchell 2007).

The aim of this chapter is to look at the United Kingdom's renewable energy policy in the context of its overall decarbonization (i.e. carbon emissions reduction) and energy policies. The chapter explores the precise nature of the failure of UK renewables policy and suggests policy changes that might be appropriate in light of the country's institutional and resource endowments. The focus is on the electricity sector in terms of both renewable generation and, to a lesser extent, the facilitating role of electricity distribution and transmission networks. The interactions among the UK's electricity, heat, and transport sectors within the overall decarbonization policy context are also examined.

The discussion suggests that the precise nature of the failure of UK policy is rather more to do with societal preferences and the available mecha-

nisms for resolving social conflict than with economic incentive arrangements. Radical changes to current policy are required, but policymakers must be careful that they are institutionally appropriate to the United Kingdom. Calls to "just do it" with respect to delivery of larger quantities of renewables are economically irresponsible and highly likely to backfire in terms of achievement of ultimate policy goals such as decarbonization and energy security.

UK renewable energy policy exists in a wider energy policy context. The country's stated energy policy can be summed up as aiming to achieve "secure, affordable and low-carbon energy" (see DECC n.d.b). It therefore has three identifiable priorities: addressing climate change, providing energy security, and keeping energy bills down. These policy objectives are naturally in tension. The first two are expensive, whereas tackling the third entails keeping prices down, if not for everyone, then for a significant minority of poor consumers. Between 1990 and 2003, residential electricity prices fell significantly in real terms in the United Kingdom, by around 30% per unit, but have risen by around 40% from 2003 to 2008 (QEP 2009). The number of households defined as being in energy (or fuel) poverty, spending 10% or more of total expenditure on heating and power, has risen from a low of 2 million in 2003 to 3.5 million in 2006 (BIS 2008), out of a total of around 25 million households (ONS 2007). This has put a strain on the ability of richer consumers to simultaneously finance poor consumers, via bill payments to company support schemes (see Ofgem 2009b),[2] and expensive policies arising from climate change and energy security objectives. European Union (EU) directives have also provided significant shape to UK energy policy, providing the basis for targets to 2020 for CO_2 reduction and renewable electricity generation share.

The chapter begins by reviewing the United Kingdom's overall decarbonization policy and potential for renewables, then its policy toward renewables since 1990, with a particular focus on recent developments. This is followed by an examination of the evidence on the performance of UK policy compared with that of other countries. Next, a new institutional economics perspective is used to discuss what sorts of policies might be right for the United Kingdom in the light of the evidence. Finally, the chapter examines the issue of overall policy toward decarbonization and the place of renewables within this.

Decarbonization Policy and the Potential for Renewable Energy in the United Kingdom

An important context for the United Kingdom's renewable energy policy is its overall decarbonization policy. The country has one of the most ambitious decarbonization policies in the world, as embodied in the 2008 Climate Change Act (OPSI 2008a).[3] This policy consists of a commitment to reducing net greenhouse gas (GHG) emissions by 80% by 2050 (from 1990 levels), with an intermediate target reduction of 26% by 2020. This target is supported by five-year carbon budgets, the first period being 2008–2012 inclusive. These budgets are formulated in the Office of Climate Change and supported by a report from the independent Committee on Climate Change (CCC). Government ministers have a statutory

duty to introduce policies that support achievement of the targets. The committee's first report (CCC 2008) was published in December 2008. This gave indicative budgets for the periods 2008–2012, 2013–2017 and 2018–2022. The budget for any period beyond this must be set at least 12 years ahead.

The report was then followed up by a significant discussion in the HM Treasury budget for 2009 of policy measures aimed at supporting the achievement of the decarbonization targets in the light of the report (see HM Treasury 2009).[4] The announced measures included support for green manufacturing, improvements to the renewable support for offshore wind, increased funding for combined heat and power, and a support mechanism for up to four carbon capture and storage (CCS) plants. The intention of the legislation is that if the government were to fail to enact appropriate policies to keep the United Kingdom on track to achieve its targets, this could result in legal action against ministers by third parties, though it remains to be seen on what grounds any action would be likely to be successful, given the less than direct link between specific government policy and impact on a national GHG target.

For reference, in 2008, UK GHG emissions were 623.8 metric tons of CO_2e (CO_2 equivalent units), which is 20% below the 1990 baseline of 779.9 tons (Defra 2008). This means the United Kingdom is the only major European country to have already met and exceeded its 2012 Kyoto target for emissions reduction target, which was 12.5% (see EEA 2006, *Table 1*). It is, however, worth pointing out that the UK target is the result of negotiations within the EU to share out the Kyoto-negotiated EU-wide target, and that the baseline date of 1990 is very favorable to the United Kingdom. This is because it coincides with the privatization of the UK power industry, leading to a "dash for gas," which resulted in an unintended environmental windfall as dirtier coal-fired plants were displaced from the system (see Newbery and Pollitt 1997). This favorable starting place in which the United Kingdom finds itself is certainly a major factor in its relative enthusiasm for decarbonization.[5] The 2009 EU Renewables Directive further commits the

United Kingdom to a 15% target for renewables contribution to total final energy consumption in 2020 as part of the EU's overall 20% renewables by 2020 target. This further target is acknowledged and accepted in the CCC report. The United Kingdom also has a specific annual target for the percentage of electricity from renewables out to 2015 as part of its Renewables Obligation Certificate scheme, discussed later in this chapter.

The report suggests that by 2020, the share of renewables could be as much as 30% in total electricity generation (CCC 2008, *208*). It also discusses the potential for the direct reduction of emissions from buildings rather than via large-scale grid-connected electricity. This involves a combination of renewable heat and microgeneration. For residential buildings, it identifies a potential contribution of 14% reduction in heat emissions via a combination of biomass, solar hot water, heat pumps, and biogas by 2020. In addition, small contributions may be made by PV and other sources for microgeneration of electricity.

Recently, the newly created responsible government ministry, the Department for Energy and Climate Change published its *UK Renewable Energy Strategy* (DECC 2009f). In line with the CCC report, this suggested that more than 30% of electricity should be generated from renewables by 2020, as well as 12% of heat and 10% of transport energy, in order to meet EU targets.

The United Kingdom's commitment to decarbonization is likely to lead to a relatively tight domestic policy with strong pressure for purchasing of renewable electricity and CO_2 permits from abroad. In 2007, the country was a net purchaser of CO_2 permits to the tune of 26 tons, or 3% of its 1990 GHG level (Defra 2009). It also purchased energy via the interconnector with France (3% of total electricity delivered), which may have displaced higher-carbon energy in the United Kingdom, and was one of the largest net importers of internationally traded bioenergy, mainly for cofiring in coal-fired power plants and for blending in gasoline (DECC 2009b; Junginger et al. 2008; Perry and Rosillo-Calle 2008). All of these have some scope for expansion in terms of achieving the net decarbonization of the UK economy.

Given the ambitious targets for decarbonization and renewable energy in the United Kingdom, it seems highly likely that nationally these targets will be missed, certainly on renewables. In these circumstances, serious consideration will be given to meeting the targets via net purchases of CO_2 or green energy certificates from abroad (e.g., funding CCS in China). Indeed, if additionality could be clearly established, this would seem to be a very sensible option given that at the margin, such purchases would be much cheaper than domestic alternatives.

A defining feature of the United Kingdom is the considerable potential it has for renewable energy relative to its demand. The country has some of the best wind, tidal, and wave resources in Europe, as well as affording opportunities for biomass and solar. The technical potential of each of these resources is very great, but the estimated economic potentials are given in Table 13.1. UK electricity supplied in 2008 was 380 terawatt-hours (TWh) (DECC 2009b, *Table 5.5*).

In addition, it is worth mentioning that the United Kingdom has up to 1,000 years' worth of storage capacity of CO_2 in the North Sea and currently generates around 13% of its electricity

Table 13.1. Estimates of the likely economic potentials for different renewable technologies in the United Kingdom

Technology category	Technology detail	Annual potential
Wind power	Onshore	50 TWh
	Offshore	100 TWh
Bioenergy	Biomass	41 TWh
Geothermal	Ground source heat pumps	8 TWh
Hydro	Large scale	5 TWh
	Small scale	10 TWh
PV	Retrofitted and building integrated	> 1 TWh
Marine	Wave energy	33 TWh
	Tidal barrage	50 TWh
	Tidal stream	18 TWh
Total		~316 TWh

Source: Jamasb et al. 2008b, *81–82*

from nuclear power (DECC 2009b). The United Kingdom has endowments of coal, oil, and gas (though all three are depleting). Thus carbon capture and storage and nuclear power are likely to compete with renewables to play a part in decarbonization of the electricity sector. The country is already committed to an auction for one demonstration CCS plant and is reviewing designs for a new generation of nuclear power plants, with an announcement in November 2009 on its preferred sites for new building (see DECC 2009c). Electricity demand growth is increasing slowly, at around 1% a year, and energy efficiency measures—such as the elimination of filament lightbulbs starting in 2011 (DECC 2009e) and the introduction of smart metering for all electricity customers by 2020—seem likely to moderate demand growth.

MacKay (2008, *109*) predicts the likely contribution of renewables to UK decarbonization in the context of delivering the current level of energy consumption of 125 kilowatt-hours per day per person. He suggests that renewables contribution is likely to be only 18.3 kWh/day/person, made up of the following: hydro, 0.3; tidal, 3; offshore wind, 4; biomass, 4; solar PV, 2 (+ 2 from solar hot water); and onshore wind, 3. Thus renewable energy would contribute around 15% toward total decarbonization. MacKay's analysis is helpful in that it illustrates that a big contribution toward current electricity provision comes in the context of electricity being the source of only about one-third of current emissions of GHGs.

The exact mix of different renewable technologies, CCS fitted to coal- or gas-fired plants, nuclear, and demand reduction in the UK energy mix will depend on the relative costs of the different technologies. Kannan (2009) shows the impacts of different assumptions on the significance of CCS in UK decarbonization and hence the implications for other sources of decarbonization. Demand reduction technologies are the cheapest GHG abatement technology at the moment (see CCC 2008, *221*), though demand reduction measures suffer from well-known institutional barriers to adoption (Grubb and Wilde 2008). Nuclear is probably the next cheapest.

Table 13.2. Examples of estimated costs of technologies for the United Kingdom in 2005

Technology	Technology detail	p/kWh
Nuclear	Generation III	3.04–4.37
Gas	CCGT[a] with CCS	3.65–6.78
Coal	IGCC[b] with CCS	3.5–5.67
Wind	Onshore	4.68–8.89
	Offshore	5.62–13.3

Source: Jamasb 2008b, *75*.
Notes: The spread of estimates reflects ranges in the discount rate, capital cost, fuel and carbon prices, and other sensitivities; p/kWh = pence per kilowatt-hour, given in 2005 values; 1 pence = 1.5 cents (U.S.) as of this writing.
[a]CCGT = combined cycle gas turbine
[b]IGCC = integrated gasification combined cycle

Among the renewable technologies in the United Kingdom, onshore wind, biomass, and offshore wind are lowest-cost at scale to 2020. Table 13.2 shows some cost sensitivities for 2005.

The table illustrates large uncertainty in the costs of building new plants, even with established technologies. For wind, this reflects the importance of exact location, which determines both building costs and the available wind. The range of costs illustrates substantial overlap under favorable versus unfavorable circumstances for any pair of technologies. However, it is important to point out that this uncertainty over actual costs for current new building does call into question projections of costs to 2020. For instance, Dale et al. (2004) assume onshore and offshore new building costs of £650 and £1,000 ($975 and $1,500) per kW, respectively, in scenarios with 25% energy from wind. The most recent (albeit prerecession) wind parks are currently costing nearer to £1,000 and £2,500 ($1,500 and $3,750) per kW (see Blanco 2009; and Snyder and Kaiser 2009). This is somewhat concerning, given a return to macroeconomic growth, for the likely projected costs of renewable scenarios to 2020, especially given that the costs of electricity (which will include cumulative subsidy commitments to renewables) in 2020 will still likely reflect, to some extent, the cumulative cost of all wind capacity installed since 2005.

Table 13.3. Costs of electricity sector decarbonization to 2020 (2008 prices)

	Conventional	Renewables scenarios		
		Lower	Middle	Higher
New generation capacity (£ billion)				
Renewable capacity	2.3	50.1	60.2	77.4
Nonrenewable capacity	14.9	12.6	12.3	12.0
Total	17.2	62.7	72.5	89.4
Network (£ billion)				
Offshore wind connection	0.0	8.4	10.6	14.1
Onshore wind connection	0.1	1.0	1.2	1.4
Other reinforcement	0.8	0.8	0.8	0.8
Total	0.9	10.2	12.6	16.3
Total grid investment costs (generation + network, £ billion)	18.1	72.9	85.1	105.7
Marginal generation cost (£/MWh)	35.9	25.0	22.6	18.9
Cost per MWh produced (£/MWh)				
Generation costs (fixed and variable)	46.8	51.9	52.6	54.5
Balancing and intermittency	1.7	6.3	7.2	8.7
Grid expansion for renewables	0.1	3.5	4.1	5.2
Total cost including network (£/MWh)	48 6	61.7	63.9	68.4

Source: SKM 2008, *8*
Note: £1 = $1.50 as of this writing

As Jamasb et al. (2008b) note, a key determinant of the relative attractiveness of different technologies will be the degree of learning in costs, and this depends on their current stage of development. Foxon et al. (2005) note that the various renewable technologies available to the United Kingdom are at different stages of development. Wind costs can be expected to fall as capacity increases significantly around the world; however, the prospects for learning in hydro and tidal barrages are low, limiting their ultimate scope for expansion. The additional costs of fitting CCS are difficult to estimate because of a lack of information, while the scope for learning may be constrained by the maturity of the different elements of the CCS process (see Odenberger et al. 2008). This is in addition to the difficulty of reconciling all the interested parties (Drake 2009). PV, tidal stream, and other marine technologies offer the greatest potential for decreases from the current costs, given low current levels of output and the implied scope for cost reduction.[6]

SKM (2008) provides estimates of the possible cost of decarbonization of the electricity sector to 2020. Under their estimates, renewables provide 34%, 41%, and 50% of electricity supply under the lower, middle, and higher renewables scenarios. Table 13.3 shows that renewables could impose significant total costs on the electricity system. The capital costs of connecting offshore wind in particular could involve up to £15 billion ($22.5 billion) of expenditure, more than the total cost of generation under a conventional scenario. The cost of balancing and intermittency could rise by up to £7 ($10.50) per megawatt-hour (MWh), or 10% of total system costs. The United Kingdom may have the wind resources, but they will have significant cost implications for the system, raising average electricity costs by up to 40% against baseline.

Policies toward Renewables in the United Kingdom

This section provides an overview of UK renewables policy since the privatization of the country's electricity supply industry beginning in 1990. Summarizing UK policy is not a straightforward task because of the large range of government initiatives toward renewable energy and the great number of policy changes that have been announced in recent years, some of which have yet to be implemented fully.[7] Discovering the exact cost of renewable energy support is not easy, as evidenced by the fact that the best sources of information are answers to parliamentary questions rather than published annual statistics. This is particularly true of the expenditure on individual technologies. The heroic efforts of Mitchell and Connor (2004), who reviewed UK renewables policy from 1990 to 2003, provided the inspiration for some of the presentation here.

In broad outline, there have been two main support mechanisms for renewable electricity and heat generation since privatization in the United Kingdom: the Non-Fossil Fuel Obligation (NFFO), which ran from 1990 to 2002, and the Renewables Obligation (RO) scheme, which began in 2002. During their period of operation, these have been the most significant forms of renewable energy support in the United Kingdom and were designed to work in parallel with liberalized electricity and gas markets.

The assessment of renewable support policies is complicated because there are two obvious metrics of success: the amount of renewables realized relative to potential (quantity); and the total cost of renewable energy support policy relative to the amount of generation actually supported (suitably discounted). These two trade off, meaning that success in one is likely to be associated with less success in the other.

The Non-Fossil Fuel Obligation

The Non-Fossil Fuel Obligation (NFFO) was originally designed as a way of financing the extra costs of nuclear power that became clear in the run-up to privatization. A non-fossil-fuel levy was introduced on final electricity prices to pay for nuclear decommissioning liabilities, and electricity suppliers were forced to buy nuclear power at higher-than-market prices in auctions for non-fossil-fuel power run by the Non-Fossil Purchas-

ing Agency (NFPA).[8] In order to avoid this being seen as a discriminatory subsidy to the nuclear industry, it was recast as a way of supporting non-fossil-fuel generation more generally, and a portion was allocated to support renewable energy (Mitchell and Connor 2004). The portion was small, but it provided a relatively significant amount of money to the industry at a time when government expenditure on new technologies was falling to a very low level, and the then Department of Energy was closing. The money was allocated to new renewable projects via a series of bidding rounds whereby renewable energy projects bid for an (inflation-indexed) per-kilowatt-hour price for initially 8 and later 15 years. Winning bids were selected by cost within each technology category.

The result was a significant number of bids in each of the auction rounds and falling bid costs in each successive round.[9] Connor (2003, 76) reports that in the five rounds of NFFO in England and Wales, onshore wind costs fell from 10 pence (15.0 cents) per kWh in 1990 to 2.88 pence (4.3 cents) per kWh in 1998, with substantial falls for the other technology bands. Although NFFO was successful in soliciting a large number of competitive bids and in ensuring that any funded projects were cost-effective for electricity customers, it failed rather spectacularly in one key respect: delivery of actual investment by the winning bidders.

Across the United Kingdom, between 1990 and 1999, out of 302 awarded wind projects covering 2,659 MW, only 75 projects were built, rated at 391 MW (Wong 2005). Spectacularly, not one of the 33 large wind projects awarded in the fifth round of NFFO in England and Wales was ever contracted. By contrast, out of 308 landfill gas projects awarded, 208 were operational in 2008, with 458 MW of capacity out of 660 MW contracted. For all the rounds of NFFO, out of 933 awarded contracts, 477 were built, representing 1,202 out of 3,639 MW (DECC 2009b, *Table 7.1.2*). The primary cause for the failure was that bidders were overoptimistic in their estimates of the actual delivery costs of the projects, often because the nature of the least-cost auction—with no assessment of likelihood of delivery—

incentivized minimization of expenditure on preparing realistic bids (Mitchell and Connor 2004).

In reviewing the failure of the NFFO policy, it is important to remember the context in which it operated. Renewables were then a very low priority for UK government policy, and it was a period of a rapid switch from coal- to gas-fired power. Prices and pollution, in terms of quantities of CO_2, SO_x, and NO_x, fell substantially. The focus on market-driven investments was good for energy and carbon-efficient combined heat and power (CHP) investment in the industrial and commercial sectors (Bonilla 2006; Harvey 1994; Marshall 1993), which had struggled prior to privatization (Jarvis 1986). UK privatization was a significant policy success in economic terms, especially when the benefits to the environment are considered (Newbery and Pollitt 1997).

The privatization and market liberalization policies ensured that the United Kingdom would easily meet its Kyoto targets for 2012 without any further action, which was not the case for other leading European countries. The mood at the time was nicely summarized by a government minister for energy in 1988, Michael Spicer, who wrote that "privatisation of the electricity supply industry should boost the commercial prospects for these [green] technologies as a free market is established" (Elliott 1992, *266*). Indeed, Friends of the Earth was optimistic that the opening up of the residential energy market to competition in 1998–1999 would give rise to demand for green tariffs and stimulate the production of green energy (Stanford 1998). It was only as the EU moved toward substantial targets for renewables that it became clear that the United Kingdom needed a policy that delivered large quantities of renewables.[10] Nevertheless, significant lessons can be learned from the NFFO experience.

Somewhat surprisingly, little quantitative analysis has been done on the bids that were successful under NFFO and the factors in their success and failure. Elliott (1992, *267*) criticized the NFFO scheme as a "somewhat half-hearted hybrid market/interventionist system" that "would still leave short-term price and market factors to shape important long term strategic choice concerning patterns of technological

development." Institutional barriers emerged early on as a critical factor in successful project implementation (McGowan 1991).

In particular, it became clear that projects had a problem with gaining the necessary consents required to start building, known as "planning permission" in the United Kingdom, and that a lack of attention was given to proper environmental impact assessments (Coles and Taylor 1993). Hull (1995) noted that in the early years, less than half of all councils, the local government bodies responsible for consents, had planning guidance for renewable energy projects, and more important, there was a lack of learning among councils. Calls came for clearer guidelines for the planning process to facilitate wind power (Roberts and Weightman 1994). Early industry views of the scheme were positive, recognizing that it did constitute a significant increase in expenditure over previous levels (Porter and Steen 1996). However, the successive rounds of auctions were thought not to provide assurance of continuity of support for renewables generally (Elliott 1994; Mitchell 1995), and some worried that although they supported near-market technologies, declines in R&D expenditure were bad for less advanced technologies such as marine (Elliott 1994).

The final years of NFFO, 1999–2001, coincided with a sharp decline in wholesale electricity prices as significant amounts of new gas-fired capacity came into the market and competition increased within the initially duopolistic generation sector (Evans and Green 2003). NFFO generators had made overoptimistic bids, and their situation was exacerbated by the end of the compulsory wholesale power pool, which had guaranteed the pool price to all generators, in March 2001. It was replaced with a contract market and a balancing market. Imbalance between supply and demand for an individual generator was now more likely to result in a financial penalty. Intermittent renewable generators were more likely to need to participate in the balancing market to balance their physical and contractual positions; because of the exogenous effects of weather, wind generators have less capacity to match supply and demand than fossil-fuel generators, who can adjust their spinning reserve. This is not necessarily inefficient, however, as generators should be incentivized to solve the imbalance problem. The impact of this effect seems to have subsided after one year of operation of the new arrangements, partly as a result of the arrival of a more generous subsidy regime when Ofgem (the independent UK agency responsible for electricity and gas regulation) found little evidence of negative impact from the change to the trading system on renewable generators (see Ofgem 2002).

The Renewables Obligation Scheme

The Renewables Obligation (RO) scheme, which replaced NFFO in 2002, uses a form of tradable green certificates (TGCs), known in the UK as Renewables Obligation Certificates (ROCs). Under this plan, the government set a minimum share of electricity to be acquired by electricity suppliers from renewable sources (larger hydro-electric schemes in operation before 2002 are

excluded). This share is steadily increasing from 2002 to 2015 (see Table 13.4). Under the RO scheme, electricity suppliers must acquire these certificates in the prescribed target share of renewable generation for each annual period. They can do this by buying or earning ROCs, which are created when renewable generators generate electricity. This essentially splits the market into two parts, renewable and nonrenewable, with renewable generators getting a price for the ROCs they create plus the wholesale price of power.[11]

The UK scheme has two important features introduced at its inception, however. One is a buyout price (i.e., a penalty price) for ROCs if not enough are created by renewable generation. This price is specified for each trading period and effectively caps the price that creators of ROCs can receive. The other is recycling of the revenue collected from the buyout sales of ROCs. This

Table 13.4. RO targets and delivery against targets

	Target renewable share in GB[a]	% delivery in UK	Nominal buyout price (£/MWh)	Total cost[b] (£ million)
2002–2003	3.0	59%	30	282
2003–2004	4.3	56%	30.51	415.8
2004–2005	4.9	69%	31.59	497.9
2005–2006	5.5	76%	32.33	583
2006–2007	6.7	68%	33.24	719
2007–2008	7.9	64%	34.3	876.4
2008–2009	9.1	65%	35.36	1,024.6
2009–2010	9.7		37.19	
2010–2011	10.4		+ inflation thereafter	
2011–2012	11.4			
2012–2013	12.4			
2013–2014	13.4			
2014–2015	14.4			
2015–2016	15.4			Estimated: ~1,733 (2008–2009 prices) assuming no demand growth

Sources: OPSI, 2009; and Renewables Obligation annual reports from Ofgem various dates.
Notes: From 2016, the share was fixed at 15.4% until 2027, now extended to 2037 for new projects; RO scheme cost is total cost including revenue recycling; £1 = $1.50 as of this writing
[a]Target share lower in Northern Ireland, but NI ROCs are tradable throughout UK. There is also a nominal distinction between Scottish ROCs (SROCs) and English and Welsh ROCs (ROCs), but these are tradable, and both are included in the GB target share.
[b]We report costs based on multiplying the buyout price by the actual ROC requirement. There appear to be small discrepancies in the actual reported payments and this figure in Renewables Obligation annual reports from Ofgem.

takes the form of allocating the revenue back to the creators of ROCs in proportion to the number they created.

The renewable energy industry was very positive about the new incentive mechanism (Hill and Hay 2004). So they should have been, because the scheme is very generous. Thus for example in 2007–2008, the buyout (penalty) price was £34.30 ($51.45) per MWh, and only 64% of the required ROCs were created by generators, meaning the buyout price was binding in the certificate market. The total payment by suppliers was the target quantity of renewables multiplied by £34.30 ($51.45) per MWh. This meant that 36% of the total ROC payment made by suppliers was available to be recycled and was divided proportionally among the generators who created actual ROCs. Accordingly, for each ROC actually presented, the renewable generators received £34.30 plus £18.65 ($27.98) (i.e., an additional 36/64 times £34.30 less costs of the scheme) This sum is in addition to the wholesale cost of power. As the total cost to suppliers of the ROC scheme was £876 million ($1,314 million), this implies that consumers overpaid, relative to what was necessary to secure the renewable generation actually supplied, by at least the value of the buyout revenue of around £315 million (36% of £876 million [$1,314 million], or 1% of the total electricity expenditure of £30.7 billion [$46 billion] in 2008) (DUKES 2009).[12] Interestingly, the government collects the associated ROC payments on the generation contracted under NFFO via the NFFO fund, which creates a surplus above the payments to generators under that program; this surplus is estimated to be around £200 million ($300 million) per year (Tickell 2008).

The RO scheme is curious for two reasons. First, it relies on underdelivery to trigger the maximum subsidy amount. If the target number of ROCs (or more) were presented, then the price would drop to zero. Second, in the case of underdelivery, the maximum amount of subsidy is paid to those actually creating ROCs. Thus the scheme assumes failure to meet the target and ensures that a fixed total subsidy is paid, given this, regardless of how few ROCs are created.

The scheme is further complicated by the introduction of "banding" starting on April 1, 2009 (see Table 13.5). This changes the exchange rate to ROCs of some renewable generation: established technologies will get less than 1 ROC per MWh, newer more. This change breaks the link between the total number of ROCs and the share of renewable energy generation and will presumably result in a reduced amount of electricity being produced from renewables if the scheme is fully successful (if the share of high-exchange-rate technologies were to take off, as it might with offshore wind). The Carbon Trust

Table 13.5. Banding of ROCs from April 1, 2009

Generation type	ROCs per MWh
Landfill gas	0.25
Sewage gas	0.5
Cofiring of biomass	
Onshore wind	
Hydro	
Cofiring of energy crops	
Energy from waste with CHP	
Cofiring of biomass with CHP	1.0
Geopressure	
Standard gasification	
Standard pyrolysis	
Offshore wind	
Biomass	1.5
Cofiring of energy crops with CHP	
Wave	
Tidal stream	
Advanced gasification	
Advanced pyrolysis	
Anaerobic digestion	
Energy crops	
Biomass with CHP	2.0
Energy crops with CHP	
Solar photovoltaic	
Geothermal	
Tidal impoundment—tidal barrage	
Tidal impoundment—tidal lagoon	

Source: DECC 2009d

(2006) recommended the move to banding to recognize the different stages of development that the technologies had reached, and hence the higher learning benefits associated with increased funding to earlier-stage technologies. Oxera (2005) points out the cost implications of allowing NFFO plants to earn ROCs once their NFFO contracts expired (around £620 million [$930 million]), giving those projects unexpected additional subsidy. Oxera calculated that as much as half the payment via ROCs was in excess of that required to ensure that the funded projects went ahead, and that existing landfill gas projects did not require any ROCs to be economically viable.

The scheme, as shown in the table, implies that the subsidy to offshore wind could be increased by £26.47 ($39.71) per MWh (50% of the 2007–2008 ROC revenue) and to tidal by £52.95 ($79.43) per MWh (100% of the 2007–2008 ROC revenue). In the 2009 budget, offshore wind was subject to an emergency rebanding provision, which saw the offshore wind ROC band go to 2 for 2009–2010 and 1.75 for 2010–2011, now increased back to 2 from 2010–2014.

Policy Costs and Delivery under NFFO and RO

Table 13.6 summarizes the financial commitments made under the NFFO and RO schemes, as well as a reference amount for the amount of public R&D expenditure reported to the International Energy Agency (IEA). The increased significance of the RO scheme is evident.

While the RO scheme is the most significant element of the United Kingdom's expenditure on renewables, it is not the only element. Table 13.7 is a summary offered in a ministerial answer to a parliamentary select committee question. It is noteworthy that significant additional amounts are still being spent by the taxpayer on supporting earlier-stage technologies outside the CO_2 price and RO support mechanisms. However, the order of magnitude of energy customer support for renewables is of the order of £1.8 billion ($2.7 billion) in 2008, in addition to £400 million ($600 million) by the taxpayer. This level of sup-

Table 13.6. Financial support (£ million) for renewables in the United Kingdom (nominal)

	R&D	RO	NFFO
1990–1991	14.7		6.1
1991–1992	17.1		11.7
1992–1993	16.1		28.9
1993–1994	15.2		68.1
1994–1995	9.1		96.4
1995–1996	9.1		94.5
1996–1997	6.2		112.8
1997–1998	4.3		126.5
1998–1999	3.3		127
1999–2000	4.6		56.4
2000–2001	4.4		64.9
2001–2002	6.1		54.7
2002–2003	10.5	282.0	-
2003–2004	11.6	415.8	-
2004–2005	19.7	497.9	-
2005–2007	36.6	583.0	-
2006–2007	49.5	719.0	-
2007–2008	41.6	876.4	-

Sources: UK government renewable R&D budget data from IEA 2009; Mitchell and Connor 2004, *1943*

port is up 47% in real terms from the figure estimated by Wordsworth and Grubb (2003) of £1.3 billion ($1.95 million) in 2002–2003.[13]

As the above discussion of the progress with the RO scheme has made clear, the development of electricity from renewables has been disappointing in terms of overall cost relative to delivery, given the United Kingdom's resource potential and ambitious targets. Table 13.8 gives the figures in terms of total electricity generation. A number of features stand out. First of all, electricity from biomass in 2008 is larger than that from wind. Hydro remains significant within the UK renewable portfolio. Connor (2003) reported estimates from 2002 that suggested the United Kingdom would meet only two-thirds of its target level by 2010. This still seems likely. However, the striking thing about the 2002 estimates is that for biomass, offshore wind, and hydro, they seem likely to be met or exceeded, though not by onshore wind. The United Kingdom is failing to meet its projections for renewables as predicted,

Table 13.7. Support for renewable energy in 2007–2009

Scheme	Description	Cost	Paid by
Renewables Obligation Certificates	Electricity suppliers must buy a proportion of their sales from renewable generators or pay a buyout charge	£874 million in 2007–2008	Electricity consumers
EU Emissions Trading Scheme	Renewable generators indirectly benefit from the increase in electricity prices as other companies pass the cost of emissions permits into the price of power	Perhaps £300 million in 2008, given current permit prices	Electricity consumers
Carbon Emissions Reduction Target	Energy companies must install low-carbon items in homes, which could include microgeneration from 2008	Total cost will be £1.5 billion over 3 years, mostly spent on energy efficiency	Gas and electricity consumers
Renewable Transport Fuel Obligation	Fuel suppliers must supply a proportion of biofuels or pay a buyout charge	No more than £200 million in 2008–2009	Consumers
Climate Change Levy	Electricity suppliers need not pay this tax (passed on to non-residential consumers) on electricity from renewable generators	£68 million to UK generators, £30 million to generators abroad in 2007–2008	Taxpayers, via reduced revenues
Lower fuel duty for biofuels	The rate of fuel duty is 20 pence (30 cents) per liter below that for petrol and diesel	£100 million in 2007	Taxpayers, via reduced revenues
Environmental Transformation Fund	Grants for technology development and deployment, including subsidies for installing renewable generation, planting energy crops, and developing biomass infrastructure.	£400 million over 3 years starting in 2008–2009	Taxpayers
Research councils	Grants for basic science research	£30 million in 2007–2008	Taxpayers
Energy Technologies Institute	Grants to accelerate development (after the basic science is known) of renewables and other energy technologies	Allocation and eventual size of budget not yet announced	Taxpayers and sponsoring companies

Source: House of Lords 2008, *Table 6 Note:* £1 = $1.50 as of this writing

but this is largely due to the failure to deliver the long-expected increase in generation from onshore wind.

Both NFFO and RO have stimulated electricity from landfill gas and cofiring of biomass and municipal waste (with fossil fuels). These technologies were near market in the early 1990s and had good prospects at that time. Brown and Maunder (1994) discuss the United Kingdom's potential for exploiting landfill gas, and Jamasb et al. (2008a) explore the prospects for waste to energy, noting it has significant further potential, especially if CHP is involved. The use of biomass for cofiring in coal-fired plants continues to be one of the most sensible uses of biomass, as it is well proven that mixes of up to 10% biomass require little adjustment to existing plants (Thornley 2006). Small hydro projects have also

had some success, with a steady increase in hydro generation from these schemes. These projects use established technology and have benefited from market-based support mechanisms. Paish (2002) highlights around 400 MW of further potential for small-scale hydro in the United Kingdom.

There also have been promising developments with offshore wind in the United Kingdom, assuming the actual delivered costs can be kept down. As of August 2009, offshore wind capacity is currently 598 MW, but an additional 1,246 MW are under construction, and a further 3,613 MW have been consented. This contrasts with 3,730 MW of onshore wind capacity, with only 930 MW under construction and 3,275MW consented (BWEA n.d.).

It seems likely, given the continuance of high levels of support via banded ROCs, that offshore

Table 13.8. Renewable electricity generation (GWh) in the United Kingdom, 1990–2008

	1990	2000	2001	2002	2003	2004	2005	2006	2007	2008
Wind										
Onshore wind	9	945	960	1,251	1,276	1,736	2,501	3,574	4,491	5,792
Offshore wind	0	1	5	5	10	199	403	651	783	1,305
Solar photovoltaics	0	1	2	3	3	4	8	11	14	17
Hydro:										
Small scale	91	214	210	204	150	283	444	478	534	568
Large scale	5,080	4,871	3,845	4,584	2,987	4,561	4,478	4,115	4,554	4,600
Biofuels:										
Landfill gas	139	2,188	2,507	2,679	3,276	4,004	4,290	4,424	4,677	4,757
Sewage sludge digestion	316	367	363	368	394	440	470	456	496	564
Municipal solid waste combustion	221	840	880	907	965	971	964	1,083	1,177	1,226
Cofiring with fossil fuels				286	602	1,022	2,533	2,528	1,956	1,613
Biomass	0	410	743	807	947	927	850	797	964	1,155
Total Biofuels and wastes	676	3,796	4,493	5,047	6,174	7,364	9,107	9,288	9,270	9,315
Total Renewables	5,857	9,828	9,516	11,093	10,600	14,147	16,940	18,136	19,646	21,597
Total Generation	319,701	377,069	384,778	387,506	398,209	393,867	398,313	398,823	397,044	389,649
% Total Renewables	1.83%	2.61%	2.47%	2.86%	2.66%	3.59%	4.25%	4.55%	4.95%	5.54%
Wind	0.00%	0.25%	0.25%	0.32%	0.32%	0.49%	0.73%	1.06%	1.33%	1.82%
Hydro	1.62%	1.35%	1.05%	1.24%	0.79%	1.23%	1.24%	1.15%	1.28%	1.33%
Biofuels	0.21%	1.01%	1.17%	1.30%	1.55%	1.87%	2.29%	2.33%	2.33%	2.39%

Source: *Digest of UK Energy Statistics*, various issues

wind will overtake onshore wind generation, albeit on the back of very disappointing delivery of onshore wind projects.

Looking at the success of the NFFO and RO schemes, NFFO did well on cost of the policy but not as well on quantity of renewables delivered, whereas RO did better on quantity delivered but much less well on cost of the policy.

Other Renewables Policies

While the main support mechanisms have favored wind and biomass, direct government funding has also helped the marine industry. A resurgence in research and demonstration funding in the last 10 years has resulted in some positive developments

(see Mueller and Wallace 2008). The first 1.2 MW tidal stream plant was installed in 2008 (Riddell 2008), and the industry is well placed internationally to exploit this and related marine technologies (Elliot 2009). The UK government is currently conducting another feasibility study of the 8.5 GW Severn Barrage, which could generate 5% of the country's current electricity demand. This is the biggest of the United Kingdom's potential tidal projects (Conway 1986), but cost and environmental issues remain to be addressed (see DECC 2009f). However, a trial with a smaller scheme first, such as a barrage across the Mersey, would seem sensible for learning that might benefit the much larger Severn project.

PV has relied on direct government support for installation programs that have involved only a small number of installations, mainly funded via the government's Industry Department (DTI, then BERR) under the Low Carbon Buildings Fund. This funding has installed only a few hundred PV systems. The degree of satisfaction with the technology among the recipients of funding has been positive (Faiers and Neame 2006), but a lack of significant sums of money and proper assessment of the learning from the policy has been noted (Keirstead 2007). This is in spite of a well-regarded R&D plan for solar being put in place in the 1990s (Stainforth et al. 1996) and work showing that significant community installations of solar would not pose any local grid problems (Thomson and Infield 2007). The government has made two very recent changes to its renewables policy, which are relevant to any assessment of the need for reform of the current arrangements (allowed for in primary legislation (OPSI 2008b)).

First, a feed-in tariff (FIT) for small-scale low-carbon generation commences in April 2010 (see www.fitariffs.co.uk/). This will be for renewable electricity generation up to 5 MW and fossil-fuel CHP up to 50 kW. Meant to encourage PV, small-scale wind (including microwind), microhydro, and micro-CHP, this policy responds to industry concerns about the lack of ambition in microgeneration policy (Lupton 2008).

The second policy is a Renewable Heat Incentive (RHI) (see www.rhincentive.co.uk). This has the potential to be a significant policy covering all scales of production: household, community, and industrial. It is intended to drive the share of renewable heat to 14% (though this is not a firm target) up from 0.6%. It could cover air source heat pumps, anaerobic digestion to produce biogas for heat production, biomass heat generation and CHP, ground source heat pumps, liquid biofuels (but only when replacing oil-fired heating systems) and solar thermal heat and hot water.

The scheme is not finalized at the time of writing and is due to commence in April 2011.

An Assessment of Renewables Policies

A 20-year view of UK renewables policy suggests a failure to translate the country's early resource-based promise into actual delivery of renewable energy. It would be wrong to suggest widespread policy failure, however. The United Kingdom is making progress on decarbonization and has strong and increasingly comprehensive policies in place, covering electricity, heat, and transport (via policies toward electric vehicles and biofuels).

Two points are worth making at this stage. First, renewable energy policy remains an expensive gamble for all countries. Second, it is unclear what part particular renewable technologies should play in decarbonization to 2050.

As Helm (2002) has pointed out, a sensibly high and stable price of carbon is the starting point for all economically feasible decarbonization policies. In the absence of this, it is virtually impossible to establish proper signals for mature technologies and near-market technologies, whose response to the proper price signal determines how fast the country needs to accelerate less developed technologies. This is particularly true for nuclear, CCS, and demand reduction investments, many of which are being delayed by low, volatile, and uncertain prices for carbon. The United Kingdom, with its diversified energy system, exposure to world energy markets, and openness to both nuclear and CCS, has keenly felt the lack of a proper carbon price signal.

As Nelson (2008) discusses, the failure to set a sufficiently tight cap on CO_2 at the EU level makes UK renewables policy meaningless as a policy for decarbonization. More renewable electricity generation within the EU Emissions Trading System (ETS) simply causes fuel switching in the fossil plants from gas to coal, not to mention delaying nonrenewable low-carbon investments in CCS and nuclear. In this context, UK renewables policy has been somewhat conservative with respect to funding levels under NFFO and to renewable energy targets under the RO and, until recently, unwilling to pick winners. As Eikeland and Sæverud (2007) point out, however, the ending of the United Kingdom's status as an energy exporter in 2003 and the associated rapid decline in oil and gas reserves have led to a reawakening of energy security concern as a major driver of UK energy policy. This is likely to explain substantially increased interest in delivering more domestic renewable capacity.

Failure to deliver large quantities of renewables so far is not a particular issue, in that delay will probably mean lower costs of exploitation (resulting from learning by doing elsewhere and learning by research) when they are finally exploited. The unfortunate aspect of the RO system is its failure to deliver cost-effectively the renewables that it has delivered. This has been a serious design flaw, and the inability of the UK government to learn and correct the flaw does not bode well for any other long-term mechanism put in place to support renewables. Nevertheless, given the targets for delivery that exist within the scheme, it is clearly important to consider why the scheme has not delivered the quantity of renewables intended. The failure of the scheme to deliver overall lies squarely with one particular technology: the failure to deliver sufficient quantities of onshore wind.

Onshore Wind and the Planning Problem

The standard reason given for the delivery failure is difficulties in getting new wind farms through local planning processes. Whereas conventional power plants can easily be built on existing sites and require national-level planning consents, wind farms are often small in terms of MW capacity and require local planning permission if less than 50 MW, which covers most onshore installations.[14] Evidence has consistently shown that gaining planning permission is a serious obstacle to the development of wind farms or, more precisely, that the costs of obtaining permission are often prohibitive in terms of imposed delays, negotiation costs, and planning restrictions on the precise nature of the final investment.

In the United Kingdom, local planning decisions typically involve an applicant, such as a wind project developer, making a planning application. This includes the submission of detailed plans and

an impact assessment to the relevant local government authority. The application is initially assessed by a local planning officer, who makes recommendations on the plans to the relevant group of elected local councilors for the area, who in turn vote on the proposal. Plans would be available for public consultation, and objections could be raised during the review period. Planning applications can be granted subject to conditions and obligations. This process might result in a number of iterations in the plans. Should permission be refused, the applicant can appeal the decision, in which case a costly public inquiry would ensue. The relevant central government department also has the right to disallow a locally approved planning application so objectors can appeal to the relevant government minister. At the national level, plans need to be submitted to the relevant government department for referral to the secretary of state for final decision. Objections can be raised to these plans according to the planning guidelines. This national-level process is being streamlined, as below.[15]

The average time for local and national planning decisions on onshore wind in 2007 was 24 months, with approval rates of 62% (Chamberlain 2008, *21*). For large projects, the Ministry of Defence, National Air Traffic Control, and civil airports were major objectors. Attempts have been made since 2007 to obligate local councils to set target levels of energy from renewables for new developments. The 2008 Planning Act (see OPSI 2008c) allows for setting up an Infrastructure Planning Commission to decide on large onshore wind farms (greater than 50 MW) as well as large offshore projects (greater than 100 MW) (see NAO 2008, *40–41*, for a discussion).

The literature has dug more deeply into the planning problem. Hedger (1995) highlights that wind power development involves a clash of planning cultures: land use versus energy supply. The first is fundamentally local, participatory, and concerned with preserving rural landscapes; the second is fundamentally national, top-down, and concerned with delivering technological solutions to national energy supply requirements. These cultures were bound to clash in onshore wind power development.

Mitchell and Connor (2004) stress that the emphasis on cost minimization, combined with the tying of subsidies to particular locations and plans, meant that many successful NFFO bids failed to get through the planning process. This was because the bidders were not able to invest in local engagement or respond to the outcome of the engagement process by modifying their proposals. Indeed, the competitive nature of NFFO meant that often the bidders had to keep prospective locations secret and did not engage in local consultations prior to bidding. Toke (2005b) found that for the projects he examined from the third through fifth NFFO rounds in England and Wales, 47 were granted planning permission, 47 refused planning permission, and 96 did not make or complete an application.[16]

The main reasons given for planning objections were visual amenity impairment and worries about noise (Eltham et al. 2008). These gave rise to concerns about economic effects on house prices and tourism. The United Kingdom is a densely populated island, with many areas of lower population and high ground located in national parks or other places that attract tourists. Increasing numbers of residents or second-home buyers have been moving to such areas for their visual amenities rather than employment reasons (see Strachan and Lal 2004 for a discussion of the debate around tourism). The decline of employment in farming and rural industries has reduced the scope for arguments based on the small number of permanent jobs that might be created in the energy sector, because increasing percentages of people living in the countryside work in nearby conurbations and are not looking for employment in local industries.

Rural environmental protection and local community action groups thus had strong incentives to organize opposition to individual wind farm projects, although in some cases tourism actually increased after wind turbines were installed, and the noise from a modern turbine that is 500 meters away is no more than in a quiet bedroom (Strachan and Lal 2004). A number of studies (e.g., Eltham et al. 2008; Warren et al. 2005) have shown that attitudes to wind farms consistently improve after construction, with

many people's fears not being realized. It is also true that in general, majority support exists for new wind farms, but there are a significant number of both local and nonlocal objectors to given schemes (Warren et al. 2005). This suggests a social gap or democratic deficit at the local level that needs to be overcome (Bell et al. 2005) in order to connect national policy delivery with legitimate local concerns.

Rather surprisingly, little systematic study has been done of success rates in individual local authority areas or by individual developers or ownership type. Only Toke (2005b) has attempted a regression analysis, looking at planning permission acceptance and refusal for wind projects based on a sample of 51 proposals. Among his findings is that if the local planning officers (who process applications and make recommendations to the local councilors who vote on the application) object, then projects are almost always refused, whereas if they accept a project, it is likely to go through on appeal. Toke also finds that if the Campaign to Protect Rural England, which campaigns "for the beauty, tranquillity and diversity of the countryside" (CPRE n.d.), objects to a project, it is likely to be opposed by the local parish council. One developer, Wind Prospect (2008), which has a joint venture with EDF, a major energy company, to develop onshore wind farms in the United Kingdom, has invested heavily in local consultation and seems to have been more successful in gaining planning permission (see Toke 2005b). Active community involvement has led to successful development in some cases, particularly when the community owns shares in the wind farm, but these are small in capacity terms.[17] However, under both NFFO and RO, there has been an unwillingness to actively involve communities in co-ownership of onshore wind developments, possibly because of the dominance of large power companies within the UK wind power sector and the high transaction costs of such engagement.

Overall, it is difficult to tell whether the full cost of developing wind power onshore is actually much higher than it would appear, given the social value of the UK countryside, or whether a feasible redistribution of the current benefits toward potential local objectors would be enough to solve the planning problem. Bergmann et al. (2008) use willingness-to-pay modeling of a sample of rural and urban dwellers in Scotland. While both groups value reduced environmental impact from power generation highly, the authors find that urban dwellers are willing to pay more for an offshore wind farm than for an equivalent large onshore wind farm and value the rural employment opportunities less than do rural people. The actual construction costs of wind farms in the United Kingdom are difficult to come by, but the information that is available suggests that simulations of the likely penetration of new projects are still based on optimistic assumptions that wind costs will be much cheaper than they currently are.[18] High actual costs may therefore be a factor delaying investment. The achieved load factors for the whole UK wind portfolio in 2008 were 27% for onshore and 30.4% for offshore (DECC, 2009b, *206*) in contrast to higher assumptions in some calculations (e.g., Dale et al. 2004, who assume 35% for both onshore and offshore wind).

No doubt smaller, more local developments would facilitate reduced planning objections, but they would come with their own higher costs. The move to FITs for such smaller developments should help increase the number of such projects. However, in examining scenario rankings from different wind actors in northwest England, Mander (2008) finds that expansion of offshore wind was the only part of a wind strategy that both pro-wind and pro-countryside lobbies could agree on, even if onshore wind became more community-driven. Attempts to streamline the planning process have been made, with significant reforms to the appeals process in 2003 (Toke 2003), giving more power at the national level; nevertheless, there is clearly still an issue of getting permission. Attempts in 2005 to streamline the planning process in Wales (under a devolved administration) have had mixed success (Cowell 2007). The Welsh Assembly designated "strategic search areas," which were assessed to be more suitable for large wind farm developments and hence more likely to be approved on appeal. These proved controversial, with both pro- and

anti-wind lobbies. The wind developers were unhappy that many proposed schemes lay outside the designated areas, and anti-wind groups were unhappy with where some of the boundaries of the acceptable areas were drawn.

Biomass

Biomass is likely to be the second-largest renewable energy source out to 2020 in the United Kingdom. Biomass is frequently cited as a significant, albeit finite contribution to UK decarbonization (of the order of up to 5%) (see Taylor 2008 for a review). Biomass policy toward waste has been largely successful because of the near-market nature of the technology and its responsiveness to both NFFO and RO subsidies. The direct burning of biocrops has also been successful, given the emerging global market in tradable biomass from countries such as Brazil, Canada, and the United States (Junginger et al. 2008).

Government support for local biocrop plants has proved problematic, however, given the technological, planning, and economic constraints. A high-profile project involving local biomass and new technology failed as a result of financing concerns (Piterou et al. 2008), and it is difficult to justify the use of local biocrops for anything other than direct burning in existing coal-fired power stations in direct competition with internationally traded biomass, which is usually produced more efficiently abroad. Nevertheless, some focus group studies have suggested that there is public support for the use of local biomass in small CHP plants and skepticism about the overall GHG impact of the use of internationally traded biomass (see Upham et al. 2007).

It is not environmentally sensible to use local biocrops to produce biofuel in the United Kingdom. Local biocrops produce more GHG impact when directly burned to produce power and heat (Hammond et al. 2008). Indeed, in the longer run, the current use of biofuels to blend with petrol and diesel may be phased out as the vehicle fleet is electrified (for current use, see Bomb et al. 2007). The difficulty of making a sensible industrial policy argument for a local crop-dedicated biomass power plant within a viable long-run decarbonization strategy is helpfully discussed by van der Horst (2005). Indeed, Slade et al. (2009) criticize UK bioenergy policy as being characterized by lots of initiatives but with a lack of clarity as to precise objectives to be delivered. If the country were to rely on internationally traded biomass as its key input, this would require better certification as to the source of the biomass (van Dam et al. 2008).

Bioenergy, with its complicated supply chain, displacement impacts, and total production cycle sustainability impacts, requires proper pricing of all its environmental effects, including GHGs and local pollutants, in order to calculate whether it is worthwhile (Elghali et al. 2007). The life cycle GHG impact of biocrops (i.e., the impact on the amount of carbon stored in the stock of growing crops) is further complicated by the carbon storage impacts of increasing the area set aside for growing them (Cannell 2003).

UK Performance versus That of Other Countries

The discussion so far indicates that comparative assessment of UK policy on renewable energy would not be straightforward. It is clear that the United Kingdom has pursued a successful decarbonization strategy to date and that relative success has been achieved in several areas, both in responding to price signals and in developing new technologies for deployment in the country. The one area of failure is in deployment of onshore wind at least cost. The net environmental impact of this failure is currently zero, given that the United Kingdom is on course to meet its GHG reduction targets. Still, this environmental performance could have been delivered at lower cost. The excess costs of the current set of policies are hard to estimate, given the diversity of support instruments. However, a lower-end estimate would be the amount of revenue recycling within the RO mechanism, as this overpayment seems largely unnecessary to deliver the observed quantity of renewables connected to the electricity sys-

tem.[19] This excess cost is significant and rising. Nevertheless, it remains small compared with the high cost of the renewable deployment strategies of some other countries, such as Germany and Spain, which have not allowed them to meet their GHG reduction targets.

It is fashionable to suggest that the root cause of the problem of underdelivery of onshore wind is the use of a tradable green certificate (TGC) scheme rather than a FIT, as used in Germany and Spain (see, e.g., Butler and Neuhoff 2008; Jacobsson et al. 2009; Lipp 2007; Meyer 2003; Toke 2005a; Toke and Lauber 2007). A more balanced assessment by the International Energy Agency (IEA 2006) of the UK renewable energy policy points out that TGCs have worked well (at least to the date of the IEA's assessment) in a number of jurisdictions, such as Texas, Sweden, Australia, and New Zealand. It is only in the United Kingdom where they seem to have manifestly failed to deliver the intended capacity.

Two common theoretical arguments have been made for the superiority of FITs over TGCs. One is that by offering a fixed price per kWh to developers, this allows new renewables to be financed more easily. The other is that FITs attract large quantities of renewables because these are not limited to the most attractive sites.

The first argument is well put by Mitchell et al. (2006), who maintain that the UK RO scheme exposes renewables to price, volume, and balancing risks, rather than just volume risks as under a FIT. Although this clearly does impose costs, it is not clear that it is suboptimal or that it explains nondelivery against the United Kingdom's renewables targets. Higher risk is relevant to nondelivery where development is small-scale and the developers have little or no credit history; here there may well be a significant market failure in the market for external finance. However, it is rather a weak argument when the ultimate developers are mostly large multinational companies making portfolio investments, and when most ROC credits are bought by the six multinational supply companies who dominate the UK market, each with generation interests and the option to invest directly in renewable capacity.

Table 13.9. Differences among leading wind countries in Europe

	1,000 mi² land per million population, 2009–2010	% onshore wind owned by utilities/ corporations	% owned by farmers	% owned by cooperatives	Wind capacity (MW), end 2008
United Kingdom	1.5	98	1	0.5	3,288
Germany	1.7	55	35	10	23,903
Spain	4.3	> 99	< 0.5	0	16,740
Denmark	2.9	12	63	25	3,160

Sources: Wikipedia, List of Countries and Dependencies by Population Density (accessed 26 March 2010); Wind Power 2009; Toke 2005a

The second argument makes less theoretical sense, because it is not clear why developing the most attractive sites first is not desirable in any case. The quantity of renewables forthcoming is clearly accelerated by offering initially high returns, but offering a margin for renewables to attract investors is a function not of whether the subsidy regime is a FIT or TGC, but of how large a quantity of renewables is required under either scheme. TGCs can set ambitious targets, as in the United Kingdom, and can deliver attractive prices. Low prices for renewables are not a problem with the ambitious RO targets.

In the end, the question becomes whether the United Kingdom would have delivered more onshore wind capacity had there been a FIT for wind energy. For community schemes, the answer is quite possibly yes, because the uncertainty of individual project cash flows may well have been an issue for funders. However, for larger schemes chiefly owned by multinational energy companies, it is hard to say. The problem has clearly been related to planning permission, and it is not obvious how changing the funding regime improves the prospects for gaining planning permission unless it is more generous and offers scope for providing attractive payments to the local community.

The literature seems to suggest that two more fundamental dimensions are of interest to explain the differences in delivery of onshore wind among the United Kingdom, Germany, Spain, and Denmark: land use constraints and local involvement in ownership, such as via local cooperatives or farmers (see Table 13.9).

Local ownership, which is very high in Denmark and also notable in Germany, is a determinant of successful strategic deployment in these countries (Szarka and Bluhdorn 2006; Toke 2007). This is important because these two countries face similar land use constraints to the United Kingdom. The development in Spain, however, has occurred with similar ownership of wind assets by multinational companies, but in the context of very little land use constraint (Toke and Strachan 2006). Thus it seems clear that these countries have different institutional and physical starting points than the United Kingdom.

Econometric modeling by Soderholm and Klaassen (2007) of diffusion rates of wind power across Europe confirms that the United Kingdom has lower diffusion (penetration) relative to other countries, and that FITs do tend to be more successful in encouraging diffusion, but that a given FIT would likely have less of an impact here than in Germany.

What is clear is that the financial cost of wind power delivered onshore is unnecessarily high in the United Kingdom. Butler and Neuhoff (2008, *1856*) show that while the NFFO schemes did result in much lower support prices for wind in the United Kingdom than in Germany, they were not that much lower once adjusted for the quality of the underlying wind resources. Under the RO, renewable support costs are estimated to have been twice as high in 2006 as they would have been under a German support tariff applied to UK wind resources (which would have been lower than the actual tariff in Germany). Toke (2005a) shows that the RO scheme with revenue recycling was more expensive per kWh than the German FIT following reductions in the size of the FIT in Germany.

Looking at Spain, where large utilities have dominated in ownership of wind generation similarly to the situation in the United Kingdom, Stenzel and Frenzel (2008) note the positive reaction of incumbent Spanish companies to wind power development in Spain in contrast with that in Germany. They highlight the importance of corporate self-interest in promoting wind power development. Wind power in Germany developed in spite of opposition from German utilities, which were forced to accommodate renewables and bear the costs of connection to the grid. In Spain, this has led the corporate generators to support investment in better prediction of wind speeds at individual wind farm sites in order to better manage the grid. In Germany, however, significant costs have been imposed on the transmission system that are not reflected in the connection incentives of wind developers. This has led to grid management issues in Germany, which will become more costly to deal with as wind capacity increases (Klessmann et al. 2008). It is even possible to suggest that the continuation of the grip of incumbents on the German power market is in significant part because of the unwillingness of the German government to liberalize the market fully, for fear of undermining the ability of the incumbents to finance the significant reinforcement costs associated with renewables expansion.

In 2008, the United Kingdom had around 13.2 GW in 195 projects that were in Great Britain's "GB Queue" (see Ofgem 2007a). These were projects that wished to connect to the power grid, but for which no firm connection right could be offered, unlike under the German FIT, where renewable capacity must be connected and paid for generated power (see Swider et al. 2008). The UK government has suggested that this is one of the barriers to the rollout of renewables (DECC 2009e). This may explain some of the slow delivery of renewable wind connection in the United Kingdom, but it certainly does not explain the most significant part of it. It is impossible to tell how economically viable many of the projects in

the GB Queue are, and Ofgem has identified only around 450 MW of wind capacity that needs to be prioritized via accelerating transmission investment (see Ofgem 2009a). It is also the case that new renewable connections should face the true costs of connection to the grid and capacity, and they should come onstream when it is at least system cost, rather than only least generation cost. Nodal pricing would seem to be a more appropriate way of signaling this, rather than the "connect and manage" approach under FITs in Germany (see Pollitt and Bialek 2008).

The correct pricing for transmission capacity also points to the need for the United Kingdom to look closely at the efficiency of utilization of transmission assets and their operational criteria. The GB transmission system in general operates under an N-2 safety standard, wherein the system must be operated in such a way that if a major link fails, it must be capable of handling another similar-size failure. This gives rise to lower rates of utilization of transmission grid assets than in countries with an N-1 safety standard and gives rise to less use of automatic voltage control equipment. This suggests that there is scope for operating the assets much more smartly in the presence of large-scale renewables. For instance, the nominal rating of Scotland–England interconnectors is around 7 GW, whereas the declared capacity is 2.2 GW; this suggests that transmission constraints could be made less in practice than they might be on paper. Ofgem's recent LENS scenario modeling (Ault et al. 2008) of the electricity transmission and distribution networks suggests that a range of network sizes and capabilities are possible by 2050, depending on how and where new generation capacity, including renewables, was connected.

Looking to other countries with TGC schemes, it is quite clear that Sweden, Australia, and New Zealand have avoided the problems of overpayment that characterize the UK RO scheme, and these jurisdictions have significantly fewer land use constraints. Kelly (2007) discusses the UK scheme in contrast to those of Australia and New Zealand. The Australian scheme, complemented by an Office of the Renewable Energy Regulator (see ORER n.d.), has much less ambitious targets than the UK scheme but does not have any revenue recycling. The New Zealand scheme has higher targets than Australia's but is voluntary. The Swedish scheme also does not have revenue recycling and is combined with carbon taxes throughout the economy (see Swedish Energy Agency n.d.). The United Kingdom would do well to examine the overall carbon reduction incentives in Sweden.

Szarka (2006) raises an important issue about policy comparison across countries in the case of renewables, suggesting that policy should be aimed at paradigm change, not just installed capacity. Clearly what matters is where the country ends up in terms of decarbonization, and what is required is radical change to the UK energy system. He maintains that the real success of German policy has been to engage large numbers of individuals in taking action on climate change, as investors in local wind farms. This is an important perspective, because it suggests that the real failure of UK policy is not gaining practical support for the sorts of changes to the energy system that are required. Failure to focus on this aspect of the problem has led to an ineffective policy on renewables deployment, which will be more expensive than it need have been, due to a combination of underdelivery and overpayment.

Another issue is the stability of policy through time. A concern of UK policymakers in setting up the RO scheme was to introduce stability in the subsidy regime over a long period, in contrast to the stop-start nature of NFFO. However, although stability is a desirable goal in itself, this has been an excuse for not facing up to the serious deficiencies of the RO scheme. Little evidence is available to indicate that the United Kingdom has had a less stable policy toward renewables than countries with high penetration rates of renewables, such as Denmark, Germany, and Spain, where responses to incentives were rapid and significant changes have occurred to support policy over time.

What Might Be Right for the United Kingdom

If a problem exists with the delivery of onshore renewable capacity in the United Kingdom, what should be done about it? Answering this question requires attention to the institutional context of the United Kingdom (following Rodrik 2008). The country's policy context is a liberalized market for a relatively small island with concerns about fuel poverty, global warming, and energy security. It is clear that what is needed is a policy consistent with a liberalized energy market and with environmental targets. By contrast, Germany is much less committed to liberalized energy markets. It also has much more of a focus on a green industrial policy aimed at promoting the manufacture of wind turbines for export. Although the United Kingdom has paid lip service to this sort of objective, the reality is that only 4,000 jobs in the country depend on the wind production industry; even in Germany, the figure is only 38,000 (EWEA 2009). It is quite clear that for an industry requiring around £1 billion ($1.5 billion) of subsidy per year, this is not a cost-effective job creation scheme.

The focus should rather be on least-cost achievement of environmental targets, which will be much more important for the competitiveness of the UK economy and for incomes and employment. The current RO scheme is clearly far too generous to existing onshore wind, and it does not guarantee cost-effectiveness for offshore wind and marine energy. It is also important that the aim of long-run cost reduction for technologies that are currently not cost-effective be maintained, and that these technologies compete with nuclear and CCS projects in a reasonable time frame. An important starting point for this is the creation of a single high and stable carbon price throughout the economy. This would immediately give clear signals to nuclear and CCS and provide the backstop technologies against which continuing subsidies can be measured. It would also provide the right incentives to biomass in terms of cofiring, landfill gas, and waste.

The principle of various levels of support for technologies at different stages of development is also well established, and recent moves in UK policy to recognize this are sensible and important. What is needed is the right mix of R&D support, competitions, and general support mechanisms such as a FIT or TGC. It seems clear that for small schemes, a FIT for small-scale wind and small hydro does offer an attractive mechanism at the current low levels of development in the United Kingdom, and hence moves in this direction are sensible, given high transaction costs in setting up such schemes and arranging finance.

For offshore wind, it would seem that a NFFO-style set of annual auctions would offer the best way of keeping prices down. NFFO arrangements could be amended to ensure actual delivery, with penalties for nondelivery. Indeed, given the scale of offshore wind's potential and the problem of finding a suitable level of support initially, relative to other sources of renewables, this would seem to be a good way forward. Bids could take the form of contracts for differences (as suggested by Ofgem 2007c for the reform of the RO scheme), whereby bids would be for a fixed price for the electricity generated, which would be paid at that price minus a reference wholesale price, with the payments being levied across licensed suppliers in proportion to their supply. This would incentivize efficient location decisions, as connection and use of system charges would still be borne by the generators, and they would be incentivized to maximize the actual wholesale price they received in the market. It would also tie in with successful experience of the use of competitions for infrastructure delivery under the private finance initiative (Pollitt 2002). As with any procurement process that is repeated with (potentially) a smallish number of bidders over time, the auctions would have to be monitored for collusion among the bidders, but given the standard nature of the investments and transparency of the bidding strategies employed by the players, actual or tacit collusion would be easy to spot. Annual bid rounds would offer the chance to adjust quantities required and other details of the auction easily over time to reflect learning.

For large-scale onshore wind, the RO mechanism could be made to work by removing the revenue recycling and adjusting the targets according to the expected amount of capacity from offshore wind. This would essentially reward onshore renewable generation with a fixed revenue supplement equal to the buyout price, assuming the target was not met or exceeded. However, it remains the case that all renewable capacity should be expected to face the full amount of transmission and distribution costs imposed on the system. This would encourage optimal siting, local generation more generally, and proper competition between renewable supply and demand reduction measures. Barthelmie et al. (2008) show that there would be benefits to learning from Spain in terms of improving the short-term forecasting of wind power availability. Improved forecasting might have increased the price of wind power received by generators by the order of 14% in 2003.[20]

In sum, the current revenue recycling within the RO mechanism is unnecessary and should be stopped. This is line with an early National Audit Office report on the RO mechanism, which warned the government that it needed "to keep a firm grip of the Obligation's cost relative to other instruments for reducing carbon dioxide" (NAO 2005, 4). The system needs to be altered with respect to offshore renewables in order to ensure least-cost delivery of an initially very expensive renewable energy source. Large onetime projects like the Severn or Thames Barrage (associated with a new London airport), if deemed necessary after appropriate cost–benefit analysis, must be auctioned rather than financed within the RO mechanism.[21] The RO scheme could further be amended to remove its all-or-nothing property by ensuring that in the unlikely event that targets were met or exceeded, the total amount of subsidy would be divided proportionately among all those presenting ROCs. This would remove the cliff-edge effect on the renewable subsidy of meeting the target.[22]

What the history of UK renewables since 1990 really tells us is that there are important institutional barriers to expansion of renewables onshore. These have to do with the lack of local benefit from renewable projects that employ a small number of people and have a significant perceived amenity impact. The key learning from Denmark and Germany is that local populations must perceive such projects as being of positive benefit to them rather than simply satisfying some distant national policy objective, which they may otherwise support. The United Kingdom must develop local energy companies that are owned by local investors or local customers or councils if the potential exploitation of local energy resources—wind, biomass, hydro, and other technologies—is to be realized. This is because virtually all renewable electricity and heat technologies involve significant local impacts in terms of siting of industrial facilities close to residential areas.

For offshore renewables, getting costs down will be the challenge. Costs need to decrease significantly in order for energy customers to be willing to support large quantities of offshore renewables. The current combination of capital grants and arbitrary ROC banding is not a satisfactory or sustainable way forward. Auctions for new capacity would be institutionally compatible with the United Kingdom's liberalized electricity market and offer the prospects of falling prices over time. They would also tie in with the auctions to build, own, and operate offshore transmission lines to the new wind farms that Ofgem is currently implementing (see Ofgem 2007b). Under Ofgem's offshore transmission auction scheme, once an offshore wind farm has a firm contract for connection to the onshore transmission grid, an auction is triggered to build the interconnection between the shore and the wind farm.

In the end, success in UK policy toward renewable deployment, relative to other countries, must be measured in terms of the net present value of the amount of renewable electricity generated scaled by the amount of subsidy. Although this success metric will be difficult to measure at any point along the pathway, in the interim, success should be measured in terms of the extent to which the maximum amount of renewable generation (adjusted for technological maturity) is being supported for the current level of subsidy. UK policy clearly is not being successful, given

the large amount of relatively cheap unexploited wind resources in the United Kingdom, in the face of overpayment to existing renewable generators.

Conclusions

The United Kingdom is struggling to develop a coherent set of policies for decarbonization following its successful experience in liberalizing energy markets. Various authors have suggested that the decarbonization policy is so ambitious that it demands radical institutional changes (Mitchell 2007; Pollitt 2008). However, little consensus has been reached on what form those institutional changes should take.

What is clear is that solutions must target least-cost, or else the whole policy is likely to fail as a result of the actual cost becoming prohibitive. On the path to this sort of ultimate policy failure, large amounts of resources are likely to be wasted, to little overall effect and for no benefit to the UK economy or the global climate. The United Kingdom has had a long history of failed government intervention in the energy market and in industrial policy in general (Pollitt 2008). It must not continue this sort of tradition. It has, however, had good experience with the role of markets, undertaking basic R&D, and the use of market mechanisms to deliver public goods. The country has also particular concerns about fuel poverty, which argues for a focus on keeping the costs of renewables policy down.

The United Kingdom agreed to an ambitious renewable generation target that was unnecessarily tough—in terms of the required speed of increase in the share—in the face of its EU CO_2 targets, which could have been met in a much more straightforward way by a combination of demand reduction and a switch from coal- to gas-fired generation (see Grubb et al. 2008). Why the country got itself into this position is not apparent, but it clearly hoped that the EU ETS would be much more effective than it has been in supporting decarbonization. Because of this, the EU Renewables Directive has become more significant for the country than it needed to be.

The United Kingdom also must resist calls to see national renewables policy as anything other than a policy for delivering learning benefits on the path to cost parity with established technologies. An industrial policy based around the employment or export potential of renewables is not a sensible use of national economic resources. No doubt some benefit will accrue to the United Kingdom from exploiting its domestic renewables potential, but this will arise naturally and should not be an objective of policy. The British Wind Energy Association (BWEA) reports that the United Kingdom is a net exporter of small-scale wind turbines, the part of the market least affected by government subsidy (see BWEA 2009). The country needs to move to a more competitive energy market wherein smaller firms compete with large incumbents to supply power and deliver national targets and the capacity to rapidly adopt new lower-cost innovations exists. This is essential if incumbent costs are to be kept down and oligopoly pricing and excessive subsidy regimes are to be avoided. The 40 years from 2010 to 2050 are very likely to see huge technological and lifestyle changes that will substantially change the potential picture of the power, heat, and transport sectors (see Ault et al. 2008). The United Kingdom must have institutional arrangements to incentivize potentially drastic innovation within the renewables sector.

The country must incorporate the learning from both its NFFO and its RO experiences into future subsidy regimes. The evidence suggests that a reformed NFFO-type auction could be a sensible way to deliver large offshore wind parks mostly built by big multinational utility companies. Onshore, it is clear that there are legitimate land use issues with renewables, which can be addressed only by smaller-scale projects for local public benefit. This policy is in line with some of the more decentralized scenarios of the future development of electricity networks, and it would have the added co-benefits of substantially reinforcing the need for paradigm change at the individual level and aiding behavioral changes that would support the optimal use of technologies that promote energy efficiency.

The United Kingdom also needs to significantly improve the quality of the information on which policy decisions are being made. There is a severe lack of analysis of the drivers of past policy outcomes, partly as a result of the lack of information on the financial characteristics of individual projects that have received subsidies. No study has been done on the actual performance of renewable projects in the United Kingdom. Foxon and Pearson (2007) highlight the need for improvements to the process of energy policymaking, whereby analysis is properly used to evaluate policy, and policy is revised in the light of analysis. One particular area for improvement is in the consistency of energy policy among heat, power, and transport fuel in terms of value of subsidies for carbon reduction, entry barrier reduction, and promoting learning.

The information available to potential, often small-scale, developers could also be improved with significantly more use of geographical information system (GIS) mapping of potential renewable energy sites and guidance on acceptable designs and siting rules. This would focus developer efforts on sites much more likely to secure local public support and obtain planning permission. This sort of proactive approach to preparing the ground for projects would seem to address some of the calls for more united government approaches (e.g., Keirstead 2007) toward energy policy in the United Kingdom. It also likely would aid in resolving resource conflicts among local community, leisure, defense, air traffic, and energy interests.

Finally, a focus on renewables must not detract from the overriding policy aim of decarbonization of the economy. This requires sensible carbon prices and the workings of the price mechanism with regards to transmission and distribution costs. In the end, it is only when locational costs and environmental externalities are properly priced that any given renewables project, with its particular characteristics, can be evaluated among the myriad alternatives. Although the UK policies toward renewables may currently be failing to deliver new capacity in sufficient quantity to hit long-term renewables targets, it is by no means clear that those countries that are doing better in this regard are any nearer to achieving long-term decarbonization.

Acknowledgments

The author acknowledges the ongoing intellectual support of the ESRC Electricity Policy Research Group. Bin Feng provided excellent research assistance. The comments of Boaz Moselle, David Newbery, Jorge Padilla, Dick Schmalensee, Steve Smith, and Jon Stern are acknowledged.

Notes

1. The definition of renewables used in this chapter is that in the EU Renewables Directive (2009/28/EC): " 'energy from renewable sources' means energy from renewable non-fossil sources, namely wind, solar, aerothermal, geothermal, hydrothermal and ocean energy, hydropower, biomass, landfill gas, sewage treatment plant gas and biogases" (European Commission 2009, *Article 2(a)*).
2. This indicates that in August 2009, 8% of a typical electricity bill and 3% of a typical gas bill was being charged to support environmental schemes, of which the most expensive were targeted toward lower-income consumers.
3. UK carbon targets are net of trading, and hence can include carbon credits purchased from abroad.
4. HM Treasury (Her Majesty's Treasury) is the UK Ministry of Finance.
5. It is worth noting that Germany also likes the 1990 baseline date, as this coincides with the collapse of the Berlin Wall and the rapid decarbonization of the former East Germany as a result of industrial decline and improved environmental standards.
6. See, e.g., DECC (2009a, *92*), which shows projected cost decreases for PV of 70% to 2050, against only 22% for coal-fired CCS.
7. NAO (2008, *17*) reports 20 government policies, strategies, and reviews on energy between 1997 and 2009, with 16 of those from 2003 onward.
8. Initially the levy was 10.6% in England and Wales, but it fell to 0.9% in 1998 when payments for

nuclear power ended. It was phased out in April 2002, having been 0.3%. The levy rate in Scotland, which was not used to fund nuclear liabilities, began at 0.5% in 1996 and reached a maximum of 1.2% (Wikipedia, s.v. "Fossil Fuel Levy").

9. England and Wales had five rounds of NFFO: NFFO-1, start date 1990, followed by NFFO-2, -3, -4, and -5 in 1992, 1995, 1997, and 1998. Scotland had three rounds: SRO-1, -2 and -3 in 1995, 1997, and 1999. Northern Ireland had two rounds: NI-NFFO-1 and -2 in 1994 and 1995. See Wong (2005, *131*). The last NFFO contract is due to expire in 2018.
10. Under the 2001 EU Renewables Directive, the United Kingdom signed up to a 10% target for renewable electricity generation, which is embodied in the successor scheme to NFFO (European Commission 2001).
11. Continuing NFFO contracts are funded via the revenue from the auction of ROCs (by the NFPA) associated with the contracts (see Ofgem 2004).
12. Assuming here that no one has invested in a renewable generation project that would be unprofitable without the "recycled" revenues. The actual reported figure for recycled revenue is £307m (Ofgem, Renewables Obligation Annual Report 2007–2008, *1*).
13. UK inflation between September 2002 and September 2008 was 15% (ONS 2009). The National Audit Office reported a figure of only £700 million ($1.05 billion) per annum for annual costs 2003–2006 (NAO 2005, *35*).
14. In May 2009, only eight operational schemes existed with a capacity of 50 MW or more onshore (DECC 2009b, *145–51*).
15. For more details on the planning process in England, see DECC (2009 n.d.b).
16. In this vein, Upreti and van der Horst (2004) have an enlightening discussion of one NFFO biomass project that, because it could not be modified as suggested by the local consultation process, eventually had to be abandoned.
17. One of the few examples of significant capital raising from the local community was the Baywind project in Cumbria, which first raised £1.2 million ($1.8 million) to form a cooperative to develop wind power (see www.baywind.co.uk).
18. Compare actual costs in Snyder and Kaiser (2009) and Blanco (2009) with cost simulation assumptions in Dale et al. (2004) and Strbac et al. (2007).
19. This is because the recycled revenue component is highly uncertain and unlikely to be a key part of the business case for a new renewables project.

20. It might be considered odd that UK wind generators have not done this already, given the financial incentive to do so, but this may be due to the currently low level of wind capacity, relative to some of the fixed costs in setting up such a system.
21. See SDC (2007) on potential tidal projects in the United Kingdom.
22. The government has considered this issue but has decided not to do anything about it at the moment, given the gap between delivery and actual (or future) targets (DECC 2008).

References

Ault, G., D. Frame, N. Hughes, and N. Strachan. 2008. *Electricity Network Scenarios in Great Britain for 2050, Final Report for Ofgem's LENS Project.* Ref. No. 157a/08. London: Ofgem.

Barthelmie, R. J., F. Murray, and S. C. Pryor. 2008. The Economic Benefit of Short-Term Forecasting for Wind Energy in the UK Electricity Market. *Energy Policy* 36 (5): 1687–1696.

Bell, D., T. Gray, and C. Haggett. 2005. The "Social Gap" in Wind Farm Siting Decisions: Explanations and Policy Responses. *Environmental Politics* 14 (4): 460–477.

Bergmann, A., S. Colombo, and N. Hanley. 2008. Rural versus Urban Preferences for Renewable Energy Developments. *Ecological Economics* 65 (3): 616–625.

BIS (Department for Business, Innovation and Skills). 2008. Fuel Poverty Statistics: Background Indicators, 2008: Annex to Fuel Poverty Strategy Report, 2008. www.berr.gov.uk/files/file48037.pdf (accessed February 22, 2010).

Blanco, M. I. 2009. The Economics of Wind Energy. *Renewable and Sustainable Energy Reviews* 13 (6–7): 1372–1382.

Bomb, C., K. McCormick, E. Deurwaarder, and T. Kåberger. 2007. Biofuels for Transport in Europe: Lessons from Germany and the UK. *Energy Policy* 35 (4): 2256–2267.

Bonilla, D. 2006. Energy Prices, Production and the Adoption of Cogeneration in the UK and the Netherlands. Cambridge Working Papers in Economics: 27–27. Cambridge, UK: University of Cambridge, Faculty of Economics (formerly DAE)

Brown, K. A., and D. H. Maunder. 1994. Using Landfill Gas: A UK perspective. *Renewable Energy* 5 (5–8): 774–781.

Butler, L., and K. Neuhoff (2008). Comparison of Feed-In Tariff, Quota and Auction Mechanisms to Support Wind Power Development. *Renewable Energy* 33 (8): 1854–1867.

BWEA (British Wind Energy Association). 2009. Small Wind Systems UK Market Report 2009. www.bwea.com/pdf/small/ BWEA%20SWS%20UK%20Market%20Report% 202009.pdf (accessed August 27, 2009).

———. No date. www.bwea.com/ukwed/index.asp (accessed August 20, 2009).

Cannell, M. G. R. 2003. Carbon Sequestration and Biomass Energy Offset: Theoretical, Potential and Achievable Capacities Globally, in Europe and the UK. *Biomass and Bioenergy* 24 (2): 97–116.

Carbon Trust. 2006. *Policy Frameworks for Renewables.* London: Carbon Trust.

CCC (Committee on Climate Change). 2008. *Building a Low Carbon Economy: The UK's Contribution to Tackling Climate Change.* London: TSO.

Chamberlain, Phil. 2008. Still Much to Be Done on Planning. *Real Power* 12 (April–June): 19–24. www.bwea.com/pdf/realpower/realpower_12.pdf (accessed February 22, 2010).

Coles, R. W., and J. Taylor. 1993. Wind Power and Planning: The Environmental Impact of Windfarms in the UK. *Land Use Policy* 10 (3): 205–226.

Connor, P. M. 2003. UK Renewable Energy Policy: A Review. *Renewable and Sustainable Energy Reviews* 7 (1): 65–82.

Conway, A. 1986. Tidal Power: A Matter of Faith, Hope and Policy. *Energy Policy* 14 (6): 574–577.

Cowell, R. 2007. Wind Power and "the Planning Problem": The Experience of Wales. *European Environment* 17 (5): 291–306.

CPRE (Campaign to Protect Rural England). No date. CPRE home page. www.cpre.org.uk (accessed February 22, 2010).

Dale, L., D. Milborrow, R. Slark, and G. Strbac. 2004. Total Cost Estimates for Large-Scale Wind Scenarios in UK. *Energy Policy* 32 (17): 1949–1956.

DECC (Department of Energy and Climate Change). 2008. *Reform of the Renewables Obligation: Government Response to the Statutory Consultation on the Renewables Obligation Order 2009.* London: DECC.

———. 2009a. *Analytical Annex: The UK Low Carbon Transition Plan.* London: DECC.

———. 2009b. *Digest of UK Energy Statistics 2009 Edition.* London: DECC.

———. 2009c. Draft National Policy Statement for Nuclear Power Generation (EN-6).

http://data.energynpsconsultation.decc.gov.uk/documents/npss/EN-6.pdf (accessed February 22, 2010).

———. 2009d. Offshore Renewables Financial Boost Kicks In. www.decc.gov.uk/en/content/cms/news/pn037/pn037.aspx (accessed August 25, 2009).

———. 2009e. *The UK Low Carbon Transition Plan.* London: DECC.

———. 2009f. *The UK Renewable Energy Strategy.* London: DECC.

———. No date, a. Energy Statistics: Prices. www.decc.gov.uk/en/content/cms/statistics/source/prices/prices.aspx (accessed August 25, 2009).

———. No date, b. Planning Process in England. www.decc.gov.uk/en/content/cms/what_we_do/uk_supply/energy_mix/renewable/planning/plan_policy/england/england.aspx.

Defra (Department for Environment, Food and Rural Affairs). 2008. Greenhouse Emissions Statistics. www.defra.gov.uk/environment/statistics/globatmos/download/ghg_ns_20090326.pdf (accessed August 27, 2009).

———. 2009. UK Climate Change Sustainable Development Indicator: 2007 Greenhouse Gas Emissions, Final Figures, www.defra.gov.uk/evidence/statistics/environment/globatmos/download/ghg_ns_20090203.pdf (accessed August 27, 2009).

Drake, F. 2009. Black Gold to Green Gold: Regional Energy Policy and the Rehabilitation of Coal in Response to Climate Change. *Area* 41 (1): 43–54.

DUKES (Digest of UK Energy Statistics). 2009. Expenditure on Energy by Final User to 2008 (DUKES 1.1.6). Available at DECC n.d.a.

EEA (European Environment Agency). 2006. EU Greenhouse Gas Emissions Increase for Second Year in a Row. www.eea.europa.eu/pressroom/newsreleases/GHG2006-en (accessed February 22, 2010).

Eikeland, P. O., and I. A. Sæverud. 2007. Market Diffusion of New Renewable Energy in Europe: Explaining Front-Runner and Laggard Positions. *Energy & Environment* 18 (1): 13–36.

Elghali, L., R. Clift, P. Sinclair, C. Panoutsou, and A. Bauen. 2007. Developing a Sustainability Framework for the Assessment of Bioenergy Systems. *Energy Policy* 35 (12): 6075–6083.

Elliott, D. 1992. Renewables and the Privatization of the UK ESI: A Case Study. *Energy Policy* 20 (3): 257–268.

———. 1994. UK Renewable Energy Strategy: The Need for Longer-Term Support. *Energy Policy* 22 (12): 1067–1074.

———. 2009. Marine Renewables: A New Innovation Frontier. *Technology Analysis and Strategic Management* 21 (2): 267–275.

Eltham, D. C., G. P. Harrison, and S. J. Allen. 2008. Change in Public Attitudes Towards a Cornish Wind Farm: Implications for Planning. *Energy Policy* 36 (1): 23–33.

European Commission. 2001. *Directive 2001/77/EC of the European Parliament and Council of 27 September 2001 on the Promotion of Electricity Produced from Renewable Energy Sources in the Internal Electricity.* Brussels: European Commission.

———. 2009. Directive 2009/28/EC of the European Parliament and of the Council of 23 April 2009 on the promotion of the use of energy from renewable sources and amending and subsequently repealing Directives 2001/77/EC and 2003/30/EC. Brussels: European Commission.

Evans, J., and R. Green. 2003. *Why Did British Electricity Prices Fall after 1998?* CMI Electricity Project working paper No. 26. Cambridge, UK: University of Cambridge.

EWEA (European Wind Energy Association). 2009. Wind Energy: The Facts. Chapter 7: Employment in the Wind Energy Sector. www.wind-energy-the-facts.org/en/part-3-economics-of-wind-power/chapter-7-employment/ (accessed August 27, 2009).

Faiers, A., and C. Neame. 2006. Consumer Attitudes Towards Domestic Solar Power Systems. *Energy Policy* 34 (14): 1797–1806.

Foxon, T. J., R. Gross, A. Chase, J. Howes, A. Arnall, and D. Anderson. 2005. UK Innovation Systems for New and Renewable Energy Technologies: Drivers, Barriers and Systems Failures. *Energy Policy* 33 (16): 2123–2137.

Foxon, T. J., and P. J. G. Pearson. 2007. Towards Improved Policy Processes for Promoting Innovation in Renewable Electricity Technologies in the UK. *Energy Policy* 35 (3): 1539–1550.

Grubb, M., T. Jamasb, and M. Pollitt. 2008. A Low-Carbon Electricity Sector for the UK: What Can Be Done and How Much Will It Cost? In *Delivering a Low Carbon Electricity System*, edited by M. Grubb, T. Jamasb, and M. Pollitt. Cambridge, UK: Cambridge University Press, 462–497.

Grubb, M., and J. Wilde. 2008. Enhancing the Efficient Use of Electricity in the Business and Public Sectors. *Delivering a Low Carbon Electricity System*, edited by

M. Grubb, T. Jamasb, and M. Pollitt. Cambridge, UK: Cambridge University Press, 229–256.

Hammond, G. P., S. Kallu, and M.C. McManus. 2008. Development of Biofuels for the UK Automotive Market. *Applied Energy* 85 (6): 506–515.

Harvey, K. 1994. The Development of Combined Heat and Power in the UK. *Energy Policy* 22 (2): 179–181.

Hedger, M. M. 1995. Wind Power: Challenges to Planning Policy in the UK. *Land Use Policy* 12 (1): 17–28.

Helm, D. 2002. A Critique of Renewables Policy in the UK. *Energy Policy* 30 (3): 185–188.

Hill, A., and M. Hay. 2004. UK Renewables: Harnessing Wind, Wave and Tide. *Refocus* 5 (2): 20–21.

HM Treasury. 2009. *Budget 2009 Building Britain's Future. Economic and Fiscal Strategy Report and Financial Statement and Budget Report.* London: Stationery Office.

House of Lords. 2008. Economic Affairs—Fourth Report. Chapter 6: Policy on Renewable Energy. www.publications.parliament.uk/pa/ld200708/ldselect/ldeconaf/195/19509.htm#a53 (accessed February 22, 2010).

Hull, A. 1995. Local Strategies for Renewable Energy: Policy Approaches in England and Wales. *Land Use Policy* 12 (1): 7–16.

IEA (International Energy Agency). 2006. *Energy Policies of IEA Countries: The United Kingdom: 2006 Review.* Paris: OECD Publishing.

———. 2009. Energy Technology RD&D Database. wds.iea.org/WDS/ReportFolders/ReportFolders.aspx (accessed August 28, 2009).

Jacobsson, S., A. Bergek, D. Finon, V. Lauber, C. Mitchell, D. Toke, and A. Verbruggen. 2009. EU Renewable Energy Support Policy: Faith or Facts? *Energy Policy* 37 (6): 2143–2146.

Jamasb, T., H. Kiamil, and R. Nepal. 2008a. Hot Issue and Burning Options in Waste Management: A Social Cost Benefit Analysis of Waste-to-Energy in the UK. Cambridge Working Papers in Economics: 24–24. Cambridge, UK: University of Cambridge, Faculty of Economics.

Jamasb, T., W. Nuttall, M. Pollitt, and A. Maratou. 2008b. Technologies for a Low Carbon Electricity System: An Assessment of the UK's Issues and Options. *Delivering a Low Carbon Electricity System*, edited by M. Grubb, T. Jamasb, and M. Pollitt. Cambridge, UK: Cambridge University Press, 64–99.

Jarvis, I. 1986. Can a successful city–wide CHP scheme be launched in the UK?', *Energy Policy*, 14 (2), 160–163.

Junginger, M., T. Bolkesjo, D. Bradley, P. Dolzan, A. Faaij, J. Heinimö, B. Hektor, Ø. Leistad, E. Ling, M. Perry, E. Piacente, F. Rosillo-Calle, Y. Ryckmans, P-P. Schouwenberg, B. Solberg, E. Trømborg, A. da Silva Walter, and M. de Wit. 2008. Developments in International Bioenergy Trade. *Biomass and Bioenergy* 32 (8): 717–729.

Kannan, R. 2009. Uncertainties in Key Low Carbon Power Generation Technologies: Implication for UK Decarbonisation Targets. *Applied Energy* 86 (10): 1873–1886.

Keirstead, J. 2007. The UK Domestic Photovoltaics Industry and the Role of Central Government. *Energy Policy* 35 (4): 2268–2280.

Kelly, G. 2007. Renewable Energy Strategies in England, Australia and New Zealand. *Geoforum* 38 (2): 326–338.

Klessmann, C., C. Nabe, and K. Burges. 2008. Pros and Cons of Exposing Renewables to Electricity Market Risks: A Comparison of the Market Integration Approaches in Germany, Spain, and the UK. *Energy Policy* 36 (10): 3646–3661.

Lipp, J. 2007. Lessons for Effective Renewable Electricity Policy from Denmark, Germany and the United Kingdom. *Energy Policy* 35 (11): 5481–5495.

Lupton, M. 2008. Chasing the Dream [Microgeneration Strategy]. *Engineering & Technology* (17509637) 3 (12): 54–57.

MacKay, D. 2008. *Sustainable Energy—without the Hot Air.* Cambridge: UIT.

Mander, S. 2008. The Role of Discourse Coalitions in Planning for Renewable Energy: A Case Study of Wind-Energy Deployment. *Environment and Planning C: Government and Policy* 26 (3): 583–600.

Marshall, E. 1993. CHP and Deregulation: The Regulator's Viewpoint. *Energy Policy* 21 (1): 73–78.

McGowan, F. 1991. Controlling the Greenhouse Effect: The Role of Renewables. *Energy Policy* 19 (2): 110–118.

Meyer, N. I. 2003. European Schemes for Promoting Renewables in Liberalised Markets. *Energy Policy* 31 (7): 665–676.

Mitchell, C. 1995. *Renewable Energy in the UK: Financing Options for the Future.* London: Campaign for the Protection of Rural England.

———. 2007. *The Political Economy of Sustainable Energy.* Basingstoke, UK: Palgrave.

Mitchell, C., D. Bauknecht, and P. M. Connor. 2006. Effectiveness through Risk Reduction: A Comparison of the Renewable Obligation in England and Wales and the Feed-In System in Germany. *Energy Policy* 34 (3): 297–305.

Mitchell, C., and P. Connor. 2004. Renewable Energy Policy in the UK 1990–2003. *Energy Policy* 32 (17): 1935–1947.

Mueller, M., and R. Wallace. 2008. Enabling Science and Technology for Marine Renewable Energy. *Energy Policy* 36 (12): 4376–4382.

NAO (National Audit Office). 2005. *Department of Trade and Industry Renewable Energy. 11 February 2005.* London: NAO.

———. 2008. *Renewable Energy: Options for Scrutiny.* London: NAO.

Nelson, H. T. 2008. Planning Implications from the Interactions between Renewable Energy Programs and Carbon Regulation. *Journal of Environmental Planning and Management* 51 (4): 581–596.

Newbery, D. M., and M. G. Pollitt. 1997. The Restructuring and Privatisation of Britain's CEGB: Was It Worth It? *Journal of Industrial Economics* 45 (3): 269–303.

Odenberger, M., J. Kjärstad, and F. Johnsson. 2008. Ramp-Up of CO_2 Capture and Storage within Europe. *International Journal of Greenhouse Gas Control* 2 (4): 417–438.

Ofgem. 2002. *The Review of the First Year of NETA: A Review Document*, Vol. 1, *July*. London: Ofgem.

———. 2004. *The Renewables Obligation: Ofgem's First Annual Report.* London: Ofgem.

———. 2007a. The GB Queue: Problems and Possible Solutions. www.ofgem.gov.uk/Networks/Trans/PriceControls/TPCR4/ConsultantsReports/Documents1/16962-The%20GB%20Queue%20-%20%20Reasons%20and%20remedies.ppt (accessed August 28, 2009).

———. 2007b. Offshore Transmission. www.ofgem.gov.uk/Networks/offtrans/Pages/Offshoretransmission.aspx (accessed August 28, 2009).

———. 2007c. *Reform of the Renewables Obligation 2006: Ofgem's Response.* London: Ofgem.

———. 2009a. Derogations to Facilitate Earlier Connection of Generation—Decision on Interim Approach. www.ofgem.gov.uk/Networks/Trans/ElecTransPolicy/tar/Documents1/20090508%20derogations%20interim.pdf (accessed February 22, 2010).

———. 2009b. Updated Household Energy Bills Explained. www.ofgem.gov.uk/Media/FactSheets/Documents1/updatedhouseholdbills09.pdf (accessed October 20, 2009).

———. Various dates. Renewables Obligation annual reports.

ONS (Office for National Statistics). 2007. Households: Rise in Non-family Households. www.statistics.gov.uk/cci/nugget.asp?id=1866 (accessed August 25, 2009).

———. 2009. CPI series. www.ons.gov.uk (accessed August 27, 2009).

OPSI (Office of Public Sector Information). 2008a. Climate Change Act. www.opsi.gov.uk/acts/acts2008/ukpga_20080027_en_1 (accessed August 28, 2009).

———. 2008b. Energy Act. www.opsi.gov.uk/acts/acts2008/ukpga_20080032_ en_1 (accessed August 28, 2009).

———. 2008c. Planning Act. www.opsi.gov.uk/acts/acts2008/ukpga_20080029_en_1 (accessed August 28, 2009).

———. 2009. *2009 No. 785 Electricity, England and Wales The Renewables Obligation Order 2009.* www.opsi.gov.uk/si/si2009/pdf/uksi_20090785_en.pdf (accessed March 26, 2010).

ORER (Office of the Renewable Energy Regulator). No date. ORER home page. www.orer.gov.au (accessed February 22, 2010).

Oxera. 2005. *Economic Analysis of the Design, Cost and Performance of the UK Renewables Obligation and Capital Grants Scheme.* Report prepared for the National Audit Office. London: National Audit Office.

Paish, O. 2002. Small Hydro Power: Technology and Current Status. *Renewable and Sustainable Energy Reviews* 6 (6): 537–556.

Perry, M., and F. Rosillo-Calle. 2008. Recent Trends and Future Opportunities in UK Bioenergy: Maximising Biomass Penetration in a Centralised Energy System. *Biomass and Bioenergy* 32 (8): 688–701.

Piterou, A., S. Shackley, and P. Upham. 2008. Project ARBRE: Lessons for Bio-energy Developers and Policy-makers. *Energy Policy* 36 (6): 2044–50.

Pollitt, M. 2002. Declining Role of the State in Infrastructure Investments in the UK. In *Private Initiatives in Infrastructure: Priorities, Incentives, and Performance*, edited by M. Tsuji, S. Berg, and M. Pollitt. Cheltenham, UK: Edward Elgar, 67–100.

———. 2008. The Future of Electricity (and Gas) Regulation in Low-Carbon Policy World. *Energy Journal*, Special Issue in Honor of David Newbery, 63–94.

Pollitt, M., and J. Bialek. 2008. Electricity Network Investment and Regulation for a Low Carbon Future. In *Delivering a Low Carbon Electricity System*, edited by M. Grubb, T. Jamasb, and M. Pollitt. Cambridge, UK: Cambridge University Press.

Porter, D., and N. Steen. 1996. Renewable Energy in a Competitive Electricity Market. *Renewable Energy* 9 (1–4): 1120–1123.

QEP (Quarterly Energy Prices). 2009. Average Annual Domestic Electricity Bills by Home and Non-home Supplier (QEP 2.2.1). Available at DECC n.d.a.

Riddell, R. 2008. Turning Tides [Tidal Power Technology]. *Engineering & Technology* (17509637) 3 (16): 46–49.

Roberts, S., and F. Weightman. 1994. Cleaning Up the World with Renewable Energy: From Possibilities to Practicalities. *Renewable Energy* 5 (5–8): 1314–1321.

Rodrik, D. 2008. Second Best Institutions. *American Economic Review* 98 (2): 100–104.

SDC (Sustainable Development Commission). 2007. *Turning the Tide: Tidal Power in the UK*. London: SDC.

SKM (Sinclair Knight Merz). 2008. *Growth Scenarios for UK Renewables Generation and Implications for Future Developments and Operation of Electricity Networks*. London: BERR.

Slade, R., C. Panoutsou, and A. Bauen. 2009. Reconciling Bio-energy Policy and Delivery in the UK: Will UK Policy Initiatives Lead to Increased Deployment? *Biomass and Bioenergy* 33 (4): 679–688.

Snyder, B., and M. J. Kaiser. 2009. A Comparison of Offshore Wind Power Development in Europe and the U.S.: Patterns and Drivers of Development. *Applied Energy* 86 (10): 1845–1856.

Soderholm, P., and G. Klaassen. 2007. Wind Power in Europe: A Simultaneous Innovation-Diffusion Model. *Environmental and Resource Economics* 36 (2): 163–190.

Stainforth, D., A. Cole, P. Dolley, H. Edwards, J. Wilczek, and M. Wood. 1996. An Overview of the UK Department of Trade and Industry's (DTI's) Programme in Solar Energy. *Solar Energy* 58 (1–3): 111–119.

Stanford, A. 1998. Liberalisation of the UK Energy Market: An Opportunity for Green Energy. *Renewable Energy* 15 (1–4): 215–217.

Stenzel, T., and A. Frenzel. 2008. Regulating Technological Change: The Strategic Reactions of Utility Companies towards Subsidy Policies in the German, Spanish and UK Electricity Markets. *Energy Policy* 36 (7): 2645–2657.

Strachan, P. A., and D. Lal. 2004. Wind Energy Policy, Planning and Management Practice in the UK: Hot Air or a Gathering Storm? *Regional Studies* 38 (5): 549–569.

Strbac, G., A. Shakoor, M. Black, D. Pudjianto, and T. Bopp. 2007. Impact of Wind Generation on the Operation and Development of the UK Electricity Systems. *Electric Power Systems Research* 77: 1214–1227.

Swedish Energy Agency. No date. Swedish Energy Agency home page. www.swedishenergyagency.se (accessed February 22, 2010).

Swider, D. J., L. Beurskens, S. Davidson, J. Twidell, J. Pyrko, W. Pruggler, H. Auer, K. Vertin, and R. Skema. 2008. Conditions and Costs for Renewables Electricity Grid Connection: Examples in Europe. *Renewable Energy* 8: 1832–1842.

Szarka, J. 2006. Wind Power, Policy Learning and Paradigm Change. *Energy Policy* 34 (17): 3041–3048.

Szarka, J., and I. Bluhdorn. 2006. *Wind Power in Britain and Germany: Explaining Contrasting Development Paths*. London: Anglo-German Foundation for the Study of Industry.

Taylor, G. 2008. Bioenergy for Heat and Electricity in the UK: A Research Atlas and Roadmap. *Energy Policy* 36 (12): 4383–4389.

Thomson, M., and D. G. Infield. 2007. Impact of Widespread Photovoltaics Generation on Distribution Systems. *IET Renewable Power Generation* 1 (1): 33–40.

Thornley, P. 2006. Increasing Biomass Based Power Generation in the UK. *Energy Policy* 34 (15): 2087–2099.

Tickell, Oliver. 2008. Robbing Us of Renewables. *Guardian*, September 6.

Toke, D. 2003. Wind Power in the UK: How Planning Conditions and Financial Arrangements Affect Outcomes. *International Journal of Sustainable Energy* 23 (4): 207–216.

———. 2005a. Are Green Electricity Certificates the Way Forward for Renewable Energy? An Evaluation of the United Kingdom's Renewables Obligation in the Context of International Comparisons. *Environment and Planning C: Government and Policy* 23 (3): 361–374.

———. 2005b. Explaining Wind Planning Outcomes. Some findings from a study in England and Wales. *Energy Policy* 33 (12): 1527–1539.

———. 2007. Renewable Financial Support Systems and Cost-Effectiveness. *Journal of Cleaner Production* 15 (3): 280–287.

Toke, D., and V. Lauber. 2007. Anglo-Saxon and German Approaches to Neoliberalism and Environmental Policy: The Case of Financing Renewable Energy. *Geoforum* 38 (4): 677–687.

Toke, D., and P. A. Strachan. 2006. Ecological Modernization and Wind Power in the UK. *European*

Environment: The Journal of European Environmental Policy (*Wiley*) 16 (3): 155–166.

Upham, P., S. Shackley, and H. Waterman. 2007. Public and Stakeholder Perceptions of 2030 Bioenergy Scenarios for the Yorkshire and Humber Region. *Energy Policy* 35 (9): 4403–4412.

Upreti, B. R., and D. van der Horst. 2004. National Renewable Energy Policy and Local Opposition in the UK: The Failed Development of a Biomass Electricity Plant. *Biomass and Bioenergy* 26 (1): 61–69.

van Dam, J., M. Junginger, A. Faaij, I. Jurgens, G. Best, and U. Fritsche. 2008. Overview of Recent Developments in Sustainable Biomass Certification. *Biomass and Bioenergy* 32 (8): 749–780.

van der Horst, D. 2005. UK Biomass Energy since 1990: The Mismatch between Project Types and Policy Objectives. *Energy Policy* 33 (5): 705–716.

Warren, C. R., C. Lumsden, S. O'Dowd, and R.V. Birnie. 2005. 'Green on Green': Public Perceptions of Wind Power in Scotland and Ireland. *Journal of Environmental Planning and Management* 48 (6): 853–875.

Wind Power (The Wind Power Wind Turbines and Windfarms Database). 2009. Wind Power Production for Main Countries. www.thewindpower.net/23-countries-capacities.php (accessed February 22, 2010).

Wind Prospect. 2008. Wind Prospect Group home page. www.windprospect.com (accessed February 22, 2010).

Wong, S.-F. 2005. Obliging Institutions and Industry Evolution: A Comparative Study of the German and UK Wind Energy Industries. *Industry and Innovation* 12 (1): 117–145.

Wordsworth, A., and M. Grubb. 2003. Quantifying the UK's Incentives for Low Carbon Investment. *Climate Policy* (*Elsevier*) 3 (1): 77.

14

Experience with Renewable Energy Policy in Germany

Hannes Weigt and Florian Leuthold

Germany now has more than 30 years of experience in supporting renewable energy sources (RES), of which almost 20 years include support for market entry. Under the Electricity Feed-In Act (Stromeinspeisegesetz, StrEG) of 1991, and continuing with the feed-in system of the Renewable Energy Source Act (Erneuerbare Energien Gesetz, EEG), the share of electricity generated by renewables increased from about 3% in 1990 to almost 15% in 2008.

This chapter summarizes the support for RES in Germany and discusses the problems and future developments regarding market design and operations. It begins with an overview, including a road map of applied mechanisms and quantitative market results. Next, it addresses the economic evaluation of the RES policy, focusing on the efficiency of the German feed-in tariff (FIT) approach and highlighting the impact of risk on investments, employment aspects of RES support, adjustment mechanisms, and interaction of RES policy with environmental mechanisms. The chapter then examines the implications for market design and future development given the high share of RES. The particular focus is on wind, as this RES technology has the highest utilization and consequently the greatest impact on the German electricity market. Topics discussed include network extension, operational issues, reserve capacities, and related long-term aspects regarding investment in conventional power plants.

Renewable Energy Policy in Germany

The German energy system largely depends on imported fossil fuels. The transport sector relies on oil imports from the North Sea, Russia, and the global market; the heating sector on oil and natural gas, the latter imported from Russia and the North Sea; and the electricity sector on nuclear, coal, domestic lignite, and a growing share of natural gas. The overall share of fossil fuels and nuclear energy in primary energy consumption in 2007 amounted to 93% (Figure 14.1). The sum total of energy imports in primary energy consumption is 60% (Bechberger and Reiche 2004).

Given Germany's import dependence, security of supply has always been an issue in developing energy policy, particularly since the 1970s oil crisis. The issue first tended to center around coal and nuclear energy. However, with the increased need to address global climate change, the environmental aspect has gained importance. It is expected that RES will play a major role in the decades ahead: DLR (2008) forecasts a gap between electricity demand and generation of 60 to 70 GW until 2030, based on the current generation portfolio. Meanwhile, the European Union has set targets of a 20% share of RES, 20% reduction of emissions, and 20% increase in energy efficiency, and the transformation of Germany's regulated electricity and natural gas markets to a competitive market framework is still in progress.

Following is a general outline of the German RES policies, highlighting the different applied mechanisms and achieved objectives in quantitative terms. It begins with the initial steps in the 1970s and 1980s, details the first major investments in wind energy in the 1990s, then discusses the breakthrough of RES support in 2000, followed by projections of expected future developments.[1]

1970s and 1980s: R&D and First Steps

The global oil crisis during the 1970s prompted the move to restructure Germany's energy sector, at first with a focus on hard coal and nuclear generation, but including RES development on the fringe. Research and development (R&D) funding for RES started in the mid-1970s. Government spending on R&D reached its peak during the first half of the 1980s, with the major share for coal and nuclear (Figure 14.2). Most of the RES

R&D was spent on off-grid systems intended for utilization in developing countries. Government-funded programs focused on prototypes, test series, and demonstrations, which mostly concentrated on the development of small- and medium-scale applications.[2] About 40 wind projects were financed during 1977 and 1989, and similar support was given to solar cell research (Jacobsson and Lauber 2006).

In addition to R&D support, a first step to foster market entry was taken when, in 1979, an RES tariff was introduced that obligated utilities to buy energy from RES based on avoided costs. The results were limited, however (Lauber and Mez 2004).

During this period, public support for nuclear energy decreased significantly, especially after the Chernobyl accident in 1986. At the same time, domestic coal became increasingly uncompetitive and required cross-subsidies via a special tax on electricity prices starting in 1975. In 1980, a commission of the German Parliament recommended efficiency measurements and RES as important cornerstones of a sustainable energy policy. The following year, the recommendation was reconfirmed by a five-year study commissioned by the Federal Ministry of Research and Technology.

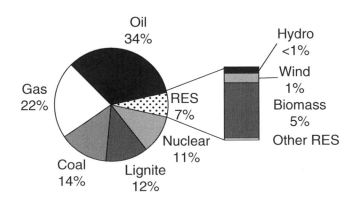

Source: BMU 2008a
Note: Total 13,993 petajoules (PJ)

Figure 14.1. Primary energy consumption in Germany, 2007

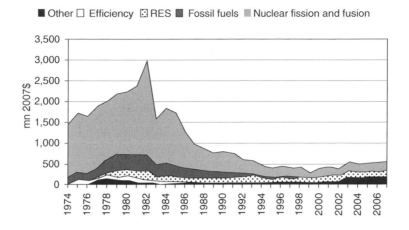

■ Other □ Efficiency ⊡ RES ■ Fossil fuels ▨ Nuclear fission and fusion

Source: IEA 2009

Figure 14.2. Energy R&D funding in Germany, 1974–2007

1990s: StrEG and Increasing Wind

As public concern about the environment grew in the late 1980s, the German government introduced a number of programs to increase support for RES. The Ministry of Research initiated two market programs. Wind energy was supported by the 100-megawatt (MW) Mass Testing Program, which was later increased to 250 MW.[3] The program included a guaranteed payment of 4 euro cents (U.S. 5.4 cents) per kilowatt-hour (kWh). Solar energy was supported via the 1,000 Roofs Program between 1991 and 1995, providing investment support that resulted in the installation of more than 2,000 photovoltaic systems and a peak capacity of 4 MW.

The most important support system was the Electricity Feed-In Act (Stromeinspeisegesetz, StrEG) in 1991; its feed-in tariff (FIT) system required utilities to purchase and pay for RES on a fixed-tariff basis coupled to the end-user tariff.[4] The StrEG, combined with the 100/250 MW Program and soft loans provided by the state-owned Deutsche Ausgleichsbank, led to a doubling of wind's installed capacities, or 4,443 MW in 1999 (Figure 14.3).

The FIT did not include a burden-sharing provision, and utilities with large shares of wind energy faced higher costs. Therefore, a so-called hardship clause was included in 1998 to address these concerns.[5] The uncertainties regarding the

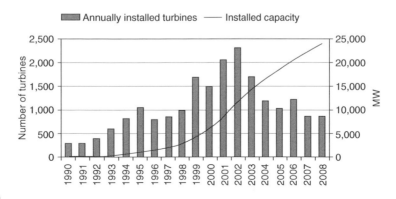

▨ Annually installed turbines   —— Installed capacity

Source: BWE 2009

Figure 14.3. Wind turbine installations, 1990–2008

FIT, as well as the end-user price decrease due to the liberalization process and the resulting revenue losses for wind generators, caused a decline in turbine installation after 1995 (see Figure 14.3). Besides wind energy, other RES did not obtain significant market share during the 1990s, as the financial support was insufficient even with the enactment of StrEG. The 1,000 Roofs Program helped increase solar penetration, yet there was no direct follow-up program.[6]

2000 and After: EEG and Breakthrough

In 1998, a change in the government[7] led to a comprehensive market program, including a reformulation of the StrEG, an ecological tax reform, further support programs for RES implementation, and the decision to phase out nuclear plants.

The most important measure for RES support was the Renewable Energy Source Act (Erneuerbare Energien Gesetz, EEG), adopted in 2000. The EEG continued the StrEG structure with respect to dispatch priority and guaranteed payments for RES generators. Whereas the StrEG tariffs varied with the end-user prices, the EEG tariff rates were guaranteed for 20 years once an investment was completed. EEG tariffs for newly installed capacity decline each year by a predetermined percentage to account for technical progress and cost savings; this should eventually align RES generation costs with competitive levels and make the support mechanism obsolete. A Germany-wide compensation mechanism was introduced to distribute the burden of RES support equally among all consumers, and the EEG included provisions regarding RES grid access (Bechberger and Reiche 2004).

The EEG had a more differentiated tariff structure than the StrEG. In addition, utilities can benefit from the EEG tariffs. For wind energy, a site-dependent tariff allows turbines at less efficient locations to obtain a higher tariff. Figure 14.3 shows the result, an increase in onshore installations. Solar rates have increased to about 50 euro cents (68 cents) per kWh, about 10 times the wholesale price of electricity in Germany. Biomass generation, landfill and similar gas-fired

units, and small-scale hydropower can obtain tariffs ranging from 7.7 to 10.1 euro cents (10.5 to 13.8 cents) per kWh depending on size and further premium options (e.g., fuel cells, fuel restrictions).

The second major policy measure to promote RES and energy efficiency was the ecological tax reform that came into force in 1999. Additional taxes were introduced on motor fuels, fuel oil, natural gas, and electricity, which have gradually increased in subsequent years.[8] Part of the tax income is used for financing RES market support.

Other programs provide investment subsidies and low-interest loans. A follow-up to the 1,000 Roofs Program, the 100,000 Roofs Program, provides soft loans with low- and fixed-interest rates and a 20-year payback period to individual homeowners and small-scale installation projects. In combination with the EEG, the follow-up program's target of 350 MW was reached within 3 years, and the government then had to increase the ceiling for solar cells receiving EEG tariffs to 1,000 MW.

Also in 1999, a general market support system was introduced with the Market Incentive Program (MAP), including direct investment subsidies and soft loans. Two other programs, the Environment and Energy Conservation Program and the Environment Program, also provide soft loans, which were particularly important for the wind energy projects because they were not covered by the MAP. The generous tariff structure of the EEG in combination with the supporting programs has increased RES generation since 2000 (Figure 14.4).[9] The major part of this increase is attributed to wind, which quintupled its installed capacity between 2000 and 2008 to about 24 GW (see Figure 14.3). Biomass also quintupled, from 600 MW to about 3,200 MW, which led to a significant increase in generation as a result of the plants' high capacity factor. Photovoltaic units represent the largest relative capacity increase, from less than 100 MW to about 5,300 MW in 2008. However, because of the low capacity factor, PV's total share in generation terms remains minor.

A useful feature of the EEG is an amendment system that allows the adaption of the law if mar-

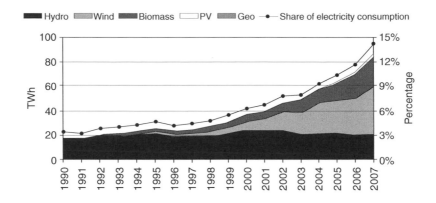

■ Hydro ▨ Wind ■ Biomass ☐ PV ▨ Geo —●— Share of electricity consumption

Source: BMU 2008a

Figure 14.4. Electricity generation from RES, 1990–2007

ket conditions change.[10] After the first progress report in 2002, the first amendment was finally passed in July 2004. It mainly included tariff adjustments (for example, offshore wind rates were reduced), further distinguished solar systems by installation type (roof, facade, or stand-alone), and improved the legal position of RES generators compared with grid companies.

Current and Future Developments

The EEG's second progress report in 2004 was transformed into an amendment that became effective in January 2009. The adjustments take into account recent developments, particularly the lack of offshore wind and geothermal investments and the cost decrease in the production of photovoltaic systems (Büsgen and Dürreschmidt 2009). The shift of the government toward a conservative–liberal coalition with the elections in September 2009 may lead to further adjustments in the EEG. Also, the abolishment of the nuclear phaseout is on the political agenda again.

Although elections almost always affect energy policy, it is expected that Germany nonetheless will continue to provide attractive investment conditions for RES. The rationale underlying the EEG has been extended to other sectors beyond electricity via the new Renewable Energy Heat Law, which should increase the share of RES in the heating sector to 14% until 2020.

The future development of RES in the German energy market is subject to uncertainty and has been analyzed in several studies, which differ in their underlying assumptions. Wischermann and Wagner (2009) compare several future projections with respect to RES development. The scenarios can roughly be clustered in business-as-usual cases, green cases with a larger focus on environmental policy, and nuclear cases in which the phaseout of nuclear plants is withdrawn. Consequently, the expansion of RES differs. The RES share of total power generation in 2030 ranges from 18% to 53% (Figure 14.5). Wind, particularly offshore, will play the largest role in future RES developments, followed by biomass. Geothermal production will most likely play a minor role in the near future, and solar shows only a moderate expansion in all scenarios, mainly driven by the EEG support.

Summary of Germany's Renewable Energy Policy

Germany has an impressive track record in increasing the share of RES in energy use. Given a system with a small share of hydroelectricity generation and hardly any other renewable energy utilization in the 1980s, the total share of RES increased to 6.9% of the primary energy consumption and about 15% of electricity generation in 2007. Germany is the market with the second-

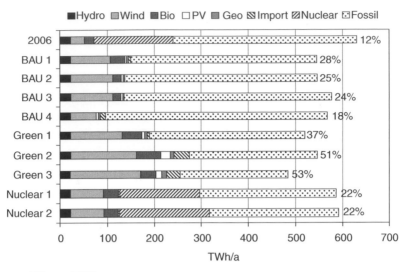

Source: Wischermann and Wagner (2009)
Note: Percentage values show the share of RES in total generation

Figure 14.5. Share of RES from total power generation in 2030 for different future scenarios

highest amount of installed wind capacity in 2008 (after the United States) and the leading market for installed photovoltaic (PV) capacity.

Taking the last decades as a benchmark, it is safe to assume that Germany will indeed obtain a further increase of RES generation and most likely reach the European Union's environmental targets until 2020. The continuous adjustment of the EEG allows the country to adapt to changing conditions and provide the investment security guaranteed by the feed-in tariffs, if the tariff level is set high enough.

Economic Analysis

As is evident by Germany's support for RES, the outcome is impressive in absolute numbers. The multitude of support mechanisms applied in the last decades allows an economic assessment of the policy's effectiveness. This section begins by examining the economic breakdown of the FIT system. Next, it shows the important role of investment security, local support, and loan policy in providing a stable, productive environment for RES generators. It then looks at the role of adjustment mechanisms to adapt to changing market conditions and analyzes the impact of

RES support on employment and general economic effects. Finally, it addresses the interaction of RES support and environmental policies, namely the emissions trading regime.

Feed-In Tariffs: Effective and Efficient?

Germany is a global leader in new wind, solar, and biomass development (Lipp 2007). Although the FIT system, unlike a quota system, does not provide a guaranteed RES share, the stated objectives of the German government could be fulfilled and even allow challenging future targets such as those discussed above to appear reasonable. However, if the government's policy appears to be effective in supporting investment in RES technologies, it is also helpful to analyze whether the policy is efficient from an economic point of view.

A FIT is often regarded as a non-market-based support mechanism, contrary to a quota or certificate system where the desired quantity is fixed and the price is determined by market participants. Consequently, the latter is assumed to be more cost-efficient in achieving specific RES targets. Under a FIT market, participants can still decide about the output, because the quantity is free whereas the price is fixed. Thus a FIT is similar to a classical ecological tax and in the same sense faces the problem of setting the right "tax level." Consequently, a FIT and a quota system can theoretically obtain the same outcome given perfect information.

In the real world, however, the condition of perfect information rarely prevails. Germany's choice of a technology-specific FIT represents a politically motivated market intervention that is likely to reduce economic efficiency, and it has many objectives, perhaps too many. The economic justification for the support of RES technologies can be seen in the external effects. On the one hand, negative external costs from carbon-emitting fuels ought to be internalized. On the other, society should benefit from positive externalities resulting from learning curves that help reduce the investment costs of RES technologies. In theory, learning effects (learning rate, progress ratio, or experience curve) result in a reduction of unit costs or increase in performance as experience with a product or process increases. Wright (1936) was the first to describe this concept when he reported that in airplane manufacturing, labor time requirements decreased by a constant percentage each time cumulative output doubled. Based on literature reviews, Abrell et al. (2009) and Wand and Leuthold (2009) find evidence for and estimate learning curve parameters within their modeling analysis for wind and photovoltaic technologies. The fact that the EEG defines different FITs for different technologies is thereby favored by policymakers who assert that political climate goals can be reached only via supporting different RES technologies. Furthermore, the actual law states that it aims to govern the development of energy supply in a way that reduces external costs and increases the share of RES energy production. The law also claims to find an economically efficient path to reach these goals. Simply stated, the EEG, its implementation, and its amendments are driven by a mixture of political and economic objectives.

As the German FIT provides specific rates for different technologies, a differentiated analysis is necessary. Today Germany has a total of about 24 GW installed onshore wind capacity, the second-largest share in power plants after hard coal, which has about 29 GW. RWI (2009) estimates the total cost borne by all consumers for the currently installed wind capacity based on the FIT at between €11 billion and €20 billion ($15 billion and $27 billion).[11] Given this cost estimate, the question is whether the policy objective to increase the share of RES could have been achieved at a lower cost. Butler and Neuhoff (2008) compare German and UK wind energy development to evaluate the performance of the UK quota and German FIT system. They suggest that the average lifetime costs of supporting wind energy have been higher under the quota system. Because of the on-average higher wind speeds in the United Kingdom, the expected return on investment for wind will be higher given similar investment costs. Butler and Neuhoff (2008) adjust for the difference in wind resources and calculate the price paid to wind generators (excluding network or balancing costs) to show that the adjusted price for wind energy in Germany would have been lower than in the United Kingdom since the mid-1990s. Furthermore, the price for the UK estimates accounts only for contracted sites, not for those actually commissioned. Particularly in the late 1990s, the average contract prices were considered not to be profitable by a majority of wind developers. Thus the price level considered by Butler and Neuhoff (2008) may not reflect the full cost coverage. They also show that the German FIT increased competition for turbine production and construction, the market segment responsible for most of the systems' cost. This increased competition could have had a significant impact on the price of wind energy.

Ragwitz et al. (2007) analyze the effectiveness of different RES support mechanisms in Europe. They measure the effectiveness of a support scheme as the increase in normalized electricity generation compared with a reference quantity. Thus the measurement does not account for the costs of the scheme. They observe the highest effectiveness in countries with a FIT system, such as Denmark, Spain, and Germany. Finon (2007) provides an efficiency estimation of wind energy support based on the data of Ragwitz et al. (2007). Using the measure of output per capita, they show that countries that apply a FIT perform better than countries that rely on a tradable green certificate (TGC) system (Figure 14.6). They also estimate the expected revenues of investors in onshore wind projects in the different countries. Under a FIT, the profits are lower than under a TGC system. The exception is Sweden, which introduced its quota in 2003 following a system of tax credits and investment subsidies.

The European Commission (2005) compares the prices for wind generation among several countries, concluding that the profit ratios of wind generators in the United Kingdom are about five times higher than in Germany. The higher price level is due to the higher risk involved in quota systems (see Toke 2005), the higher administrative costs (European Commission 2005), and the fact that increasing market prices are not reflected in a FIT system. The EC also determined that the FIT system provides better incentives for innovation and dynamic efficiency. Thus for wind energy, the German approach has been effective in terms of quantity and is cost-efficient compared with the existing quota systems.

To our knowledge, there have been no extensive empirical analyses for biomass, landfill gas, and geothermal production. Similar to the support for wind energy, however, the European Commission estimates a cost advantage compared with the United Kingdom for biogas and small-scale hydropower plants (European Commission 2005). A further, not yet quantified, aspect of

biomass is its impact on the German heat market. Because of its diversity, biomass provides several options for heat production, and RES are expected to provide a significant share of the German heat demand in the future, with biomass providing the largest part (BMU 2006). Bürger et al. (2008) analyze several possible support instruments for promoting RES usage in the heat sector, providing first quantitative projections. However, an economic assessment of the 2009 Renewable Energy Heat Law is not yet possible.

Finally, Germany's support for solar energy remains to be evaluated. PV generation has the highest FIT, accounting for roughly 5 to 10 times the wholesale price of electricity. Although the cost of solar power decreased by 60% between 1990 and 2000, reductions have been less significant since, and German customers pay more for photovoltaic modules (retail) than in Japan or the United States (Wüstenhagen and Bilharz 2006). RWI (2009) estimates the costs for the 5.3 GW of installed PV capacity in Germany at €35 billion ($48 billion), given the 20-year feed-in guarantee. Assuming a further increase of capacity until 2010 similar to recent investments levels, the costs will rise to €53 billion ($72 billion). RWI also provide an assessment of the emissions abatement costs using photovoltaic generation based on an average emissions factor of the German power plant mix of 0.58 kilograms of CO_2 per kilowatt-hour (kg_{CO2}/kWh). They obtain abatement costs of

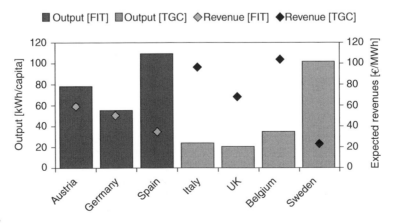

Source: Finon 2007

Figure 14.6. Annual average wind output, 2000–2004, and expected revenues for onshore wind

more than €700 ($954) per metric ton of CO_2 (t_{CO_2}), which is still below the IEA (2007a) estimate of €1,000 ($1,362) per t_{CO_2}. The numbers highlight PV generation's significant cost disadvantage as a result of high investment costs and low utilization factors. A comparison of subsidy costs under different systems and solar resources is not yet available. Witzmann and Kerber (2007) analyze the impact of increased solar generation in Germany's distribution network and conclude that despite the decentralized RES generation, and thus a more equalized generation distribution, grid investment will be necessary.

The additional burden of RES subsidies is collected from electricity end users via an additional tariff payment. Despite the large total cost, however, the end-user price increase is moderate. In 2006, the surcharge was about 0.75 euro cent (1.02 cents) per kWh. With the expected growth of RES in coming years, this charge will steadily increase by about 1.5 euro cents (2 cents) per kWh and continuously decrease after 2020 (Büsgen and Dürrschmidt 2009).[12] Compared with other taxes that consumers pay on electricity prices, the EEG surcharge does not represent an excessive fee: the concession fee amounts to 1.32 to 2.39 euro cents (1.8 to 3.26 cents) per kWh,[13] depending on the community size, and the energy tax amounts to 2.05 euro cents (2.79 cents) per kWh. However, the overall share of government charges in the German household electricity price sums to about 40%.[14]

Finally, the expenses for RES can be compared with governmental spending for fossil energy (see Jacobsson and Lauber 2006). Adding to the financial flow caused by the FIT, German RES received about €1.6 billion ($2.2 billion) in R&D funds between 1975 and 2002, plus additional millions for support measurements such as the 100,000 Roofs Program. The total R&D spending for coal is €2.9 billion ($3.95 billion) in the same period; subsidies for the uncompetitive German hard coal are between €80 billion and €100 billion ($109 billion and $136 billion) since 1975. Nuclear fission received about €14 billion ($19 billion) in R&D, and the fusion program has expenses of about €3 billion ($4 billion). In sum-

mary, governmental support for RES is comparable with support for conventional fuels.

Given this fiscal record and the political goal to increase the RES share, German support has been effective and cost-efficient for wind and most likely for biomass. For solar energy, the picture is less optimistic. Although in quantitative terms the increase of solar capacity is impressive, the cost burden on society is high. This evaluation does not draw any conclusion whether the postulated objective of increasing the RES share to specific targets is in itself economically reasonable.[15]

The economic justification for RES often emphasizes future expectations, however, such as for structural cost changes through learning effects. A study commissioned by the Ministry for the Environment (BMU 2008b) evaluates the impact of German RES support on the economy, estimates the occurring cost burden, and provides future development scenarios.[16] The estimate of the differential costs[17] resulting from the German RES support in the coming years finds that as a result of the increased share of RES, costs will increase until 2015 and steadily decrease after, because of learning-curve effects and the fossil fuel price increase. From about 2025 on, RES will lead to a price-reducing effect (Figure 14.7). The resulting differential costs can be compared with the avoided external costs and further positive impacts of RES generation. These include environmental damages due to global warming and pollution effects on health, crops, and materials.[18] The BMU assumes that the avoided external costs are already higher than the occurring differential costs.

Although the neutrality of the BMU concerning RES can be doubted, the general trend of its study is similar to other studies conducted. Wischermann and Wagner (2009), who provide an overview and comparison, find that the projected differential costs all show a peak around 2015, ranging from €2.5 billion to €6.2 billion ($3.4 billion to $8.4 billion), and negative differential costs after 2040 at the latest. The studies do not answer whether the expected cost advantage of RES in the future justifies the current support expenses or whether the efficiency gains are partly destroyed by the effects on the conventional generation fleet.

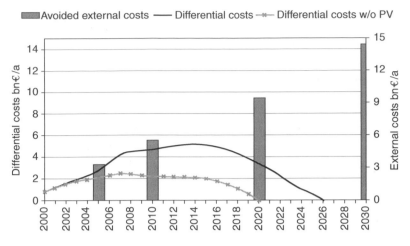

Source: BMU 2008b

Figure 14.7. Estimated differential costs and avoided external costs as a result of German RES production

Risk, Supporting Mechanisms, and Local Support

The German support policy aims at a maximum of RES expansion. Hence the schemes were designed such that potential investors are incentivized to invest as much and as early as possible. One important way to entice investors is a combination of direct financial support (the FIT schemes) and an indirect benefit, the reduction of uncertainty and exposure to market risks. The weakness of this approach is that particularly the latter benefit for investors causes costs within the system that cannot be quantified easily. The costs are basically shifted from the RES investors and borne by the customers. A study commissioned by the Ministry for the Environment (BMU 2008b) shows that most of the entrepreneurs in the RES segment are satisfied with the German FIT and view it as the major contributor to successful development.

Contrary to a quota system, the German FIT schemes provide investors with a hedge against three different types of risks: price, volume, and balancing risk (Mitchell et al. 2006). First, the guaranteed feed-in tariffs provide RES investors with price security regarding the sales price. They also provide RES generators with a perfect and cost-free hedge against price volatility, which is relatively high in liberalized electricity markets.

The volume risk is eliminated by the priority of the RES feed-in. Because the system operator is obliged to accept the supplied renewable generation, sales will largely equal the potential production. Finally, balancing risk is eliminated by the FIT as well as by the exemption from balancing requirements. Other market participants in a liberalized electricity market are typically penalized if the projected and actual load profiles diverge. In Germany, the generator is not penalized for fluctuating generation, but the costs are passed through to end users. This protection from balancing risk on the generation level does not provide incentives to improve the reliability of RES generation and thus may induce higher social costs in the long run.

As a consequence, the low-risk situation increases the ability of investors to finance their projects via the financial markets, reduces the costs of capital, and provides long-term stability, incentives, and resources for innovations (Mitchell et al. 2006). Ragwitz et al. (2007) compare the effectiveness of different support mechanisms with the expected profit for RES investors. They show that for Spain and Germany, despite low producer profits, the effectiveness in quantity terms is best. This is due to the low market risk faced by investors.

Another important risk- and cost-reduction factor of the German RES scheme is the shallow grid connection charges. RES investors have to pay only for the connection to the nearest grid connection point. The system operator must realize necessary grid reinforcement investments, and the occurring costs are redistributed to end users via the network charges. After taking into account the opposing social effects of shallow grid connection charges, this procedure tends to be a simple redistribution of costs within the system. According to Klessmann et al. (2008), in case of shallow grid connection charges, social cost could be lower than when the RES investor would need to raise capital for the investments because of lower capital costs. However, the issue of regulated network expansion must then be revisited, which raises questions about regulatory inefficiencies and the realization that shallow connection charges do not provide a decent investment signal for plant siting.

Although, the FIT of the StrEG and EEG provided the basis of the German RES support, the guaranteed tariffs alone would not have led to the observed capacities in the market without additional measures. The different supporting programs mainly provided investors with access to low-cost loans. For solar energy, the 1,000 and 100,000 Roofs Programs were crucial in providing private investors with the required capital. The programs aimed at individuals, associations, foundations, and small-scale enterprises and guaranteed a long-term loan with very low- and fixed-interest rates (Bechberger and Reiche 2004). The high remuneration of the EEG alone proved insufficient as the investment process significantly slowed in 2003 with the phaseout of the 100,000 Roofs Program.

For other RES projects, the MAP was particularly important. Financial support, in the form of direct investment subsidies and soft loans, was available for solar thermal, biomass and biogas, small-scale hydro, and geothermal plants (Bechberger and Reiche 2004). The success of the program led the Ministry of Environment to continue it after the planned expiration in 2003. For wind energy, the Environment and Energy Conservation Program and the Environment Program were crucial elements because MAP did not support wind. The programs particularly targeted

small enterprises, local companies, and public–private partnerships. The importance for wind energy is highlighted by the fact that between 1990 and 2002, 95% of the granted €10 billion ($13.6 billion) went to wind projects (BMU 2003).

Local and public support for RES should not be underestimated. From the beginning, the development of the RES sector was closely connected to associated companies and the local population (Bechberger and Reiche 2004). In the early 1990s, municipal utilities and market introduction programs at the federal level formed the basis of the sector. They bridged the gap between the first government programs in the 1980s and market support. The large number of local feed-in laws also highlights the public's interest in RES (Jacobsson and Lauber 2006), and Germans have widely supported the increase in RES capacity expansion (Zoellner et al. 2008).

About 50% of the installed wind capacity in the country is locally owned. Local initiatives reduce possible "not-in-my-backyard" (NIMBY) resistance to the erection of new facilities, are cheaper than corporate projects with a higher overhead, and consequently lead to a higher installed overall capacity (Toke 2007). Further, German municipalities have to identify possible areas for wind farms in their spatial planning processes; this in turn speeds up the investment process and additionally reduces local resistance because municipalities are free to choose where to build (Reiche 2002).

From the above, it can be argued that components exist in the German support scheme that more or less do not affect welfare but do shift costs from RES producers to other marketers, such as in the case of shallow grid connection charges. Other components, such as the merit-order effect (see the section titled Operational Aspects below) and the indirect benefits from reduced risk exposure, are likely to have welfare effects, particularly in the long term. The economic problem of the indirect benefits for RES investors becomes apparent when examining the extent to which RES can replace conventional capacities. This capacity replacement potential, or capacity credit, is defined as the fraction of RES energy by which conventional capacity can be reduced without a loss in security of supply. The capacity factor of wind energy is estimated to be rather low (compare the discussion in the section titled Strategic Aspects below). Consequently, the reduction in risk exposure incentivizes investments in RES capacities that are basically added to the existing generation fleet but cannot replace existing units.

Adjustment Mechanisms and Political Conditions

RES are assumed to have significant learning-curve effects that will decrease future investment costs. An inflexible feed-in scheme with fixed tariffs would lead to an excessive burden for consumers, because the benefit of reduced generation costs would only increase the producers' rent. Furthermore, a fixed feed-in payment could hamper innovation and lead to inefficiencies during changing market conditions.

To avoid these effects, the German FIT incorporates two mechanisms. First, the guaranteed tariff is reduced each year by a predefined percentage level for newly installed capacity.[19] Thus the generation costs of RES have to decrease to remain profitable. In the long term, the support can be stopped, as it will become more profitable for RES generators to participate in the open electricity market. As an example, wind generation currently receives an average feed-in tariff of about 9 euro cents (12 cents) per kWh (based on 2007 values). The price for a yearly electricity peak-load future in 2008 topped €100 ($136) per megawatt-hour (MWh) as a result of increased fuel prices (VIK 2009). Consequently, a wind farm owner could possibly earn a higher profit in the wholesale market than under the FIT, but at a higher risk because of wind's intermittent generation. High electricity prices due to either increased fuel costs or tighter emissions restrictions will most likely render RES generation competitive in the future.

The second mechanism is the periodic revision process of the EEG, which evaluates progress and allows the government to adapt to changes in the market environment. This amendment process theoretically ensures that political expectations

and actual market forces correlate; for example, the reduction of the feed-in tariff for solar generation in the last amendment accounts for the cost reduction in recent years, and similarly, the increase for offshore wind generation accounts for the lack of project progress. However, the experience with the two amendments so far also shows that the process is lengthy, influenced heavily by lobbyists, and produces a high degree of uncertainty (Agnolucci 2006). This last point is a problem for investors and could possibly result in stop-and-go behavior.

Institutional arrangements assume an important role in the stable development of RES support, particularly regarding who holds responsibility for RES. With the shift in 2002 from the Ministry of Economics, which traditionally is more aligned with industry, to the Ministry of Environment, the German RES policy has stronger political support, which was lacking when the FIT was introduced (Lipp 2007). In 1999–2000, the Ministry of Economics delayed the FIT draft bill several times until the parliamentary parties presented their own bill to speed up the process (Bechberger and Reiche 2004). Other important administrative support for RES can be seen in the decision to phase out nuclear energy in Germany, which will lead to a higher demand for RES investment in the middle and long run. However, this decision has reappeared on the political agenda after the election in September 2009.

Employment Effects and Economic Impacts

Support for RES has led to expanded investments in production and construction of RES generation technologies that would not have been profitable without the support. Such investments have led to positive gross employment effects in a country where unemployment hovers at up to 10%. As a result, politicians have increasingly stressed the employment effects of RES support. Particularly the Green Party claims a positive impact of supporting RES and a sustainable economy on both the employment situation in

Germany and the competitiveness of German industry in the global economy (Bündnis 90/Die Grünen 2009).

There are also negative effects, however, such as increased energy costs for consumers because of the refinancing of RES support and adjustments in production and transport (Hillebrand et al. 2006). Second, investments in RES generation will reduce investments in fossil generation, and a portion of the newly formed jobs will be offset by additional unemployment in the conventional energy sector. Also, the lower public budget as a result of RES support will have a negative impact on government investment and spending (Lehr et al. 2008).

The gross effect of RES support is easy to assess. A study commissioned by the Ministry of Environment (BMU 2007) quantifies the overall employment numbers in the RES sector to about 250,000 people employed in 2007 (Table 14.1). The ministry expects the subsequent trending increase to result in about 400,000 employees in 2020, although not all sectors will have a similar development; for example, the photovoltaic and biofuels sectors are assumed to have reached their peaks (BMU 2007).

The net effect of RES support is less clear and difficult to estimate, however. BMU (2007) assumes that the net employment effect will be in the range of 50,000 to 120,000 additional jobs, depending on assumptions about the export capability of the German RES industry. Pfaffenberger et al. (2003) estimate a cumulative net loss of about 20,000 jobs within a 20-year period. Hillebrand et al. (2006) analyze the net effects of

German RES support with econometric methods. They observe that the positive overall effect of the first years as a result of investments will even out and eventually become negative. Lehr et al. (2008) develop an input–output vector for RES and several policy scenarios. They show that the net effect is positive throughout the scenarios and that exports in particular are an important driver of future development, whereas domestic investments lead to a rather small positive labor effect.

Thus the net employment effect of RES policies appears slightly positive at best, contrary to political perception. Furthermore, the argument that labor-intensive energy generation is favorable is part of the discussion (Michaels and Murphy 2009). Note that local employment impacts regardless of the overall economic effect are always important for elected officials. A large proportion of RES investments in generation and facility production occurs in areas with high unemployment rates, particularly eastern Germany (Handelsblatt 2007), and thus contributes to the industrial development of those regions. Finally, the German RES policy provides other countries that supply the German market with a positive net employment effect.

Interaction of Environment Policies

RES support in Germany embraces several instruments to support the market entry of RES suppliers. Beside pure support systems, accompanying environmental aspects have gained increased attention, finally culminating in the establishment of the European Union Emission Trading System (EU ETS). Environmental policies that target energy markets have overlapping objectives and interact to a specific degree with the RES support mechanism.[20] This interaction produces both synergies and conflicts (Gonzáles 2007).

The main interaction of the EU ETS and RES support instruments is the impact on the CO_2 emissions level. The ETS introduces a price on emissions that in turn increases the electricity price. In contrast, RES support desires to increase the share of renewable generation and thus indirectly leads to a reduced emissions level. A larger share of RES reduces the demand for emissions

Table 14.1. Gross employment figures of the RES sector in Germany

	1998	2002	2004	2006	2007
Wind	16,600	53,200	63,900	82,100	84,300
Solar	5,400	12,700	25,100	40,200	50,700
Hydro	8,600	8,400	9,500	9,400	9,400
Geothermal	1,600	2,400	1,800	4,200	4,500
Biomass	25,400	29,000	34,200	45,200	44,200
Total[a]	66,600	118,700	160,490	235,640	249,300

Sources: BMU 2007, 2008c
[a]Including biofuels, services, and publicly financed positions

allowances and thus has a decreasing effect on allowance prices and in turn on electricity prices. However, the allowance price reduction is obtained by using abatement technologies (RES) that typically would not be cost-efficient in a pure ETS scheme.

Rathmann (2007) analyzes the impact of wind energy on emissions allowance prices and its feedback on market prices, concluding that in the presence of an ETS, additional wind generation can reduce allowance prices (and thus electricity prices). For the first trading period between 2005 and 2007, he estimates a reduction of electricity prices by €6.4 ($8.7) per MWh for Germany solely by reduced emissions prices, not taking into account price impacts as a result of a changed dispatch. The savings are higher than the increase in electricity prices of €3.8 ($5.2) per MWh from the feed-in tariffs.

Traber and Kemfert (2009) analyze the combined impact of the German FIT and the ETS on the electricity market using a bottom-up model approach with strategic company behavior. They show that the FIT has a total additional burden of about €5 ($6.8) per MWh, of which the producer price decrease is the largest share. The decrease can be divided into a substitution effect and a permit price effect of roughly the same size, illustrating the feedback effect of the ETS. They also demonstrate that the emissions reduction in Germany as a result of the EEG has no impact on the overall European emissions level; the additional reduction in Germany reduces the burden only for other member states.

Abrell and Weigt (2008) analyze how the EU ETS and renewable support mechanisms influence one another by applying a static open economy computable general equilibrium (CGE) model of Germany incorporating different conventional and renewable generation technologies. They test the impact of a pure ETS scheme, a green certificate scheme, and the combination of both schemes on generation investment and market prices. They observe that the restrictions imposed by the ETS and a quota are achieved by reducing the output of electricity and shifting generation to green or emissions-free technologies, or both. If both environmental restrictions

are regarded simultaneously, a lower CO_2 price can be observed. The lower carbon price in turn supports "dirty" generation from fossil fuels and reduces the investments in CCS technologies, which aligns with the findings of other studies (e.g., Böhringer and Rosendahl 2009; Pethig and Wittlich 2009). The three environmental policy cases analyzed in Abrell and Weigt (2008) lead to a welfare decrease of about 0.6‰ compared with an unrestricted benchmark (Table 14.2).

A study commissioned by the Ministry of Environment (BMU 2008b) evaluates the interaction of German RES support with other climate and environmental instruments. Regarding emissions trading, the study highlights the importance of considering RES generation when setting the target cap. In contrast, Germany's ecological tax reform shows little interaction with RES support. Particularly in the electricity sector, the impact of taxes is negligible, because energy from RES is taxed similarly to fossil energies concerning end usage. Also, differentiated taxes on fuels for electricity generation have been annulled by European guidelines. Thus the possible regulating effects in the fuel choice in favor of RES are not achievable. Finally, an introduction of specific non-RES taxes would not induce any further investments in RES, as these are defined by the unaffected FIT. Support for combined heat and power production (CHP) shows no direct interaction, because plants can profit from only one support scheme. Conflicts can arise in the priority feed-in of both RES and CHP electricity in cases of network congestion.

Table 14.2. Impact of emissions trading and RES support on the German economy

	BAU	ETS	Quota	ETS + quota
Electricity price (%)	100	107.58	103.48	107.42
Carbon price (€/t$_{CO2}$)	—	10.04	—	7.29
Green certificate price (€/MWh)	—	—	26.1	12.1
Welfare (‰)	0	−0.598	−0.602	−0.64

Source: Abrell and Weigt 2008
Note: €1 = $1.36 as of this writing

Last but not least, all measures show an indirect impact, because they all represent an additional burden for consumers and lead to price increases, which induce consumption effects.

Summary of the Economic Analysis

The German RES policy based on fuel-type-specific FITs and investment programs provide investors with a strong framework that has led to a large increase in total numbers. The approach was clearly effective but lacks efficiency. For wind energy, Germany's support payments are less expensive than in other countries, whereas they are extremely expensive for solar. The implementation of a technology-specific FIT has been driven not only by economic factors, but also by a mix of economic and political reasons, including learning-curve expectations. The political argument for the implementation of more than one FIT is that learning for more than one technology can be achieved, which hedges uncertain outcomes and addresses the issue of security of supply.

Market Implications of RES Support: The Case of Wind Energy

Because of its development, wind energy represents the renewable source with the largest impact on market operations. This section focuses on Germany's experiences with wind energy. The experience from wind integration can be largely transferred to solar generation and is characterized by its stochastic nature. They differ only in the stochastic production profile. In contrast, biomass, hydro, and geothermal production can be operated just as conventional generation plants; hence their impact on electricity market operations will not be stressed here.

This discussion begins by briefly highlighting the characteristics of the German wind energy sector. This is followed by an analysis of the effects of wind energy on operational aspects in the short term and strategic impacts in the long term. It is argued that the integration of wind generation necessitates transparent market structures for all energy market segments: spot, forward, and balancing. Furthermore, efficient locational price signals are required in order to support efficient congestion management and extension planning for both network and RES generation locating.

Wind Energy in Germany

Wind has been the fastest growing RES source in Germany. This strong growth was made possible by the support scheme of the German government, discussed earlier in this chapter. The major breakthrough for RES technologies, particularly for wind, came with the EEG in 2000. As a result of the EEG feed-in tariffs, installed wind capacity grew from about 2 GW in 1997 to about 24 GW in 2008 (BWE 2009). The tariffs were readjusted in 2004 and 2008. Table 14.3 displays the feed-in tariffs as stipulated in the EEG. The tariffs are guaranteed for a period of 20 years, during which they change from higher initial tariffs to lower-end tariffs according to the yield of the unit. These numbers are known by the investor in advance. The tariffs decrease beginning with the year in which the law became effective, such that turbines that go online earlier receive higher support. Hence the EEG fosters the growth of wind in two ways: the investor does not have uncertainty about the electricity price, because it always receives the guaranteed tariff; and the EEG stipulates a priority feed-in for RES-generated electricity, which means that the Transmission System Operator (TSO) always accepts and dispatches electricity from wind turbines first.

Germany has both onshore and offshore wind potential. For the time being, increased wind generation has been achieved by onshore technology, but for future developments, it is estimated that offshore technology will be of greater importance (DEWI et al. 2005). Germany treats wind energy as intermittent base load generation (Klessmann et al. 2008). Even with larger turbines (compare the discussion of StrEG earlier in this chapter), however, a single turbine cannot replace an entire fossil plant. Therefore, wind generation takes place by building so-called wind farms,

Table 14.3. Feed-in tariffs in Germany to EEG 2008 and EEG 2004 (in €/MWh)

	EEG 2008	EEG 2004
Wind onshore	Annual decrease: 1%	Annual decrease: 2%
Initial tariff	92	78.7
End tariff	50.2	49.7
Wind off-shore	Annual decrease (from 2015): 5%	Annual decrease (from 2008): 2%
Initial tariff[a]	130	87.4
End tariff[a]	35	59.5

[a]Commissioning until 2015: bonus of 20 €/MWh
Note: €1 = $1.36 as of this writing

which are an agglomeration of turbines. The generated energy is collected locally at a bus, which then connects the facility to the distribution or transmission grid. Nevertheless, onshore wind usage leads to a rather decentralized generation structure, because the farms are widespread over northern and central Germany. The exploitation of feasible onshore wind farm locations is already high in Germany. Hence associated operational market issues can be easily observed and addressed.

Operational Aspects

Integrating wind in the existing German market structure is challenging, because wind energy has to be treated differently in the market than the "classical" generation technologies. Major fields of the energy market organization that have to be considered in order to assess the market impact of wind are the applied support scheme, grid code, balancing regulations, and collateral market regulations (Klessmann et al. 2008). These fields of interest are the distinctive criteria when comparing country examples.

The German market design distinguishes a forward market and a balancing market. A real-time market has only recently come into force. The term "spot market" is also used, but it refers to the day–ahead market. Thus most market transactions concerning energy delivery within one day (intraday) have to take place via balancing, which is managed by the TSOs. Wind energy

operators are exempt from the balancing requirement. Consequently, three elements are particularly important for the integrated operations of electricity markets with extensive wind energy production: economic integration in forward markets (ahead of delivery); operational integration in forward markets; and operational integration in balancing markets (compare Klessmann et al. 2008).

The forward market in Germany is divided into bilateral over-the-counter (OTC) and standardized future trades. The future trades are managed by the European Energy Exchange (EEX). The market is dominated by OTC transactions, whereas the EEX made up only about 19% of the market in 2007 (Schöne 2009). The balancing market is required because electricity is highly inelastic in a short-term perspective. Hence the demand for electrical energy must be balanced with the supply (generation) at each point in time, or otherwise the system will collapse. Although concepts such as demand-side management and interruptible load programs exist, for the time being balancing has to be achieved to a large extent by supply-side effects. The balancing service comprises primary reserve, secondary reserve, and tertiary reserve. The system operator provides these balancing services to compensate physically for flows that deviate from the schedules.[21] Klessmann et al. (2008) state that balancing wind normally requires the cheaper tertiary reserve.

This is partly due to the way wind is integrated in the German market. Regular market players such as traders and fossil generators have to announce their schedules a day ahead and send them to the system operators. These marketers are obliged to pay if their actual flow deviates from the schedule that is specified in the imbalance settlement rules. Wind, however, is exempt from this rule. Additionally, wind generators do not have to provide primary reserve. The TSO assumes many obligations of the wind operators that a regular market participant would have to fulfill individually. The TSO integrates the stochastic generation profile of the wind producers in the merit order of the entire plant fleet. For this purpose, the TSO defines monthly standard profiles of wind production based on its wind predictions. These profiles are sold to all players that deliver electrical energy to final customers. For them, the profiles are constant. The cost associated with converting intermittent wind generation into a constant profile are borne by the TSO and passed through to all network users via a system usage charge. Consequently, distribution and transmission system operators pay the feed-in tariffs to the wind generators. These costs are then in turn socialized over all network users. Hence German consumers support the extension of wind capacity by directly bearing the costs resulting from the feed-in tariff and assuming the costs resulting from some of the uncertainties associated with wind operation, particularly forecasting, scheduling, and balancing. The advantage of this approach is that the TSO manages a large number of wind farms and can hedge stochastic wind input geographically. It could also realize certain economies of scale in forecasting and minimizing forecast errors. Thus the TSO manages to integrate the stochastic generation profiles in the fossil dispatch partly by day-ahead settlement and partly by balancing. However, only for wind-caused balancing, the German TSOs have introduced an own tender in addition to the regular reserve tender, which shows one of the system's disadvantages. In addition, in October 2006, the EEX introduced an intraday market. Nevertheless, the traded volumes are still low, and empirical data on the impact of this development are absent. The late establishment and illiquidity of the intraday market means that wind forecast errors are relatively high, because most of the forecast must be conducted 24 hours ahead.

The major problem in Germany, however, is that there are misleading incentives for several reasons. First, the market structure for balancing services, consisting of basically four different tendering systems, causes low liquidity and high price levels (Klessmann et al. 2008). In addition, the costs of converting the stochastic wind input into synthetic constant profiles appear too high. For example, LBD (2007) estimates that the costs range between €3.4 and €5.4 ($4.6 and $7.4) per megawatt-hour of renewable energy (MWh_{RES}), whereas the average cost charged by network operators is about €8.3 ($11.3) per MWh_{RES}.

Another reason is the congestion management mechanism. Currently, Germany has a single electricity price at the wholesale market (EEX), which is determined independently of the location of demand and supply, thus ignoring congestion in the network. Leuthold et al. (2008) model the German electricity market and show that this uniform pricing scheme is less efficient from a welfare perspective than a full nodal pricing approach, which assigns a price to each node of the network taking into account all relevant market and capacity information. Because of the single price in Germany, the schedules that are announced to the TSOs often are not feasible from a technical load flow perspective. In this case, the TSO has the right to change the dispatch of the power plant, deviating from the market equilibrium at the EEX ("redispatch"). This redispatch is cost-based in Germany, which means that the costs that occur can be socialized by the TSO via the network charges. An alternative does exist, however, in the form of market-based redispatch or countertrading. In the latter case, an own merit order is determined for the redispatch by an independent coordination office or exchange, which is a more transparent approach because the order books can be made public after the market clearing, whereas in the current scheme the TSOs individually decide what is to be redispatched (Wawer 2007). In the case of congestion, wind energy has the priority right, meaning that it is dispatched first or curtailed last compared with fossil units. Regarding the political wish to expand wind, locational price signals can have opposing effects. Klessmann et al. (2008) argue that the problem of not having locational price signals provides no incentives for wind to locate efficiently, which leads to efficiency losses as a result of reduced market response and less system-optimized behavior. On the other hand, locational price signals impose market risk on wind operators that they do not bear now, which brings efficiency gains as a result of lower risk premiums and the lower required support payments. This argument ignores the efficiency effect, however: a more efficient congestion management scheme would affect the entire market outcome, including fossil production. From an economic point of view, the introduction of locational price signals should be mandated, because they improve incentive structure in the network. Higher FITs could compensate for the different risk situations for wind operators.

Klessmann et al. (2008) find that in 2005, the loss through curtailment of wind turbines caused by network congestion accounted for 5% of the annual yield. Jarass and Obermair (2005) show that there is an increasing tendency to wind production curtailment. This fact leads to the last point of the operational aspects: grid connection of wind facilities. In Germany, a wind farm investor now pays for the connection to the nearest grid access point. If other grid reinforcements are required to transport the generated electricity to the demand locations, they are carried out by the system operator. This is a so-called "shallow" cost allocation method (e.g., Rious et al. 2008), because the generator does not take into account the effect of its investment on the overall grid congestion situation. Other than building a wind farm, the planning and construction of new high-voltage lines are a long-term issue and will be addressed in the next section.

Strategic Aspects

The strategic or long-term aspects of integrating wind production into the German electricity market mainly affect investment. One issue concerns grid investments. Looking at the continental European region managed by the Union for the Co-ordination of Transmission of Electricity (UCTE), including Germany, Leuthold et al. (2009) analyze the impact of wind capacity extensions on the grid. The wind extension scenarios for Europe are ambitious, with 114.5 GW (IEA 2007b) and 181 GW (Greenpeace International/ EWEA 2005) of installed capacity. Based on a welfare maximization approach and using the nodal pricing methodology, the optimal investment strategy is determined. Leuthold et al. (2009) show that the remarkable extension of wind capacity leads to an increase in total European welfare compared with a current fuel mix scenario. They conclude that developing the network at existing bottlenecks—mainly cross-

border connections—should be encouraged now by regulatory authorities. With a more moderate wind expansion of 114.5 GW, the optimal grid investments are smaller. If the additional wind capacity becomes too great (181 GW), the needed grid extensions will increase compared with the actual situation. Although the grid extensions determined are most likely feasible from economic and political viewpoints, their study rests on two strong assumptions: the wind capacity extension is supposed to occur throughout Europe and not be concentrated within a single or only a few countries, such that additional cross-border flow issues due to wind are minor; and the stochastic nature of wind production is neglected, which may lead to an underestimation of balancing costs. The first constraint is important for Germany and its neighbors, as Germany plans to develop large-scale offshore wind. DEWI et al. (2005) estimate that Germany will have 30 GW installed offshore capacity in 2030. Based on this assumption, Leuthold et al. (2008) and Weigt et al. (2010) model the economic impact of offshore wind expansion on Germany using nodal pricing as an analysis tool for the German market. Leuthold et al. (2008) assume that the entire offshore wind capacity will be erected in the North Sea and connect to the grid at the best possible node on the German coast. They find that the offshore capacity has a price-decreasing and welfare-increasing effect. However, the present grid cannot transmit the 30 GW input to the load centers; absent extensive grid expansion, only 8 to 13 GW appears feasible. Additionally, in times of high wind production, serious congestion might occur to and within the Benelux countries. In contrast, Weigt et al. (2010) assume that the offshore wind can be connected to the well-meshed parts of the grid in central Germany via high-voltage direct current (HVDC) technology. In their scenario, the price-decreasing and welfare-increasing effect of wind can be realized at the German demand centers without additional serious congestion problems.

The two studies assume, however, that the wind energy can be sufficiently backed up by other generation such that there will be no balancing or network stability problems. This assumption is valid as long as the considered time periods are within the lifetime of the existing fossil plant fleet. In this case, increasing balancing requirements might lead to increasing balancing costs, but contingency issues appear to be minor. Hence there are decreasing effects on price and CO_2 emissions. In the short-term, these effects have been quantified by some studies. Sensfuß et al. (2008) find that the price effect ("merit order effect") of wind input can range from €0 per MWh during low load periods up to €36 ($49) per MWh during peak load periods. Weigt (2009) finds that the average electricity price in Germany is about €10 ($13.6) per MWh lower in 2006–2007 because of wind input. When subtracting the average support expenses of €5.4 ($7.4) per MWh in 2006 and €7 ($9.5) per MWh in 2007, he concludes that Germany still realizes a net benefit of wind energy, even when possible additional gains of reduced emissions allowance prices are not accounted for. Based on a literature review, Klessmann et al. (2008) determine that the minimum average price advantages are €3 ($4.1) per MWh in 2005 and €6 ($8.2) per MWh in 2006. Thus a short-term advantage of increasing wind capacities appears to be proven as a result of the extremely low marginal cost (almost €0 per MWh) of wind production.

The long-term aspect is less clear, however. As wind production has marginal costs near zero and is exempted from the balancing requirements but has an intermittent character, the structure of the conventional plant fleet is likely to change. Investors in conventional technology face higher uncertainty regarding the full load hours and probability to be dispatched in the future. The existing base load technologies in Germany, nuclear and lignite, are characterized by high capital and low fuel costs, which require high full load hours to recover their fixed costs. Therefore, these types of technology will be associated with higher investment risk in a long-term perspective with constantly high or even increasing wind energy production. Hence a shift in fossil generation technologies to plants with higher variable costs but lower capital costs could be a consequence. The effect of this development could be lower electricity prices on average, but with very high price spikes during peak load times accounting for the higher marginal cost of the conventional generation fleet.[22] In addition to the described price and emissions effects, another issue is the capacity credit of wind energy. Weigt (2009) estimates that the present installed wind capacity does not allow a significant reduction of installed conventional capacity, because the lower boundary of Germany's wind capacity credit is only about 1%, which means that for the time being, basically the entire installed wind capacity must be backed up by conventional technologies.

Summary of the Market Implications

Regarding the operational aspects of integrating large amounts of intermittent renewable generation such as wind energy into electricity markets, it can be concluded that wind producers enjoy low market risk and reasonable financial support via FITs. This appears to be a major driver for the country's extensive wind capacity expansion. The reduction of uncertainty specifically appears to be a crucial aspect in the German feed-in system. It is sometimes argued that a quota system is preferable, because the market can then determine the optimal technology investment strategy. Some studies show, however, that in the presence of certain framework factors, the optimal policy choice can deviate from the theoretically favorable instrument. One of these factors appears to be the presence of uncertainty (compare Fischer et al. 2003). However, shortcomings in the German system derive from the opacity and inefficiency of associated regulatory issues:

- The balancing market is an administrative entity and is thus illiquid and inefficient; the same is true for the process of integrating wind into the electricity market, which is done by converting intermediate wind input into synthetic constant profiles.[23]
- The long absence and present illiquidity of the intraday market means that the wind forecast errors are relatively high, as most of the forecast has to be conducted 24 hours ahead; shorter gate closure or handling time would help decrease forecast error.[24]

- The German congestion management scheme does not provide locational price signals and therefore does not offer incentives to TSOs or wind farm operators to optimize their locations.

Regarding the strategic aspects of integrating wind energy production into electricity markets, the question arises how to account for the low capacity credit of wind capacities in an economic assessment. This could be accomplished by including the required incremental capital cost of conventional backup in the investment calculation of additional wind capacity expansion. It is questionable, however, whether society will accept additional large-scale expansions of both wind and conventional capacities even if it should appear to be economic. Technological innovation could help overcome this problem. A major driver to increase the capacity credit of wind is decentralized storage facilities. Using these facilities, large wind farms could handle the intermittency on the spot and act as a constant generator. This could be particularly interesting in the context of offshore expansion, where large amounts of wind are transmitted from only a few power bus bars offshore. However, storage facilities are not yet available at reasonable cost. Another long-term aspect is grid investment issues. To address these issues, the aspect of locational price signals is important. Based on these signals, socially favorable grid enforcements could be identified more easily and transparently. The introduction of financial transmission rights or similar financial products can be used to support this process. These rights could also help determine the real network cost of certain grid connection projects. Furthermore, the integration of today's national and regional electricity markets in Europe can help increase the capacity credit of wind energy as a result of greater geographic coverage.

Conclusions

When reviewing the case of Germany, it can be seen that the record of renewable energy programs is remarkable. In 2007, the total share of RES in Germany accounted for 6.9% of the primary energy consumption and about 15% of electricity generation. In 2008, Germany had the second-highest amount of installed wind capacity, after the United States, and was the world leader for installed photovoltaic capacity. One reason for that is that Germany provides a strong framework for investors which means that society bears most of the market risks, as the FITs are guaranteed for 20 years and RES units are exempted from balancing requirements. Another reason appears to consist in the technology-specific German FIT scheme.

However, the evaluation of the system's economic efficiency is ambiguous. Germany's support payments for wind are less expensive than in other countries, but they are very expensive for solar, presumably because of environmental factors. Also, the implementation of a technology-specific FIT is driven by a mix of economic and political reasons. The economic argument in support of RES technologies is that learning effects can be achieved that produce positive external effects. The political argument for the implementation of more than one FIT is that learning for more than one technology can be achieved, hedging uncertain outcomes and addressing security of supply.

Another conclusion from the German example is that nonintermittent production (e.g., biomass, geothermal) can be easily integrated into the existing market structure as they can be treated the same as other conventional units. Intermittent production (e.g., wind, solar), however, must be backed up by conventional units; hence the capacity credit of these RES technologies is currently low. Nonetheless, there are short-term and long-term effects. In the short term, the RES production from sources with low marginal costs had a price-decreasing effect in recent years, whereas in the long term, the conventional plant portfolio is likely to gravitate to more flexible units with lower fixed and higher variable cost components, which would then lead to increasing prices on average.

In addition to that effect, evidence for other market inefficiencies could be found. However, the causes of inefficiencies within the system integration process appear to be manifold, and costs cannot be allocated clearly. The balancing market is important in the case of intermittent production. However, Germany's balancing market is not a real market, but rather an administrative entity, and as such it is illiquid and inefficient. Additionally, the long absence and present illiquidity of the intraday market means that wind forecast errors are relatively high, as the majority of forecasts must be conducted 24 hours ahead; shorter gate

closure or handling time will reduce forecast errors. Lastly, Germany's congestion management scheme does not provide locational price signals; therefore, it does not offer incentives to either TSOs or wind farm operators to optimize their locations. Hence, it is not always possible to distinguish between costs and inefficiencies caused by renewable energy integration and failures in the structure of the different sub-markets for electricity.

Appendix

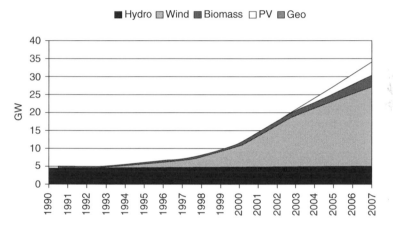

Source: BMU 2008a

Figure 14.8. Installed RES generation capacities, 1990–2007

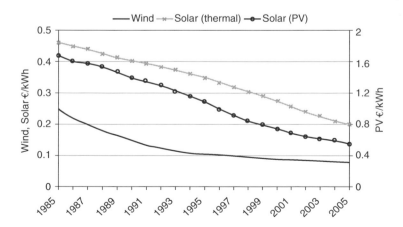

Source: BMU 2008b

Figure 14.9. Cost reduction for RES generation

Notes

1. This case study is based on Bechberger and Reiche (2004), Büsgen and Dürrschmidt (2009), Gan et al. (2007), Jacobsson and Lauber (2006), Lipp (2007), and Toke and Lauber (2007).
2. Other programs, such as the GROWIAN project to develop a wind turbine with several megawatts, were only demonstration projects.
3. With the start of the program in 1989, 20 MW of wind energy were installed.
4. Wind and solar power obtained 90% of the end-user tariff; all other small-scale plants (< 500kW) obtained 80%, and large-scale plants (500 kW to 5 MW) obtained 65%.
5. The clause provided a twofold 5% cap. The first cap was at the utility level and allowed a cost pass-through to the Transmission System Operator (TSO) if the amount of purchase obligations exceeded 5% of the utilities' total deliveries. The second cap was at the TSO level and withdrew the dispatch obligation for the TSO (Agnolucci 2006).
6. Further support for RES was initiated at the municipal level, as the 1989 tariff regulation allowed utilities to sign contracts with RES in excess of their long-term avoided costs. Several German cities adopted this model. Additional support came from state governments that adopted specific support programs highlighting the still high public support for RES (Jacobsson and Lauber, 2006).
7. The conservative–liberal coalition was replaced by a social democratic–green coalition.
8. To reduce the burden for the domestic companies, energy-intensive industries and transportation paid reduced taxes. Because biofuels were exempt from the tax, they obtained an advantage of 14.2 euro cents (19.3 cents) per liter, which led to an increase in biodiesel production (Bechberger and Reiche 2004).
9. For installed capacities, see Figure 14.8 in the Appendix at the end of this chapter.
10. This amendment process became more administration-led with the shift of responsibility for RES from the Ministry of Economic Affairs to the Ministry of the Environment after the share of the Green Party in the government coalition increased in the 2002 elections (Wüstenhagen and Bilharz 2006). This shift of responsibility also strengthened the general position of RES, as the Ministry of Economic Affairs tended to support the incumbent energy companies.
11. Wind turbines receive a site-dependent premium, so the actual FIT varies for each turbine. The value of €11 billion ($15 billion) represents the lower boundary, assuming no extra premiums, and the upper value represents the extreme case that all turbines receive the full premium.
12. These numbers are derived using the EEG amendment of 2004. They will likely increase as a result of the higher remuneration for offshore wind with the amendment of 2009, and further amendments may provide additional burdens or offsets.
13. The concession fee is a levy by the municipality for the right to build a network in the municipality.
14. End-user prices in Germany range from 16 to 20 euro cents (22 to 27 cents) per kWh.
15. See also Finon (2007) and Fouquet and Johansson (2008) for a general assessment of different support mechanisms.
16. An estimate of the cost reduction in RES investments is presented in Figure 14.9 in the Appendix at the end of this chapter.
17. The differential costs estimate the cost burden as a result of the RES fee compared with the supply costs without the feed-in requirement.
18. The estimates are based on cost projections by Krewitt and Schlomann (2006): external costs in €/t [$/t] for CO_2 (70 [95]), SO_2 (3,280 [4,468]), NO_x (3,320 [4,523]), PM_{10} (12,000 [16,348]), and NMVOC (870 [1,185]).
19. A RES plant constructed in 2007 receives the 2007 FIT for 20 years, whereas a plant constructed in 2008 receives the lower 2008 FIT for 20 years, and so on.
20. For effects regarding the interaction with energy-efficiency targets, see Meran and Wittmann (2008) and Sorrel and Sijm (2005).
21. In Germany, each running unit with an installed capacity of 100 MW or more must be capable of providing primary reserve. The primary reserve must be available within 30 seconds and for at least 15 minutes. The primary reserve market is structured as a monthly tender. The market clearing is based on a primary reserve merit order, which in turn is based on a capacity price, and the pricing follows the pay-as-bid rule. The secondary reserve units must be available within 5 minutes and have at least a gradient of 2% per second of their capacity, which means they must reach full load after 50 seconds at maximum. Depending on the type of provider, the secondary reserve must be made available for several hours, e.g., 4 hours for

pumped storage plants. The secondary reserve market is also structured as a monthly tender. The market clearing is based on a secondary reserve merit order, which in turn is based on a capacity price, and the pricing follows the pay-as-bid rule. The tertiary reserve (also called minute reserve) must be available within 15 minutes and must also be able to be switched off within 15 minutes. The contracted capacity must be available for the entire time slice. The time slices are 4 hours, resulting in 6 predefined periods over the day. The tertiary reserve market is structured as a daily tender. The market clearing is based on a tertiary reserve merit order, which in turn is based on a capacity price, and the pricing follows the pay-as-bid rule. In addition to the capacity payment, an energy payment is provided in the event of usage. Klessmann et al. (2008) state that the economic value of the different balancing services decreases in the same order, from primary to tertiary.

22. The same effect is likely to occur in times of low wind energy production.

23. See Vandezande et al. (2010) for a recent discussion on balancing market designs.

24. See Weber (2010) for a recent discussion on intraday market issues.

References

Abrell, J., J. Herold, and F. Leuthold. 2009. Modeling the Diffusion of Carbon Capture and Storage under Carbon Emission Control and Learning Effects. Innovations for a Low-Carbon Energy System Working Papers, WP-RD-04. Dresden, Germany: Dresden University of Technology.

Abrell, J., and H. Weigt. 2008. The Interaction of Emissions Trading and Renewable Energy Promotion. Economics of Global Warming Working Papers, WP-EGW-05. Dresden, Germany: Dresden University of Technology.

Agnolucci, P. 2006. Use of Economic Instruments in the German Renewable Electricity Policy. *Energy Policy* 34 (18): 3538–48.

Bechberger, M., and D. Reiche. 2004. Renewable Energy Policy in Germany: Pioneering and Exemplary Regulations. *Energy for Sustainable Development* 8 (1): 47–57.

BMU (Federal Ministry for the Environment, Nature Conservation and Nuclear Safety of Germany). 2003. *Entwicklung der erneuerbaren Energien—Stand: August 2003.* (Development of Renewable Energies – As of: August 2003.) Berlin: BMU.

———. 2006. *Eckpunkte für die Entwicklung und Einführung budgetunabhängiger Instrumente zur Marktdurchdringung erneuerbarer Energien im Wärmemarkt.* (Key Points for the Development and Implementation of Budget Independent Instruments for the Market Penetration of Renewable Energies on the Heat Market.) Berlin: BMU.

———. 2007. *Erneuerbare Energien: Arbeitsplatzeffekte 2006.* (Renewable Energies: Employment Effects 2006.) Berlin: BMU.

———. 2008a. *Development of Renewable Energy Sources in Germany in 2007: Graphics and Tables.* Berlin: BMU.

———. 2008b. *Analyse und Bewertung der Wirkungen des Erneuerbare-Energien-Gesetzes (EEG) aus gesamtwirtschaftlicher Sicht.* (Analysis and Evaluation of the Effects of the Renewable Energy Law (EEG) in Welfare Terms.) Berlin: BMU.

———. 2008c. *Bruttobeschäftigung 2007 -eine erste Abschätzung-.* (Gross Employment 2007 – A First Estimation.) Berlin: BMU.

Böhringer, C., and K. E. Rosendahl. 2009. Green Serves the Dirtiest: On the Interaction between Black and Green Quotas. Discussion paper no. 581. Oslo: Statistics Norway.

Bündnis 90/Die Grünen. 2009. *Der grüne neue Gesellschaftsvertrag.* (The Green New Social Contract.) Berlin: Bundestagswahlprogramm.

Bürger, V., S. Klinski, U. Lehr, U. Leprich, M. Nast, and M. Ragwitz. 2008. Policies to Support Renewable Energies in the Heat Market. *Energy Policy* 36 (8): 3150–59.

Büsgen, U., and W. Dürrschmidt. 2009. The Expansion of Electricity Generation from Renewable Energies in Germany: A Review Based on the Renewable Energy Sources Act Progress Report 2007 and the New German Feed-In Legislation *Energy Policy* 37 (7): 2536–45.

Butler, L., and K. Neuhoff. 2008. Comparison of Feed-In Tariff, Quota and Auction Mechanisms to Support Wind Power Development. *Renewable Energy* 33 (8): 1854–67.

BWE (Wind Energy Association). 2009. *Anzahl der Windenergieanlagen in Deutschland.* (Number of Wind Turbines in Germany.) www.wind-energie.de/de/statistiken/ (accessed June 2, 2009).

DEWI (Wind Energy Institute), E.ON Netz, EWI (Institute of Energy Economics), RWE Transportnetz Strom, and VE Transmission. 2005. *Energiewirtschaftliche Planung für die Netzintegration von*

Windenergie in Deutschland an Land und Offshore bis zum Jahr 2020. (Energy-Economic Planning of the Network Integration of On- and Offshore Wind Energy in Germany until 2020.) Berlin: German Energy Agency (DENA). www.dena.de/de/themen/thema-kraftwerke/projekte/projekt/netzstudie-i/, accessed January 31, 2009, (in German).

DLR (German Aerospace Center). 2008. *Leitstudie 2008: Weiterentwicklung der Ausbaustrategie Erneuerbare Energien vor dem Hintergrund der aktuellen Klimaschutzziele Deutschlands und Europas.* (Pilot Study 2008: Improvement of the Extension Strategy of Renewable Energies in the Context of the Current Climate Policy Objectives of Germany and Europe.) Berlin: BMU.

European Commission. 2005. *The Support of Electricity from Renewable Energy Sources.* Com(2005) 627.

Finon, D. 2007. *Pros and Cons of Alternative Policies Aimed at Promoting Renewables.* EIB Papers. Kirchberg, Luxembourg: European Investment Bank, Economic and Financial Studies.

Fischer, C., I. W. H. Parry, and W. A. Pizer. 2003. Instrument Choice for Environmental Protection when Technological Innovation Is Endogenous. *Journal of Environmental Economics and Management* 45 (3): 523–45.

Fouquet, D., and T. B. Johansson. 2008. European Renewable Energy Policy at Crossroads – Focus on Electricity Support Mechanisms. *Energy Policy*, 36(11): 4079–4092.

Gan, L., G. S. Eskeland, and H. H. Kolshus. 2007. Green Electricity Market Development: Lessons from Europe and the US. *Energy Policy* 35 (1): 144–55.

González, P. D. R. 2007. The Interaction between Emissions Trading and Renewable Electricity Support Schemes. An Overview of the Literature. *Mitigation and Adaptation Strategies for Global Change* 12: 8.

Greenpeace International/EWEA. 2005. *Wind Force 12: A Blueprint to Achieve 12% of the World's Electricity from Wind Power by 2020.* Brussels: Global Wind Energy Council.www.gwec.net/fileadmin/documents/Publications/wf12–2005.pdf (accessed February 15, 2009).

Handelsblatt. 2007. *Solarindustrie bringt Jobs für Ostdeutschland.* (Solar Industry provides Jobs for Eastern Germany.) www.handelsblatt.com/unternehmen/industrie/solarindustrie-bringt-jobs-fuer-ostdeutschland;1370712 (accessed October 15, 2009).

Hillebrand, B., H. G. Buttermann, J. M. Behringer, and M. Bleuel. 2006. The Expansion of Renewable Energies and Employment Effects in Germany. *Energy Policy* 34 (18): 3484–94.

IEA (International Energy Agency). 2007a. *Energy Policies of IEA Countries: Germany, 2007 Review.* Paris: OECD Publishing.

———. 2007b. *World Energy Outlook 2006.* Paris: OECD Publishing.

———. 2009. *Energy Technology R&D Statistics.* www.iea.org/textbase/stats/rd.asp (accessed June 2, 2009).

Jacobsson, S., and V. Lauber. 2006. The Politics and Policy of Energy System Transformation: Explaining the German Diffusion of Renewable Energy Technology. *Energy Policy* 34 (3): 256–76.

Jarass, L., and G. M. Obermair. 2005. Wirtschaftliche Zumutbarkeit des Netzausbaus für Erneuerbare Energien. (Economic Reasonability of Network Extensions for Renewable Energies.) *Zeitschrift für Energiewirtschaft* 29 (1): 3–10.

Klessmann, C., C. Nabe, and K. Burges. 2008. Pros and Cons of Exposing Renewables to Electricity Market Risks: A Comparison of the Market Integration Approaches in Germany, Spain, and the UK. *Energy Policy* 36: 3646–61.

Krewitt, W., and B. Schlomann. 2006. *Externe Kosten der Stromerzeugung aus erneuerbaren Energien im Vergleich zur Stromerzeugung aus fossilen Energieträgern.* (External Costs of Electricity Generation with Renewable Energies in Comparison to Generation with Fossil Fuels.) Stuttgart: BMU.

Lauber, V., and L. Mez. 2004. Three Decades of Renewable Energy Politics in Germany. *Energy & Environment* 15 (4): 599–623.

LBD. 2007. *EEG-Gutachten: Gutachten zur Angemessenheit der Aufwendungen für die Veredelung des EEG-Stromaufkommens durch die Übertragungsnetzbetreiber.* www.lbd.de/cms/pdf-gutachten-und-studien/0710-LBD-Gutachten-EEG.pdf (accessed August 24, 2009).

Lehr, U., J. Nitsch, M. Kratzat, C. Lutz, and D. Edler. 2008. Renewable Energy and Employment in Germany. *Energy Policy* 36 (1): 108–17.

Leuthold, F., T. Jeske, H. Weigt, and C. von Hirschhausen. 2009. When the Wind Blows over Europe: A Simulation Analysis and the Impact of Grid Extensions. Electricity Markets Working Papers WP-EM-31. Dresden, Germany: Dresden University of Technology.

Leuthold, F., H. Weigt, and C. von Hirschhausen. 2008. Efficient Pricing for European Electricity

Networks: The Theory of Nodal Pricing Applied to Feeding-In Wind in Germany. *Utilities Policy* 16 (4): 284–91.

Lipp, J. 2007. Lessons for Effective Renewable Electricity Policy from Denmark, Germany and the United Kingdom. *Energy Policy* 35 (11): 5481–95.

Meran, G., and N. Wittmann. 2008. Green, Brown, and Now White Certificates: Are Three One Too Many? A Micromodel of Market Interaction. Discussion paper 809. Berlin: German Institute for Economic Research.

Michaels R., and R. Murphy. 2009. *Green Jobs: Fact or Fiction?* Washington, DC: Institute for Energy Research.

Mitchell, C., D. Bauknecht, and P. M. Connor. 2006. Effectiveness through Risk Reduction: A Comparison of the Renewable Obligation in England and Wales and the Feed-In System in Germany. *Energy Policy* 34 (3): 297–305.

Pethig, R., and C. Wittlich. 2009. Interaction of Carbon Reduction and Green Energy Promotion in a Small Fossil-Fuel Importing Economy. Working paper no. 2749. Munich: CESifo.

Pfaffenberger, W., K. Nguyen, and J. Gabriel. 2003. *Ermittlung der Arbeitsplätze und Beschätigungswirkungen im Bereich erneuerbarer Energien.* (Estimation of Employment Effects in the Renewable Energies Sector). Düsseldorf: Hans-Böckler-Stiftung, Bremer Energie Instituts.

Ragwitz, M., A. Held, G. Resch, T. Faber, R. Haas, C. Huber, P. E. Morthorst, S. G. Jensen, R. Coenraads, M. Voogt, G. Reece, I. Konstantinaviciute, and B. Heyder. 2007. *OPTRES. Assessment and Optimisation of Renewable Energy Support Schemes in the European Electricity Market.* Final Report. Karlsruhe, Germany. www.optres.fhg.de/ (accessed August 24, 2009).

Rathmann, M. 2007. Do Support Systems for RES-E Reduce EU-ETS-Driven Electricity Prices? *Energy Policy* 35 (1): 342–49.

Reiche, D. 2002. Renewable Energies in the EU Member States in Comparison. In *Handbook of Renewable Energies in the European Union*, edited by D. Reiche. Frankfurt/Main: Verlag Peter Lang, 13–24.

Rious, V., J.-M. Glachant, Y. Perez, and P. Dessante. 2008. The Diversity of Design of TSOs. *Energy Policy* 36 (9): 3323–32.

RWI (Rhine-Westphalia Institute for Economic Research). 2009. *Die ökonomische Wirkung der Förderung Erneuerbarer Energien: Erfahrungen aus Deutschland.* (The Economic Impact of Renewable Energy Support: Experiences from Germany). Essen, Germany: RWI.

Schöne, S. 2009. *Auctions in the Electricity Market.* Berlin: Springer-Verlag.

Sensfuß, F., M. Ragwitz, and M. Genoese. 2008. The Merit-Order Effect: A Detailed Analysis of the Price Effect of Renewable Electricity Generation on Spot Market Prices in Germany. *Energy Policy* 36 (8): 3086–94.

Sorrel, S., and J. Sijm. 2005. Carbon Trading in the Policy Mix. *Oxford Review of Economic Policy* 19 (3): 420–37.

Toke, D. 2005. Are Green Electricity Certificates the Way Forward for Renewable Energy? An Evaluation of the United Kingdom's Renewables Obligation in the Context of International Comparisons. *Environment and Planning C: Government and Policy* 23 (3): 361–74.

———. 2007. Renewable Financial Support Systems and Cost-Effectiveness. *Journal of Cleaner Production* 15: 280–87.

Toke, D., and V. Lauber. 2007. Anglo-Saxon and German Approaches to Neoliberalism and Environmental Policy: The Case of Financing Renewable Energy. *Geoforum* 38 (4): 677–87.

Traber, T., and C. Kemfert. 2009. Impacts of the German Support for Renewable Energy on Electricity Prices, Emissions and Firms. *Energy Journal* 30 (3): 155–78.

Vandezande, L., L. Meeus, R. Belmans, M. Saguan, and J.-M. Glachant. 2010. Well-Functioning Balancing Markets: A Prerequisite for Wind Power Integration. *Energy Policy*, 38 (7): 3146–3154.

VIK (German Association of Industrial Energy Users and Self-Generators). 2009. Die Entwicklung am EEX-Terminmarkt. www.vik-online.de/fileadmin/vik/EEX/Terminmarkt.pdf (accessed June 2, 2009).

Wand, R., and F. Leuthold. 2009. Feed-In Tariffs for Photovoltaics: Learning by Doing in Germany? Innovations for a Low-Carbon Energy System Working Papers WP-RD-03. Dresden, Germany: Dresden University of Technology.

Wawer, T. 2007. Konzepte für ein nationales Engpassmanagement im deutschen Übertragungsnetz. (Concepts for a National Congestion Management Scheme in the German Transmission System). *Zeitschrift für Energiewirtschaft* 31 (2): 109–16.

Weber, Christoph. 2010. Adequate Intraday Market Design to Enable the Integration of Wind Energy into the European Power Systems. *Energy Policy* 38 (7): 3155–3163.

Weigt, H. 2009. Germany's Wind Energy: The Potential for Fossil Capacity Replacement and Cost Saving. *Applied Energy* 86 (10): 1857–63.

Weigt, H., T. Jeske, F. Leuthold, and C. von Hirschhausen. 2010. Take the Long Way Down: Integration of Large-Scale North Sea Wind Using HVDC Transmission. *Energy Policy* 38 (7): 3164–3173.

Wischermann, S., and H.-J. Wagner. 2009. Renewable Energy in Energy Scenarios for Germany. Paper presented at 10th IAEE European Conference, Energy, Policies and Technologies for Sustainable Economies. September 2009, Vienna, Austria.

Witzmann, R., and G. Kerber. 2007. Capacity of Distribution Networks due to Power from Photovoltaic. *EW: Das Magazin für die Energiewirtschaft* 419 (4): 50–54.

Wright, T. P. 1936. Factors Affecting the Cost of Airplanes. *Journal of the Aeronautical Sciences* 3: 122–28.

Wüstenhagen, R., and M. Bilharz. 2006. Green Energy Market Development in Germany: Effective Public Policy and Emerging Customer Demand. *Energy Policy* 34 (13): 1681–96.

Zoellner, Jan, P. Schweizer-Ries, and C. Wemheuer. 2008. Public Acceptance of Renewable Energies: Results from Case Studies in Germany. *Energy Policy* 36 (11): 4136–41.

15

Renewable Electricity Support: The Spanish Experience

Luis Agosti and Jorge Padilla

As in many other countries, the policy of the Spanish government toward the electricity sector has had three sometimes conflicting objectives: low prices, security of supply, and environmental sustainability. Over the last few years, the government has promoted investment in renewable energy, both wind and solar, with those objectives in mind. The expansion in low-marginal-cost renewable capacity was expected to push wholesale prices (excluding subsidies) downward; reduce the traditional dependency of the Spanish economy on imported primary energy sources; and meet the government's emissions reduction targets.

Investment in renewable generation has been supported by means of a dual feed-in tariff (FIT) scheme.[1] Renewable generators can choose whether to sell their energy at a regulated fixed price or to sell at the market price and receive an additional premium. Investors in renewables also benefit from low administrative and regulatory barriers and relatively favorable grid access conditions in Spain in comparison with other countries.

The policy of the Spanish government has some aspects to commend but can also be criticized on a number of fronts. The European Commission's assessment of renewable energy support schemes relies on two indicators relative to their effectiveness and efficiency. The effectiveness indicator shows for each technology the increase in renewable generation compared with its estimated midterm realizable potential.[2] The efficiency indicator compares the support received with the generation cost of the generation units covered by the scheme. The scheme is considered more efficient when that difference is small.

The government's support scheme has proved to be effective. In 2008, renewable capacity accounted for 42% of all generation capacity and 22% of total electricity production. Today Spain is the second-largest wind power generator in the European Union (EU). In November 2009, wind generation reached record output levels, representing 50% of total demand for several hours. Solar photovoltaic (PV) generation has experienced an extraordinary increase in recent years, from 146 megawatts (MW) installed capacity in 2006 to 3,342 MW in 2008. Indeed, Spain installed more than 40% of the world's total solar units in 2008.

Regarding wind generation, the policy has been both effective and efficient. Figure 15.1 shows the effectiveness and efficiency—expected profit, in terms of the cost of renewable support measured in euro cents per kilowatt-hour (kWh)—of the promotion schemes used by various EU member states in connection with wind

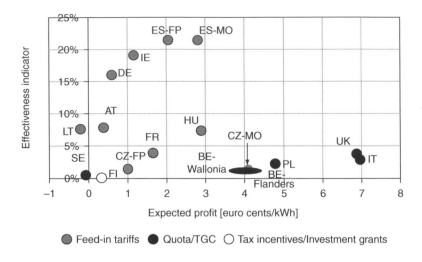

Source: European Commission 2008
Notes: MO = market option; FP = fixed price option

Figure 15.1. Effectiveness and efficiency of support schemes for onshore wind generation in Europe in 2006

generation. The support scheme in Spain is the most effective, while the cost of the scheme is no greater than the average of the member states. The picture for solar generation is somewhat different. The rapid growth in solar deployment described above is in part the result of an extremely generous FIT. As the number of solar units in the market increased well above what was planned, the Spanish government found itself committed to pay billions of euros over a 20-year period. Inevitably, this led to a sudden reduction of the feed-in tariffs for this technology in 2009.

The current debate in Spain concerns the impact of the current policy toward renewable generation on the future performance of the country's electricity sector, in particular, on wholesale and retail electricity prices, system operation, and security of supply. Has the Spanish government gone too far in its support of renewable energy? Has it sacrificed the goals of economic efficiency and security of supply to the environmental objectives?

This chapter seeks to answer these questions by describing the current status and future challenges of the policy of support to renewable generation in Spain. It also explores potential solutions to the problems identified. The discussion

begins with an examination of the current regulatory framework for renewable energy, as well as a detailed description of existing renewable capacity and its expected development. The chapter then looks at the challenges affecting the future expansion of renewable capacity in Spain—in particular, the effects that large volumes of renewable energy have had, and are expected to have, on the operation of the Spanish electricity market, investment incentives for different technologies, and retail prices. Finally, it gives possible solutions to the problems posed by large-scale deployment of renewable generation.

Renewable Energy in Spain Today

Renewable energy production is part of the Régimen Especial (Special Regime, or SR), which includes all electricity produced from renewable sources, combined heat and power (CHP), and solid waste from units below 50 MW. Conventional units—nuclear, large hydro, coal, and combined cycle gas turbines (CCGTs)—operate under the Régimen Ordinario (Ordinary

Regime, or OR). In 2008, the SR was responsible for 23% of electricity generated and represented 32% of total installed capacity, as described in Table 15.1.

Table 15.1. Generation mix in Spain, December 2008

Technology	Electricity generated		Installed capacity	
	GWh	%	MW	%
Hydro (> 50 MW)	21,428	7.5	16,657	18.3
Nuclear	58,973	20.6	7,716	8.5
Coal	46,275	16.1	11,359	12.5
Fuel/gas	2,378	0.8	4,418	4.9
CCGT	91,286	31.8	21,675	23.9
Ordinary Regime	220,340	76.9	61,825	68.0
Hydro (< 50 MW)	4,416	1.5	1,979	2.2
Wind	31,393	11.0	15,874	17.5
Other renewables	7,183	2.5	4,069	4.5
Nonrenewables[a]	23,308	8.1	7,132	7.8
Special Regime	66,300	23.1	29,054	32.0
Total	286,640	100.0	90,879	100.0

Source: REE 2008
[a]Include CHP and solid waste

Figure 15.2 shows the volumes of renewable capacity (excluding large hydro units) in several EU countries, based on 2007 data. In absolute terms, Spain ranked second in renewable capacity, after only Germany. In relative terms, renewables represented 21% of total capacity in Spain, the second-highest proportion after Portugal.

Among the different technologies included in the SR, wind generation has a predominant role. As shown in Table 15.2, onshore wind capacity has grown from 886 MW in 1998 to 15,709 MW in 2008. Wind generation, together with CCGT, has dominated the evolution of the Spanish generation mix in the last decade. These two technologies together accounted for 94% of all capacity installed between 2003 and 2008. Solar PV represents only 3% of total capacity, although the pace of investment in the last two years has been extraordinary.

As a result of the growth in installed renewable capacity, output from the SR has experienced a substantial increase in recent years. As Figure 15.3 shows, the combination of increased output and a recession-induced drop in demand meant that during 2009, SR generation represented more than 30% of electricity demand—a figure that rises to above 40% if the production from large hydro units that operate in the OR were added in.

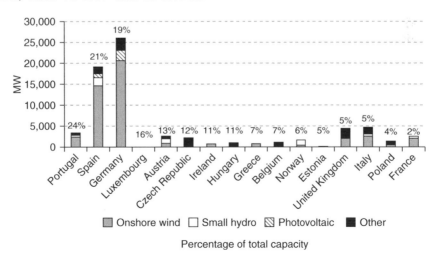

Source: CEER 2008
Note: Figures exclude large hydro capacity

Figure 15.2. Renewables mix in EU countries, 2007

Table 15.2. Evolution of installed renewable and other SR capacity (MW)

Year	Biomass	Solar	Wind	Hydro (< 50 MW)	Hydro (> 50 MW)	CHP	Solid waste	Solid waste treatment
1998	81	1	886	1,300	16,454	3,673	334	N/A
1999	88	2	1,686	1,439	16,526	4,206	351	29
2000	144	2	2,296	1,469	16,526	4,929	339	81
2001	230	4	3,508	1,562	16,588	5,352	449	157
2002	352	8	5,066	1,594	16,587	5,567	461	324
2003	454	12	6,324	1,666	16,658	5,628	468	420
2004	469	23	8,522	1,708	16,657	5,694	585	469
2005	499	48	10,097	1,765	16,657	5,706	585	538
2006	540	146	11,891	1,893	16,657	5,836	579	624
2007	557	695	14,423	1,913	16,657	6,060	569	527
2008	582	3,342	15,709	1,965	16,657	6,168	579	554

Source: CNE 2009b
Note: SR includes renewable, CHP, and solid waste and excludes large hydro generation

Policy Goals

The key goal of the renewables policy of the Spanish government is the reduction in CO_2 emissions. In 2008, the production of electricity from renewable sources, excluding large hydro units, saved more than 15 million tons (Mt) of CO_2,[3] which represents approximately 4% of yearly emissions (MARM 2009). Current annual CO_2 emissions represent a 52% increase with respect to base-year emissions, or almost 37%

above the Spanish target under the Kyoto Protocol. The policy of support to investment in renewables is a natural response to the significant increase in CO_2 emissions.

Another fundamental goal is the reduction of primary energy dependence. Domestic primary energy production (including nuclear power) currently accounts for just 19% of total primary energy supply in Spain. With hardly any natural gas or oil production, the country relies on nuclear and coal production for the bulk of

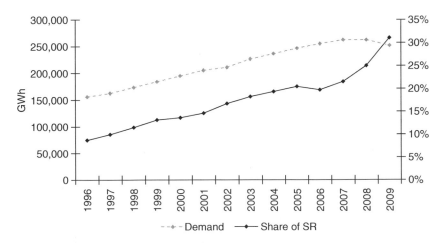

Source: CNE, 2009b

Figure 15.3. Evolution of demand and share of the SR

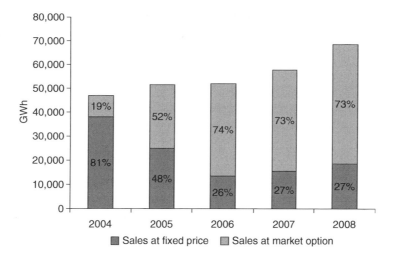

Source: CNE 2009b

Figure 15.4. Distribution of SR production between fixed price and market options

domestic energy sources, both under pressure to be reduced in coming years.[4] The current government has clearly stated its intention to abandon nuclear power in favor of renewable energy. In the case of coal, mining activity is for the most part heavily subsidized and likely to disappear in the medium term.[5] Renewables will then be the sole sources of indigenous energy. Only if renewable generation grows at above 8% per year from 2008 onward will Spain be able to maintain its energy dependence below the current level of 80%. Without the contribution of renewables, final energy dependence would be above 90% by 2020.[6]

A third goal of the renewables policy in Spain concerns electricity prices. The expansion in renewable generation, which is characterized by low variable costs and intermittency, was expected to exert downward pressure on wholesale electricity prices, at least in the short and medium terms. Provided that additional capacity was owned by nonincumbent generators, it would contribute to address the government's repeatedly stated concerns about the use and abuse of market power in the electricity generation market. The effect of this expansion in capacity on market prices was also seen as a way to partly offset the cost of the subsidies to renewable generation.

Renewable Regulation

The legal framework of the SR has evolved substantially over the last 15 years. The first major push for the promotion of renewable energy came with the enactment of the Spanish Electricity Law in 1997 and Royal Decree (RD) 2818/1998, which established a reward scheme for each technology, consisting of a fixed premium over the monthly average market price.

In 1999, the government approved the Plan de Fomento de las Energías Renovables (Plan to Promote Renewable Energy, or PFER), setting investment objectives for each technology with the aim of meeting 12% of primary energy consumption in 2010 from renewable sources (including large-scale hydro). It also approved several measures to encourage market participation by renewables. Renewables units were allowed to sign bilateral contracts with retail companies and also became eligible to receive a capacity payment for participating in the market. This was removed in 2007.

In 2004, this regime was modified by RD 436/2004, which allowed renewable generators to choose either to sell their output to a distribution company at a fixed feed-in tariff or to go to the market and receive the market price plus a premium, and in some cases a further incentive.[7]

The possibility of choosing between these two options was in itself a significant advantage compared with RD 2818/1998. In addition, RD 436/2004 implied an increase in terms of absolute compensation, quite large in some cases. As a result, after its enactment, most of the SR production switched from the fixed feed-in tariff to the market option, as shown in Figure 15.4.

A 2005 review of the PFER showed that the observed growth in renewable energy was insufficient to meet the goals defined under the plan. As a consequence, the PFER was updated in 2005 with the Plan de Energías Renovables (Renewable Energy Plan, or PER) 2005–2010. According to that plan, by 2010 at least 12% of primary energy consumption and 29.4% of the total generation of electricity should come from renewable sources. The PER 2005–2010 argued the need to reinforce the government's support of renewable energies through various measures, including stronger economic incentives.

This gave rise to RD 661/2007, which provides the current framework for the promotion of renewables. The economic regime is similar to that under RD 436/2004. Each unit may choose between the fixed tariff and the market option,

and a generation plant operating within the SR can change from one alternative to the other if it stays with the chosen alternative for at least one year. The level of subsidies is somewhat higher than provided by RD 436/2004.

Table 15.3 shows the evolution of the premiums and fixed prices under the different royal decrees. As can be seen, RD 436/2004 already represented a large increase in the value of the incentives, especially in the case of solar PV and solar thermal generation, which were subsequently increased with RD 661/2007. In order to limit the potential cost of the support schemes, RD 661/2007 introduced a cap-and-floor mechanism for the market option premium of some technologies, with the intention of both reducing the risk for investors and limiting the maximum cost of subsidizing renewables. RD 661/2007 also established that once 85% of the 2010 capacity targets for each technology had been achieved, the remuneration scheme for additional capacity would have to be redefined. In the case of solar PV, the 2010 goal was exceeded in 2008. Installed capacity in 2008 equaled 3,342 MW, compared with a 2010 target of 371 MW.

Table 15.3. Evolution of incentives for renewable generation

RES technology	RD 2818/1998 1998 Premium (€/MWh)	RD 436/2004 2004		RD 661/2007 2007	
		FIT (€/MWh)	Premium (€/MWh)	FIT (€/MWh)	Premium (€/MWh)
PV < 100 kWp	60.0	414.4	N/A	440.0	N/A
PV > 100 kWp	30.0	216.2	187.4	[229–417]	N/A
Solar thermal electricity	20.0	216.2	187.4	269.0	254.0
Wind < 5 MW	31.6	64.9	36.0	73.0	29.0
Wind > 5 MW	31.6	64.9	36.0	73.0	29.0
Geothermal < 50 MW	32.8	64.9	36.0	69.0	38.0
Mini hydro < 10 MW	32.8	64.9	36.0	78.0	25.0
Hydro 10–25 MW	[0–35.8]	64.9	36.0	[66–78]	13.0
Hydro 25–50 MW	[0–35.8]	57.7	28.8	[66–78]	13.0
Biomass (biocrops, biogas)	28.0	64.9	36.0	[107–158]	[61–115]
Agriculture residues	28.0	57.7	28.8	[96–130]	[30–97]
Municipal solid waste	22.0	50.5	21.6	[38–53]	[30–97]

Notes: For some technologies, the value of the subsidies varies with the size of the installation; brackets indicate the minimum and maximum value of the subsidy; €1 = $1.36 as of this writing

The government therefore established a new remuneration scheme for solar PV units in RD 1578/2008.

In 2009, the renewable sector reduced its expansion significantly as a result of various factors, including new administrative barriers, uncertainty about the economic framework that will apply once the targets for 2010 are accomplished, and the economic recession. Investment in wind and solar developments has almost ceased.

There is little doubt, however, that the sector will resume its expansion in the future. Spain is obliged to implement European Directive 2009/28/EC on the promotion of the use of energy from renewable sources,[8] which requires it to produce 20% of final energy consumption from renewable sources by 2020. Moreover, the Spanish government has made the promotion of renewables a national priority. It is currently preparing a new Law on Energy Efficiency and Renewable Energies, which will translate into Spanish law the EU regulations on energy and climate change, and a new 2011–2020 Plan on Renewable Energies, which will establish individual targets for each type of technology and the corresponding measures that will have to be adopted in order to attain those targets.

Data for 2008 show that Spain is well positioned to meet the 2020 challenges resulting from the European directive in electricity, but not so in heating and transport. In 2008, the share of final energy produced by renewables was approximately 9%, with 5% corresponding to the electricity sector and 4% to the heating and transport sectors (MITYC 2009a). According to the Spanish government, the 2020 scenario would require 40% of electricity to be produced from renewable sources, which corresponds to 9% of total energy consumption.[9] The remaining 11% necessary to meet the 20% target would have to be achieved by the heating and transport sectors. These estimates involve rapid annual growth rates of 6% for electricity and 11% for heating and transport, as shown in Figure 15.5.

Assessing Current Policy

Has the support scheme implemented by the Spanish government successfully contributed to

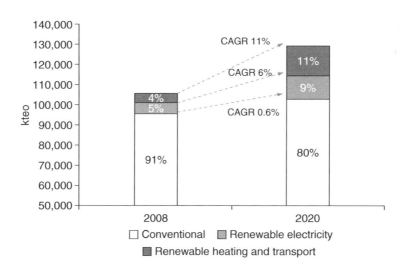

Source: Author's estimates, assuming 40% of electricity coming from renewables in 2020
Notes: Final energy consumption growth 1.8% per annum as estimated for Spain during the period 2007–2016 in IEA 2009; ktoe = kilo tons of oil equivalent; CAGR = compound annual growth rate

Figure 15.5. Renewable energy growth till 2020 and contribution to final energy consumption

its three main policy goals of environmental sustainability, lower electricity costs, and security of supply? As explained in detail in the following discussion, the current support scheme has proved effective but quite expensive, is likely to have caused an increase in electricity prices, and raises several concerns in relation to the operation of the system and its reliability, especially in the long term.

Environmental Sustainability: Effectiveness and Efficiency

As noted above, the Spanish renewable electricity support scheme has proved to be highly effective. Its overall 2010 target is within reach, even if some of the subtargets for individual technologies defined in PER 2005–2010 and RD 661/2007 will likely be missed, as shown in Table 15.4. The increase in renewable capacity has significantly contributed to reducing the high level of CO_2 emissions.

The effectiveness of the scheme has come at considerable cost, however. As shown in Table 15.5, in 2008 the average subsidy received by SR production units per MWh produced was 75% of the average market price. Subsidies to the SR are expected to reach €4.7 billion ($6.4 billion) by the end of 2009 (CNE 2009c). Notably, 40% of that amount will go to solar PV units, which represent only 3.7% of total SR generation.

Table 15.4. Capacity targets and current deployment status, September 2009

	September 2009 (MW)	Target for 2010 (MW)	% accomplished
CHP	6,464	9,215	70%
Solar PV	4,824	371	1,300%
Solar thermal-electric	82	500	16%
Wind	17,269	20,155	86%
Wind repowering[a]	0	2	0%
Hydro (< 10 MW)	1,414	2.4	59%
Biomass	674	1,567	43%
Residuals	269	350	77%
Total	30,996	36,558	85%

Source: CNE 2009b
[a]Repowering involves replacing first-generation wind turbines with modern multimegawatt wind turbines

Lower Electricity Costs

In 2009, a combination of factors—increased renewable capacity, reduced demand, and high levels of available hydro production—led to a rapid increase in the share of energy produced by the SR, which represented 28% of total generation in January–October 2009. The increased role of renewable energy has had major implications for the performance of the Spanish electricity system. In particular, the surge in renewable genera-

Table 15.5. Implicit subsidies for the SR, 2008

	Capacity (MW)	Energy (GWh)	Total price received (€/MWh)	Market price (€/MWh)	Implicit premium (€/MWh)	Premium over market price
CHP	6,136	21,088	99.2	64.5	34.7	54%
Solar	3,454	2,541	453.0	64.5	388.6	603%
Wind	15,982	31,869	100.4	64.5	36.0	56%
Small hydro	1,945	4,632	96.2	64.5	31.8	49%
Biomass	583	2,487	116.5	64.5	52.0	81%
Solid waste	569	2,732	87.8	64.5	23.3	36%
Solid waste treatment	573	3,156	111.4	64.5	47.0	73%
Total SR	29,242	68,504	113.4	64.5	49.0	76%

Source: CNE 2009b
Note: €1 = $1.36 as of this writing

tion has had an impact on the electricity prices faced by end users. Measuring that impact is a complex exercise, however, because the increase in renewable generation produces several effects that may operate in opposite directions.

First, consumers of electricity pay the high subsidies received by renewable generators via higher regulated network access tariffs. These tariffs are set by the government periodically and are paid by all consumers that have access to the electricity grid. They are set taking into account the costs of the transmission and distribution grids, other costs of the system, and the subsidies paid to the SR.[10] The weight of these subsidies in the calculation of the access tariff is significant. Not surprisingly, the policy of subsidizing investment in renewable generation has led to increases in the access tariffs paid by the average consumer. Those tariffs have increased from €15.70 ($21.29) per MWh in 2008 to €33.30 ($45.16) per MWh in 2009—an increase of 112%, half of which is caused by the renewable electricity support scheme.[11] As these charges account for around 50% of final prices paid by end consumers, the increase in the access tariffs has had a significant impact on the overall cost of electricity and hence on consumer welfare (CNE 2009a).

Second, the increase in renewable generation can reduce wholesale market prices in the short term. In Spain, most of the production of all OR and SR units is sold in a day-ahead market, which is a pool-type market in which all generators receive the marginal prices of hourly auctions, provided they submit supply offers at prices below the clearing price of the market. Conventional units are expected to submit bids based on their variable costs. Renewable SR units, whether they have opted for the FIT or the market price plus premium option, bid in all their production at zero, as in most cases this is close to their marginal cost, and because they need to ensure that all their production is sold in the market. As a result, all output from the SR, including the output of renewable units, is cleared, reducing the residual demand faced by the OR units. An increase in the output supplied by the SR reduces the demand faced by the only price-setting units in the day-ahead market—those within the OR. As a result,

the increase in SR supply results in lower wholesale prices (Sáenz de Miera et al. 2008).

Note, however, that any reduction in spot prices would reduce the remuneration received by existing production units. The adoption of a policy aimed at promoting renewable generation causes an adverse shock to the actual and future profitability of those units which may render the investment made on them unjustified. To the extent that that policy, or at least some of its central elements, could not have been anticipated by market participants at the time their investment decisions were made, the adverse impact of the policy on the profitability of incumbent plants may be seen as a form of regulatory taking which should be compensated. Note, in addition, that the exit from the market of inadequately remunerated plants would bring prices up and undermine the price goal of renewable promotion. So it appears that an aggressive renewables policy may have to go hand in hand with some form of compensatory measures aimed at compensating incumbent players for unamortised investments made before the new regulations were adopted. Those compensations may be defended on both fairness and efficiency grounds.

The net effect of an increase in renewable capacity on end-user prices is therefore ambiguous. As illustrated in Figure 15.6, the net effect could be higher or lower end-user prices, depending on the slope of the supply curve in the day-ahead market and the magnitude of the above-market premium paid to incentivize investment in renewable capacity.

Figure 15.6 depicts two styled examples. In both Case 1 and Case 2, the production of the SR, Q_{SR}, reduces the demand faced by OR generators from Q_T to Q_{OR}, which causes a reduction in the wholesale market-clearing price from P_T to P_{OR}. As OR units are remunerated at the market-clearing price, the reduction in that price results in a reduction in the wholesale cost of electricity given by area A. On the other hand, the SR units are remunerated at a price equal to P_{RE}, irrespective of the market-clearing price. A lower market-clearing price simply translates into a greater premium for the units operating under the SR. Hence an increase in the production of the

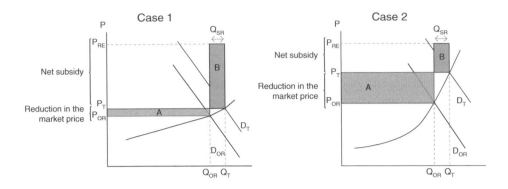

Figure 15.6. Effect of renewable energy promotion in the wholesale generation market

SR results in extra payments to the SR equal to area B. The net result of the increased production of the SR will be a reduction (increase) in the wholesale cost of electricity when area A is larger (smaller) than area B. In Case 1 the cost of the renewables subsidy is greater than the savings derived from the reduction in the wholesale market-clearing price. In Case 2, on the contrary, the cost of the subsidy is more than offset by the reduction in the wholesale market-clearing price. Case 1 is characterized by a relatively flat supply curve, whereas Case 2 involves a relatively steeper curve.

The net effect of the policy of supporting investment in renewables via FITs in Spain is likely to have increased the cost of electricity, and hence the price paid by end users. This is because at present, the supply curve in the Spanish day-ahead market is quite flat at the margin, as a result of the large number of CCGTs competing in the same range of costs. Thus the impact of the increase in renewable capacity on the day-ahead market price can be expected to be fairly small—in any event, smaller than the overall cost of the subsidies paid to the owners of renewable electricity assets. Note in this respect that during the first half of 2009, the day-ahead market price ranged between €35 and €40 ($47 and $54) per MWh, which, given that the floor value of the FIT for wind production is €71.30 ($96.70) per MWh, implies a very large premium. Moreover, the intermittent nature of wind and solar technology imposes additional pressure on electricity prices. The production of wind plants is highly

volatile and requires thermal capacity to be available for backup, which increases requirements for spinning reserves,[12] and these have to be appropriately remunerated.

The Spanish renewable electricity support policy is likely to lead to additional increases in electricity prices in the medium term and even more so in the long term. In the medium term, unless a significant reform of the FITs occurs, the overall cost of the subsidies to the SR will increase in direct response to the increase in renewable capacity. Moreover, the impact of further additions of renewable capacity on day-ahead prices is likely to decrease as installed capacity goes up and market prices approach the competitive benchmark.

In the long term, the increase in renewable capacity will likely crowd out some thermal capacity, causing prices to increase. Note in this respect that the expansion of renewable capacity has already resulted in a significant reduction in the production of conventional thermal units. From November 2008 to October 2009, output from CCGTs and coal plants was 17% lower than in the previous 12 months. Some of this reduction is the result of a fall in electricity demand, but some of it (no less than 7%) is the direct consequence of the increase in SR production.[13] The reduction in the production of conventional thermal units has led to lower utilization rates, which have fallen from 53% in 2008 to around 44% in 2009.

Security of Supply

The significant increase in renewable capacity has implications for the operation of the system in the short term as well as for its performance in the medium and long term.

As is well known, the integration of a large volume of intermittent generation into an electricity system poses several operational challenges. Red Eléctrica de España (REE), the Spanish system operator, has made considerable efforts to integrate the production of wind and solar units efficiently and reliably. For instance, in 2006, REE created the Centre for the Control of the Special Regime (CECRE), with the specific mission of maximizing renewable generation, especially wind generation, while ensuring system security.

CECRE's mission is made difficult by the volatile nature of the production of wind (and also solar) plants. According to REE, forecasting the production of wind plants 24 hours ahead typically involves average forecasting errors of about 20% (Rodríguez 2007). These errors require considerable additional reserves. When forecast production is above actual production, the system requires upward reserves. When, instead, forecast production is below actual production, the proper operation of the system demands downward reserves.

Managing wind plants in Spain is particularly cumbersome, as their production is negatively correlated with electricity demand: production is low during the summer and winter peaks, but it results in energy "spills" during off-peak hours.[14] For example, as shown in Figure 15.7, on November 2, 2008, wind production was 3,200 MW above forecast. With a low demand, 20,000 MW, the system ran out of downward reserves very rapidly. To balance the system, the REE had to reduce wind production by 2,400 MW between 7:00 and 9:00 a.m.

Another common problem occurs when large numbers of wind turbines need to be shut down because of high wind speeds. For example, on January 23–24, wind turbines in the north of Spain experienced wind speeds above 200 kilometers per hour and had to be disconnected. As a result, the difference between forecast and actual production was above 5,000 MW, as shown in Figure 15.8. The system operator had to cover this difference by quickly switching production to CCGTs.

In summary, wind, and to some extent also solar, generation has introduced significant uncertainty in the operation of the system. As a result, REE has had to increase the reserve margin so as to be able to respond in a timely and efficient manner to potential variations in renewables production. In particular, REE has relied on a combination of gas fired and hydroelectric generation to provide the necessary reserves.

The reliability of the system on a forward-looking basis will hinge on a number of factors.

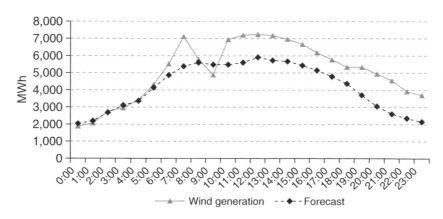

Source: Data obtained from REE database.

Figure 15.7. Actual versus forecast generation from wind, November 2, 2008

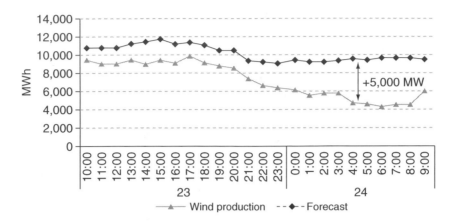

Source: Data obtained from REE data base.

Figure 15.8. Actual versus forecast generation from wind, January 23–24, 2008

The size and availability of the CCGT fleet is perhaps the most important of all. This is a reason for concern, however, because the profitability of CCGT plants fell dramatically in 2009, and their prospects in the near future are not particularly bright either. As explained above, the increase in renewable capacity has led to a reduction in the utilization rates of the CCGTs, as well as a drop in the prices received when they operate. The reduction in the number of hours of operation has also caused unit variable costs to rise as a result of, among other things, the increased maintenance costs resulting from more variable operating patterns and the "take or pay" obligations that force CCGT operators to pay for gas volumes they purchased under long-term contracts regardless of whether those volumes are effectively consumed. The forecast evolution of renewable capacity, which could be large enough to cover almost 100% of the demand sometimes, suggests that the utilization rates and profitability of the CCGTs currently in operation will remain low in the near future.

The implication of this is that the availability of backup thermal capacity may be at risk. Incumbent CCGT operators will be tempted to close down or "mothball" some of their existing capacity. Moreover, they (as well as other potential entrants) will no longer have the incentive to introduce additional thermal capacity into the system. The evidence shows that this is indeed the

case: several investment plans have been discontinued, which means that CCGT capacity in the future will fall short of what was expected not long ago. Tighter supply conditions may lead to higher spot prices at times when wind output is low, and that may allow the conventional units that remain in the market to operate profitably. Nevertheless, what constitutes a rational response from a private point of view could have disastrous effects from the viewpoint of the system's security of supply.

Other factors that may also contribute to integrating renewable generation efficiently include the ability of the system to manage demand fluctuations, the availability of hydro pump units whose operation can be optimized to provide additional energy storage, the development of interconnections with neighboring countries, and the existence of a transportation grid that can successfully accommodate the deployment of renewable units in areas that are not necessarily located where the demand is. Unfortunately, Spain is not terribly well placed with respect to any of these factors, which limits the ability of REE to avoid energy spills and minimize reserve requirements. For example, the interconnections with the neighboring countries, especially with France, represent a negligible proportion of peak demand, and the transmission grid is designed to reflect the generation fleet in place prior to the deployment of wind generation units.

Policy Recommendations

The renewable electricity support scheme adopted by the Spanish government no doubt has contributed positively to achieve its environmental objectives, but it has done so at a high cost in terms of both the efficiency and reliability of the Spanish electricity system. From an efficiency standpoint, as explained above, the drastic expansion of renewable capacity in Spain is likely to have raised the cost of electricity in the short term, and its medium- and long-term effects on prices are bound to be adverse from the viewpoint of end users. Regarding security of supply, the policy of the Spanish government has contributed to reducing the dependency of the system on imported energy sources. On the other hand, an electricity system where a significant proportion of electricity demand is covered by wind and solar generation units can work reliably only if there is sufficient thermal capacity in reserve. This in turn requires remunerating that backup capacity appropriately in a market context where, precisely because of the expansion of renewable generation, the output of those thermal units and the price received by them are bound to fall.

The Spanish government has no room to renegotiate its environmental commitments. What it can do, however, is rethink its current policy to ensure that those commitments are made compatible with the efficient and reliable operation of the system in the short, medium, and long term. Otherwise, the environmental policy of the government may come into question.

What should be done, then? First, and most important, the Spanish government should carefully consider the extent and cost of its support scheme. It should investigate whether its environmental objectives can be more cheaply achieved by means of policies aimed at promoting energy efficiency. It should revisit its forecasts regarding future electricity demand and generation capacity in order to rigorously assess how much support to offer the deployment of renewable generation capacity, taking into account its potentially adverse effects on economic efficiency and security of supply, as discussed above.

The available evidence suggests that this is precisely what the government is starting to do. The Spanish government is taking steps to limit the costs of its support policy, even when that may imply curtailing the expansion of renewable generation. Thus, for example, Royal Decree-Law (RDL) 6/2009 imposes additional administrative burdens on the installation of renewable capacity. Only those production units with the necessary authorizations and credible construction plans will be eligible to register into the SR. In promulgating this RDL, the government explicitly acknowledged that if the expansion of renewable capacity were to follow the observed trend, the economic and technical viability of the whole electricity system could be seriously jeopardized. The government has now imposed yearly caps on the expansion of certain technologies (Secretaría de Estado de Energía 2009). Wind generation capacity will not be able to increase by more than 1,855 MW in 2010 and 1,700 MW in 2011 and 2012. Solar PV capacity expansions will be capped at 500 MW until 2012. The premium paid to solar PV units has also been significantly reduced, from €442 to €320 ($599 to $434) per MWh.

These measures may nonetheless prove insufficient. It thus makes sense for the Spanish government to look for alternative ways to achieve its environmental objectives at lower cost. One obvious recommendation is to proceed further in reducing support for solar PV, which despite the reduction noted above remains extraordinarily high and is hard to justify on environmental or industrial policy grounds. Some of the savings could be invested in research and development (R&D) into solar energy. Given the current state of knowledge regarding solar energy, investing in R&D is likely to prove more effective and efficient than investing in installations that can soon prove obsolete.

Second, the Spanish government should also assess whether the overall cost of meeting its 2020 targets can be lowered by placing increased emphasis on renewable energy in the heating and transport sectors, such as through the promotion of biofuels, and also on the promotion of energy efficiency. The current situation of renewables in these sectors suggests great potential for improvement, especially in the transport sector, where renewable energy represents less than 2% of total consumption (as compared with the 10% target set for 2020).

Some estimates indicate that biomass and solar thermal heating are much more economic means of reducing emissions than other technologies such as wind or hydro generation (IEA 2009, *96*). Policies aimed at increasing energy efficiency should also be a priority (European Commission 2009). The current strategy of achieving significant emissions reductions by focusing almost exclusively on the supply side of the electricity system is too costly. A multipronged approach involving demand-side interventions in the electricity markets and actions in heating and transport may prove more effective and efficient.

Third, once the government has decided how much renewable generation to promote, it should consider reforming the generation market so as to ensure that the increase in renewable capacity does not distort the operation of the system or create security of supply concerns. In this respect, the government should assess how to reward the availability of backup capacity in the form of CCGTs and open cycle gas turbines. The government should perhaps increase the capacity payments made to CCGTs and other flexible backup units. Currently, the value of the capacity payments is fixed at €20,000 ($27,126) per MW per year for the existing conventional units and limited to 10 years. In the case of capacity payments for future investments, the value of the capacity payment is calculated according to the value of an index that measures the excess of capacity of the system. This capacity payment has a cap of €28,000 ($37,976) per MW per year and is awarded for only 10 years as well. These figures may be insufficient to remunerate generation units that will run only at peak or as backup capacity. A more definitive conclusion on the appropriate level of payments would require further research.

Also, the government could introduce a market for short-term backup capacity, which can send the appropriate signals to investors considering whether to enter the market to cover the flexibility needs of a system with significant amounts of intermittent capacity.[15] Or if none of this works, it could consider raising or removing the cap on the electricity price of the day-ahead market, currently set at €180 ($244) per MWh. This very low value, which is below any estimates of the value of lost load, clearly risks limiting the ability of peaking units to earn their cost of capital. If it fails to undertake any of these measures, the Spanish electricity system will face a considerable risk of underinvestment in thermal units, particularly combined cycle and peak gas turbines, which could eventually undermine its ability to reliably meet electricity demand.

Fourth, the government should promote investment in the development of new grid infrastructures, subject to appropriate cost–benefit analyses, so that the generation of wind and solar units can be transported and distributed more efficiently to those areas of the country where demand is located. According to REE, its investment plans would make it technically possible for the Spanish grid to connect and serve more than 40,000 MW of wind power and more than 8,000 MW of solar thermoelectric capacity by 2016, in comparison with 15,800 MW of wind power and 82 MW of solar power in 2008.

Fifth, the government should also revisit the question of how to pay for the support offered to the SR. Who should contribute to fund the government's environmental policy? Should the cost of that policy be borne exclusively by end users of electricity in proportion to their usage? This is not a for-gone conclusion. For one thing, the benefits of that policy are spread over the entire population. For another, by distributing the burden in a way that is unrelated to usage, the government would be minimizing the impact of its environmental policy on the competiveness of energy-intensive manufacturing and services industries.

Conclusions

The Spanish government has made investment in renewable electricity generation a national priority and believes it will be one of the key drivers of economic development in the coming years.[16] Its policy has no doubt been effective. Spain is one of the countries in the world with more wind and solar PV electricity generation units in absolute and relative terms. Expanding renewable capacity has also been fairly costly and has raised concerns regarding the efficiency and reliability of the Spanish electricity system. This chapter has identified and explained the related problems and proposed how some of them might be addressed successfully. The Spanish government should proactively tackle the problems generated by its renewable electricity support power as a matter of urgency. The country's economy could be seriously damaged if its electricity power system were unable to meet its needs efficiently and reliably. The environmental objectives of the government cannot and should not be achieved at the expense of the competitiveness of the Spanish industry.

Notes

1. FIT schemes are widely regarded as particularly effective. See, e.g., CEER (2008); IEA (2008, 2009).

2. The realizable potential represents the maximum achievable potential, assuming that all existing barriers can be overcome. The assessment of the realizable midterm potential of renewable technologies for European countries up to 2020 was carried out using the Green-X model. See Ragwitz et al. (2005).

3. Relative to a counterfactual scenario where the same levels of generation were provided by CCGTs.

4. According to the IEA methodology, the primary energy form for nuclear energy is not the heating value of the nuclear fuel used, as this is difficult to establish unambiguously. Instead, the heat content of the steam leaving the reactor for the turbine is used as the primary energy form, and it is therefore considered as a domestic source of energy.

5. The plan for the support of domestic coal requires the reduction of coal production to 9.2 Mt by 2012. See European Commission (2006, 2009).

6. This scenario assumes that primary energy grows at an annual rate of 1.3%, as assumed in the IEA energy balances for Spain, and that outputs from nuclear and domestic coal remain at 2008 levels.

7. Under the fixed feed-in tariff option, generators sell their output at a fixed price regardless of the price in the wholesale electricity market; under the premium option, they receive a price equal to the market price plus a premium. The values of the fixed feed-in tariffs, premiums, and incentives were fixed in relation to the tarifa media de referencia (TMR; average reference tariff), which measures the average cost of electricity in a given year.

8. Directive 2009/28/EC of the European Parliament and of the Council of 23 April 2009 on the promotion of the use of energy from renewable sources and amending and subsequently repealing Directives 2001/77/EC and 2003/30/EC.

9. The Ministry of Industry, Tourism and Trade has suggested on several occasions that the 2020 objectives require 40% of electricity to have renewable origin by 2020. See, e.g., MITYC (2009b).

10. These include inter alia the costs of the system operator (REE), the market operator (OMEL), and the electricity regulator (CNE).

11. Average access tariffs, excluding the ex ante deficit, as described in CNE (2009a).

12. On average, wind generation in Spain requires over 600 MW of additional and expensive reserves.

13. This assumes that 100% of the demand reduction is compensated by a reduction in CCGT production. This is a conservative assumption, as the ordinary regime production, excluding coal and CCGTs, has also decreased in comparison with 2008.

14. According to REE, if the current trend continues, energy spills will become a constant in the Spanish system. The report estimates that from 2014 onward, energy spills will reach between 0.4 and 2.3 TWh for 3% to 10% of hours in a year, or between 0.6 and 3.6 TWh from 5% to 12% of hours, depending on the scenario. See Secretaría de Estado de Energía (2009).

15. Currently, no such market exists. The tertiary reserves market comprises the reserves required to increase or decrease production within a time frame of 15 minutes for a period above 2 hours. Additionally, this service rewards only production and not capacity. With the modification of the capacity payments in 2007 (see Orden [Order] ITC/2794/2007, Annex III), the system operator was expected to develop a short-term capacity market or availability service, which was intended

to incentivize thermal capacity availability during peak hours by having the the the system operator and generators sign bilateral contracts. However, this market has not been developed yet, nor is it expected to be developed in the short term.

16. A number of agents and institutions have analyzed this belief and reached different conclusions. For example, the Spanish renewable energy association, APPA, concludes that the contribution of renewables to economic growth is positive in terms of employment and economic growth (APPA 2009). On the contrary, the Instituto Juan de Mariana finds that the renewable policy in Spain destroys 2.2 jobs for each green job created (Calzada Álvarez 2009). However, it does not appear that any rigorous economic analysis has been done of the issues.

References

APPA (Association of Producers of Renewable Energy). 2009. Estudio del Impacto Macroeconómico de Las Energías Renovables en la Economía Española. (Macroeconomic Impact of Renewable Energy in the Spanish Economy). www.appa.es/descargas/NP_APPA_Estudio_Impacto_ER_Espana.pdf (accessed February 22, 2010).

Calzada Álvarez, Gabriel. 2009. Study of the Effects on Employment of Public Aid to Renewable Energy Sources. www.juandemariana.org/pdf/090327-employment-public-aid-renewable.pdf (accessed February 22, 2010).

CEER (Council of European Energy Regulators). 2008. Status Review of Renewable and Energy Efficiency Support Schemes in the EU. Brussels: CEER.

CNE (National Energy Commission). 2009a. *Boletín Mensual de Indicadores Eléctricos y Económicos, Octubre 2009.* (Monthly Bulletin on Economic and Electric Indicators, October 2009) www.cne.es/cne/doc/publicaciones/iap_indicadores-oct09.pdf (accessed February 22, 2010).

———. 2009b. *Información Estadística sobre las Ventas de Energía del Régimen Especial.* (Statistical Information on Special Regime Energy Sales.) www.cne.es/cne/Publicaciones?id_nodo=143&accion=1&soloUltimo=si&sIdCat=10&keyword=&auditoria=F (accessed February 22, 2010).

———. 2009c. *Informe 19/2009 de la CNE sobre la Propuesta de Orden Ministerial por la que se Revisan las Tarifas de Acceso Eléctricas a Partir del Día 1 de Julio de 2009.* (Report 19/2009 from the CNE on the Proposal about the Ministerial Order to Review Electricity Access Tariffs from July 2009 Onwards.) www.cne.es/cne/doc/publicaciones/cne86_09.pdf (accessed February 2, 2010).

European Commission. 2006. National Plan of Strategic Reserve of Coal 2006–2012. NN 81/2006. http://ec.europa.eu/competition/state_aid/register/ii/by_case_nr_nn2006_0060.html (accessed March 2, 2010).

———. 2008. The Support of Electricity from Renewable Energy Sources. http://ec.europa.eu/energy/climate_actions/doc/2008_res_working_document_en.pdf (accessed March 2, 2010).

———. 2009. Study on the Energy Savings Potentials in EU Member States, Candidate Countries and EEA Countries. Final Report. http://ec.europa.eu/energy/efficiency/studies/doc/2009_03_15_esd_efficiency_potentials_short_report.pdf (accessed February 22, 2010).

IEA (International Energy Agency). 2008. *Deploying Renewables: Principles for Effective Policies.* Paris: OECD Publishing.

———. 2009. *Energy Policies of IEA Countries: Spain 2009.* Paris: OECD Publishing.

MARM (Ministry of the Environment and Rural and Marine Affairs). 2009. *Inventario de Emisiones a la Atmósfera de España, Edición 2009, Serie 1990–2007, Sumario de Resultados de GEI.* (Inventory of Emissions to the Spanish Atmosphere, 1990–2007 Series. Summary of GEI Results.) www.mma.es/secciones/calidad_contaminacion/pdf/Sumario_Inventario_de_Emisiones_GEI-_serie1990–2007.pdf (accessed March 2, 2010).

MITYC (Ministry of Industry, Tourism and Trade). 2009a. *La Energía en España 2008.* (The Energy in Spain, 2008) www.mityc.es/energia/balances/Balances/LibrosEnergia/ENERGIA_2008.pdf (accessed March 2, 2010).

———. 2009b. Sebastián: "España tiene un compromiso firme y ambicioso con las energías renovables". June 5, 2009. www.mityc.es/es-ES/GabinetePrensa/NotasPrensa/Paginas/Rusia050609.aspx (accessed March 2, 2010).

Ragwitz, Mario, Joachim Schleich, Claus Huber, Gustav Resch, Thomas Faber, Monique Voogt, Rogier Coenraads, Hans Cleijne, and Peter Bodo. 2005. *FORRES 2020: Analysis of the Renewable Energy Sources' Evolution up to 2020.* Stuttgart: Fraunhofer IRB Verlag.

REE (Red Eléctrica de España) 2008. Informe del Sistema Eléctrico.

Rodríguez, Juan M. 2007. REE (Red Eléctrica de España), Integración en el Sistema y Operación. (Integration and Operation in the System). Presented at CNE's Jornadas sobre la Perspectiva Actual y Evolución de las Energías Renovables en España (Conference on Current Perspective and Evolution of Renewable Energy in Spain). December 2007, Madrid.

Sáenz de Miera, Gonzalo, Pablo del Rio González, and Ignacio Vizcaino. 2008. Analysing the Impact of Renewable Electricity Support Schemes on Power Prices: The Case of Wind Electricity in Spain. *Energy Policy* 36 (9): 3345–59.

Secretaría de Estado de Energía (Secretary of State for Energy). 2009. Resolución de 19 de noviembre de 2009 (Resolution of November 19, 2009). http://noticias.juridicas.com/base_datos/Admin/res191109-itc.html (accessed March 2, 2010).

Conclusions: Whither Renewable Generation?

Boaz Moselle, Jorge Padilla, and Richard Schmalensee

The authors of this book have assessed the current use and future potential of renewable energy technologies for electricity generation. These are technologies that, as Godfrey Boyle puts it in Chapter 2, "enable constantly replenished renewable energy flows to be harnessed to produce power in forms useful to humanity on a sustainable basis." In particular, the authors have addressed the following two questions: What is the case for promoting renewable energy? and What are the implications for power markets and systems of the widespread adoption of renewable generation? In this concluding chapter, we sum up the answers provided in preceding chapters and discuss some possible policy implications.

The Case for Promoting Renewable Power

Kenneth Gillingham and James Sweeney argue in Chapter 5 that the transition from carbon-based technologies to renewable energy is inevitable in the very long run. As noted by Erin Mansur in Chapter 3, we are likely to see a significant increase in the role of renewables in meeting electricity demand in most developed countries in coming decades. Recent experience surveyed in this book, notably Germany (by Hannes Weigt and Florian Leuthold in Chapter 14) and Spain (by Luis Agosti and Jorge Padilla in Chapter 15), is consistent with this trend. The goal of the European Union is to achieve significant reduction in carbon intensity by 2020, with renewable generation playing an important role. As explained by Christopher Jones in Chapter 12, about 60% of the world's wind capacity was installed in Europe at the end of 2007, and the EU is committed to a 20% share for renewable energy in its total energy mix by 2020, compared with about 8.5% in 2005.

The growth in renewable generation is not—and, for the foreseeable future, is not likely to be—driven by market forces, but is largely the result of government intervention. As described by Richard Schmalensee in Chapter 11, there are four basic kinds of support schemes targeted specifically at renewable generation: feed-in tariffs, output subsidies, investment subsidies, and output quotas. Feed-in tariffs guarantee a predetermined, above-market price for power over a period of years. They have been used widely within the EU, notably in Germany and Spain, and have proved to be a powerful mechanism to promote investment, minimize costs to consumers (for a given level of output and mix of renewable technologies), and maximize production. Output subsidies paid on top of market price, though not as widely employed, can be shown to be as effective as, and less distortionary than, feed-in tariffs. Investment subsidies are less efficient than feed-in tariffs or output subsidies yet are widely used all over the world to promote the deployment of renewable power plants. Finally, output quotas typically require agents operating in power markets to generate or procure a minimum fraction of energy from renewable sources.

Renewable generation support schemes, whether feed-in tariffs, output subsidies and quotas, or investment subsidies, are commonly justified as a means of curbing CO_2 emissions and therefore as part of the overall response to global warming. Indeed, U.S. and especially EU energy policies place renewables at the forefront of the fight against climate change (see Chapters 11 and 12). Climate change is expected to adversely affect many economic sectors and natural systems and increase human mortality and morbidity. The need to address this threat is beyond dispute. With respect to renewable generation, the relevant and difficult question from an economic perspective is whether current and planned support schemes represent an efficient response to the challenges posed by climate change.

From an economic viewpoint, the starting point for designing an efficient climate policy is a market-based mechanism to internalize the externalities associated with emissions of greenhouse gases, such as a carbon tax or emissions trading (cap-and-trade) system. A properly designed carbon tax or cap-and-trade system can in theory reduce emissions at least cost.

Those market-based instruments are by definition technology-neutral.[1] That is, they affect different technologies in terms of their greenhouse emissions only, and therefore do not favor one technology (e.g., renewable technologies) over other low-carbon forms of generation (e.g., nuclear power or energy efficiency) on a priori grounds. Under those mechanisms, technologies compete on their merits and electricity is generated efficiently, using those technologies that are more economical on the basis of both their actual costs of production and the market cost of their emissions. Investment in renewable energy may

be an efficient response to those market-based interventions, but there is no guarantee that this is the case.

Market-based solutions would also affect all CO_2-emitting sectors in a similar way and would not place the entire decarbonization burden on the electricity sector. Most of the jurisdictions analyzed in this book have committed to ambitious renewable generation targets even though they perhaps could have more easily and economically achieved the decarbonization of their economies through a properly designed carbon tax.

Governments almost universally have adopted specific policies to promote renewable generation rather than relying on market-based solutions, however. This is so even though alternative technologies may offer the same environmental benefits at lower cost. Of course, policy choices are the outcome of political processes that are often complex, and it would be naive to expect that those outcomes generally coincide with the recommendations of economics textbooks.

Existing renewables policies and future policy proposals have been defended using both economic and noneconomic arguments. The various chapter authors have a range of views regarding those justifications and the necessity or desirability of specific support mechanisms for renewable generation. The view of the book editors is derived from three observations.

First, it is plausible that the true size of the negative externality associated with CO_2 emissions—the social cost of carbon—is higher than the current price of CO_2 emissions (e.g., in the EU Emission Trading System, or ETS), and that, as Boyle argues in Chapter 2, the difference exceeds the incremental cost of renewable generation relative to conventional generation. This is a necessary condition for supporting renewable generation, though by no means sufficient (for example, one might be able simply to raise the price of CO_2 emissions).

Second, it is also plausible that other forms of emissions reduction—such as nuclear, carbon capture and storage (CCS), or energy efficiency policies[2]—are either more costly (at the relevant margin) than renewables or constrained by noneconomic factors, such as the public acceptability issues around nuclear power.

The third observation is an empirical one, for which Part IV of this book provides ample support: political processes do not easily deliver outcomes that resemble the first-best outcome of technology-neutral, market-based mechanisms to reduce greenhouse gas emissions. Why this is so raises many interesting questions of political economy, but it is clear that governments face great difficulty in credibly committing to a long-term carbon price that is close to the social cost of carbon or high enough to support significant investments in low-carbon technologies. Even the EU ETS, which is an impressive and unique achievement, has to date given a level of carbon prices that induces switching from coal to gas-fired generation but is not high enough to support such investments.

Drawing these three observations together, the editors therefore recognize that the need to respond to the challenges posed by global warming, combined with real-world constraints on policymaking processes, may provide a valid justification for specific support mechanisms for renewables, especially for less costly forms. However, no plausible combination of assumptions justifies a "pay whatever it takes" approach. The shadow value of investing in a given technology is finite, limited, if by nothing else, at least by the opportunity cost of investing more in lower-cost technologies. In particular, it is hard to justify extensive investment in deploying extremely expensive forms of renewables, such as solar photovoltaic in Spain, Germany, and parts of the United States and offshore wind in the United Kingdom.

This logic for supporting some specific measures to promote renewable generation does not depend on the kinds of market failure arguments that are often cited in favor of such measures. Although it is possible in theory to identify many such market failures (see Chapter 5), in most cases they appear unlikely to be material enough to justify the kind of large-scale interventions they are used to support. In general, the claimed "non-climate-change externality" arguments for renewables support appear rather weak.

For example, investing in renewables to create jobs seems like poor economic policy. This is because electricity generation is generally highly capital-intensive, the time frame for investment is too long to allow for a temporary boost in employment in the short run (during a recession), and in the long run the level of employment depends on structural macroeconomic factors and is unlikely to be affected by policies of this nature. As an illustration, in Spain, the rapid growth of renewable generation before and after the Great Recession has had, at most, a *de minimis* impact on its labor markets and has not offset in any meaningful way the growth of unemployment during the current crisis.

With regard to industrial policy, almost every major government in the developed world seems to believe that it will become a world leader in new energy technologies, and that such leadership will generate positive externalities on other companies within the energy sector as well as on other industrial and services sectors. As yet, however, evidence is slim in support of that claim for any nation. In particular, little evidence exists that extensive deployment of renewables creates learning-by-doing (or knowledge) spillovers that cannot be captured within firms (see, e.g., Chapter 5). Moreover, as in other industries, it is likely that these positive externalities are much stronger at the R&D level. Subsidies for wide-scale deployment of expensive renewable technologies are therefore unlikely to be justified on the basis either that the cost is overestimated (because they will bring down future costs) or that they will stimulate an infant industry.

An alternative justification for existing and proposed support schemes for renewables concerns their impact on security of supply. In most markets, individual participants deal effectively and efficiently with uncertainty regarding demand and supply through price incentives, bilateral insurance contracts, and related devices. The conclusion that supply insecurity justifies government action here must rest on the identification of one or more specific externalities that can be corrected by nonmarket intervention.

From a U.S. perspective, Gillingham and Sweeney point out in Chapter 5 that an important externality may relate to the costs associated with national security, but this concerns oil and has little relevance to renewables other than biofuels. Looking at the EU, where security of supply is high on the political agenda and is routinely cited as a justification for renewables subsidies, Boaz Moselle in Chapter 4 identifies significant externalities in the context of the key relevant security-of-supply issue: dependence on Russia and Algeria for natural gas. Although EU policymakers often refer to generalized import dependence, few security issues appear to exist around the use of imported coal, given that many diverse and historically friendly countries have enormous coal reserves. Moselle discusses the extent to which renewable generation in the EU, as opposed to other energy sources, may replace Russian and Algerian gas. He concludes that dependence on imported gas gives rise to real security-of-supply issues in the EU, especially in eastern Europe, and that market outcomes may not provide an efficient response to those risks because of "moral hazard" types of concerns that give rise to externalities. He argues, however, that these externalities do not justify the specific promotion of renewables, because it is not clear how much Russian or Algerian gas would be displaced by renewable generation, and because other forms of low-carbon generation could have similar or greater impact on security of supply.

In summary, then, although the environmental benefits of renewable generation are clear, the editors are skeptical of economic and geostrategic justifications for policies specifically aimed at promoting renewables. They do, however, recognize a political rationale for existing renewable support schemes: subsidizing renewables may be politically more acceptable than taxing firms and consumers for polluting. As in many other instances, first-best economic policy choices may not be politically feasible. In such cases, we need to look for second-best policy responses. Existing and planned support schemes can be rationalized only as second-best responses to the challenges posed by climate change. Yet the authors widely agree that current and anticipated policies need considerable fine-tuning before they can be properly regarded as the right policy instruments even in a second-best world. The editors would add that the constraints that lead to second-best policy outcomes can change, and as the true cost of not using technology-neutral, market-based mechanisms becomes clearer over time, the opportunity may arise to move closer to first-best.

Renewable Generation and Power Systems in Practice

Current policies toward greenhouse gas abatement in the electricity generation sector in the EU, in many EU member states, in some U.S. states and regions, and under serious consideration at the federal level in the United States combine a technology-neutral market-based mechanism (e.g., the EU ETS and similar cap-and-trade schemes in California and the U.S. Northeast) with technology-specific interventions for renewables, nuclear, and CCS. This mix of policies has profound implications for wholesale power markets.

Existing and planned policies may raise questions about the current model of liberalized power markets. A large part of the benefits from liberalization have come about through improved investment decisions. In fact, dynamic efficiency considerations underlay the move from regulated to liberalized generation. However, current policies mean that market forces will have limited impact on future investment decisions, as those will be driven, to a large extent, by the environmental and security-of-supply concerns of governments. In the United Kingdom, for example, choices for new investment are affected by a very large number of different environmental programs (as discussed by Michael Pollitt in Chapter 13), whose cumulative effect is likely to be determinative.[3]

At a more concrete level, existing and planned policies are bound to have a significant impact on the economics of conventional generation plants. As shown by James Bushnell in Chapter 9, the exploitation of wind resources will have a significant impact on market prices. It will also affect the net load shape, the difference between load and supply from intermittent sources. This is likely to exhibit relatively higher spreads between peak and average demand for thermal production. As a consequence, the equilibrium investment mix of nonwind resources will shift toward less base load and more peaking capacity. The experiences in Spain and Germany show that the widespread deployment of intermittent generation (wind) leads to increased price volatility, with very low (on occasions even zero or negative) prices when wind patterns make for high levels of output at times of low load (see Chapters 14 and 15).

This combination of spot price volatility and the need for large numbers of peaking plants with very low utilization is likely to significantly exacerbate the "missing money" problem that can already arise in wholesale power markets, where a combination of the lack of real-time pricing for many consumers, transmission system operator (TSO) behavior, explicit regulatory interventions (price caps), and implicit regulation means that markets do not provide the right signals to get sufficient peaking capacity.

Essentially three approaches can be taken to this problem. The first is to observe that markets are quite capable of dealing with problems of this sort via the price mechanism, including for goods that are not storable. For example, demand for accommodation on or near a ski slope is highly weather related. High prices for that accommodation at times of peak demand (e.g., around Christmas and during school holidays in winter) ensure a high level of investment and the absence of lines outside ski chalets. Similarly, if there are no price caps and investors do not expect future government intervention, then they should be expected to build sufficient capacity to cope with demand, investing in backup plants that would tend to run infrequently, on the basis that the spot prices when they did run would be high enough that they could recover their fixed costs over time. At the same time, demand should become more responsive to short-term price signals as the prevalence of price spikes makes it worthwhile to devote time and make necessary capital investments so as to be able more easily to reduce or shift demand at times of peak load.

In many (probably most, and perhaps all) jurisdictions, however, governments lack the ability to credibly commit not to intervene in energy markets when prices are high. Indeed many liberalized energy markets, including several in the United States and in a number of EU member states, already have explicit price caps in place. These caps in part reflect political sensitivities but are also a reaction to well-founded concerns that wholesale power markets are more susceptible than many others to market abuse.

In those circumstances, the second approach to dealing with intermittency, price spikes, and the need for backup is to provide a subsidy to investment in generation (and on efficiency grounds, perhaps also to flexible load) in the form of "capacity payments". A number of design issues around the capacity markets determine these payments, which have been widely explored (in theory and in practice) in the United States, much less so in the EU, where few jurisdictions currently have any form of capacity payment in place. Getting those payments at the right level appears to be key to ensuring that the move toward renewable energy does not compromise the reliability of electricity systems.

The third approach would be to conclude that measures of this kind are ineffective, and that competitive markets with a significant proportion of intermittent (and low-marginal-cost) renewable energy are not able to deliver the necessary rents to induce adequate investment in peaking capacity. From the discussion above, it should be clear that the editors do not share that conclusion. The prospect of re-regulation of electricity aimed at ensuring generation adequacy, while at the same time giving governments more direct control over technology choices, is nonetheless a real prospect,[4] though in the editors' view, it is problematic and potentially worrisome.

That the shift to renewable energy may lead to new market distortions and regulatory challenges does not justify giving up on markets. No doubt regulators will have to adapt their tools to accommodate the environmental and security-of-supply concerns of governments, but they should do so without throwing off the discipline that a competitive market imposes not only on firms and consumers, but also on policymakers. Bad policies, like poorly managed firms, tend to fail the market test quickly.

Power markets that integrate large amounts of wind face several other policy issues. First, apart from the investment issue discussed above, increasing penetration of intermittent generation gives rise to operational concerns because of the difficulty of predicting output ahead of time. However, significant improvements have taken place in forecasting wind generation output over time (see Chapter 2). Moselle argues in Chapter 4 that as a result, the operational issue can in principle be made relatively straightforward and, subject to solving the problem of providing investment incentives to ensure sufficient availability of peaking plants, the problem becomes simply a further cost element, albeit potentially a very material one, rather than a security-of-supply concern.

Second, a subsidy per megawatt-hour of renewable generation distorts price signals and can lead to inefficiencies. For example, the massive introduction of wind generation can lead to negative prices, reflecting an inefficient outcome where wind generators, which could stop running at zero social cost but at the expense of losing their feed-in tariff payments, pay others (e.g., nuclear generators) to incur real costs to produce less electricity (Schmalensee reports on negative spot prices in west Texas in Chapter 11). Other inefficiencies may arise when the level of payment is unrelated to the market price (e.g., the absence of an incentive to produce at peak hours or at peak times of the year).

A third problem concerns the potential need for new investment in transmission, as new patterns of generation, reflecting different patterns of location for new installed capacity, lead to changing flow patterns in transmission systems. Christian von Hirschhausen explains in Chapter 10 that the complexities of harnessing renewable energy to generate electricity are relatively simple in comparison to transporting that electricity over long distances to large demand centers. He also describes the many market and institutional problems, including regulatory and technological risks and rent-sharing issues, which make it difficult to overcome the transmission bottlenecks that limit

the effective deployment of renewables. If renewables are to play a more important role, policymakers must address these difficult problems.

The location of large-scale renewable generation will depend on a number of factors, including the location of appropriate resources, such as water, wind, sunshine, and sources of biomass; the relevant transportation costs for some of these resources; issues around siting; and the costs of developing the necessary distribution and transmission systems. Efficient locational pricing, as discussed by William Hogan in Chapter 7, will help provide incentives for efficient decisions concerning the location of generation and transmission facilities, such as by ensuring higher prices in areas where transmission bottlenecks exist. However, it would be daunting even in theory to attempt to fully decentralize transmission investment decisions via locational pricing, if only because transmission investments are lumpy and commonly eliminate the nodal price differences that justified the investments. In practice, therefore, more extensive work is needed on developing and implementing appropriate methodologies for transmission planning.

Moreover, one effect of the need to locate generation close to renewable resources, and far from NIMBY-minded citizens, is likely to be a much greater mismatch between the locations of generation and load. New arrangements for transmission planning thus need to include arrangements to coordinate planning among multiple transmission owners. U.S. experience suggests that electricity systems operated by regional transmission operators (RTOs) and independent system operators (ISOs) are more effective in integrating wind generation. Those systems leverage their operational and transmission integration to facilitate deployment of renewable generation (see Chapter 11). A new approach to infrastructure planning is foreseen in Europe. Under the third internal market package, two new European organizations, the Agency for the Cooperation of Energy Regulators (ACER) and the European Network of Transmission System Operators for Electricity (ENTSO-E), will have to cooperate and coordinate to put in place new infrastructure and grid access rules to ensure that the growth in renewable energy is sustainable and the available capacity is used efficiently (see Chapter 12).

Finally, large-scale deployment of renewable generation raises questions as to the nature of regulation. Richard Green maintains in Chapter 8 that energy regulation will need to adjust, for example by recognizing the need for new regulated investments (e.g., in "smart grids" to complement distributed generation), but that there should be no step change in the fundamental scope of energy regulation. He also suggests that regulators should continue to focus on the promotion of competition, and indeed that competitive models will have extra advantages in the context of a transition to renewables because of their superior performance in stimulating innovation.

Conclusion

Except possibly for nuclear terrorism, global warming is widely regarded as the most important challenge to our globalized society. Policymakers are considering ways of confronting this challenge and are also putting a substantial amount of money on the table. A significant share of that money is being allocated to renewable generation support schemes. For a variety of reasons, a lot of that money will be spent inefficiently. Because the sums involved are very large, it is imperative that we discuss how to move toward a decarbonized electricity system at the least possible cost. This requires moving away from generic and arcane debates about policy goals and toward analyzing the design and implementation of renewable generation support schemes, as well as the relative merits of renewable generation policies in comparison with other decarbonization policies. It is hoped that this book represents a nontrivial step forward in that direction.

Notes

1. A "market-based instrument" is defined in this context to refer to an instrument that puts a price on greenhouse gas emissions (or at least on CO_2 emissions), either directly via a tax or indirectly via cap-and-trade. Under this definition, therefore, an instrument like tradable renewables certificates (or, hypothetically, a tax on all nonrenewable generation) does not qualify as a market-based instrument.

2. In industrialized countries, as explained by José Goldemberg in Chapter 6), energy efficiency will be an attractive, though limited, alternative to renewable generation. In developing countries, energy efficiency programs are less likely to substitute for the promotion of carbon-free or low-carbon technologies. In those latter countries, energy demand is bound to grow and should be met by deploying clean and efficient technologies early in the process of development.

3. These programs include the EU ETS; the national UK Emissions Trading Scheme; the Renewables Obligation Certificates, which fund renewables deployment differentially by technology; investment subsidies for renewables, known as capital grants; feed-in tariffs for new microrenewables; support for cogeneration; new support measures currently being developed for nuclear and CCS; obligations on suppliers to install energy efficiency measures to meet the Carbon Emissions Reduction Target (CERT); as well as a number of other measures.

4. Recent proposals from the British energy regulator (formerly a leading advocate of liberalized energy markets) include, at one extreme, the creation of a single central buyer responsible for procuring wholesale power and contracting to procure new generation investment, which it would secure against long-term contracts (see Ofgem 2010).

Reference

Ofgem. 2010. *Project Discovery: Options for Delivering Secure and Sustainable Energy Supplies*, February 3. London: Ofgem.

Index

Note: Page numbers in italics indicate figures and tables. Page numbers followed by an 'n' indicate notes.